Pau–Brasil Culture
When Lúcio Costa Met Mário de Andrade, Oswald de Andrade and Tarsila do Amaral

Abilio Guerra

Latin America: Thoughts

Romano Guerra Editora
Nhamerica Platform

Management Coordination
Abilio Guerra
Fernando Luiz Lara
Silvana Romano Santos

Translation
Odorico Leal

Translation Review
Noemi Zein Telles
Irene Nagashima

Pau–Brasil Culture
When Lúcio Costa Met Mário de
Andrade, Oswald de Andrade and
Tarsila do Amaral
Abilio Guerra
Brasil 8

Editor
Abilio Guerra
Fernando Luiz Lara
Silvana Romano Santos

Graphic Design and Formatting
Dárkon V Roque

To Silvana Romano Santos and
Valentina Moimas who, each in their
own way, made this book possible.

Cultural Support

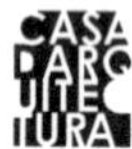

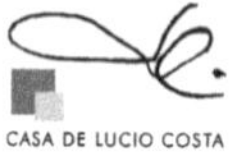

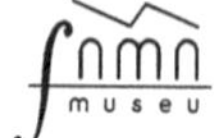

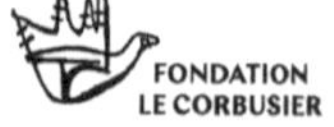

Pau-Brasil Culture

When Lúcio Costa Met Mário de Andrade, Oswald de Andrade and Tarsila do Amaral

Abilio Guerra

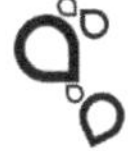

Romano Guerra Editora
Nhamerica Platform

São Paulo, Austin, 2023
1st edition

Summary

Introducing Pau-Brasil Culture

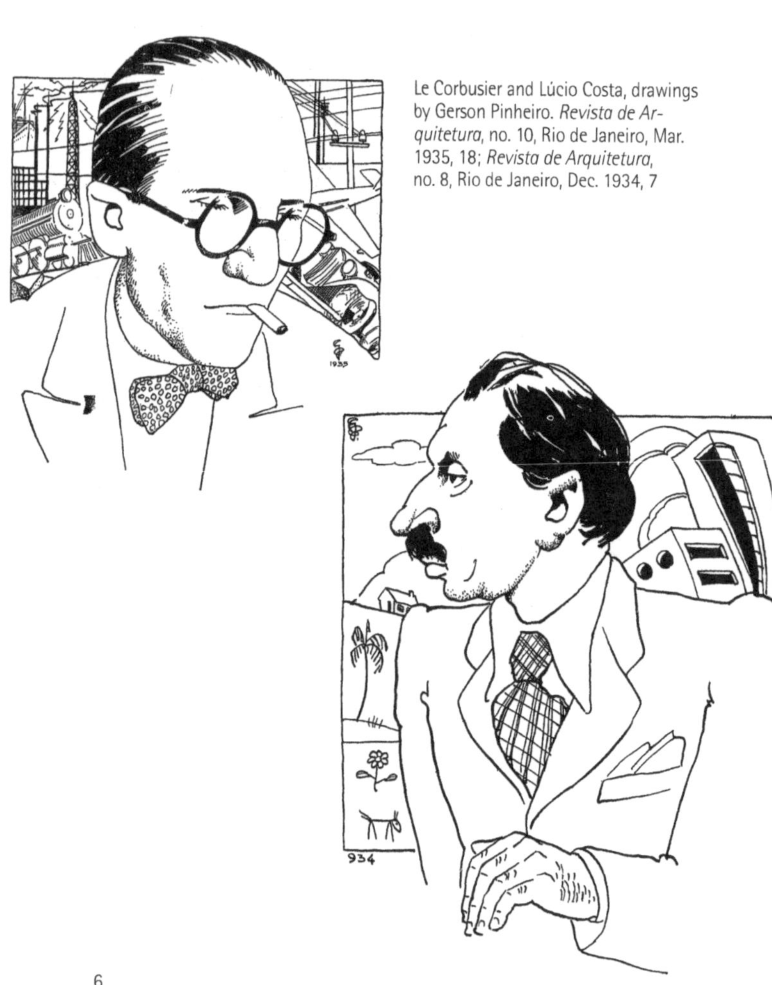

Le Corbusier and Lúcio Costa, drawings by Gerson Pinheiro. *Revista de Arquitetura*, no. 10, Rio de Janeiro, Mar. 1935, 18; *Revista de Arquitetura*, no. 8, Rio de Janeiro, Dec. 1934, 7

An Indian will descend from a bright and colorful star
landing with dizzying speed
in the heart of the southern hemisphere
he will land in America, in a clear instant [...]
and what will be revealed
shall surprise everyone, not for being exotic,
but rather for managing to stay hidden
while being quite obvious.
Caetano Veloso, Um índio, 1977

A well-woven tale

In a well-known debate with Geraldo Ferraz in 1948, Lúcio
Costa argued that modern architecture as practiced in Brazil
only became truly interesting when the functional grounds
of this new architecture - bequeathed to us by Le Corbusier
- were incorporated and developed by the national genius.
From then on - the argument goes -, we could actually be
proud of an architecture that was authentically ours, deeply
rooted in a tradition that went back to the colonial baroque
style from Minas Gerais. Moreover, in our modern architectural production, Oscar Niemeyer played a role equivalent
to that of Aleijadinho, embodying to the highest degree the
latent possibilities of "Brazilianness". "There is much more
affinity" - Lúcio Costa insisted - "between Oscar's work, as
seen in the admirable Pampulha ensemble, and Aleijadinho's
masterpiece — the church of São Francisco de Assis, in Ouro
Preto — than between Oscar's work and that of Warchavchik
- which is, in my view, a quite significant fact."[1]

Even more significant than that is the formula Lúcio
Costa applies when he's sorting out affinities and pushing
the premise that the *national* element in this new architecture is actually more vigorous than the *modern* one. He
argues that, on the one hand, there are genuine, innovative
works — seeds that sprout beautifully in our tropical soil,
nurtured by the most authentic native sap; on the other

hand, we also find imitations devoid of any ties to our traditions; these are second or third-hand copies, like exotic trees transplanted after full maturation somewhere else. Lúcio Costa's words, pregnant with meanings, implications and commitments, outlines a distinction that has enjoyed a long history among us, that is: the distinction between *Brazilian modern architecture and modern architecture in Brazil.*

Having been repeated so many times, Lúcio Costa's sentence has long become an untouchable axiom. As Otília Arantes says, the construction of a "miraculous" image of Oscar Niemeyer operates as a "perfect background story", a kind of "well-woven tale", a "precise fantasy that has since taken on mythological proportions, such was the success with which each work of Modern Brazilian Architecture, whether momentous or not, reinforced the legend of its own supernatural origin."[2] This phenomenon was only possible because, when it came to the cultural business, Lúcio Costa moved on both sides of the counter: he was a practicing architect who guided the group of young Brazilians who would bequeath to the world the first modern skyscraper built according to the principles outlined by Le Corbusier: the headquarters of the Ministry of Education and Health – MES, in Rio de Janeiro; yet he was also the main theorist of the group, the intellectual author of the vision framing the history of national architecture as an interplay between tradition and modernity. On the occasion of the release of Lúcio's book/testament, *Record of an experience*, Otília points out the enigmatic character of the old master's intellectual construction: "despite numerous additions and recent comments that punctuate the texts, this last record adds very little beyond this diffuse feeling that, at each time the script takes a look back, something yet to be clarified remains hidden, eluding each new attempt, which invariably seems to return to the same point."[3]

During the period in which Costa's postulates were taken as historical truths, the commitments and compromises that, being so extensive and profound, guaranteed architecture a leading role in the country's history were rarely considered. The architects' task in this period covers an extensive arc, from the aesthetic embodiment of raciality to the adequate installation of the Brazilian man in the tropical territory. These beliefs were not shared only by the people in the métier: they spilled over into society and were instrumented by men in power. We're talking about a quarter century of total supremacy. The construction of Brasilia is based on the faith in the capacity of our national architecture to carry out such projects as well as in its power to reorder the political, social and economic structure of the country. However, modern thinking in architecture, as structured from the mid-1930s onwards, owes a great deal to previous debates that took place in the country not only in the strict disciplinary field of architecture, but in the broader territory of art and culture.

The narrative presented here seeks to unveil the mechanisms that informed and engendered Lúcio Costa's discourse, which pays heavy tribute to the 1920s modernism that flourished in São Paulo. If the 1922 Modern Art Week works as an inaugural milestone, the Andrades – writers Oswald and Mário – and painter Tarsila do Amaral are the leading figures. In the art field, the aesthetic experimentalism inspired by the European avant-garde, which was predominant during the early stages, gradually gives way to a nativism of a romantic bent, casting a glance towards the heartland of the country. The famous manifesto,[4] the "*Pau-Brasil*" poetry and painting of Oswald and Tarsila, Mário de Andrade's *mata-virgismo* ("woodland virginism"), the radicalization of the 1928 "Anthropophagic Manifesto"[5] and later manifestos and artistic directions of the period established the urban front of this artistic renewal, its rural mirroring being the expeditions of apprentice tourists reporting on cities and landscapes of the interior of the country.

The narrative montage this book intends to decipher crosses over to different areas, especially architecture, literature, painting and music. In all of them, there is this contradiction between the desire to catch up with European artistic production and to reconnect with the roots of nationality. In all of them, the aesthetic-cultural project seeking to merge these antagonisms – *being Brazilian and modern at the same time* – becomes visible. The raw material of this book – the propositions, actions and works of the protagonists of the 1920s and 1930s – are to be understood in two senses: first, as a human phenomenon that has actually taken place – what historians usually call "ontological facts" – and which can be verified as false or true; second, there's the interpretation of these facts, a plausible or implausible explanation for causal relationships between them, the extent to which an idea can unfold into an act, the extent to which that act can then unfold into new ideas. At first glance, the primary sense seems unimportant; however, those who depend on accurate descriptions are well aware that correct datings may lead to new interpretations. On the other hand, the idea that all explanations are equivalent because they cannot be verified as to their falsity or veracity – an argument can only be credible or not, according to epistemology – is not acceptable. Not all arguments are born equal, to use a familiar expression. A well-built one, with proven facts and an interpretation that retraces the specular process that transmits and modifies an idea, will always be more credible than an argument based on guesswork or simply without any basis.

The silence of the sphinx and the song of the siren

This book is based on a doctoral dissertation defended in 2002,[6] thus, its publication deserves some consideration, which will be restricted to this section. We believe there are three reasons to publish this dissertation two decades later. The first one is theoretical. During this period, developments

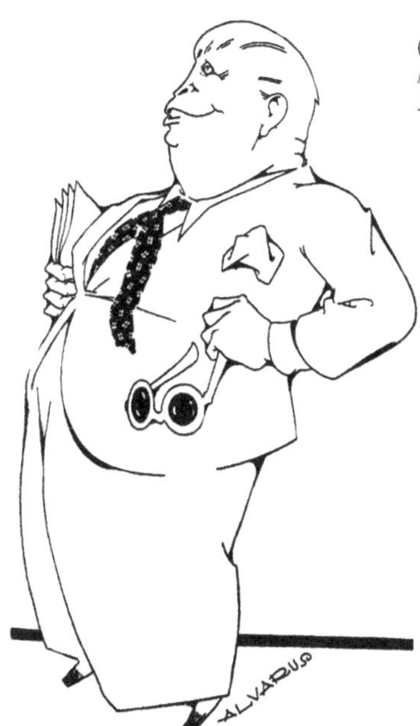

Oswald de Andrade, drawing by Alvarus. *Vamos Ler!*, no. 333, Rio de Janeiro, Dec. 17, 1942, 61

in this particular area of studies occurred mainly in the scope of graduate courses in architecture schools, where the transdisciplinary vision is little considered; thus, deeper research into specific themes – monographs by architects, particular episodes or small extracts from broad contexts – and more horizontal explanations for comprehensive phenomena are carried out respecting the demarcation of the specific area of architecture and urbanism. Overlaps do exist, of course, but they generally consider the legal, social and political spheres, which are understood as determinants for the production of built space. So, there is a perception that, despite the time that has elapsed, many of the issues presented here will be seen as new or even unique. Many others, although not unprecedented, may prove useful in order to better clarify what is already known. The attested symmetry between the thought and work of Mário de Andrade and Lúcio Costa, which has been suggested by some researchers,[7] gains here, one hopes, documentary evidence and an unexpected conceptual analysis.

There is yet another methodological aspect at play. To properly analyze the discourse of others, it is often necessary to really bring it into the spotlight so that it presents itself with its peculiar constructive beauty and persuasive rhetoric. In writing methodology, this means making cuts and combinations. In the practice of reading, it means interpreting and differentiating. In theoretical terms, there is a bet on the ability of the aesthetic-cultural discourse to propagate itself through the social fabric and on its *effectiveness* in transforming the world, even when it is structured on uncertain bases. At every step, we kept in mind Jean-Pierre Faye's reminder: "It would be legitimate to show that the interlacing of language simply emanates from conflicting social groups and, ultimately, from social classes. To conclude, however, that the analysis should refer to the social groups themselves, without dwelling on the secondary level, that is, the level of language, is naive. It would be like saying that, for ideological reasons, physical research should focus on matter itself, without taking into account luminous phenomena, which would be superfluous."[8]

These theoretical and methodological concerns regarding our theme – which is the engendering of the notion of a cultural synthesis between the modern element and the traditional element both in the context of avant-garde modernism and of a stabilized modern style, present in Brazilian culture – entails the following situation: all concepts, notions and identities that underlie this historical processing are artificial constructions, but they cannot be naively classified as historical falsehoods. What marks the ideological representation of national identity is its effectiveness in giving what is artificially constructed a status as a result of organic processes. And this phenomenon, with secular precedents, is established precisely during the period that interests us: the

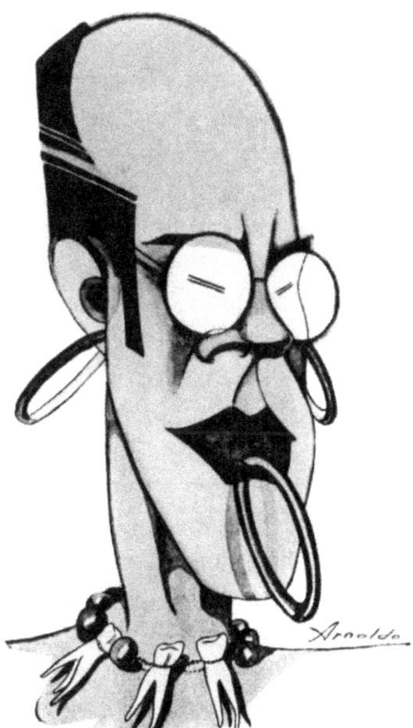

Mário de Andrade, drawing by Arnaldo. *Paratodos*, no. 509, Rio de Janeiro, Sept. 15, 1928, 15

1920s and 1930s, when the conventions of what should be the Brazilian man are processed in an arc that encompasses culture, art, politics, sociology, history and anthropology. Jessé Souza comes to our rescue to clarify what is at stake here: "Regardless of whether this set of attributes is true or false – national identity is not defined by its truth value, but by its effectiveness in producing an imaginary community that perceives itself as unique."[9]

When pursuing so closely, in time and in the interstices of art and culture, an object so elusive and powerful, we often unintentionally fall for its charm. Now that the work is complete, we notice that we have often deceived ourselves when trying to do what Ulysses taught us: to tie ourselves to the safe trunk of reason, so that we can let ourselves be seduced by the tender song of the sirens, while avoiding, however, the risk of destruction. But there is no way, when dealing with history, to act like a privileged and manipulative spectator. When considering everybody who preceded us – and so many of them were much more astute and cultivated –, it's easy to see that, despite these combined efforts, the sphinx remains silent. We can only hope that, at certain, perhaps numerous moments, the lucidity of the analysis has managed to impose itself.

The second justification relates to the sense of opportunity in presenting this work to a broader public as we celebrate two occasions: the bicentennial of Brazilian Independence and the centenary of the Modern Art Week in São Paulo. The subtext here is the feeling that this extensive and intense research garnered limited attention at the time, even though it has been read by many over the years. Some of the hypotheses launched here actually spread through our field, either because they jumped from our pages – sometimes with no proper credit – or because they were figured out by others who consulted the same sources. In both cases, the presence in other works of the ideas developed here evokes two feelings: a feeling of pride, for having collaborated to some extent for the construction of our field, and also of relief, when one recognizes that synapses recorded way back then were actually sound. Nevertheless, frankly speaking, while revisiting the work two decades later, we are faced with too many gaps and redundancies beyond the acceptable. We have now tried to solve these problems, considering that the theoretical-methodological input has accompanied us to this day and that the past – or that which we see in the past – remains fairly the same, for better or for worse. On the other hand, any updates to the current debate are mostly located in footnotes and bibliographic suggestions, including a few other studies I myself have written.

Besides this more personal dimension, the celebration of Brazilian independence highlights once again the moment when the territory known today as Brazil had to take on the challenge of national construction. Although it is a more

symbolic than real milestone – the process of building an
actual federation of states under the control of a central
Republican power only takes hold during the Vargas period,
a political turn with cultural and aesthetic implications –,
the ambition of a unifying national culture, which gained its
first contours during the romantic era in the 19th century, is
also the touchstone for the modernism of the 1920s. In the
year in which this doctoral dissertation was defended – 2002
–, the country was experiencing enormous optimism, with a
popular government that would manage to coordinate economic growth and a series of policies that gave poor popula-
tions access to services and education, breaking, even if partially – or provisionally, as it's pretty clear today – the vicious
circle of exclusion. A work which dealt with utopias seemed
out of place when people were finding so much satisfaction
in everyday life. Considering the bleak picture today, perhaps now our research will be able to garner greater interest
amidst the contemporary debate.

The third justification is the most important when considering the world today, shaken by crucial doubts and visceral fears concerning what the near and distant futures may
hold for us. The rise of right-wing parties on all continents;
the globalization of problems that used to to be local, such
as diasporas motivated by hunger and other ills; the agony
of the environment, perhaps already irrevocably doomed; the
ever growing poverty, democratically distributed in virtually
all countries; the ever greater concentration of wealth in the
hands of only a few people and corporations increasingly
shielded and alienated from the real world; the Covid-19
pandemic, which accentuated the general picture of structural imbalances in financial capitalism – these and many
other ongoing processes, some of them in rapid acceleration,
unravel an apocalyptic world. However, in the last twenty
years in which these problems have worsened, we have also
witnessed the emergence and consolidation of organically
constituted groups apt to discuss exclusion from the point of

view of the excluded. At least two groups interest us closely, for they are at the heart of our original research, although unfortunately more as themes than flesh-and-blood contributors. Currently, what we see are black people talking about racism and its consequences, and also indigenous people talking about the genocide of ethnicities and the extermination of languages and cultures. There is no longer a need for a "symbolic attorney" to defend the rights of such minorities. The Jessés and Krenaks of today are black and indigenous – and also Brazilian; they come from the social base, but they are intellectuals too; they can live in their own communities and teach at federal universities in Brazilian capitals. The Jessés and the Krenaks are now being heard as never before.

Black people in Brazil have a remarkable tradition in music and sports; however, their potential for protagonism was practically limited to these particular fields of activity. Nowadays, a black intellectual elite has emerged in virtually all areas, beneficiaries of inclusive policies promoted by progressive governments, highlighting the low political and economic representation of this social group – in other words, the structural racism of our society. Jessé Souza explains how, in the first decades of the 20th century, theories explaining social history based on racial differences were assimilated by culturalism, which was supposed to overcome old prejudices. From then on, the unevenness of economic development between countries and social strata would be explained by cultural inequalities. Cultural modernization and economic progress, never contested and seen as natural phenomena of social evolution, became the measure of societies, legitimizing the dominance of the white – especially Protestant – society. According to this world view, *primitive* and *backward* societies, averse to the rational and productivist codes of the contemporary world, would be condemned to a subordinate role in the general concert of nations. Dismantling this interpretation is a complex enterprise, as it is necessary to dig deep into its theoretical artifices and discursive practices.

Indigenous peoples, in turn, who for centuries were considered incapable of taking hold of their own destiny, were tutored by the state until recently. However, the broad mobilization of its leaders, overcoming ancestral disagreements, managed to secure their fundamental rights in the 1988 Constitution, such as self-government and the original and inalienable right over the lands they traditionally occupy: "the social organization, customs, languages, beliefs and traditions of the Indians are unacknowledged here, as well as the original rights over the lands they traditionally occupy, and it is up to the Union to demarcate them, protect and ensure respect for all their assets,"[10] says the Constitution. Therefore, just as it is up to the state to guarantee the institution of private property in urban and rural societies, the same must be pursued as to the land that indigenous peoples have traditionally occupied. However, the federal government's negligence in complying with constitutional norms dealing with the safeguards of native peoples is widely known, especially in recent years. Rights conceived in *spirit*, and enshrined in the *letter of the law*, are increasingly vilified by the overwhelming power and excessive arrogance of invaders – agribusiness, miners and prospectors, deforesters etc. –, which end up protected by the inaction of the state power. It would be up to the so-called fourth power – the Public Federal Ministry – to play a leading role in the defense of these instituted rights, which has also not been observed.[11]

Running counter to the violence of economic power against indigenous communities, there is a growing interest in the worldview of these cultures – what Eduardo Viveiros de Castro has called "Amerindian perspectivism" –, which has among its features the "Amerindian multinaturalism" marked by a deep regard for nature, both organic and inorganic.[12] This original philosophy is also expressed as a poetics, a sort of art of living, where an archaic wisdom battles the desacralization of the world and survives by coexisting with the visible and the invisible. In the presentation of the book *The falling sky*, Eduardo Viveiros de Castro warns us that it is high time we hear what this *other* has to say: "How appropriate that this message comes from way out in the boondocks, from this indigenous Amazon that continues to resist, albeit weakened, to successive assaults; that it comes, then, from the Yanomami, this message, this prophecy, a note from the forest warning us of the betrayal we are committing against our fellow earthlings."[13] In this magnificent book, where the French anthropologist Bruce Albert codifies in "civilized" language the magic words of the Yanomami shaman David Kopenawa, we find this passage, a "note from the forest", which show us how pride might hide a good deal of ignorance:

> "In the forest, ecology is us, humans. But so are the *xapiri*, the animals, the trees, the rivers, the fish, the sky, the rain, the wind and the sun! It is all that came into being in the forest, away from the whites; everything that is not yet surrounded by fences. The words of ecology are our old words, the ones that *Omama* gave our ancestors. The *xapiri* have defended the forest for as long as it has existed. They have always been on the side of our ancestors, which is why they never devastated it. The forest is still very much alive, isn't it? Whites, who were previously ignorant of these things, are now coming to understand. That's why some of them invented new words to protect the forest. Now they call themselves ecology people because they are worried, because their land is getting warmer and warmer. Our ancestors never had the idea of deforesting or excavating the earth in an unrestrained way. They just thought it was beautiful, and that it should stay that way forever. Ecology, for them, was to think that *Omama* had created the forest for humans to live in without mistreating it.

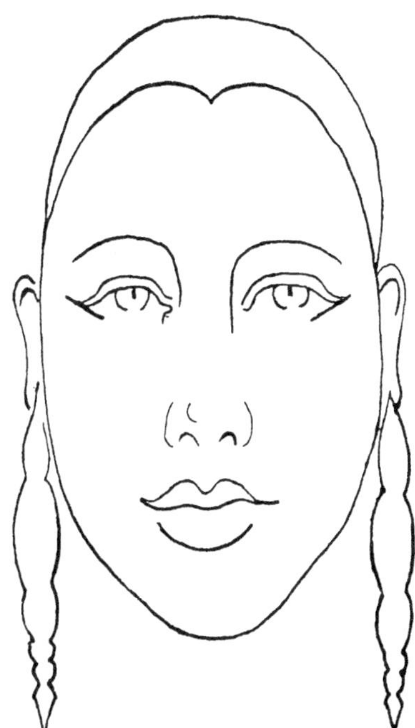

And that's it. We are the inhabitants of the forest, we were born in the very center of ecology and that's where we grew up."[14]

Amerindian thought questions the culturalism of positivist bent that sees progress and modernization at all costs as inevitable. Even when it harms the body of nature and the soul of humanity. According to Viveiros de Castro, the current Brazilian federal government aims to abolish all legal protection associated with public lands and those occupied by traditional peoples, which remain separate from the logic of private property, "in order to make these lands 'productive', that is, profitable for its claimants, the great contractors of agribusiness, mining and land speculation."[15] Indigenous leader Ailton Krenak points out that the native peoples "have resisted with all strength and courage in various regions of the planet so as not to be completely engulfed by this utilitarian world. The native peoples resist this attack by the white man because they know he is wrong."[16] The intersection between these points of view – the one looking from the city towards the forest, and the one looking from the forest towards the city – illuminate reality like a lightning bolt cutting through the night sky. Sadly, after the thunder, reality recedes back into darkness, driven by diabolical forces.

The worldview that native peoples offer us through the simple fact of resisting – or (re)existing, as José Celso de Martinez Correia would say – has gradually gained recognition in "literate thinking". Philosophers Michael Hardt and Antonio Negri, for example, in assessing the state of human rights in today's world, which are increasingly constrained by the overwhelming forces of global capital, put forward the hypothesis of a new understanding of the common good that would move beyond the traditional divide between the public and the private in order to give everyone the right to the essentials of life, such as the enjoyment of nature. Among the various forces of resistance and creativity, they introduce Amerindian thought via Eduardo Viveiros de Castro as a contribution to the shaping of a *new biopolitical reason*: "We are now in a position to provisionally offer three features that a biopolitical reason would have to fulfill: setting rationality in the service of life; technique in the service of ecological needs – ecological here understood not only as the preservation of nature, but as the development and reproduction of 'social' relations, as Viveiros de Castro says, between humans and non-humans; and, finally, the accumulation of wealth in the service of the common good."[17]

More recent works pick up on the power in Brazilian thought and art from the period with which we are concerned here, taking up an alternative point of view – the point of view of the *other*, that can be incorporated into an updated hybrid thought, both modern and primitive, or "savage", as Paola Berenstein Jacques puts it: "The artistic discussion, present above all in Tarsila's drawings and paintings and in the poems by Oswald and Cendrars, which were published together (texts/images), brought about an artistic revolution in the country, not only by blending modern – or 'modernist', as the artists declared themselves – thinking with the primitive or wild – conceived here as thought in a wild state –, but also by exercising impure montages."[18] In line with our own way of going about this issue, the author favors an articulation between form of expression and form of content in which these dimensions cannot be taken separately.

What we want to retrieve from modernism is the inversion of a series of ingrained value judgments regarding blacks, natives, mestizos and also dispossessed whites in order to give them visibility and take them as vectors of a new possible society – not a "pure", regressive one, but a mixed-race, advanced, democratic society. *Macunaíma*, by Mário de Andrade, *A favela*, by Tarsila do Amaral, and the project for Vila Monlevade, by Lúcio Costa, are all examples of the aesthetic grandeur that such a formula might achieve by blending foreign expressive forms with subject matter that is rooted in local tradition.[19] It is still a white perspective, but one that tries to find nourishment in other people's food. Thus, it might make sense at this point to go back to the utopia this perspective aims at, turning that nourishment into energy for the new world that we still need to build.

What follows is an attempt to sew by unsewing – from the multiple discourses and works of intellectuals and artists from a century ago – a single representative conception of what we call *Pau-Brasil culture*. In a sphere where metaphors are as operative as the ideas and forms they represent, the image of a patchwork quilt, made of pieces of cloth that one finds here and there, many of them still detached or only partially stitched to the ensemble, may perhaps suggest what we have in mind.

Notes Introduction

1. Lúcio Costa's answer – the "letter/testimony" –, dated February 20, 1948, was included by Geraldo Ferraz in the article published in *O Jornal*, 14 Mar. 1948, quoted in Geraldo Ferraz, "Depoimento do arquiteto Lúcio Costa sobre arquitetura moderna brasileira." Quotes were taken from: Lúcio Costa, *Lúcio Costa: registro de uma vivência*.

2. Otília Beatriz Fiori Arantes, "Lúcio Costa e a *boa causa* da arquitetura moderna," 126.

3. Ibid., 117.

4. See: Oswald Andrade, "Manifesto da poesia Pau-Brasil." Originally published in the Rio de Janeiro newspaper *Correio da Manhã*, in 18 Mar. 1924.

5. In my master's thesis entitled *The primitive man: origin and conformation in the Brazilian intellectual universe (19th and 20th centuries)*, we sought to establish the differences between the pau-brasil manifesto and the anthropophagic manifesto. In the present work, however, we are taking those texts mostly as complementary works, pointing out only the unavoidable distinctions. Quotes were taken from the book: Abilio Guerra, *O primitivismo em Mário de Andrade, Oswald de Andrade e Raul Bopp: origem e conformação no universo intelectual brasileiro.*

6. Abilio Guerra, *Lúcio Costa, modernidade e tradição: montagem discursiva da arquitetura moderna brasileira.*

7. Among them, it is worth highlighting the article by Guilherme Wisnik, which adopts another perspective and has only a few points of contact with our work. Guilherme Wisnik, Plática e anonimato: modernidade e tradição em Lúcio Costa e Mário de Andrade.

8. Jean-Pierre Faye, *Los lenguajes totalitarios*, 116.

9. Jessé Souza, *A elite do atraso: da escravidão à lava jato*, 19.

10. Constitution of the Federative Republic of Brazil, from 1988, Chapter VIII, article 231. The rights of the indigenous peoples are laid down in Chapter VII, which subdivides in articles 231 e 232. The six paragraphs from article 231 give us a good idea of the scope of the acquired rights: "Paragraph 1. Lands traditionally occupied by Indians are those on which they live on a permanent basis, those used for their productive activities, those indispensable to the preservation of the environmental resources necessary for their well-being and for their physical and cultural reproduction, according to their uses, customs and traditions. Paragraph 2. The lands traditionally occupied by Indians are intended for their permanent possession and they shall have the exclusive usufruct of the riches of the soil, the rivers and the lakes existing therein. Paragraph 3. Hydric resources, including energetic potentials, may only be exploited, and mineral riches in Indian land may only be prospected and mined with the authorization of the National Congress,

after hearing the communities involved, and the participation in the results of such mining shall be ensured to them, as set forth by law. Paragraph 4. The lands referred to in this article are inalienable and indisposable and the rights thereto are not subject to limitation. Paragraph 5. The removal of Indian groups from their lands is forbidden, except ad referendum of the National Congress, in case of a catastrophe or an epidemic which represents a risk to their population, or in the interest of the sovereignty of the country, after decision by the National Congress, it being guaranteed that, under any circumstances, the return shall be immediate as soon as the risk ceases. Paragraph 6. Acts with a view to occupation, domain and possession of the lands referred to in this article or to the exploitation of the natural riches of the soil, rivers and lakes existing therein, are null and void, producing no legal effects, except in case of relevant public interest of the Union, as provided by a supplementary law and such nullity and voidness shall not create a right to indemnity or to sue the Union, except in what concerns improvements derived from occupation in good faith, in the manner prescribed by law."

11. Article 232. "The Indians, their communities and organizations have standing under the law to sue to defend their rights and interests, the Public Prosecution intervening in all the procedural acts."

12. Among others, see: Eduardo Viveiros de Castro, *Arawete: os deuses canibais.*

13. Eduardo Viveiros de Castro, *O recado da mata*, 23.

14. Davi Kopenawa and Bruce Albert, *A queda do céu: palavras de um xamã yanomami*, 480. This extract was highlighted by Eduardo Viveiro de Castro in his introduction, but our quote is a bit longer.

15. Viveiros de Castro, *O recado da mata*, 19.

16. Ailton Krenak, *A vida não é util*, 112. From the same author, see: Ailton Krenak, *Ideias para adiar o fim do mundo.*

17. Michael Hardt, and Antonio Negri, *Bem-estar comum*, 147.

18. Paola Berenstein Jacques, *Pensamentos selvagens: montagem de uma outra herança*, 259.

19. In the famous chapter 7, "Macumba", Macunaíma resorts to black religiosity to face the giant Paimã: "The other day the weather was completely cold and the hero decided to take revenge on Venceslau Petro Pietra by hitting him to warm up. However, this was due to not having strength, what he had was very afraid of the giant. Well then he decided to take a train and go to Rio de Janeiro to help himself from Exu the Devil in whose honor a macumba was held the other day". Mário de Andrade, *Macunaíma: o herói sem nenhum caráter*, 56-57.

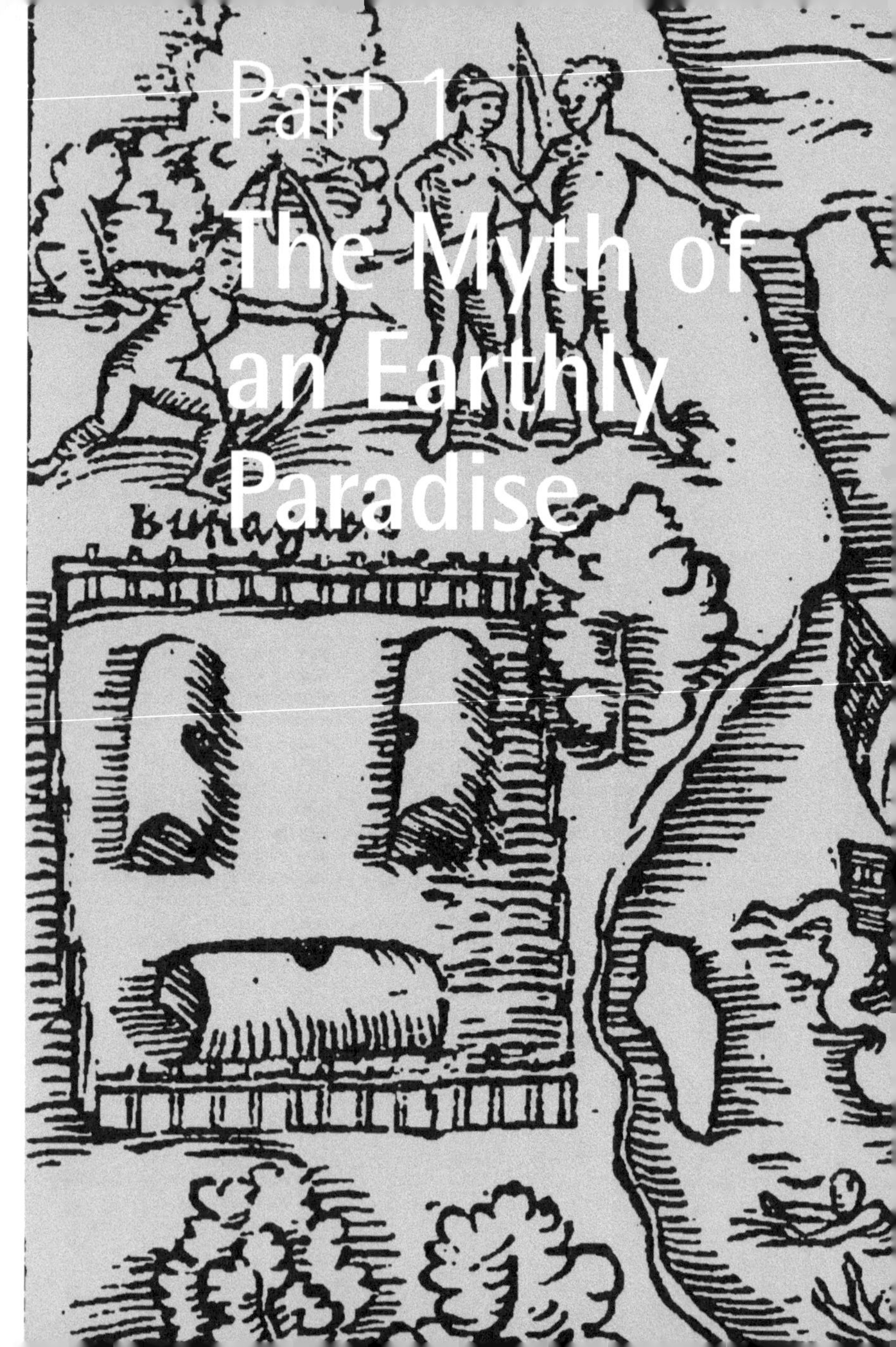

Part 1
The Myth of an Earthly Paradise

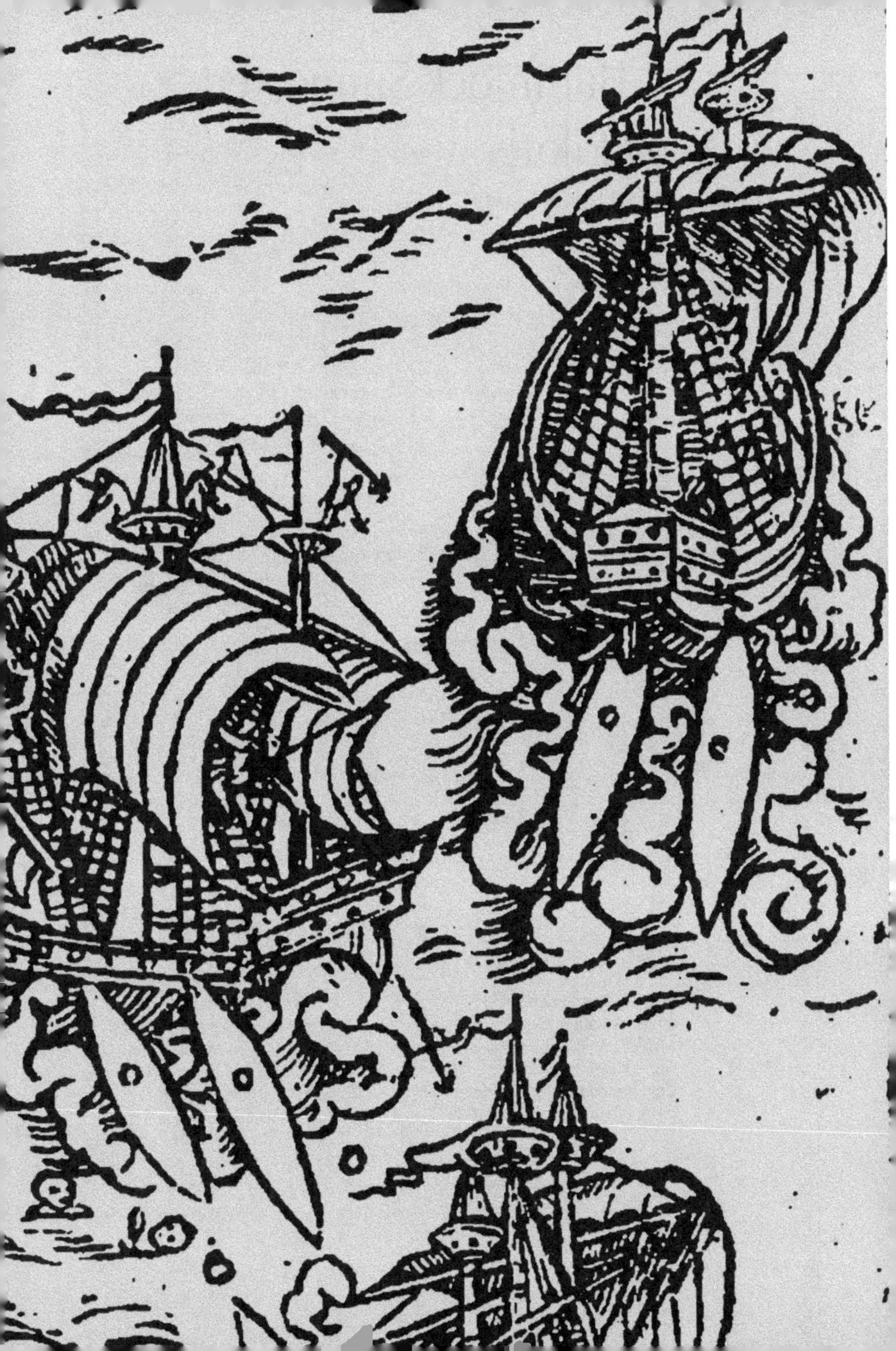

A Hammock Supported by Pilotis

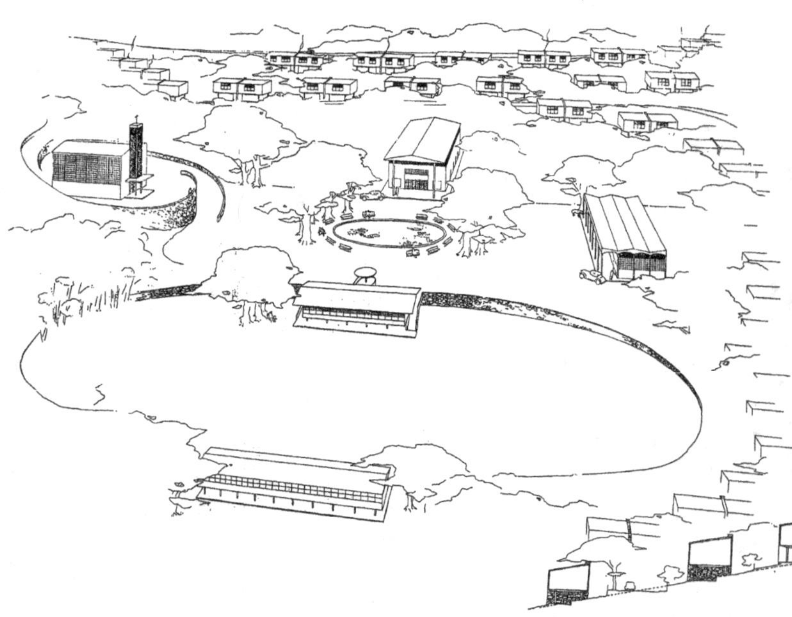

Vila Monlevade, general implementation perspective, Monlevade MG. Lúcio Costa, 1934. *Revista da Diretoria de Engenharia da Prefeitura do Distrito Federal*, vol. III, no. 3, Rio de Janeiro, May 1936

On the two previous pages Navios europeus na costa brasileira (European ships on the Brazilian coast), detail. STADEN, Hans. *Warhaftig Historia und beschreibung eyner Landtschafft der Wilden*, 1557, 27

*The hero lived a quiet life, happily lazing away the days
in his hammock, killing sugar ants and taking little noisy
sips of* pajuari; *when he felt like singing, accompanying
himself with his* viola-de-cocho, *woods resounded with
delight, lulling to sleep all such pests as snakes, ticks,
mosquitoes, ants and malignant gods. At night Ci would
return and, reeking with the balsam she smeared on her
bleeding wounds, she would climb into the hammock
she herself had woven with strings of hair. The pair
would fool around, giggling and teasing each other.
They went on giggling, close together, for a long time.
Ci exhaled such smells that Macunaíma felt dizzy and
weak.*
Mário de Andrade, *Macunaíma*, 1928[1]

In 1934, the Belgo-Mineira Steel Company ran an architectural and urban design competition for the construction
of a small town that would house its employees. Among the
competitors we find Lúcio Costa (1902-1998), who showed
up with nothing but a text and a few sketches to the jury,[2]
thus anticipating by twenty years the radical gesture that
marked his participation in the competition for the Brasília
Pilot Plan. The relevance of this later competition – entailing nothing less than the construction of the new capital
of Brazil – led most competitors to come up with drawings
and memorials of exquisitely technical and formal precision.
Lúcio Costa, on the other hand, presented a short written
document describing the spatiality of the new city and the
daily life of its inhabitants along with a series of freehand
sketches.[3] He was hoping that the jury would be able to
discern and pick up among the many proposals the vigorous
idea to be developed satisfactorily at the appropriate time.
His victory granted him the rare glory of designing the capital of his own country and actually seeing it built.

His success here contrasts with the results of the competition promoted by the Belgo-Mineira company in the 1930s.

At the time, his work was ignored and ranked last.[4] Had it not been published two years later by the *Revista da Diretoria de Engenharia*, associated with the Federal District's municipal government, it would likely have fallen into oblivion. The periodical, which would become the main publication to promote Brazilian modern architecture in the 1930s, had among its founders engineer Carmen Portinho (1903-2001), who would later become famous as a structural engineer, building the works of her husband, Affonso Eduardo Reidy (1909-1964). The influence that Lúcio Costa already enjoyed at the time on young architects who advocated for this new architecture was perhaps reason enough for the publication of the Vila Monlevade project. However, the fact that Lúcio Costa – known for his introspective temperament and propensity for solitude – agreed that a work despised by the jury should nevertheless be made public points to the author's keen desire to publicize the ideas contained therein. Two years after the publication, when dealing with the traditional architecture of the colonial past, Lúcio Costa mentions his proposal, betraying a bit of resentment for the neglect with which it had been treated:

> "The ingenious process by which they are made – clay reinforced with wood – has something of our reinforced concrete; with due care, shifting the floor away from the terrain and conveniently whitewashing the walls to avoid humidity and kissing bugs, it should be adopted for summer houses and economic constructions in general. This is what we sought to do for the working-class village of Monlevade, near Sabará, at the invitation of the Belgo-Mineira Steel Company – however, the project was not taken seriously, as you can see."[5]

Lúcio Costa's Vila Monlevade would benefit from recent advances in modern urbanism, with the functional layout of the buildings based on their programs, marking a clear

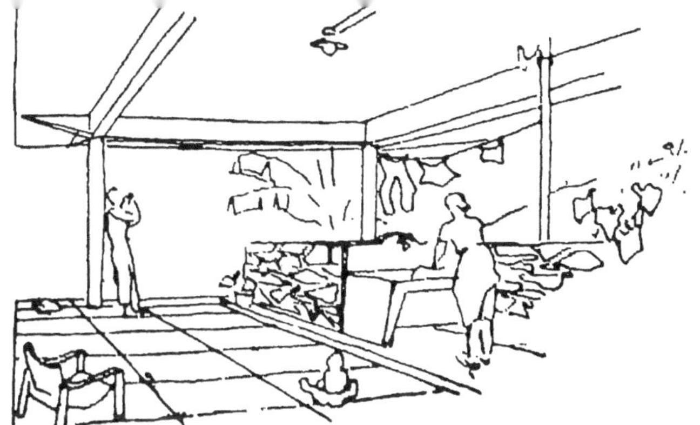

Vila Monlevade, worker housing, laundry area, Monlevade MG. Lúcio Costa, 1934. *Revista da Diretoria de* *Engenharia da Prefeitura do Distrito Federal*, vol. III, no. 3, Rio de Janeiro, May 1936

distinction between the housing area and the civic center, where collective equipment – cinema, church, market, school and social club – would be located. On the other hand, the workers' village should retain that typical aspect of small Brazilian towns, marked by improvisation, irregularity and dispersion: "*streets* should preserve, as much as possible, those unpretentious features peculiar to *roads* – instead of sidewalks, there should be simple paths made out of concrete slabs with grass joints in order to avoid future cracks: an update on the old *capistranas*."[6]

Here *simplicity* and *clarity* should not be confused with poverty or paucity. These are rather noble values that inform a good synthesis between material goods – buildings, equipment, objects – and individual and collective values of a moral and psychic order – tranquility, familiarity and companionship. This simplicity and clarity are present above all in the houses, irregularly arranged amongst the trees, yet they are also dispersed throughout the envisioned scenario, as though they were positive values to be conquered: "Regarding the plans for the other buildings – warehouse, school, club, cinema, church –, it is not necessary to comment on them here: the drawings express them more effectively; we must only call attention to the their *simplicity* and *clarity*, qualities that, of course, are reflected in the cuts and elevations. While attributing a purpose-based character to each building, we try to maintain, in all of them, that unity, that *familiar aspect* to which we have already pointed and which, we repeat, is the staple of authentic styles."[7] In this search for familiarity, primitive simplicity and modernist clarity act as antidotes to the disruptive complexity and convulsive estrangement of modern life. The secret for a happy community lies in its ability to revive, from positive modern elements dispersed in the contemporary world, the utopian essence of a distant past transmitted to us by tradition.

Lúcio Costa's urban plan meets three requirements: escape from any rigidity in the design so as to better adjust the implantation in the local topography; cost saving, as fewer areas needed to be leveled; and the least possible damage to the natural beauty of the place. The adoption of the structure of Maison *Dom-Ino*[8] by Le Corbusier for the buildings mostly preserves the conditions of the natural terrain, as the use of *pilotis* maintains the natural slopes, particularly in the houses. While in Corbusier the suspension of the volumes aims at a functional hierarchy of paths as well as the use of the unoccupied areas, Lúcio Costa has in mind the beauty of the landscape and the integration of the built set with the surrounding nature. It is, therefore, an adaptation of a foreign constructive system to a particular way of accommodating man in the territory. While for Le Corbusier the *pilotis* is a functional urban artifact, for Lúcio Costa it fulfills a purpose associated with the cultural dimension of the landscape. The good relationship between man and his natural habitat – necessary for the constitution of a rooted and consistent culture – becomes viable thanks to the correct choice of a modern constructive element.

What is sought is to integrate the artifacts of modern civilization with a primitive spiritual and cultural foundation,

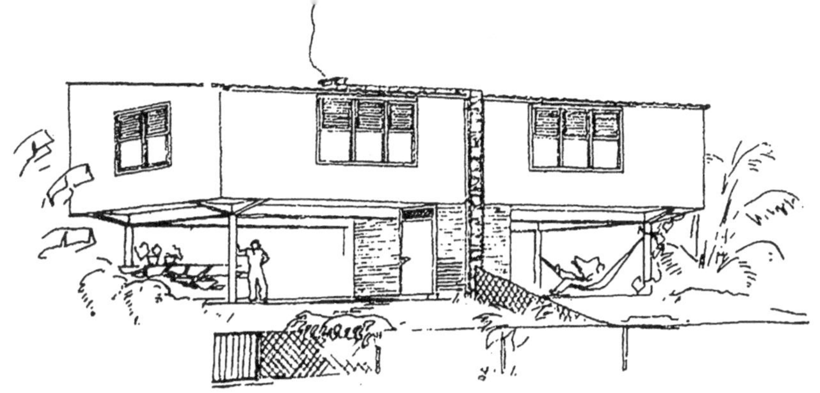

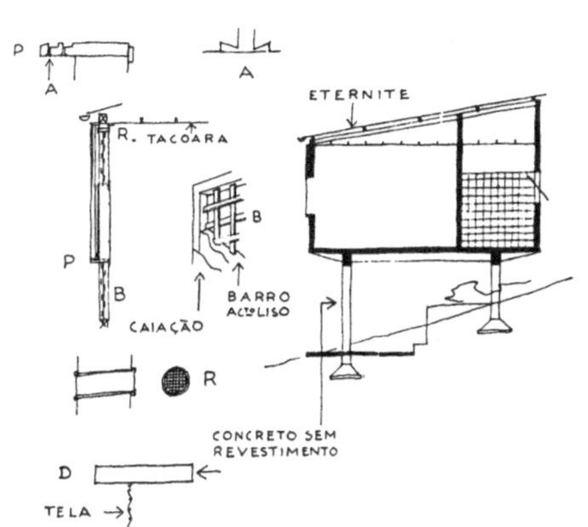

Vila Monlevade, worker housing, perspective, technical details, and floor plans of the ground and first floors. Monlevade MG. Lúcio Costa, 1934. *Revista da Diretoria de Engenharia da Prefeitura do Distrito Federal*, vol. III, no. 3, Rio de Janeiro, May 1936

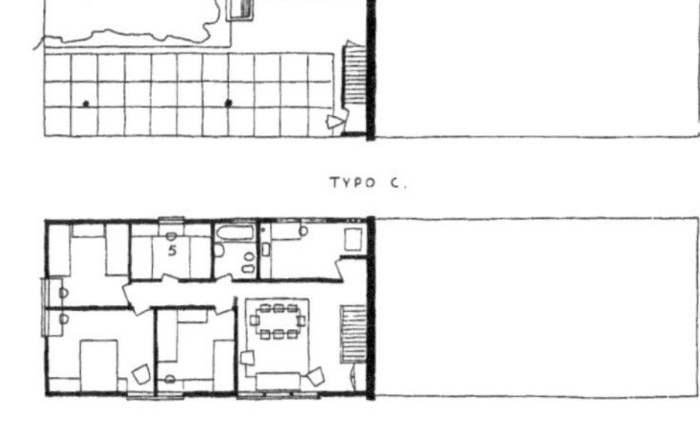

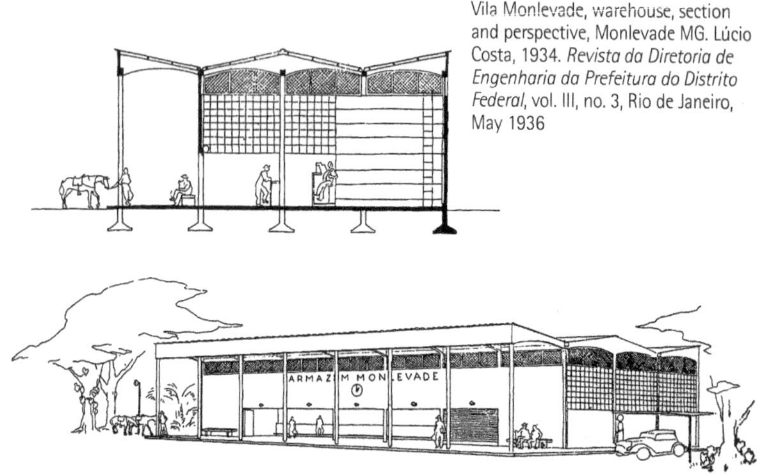

Vila Monlevade, warehouse, section
and perspective, Monlevade MG. Lúcio
Costa, 1934. *Revista da Diretoria de
Engenharia da Prefeitura do Distrito
Federal*, vol. III, no. 3, Rio de Janeiro,
May 1936

sheltering contemporary man amidst the exuberant and
portentous natural environment of the tropics. From a
technical point of view, the workers' residence is a sum that
adds structures in reinforced concrete, roof with Eternit
tiles, reinforced clay as a sealing element and openings with
wooden shutters on the windows. For the daily comfort of
its residents, each unit has a bathroom, standard furniture
and simple and effective household items. On the other
hand, the adoption of semi-detached houses irregularly
arranged on the plot guarantees, from a spiritual point of
view, greater intimacy and relative isolation for the residents.
This housing model thus fulfills the twofold role of assuring
the Vila Monlevade worker access to the undeniable benefits
of industrial society while also enjoying the pleasures of a
natural environment.

The other buildings – club, school, warehouse, cinema
and church – are architectural objects of a simple and synthetic nature, marked by the use of reinforced concrete
structures, reinforced clay as sealing element and window
shutters. Larger buildings, with diversified programs, exhibit

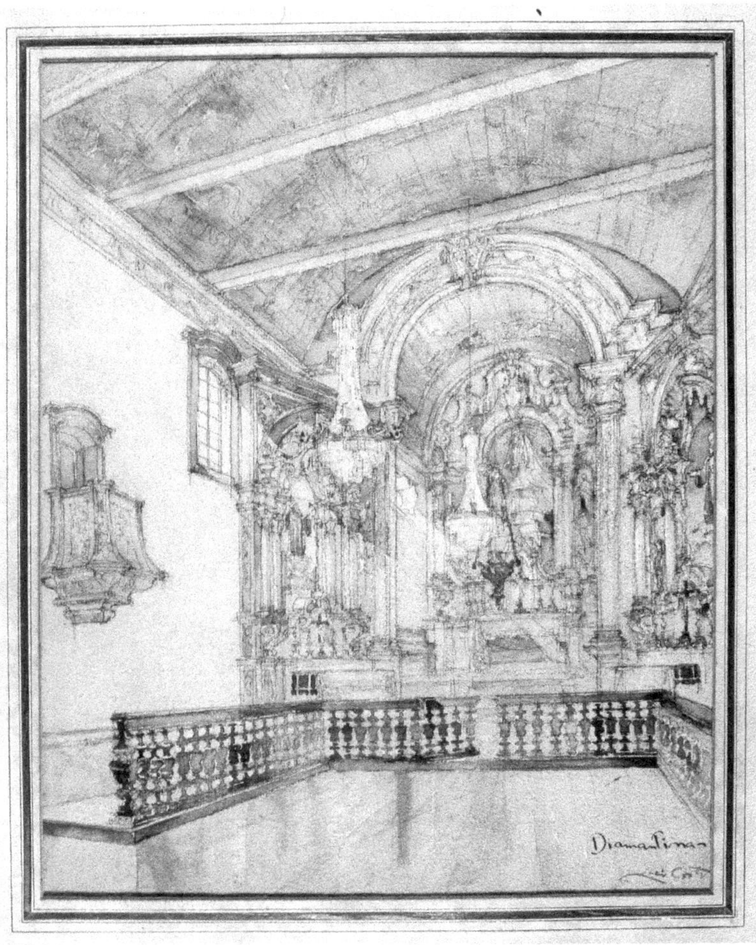

Igreja do Carmo, interior, Diamantina
MG. Lúcio Costa, 1922. Casa da
Arquitectura Archive

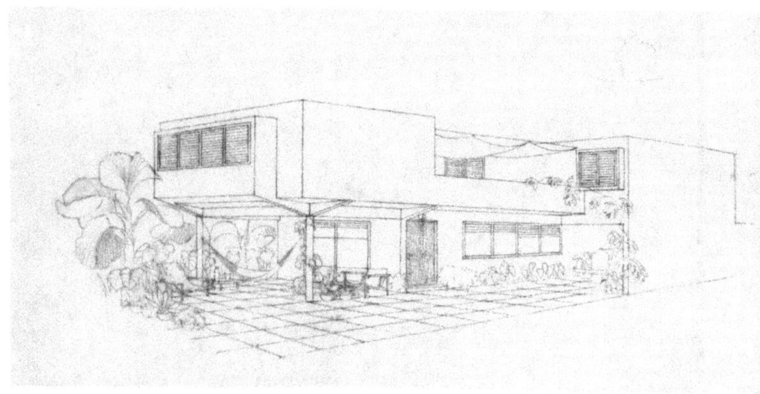

Ownerless Houses 1 and 3,
perspectives. Lúcio Costa, 1932–1936.
Casa da Arquitectura Archive

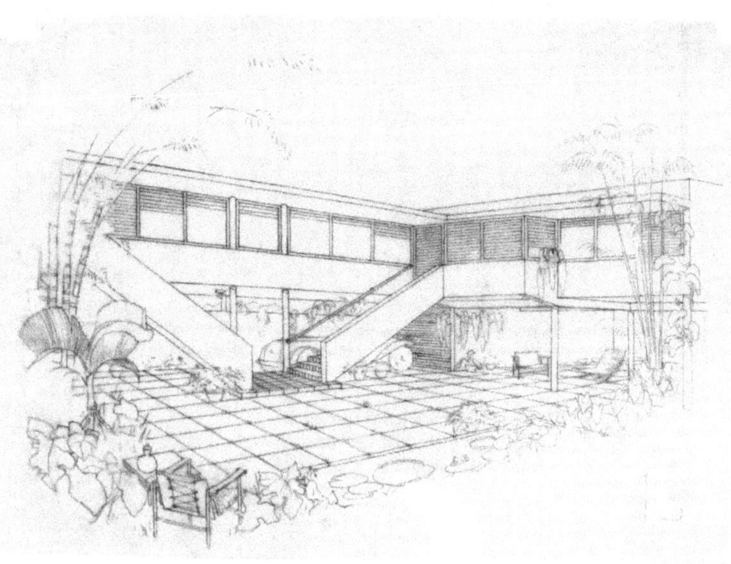

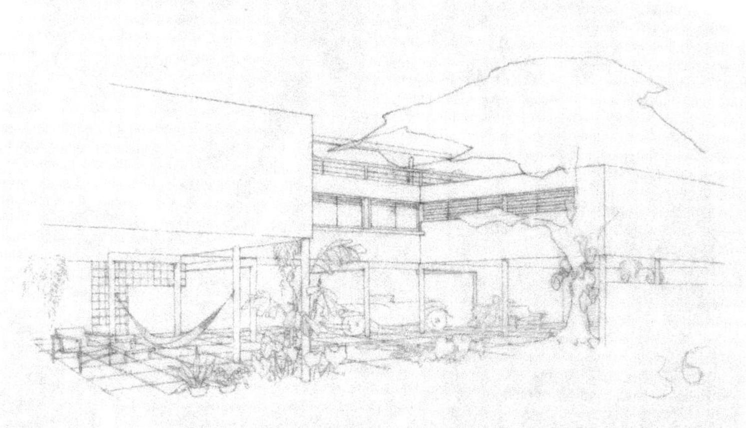

Ownerless House 2, perspective.
Lúcio Costa, 1932-1936; Park Hotel,
ground and first floor plans, Nova

Friburgo, RJ. Lúcio Costa, 1940. Casa
da Arquitectura Archive

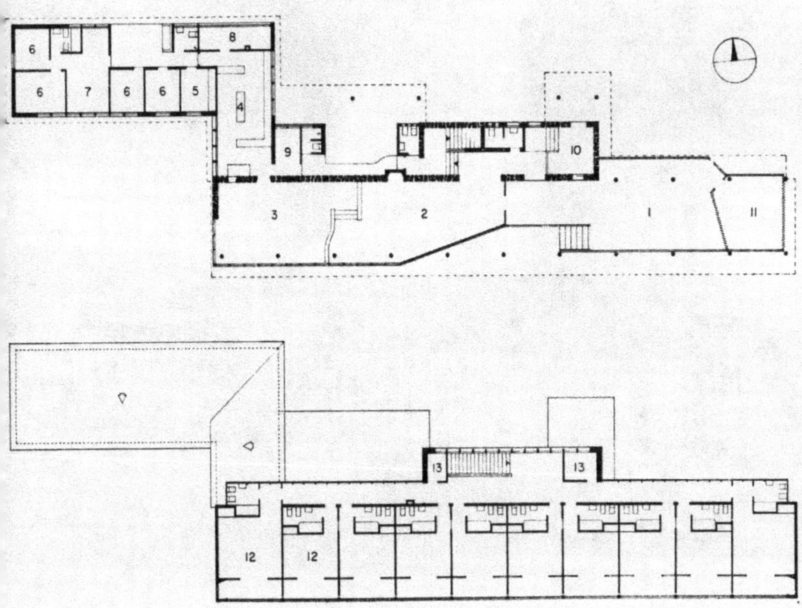

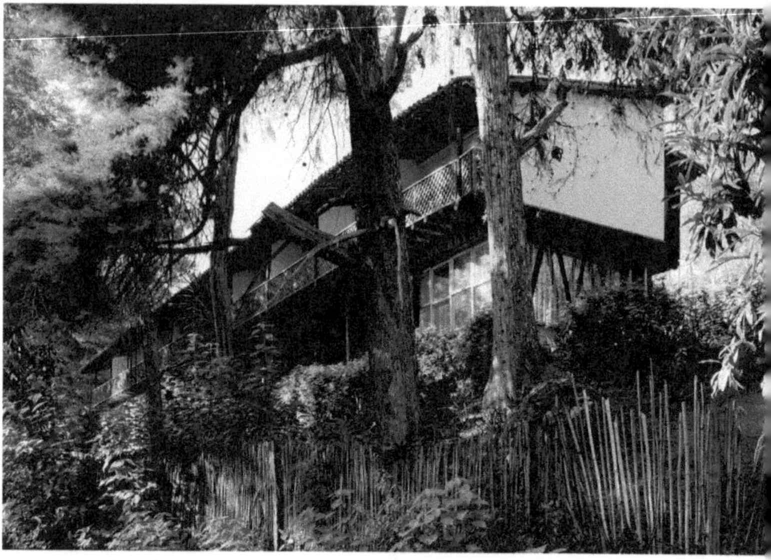

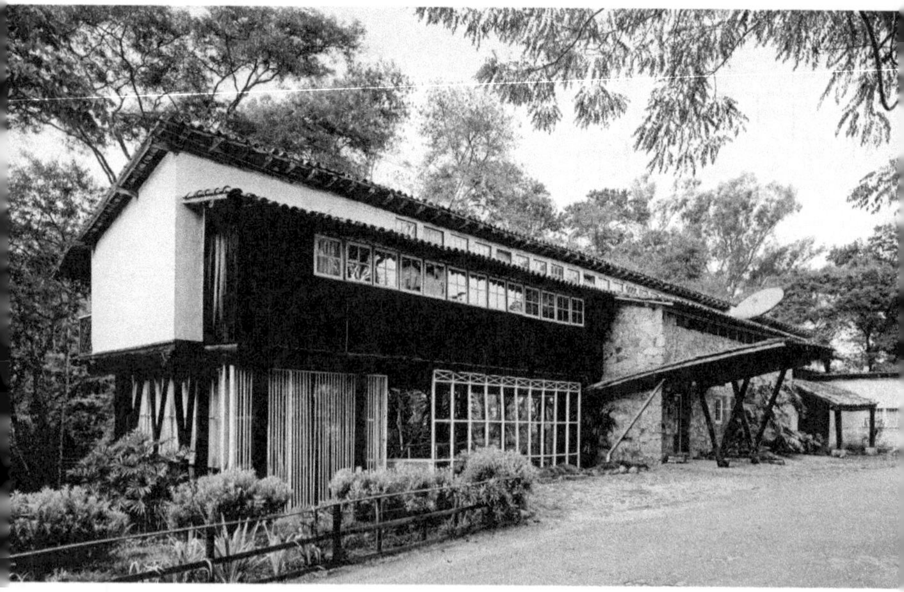

Park Hotel, Nova Friburgo, RJ. Lúcio
Costa, 1940. Photos by Nelson Kon

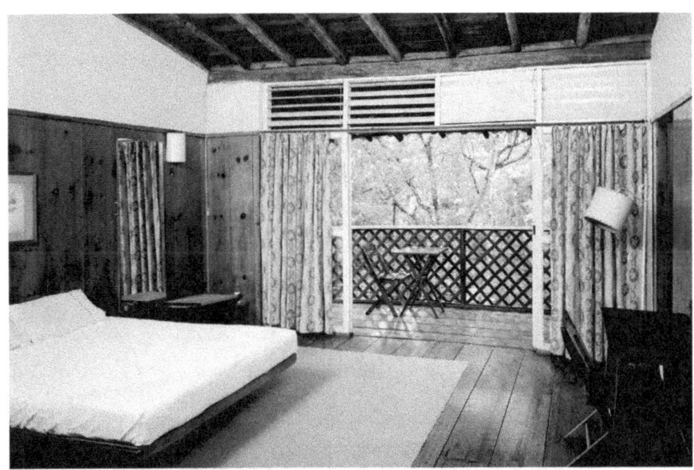

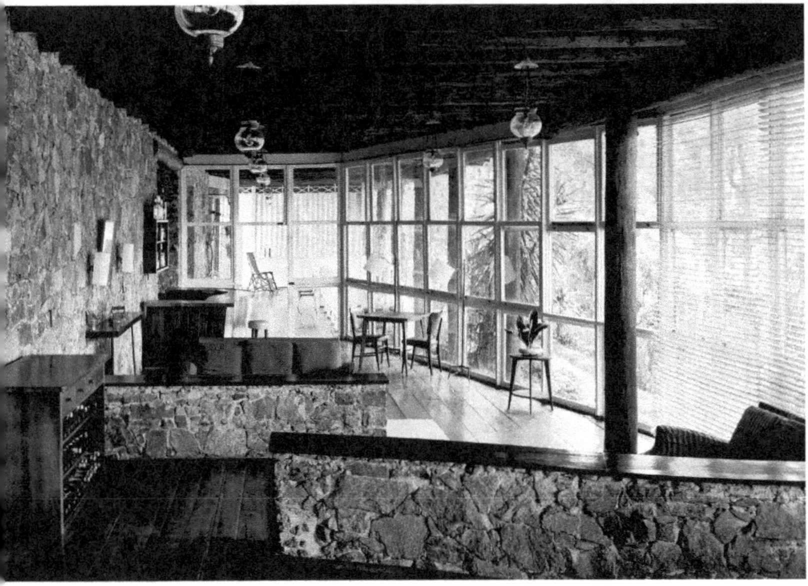

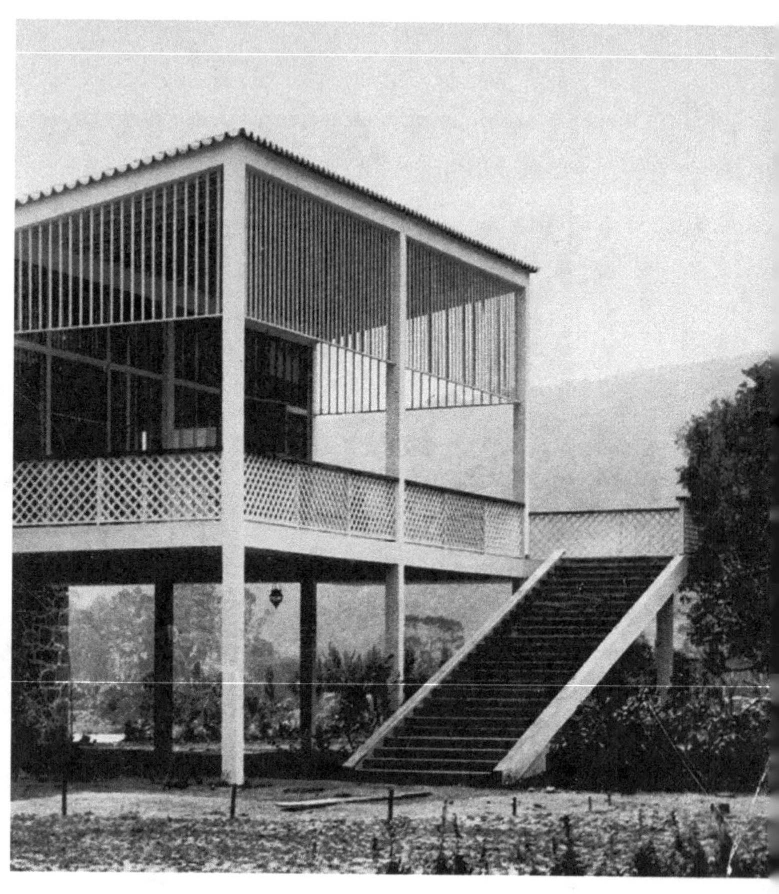

Saavedra House, photo of the balcony
and drawings of details and balcony,
Corrêas RJ. Lúcio Costa, 1940's. Casa
da Arquitectura Archive

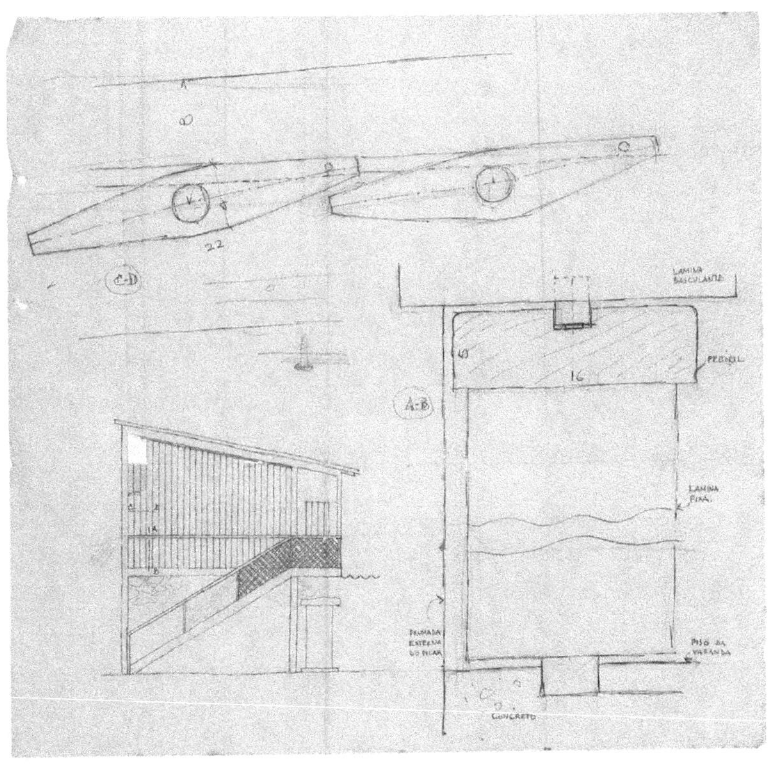

Saavedra House, perspective, elevation,
and photo of the balcony, Corrêas RJ.
Lúcio Costa, 1940's. Casa da Arquitectura
Archive

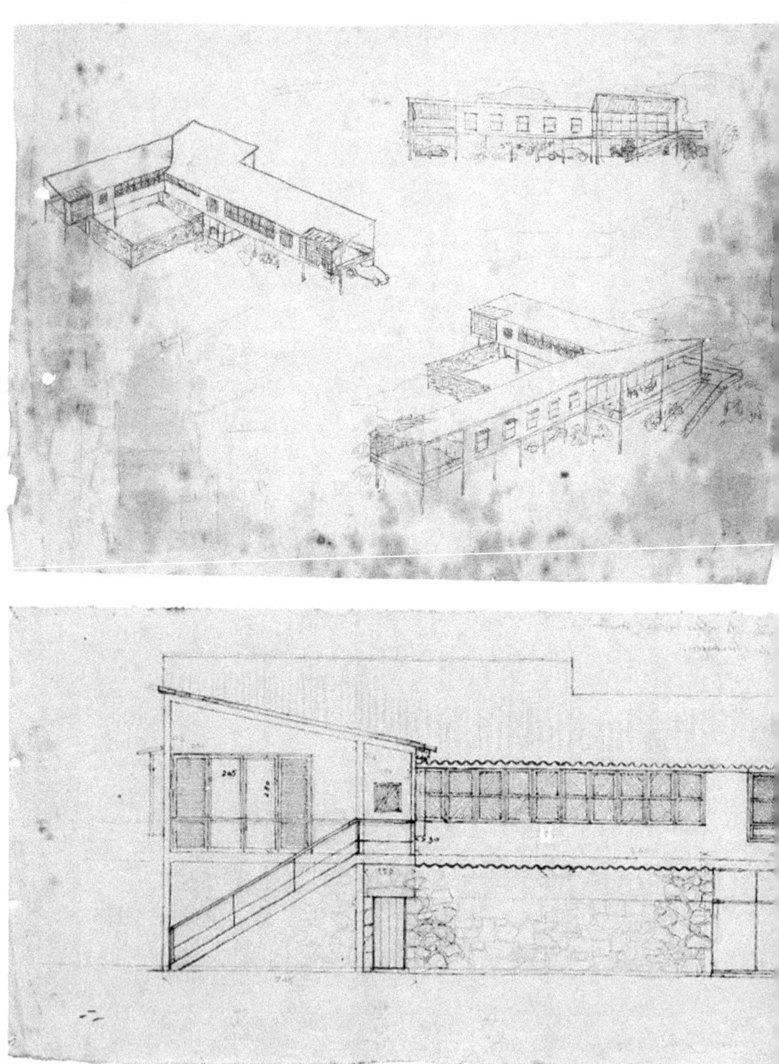

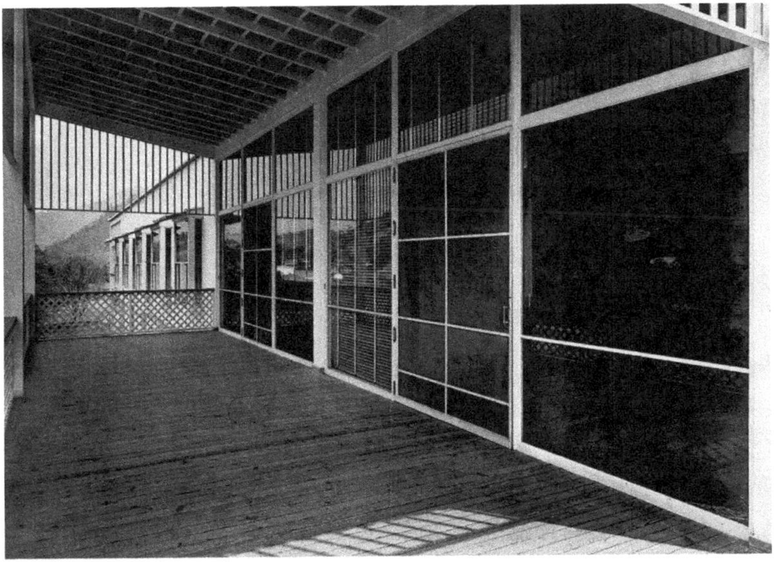

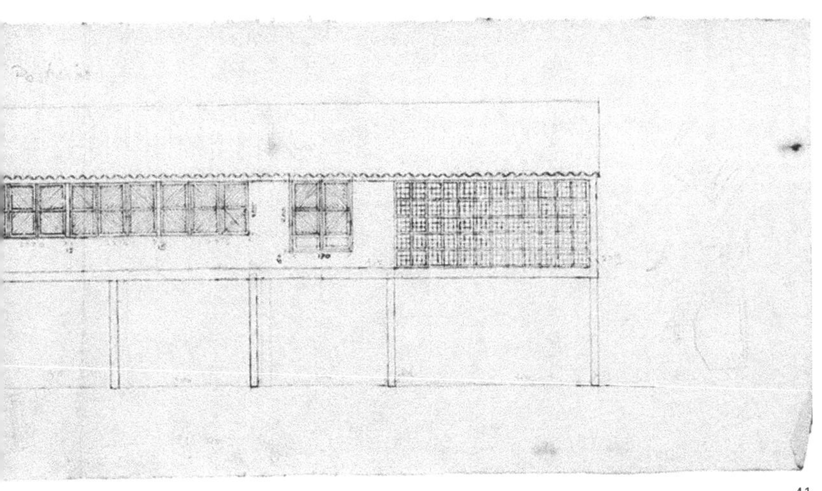

Student House, site plan, perspectives, and floor plans of the ground, standard, and first floors, University City, Paris. Lúcio Costa, 1952. Casa da Arquitectura Archive

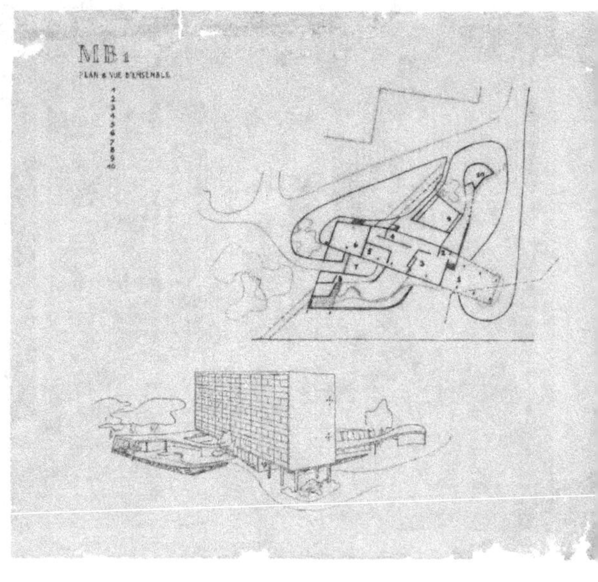

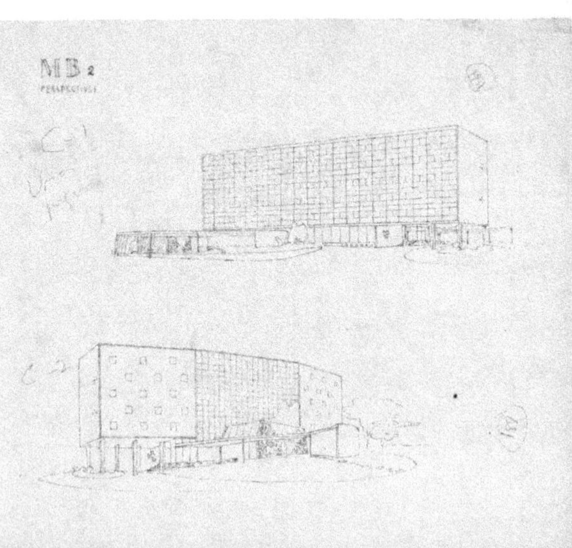

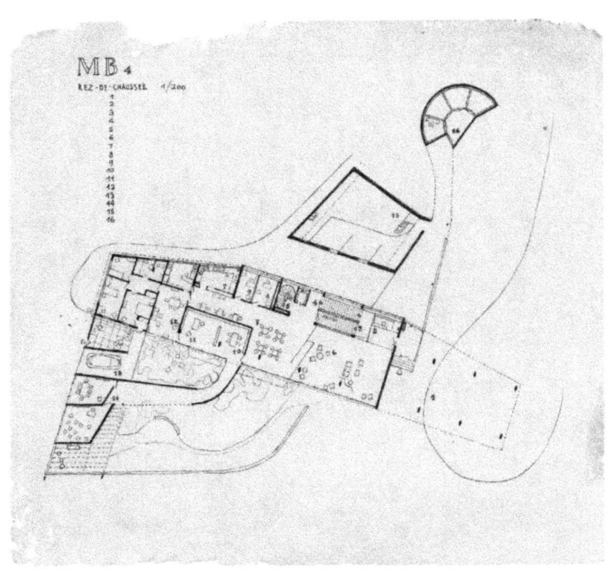

MB 4
REZ-DE-CHAUSSÉE   1/200

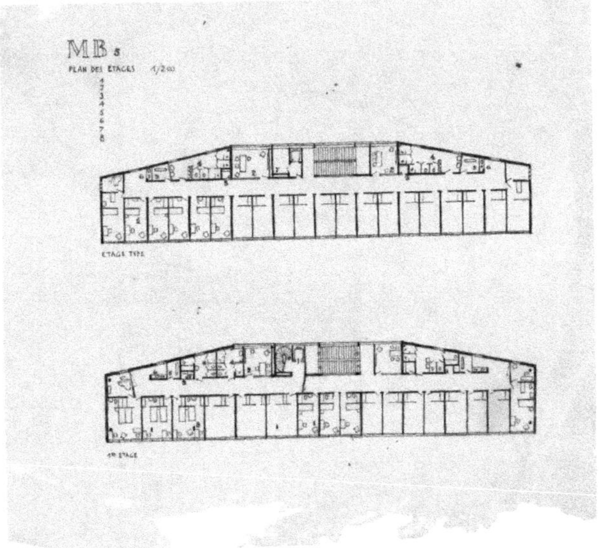

MB 5
PLAN DES ÉTAGES   1/200
ÉTAGE TYPE
1er ÉTAGE

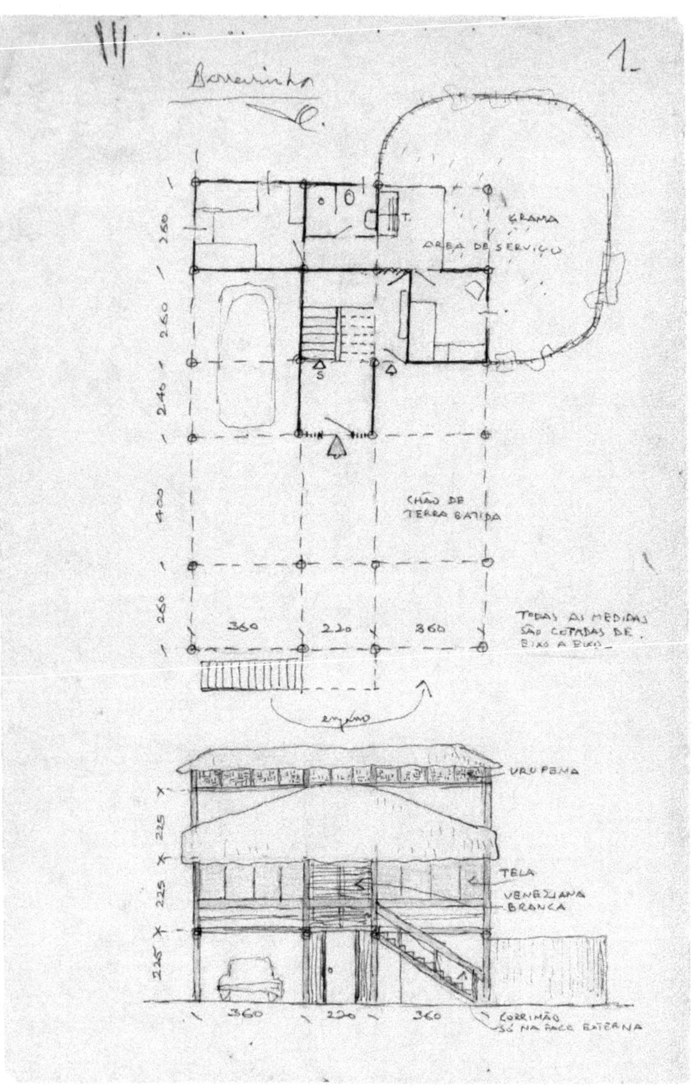

Barrerinha
GRAMA
ÁREA DE SERVIÇO
T.
S
CHÃO DE
TERRA BATIDA
TODAS AS MEDIDAS
SÃO COTADAS DE
EIXO A EIXO
360
220
360
2.60
2.60
2.40
4.00
2.60
URUPEMA
TELA
VENEZIANA
BRANCA
225
225
225
225
360
220
360
CORRIMÃO
SÓ NA FACE EXTERNA

44

Thiago de Mello House, ground floor
plan and elevation; section and
perspective, Barreirinha AM. Lúcio
Costa, 1978. Casa da Arquitectura
Archive

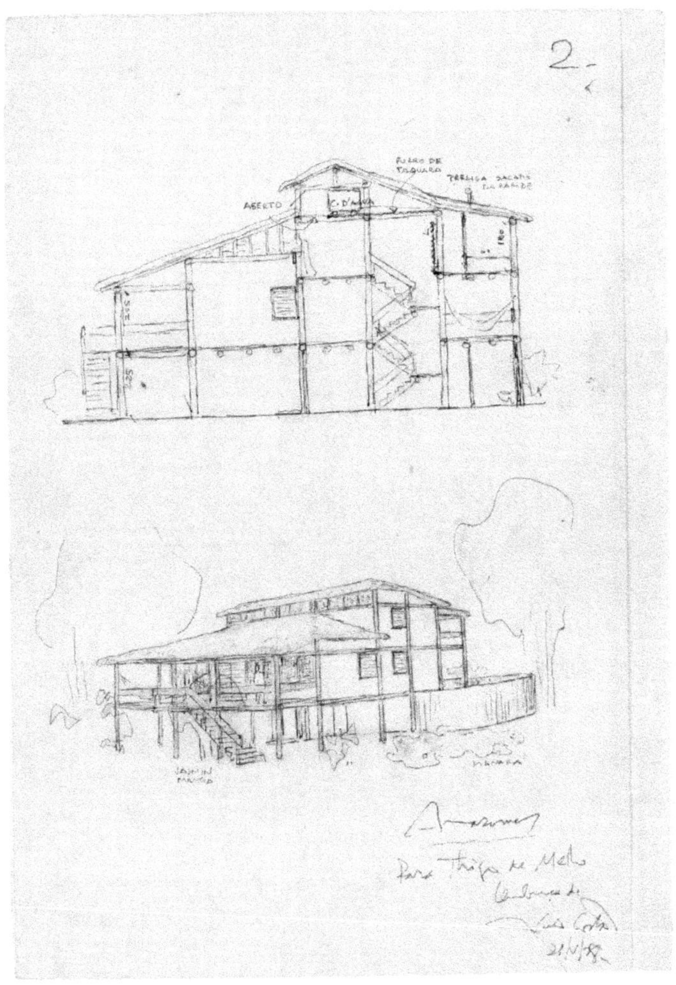

Thiago de Mello House, first floor plan
and section; second floor plan and
elevation, Barreirinha AM. Lúcio Costa,
1978. Casa da Arquitectura Archive

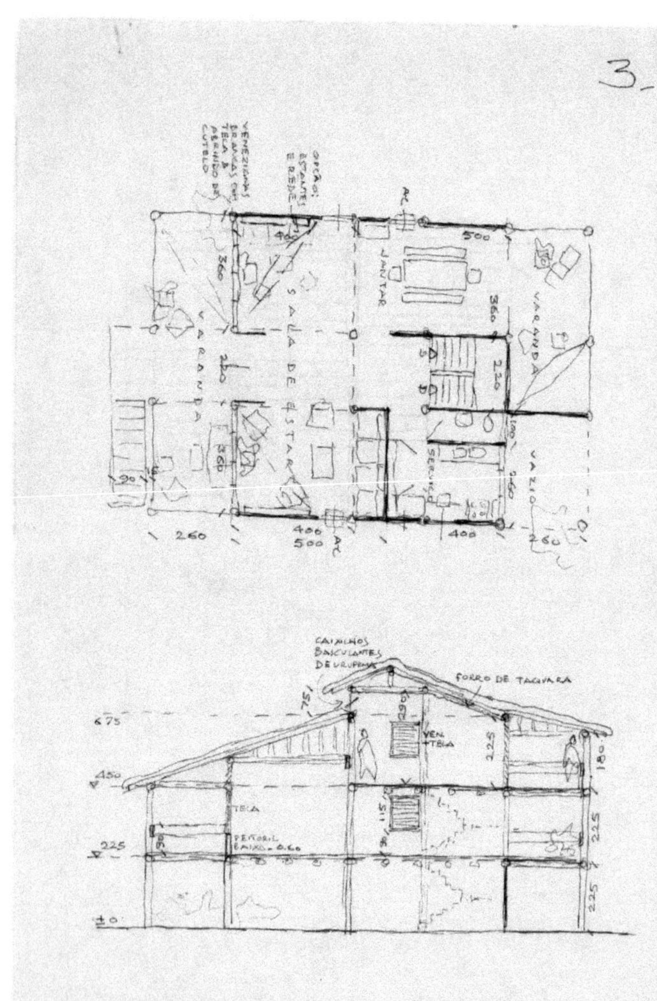

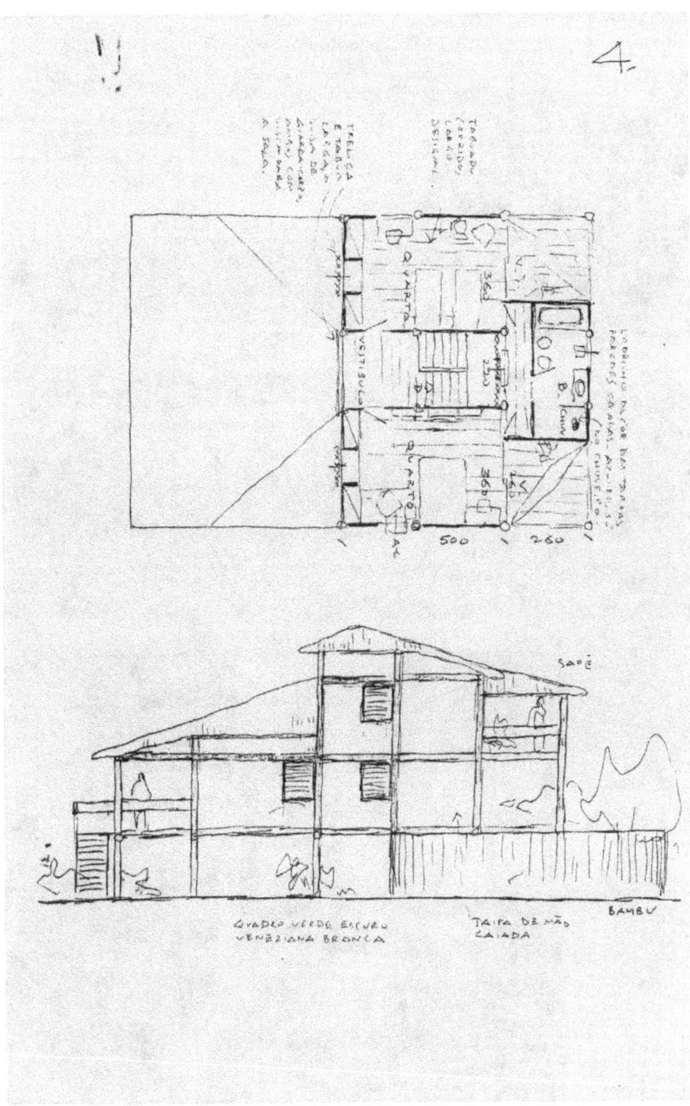

QUARTO
VESTÍBULO
B. CHUV
500
260
SAPÉ
QUADRO VERDE ESCURO
VENEZIANA BRANCA
TAIPA DE MÃO
CAIADA
BAMBU

Thiago de Mello House, Barreirinha AM.
Lúcio Costa, 1978. Photos by Hugo Segawa

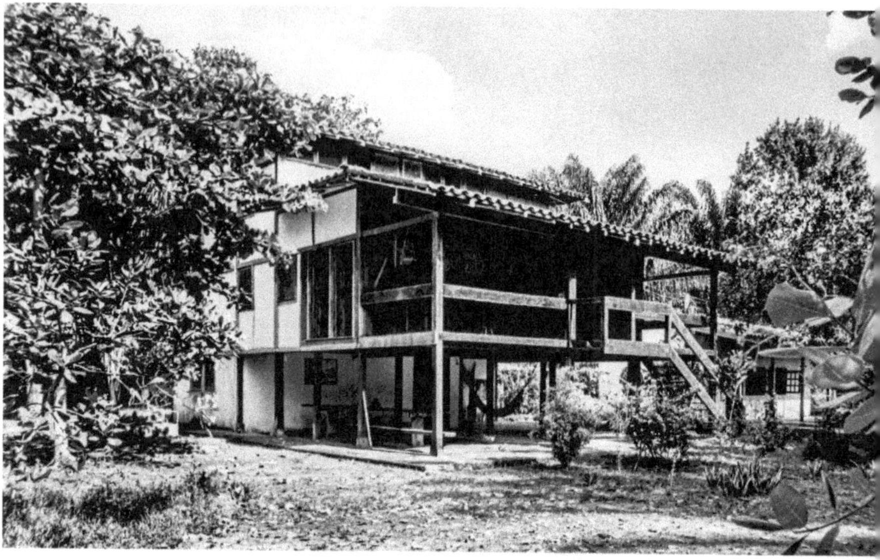

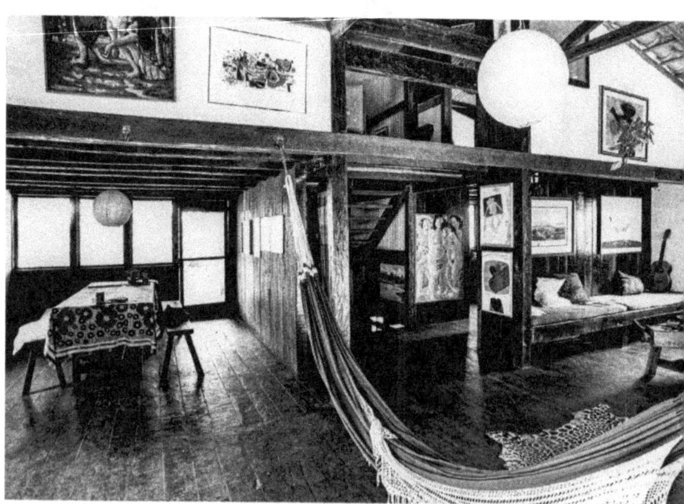

greater variation in the closings – hinged windows, wooden gratings, sash windows – and in the accesses, with ramps, bridges and staircases. Here, too, one can attest to the goal of adapting the buildings to the irregular topography: "For the social club and the school we had in mind the possibility of access from different levels, thus making it easy to adapt them to the place."[9] The quite simple detailing and finishing of the social club suit both everyday use and festive moments: "the ballroom would be entirely whitewashed, with the casings painted in blue, keeping the shutters and door frames in the natural color of the cedar, finished only with boiled oil. Decoration for parties would be made with paper flowers, streamers, etc., creating large festoons hanging from the ceiling, thus seeking to preserve that somewhat clumsy *charm*, peculiar to countryside festivities."[10] Addressing a program consistent with modern life – through access to goods, services and entertainment that only exist in cities of a certain size –, the buildings are accommodated in the territory in a calm and peaceful way, without any grandiloquence jeopardizing the simple life of the its residents.

The attempt to induce the residents of the village to a particular type of individual behavior and collective coexistence is visible. In the functional plans for the different architectural programs, in the unconditional use of standard furniture and in the prohibition against *bizarre* pruning of trees and shrubs proposed by Lúcio Costa to the future managers of Monlevade, one can glimpse a pedagogical vision similar to that of the European avant-garde, which sees in the conditioning of habits and sensibilities a powerful lever for the reconciliation between the industrial city and collective and individual human values. Faced with the brutal transformation of cities and the new experiences that it brought about, a belief emerges regarding the obsolescence of traditional forms of knowledge transmission and the need for new educational approaches and methods to deal with problems and demands that did not exist before and that were now being

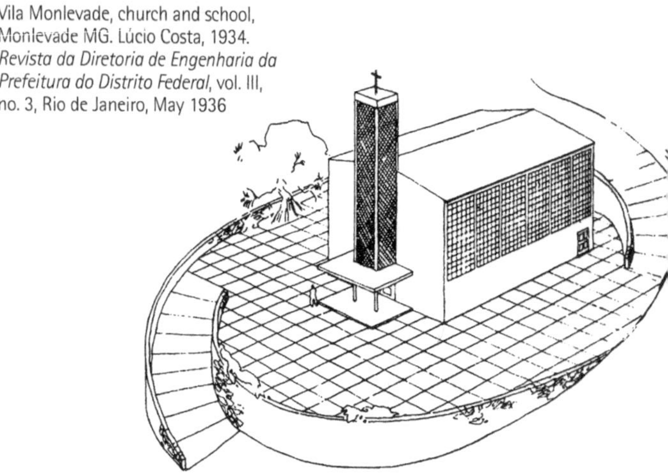

engendered by the new *status quo*. In Europe, the most
widespread expression of this eagerness to teach how to live
in the new world is represented by the Bauhaus collective,
but several other pedagogical formulations were in vogue,
with greater or lesser penetration.[11] Here lies a deep distrust
regarding the ability of the common man to deal with the
urban and existential problems in which he finds himself
entangled. Almost two decades after Monlevade, Lúcio Costa
maintains this disbelief:

> "The relevant populations ignore both the general princi-
> ples on which this new urban design is based, as well as
> the comprehensive and detailed solutions that contem-
> porary technology offers to resolve the housing issue;
> ignoring these principles and solutions, the public is not
> in a position to foresee with the necessary objectivity
> and clarity this different style of living — a balanced and
> serene style, precisely the opposite of the feverish agi-
> tation erroneously associated with the idea of *modern
> life*. And if they do not foresee it, they cannot yearn for

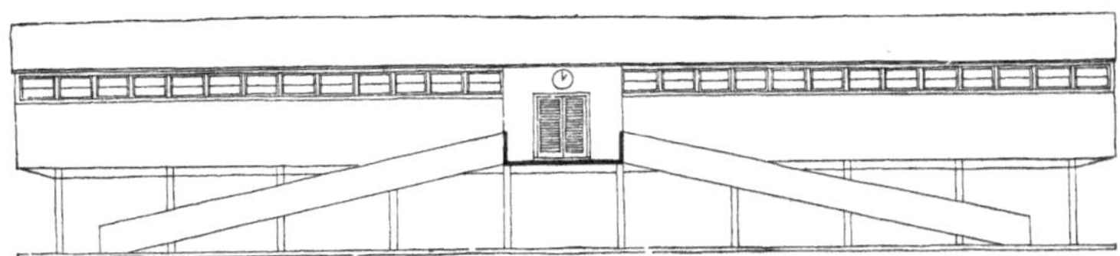

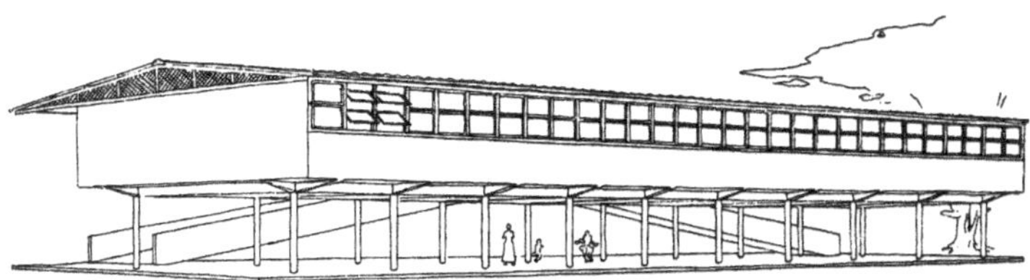

it; if they do not yearn for it, they will have no reason to claim what is rightfully due to them".[12]

Thus, the small town idealized by Lúcio Costa is the product of a synthesis between seemingly disparate elements and values: concrete and clay, asbesto ceiling tiles and wooden shutters, pilotis and mashrabiya, countryside festivities and standard furniture, rural roads and modern urbanization principles... This scenario is inhabited by a man who is both bucolic and urban, with a humble, almost rustic disposition, and yet engaged with the achievements of the new age. This is a microcosm where a silent and somewhat melancholic happiness reigns, where *new elements* appear as if touched by solitude and nostalgia for a world perhaps buried in a forgotten past. The vision of an earthly paradise that settlers and explorers cast over the unknown land, this lush empire of virgin woodland, resonates in this search for peace and warmth. We can discern here some of the elements, conceptions and motifs coming from different traditions which the late Middle Ages and the Renaissance blended in

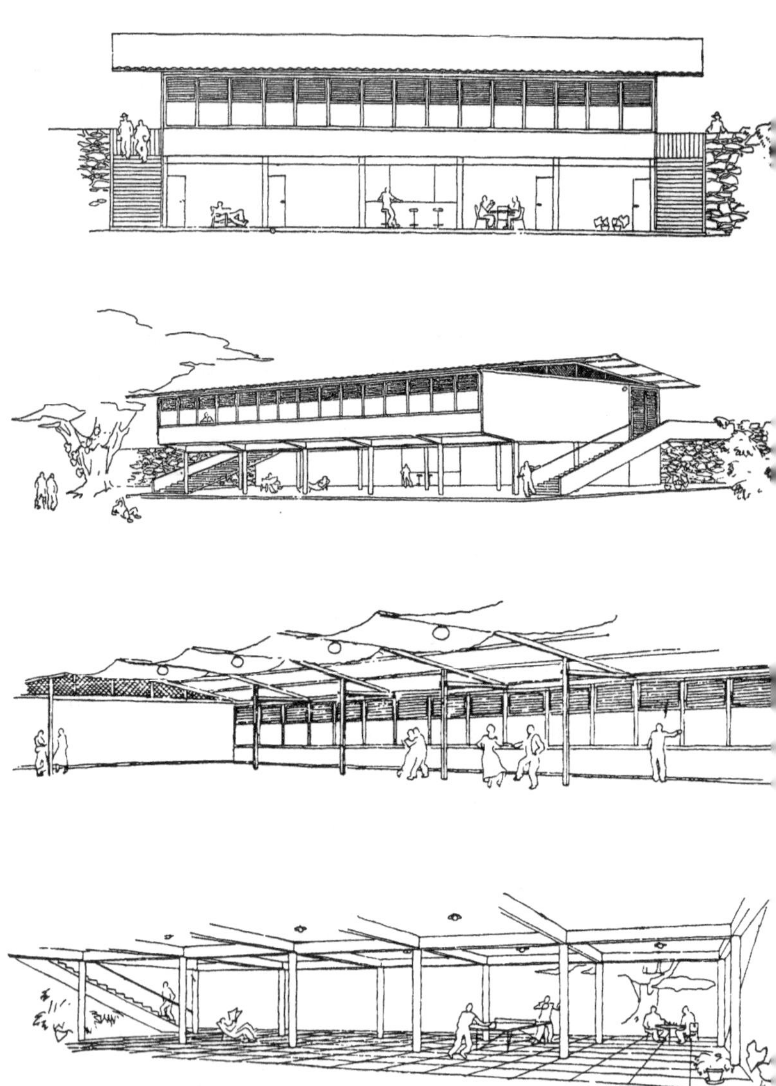

order to describe the paradisiacal locus: it is neither cold nor hot; its inhabitants laze away in their hammocks enjoying the "perennial spring or a temperature that is always the same, free from the variety of seasons found in the European climate, with leafy forests of tasty fruits and fertile meadows, eternally green or sprinkled with multicolored and scented flowers, crisscrossed by copious waters."[13]

The ensemble echoes a certain *ethos*, a certain way of going about life, which oscillates between tropical laziness as expressed in the Tupi-Guarani hammock and the electrifying modern enjoyment of ballrooms and movie goers. The people of Monlevade enjoy a life where the *simplicity* of spiritual values and the *clarity* of everyday gestures prevail, and the sum of each individual intimacy makes up a community that peacefully enjoys the leisure of non-working hours. "The only possible happiness for those who will certainly have to live there all their days, silently contributing to the well-being of so many others."[14] A small world, perfect and serene, insulated from historical corruption and decay, a sort of monad tributary to different worldviews, almost always seen as incompatible or irreconcilable.

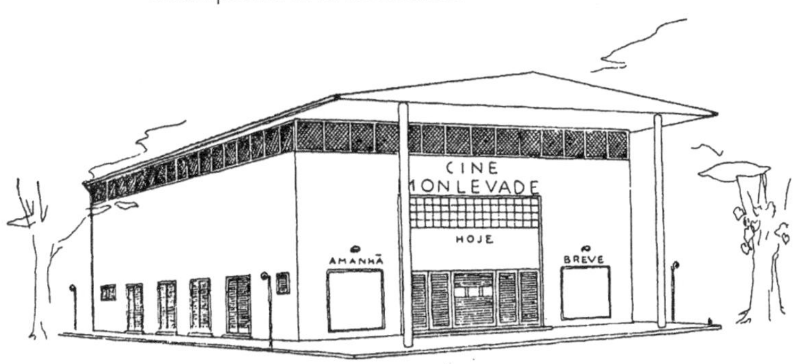

Vila Monlevade, social club and
cinema, Monlevade MG. Lúcio
Costa, 1934. *Revista da Diretoria de
Engenharia da Prefeitura do Distrito
Federal*, vol. III, no. 3, Rio de Janeiro,
May 1936

The Brazilian Roots of the Universe

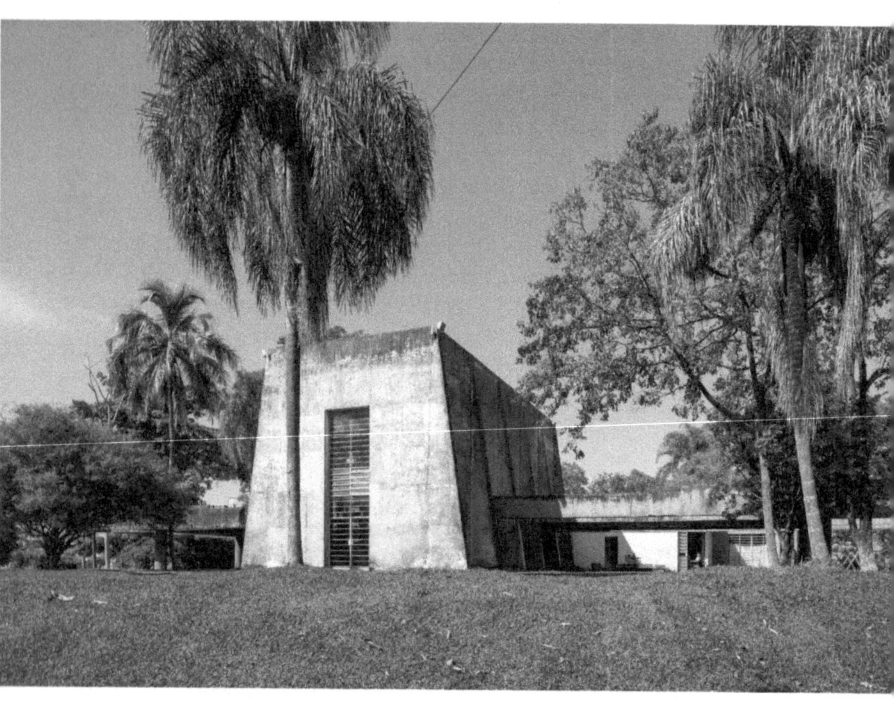

Capuava Farm Headquarters, Valinhos
SP. Flávio de Carvalho, 1938. Photo by
Nelson Kon

*In my night with my stars over my land I behold my
own cross: my cross of stars, my sloppy cross, my imperfect cross, my cross under whose light three races have
crossed, three drops of blood from three crucified.*
Guilherme de Almeida, *Raça*, 1925[15]

In 1948, in an article published in a widely circulated
São Paulo newspaper, journalist Geraldo Ferraz (1905-1979)
contested the label of *pioneer of contemporary architecture
in Brazil* attributed to Lúcio Costa by a magazine published
by students from the state of Rio Grande do Sul.[16] Ferraz
demanded a statement from the architect that could rectify
what he described as "informative distortion", a "cover-up of
historical truth", the latter expression being used four times
with minor variations.[17] In a quarrelsome tone, Ferraz points
to the precedence of Russian emigrant Gregori Warchavchik
(1896-1972) and Flávio de Carvalho (1899-1973), who, in
a lowbrow and hostile cultural environment,[18] facing the
sordid ignorance of detractors, still managed to conceive and
build the first modern buildings in the country, including
in the capital. "It is Flávio who, in a public contest, presents
for the first time in Rio the project for the new Embassy
of Argentina. In turn, it was Warchavchik who built the
first modern house in Rio, the one at Toneleros Street, in
Copacabana."[19] At the end of the 1920s, these two were the
legitimate Brazilian representatives of the European avant-
garde, therefore, the honorific title of pioneers belonged
to them. While the famous *Brazil Builds* catalog, which
had also committed the sin of omitting the precedence of
Warchavchik and Carvalho, could be partly excused for being
a foreign publication, this gross misunderstanding coming
from Brazilian students was inexcusable and required a
retraction.
Lúcio Costa does not shy away from the debate, and
his answer is actually disconcerting: setting aside his typical
politeness and completely reorienting the discussion, he says

that "architecture is not a Far-West" and that time should not be wasted "looking for pioneers."[20] In Costa's view, what is essential is not to determine which is the first modern building or which architect suffered the most from conservative or reactionary hostility, but rather to verify where lies the singular contribution that sets modern architecture in a peculiar trajectory in our country. There's a nuance here, one that will enjoy a successful career in Brazilian criticism and history: on the one hand, we have a *modern architecture* that, despite being *made in Brazil*, is developed according to principles established in Europe, principles which were imported and applied *en bloc* and which could have easily risen in any other country in the world; on the other hand, there's Brazilian modern architecture, something unusual and surprising, which sprouts and thrives here and solely here, coming up with unusual plastic solutions and commanding, for this reason, the interest and praise of foreign critics. Lúcio Costa would better conceptualize what this genuinely Brazilian modern architecture would be – trying to accommodate the contradictions involved – in a text from 1951.[21] The curious thing about this parochial dispute is the opinion that Mário de Andrade (1893-1945) expressed seven years earlier, anticipating Lúcio Costa's arguments and confirming their like-minded nature:

> "The first manifestation of modern architecture in Brazil, as is the case with other arts, also took place in São Paulo. It was a house by architect Warchavchik, much discussed in magazines at the time. But the modern in architecture had to concede here. The first school, the one that can legitimately be called a 'school' of modern architecture in Brazil, was that of Rio, led by Lúcio Costa, who is still unparalleled to this day. I say unparalleled, because, although other architects from the Rio de Janeiro school may have already had the opportunity to obtain more stunning architectural results than Lúcio

Costa, he continues to be a force of craftsmanship, a force of principle, reason and especially balance, avoiding experimentation that wastes time and money, which I consider to be a basic property of architecture."[22]

Ferraz's two protégés are actually culture heavyweights. Flávio de Carvalho, born in Rio de Janeiro, studied in Europe and graduated as an engineer in England. Upon his return to Brazil, he settled in the state of São Paulo, working between São Paulo and Valinhos, a small town close to Campinas. A pioneer modernist, his work as an architect, however, is quite rare, with only two works built: the main house at Fazenda Capuava, his residence in Valinhos, and a residential complex in Jardim Paulista, São Paulo. His inclination towards polemics and confrontation leads him to participate in several architectural competitions with projects marked by partisanship. The first of them – the project for the São Paulo State Government Palace, from 1927 – elicits three articles by Mário de Andrade, who shows sympathy for the theoretical substrate, but makes a few criticisms, mainly against the rigid symmetry of the composition.[23] Even though Mário de Andrade's criticism is correct, Carvalho has the merit of drawing attention to the architectural renovation underway in Europe. His contribution will be more significant in the visual arts and scenography, but his fame will mostly be due to controversial initiatives, especially the behavioral experiments in public that anticipate North-American happenings.

A Jew of Russian origin, Gregori Warchavchik studied architecture in Italy, then migrated to Brazil, where he worked at the Companhia Construtora de Santos (Santos Construction Company), owned by Roberto Simonsen, a position later held by architect Rino Levi.[24] Warchavchik settles in São Paulo, where he maintains an active office for several decades, with a brief interlude in the early 1930s, when he moves to Rio de Janeiro to teach at the Escola de Belas Artes (School of Fine Arts) at the invitation of Lúcio

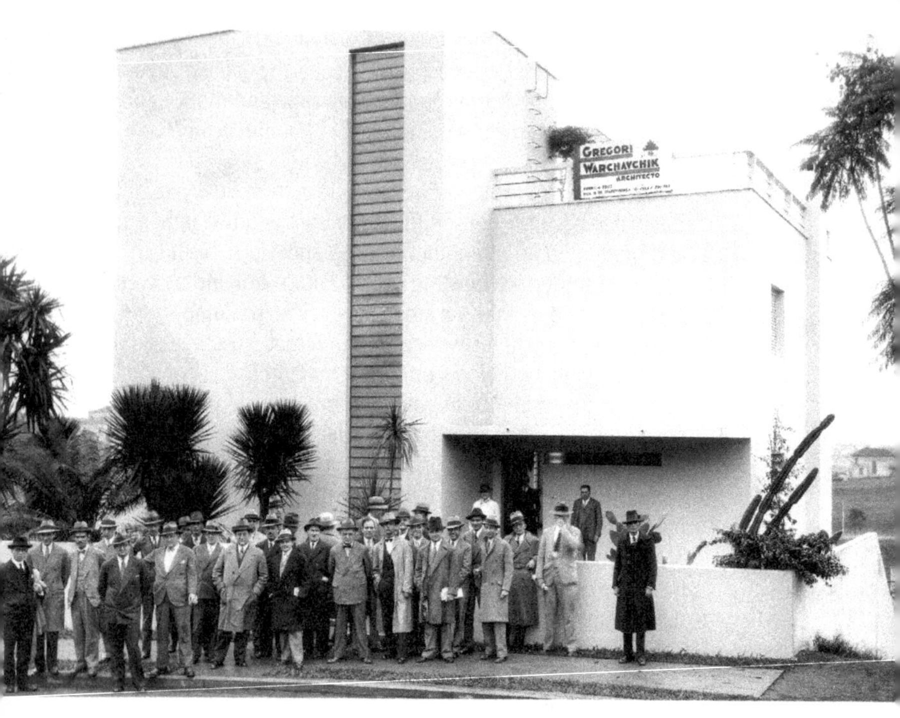

Costa, who was the intervening director at the time. Between 1931 and 1933, the two partnered up in a short-lived firm. After returning to São Paulo, the Russian architect continued to design and build houses strongly influenced by the emerging European modern architecture, causing sensation and uproar for the boldness of his designs, which defied the dominant taste. As proof of the resistance that the architect had to face, one might mention the fact that the authorities in São Paulo did not approve the project for his own residence for lack of decorative elements that followed the standards of the neighborhood. "His strategy – narrates Agnaldo Farias – consisted of sending a design of the façade filled with cornices and other ornaments in vogue at the

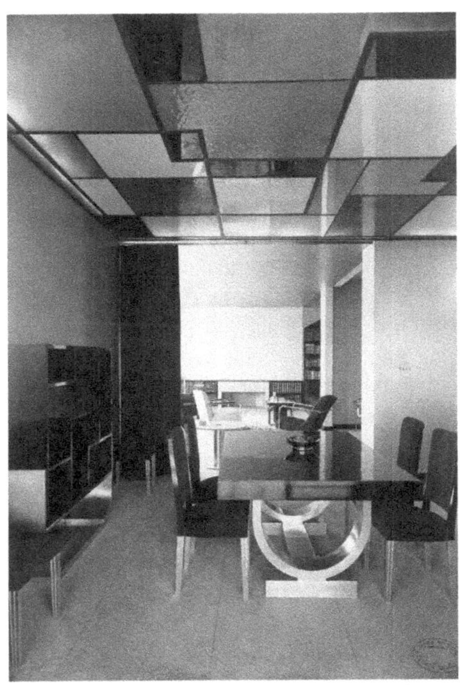

Modernist House on Bahia Street,
guest visit and interior, São Paulo.
Gregori Warchavchik, 1930.
Warchavchik family collection

time only to allege lack of money as a way of justifying their absence in the finished building."[25] The houses on Santa Cruz, Itápolis and Bahia streets – designed and built in the late 1920s and early 1930s – became visiting points for São Paulo modernists participating in the 1922 Modern Art Week and their alien guests, both from other states and abroad. In 1930 Warchavchik presents the "Exhibition of a Modernist House" in the newly built house on Rua Itápolis. Decorated with works by Tarsila do Amaral, Anitta Malfatti, Victor Brecheret, Di Cavalcanti, Lasar Segall and John Graz, pillows and bedspread by Regina Gomide Graz, with furniture, lamps and other design pieces conceived and built by Warchavchik himself. The exhibition, open to the public, was a success.[26]

From Lúcio Costa's point of view, however, the works of Gregori Warchavchik and Flávio de Carvalho are examples of *a modern architecture* which, although *made in Brazil*, is not quite *Brazilian*, deriving from exotic models. It differed from the other lineage, the authentic fruit of our land, which blends two distinct features: *affiliation to modern European ideas and national originality.* Such is the hallmark of the major works, those of Oscar Niemeyer (1907-2012) being the most expressive: while "his work sprang directly from that of Le Corbusier,"[27] it was also "our own national genius expressed through the chosen personality of this artist."[28] In Lúcio's view, the double influence exerted on our greatest architect – the external influence, coming from modern principles; and the internal one, coming from the traditional elements of the nation – is amalgamated in the plastic exuberance conquered through reinforced concrete. It is remarkable that, in Lúcio Costa's response, the superior quality of Oscar Niemeyer's work is not only a matter of innovative aesthetics; it is also a *moral imperative.* By embodying atavistic and exotic cultural vectors, it fulfills a destiny that goes beyond any vicissitude or personal preference. The aesthetic phenomenon, from this perspective, is deeply rooted in a collective historical experience of a given society, where novelties can bear fruit, but only on the solid ground of tradition. Although his theoretical reasons for praising Niemeyer are justifiable, Lúcio Costa's veto against Warchavchik's work, however, is somewhat problematic, as will be seen later.

The connections between the 1922 Modern Art Week and the modern architecture that would develop later – Rio de Janeiro being the main center of diffusion from 1930 onwards – are not so evident. Among the multiplicity of reasons that explain the frayed or broken nexus between the two moments, one gains special relevance: the originality of the local manifestation of national architecture, defended by architects, critics and historians. An episode specific to the architecture scene in São Paulo shows how the theme

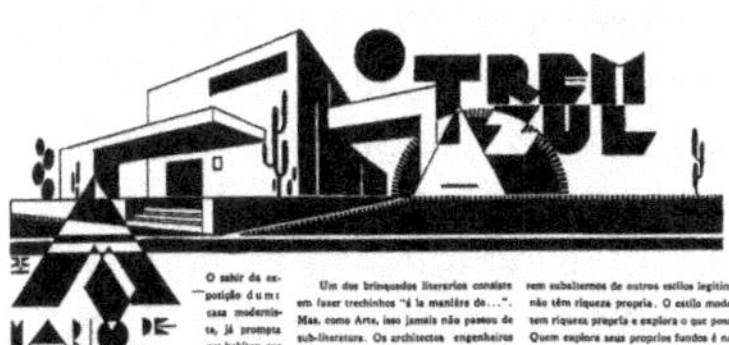

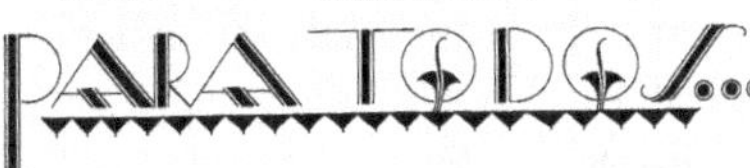

O sahir da exposição d'uma casa modernista, já prompta pra habitar, que o architecto Gregori Warchavchik organizou no bairro-jardim do Pacaembú, eram tantos meus pensamentos decididos!... Estava sem geito para contar o que vira. Imaginava aos golpes só:

Ha duas especies de pessoas constructoras de casas: os architectos engenheiros e os architectos enfeitados.

Os architectos enfeitados multiplicam os arrebiques e tapetes de todos os estylos nas suas casas, na intenção de dar uma personalidade pra ellas. Se esquecem que a architectura já tem uma personalidade propria: a engenharia.

Existe uma architectura actual: a que em São Paulo as casas de Gregorio Warchavchik e poucos mais, representam. Os architectos enfeitados que vivem fabricando o estylo grego, o florentino ou o Luiz XVI, elles mesmos se recusam a acceitar que estejam fazendo estylo grego, florentino ou Luiz XVI. Dizem que "se inspiram" nesses estylos, ou que "fazem uma adaptação" delles ás necessidades contemporaneas. Mas si já existe uma architectura contemporanea e essas senhores não a estão fazendo, nem fazem architectura grega, nem florentina, nem Luiz XVI, que architectura fazem então?

Os pseudo-estylos imitativos, com se-

Um dos brinquedos literarios consiste em fazer trechinhos "à la manière de...". Mas, como Arte, isso jamais não passou de sub-literatura. Os architectos engenheiros fazem architectura. Os architectos enfeitados vivem fazendo "à la manière de...": sub-architectura. Isso não é serio.

Em architectura, toda subalternidade é a perdição. Os pseudo-estylos imitativos, o néo-colonial, o néo-florentino, etc., são estylos subalternos. Por isso nós lhes tiramos as riquezas e as damos aos donos legitimos. São estylos que pagam divida de colonia: e todos sabem que o nosso ouro setecentista foi parar em Portugal. O estylo actual não é subalterna de ninguem, não tem quintos a pagar. As suas riquezas lhe são proprias.

Os estylos grego, egypcio, renascente, bizantino, foram estylos que passaram. Mas os architectos engenheiros voltam sempre a elle para delles tirar ensinamentos e normas. Tambem os architectos enfeitados voltam a elles pra "se inspirar", pra "adaptal-os", fazendo desses estylos não dados instrutivos do tempo, mas ideaes! Os architectos engenheiros com ensinamentos e normas estão construindo um estylo novo geral. Os engenheiros enfeitados constroem uma coisa que não é nem actual nem é bem do antigo, é apenas um pseudo-estylo, particular a cada um, romanticamente individualista. O Art-Nouveau tambem foi um pseudo-estylo individualista. Mas não passou, como os estylos verdadeiros. Se acabou. Em Arte os estylos verdadeiros passam, os pseudo-estylos acabam.

Os pseudo-estylos imitativos, com se-

rem subalternos de outros estilos legitimos, não têm riqueza propria. O estilo moderno tem riqueza propria e explora o que possue. Quem explora seus proprios fundos é negociante. Quem explora fundos alheios não passará jamais dum "explorador". No sentido pejorativo da palavra.

Quando vejo uma casa neo-colonial tenho uma impressão de "gostoso"; quando vejo uma casa neo-florentina tenho uma impressão de "chique"; quando vejo uma casa de Gregorio Warchavchik tenho uma impressão de "casa".

Em architectura, mais do que em nenhuma outra arte, a Beleza não é um fim, é uma consequencia.

O neo-colonial, que é o unico justificavel dos pseudo-estilos do Brasil, foi tão mal orientado que ainda não criou uma forma. No entanto o Brasil-Colonia criou formas: a igreja de Aleijadinho em principal. O colonial foi uma architectura. O neo-colonial é uma arte decorativa. Como Architectura ainda não tingiu a malhas e o papira, que são formas da engenharia amerindia.

Entre o anjo, e o espirito invocado pelas mesas espiritistas, existe a mesma diferença que entre um estilo verdadeiro de Architectura e um pseudo-estilo imitativo de qualquer coisa. Os anjos são espiritos puros, ao passo que... os outros são espiritos vagantes em busca de purificação. O povo é que distingue bem as duas especies, a uns chamando-lhes "anjos", a outros "assombração".

Article "O trem azul", by Mário de Andrade. *Para Todos*, year 12, no. 593, Rio de Janeiro, Apr 26, 1930, 9

is ideologically contaminated. In a text written in 1977 – *Semana de 22 e a Arquitetura* (1922 Modern Art Week and the Architecture)[29] –, at a mature stage in his career, Vilanova Artigas (1915-1985) contradicts two statements that he had put forward in a famous text from 1952 – *Os caminhos da arquitetura moderna* (Pathways of Modern Architecture).[30] The first dealt with the supposedly fake radicalism of modernist artists led by Mário de Andrade in the 1920s, who would have "created a 'revolutionary' halo that increased or decreased according to the needs of the ruling class,"[31] a fact that would supposedly be evidenced by the subsequent co-optation of these false leftist intellectuals by the reactionary government of Getúlio Vargas. [32]

In the later article, however, taking into account the modest role of architecture in the Modern Art Week that took place in São Paulo in 1922, the link established by Artigas between this artistic event and Brazilian modern architecture, which would emerge at least a decade later in a different scenario – Rio de Janeiro – becomes quite telling. Dominated by the fine arts and literature, the Modern Art Week could not provide architecture with formal solutions in an immediate way, but only in a *mediated* way. When Artigas argues that "the cultural terrain was mostly prepared,"[33] he refers to the modernist effort in order to "discover the *Brazilian roots of the universe*,"[34] which is in line with the vision that Lúcio Costa had of the period: "Unlike what happened in most countries, here in Brazil it was precisely those few who insisted on opening up to the modern world who also delved into the country in search of its roots, its tradition, both in São Paulo in the 1920s and in Rio, Minas, in the South and Northeast in the 1930s, always advocating for the defense and preservation of our valid past (Sphan)."[35] The intellectuals of 1922 and 1936, in the similar assessment of Lúcio Costa and Vilanova Artigas, shared the same spirit of synthesis between *renovation* and *preservation*. Decades later, Lúcio Costa reiterates the same understanding, with a more precise view of what was at stake:

> In Brazil, both in 1922 and 1936, those committed to 'renovation' were the same who were committed to 'preservation', while elsewhere, at the time, one would find people from antagonistic backgrounds who opposed each other. In 1922, Mário, Tarsila, Oswald and Cia., while internationally reforming our obsolete culture, also roamed the ancient cities of Minas and traveled North, in an 'anthropophagic' search for our roots; In 1936, the architects who were fighting for architectural adaptation to the new construction technologies were the same who committed themselves with Rodrigo M. F. de Andrade to the study and safeguard of the permanent testimony of our authentic past.[36]

The second statement revised by Artigas concerns the historical role of Le Corbusier (1887-1965), to whom Artigas, in the 1952 text, attributes the sordid role of acting in the service of the North American business community to try to "convince the bourgeoisie that there is still something to be done, that it is possible to postpone the date of the collapse."[37] However, in the 1977 article, Artigas gives Le Corbusier a strategic role in the emergence of modern architecture in Brazil, while also emphasizing the preparation carried out by the local cultural environment: "Le Corbusier's contribution to the Ministry building project is undeniable. It has been affirmed and reaffirmed so many times that it is not worth detailing. It should be noted, however, that the cultural terrain was, as it were, prepared, dominated by figures who were able to lucidly value and assimilate the artistic experience of the French master, conforming it to the nationalist and reforming ideals of the 30's revolution."[38]

The scathing criticisms directed by Artigas in the early 1950s to the modernists and Le Corbusier were made from a political framework in which an orthodox stance of the Brazilian Communist Party – PCB, then unaware of the "bad news" coming from Eastern Europe, prevailed. At that moment, when the socialist revolution seemed like a palpable reality, Corbusian functionalism and Brazilian modernist culturalism were taken by the São Paulo architect as ideological and diversionist mechanisms. His point of view changed after a political-ideological reorientation, where he abandoned the internationalist perspective in favor of the country's economic and cultural autonomy. From this new perspective, the civilizational advance and the synthesis between modernity and the roots of Brazilian culture sought by the modernists of São Paulo in the 1920s became justifiable, as well as admirable and praiseworthy, these lessons being digested and adapted by the carioca architects in the following decade. Modern architecture, seen at first as an expression of the ruling class, takes on a transformative role

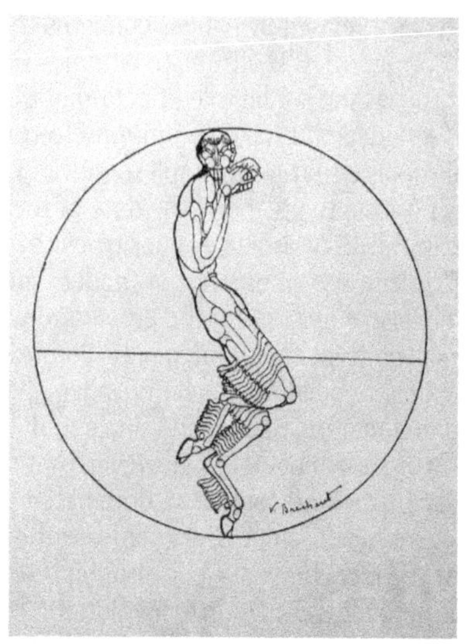

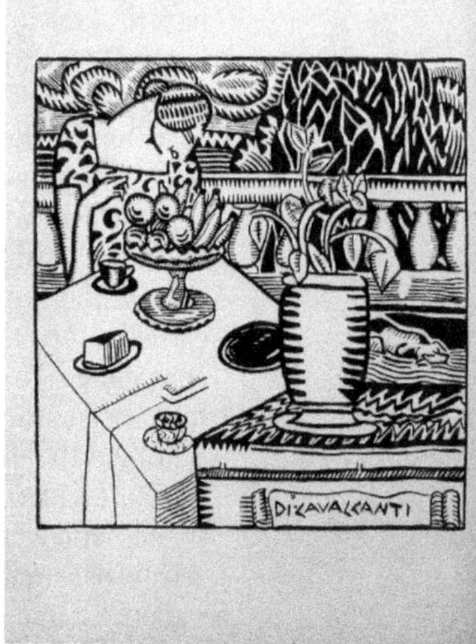

in Artigas's most up-to-date perspective by characterizing a genuinely national architectural tradition, which combines two positive and essential vectors: *cultural independence* and *technological autonomy*.

Although both historical judgments derive from political attitudes – proving that, for Artigas, art and architecture must always be at the service of a political project that transcends particular interests[39] –, his initial refusal to engage in an aesthetic discussion is overturned by an emphasis on *Brazilian formal memory* and by the praise of Oscar Niemeyer's *genius*, endorsing the words that Lúcio Costa would repeat for almost his entire life: "With the Pampulha ensemble, Oscar Niemeyer shaped the synthesis necessary to guide Brazilian architecture towards the safe route that now characterizes it. Lúcio Costa has already called his presence a miracle. The strength of his genius, based on the works of Pampulha, led Brazilian architecture to broad and fruitful paths, inaugurating a vast cultural field for formal research

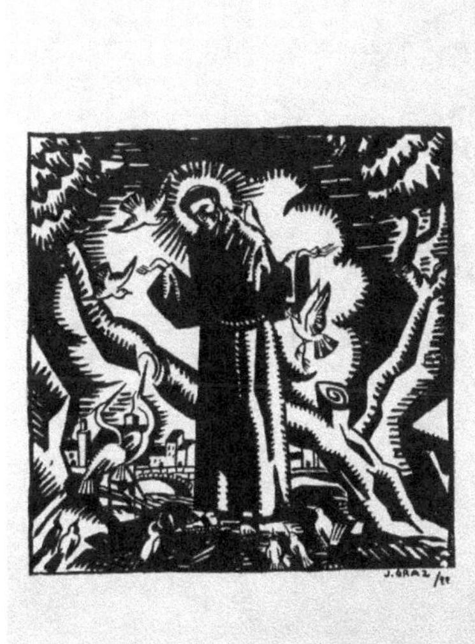

Illustrations: Victor Brecheret. *Klaxon*, no. 1, May 15, 1922; Di Cavalcanti. *Klaxon*, no. 2, June 15, 1922; John Graz. *Klaxon*, no. 7, Nov 30, 1922

by younger people."[40] That is, while the first stance obliterates the aesthetic analysis, condemning the phenomenon from the onset, the second opens up to the materiality and expressiveness of form, leading to the understanding of the mechanisms that made possible "new symbols, such as, for example, the Alvorada Palace column, which Malraux has described as a *caryatid*."[41] Artigas' revaluation is conditioned by the accommodative stance adopted by the Communist Party, and yet it has consequences for the Brazilian cultural debate, as it aligns itself with the main current of the historical and ideological construct articulated by Lúcio Costa.

Being Regional and Pure in your Own Time

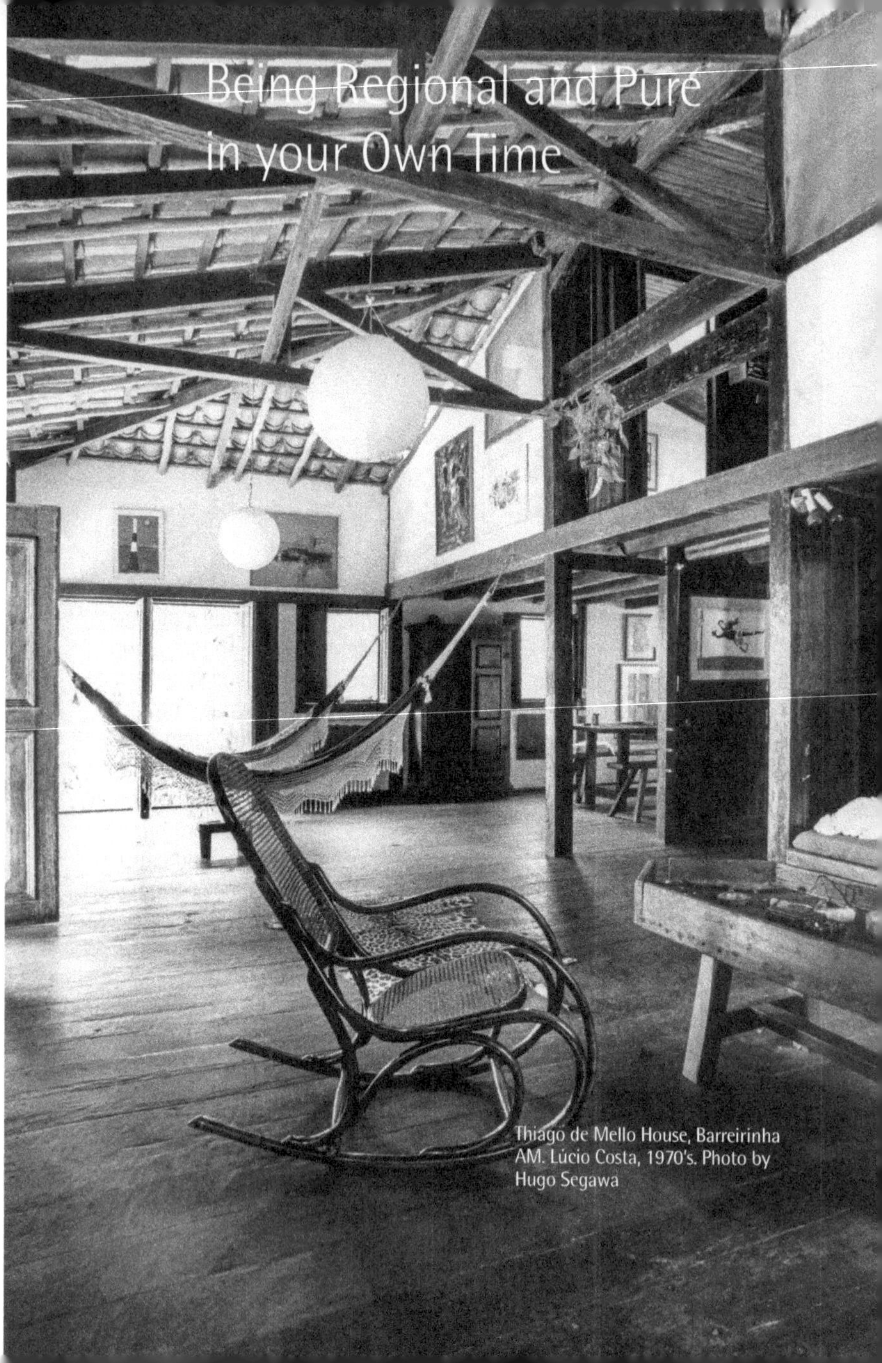

Thiago de Mello House, Barreirinha
AM. Lúcio Costa, 1970's. Photo by
Hugo Segawa

Oswald de Andrade, "Manifesto da poesia Pau-Brasil,"
1924[42]

The short text by Artigas, published in 1977 in the
Modulo magazine, does not mark the birth of the debate
on the paternity of our modern architecture. However,
since it is being addressed by such an emblematic personality in the national architectural scene, the resurgence of
the issue becomes evident, taking part in the architectural
debate of the 1970s and 1980s. In 1981, not long after
Artigas' text, the best known – and also the most comprehensive – study on our modern architecture was published:
Arquitetura contemporânea no Brasil (or *Contemporary
Architecture in Brazil*, in free translation), by French artist
Yves Bruand. Originally a doctoral dissertation defended in
1971, *L'Architecture Contemporaine au Brésil* narrates the
epic of our architecture with a *script* based on the ideas of
the people who produced it – *Brazilian modern architects*
themselves. What we find here is a perfect harmony between
the historical reassessment carried out by Vilanova Artigas
and the reestablishment of the nationalist perspective in the
research on the history of Brazilian architecture.

With regard to one of the themes discussed here – the
theoretical framework and architectural practice of Lúcio
Costa in the shaping of a lineage of Brazilian architecture –,
Yves Bruand sees quite perceptively the general meaning of
the work of the architect and urbanist from Rio de Janeiro
and his profound and inspiring presence in Brazilian architecture: "All the attempts he made to find a new vocabulary,
both international and local, modern and yet linked to the
past, were soon studied, inspiring an active movement of
research in this direction, which is one of the most striking

features of the new Brazilian architecture. His influence was profound and diffuse".[43] Bruand highlights that Lúcio Costa's influence did not entail restriction, which could lead to repetitive and stereotyped creations. On the contrary, his line of thought "provided a flexible framework"[44] where the many architects who followed him were able to find a personal solution to address each problem.

Several personal developments pick up on the ideas of Lúcio Costa, as is the case with architect Francisco Bolonha. Bruand points out, however, that Bologna merely *juxtaposes* traditional and modern techniques, while Lúcio Costa goes for complete *integration* – a concept or idea that Bruand does not develop –, obtaining a unitary set. The French author lists a few other architects, discerning in personal variations a few formal constants that allow him to envision two currents: "one that seeks to explore local conditions by accentuating a rustic character, and another one looking for a new vocabulary through contemporary technique, a current which, while employing resources entirely different from those employed in the past, subscribes to the same line and subtly evokes that past."[45] According to Bruand, these two currents constitute variations within the same school – that of the southern region of the country. A second school, also born from the fusion between the traditional and the modern, develops with great autonomy in the Brazilian Northeast, especially in the states of Pernambuco and Bahia, with emphasis on the works of Paulo Antunes Ribeiro, Delfim Moreira and Luís Nunes. This second current eludes the direct influence of Lúcio Costa, which is a situation analogous to that of the Roberto brothers, who took part in the first current, but whose work actually developed in parallel with that of the carioca master.

The correct evaluation of works and architects carried out by Bruand spots personal nuances and group proximities, which allows him to both highlight the contribution of each individuality and propose "currents", "movements" and

"schools". Bruand attributes to personal choices the finding
of a more or less successful formula for the *fusion between
the traditional and the modern* within the "flexible frame"
provided by Lúcio Costa. The relative autonomy of his field of
knowledge privileges the work of art, its structural coherence
and its correspondence to the artist's worldview. The method
is consistent with an aesthetic-materialist history of architecture, as it considers – just as Yves Bruand and many other
historians do – the net of influences among the participants
of a cultural movement, the hierarchical relations that help
convey authority to opinions and arguments, the personal
and formal affinities that result from these relations, the set
of discourses that, through interaction, push forward the diffusion of ideas and formal solutions. However, Bruand's strict
focal point neglects the communicating vessels through
which architecture gets to engage with the other arts and
culture in general, disregarding the fact that subjective
invention springs from a field of possibilities objectively conditioned by the historical period in which the artist moves.[46]
The "flexible frame" encompasses the wider field of culture,
not being endogenous to a particular métier. Bruand grasps
this limitation in his own method when he refers more than
once to a vague "kinship of spirit"[47] between Brazilian modern architecture and colonial architecture.

Lúcio Costa's intellectual project transcends any personal
preference for a particular architectural style or current. It
is rather a personal version – the most sophisticated and
far-reaching in Brazilian architecture and urbanism – for
a cultural project with very broad ambitions that spread
throughout the country since its inception in the São Paulo
modernism of the 1920s. This is an aesthetic project that
claims both the right and the obligation to solve very deep
problems of our collective existence and which has as its
main goal the formulation of a *national character* harmoniously expressed by the organic articulation between an
authentic local culture and an elite art. Thus, the *integration*

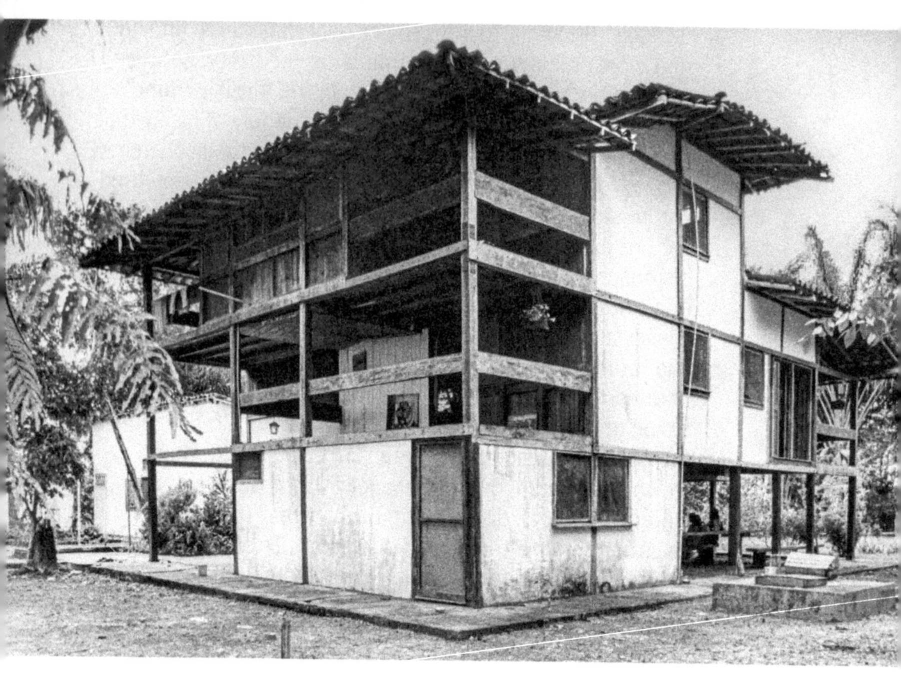

Thiago de Mello House, Barreirinha
AM. Lúcio Costa, 1970's. Photo by
Hugo Segawa

between tradition and modernity is no longer an aesthetic
choice of a personal nature, for it gains a collective status
– perhaps the most viable in those circumstances – in the
constitution of our nationality. The fact that this discursive
structure is an artificial conceptual construction does not
reduce its effectiveness, since one of its features is precisely
the need to be organically linked to the national territory and
Brazilian society.[48]

The importance of Lúcio Costa's work lies not only in
the intrinsic quality of his projects or texts, but also in how
he accommodates a worldview that was not originally

conceptualized within his own discipline. When we see
him as the cultural promoter that he had always been, the
peculiarities of his career – his early involvement in teaching
initiatives, the insistence on fostering collective production
despite his own propensity towards isolation, his engage-
ment in the preservation of national architectural heritage,
the indirect roles in the inner workings of political powers
and also his decades-long struggle to elevate Oscar Niemeyer
to the status of genius of our architecture – no longer seem
to be isolated or complementary aspects of his professional
performance, but rather genuine facets outlining the very
same worldview. This vision pays heavy tribute to São Paulo
modernism, as he never failed to acknowledge, returning
several times to this issue, as in the justification for the 1931
Salon: "Hence the idea of breaking away from the tiresome
monotony of the previous exhibitions by inviting – to participate of the Official Salon – those artists who were somehow
committed to the 1922 Modern Art Week, whose true purpose, in essence, was to engage our most authentic native
sap, our very roots, with the plethora of new ideas coming
from that fruitful 19th century – ideas that were already
going through a third wave in Europe at the time. The objective was to carry out here, albeit belatedly, a lucid and necessary renovation."[49]

The arguments developed by Yves Bruand in 1971
take part in a poorly considered but vigorous intellectual
genealogy, which includes a book from 1956, published
in Portuguese for the first time only in 1999: *Modern
Architecture in Brazil*,[50] released in English around the time
the construction of Brasília began, with French and German
editions in subsequent years. The author, renowned architect
Henrique Mindlin (1911-1971), maintained for many years a
fruitful association with Italian architect Giancarlo Palanti.
Coming to light at the end of the heroic period of the constitution of our modern architecture – the construction of the
new Brazilian capital in the heart of the country –, Mindlin's

book has as an explicit goal the worldwide dissemination of a specific national approach regarding the materialization of the modern principles – that is, the "Brazilianness" of our architecture.

It was on a trip to the United States in 1943, shortly after the opening of the *Brazil Builds* exhibition promoted by the Museum of Modern Art of New York – MoMA, that Mindlin learned about an expression created by the North-Americans and which would enjoy a long history in international criticism: the *Brazilian School*.[51] Excited with the exhibition and its repercussions, of which he would actually take part by writing his own book, Mindlin went on to conceive a few years later a publication that intended to be a follow-up to the catalog produced at the time: "This work was conceived as a supplement to Philip E. Goodwin's *Brazil Builds*, a magnificent presentation of old and new architecture in Brazil, published by the MoMA featuring splendid photographs by G. E. Kidder Smith." However, the book turns out to be even more comprehensive: "As *Brazil Builds* has been out of print for several years, it was later decided to include here some of the major examples which were previously featured there. Thus, it will be possible to give a fuller picture of the development of modern architecture in Brazil, from its inception in the late 1920s to the present day."[52]

This self-confessed follow-up to *Brazil Builds* by Henrique Mindlin – *Modern Architecture in Brazil* – inherits from the original work some structural and stylistic aspects, especially the rhetoric exploring the spiritual nexus between modern and colonial architecture and inflating the notion of a *national tradition* in perfect harmony with Lúcio Costa's point of view. Both in the text by the architect-author and in the preface signed by Sigfried Giedion – who would also write a preface for a book about Affonso Eduardo Reidy published in Germany in 1961 – there are several statements regarding the vicissitudes – mostly positive – of our modern architecture, particularly its roots in our cultural past and the ability to merge elements from the colonial constructive tradition with the technical and functional aspects of European ideas. In order to justify such singularity, Giedion and Mindlin mobilize a few notions which seem quite alien to the architectural discourse, such as the issue of *Brazilian racial miscegenation*, the *mental elasticity* of our people and the *integration with tropical nature*...

Perhaps because more than a decade had passed since the release of the original work that had inspired him to write his own book, or perhaps because he was an active architect, more prone to practice than discursive constructions, the fact is that the opening text written by Mindlin goes over the old premises only to abandon them at the final stage of his argument. When trying to point out factors that explain the advancement of modern architecture in Brazil, he picks up two historical events of a much more prosaic nature, associated with the material stage of our civilization: first, the "research on the problems of insolation,"[53] associated with the scientific and academic contributions of Lúcio Rodrigues Martins at the Polytechnic School of São Paulo and later developed in Rio de Janeiro by other specialists; secondly, the "development of an advanced technique for the employment of reinforced concrete, which resulted not only in lighter and more elegant structures, but also in a significant cost reduction, compared to other countries."[54] Thanks to the solid training of our engineers, among them Emílio Baumgart and Joaquim Cardozo, both notoriously capable of translating the problems of architectural form into adequate practical solutions, the second phenomenon became possible. Mindlin then concludes: "These two factors are directly associated with two of the most notable features of modern architecture in Brazil: the use of large glass surfaces, protected, when necessary, by brise-soleil, and the use of free structures supported by pilotis, featuring an open ground floor whenever possible. These two characteristics also show the marked influence of Le Corbusier."[55]

The mesological and culturalist concepts, which in Henrique Mindlin only appear in an incidental and peripheral way, are central for the argument developed in the preface by Sigfried Giedion, who is surprised by the contrast between Brazil's economic-social paucity and the strength of the architecture.[56] Faced with the absence of a civilizational foundation consistent with the ongoing architectural aesthetic manifestation, Giedion states that "there is something irrational in the development of Brazilian architecture."[57] He also extends his perplexity to the much-vaunted Corbusian influence: "Without a doubt, the arrival of Le Corbusier to the country, in 1936, prompted Brazilian inclinations to find their own path. But Le Corbusier had visited many other countries and nothing ever came of it except for hostile headlines in the newspapers, as happened once in New York."[58] In the absence of a robust material evidence that could explain the rapid development of reinforced concrete architecture in Brazil, Giedion appeals to a mediated and previously codified explanation: "the prodigy of Brazilian architecture *flourishes* like a tropical plant"; "in Brazil, contemporary architecture took *root* in the tropical soil"; "Mindlin's book makes evident the *flowering* of Brazilian architecture from the 1930s onwards."[59] This organic metaphor gives the explanation a vague character, implying a somehow inexorable and spontaneous blooming. References to Gilberto Freyre (1900-1987) and Hermann von Keyserling (1880-1946) also frame social, anthropological and psychological themes as relevant to the understanding of our architectural phenomenon.[60] Finally, the link between modern architecture and tradition is not forgotten: "Brazil already had a tradition of enhancing the surface of its facades, so subjected to the pressures of the tropical climate, through the structural treatment of flat surfaces. Contemporary architects have reworked this tradition, including in their projects perforated external panels, *cobogós* (see Bristol building by Lúcio Costa, 1948), tiles employed in a quite innovative way and brise-soleil".[61]

If the prefacer Giedion calls into question the influence
of Corbusier in 1936, the main author will be even more
radical: "when Le Corbusier first passed through São Paulo
and Rio in 1929 on his way back from a trip to Argentina and
Uruguay, Brazilian architects had already laid the groundwork."[62] Going a step further than Giedion, Mindlin links
Brazilian modern architecture to a specific genealogy, that of
São Paulo modernism: "The Modern Art Week brought with it
the germ of an authentic renaissance that, over time, would
establish a connection with the highest values of Brazilian
life, with the sources of the past, the land and its people."[63]
Still strong, though somewhat faded by the presence of more
consistent material elements, Mindlin's arguments, which
appeal to the flourishing of modern architecture in our cultural soil, echo words he himself had put forward in 1945
– more than a decade prior to the publication of his book –
which reveals how much he paid tribute to this worldview:

"The roadmap for the new architecture in Brazil is
already laid down. Just as in other countries, where
the work of good architects, evolving from the strict
functionalism of twenty years ago, is now marked by a
healthy regionalism, also among us free-spirit architects
are creating a new vision, a new architectural language.
It is not a question of narrow regionalism, but rather of
a profound adaptation to the land and the environment.
Starting from the complete identification with the spirit
of the age, on the broad foundation of spiritual freedom — a tradition of our culture —, and carried forward
by a lyricism that mirrors our collective soul, the new
architects of Brazil are creating the architecture of the
sun. From the sun, because it was in the study of light as
the primary factor in controlling insolation that the first
concrete achievements of our architecture were based.
This is how the ABI, the Ministry of Education, the Hidros
Station were born, as well as many other works that

international critics have identified as a Brazilian school. It was from the courageous employment of a point of view uncompromisingly associated with our own local problems that these buildings emerged, full of light and breeze, now being treated in all countries as examples for contemporary architects. This prestige that Brazilian culture has come to enjoy, due to the international consensus that such works currently constitute Brazil's highest contribution to universal heritage, this general recognition that our new architecture is of interest to the whole world, must at least point out the path to those who wish to study architecture."[64]

In 1945, it was already clear to Henrique Mindlin that the heart of our modern architecture resides in its regional singularity, supported by mesological, rational and culturalist determinants, themes of enormous relevance in the Brazilian cultural debate since the second half of the 19th century. The presence of the same arguments in his work aimed at the general public is as relevant as his desire to celebrate our architecture for a wider audience. *Modern architecture in Brazil* does not limit itself to new projects by established architects, going for a much larger number of authors and projects. Alongside Oscar Niemeyer, Lúcio Costa, Affonso Reidy, the Roberto brothers, Álvaro Vital Brazil, Atílio Correa Lima and Rino Levi – all featured in *Brazil Builds* –, we also find Francisco Bolonha, Sérgio Bernardes, Eduardo Corona, Hélio Duarte, Ícaro de Castro Mello, Olavo Redig de Campos and others. By insisting on the role of tradition, alongside research on insolation and reinforced concrete, in the constitution of modern Brazilian architecture, Mindlin makes his personal contribution to the collective processing that will transform this particular point of view into an axiomatic explanation. One more stitch in the discursive fabric that reveals the national character of the new architecture.

When investigating the fundamental texts on Brazilian modern architecture – articles, lectures, books, etc. –, Hugo Segawa's contribution must not be overlooked. In *Arquiteturas no Brasil 1900-1990 (Architectures in Brazil 1900-1990)*, from 1998, the São Paulo author sets himself two challenges: stripping Yves Bruand of the privilege of having authored the only manual on Brazilian architecture in the 20th century and correcting the mistaken perspective adopted by the French author. The laudatory and apologetic approach to modernism carried out by Bruand and the deep-rooted prejudice that Brazilian modern architects felt against other styles did not go unnoticed by Segawa.[65] To this lack of distancing Segawa responds with a more neutral critical path, carefully considering each manifestation in progress. Hence the plural in the title: *Architectures in Brazil* must meet the basic observation that "there is no univocal definition of modernity,"[66] but multiple *modernities*. Here we have a conscious withdrawal from the trenches of the history of art and architecture – where the term "modernism" is legitimized – in favor of a broader approach to the historical phenomenon, with the introduction of the concept of "modernity". The categories adopted by Hugo Segawa – "the search for some modernity", "pragmatic modernity", "current modernity", "episodes of a great and modern Brazil" – confirm the prevalence of a vision of history supported by the general vectors of social evolution. As a result, these generic labels justify the homogenization of the various *Brazilian architectures* that, within their possibilities, take part with the same commitment in the technological and social modernization of the country.

Hugo Segawa's criterion for periodization is how much each development relates to the country's technological and social modernization process. The first period – that of Gregori Warchavchik and Flávio de Carvalho –, paying tribute to European avant-garde functionalism, is called "programmatic modernism", since it stuck to imported ideas, lacking

the technical knowledge and the technological appropriation capacity to put it into practice. Running alongside this
engaged modernism, we have "pragmatic modernity": a
countless number of constructive experiences from the most
diverse areas – Roberto Simonsen's industrialism, the modern *a la Perret*, the Art Déco skyscraper – whose common
denominator is the modernization of construction. Finally,
the historical processing brought about by the encounter
between Le Corbusier and Lúcio Costa's group, Segawa calls
"current modernity", the adjective suggesting the hegemony of this particular current in relation to alternative
modernities.

When characterizing the hegemonic current of modernity, Hugo Segawa sets a series of episodes in chronological
order – reform of the School of Fine Arts, Corbusier's visit,
the presence of Juscelino Kubitschek etc. – and the relevant
modern buildings derived from such historical circumstances
– the Brazil Pavilion in New York, MES, Pampulha, etc. His
concerns do not explore the reason for this hegemony, just
as he does not focus on the synthesis between primitivism
and modernization featured in the "current modernity". The
lack of interest for such questions – as has been said, he
focuses on attesting to the variety of contributions to the
shaping of 20th century Brazilian architecture – does not
detract from the excellent survey of sources and the characterization of diverse architectural lineages that mark the
work carried out by Hugo Segawa, on which our present
work constantly relies.

The North-American Path

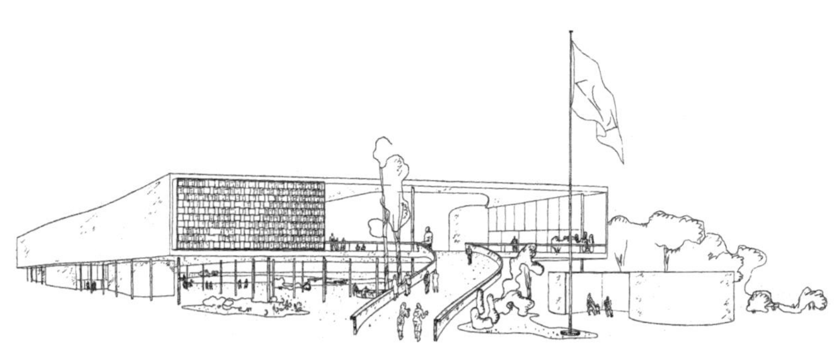

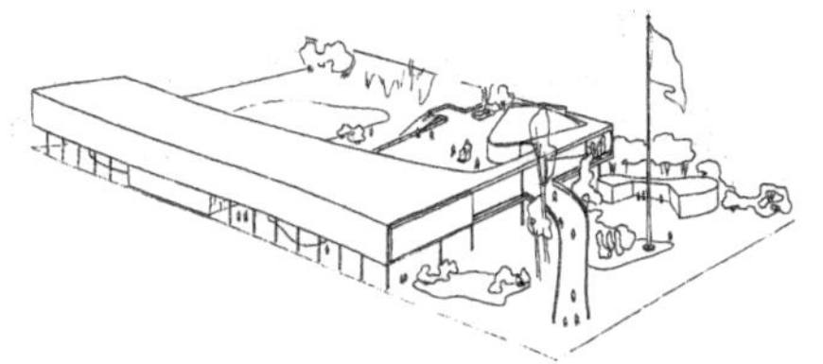

Brazil Pavilion at the New York World's Fair. Lúcio Costa and Oscar Niemeyer, 1939. Casa da Arquitectura Archive

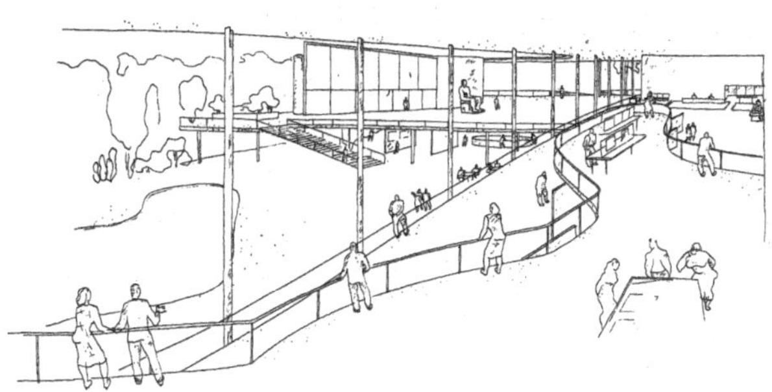

The British and Americans fear for us. We are tied to their fate. We owe everything, what we have and what we don't have. We have mortgaged palm trees... waterfalls. Cardinals!
Oswald de Andrade, *O rei da vela* (*The Candle King*), 1937[67]

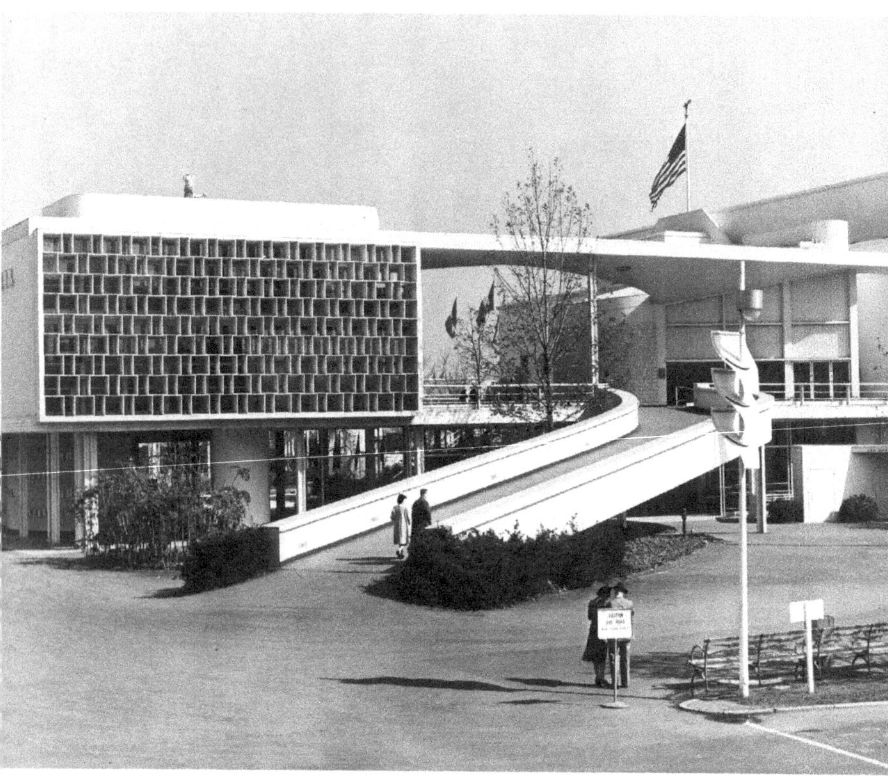

Brazil Pavilion at the New York World's Fair. Lúcio Costa and Oscar Niemeyer, 1939. New York Public Library Collection

The Brazilian Pavilion at the New York World's Fair in 1939 and the whole *Brazil Builds* episode – both the exhibition held at the MoMA in 1943 and the Philip Goodwin and Kidder Smith catalog – constitute the *North-American path* that invites the European recognition of Brazilian modern architecture. In the midst of the Second World War, these events presented to the American public not only the current state of our architecture, but also the current stage of Brazilian economic development as well as the relevant facts of the country's history.

In the specific case of the 1943 event, in addition to the current examples of modern architecture, Goodwin selects – and Kidder Smith photographs – dozens of works from the colonial period, ignoring, however, any building in neoclassical or neocolonial style. Even the first instances of modern architecture made in the country, designed by Flávio de Carvalho and Gregori Warchavchik, are overlooked: no work by the former is featured, even though his name is mentioned in the acknowledgment list; the latter, besides also being present in the acknowledgment list, gets three quick references: a photo of an apartment building from 1940, located in Alameda Barão de Limeira in São Paulo; another photo of a "simple house in São Paulo" with gabled roof, without further references; and a photo of the house on Rua Bahia, with an incorrect caption describing it as "the first modern house built in São Paulo."[68] The house on Rua Bahia dates from 1930; at least two others were built by Warchavchik before that: the house on Rua Santa Cruz, from 1927, is "consecrated as the first modernist house built in São Paulo,"[69] and the house on Itápolis Street, also from 1930, which elicits enthusiastic articles from Mário de Andrade, Oswald de Andrade (1890-1954) and Flávio de Carvalho,[70] as well as the nickname *Casa Modernista* (*Modernist House*), "thanks to the buzz that followed its inauguration" and the consequent influx of the public, which would have reached the respectable mark of 20,000 visitors, according to the newspapers of the time."[71]

The discreet presence of the two modern architects from São Paulo at *Brazil Builds* is at odds with the prominence they elicited from the media in the 1920s and 1930s, but it is understandable when one considers the circumstances surrounding the exhibition and the catalog, both the institutional circumstances – which will be discussed later – as the conceptual ones. The historical selection featured in *Brazil Builds* derives from the theoretical elaboration of Lúcio Costa, who attributes to modern architecture a spiritual connection with colonial architecture, both in the highbrow version of Aleijadinho's baroque churches and in the prosaic iterations of civil architecture carried out by anonymous tradesmen.[72] From this point of view, the first manifestations – in this case, those put forward by Flávio de Carvalho and Gregori Warchavchik – seemed too attached to European models, failing to incorporate traditional elements.

In Lúcio Costa's own words, Warchavchik's work suffered from a "stylized modernism", lacking a clear understanding of "Corbusian principles"; its value as a pioneering work, however, was unquestionable,[73] having contributed to the upgrading of ideas at a time when a proper modern thought was being established, but not as organic manifestations of Brazilian culture. Lúcio Costa seems to be unaware, or perhaps he chooses to ignore, that Warchavchik did see in his work an effort to adjust to the local reality, both in the use of colonial tiles and in the deployment of tropical vegetation. Commenting on his house on Itápolis street, the Ukrainian architect says:

> "Inspired by the charm of Brazilian landscapes, and seeking to avoid copying what is currently being done in Europe, I tried to create an architectural character that would adapt to this region, to the climate and also to the old traditions of this land. Alongside straight, clear,

vertical and horizontal lines, which, in the form of cubes
and planes, constitute the main element of modern
architecture, I made use of the quite decorative and
typical colonial tiles, managing, I believe, to conceive
a very Brazilian house, due to its perfect adaptation to
the environment. The tropical garden around the house
contains all the richness of the typical Brazilian flora. My
lady, Mrs. Mina Klabin Warchavchik, collaborated in the
creation of this garden, as well as in the final internal
arrangements."[74]

Regarding *Brazil Builds*, Hugo Segawa attributes to the
author a strategic importance in steering the discussions
taking place here in Brazil: "Goodwin put together a publication dedicated to a Brazilian architecture that Brazilians
themselves were unaware of, as can be attested by Mário
de Andrade's comments. The *ancient/modern* dichotomy
reanimated the debate concerning tradition/modernity in
the discourse that was being established among modern
architects in Rio de Janeiro."[75] It is possible and even likely
that the eternal inferiority complex that plagues Brazilian
intelligence felt catered to with this foreign praise, which is
the theme of Mário de Andrade's article implicit in Segawa's
commentary.[76] However, even though Lúcio Costa was yet to
produce some of his most important articles at the time of
the release of the catalog – therefore, he had not yet systematized his theory regarding the deep connection between
tradition and modernity –, there are many allusions to this
issue in the many texts he wrote around that time, and these
allusions, and certainly not the catalog, are the true force
steering not only the ongoing discourse among the Rio de
Janeiro architects alluded to by Segawa, but Philip Goodwin's
own discourse. In turn, Lúcio Costa's argument is very closely
related to that of the São Paulo modernists, especially Mário
de Andrade, who had been arguing for the synthesis between
modernity and national roots since the 1920s. There is,

therefore, at that moment, a broader and more articulated discursive framework that supports both Goodwin's statements as well as those of the "*carioca*" *architects*, with Lúcio Costa's voice being the one that stands out the most. With a lyrical spirit similar to that of the 1936 *Vila Monlevade Memorial*, Lúcio Costa closes his presentation of the Rio de Janeiro University City – a project developed by him and his project team, with Le Corbusier as a consultant – pointing out the accommodation of the precepts of the international modern architecture to the simplicity of our local character:

> "The project follows contemporary technique by its eminently international nature – however, thanks to the particularities of the floor plan, such as the open galleries, the patios etc., the choice of materials and the respective finishes (rustic stone masonry walls, smooth gneiss slabs, tiles under pilotis, whitewashing or suitable painting on exposed concrete, etc.) and, finally, thanks to the use of appropriate vegetation, the project will be able to acquire an unmistakable local character, whose simplicity, quite lush and unpretentious, owes a lot to the good principles of old constructions with which we are familiar."[77]

If *Brazil Builds* introduced the world to modern and colonial Brazilian architecture through photographs, drawings and models, the 1939 New York World's Fair exhibits an actual iteration of modern architecture in the Brazilian way: the Brazilian Pavilion by Lúcio Costa and Oscar Niemeyer, with the collaboration of North American architects Paul Lester Wiener and Thomas Price in the interior and landscaping projects, respectively. Yves Bruand mentions the criteria adopted by the jury, guided by the national character: "The jury, made up of architects nominated by the Institute of Architects of Brazil alongside employees of the Ministry of Labor, which was sponsoring the competition, decided to rate the preliminary projects following two criteria: first and foremost, the national character, and, then, the technical conditions, which had to be consistent with an exhibition pavilion. It is important to note that the national character was not seen as an imitation of the past, but as research on *an architectural form that could translate the expression of the Brazilian environment*."[78] The extraordinary fact following the announcement of the winner is well known: "Judging that the work that was ranked second was superior to his own, Lúcio Costa rejected the result, being then authorized by the commission to develop a new project, now in partnership with Niemeyer."[79] This created the possibility of a new collaboration between the pair, now no longer according to a mentor/assistant dynamics, as during the project for the Ministry of Education and Health in 1936, but on equal footing – or, according to Lúcio Costa, with the creative predominance of the former disciple.

Carlos Eduardo Comas, in an article from 1989, understands that the Brazilian Pavilion project coherently meets the political and cultural demands established by the competition, especially the concerns of the Vargas government's *intelligence* in shaping the hegemonic nationalist ideology. The building's program was established by a commission under the coordination of the Ministry of Labor, Industry and Commerce, indicating that the pavilion should "highlight the unity, originality and dynamism of Brazilian culture, as well as the agricultural and mineral riches, which were the basis for the country's qualification as an exporter."[80] The specific way that Lúcio Costa and Oscar Niemeyer interpreted the problem – the pavilion should be both representative of the national character and an example of the country's development – resulted, according to hegemonic narratives, in an original building, the architectural qualities of which expanded the international recognition of the Brazilian architects, still at an early stage.

According to Comas, the intellectual mechanisms that resulted in the first project of Brazilian architecture to embody the "lightness that would become the dominant trademark"[81] are explained by the specific interpretation of Le Corbusier's work carried out by Lúcio Costa and Oscar Niemeyer. Such an interpretation is based on aesthetic convictions they picked up in the academic tradition — an intellectual environment the two had shared —, with Corbusian principles being appropriated as a *style* and the problems of *composition*, typical of classical and neoclassical formal operations, gaining new directions and new possibilities of resolution.

Relying on a text by Julien Guadet, with which Lúcio Costa was certainly familiar, Comas recalls that the "idea of composition implied acceptance and deliberate manipulation of defined formal elements, schemes and principles,"[82] entailing two types of elements: "on the one hand, the material components such as walls and windows that alone could not configure closed volumes, but which could still be considered architectural elements or primary elements of composition; on the other hand, the compositional elements *per se*, those volumes that were virtual or literally closed, such as rooms, circulations and porticos."[83] Bearing in mind these principles, which were present in their academic background, Comas states that Oscar Niemeyer and Lúcio Costa adopted Le Corbusier's independent structure – the Dom-ino structure – as the technical foundation of the "modern style". The total independence between "walls", "supporting elements" and "slabs" – the most important elements of modern architecture – facilitated a number of compositional possibilities unimaginable within previous constructive parameters, which led to a freer and more abstract geometric syntax. In practice, it meant that the Corbusian configuration could be greatly tampered with, as it indeed came to be, without the compositional principles inherent to it being defiled.

The formal contribution of the Brazilian Pavilion, in Comas' assessment, lies in the innovative solution for the Dom-ino structure, where the *planar perception* (from the Greco-Latin tradition, which results in the *Classical* style) and the *volumetric perception* (from the gothic-oriental tradition, which results in the *baroque* style) coexist without canceling each other out. The *crystal* – a metaphor for classicist and mechanistic tendencies – and the *flower* – a metaphor for organicist and romantic tendencies – could coexist within the same aesthetic conception, that is, Brazilian modern architecture, and the Brazil Pavilion for the New York World's Fair is a first example and proof of its possibility of materialization. The curved shapes and various compositional elements are in tune with the baroque inclinations of our colonial past, while the orthogonal shapes and the constructive system point to the modern world of the industrial age.

According to Comas, a second concept is fundamental in Costa and Niemeyer's theory and practice: the concept of *character*. Once again relying on Guadet's words, the "*gaucho*" author points out two varieties of character: "typological or programmatic character" and "generic character". The former "seeks to reveal the purpose of the building and the values related to that purpose – taking into account the influence of the climate and the nature of the site and the place"; the latter "seeks to represent civilization and culture in temporal and geographic coordinates. The spirit of the times or the spirit of the place."[84] However, Comas makes it clear that Guadet does not offer an objective solution regarding the combination of the two varieties of character, leaving Brazilians to formalize the "national identity and traditions"[85] amid the universalizing winds. Thus, local architecture would be a manifestation within a broader and more widespread historical advance: "Brazilian nationality and culture are calmly asserted, located in the broader framework of Western culture and civilization, either in terms of the past, or of the present and future."[86] The reasoning comes to a close: the Brazilian Pavilion – the fruit of the "spirit of the time" – is pregnant with *tradition* and *modernity*, hence its quality and value.

Within the perspective of the present work, the statements of Carlos Eduardo Comas run against the hypothesis that Brazilian modern architecture springs from a well-articulated discourse that seeks a synthesis between *modernity* and *tradition*, that there is a cultural desire that precedes the architectural form. The affiliation of Lúcio Costa's thought to the academic tradition pointed out by the *gaucho* author joins other elements to illustrate the contamination of Brazilian modernist thought by previous worldviews.[87] The concept of character originating from the academic tradition is operative in Lúcio Costa's thought and has a strategic role, mainly because there are much broader concerns than its aesthetic-formal aspect. Nevertheless, the theme of a national character is the touchstone of modernism in the 1920s and 1930s and entails a series of diffuse aspects – racial and mesological, in particular –, also present in Lúcio Costa's architectural conception.[88] When developing his argument, Comas even refers to an intellectual debate external to architecture, although he does not delve into this connection: "Dialecticism, ambivalence and inclusivity could also be considered emblematic attributes of a country that, at that moment, became aware of its culture as a product of the interaction between different races through works by Gilberto Freyre and Sérgio Buarque de Holanda: *Casa-grande e senzala* and *Raízes do Brasil*, respectively."[89]

The ideas of Freyre and Holanda mentioned by Comas, centered on the relationship between raciality and culture, as well as the various versions of their discourse in the architectural field, are late developments of an intellectual debate that dates back to the 19th century and that had several chapters in the modernist environment of the 1920s. Published respectively in 1933 and 1936, *Casa-grande e senzala*[90] and *Raízes do Brasil*[91] adopt a much more scientific stance for the analysis of Brazilian reality, supported by new anthropological and sociological methodologies that the authors came into contact with in Europe and in the United States. If it is true that the work of the two intellectuals far exceeds the impressionist criticism that had prevailed until then, it is also true that both Sérgio Buarque de Holanda, born in São Paulo, and Gilberto Freyre, born in Pernambuco, pay tribute to the previous discussions that took place in the modernist scene, a movement that already considered racial fusion – and the consequent blending of habits, beliefs and customs – as strategic in understanding and consolidating the Brazilian cultural and civilizational phenomenon. Thus, taking into account the very direction of the debate, the ties of friendship and intellectual affinity that the architects maintain with other relevant personalities, the ideological and even political commitments that motivated them, for all this confluence of factors, it would be more prudent to consider that academic aesthetic principles participate only in a subsidiary way in the aesthetic commitments and project decisions of Lúcio Costa and Oscar Niemeyer.

The success of the Brazilian Pavilion at the New York World's Fair, so publicized over the years, dates back to Philip Goodwin's book *Brazil Builds* – "there were excellent modern buildings at the New York Fair, but none of such elegant lightness as the Brazilian Pavilion"[92] – and has been reinforced over time by several critics. In *Modern Architecture in Brazil*, Henrique Mindlin highlights its international repercussion: "this pavilion attracted worldwide attention to the work of Brazilian architects who, at that time, had few finished works to showcase."[93] Yves Bruand focused on the exceptional qualities of the project: "plain in appearance, despite the diversity, and modest in dimensions, the Lúcio Costa and Niemeyer pavilion stood out for its lightness, harmony and balance, for its elegance and distinction."[94] Carlos Eduardo Comas links the international reverberation to the quality of the project: "Lúcio and Oscar owe their first international recognition to the undeniable originality of the Pavilion."[95] Hugo Segawa is emphatic about the repercussion: "the Brazilian pavilion at the New York World's Fair was considered one of the highlights of the entire exhibition. [...] The international success of the Brazilian pavilion can be credited to a serene stance on the meaning of Brazil and Brazilian architecture in the global context."[96] Fernando Lara, when analyzing the repercussion of Brazilian architecture in the international media, states that "the first relevant external conjunctural factor is the end of the Second World War (1945), when the enchantment with Brazilian modern architecture — which was already occupying spaces abroad ever since the Brazilian Pavilion at the New York World's Fair — adds to the repressed demand for architectural articles and magazines."[97] These are just a few examples; the notoriety of Oscar Niemeyer and Lúcio Costa's project results from its success in the media, echoed by texts, lectures and classes.

But is the "international success" of the Brazil Pavilion at the New York World's Fair an undisputed fact? Where's the evidence? Hugo Segawa mentions only two articles, one published in the magazine *The Architectural Forum*, the other in the Brazilian magazine *Arquitetura e Urbanismo* – which, in turn, mentions two other non-specialized foreign publications, *The Magazine Art* and *Fortune* – to attest to "the international success" of the pavilion. In the case of Fernando Lara, it is difficult to know – without access to the detailed statistical surveys he mentions – whether the international interest in Brazilian architecture is due to the success of the Pavilion or whether the phrase is rhetorical and motivated by a coincidence of dates. Lara points to a vertiginous growth of publications on Brazilian architecture in the mid-1940s, but the phenomenon may have been prompted by other episodes – the circulation of the *Brazil Builds* catalog or the news regarding the inauguration of the Ministry building in Rio de Janeiro – and not the pavilion.

The lack of documentary evidence allows the Argentine critic Jorge Francisco Liernur to contest both the success and the very originality attributed to the project developed by Lúcio Costa and Oscar Niemeyer: "I believe that it is possible to affirm that its critical popularity, and especially its singularity, is a later historiographical construction carried out in the context of the consecration encouraged by the MoMA in 1943. Back in1939 the exceptionality of the work was not noticed either by the public or by the critics, for whom the Brazil Pavilion occupied a place similar to other countries such as Finland, Sweden, Argentina and Venezuela."[98] To prove his assertion, the author continues in a footnote: "according to a Gallup poll published in May 1939, 'the visitors of the Fair like the following exhibition places: General Motors, the Theme Center (Democracity), the American Telephone and Telegraph, Ford Motor Company, the Soviet pavilion, the British pavilion and the Rail Transport Exhibition.'"[99]

The subject in question – the real or fabricated success of the Brazilian Pavilion at the New York World's Fair[100] – would be of no interest if its demystification by Liernur were not accompanied by an interesting presentation of the historical and cultural circumstances that triggered this discursive montage. There are two arguments. The first suggests that the strong Brazilian cultural presence in the United States – *Brazil Builds* at MoMA, Zé Carioca at Disney, Carmem Miranda at Broadway and in Hollywood – is encouraged by the US Department of State to facilitate US agreements with Latin American countries, especially Mexico and Brazil, during the Second World War. These are facts widely publicized over the years in academic publications aimed at the general public. Even some of the authors mentioned here, although they have not given greater importance to the fact, have already dealt with it.[101]

The second argument deals with the central concern of this work: the relationship between Brazilian modern architecture and the discursive montage combining *modernity* and *tradition*. Regarding the 1939 Pavilion, Liernur gets straight to the point:

> "What kind of Brazil would be showcased in New York? A large country with numerous natural resources (quite useful for the United States), but also a country with a modernizing vocation and a strong, independent personality. The main distinguishing feature that the Pavilion indicated to its North American hosts was the priority given to the sensitive over the calculated or the utilitarian. If the United States or other industrialized countries could impress visitors with their advanced technology or organizational skills, Brazil would proudly exhibit an ineffable sense of sensual enjoyment of life: a friendly, joyful, and vital giant. Therefore, the Pavilion displays, on the one hand, an idea of Brazilian nature, rich in resources, and on the other, a set of activities for the enjoyment of the senses: hearing, sight, taste, smell, touch."[102]

The sensorial appeal that moves beyond the utilitarian, according to Liernur, entails an architecture that departs from the rational and functional principles of the modern movement: "the curves of the Brazilian Pavilion are absolutely arbitrary. It is true that its use is determined in the plan by the conditions of the terrain, but once this theme is discovered, its repetition in the entire pavilion score ceases to be explained by functional, economic or symbolic reasons, displaying itself as a gratuitously exquisite product of the talent of its creators."[103] This expressive preciosity, which values creative individuality, had already been observed by Max Bill (1908-1994) on a visit to Brazil in 1954, when he strongly criticized the Industry Pavilion in the brand new Parque Ibirapuera. Bill's sour words against the now Biennial Pavilion, projected by Niemeyer, were highlighted by Frampton and Segawa:

"I saw shocking things there: modern architecture shipwrecked in the depths, a seditious antisocial waste devoid of any sense of responsibility to either the commercial occupants or their customers. [...] Thick pilotis, thin pilotis, bizarrely shaped pilotis, all without rhyme or reason, taking over all the space. [...] It is disconcerting to explain the existence of such barbarism in a country where there is a group associated with Ciam, a country that holds conferences on modern architecture, where a magazine like *Habitat* is published and where an architecture biennial takes place. These works are born of a spirit devoid of any decency and responsibility towards the human needs. It is the spirit of decoration, something diametrically opposed to the spirit that animates architecture, which is the art of construction, the social art par excellence."[104]

"The free forms are purely decorative [...]. Initially the pilotis were straight, but now they are starting to take on very baroque shapes. Good architecture is one where each element follows a purpose and no element is superfluous. To achieve this, the architect must be a good artist. He must be an artist who doesn't feel the need to be flamboyant so as to get attention; someone who, above all, is aware of his responsibility towards the present and the future."[105]

In Max Bill's assessment, this expressive preciosity lays bare the formalism that contaminates the work of Oscar Niemeyer and much of Brazilian modern architecture.[106] The discomfort these statements caused in the national architectural milieu found in Lúcio Costa an appropriate retaliation. In his response, Costa says that Bill, on his visit to Brazil, disliked all aspects of our architecture, from the bourgeois apartments of Parque Guinle to the *useless* and *harmful* Portinari tiles on the ground floor of the Ministry of

Education and Health – and even its lack of human proportion. After pointing out the ill will and prejudices of the Swiss artist and critic, Costa proceeds to defend his work: "Now, the tile covering on the ground floor and the fluid sense adopted in the composition of the large panels have the very clear function of softening the density of the walls in order to curb any sense that they fulfill a supporting function, as the upper block does not rest on them, but on the columns. As the tile is one of the traditional elements of Portuguese architecture, which was ours, it seemed to us quite appropriate to renew its employment."[107] Only Affonso Reidy is spared by the Swiss artist: his project for the Pedregulho housing complex is emphatically praised.[108] In Lúcio Costa's view, however, the purpose of this praise is to criticize Pampulha: "On one point, however, we are in complete agreement. That's when he correctly highlights the splendid achievement of Pedregulho. But even here the critic's ulterior motives are revealed when, on the other hand, he belittles Pampulha. Now, without Pampulha, Brazilian architecture as we currently know it – including Pedregulho – would not exist. This was the work that defined its distinctive features."[109] Lúcio Costa passionately defends the *gracious "dengo"* present in the sensual curves of Oscar Niemeyer's work and shared by a substantial part of Brazilian modern architecture, including that of Affonso Reidy.

Advocating for creative freedom and the use of traditional elements, Lúcio Costa explains the peculiarity of Brazilian modernism: while faithfully following the core principles of Le Corbusier's doctrine, Brazilian modern architecture incorporates elements of the national tradition. In a "world still wounded and brutalized by the self-flagellation of war,"[110] one arrives at the synthesis between the functional meaning and the plastic intention that make Brazilian architecture famous. Where Max Bill sees an irresponsible distortion of modern principles, mainly due to the abandonment of social commitment and ethical restraint in the use of plastic and constructive resources, Lúcio Costa sees a conscious and constructive deviation, the very core of the Brazilian contribution to the development of modern architecture worldwide.

Although he takes into account Max Bill's ethical and aesthetic objections, Jorge Francisco Liernur shifts his interest to another point: how the process sanctioning the discourse that sees Brazilian modern architecture as an expressive branch of world architecture takes place. According to Liernur, behind the *Brazil Builds* episode, which is explained by North-American strategic interests, we find Lúcio Costa's theoretical assumptions, the complexities and incongruities of which the catalog proceeds to flatten in favor of a more synthetic and harmonious view of the national architecture. "Although in some aspects the approach is indeed suggestive of his influence, the book does not exactly reproduce Lúcio Costa's position. *Brazil Builds* picks up the dominant lines of the debate and reduce its contradictions to an apparent unity, marking a first step towards the imposition of an idea – the baroque inclination as a particularity of Brazilian modern architecture –, an idea that was not yet fully accepted in 1942."[111] Liernur argues that only a few years later would Lúcio Costa integrate baroque excesses into his theoretical synthesis, when, following the "American path" for our architecture, his priority shifts to reconciling the modern architecture of Corbusian bent and the routine architecture of the tradesmen of the colonial period: "It was there, in the answers found and continued by the anonymous builders of the villages, that one could verify the uninterrupted line of identity that would connect modern architecture to the eternal and immutable Brazilian spirit."[112]

However, in a text published a year before the Brazil Pavilion at the New York World's Fair – "Necessary Documentation", 1938 –, Lúcio Costa argues for the systematic study of the anonymous production of Portuguese architecture accommodated to the colonial scene, highlighting the scarcity of studies on religious and civil architecture and directing positive words to Aleijadinho: "If there is already something about the main churches and convents – very little, in fact, and most of it revolving around the work of Antônio Francisco Lisboa, whose personality, rightfully so, has been the first to attract attention –, nothing or almost nothing has been done with regard to civil architecture and particularly to houses."[113] Although noting the scarcity of studies on the subject, Lúcio Costa feels comfortable stating that in this architecture "one observes the softening mentioned by Gilberto Freyre, dropping, in order to adapt to the local environment, a bit of that "*carrure*" so typical of Portugal."[114] According to him, the simplicity of customs preserved the colonial scene from "certain precious and somewhat pompous mannerisms"[115] found in the metropolis. The mention of the sociologist from Pernambuco brings up the cultural environment and is followed by references to racial issues – blacks, indigenous peoples and white Europeans – and mesological issues – the grandeur of the territory. In another text from the same period regarding the University City of Rio de Janeiro, Lúcio Costa on several occasions imagines reconciling Corbusian principles to the local reality, with the inclusion of traditional balconies[116] and the use of pilotis to create free spaces integrated with nature: "After passing through the entrance, the mass of students is still not inside the school, but below it – in a patio among the vegetation."[117] The arguments present in the two texts by Lúcio Costa written in the second half of the 1930s attest, therefore, to Liernur's statements about the architect's concerns during this period, which aimed at placing Corbusian modern architecture and anonymous colonial architecture on the same agenda.

Still regarding *Brazil Builds*, Liernur also notes that taking the idea of a homogeneous and original national identity as a fundamental reason for the success achieved by the Brazilian architecture exposed in New York was an inconsistent position for a variety of factors, such as: the

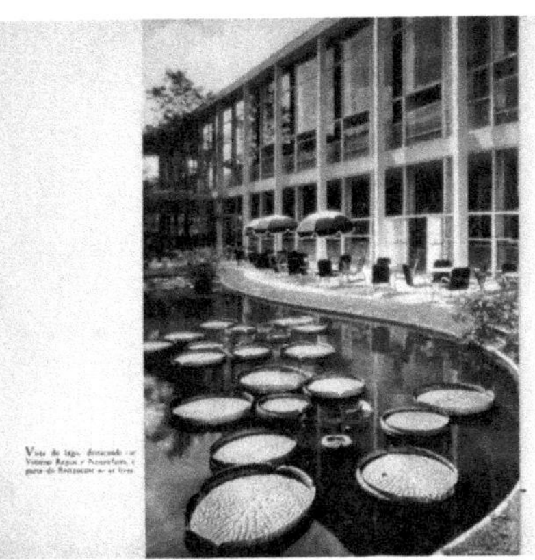
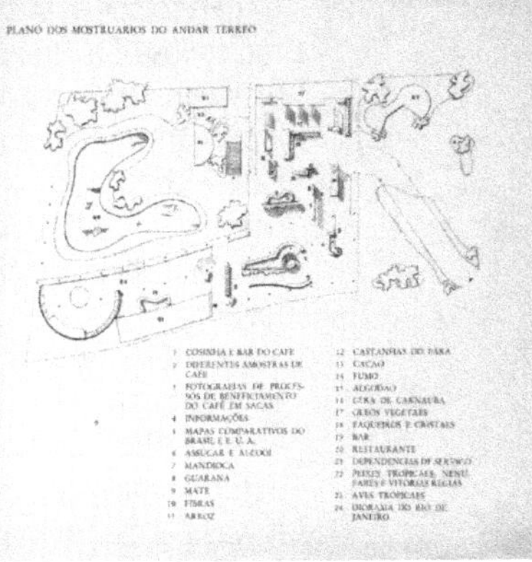

Catalog of the Brazil Pavilion, New York World's Fair, USA. Lúcio Costa and Oscar Niemeyer, 1939. FAU USP Library Collection

presence of foreign architects like Gregori Warchavchik; the diffuse foreign influences that are inevitable in the face of such presences, such as the *Italian character* of Bernard Rudofsky's patios; the diverse regionalisms that emerged within modern architecture, as can be seen in Scandinavia, Central Europe and the Mediterranean countries; the survival of primitive aspects in places other than Brazil, as is the case in virtually all Latin-American countries and even in different regions around the world; the absence of works that could be identified as precursors, which gave the impression that "the modern buildings that the book presented seemed to have emerged abruptly, without any transition, from a fusion between international principles and a 'local soul' at last recovered,"[118] and, finally, the fact that the formal characteristics generically attributed to Brazilian architects are found almost exclusively in the works of Oscar Niemeyer... On the whole, such objections say a lot about undue and ideologically compromised generalizations. To conclude, Liernur explicits the incongruities, limits and problems of such an intellectual montage:

"I tried to show, in short, not only or not so much that the *topos* of a 'Brazilian architecture' was constructed between 1939 and 1943, but that the image of this 'Brazilian' architecture was associated for the most part with the *extraordinary* individual talent of Oscar Niemeyer. For that reason, what came after that should inevitably bear the imprint of his particular *manner*, and for that very reason could not secure, in the long run, any continuity, only frustration. As the identification of the totality of architecture in Brazil with Niemeyer's architecture was artificial, it would be necessary to deform reality to process it in this scheme. As a result, it was necessary to put aside a large amount of highly valuable ferments, ideas and experiences – including those of Costa himself – which, had it emerged free from the weight of the *monumental construction* set up by the MoMA operation, would certainly have been able to flourish in as many new and multiple directions as all those that the real Brazil had inevitably produced until then throughout its complex and rich history."[119]

Catalog of the Brazil Pavilion, New York World's Fair, USA. Lúcio Costa and Oscar Niemeyer, 1939. FAU USP Library Collection

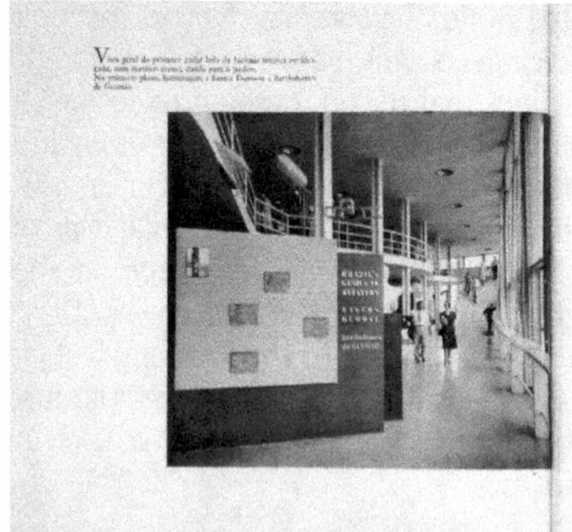

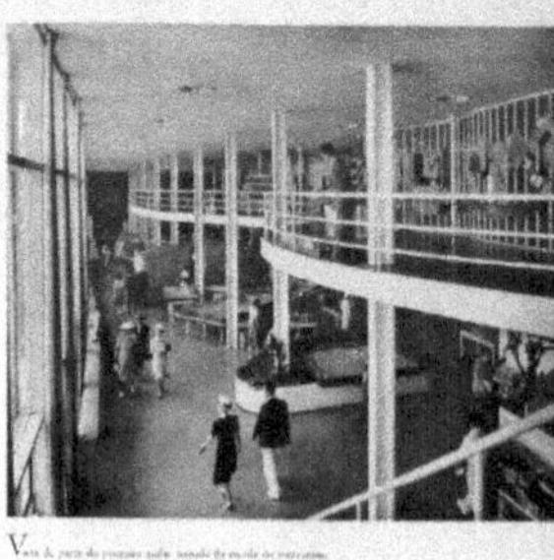

Liernur spots a key issue for understanding the later course of Brazilian architecture. Smoothing out the contradictions in the discourse set forth by *Brazil Builds* has the immediate consequence of spreading a simplified version of Lúcio Costa's theoretical vision for a modern architecture that incorporates tradition. The stark differences between Vila Monlevade and the Park Hotel in Nova Friburgo, designed by Costa, and Niemeyer's Pampulha ensemble or Casa das Canoas end up overlooked as products of the same architectural lineage – the Brazilian School. Lúcio Costa himself will be captured by this discursive trap, increasingly giving Oscar Niemeyer a central role, to the point of elevating him to the status of a genius on par with Aleijadinho.[120] His discourse becomes more ambiguous in order to accommodate these differences, seeking to enlist in the same definition of modern Brazilian architecture both the Niemeyer lineage, heir to the baroque tendency, and his own version, more in line with the architecture of anonymous master craftsmen. Cultural heritages of a distinct character will unfold in equally distinct modern works, encompassed, however, by a unitary and contradictory discourse.

The acute analysis by Jorge Francisco Liernur, who methodically scrutinizes the different directions contained within the same concept of "Brazilianness" – even when this Brazilianness is clearly non-existent – does not provide a satisfactory answer to a fundamental question: faced with such a vast menu, why did the ideologues of Brazilian modernism, especially Lúcio Costa, choose Le Corbusier's principles as the external element to be incorporated into the national tradition? Liernur's quick allusion to the issue – "the demand for a specific plastic role for architecture placed Costa in the current represented by Le Corbusier and opposite to that led by the Germans of the so-called *hard line* of functionalism"[121] – is correct, but excessively generic. There is something to be explored here.

The Technized Barbarian

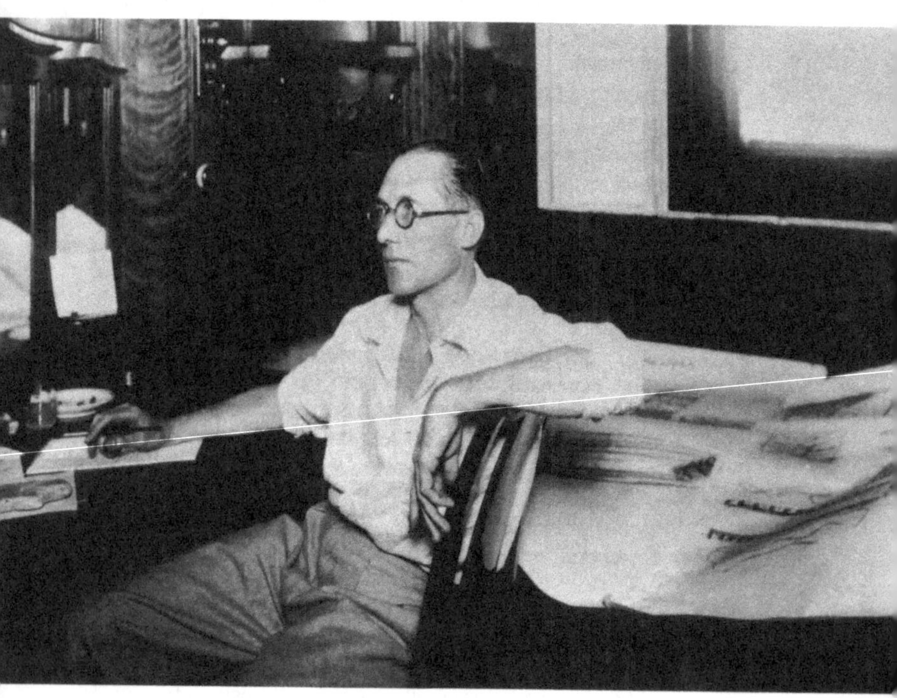

Le Corbusier's return to France aboard
the ship Lutetia, 1929. Collection of
the Foundation Le Corbusier

The sky is a raw blue
The wall in front is a raw white
The raw sun knocks me on the head
The black woman on a small porch is frying   little fish
on a stove made from an old cookie tin
Two little black kids suck a piece of sugar cane
Blaise Cendrars, "Peixinhos"[122]

In the same issue of *Block* magazine in which the article by Jorge Francisco Liernur appears, we find a text by Carlos Alberto Ferreira Martins that interests us a lot for its important contribution to the understanding of the intellectual montage that shapes Brazilian modern architecture. Martins also points out the relevant role of the *Brazil Builds* catalog/exhibition promoted by MoMA of New York in 1943: "Goodwin's work is important for the international projection it gives to Brazilian architecture, but also because it inaugurates an interpretation that will become recurrent in historiography."[123] While Liernur focuses his analysis on North-American events, Martins looks into the association between the intellectual motivations of the episode and the ideas previously disseminated by Lúcio Costa:

"It is known that Goodwin's book triggered a wave of international dissemination of Brazilian architecture. But its fundamental contribution was undoubtedly to inaugurate a narrative argument that would become recurrent in historiography, based essentially on the idea of the inseparability between the 'originality' – and the consequent international recognition – of Brazilian architecture and its identification with a project blending modernity and tradition, which was sustained and supported by the expansion and the need for ideological affirmation of the Vargas state apparatus. The ties to the theoretical scheme proposed and developed by Costa, since his famous text 'Reasons for the new architecture', are not, as we well know, mere coincidences."[124]

Martins establishes the affiliation of Goodwin's arguments to those of Lúcio Costa, demonstrating how the same convictions propagate over time. Henrique Mindlin and Yves Bruand's books, the main followers and promoters, start from the same assumptions and reach the same conclusions regarding the existence of a specific modern architecture, of regional character, developed in Brazil, and whose main characteristic is precisely the synthesis between modernity and tradition. The weaving of such a "narrative thread", as the author calls it, cannot be carried out without erasing destabilizing elements that jeopardize the clarity and coherence of the argument. He mentions as examples the disregard for instances of neoclassical inclination and the little attention given to Gregori Warchavchik and Flávio de Carvalho, as well as further evidence already covered in the course of this book.

The revelations concerning the contradictions and omissions of these authors prove to be effective tools in the hands of Martins, who finds in Geraldo Ferraz's book on Gregori Warchavchik a precious argument: on his visit to Brazil, Le Corbusier actually praised the pioneering works by the Ukrainian architect based in São Paulo, highlighting precisely the *regionality* of his projects and saying that his is "the best adaptation of the constructive guidelines of modern art to the tropical landscape of South America."[125] The characterization of Warchavchik as the author of a modern architecture not yet acclimatized to the tropical soil – a crucial argument for the paternity of true Brazilian modern architecture to be attributed to the carioca branch – is affirmed with no mention of the assessment put forward by Le Corbusier himself, the guru of Brazilian modern architects. In Ferraz's verdict – corroborated by Martins, despite pointing out the local bias behind the author's motivations –, the reason for Warchavchik's exclusion from official historiography is his relative marginality after returning to São Paulo and the reduced scale of his buildings, when compared to the official buildings constructed by the architects from Rio de Janeiro.

The interplay between the international and regional dimensions of modern architecture was very present in Warchavchik's worldview. At the 4th Pan-American Congress of Architecture held in Rio de Janeiro in 1928, he made a specific digression on the theme: "We will perhaps have an European architecture, a South American architecture and an American architecture. Eventually, together they will form a single world style, prompted by the same demands of life"; however, this "architecture will be as regional as possible, because its first and main requirement will be to adapt to each region, each climate and to the customs of each people."[126] In the same year, in a text concerned with the ongoing verticalization in the federal capital, Lúcio Costa associates architectural development with raciality and culture, presenting an unexpected derogatory view of the Brazilian man: "All architecture is a matter of race. As long as our people continue to be this exotic thing that we see on the streets, our creations are bound to be something exotic. This is not about half a dozen people who travel and dress in *rue de La Paix*, but about the anonymous crowd on the trains in the Central and Leopoldina stations, people with livid faces, who makes us feel ashamed everywhere. What can we expect from such people when it comes to architecture?"[127] The derogatory and unbacked judgment present in this 1928 text reveals Lúcio Costa's cultural lag not only in regard to Warchavchik, but also to the modernists in São Paulo: in that same year Mário de Andrade, Oswald de Andrade and Raul Bopp published a series of exceptional modernist works – a rhapsody, a poetic manifesto and a series of poems – celebrating the positive aspects of the Brazilian man. There is an asynchrony of more or less a decade between the nationalist projects of Mário de Andrade and Lúcio Costa, which prevents a complete symmetry between them.

Picking up that line of argument, Martins highlights a second point of interest: the significant amount of good works of modern architecture spread across the country, designed by many architects, mentioned in the preface to *Brazil Builds* and in the introductory text of *Modern Architecture in Brazil.* The works that will later be canonized for their brilliant qualities, designed by a select group of architects, constitute only a narrow cut from the names featured in the lists by Giedion and Mindlin. Such fondness of historiography for the exceptional deserves clarification and, according to Martins, "understanding the logic behind this montage of the historiographical narrative entails reconstituting the construction of the supremacy of a particular project that became a *Brazilian project.* Consequently, it is important to avoid getting trapped in a discourse that takes for granted the spontaneity of that course."[128] Lúcio Costa's worldview, which gets diluted by widespread diffusion, obscures alternative modern iterations in Brazil, and its constant repetition crystallizes into an indisputable version.

The third point highlighted by Martins – one strategically important in the arguments developed throughout this work – is Yves Bruand seeing a harmony of worldviews in the fondness of modern Brazilian architects for Corbusian principles. Le Corbusier's prophetic discourse, his visionary enthusiasm, is in line with the anarchic individualism typical of Brazilians, just as the latent authoritarianism of the Swiss-French was naturally assimilable in an environment extremely respectful of social hierarchy. According to Martins, Bruand notes Le Corbusier's suggestion for the use of tiles and imperial palm trees in modern Brazilian architecture, a fact always remembered by Lúcio Costa: "We accepted his recommendations to use tiles on the walls of the ground floor areas and the gneiss in the framings and gables, as well as his preference for a sculpture by Celso Antonio different from the one we had chosen, – the *Sitting Man.*"[129] In other words, the synthesis with tradition – so dear to our architects

– was actually shared by the master, which reveals an unsuspicious acceptance and promotion on his part of regional solutions in local modern output.

Martins' article is a compendium of the arguments presented in his master's thesis, a pioneering work for the understanding of the hegemonic historical plot governing the interpretation of Brazilian modern architecture. Martins mentions in the thesis the *ideological convergence* between "some basic principles and doctrinal conceptions of the modern movement in Brazil and the fundamental features of what is conventionally described as the country's penchant for authoritarian thinking."[130] In this sense, the Corbusian assumptions, where we can spot traces of a despotic positivism, are suitable for Brazilian architects, who come up with a project of convergent action under the tutelage of an authoritarian State. The role of architecture and the architect himself in achieving and managing social well-being is impregnated with an authoritarian and simplifying vision of society:

> "Partially in Corbusier, but fully developed in Brazilian theorists, we have a conception of society basically structured from the relationship between four sectors or social agents: landowners, industrialists, the *masses* and intellectuals. A particular relationship is established between the latter and the State, based, on the one hand, on the benefactor character of the State, erected as a social agent capable of overcoming the irrationality resulting from the mismatch between technical production and the unfair distribution of its benefits and, on the other hand, on the specific character of this sector of intellectuals, whose interests would be identified with those of the new society as a whole."[131]

Martins' premises lead to an important conclusion: the advent of modern Brazilian architecture is not a miracle, as

Lúcio Costa previoulsy suggested, nor is it irrational as advocated by Giedion. Furthermore, the choice for Le Corbusier is not random or a matter of personal preference, but the result of a deep identity of values and discourses, in addition to a subjective sympathy provoked by the strong personality of the Swiss. Le Corbusier's prophetic vision, which imagines a new city planned for the machine age, made a lot of sense in a society like Brazil's, which was undergoing profound changes brought about by the political and cultural rearrangements emanating from the historical episode of the so-called Revolution of 1930. "It was a permanent modernization", says Lúcio Costa, "with total conviction. At the time, we were all convinced that this new architecture we were making, this new approach, was linked to social renewal. It seemed that the world, the new society, as well as the new architecture, were twins, closely tied."[132] The reasons for Lúcio Costa's predilection for Le Corbusier, at least the most prominent in consciousness, are evident in the comparison made with Walter Gropius:

> "Gropius was an exceptional figure and his work had
> an exceptional quality as well. A learned man, married
> to a very intelligent and beautiful woman. During the
> first war he was in the cavalry, he was a ulan, he told
> me himself. A splendid figure. I spent a lot of time with
> him in Paris, and then here at home. He liked Leleta
> very much, who took him to the Botanical Garden. But
> Le Corbusier was the only one who faced the problem
> from three angles: the sociological one – he gave great
> importance to the social dimension –; the question
> of adapting to new technology; finally, the plastic
> approach. This is what impressed me the most, what
> set him apart from everyone else, even though Gropius
> had organized a stupendous thing at Bauhaus. Today,
> many people see the Bauhaus movement as a very rigid
> and restrictive thing, but we cannot forget the fabulous

structure that Bauhaus was at the time – Kandinsky, Klee, etc. But Le Corbusier's approach was more seductive. He was good with words, and the text of his publications, together with the peculiar layout, was appealing. It was that faith in the new, in the good sense, a force that spoke to young people."[133]

Carlos Alberto Ferreira Martins' argument reveals not only the existence of the discursive montage, but also the political and ideological motivations that inspire it. This book attempts to take a distinct, but not contradictory path. We believe that as important as recognizing the existence and the motives behind a historical phenomenon is understanding the materiality engedering this phenomenon, explaining how a set of discourses dispersed in the cultural sphere get processed, transformed, adapted and/or distorted so that they fit a certain purpose. The effectiveness of discourse is not a matter of veracity, but of its ability to evoke, mostly unconsciously, latent forces within a community. Discourses give shape to the formless, picking up drives and impulses spread throughout society and transforming them into operative energy by creating mental scenarios where they gain meaning and direction. The discursive montage concerning modern Brazilian architecture obeys a historical purpose towards which many interests converge; these interests, albeit diverse, are amenable to accommodation. Understanding how this is possible might be the particular contribution of this work.

Following Le Corbusier's trips to Brazil is another way of understanding the friendliness with which he was received in the country and the intellectual and affective identification with modern Brazilian architects that he established over time. This Le Corbusier who so deeply intoxicated the young modernist intellectuals is not yet the great artist with a polished and stabilized thought, but rather the young architect – at that time mostly a proselyte of modernist promises with no great achievements to offer – who came to Latin America at the end of the 1920s to be dazzled by the immensity of the territory and the splendor of the virgin forest.[134] The tradition of European travelers, who arrived here during the colonial and imperial periods to portray us, was taken up by the São Paulo modernists, who, among others, brought Filippo Tommaso Marinetti, who ended up being somewhat snubbed by Mário de Andrade, and Blaise Cendrars (1887-1961), who maintained contact with São Paulo intellectuals for a long time. It is on the 1924 trip to Brazil that Cendrars learns about the Brazilian government's plans to build a new capital for the country, soon passing along the information to his friend Le Corbusier,[135] who in turn promptly contacted Paulo Prado (1869-1943), one of the promoters of the 1922 Art Week and friend of the Belgian poet, whose visit to Brazil he had facilitated. Corbusier offered his services to carry out the project, saying that he was willing to visit Brazil immediately. Prado seems to have encouraged the young architect, as the correspondence between the two continues, with the architect's visit to Brazil and the new capital as the main subjects. Formal, but sincere in his interests, Le Corbusier writes to Paulo Prado: "Dear Sir, I left Paris without having had the pleasure of meeting you. I will return around the 20th of August. Will you still be here? In any case, I would very much like to be able to lay the groundwork for my trip to Brazil. [...] Indeed, the dream of 'Planaltina' won't leave my mind: I would like to be able to build in these virgin territories of yours some of the great projects on which I have been working here, whose consummation the continental lethargy will certainly never allow."[136]

The fact that it is Paulo Prado who set up Le Corbusier's visit in 1929 shows that São Paulo modernism was still leading the struggle for cultural renewal in the country. This state of affairs changed radically soon after, with the rise of Getúlio Vargas to power in 1930, the strong centralization of political power in Rio de Janeiro and the consequent transfer of the cultural headquarters. The Swiss-French architect arrived in Brazil in 1929, after a stay in Argentina and Uruguay, to make public appearances in São Paulo and Rio de Janeiro. He then had the opportunity to describe the magnificent trip between Buenos Aires and São Paulo: "From the plane I witnessed spectacles that I could describe as cosmic. What an invitation to meditation, what an evocation of the fundamental truths of our land!"[137] Unlike past travelers, Le Corbusier saw us from above, which, for an urban planner, meant encompassing the territorial immensity of Brazil.[138] The profusion of drawings, sketches, notes, letters and texts testifies to the dizzying intellectual clash that Corbusier experienced, driven by a "foreign gaze" that sees tropical reality as if it were still enveloped in a primordial atmosphere:

> "The Earth is not uniformly green, it has all the stains and differences in color of a putrefying body. Elegant palm trees, blooming fields, majestic rivers, or enchanting streams, virgin woodland – grandeur that, whether down below or at close range, gives us a feeling of nobility, of exuberance, of opulence, of life – you tree, you all, seen from the sky, you are nothing but an apparent mold. And you Earth, oh! Desperately damp earth, you are nothing but mold! And your water, either as vapor or liquid, maneuvered by a distant fire star, you draw everything to you at the same time, joy or sadness, abundance or misery."[139]

> "Everything follows the scriptures: the virgin forest, the Pampas. [...] There are immense snakes [...]. We don't see them. The dam is full of crocodiles. We don't see them."[140]

This aquatic, humid, nocturnal universe, full of reptiles, pregnant with original life that emerges from Le Corbusier's pen, so exotic and primeval that it can be compared to biblical creation, maintains enormous similarities with the considerations of Hermann Keyserling, a German philosopher who visited South America between 1929 and 1930, the same period as the Swiss-French architect. Anchored in a historical overview of romantic inclination developed by Oswald Spengler,[141] Keyserling argues, in 1926, that "all previous cultures had their center of gravity in the irrational, impulsive, sensitive, illogical, erotic."[142] The book in question, *Le monde qui nait* (*El mundo que nace*) excited Mário de Andrade and Oswald de Andrade and is a fundamental reference in their work from 1928 onwards.[143]

A second book by Keyserling – *Meditaciones suramericanas* (*South-American Meditations*)[144] published in 1932 – bears striking similarities to the ongoing debate in Brazil at that time. For the German author, South America was the continent of the third day of creation, the incarnation of that primordial world where the cosmic environment and the telluric energies shape a life still quite precarious. An original world full of life, where the limitless extension is waiting for a satisfactory accommodation of human culture and civilization. "The continent of the third day of creation", title of the first chapter of the book, is a recurrent phrase to designate South America. According to Genesis, on the third day God separated the water from the land and created the continents and the seas. Then, on solid ground, he created herbs that bore seeds and fruit trees that bore fruit containing the seeds themselves. Before the third day, God had already created the light, the firmament, the night and the day; contradictorily, he had created neither the sun nor the moon. Earth is created on the third day, a nocturnal and aquatic land. The biblical image, used by Keyserling as an allegory to express the idea of a world at the beginning of evolution, is replaced in another passage by another image, now a dreamy one, illustrating the primordial world:

When, still in Europe, I had been meditating the first
South American souls I had met, I was assailed by visions
of snakes; before my eyes arose mottled or tiger-spotted
fragments of trunks of huge pythons, flecked by flashes
of light filtering through the tree-tops ; bodies welling
up and rolling forth out of a bottomless opaque pond.
In its native landscape this netherworld which lifted to
the surface its inner correspondence within me, took its
original elementary shape and mould. All colours paled,
all firm lines faded into each other. I felt encircled and
begirdled on all sides by coils of writhing larvae; the first
time I saw them, the awe-inspiring music of the Dance
of the Shades of Gluck's Orpheus sounded within me,
as though it were the necessary accompaniment of the
vision. And so it is; only in the pace was the great seer
mistaken. With slow move- ments, like the chameleon of
to-day, the brood of the netherworld creeps and crawls
around in a circle within an infinite yet closed space.
And least of all do these larvae resemble the shades of
humans. They are not real snakes, but they are like unto
snakes; they are most akin to the glass-eel, that earliest
form of the eel after it has shed its larva; only they are
pervious not to light, but, as it were, to darkness. When
first I saw those cold, slimy bodies crawling towards me,
and the innumerable staring glassy basilisk-eyes fixed
upon mine, I was horror-struck. I felt abandoned to
evil. But soon I realized that neither were they crawling
towards me, nor did they stare at me; they were ever
moving yet without direction nor aim, and with eyes
phosphorescent and wide-open they were blind. And
then it was revealed to me that what had first evoked
in me the idea of evil is simply life primordial; the
association with Evil is due to the fact that a distorting
mirror receives its reflection. And then I understood,
moreover, why nethermost Life must needs be reflected
in daylight consciousness in the form of the snake, as

indeed the Chaldeans had but one word for Serpent
and Life. Our consciousness can only reflect what par-
takes of the quality of light. But the netherworld is
shrouded in darkness eternal. Thus, its projection onto
the surface appears, if it does appear, in the shape of a
counter-shadow, as the opposite of a shadow: the blind
as seeing, the inert as swift of movement, the invisible
as shining. Thus, that which 'in itself' is the primordial
worm, for ever incapable of rising, glistens forth as the
cunning, wicked and gem-like snake.[145]

Although only in passing, it is worth mentioning how
close this description is to the gestational forest present in
the Amazonian texts of Euclides da Cunha as well as in the
anthropophagic work of Tarsila do Amaral (1886-1973).
While in the first case we might attribute any similarity to
a curious communion of worldviews, the attested influence
caused by Keyserling's work within the hosts of São Paulo
modernism allows us to suppose that, in Tarsila's case, the
influence operated through more direct and conscious
mechanisms. The "technized barbarian of Keyserling" referred
to by Oswald de Andrade in the "Manisfesto Antropófago",
published in 1928[146] – a period of loving, intellectual and
artistic partnership between him and Tarsila –, comes directly
from the book *Le monde qui nait*, by the German author.[147]
In turn, Telê Porto Ancona Lopez, in a seminal text on the
work of Mário de Andrade, deals specifically with the deep
impression caused by the German's considerations on the
Brazilian's work:

"For this reason, in 1927, it is by stepping out of a
Marxist path that [Mário de Andrade] seeks to conceptualize the destiny of the Brazilian man, calling Keyserling
(*Le monde qui nait*) to his aid. That same year, by the
way, he leaves São Paulo for a three-month stay in
the north of the country. It is when he sets his critical

view of the Brazilian people, outlined for the novel *Macunaíma*, in contact with the reality and problems of a true tropical environment. He discovers the Amazon, where man could live without contradictions with his geography, freed from an imported civilization, realizing himself as the *Sein* of Keyserling. The Amazon reinforces his certainty of the legitimacy of laziness as creative leisure, which he had been exploring since his youthful readings of the Greek classics, from Virgil to Horace."[148]

The point of contact between the views on Brazil featured in Mário de Andrade, Tarsila do Amaral, Le Corbusier and Keyserling – the luxuriant, impenetrable, primordial and imposing nature – is the basis for much mistrust regarding the possibilities for a satisfactory establishment of man in the Brazilian territory, at least along the same lines established by the Europeans.[149] With the temperament of an architect and urban planner, Le Corbusier points out as a major issue the need to confront the territory, how to overcome a destiny, the product of random brutal forces, and take control of the civilizing process.

Like previous foreign travelers, Le Corbusier expresses serious doubts about man's chances of conquering this tropical nature. Upon arriving in Rio de Janeiro, he had the feeling that "everything would be absorbed by this violent and sublime landscape."[150] A few days earlier in São Paulo, in a meeting with the group of Oswald de Andrade, Tarsila do Amaral and Raul Bopp, he had already spoken about the enormous challenge that awaited them: "Young people from São Paulo, presenting themselves as anthropophagic, want with this to express that they mean to put a fight against international dissolution, adhering to heroic principles whose memory is still present. Such a leap of courage is not negligible in America. I told them many times: you are shy and fearful, you are afraid. We, the members of the Paris team, are much more intrepid than you, and I will explain why: in

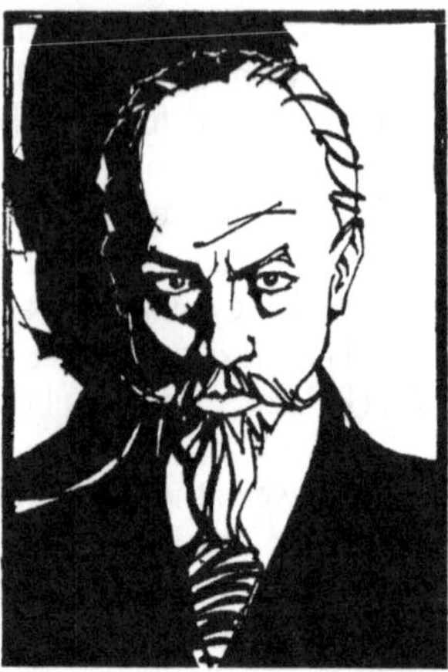

Hermann Keyserling, illustration for the column "Panorama literário". *Vamos Ler!*, no. 37, Rio de Janeiro, April 15, 1937, 23

your country the problems are so numerous, so immense, the interiors yet to be colonized are so large, that your energies are immediately diluted in these dimensions, quantities and distances."[151] The enormity of our territory and the savage violence of our nature deserve an equally powerful civilizing effort. The timorous shyness that he sees in our modernists seems to him to be devoid of the gigantism and radicalism necessary for the enterprise.

The convergence of Keyserling and Le Corbusier's points of view – so similar and so close historically – in our modernist environment, far from European centers, is not a neglectable coincidence and points to an uncomfortable node in our social existence. The theme of the prodigious tropical nature has informed visions of Brazil ever since its discovery. Originally associated with paradise, over centuries of discursive changes, it ended up reduced, at the end of the 19th century, to a somber argument featured in many theories concerning our civilizational infeasibility. Along with the mesological determinism, there is also a very unedifying view of the character of the Brazilian people, which would be the result of a supposedly degrading racial fusion taking

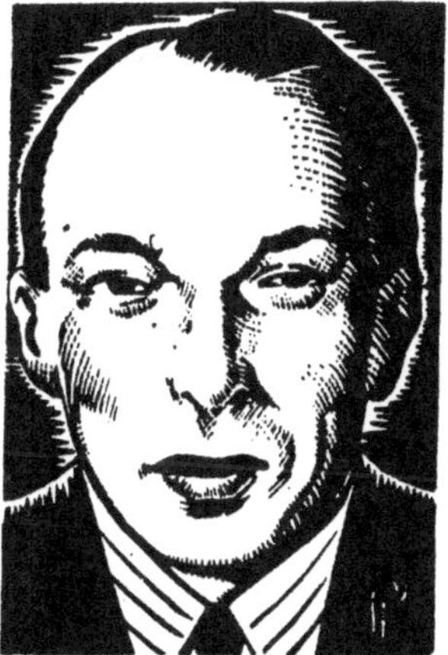

Raul Bopp, illustration for the column "Panorama literário". *Vamos Ler!*, Rio de Janeiro, January 22, 1942, 15

place in an inhospitable environment. When they return to the theme, however, both Keyserling and Le Corbusier, even if they partially reproduce the pessimistic prediction, introduce redemptive possibilities — shared by our young modernists — by recognizing in the "primitive" the potential for the "new". How much the pessimistic view is ingrained in the local mentality is shown in this passage by Le Corbusier: "High-ranking Brazilian characters were furious when they learned that I had visited the hills where the blacks lived in Rio: 'It's a shame for us, civilized people!' I calmly explained that, to begin with, I thought these Negroes were fundamentally good; good-hearted people. Not to mention the fact that they're beautiful, magnificent." Much to the surprise of his astonished audience, Le Corbusier, besides praising the native cordiality, points out civilizing qualities arising from the tender nature of this humble people: "their care-free attitude, the limits they wisely impose on their needs, their inner capacity for fantasy, their candor, made their houses always admirably well placed on the ground, the window surprisingly open to magnificent spaces, the smallness of the pieces abundantly effective."[152]

The City and the Country are Aesthetic Facts

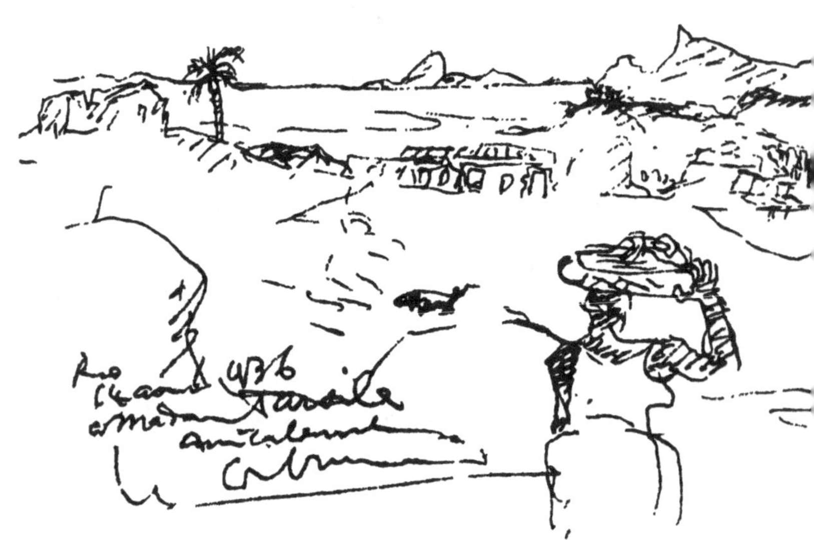

Drawing by Le Corbusier, with the dedication "Rio, August 14, 1936. To Mrs. Tarsila, fraternally, Le Corbusier". AMARAL, Aracy. *Tarsila: Her Work and Her Time*, 254.

Drugstore
Hypodermic jabs against retrograde aesthetics
And a vaccine against the new...
Chemical laboratory
Crucibles retorts balloons glasses cups thermometers
tubes
Pots and stills
Large chemical factory on the Tietê River
Large water pipelines with special reservoirs and tanks
Bridges that close and open
Elevators and chimneys
Wheels pulleys boilers reels
Wagon turbines pipes electrical machinery and
appliances
Special railroad key
Internal trains for industry exclusive use
Telephone and electrical wires, a whole network over the
factory...
The world is too narrow for my industrial facility!...
Luis Aranha, "Drogaria de éter e sombra", 1922[153]

In 1936, during his second trip to Brazil, Le Corbusier presented Tarsila do Amaral with a drawing, a record of an everyday scene in Rio de Janeiro. The sketch, entitled "Panorama of the city" and dated August 14, 1936, shows a black woman in the foreground with her back to us, carrying an indefinite volume on her head, perhaps a bundle of clothes to wash or products to sell; in the background, the carioca landscape, the Pão de Açúcar mountain, the sea and a coconut tree. The quick stylized representation shows homogeneous and simple houses, peacefully settled in the territory.[154] Daily life in the favelas of Rio de Janeiro was documented twice by Le Corbusier on his first visit to Brazil, back in 1929. In the first drawing ("Favela", 1929), three black women carry something on their heads – one of them carries a can of water, while the other two carry undefined volumes.

The second ("A favela", 1929) bears even more striking similarities with the little gift offered to Tarsila. A black man (or is it a black woman?) with his back to us in the foreground faces the low, homogeneous group of houses; the lower edge of the drawing cuts the figure at shoulder height; in the background, the coast and the Pão de Açúcar mountain can be seen. In the three scenes, the same microcosm: the quiet life of simple people in a habitat quite precarious, yet peaceful, pleasant and harmonious.[155]

More than copying what he sees, these drawings register a structural re-elaboration of reality, or, in other words, a kind of potential new world. It lacks both the terrible living conditions of ex-slaves and the buildings and symbolic spaces of political and religious power – palaces, gardens and imperial parks. However, a certain formal schematism emanates from these pieces, which we can attribute to the persistence of cultural conventions. There is no formidable discovery in the scenes recorded by Le Corbusier on his first visit to Brazil. It seems more like him *revealing* to himself thoughts and convictions ingrained in his spirit. The excessive artificiality of Western civilization and the resulting evils in its psychic economy had already been outlined in previous texts and lectures, but nothing compares to the visceral diagnosis of his South American texts:

> "If I think of architecture as 'the houses of men', I feel more in line with Rousseau: 'Man is good'. But if I think of Architecture as a 'house of architects', I become skeptical, pessimistic, Voltairian, and I say: 'Everything is wrong, in the most detestable of worlds' (Candide). This is where architectural exegesis leads, architecture being the result of the state of mind of an era. We have reached a deadlock, the social and moral mechanisms are jumbled. We have the thirst of a Montaigne and a Rousseau going on a journey to question the *naked man*. The reform to be undertaken is profound, for it is

hypocrisy that reigns: love, marriage, society, death; we are totally and utterly fake, we are *fake*!"[156]

There is a certain proximity between Le Corbusier's thought and the Romantic tradition, especially in its positive valuation of pre-industrial purity and simplicity, which informs his ambiguous assessment of modern society and its promises of unlimited material satisfaction. However, after his tropical rendezvous, the contradictions in his work accentuate, giving a new direction to theoretical and formal considerations. The drawings from his first visits to Brazil in 1929 and 1936 show a surprising connection with the intellectual and artistic production of São Paulo modernism. This proximity is not just a matter of theme – tropical nature, raciality and civilization –, it also points to a common worldview, associated with the ambiguous valuation of modernity. However, the greater radicalism of Brazilian production suggests that the European architect may have suffered an unexpected influence during his first stay in Brazil, when he learned and was surprised by the ideals of the group led by Oswald de Andrade.[157] More accurate research could perhaps elucidate the suspicion put forward by Kenneth Frampton regarding the turnabout in the work of Le Corbusier: "For some reason the ultimate foundations of which we do not know, the fact is that primitive technical elements began to appear in his work with increasing frequency and freedom of expression from 1930 onwards."[158] In order to test this hypothesis, it would be necessary to challenge the omission, in critical and historical texts on the Swiss-French architect, of personal, epistolary and work exchanges that he had with Brazilian intellectuals, artists and architects since the 1920s and that continued throughout his life.[159] Instead of a one-way influence, we could conceive of a bilateral exchange, with mutual benefits.[160]

In the genealogy of this shared worldview, we might point to the works of the two philosophers mentioned both

by Corbusier and by Oswald's group: the *Essays*, published
by Michel de Montaigne in 1580 – particularly chapter 21,
"Dos canibais" ("Of Cannibals")[161] –, and the *Discurso sobre a
origem e os fundamentos da desigualdade entre os homens*
(*Discourse on the origin and basis of inequality among men*),
published by Jean-Jacques Rousseau in 1754.[162] It is remarkable that Le Corbusier summoned for his arguments in the
"American Prologue" of 1929 the very same authors present
in the "Anthropophagous Manifesto" of 1928, authored
by the very same group of intellectuals that guided him in
São Paulo.[163] The works of these French philosophers triggered Oswald de Andrade's imagination and his manifestos
stimulated his group, made up of both visual artists and
writers, who express through texts and images the harmonious relationship between man and the environment, the
idealization of the natural state as a place of freedom and
equality, untouched by repressions and interdictions, a paradisiacal setting where primitive man lives.[164] The concept of
the "naked man" referred to by Le Corbusier in his "American
Prologue" would be radicalized two years later in an anthropophagic way by Flávio de Carvalho in the1930 text-man-
ifesto *The city of the naked man*,[165] a dislocation of the
Swiss-French architect's urban vision reiterated by Oswald de
Andrade's ironic comment.[166]

Le Corbusier and the Brazilian modernism of the 1920s
shared the belief that it was possible to dissociate the technical aspects of modern society from the social aspects in
order to trigger different developments. For the European
architect, it made it possible to praise the technique as
well as denounce the inauthentic nature of "social and
moral mechanisms". In the Brazilian case, Oswald's manifestos, both the 1924 *Pau-Brasil Manifesto*[167] and the 1928
Anthropophagous Manifesto, operate a distinction between
culture and *civilization* – European concepts in vogue in
Brazil since the end of the 19th century. On the one hand,
the gathering of traditions, habits and customs; on the other,

material conquests against nature. The anthropophagic plunder proposed by Oswald goes after the civilizational dimension – especially technical-scientific aspects –, disregarding the cultural dimension, which was ridden with prohibitions. For Oswald, we already had our own culture to add to the new synthesis: "Elevator projectiles, skyscraper cubes and the wise solar sloth. The prayer. The carnival. The intimate energy. The song-thrush. Hospitality, slightly sensual, affectionate. The yearning for shamans, and the military airfields. *Pau-Brasil*."[168]

While he firmly believes in the technical achievements of the modern world – the automobile, the ocean liner, the highway, the skyscrape... –, Le Corbusier, on the other hand, fears that this unlimited advance might jeopardize the human dimension of progress. Throughout his life, one of his answers to this dilemma was an appeal to some sort of *Authority* that could dampen and control the anonymous and irrational power of the productive forces: "All we need is an authority – a man – lyrical enough to start the machine, dictate a law, a regulation, a doctrine: and then the modern world would begin to leave behind the gruesomeness of its hands and working face, and it would smile, powerful, content, hopeful."[169] Such an appreciation for political personalism leads him, throughout his life, to flirt with extremist governments on the right and on the left, hoping that the dictator on duty would be *lyrical enough* to lead society to order and balance with the environment. It is difficult to discern opportunism from gullibility, but the fact of the matter is that the subtraction of political-ideological issues from the discourse results in a visionary and voluntarist militancy, which promises an organized world rid of conflicts. An idealized world, which can be offered to society through the work and grace of the architect: "Architecture? But it is in what we see and feel that the morality of architecture resides: truth, purity, order, the instruments... and adventure."[170]

Historian and architectural critic Kenneth Frampton is well aware of the ambivalence with which the Swiss-French architect addresses the essential issues of machine-age society. To prove his point, he mentions a passage by Robert Fishman, which is reproduced here:

> Le Corbusier's quest for authority in the thirties reflects his deeply ambivalent attitude toward industrialization. His social thought and his architecture rested on the faith that industrial society had the inherent capacity for a genuine and joyous order, but behind that faith there was the fear that a perverted, uncontrolled industrialization could destroy civilization. As a young man at La Chaux-de-Fonds he had seen ugly, mass-produced timepieces from Germany virtually wipe out the watchmakers' crafts. The lesson was not forgotten.[171]

This passage is quite precious. The fear that scientific pride might produce a "perverted industrialization" that would rise up against its creator is one of the great myths of the Romantic Age, which gave us at least one masterpiece: *Frankenstein*, by Mary Shelley, published in 1818. The great dystopias of the 20th century will add the dread of totalitarianism to the 19th century theme. *Metropolis*, a German production directed by Austrian film-maker Fritz Lang, released in 1927, inaugurates a futuristic-gothic take on the subject. The story takes place in 2026, in the great city of Metropolis. The social split between rich industrialists who enjoyed the pleasures and abundance of the technological society and poor workers who carried along the production of goods and energy is reproduced in the very materiality of the city, which contrasts the skyscraper realm bathed in light and the hellish underground world of production. It is curious that Le Corbusier's reservations regarding industrialization were not accompanied by fear of political extremism.

The ambivalence with which industrialization was viewed in Europe had different contours in Brazil. São Paulo modernism in the early 1920s saw technology with optimism or as an inevitable phenomenon. One of Mário de Andrade's last poems, "Meditation on the Tietê River", blends a diffuse melancholy and the naive wonder at the modern city so characteristic of the young participants of the 1922 Modern Art Week:

> *It is night. And all is night. Beneath the splendid arch of the*
> *Bridge of the Flags the river*
> *Murmurs in a swirling of heavy and oily water.*
> *It is night and all is night. A patrol of shadows,*
> *Silent shadows, fill with a night so vast*
> *The breast of the river, which is as if the night were water,*
> *Nocturnal water, liquid night, drowning with apprehensions*
> *The high towers of my exhausted heart. Suddenly*
> *The oily water gathers the shimmering lights,*
> *It scares me. In a moment the river*
> *Glows with countless lights, homes, palaces, and streets*
> *Streets, streets, where the dinosaurs hobble,*
> *Now brave skyscrapers from which they spring,*
> *the blue creatures and the punishing green cats,*
> *In song, pleasures, works and factories,*
> *Lights and Glory. It's the city...*[172]

In the context of São Paulo modernism, the theme of industrialization is a main concern for Tarsila do Amaral. Her days in Europe put her in direct contact with the pioneers of modern painting. Her greatest affinity is towards Fernand Léger's cubism. During her long stay in Europe in 1923 – she was in Paris for the most part –, already as Oswald de Andrade's partner, Tarsila frequently visited the French

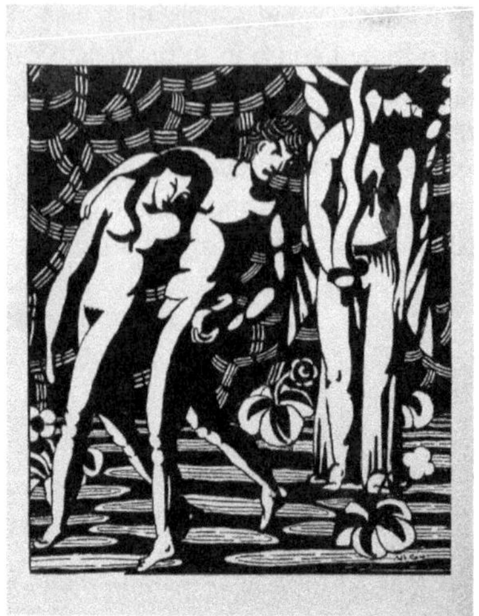 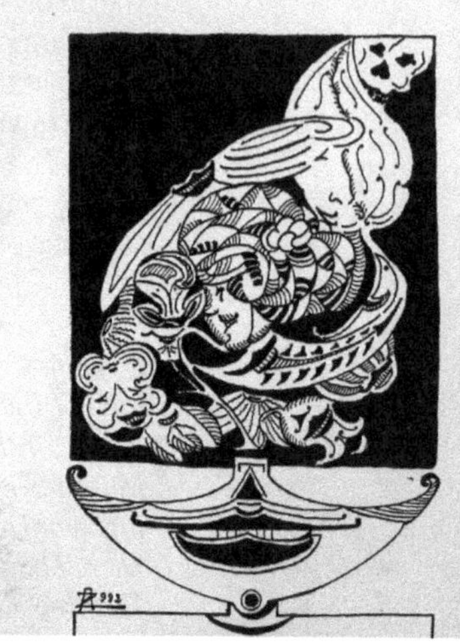

painter's studio. According to Carlos Zílio, "Léger's work, in its connection with the machine model, produces objective or non-objective images that stand for a new mythology of industrialization."[173] The industrial city with its machines well-adjusted to the new chronometer of everyday life is a model for the French painter, who aimed not at a naturalistic record, but a rational representation of industrial society. "In this procedure, Léger abolishes any ties to appearances, trying to integrate into painting the very functional logic of machines, like gears producing through a precise choreography a particular effect, which in art would be an aesthetic one."[174] Tarsila, in addition to the work of Léger, learns about the primitivist experiences of Matisse and Picasso, following Gauguin. Primitivism here plays the role of countering European egocentrism by implying a subjective adventure into the wild, a quest for the very essence of human experience. In a certain sense, it participates in the process of destroying the "aura" of art along with the championing of popular culture.

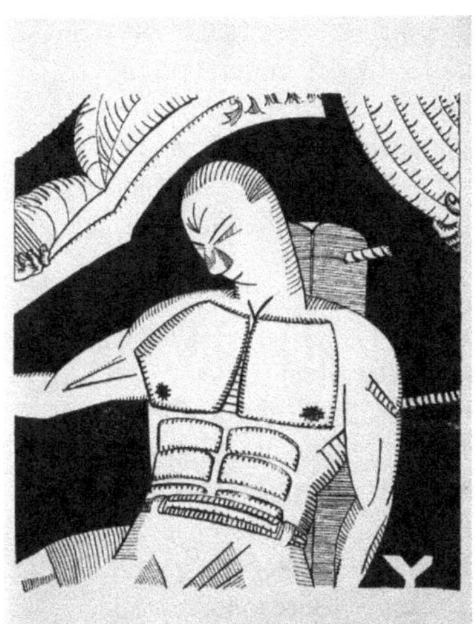

In Brazil, unlike Europe, the popular and the primitive are already mixed, which explains the loyalty to the common man – expressed not so much through aesthetic choices, but certainly through intellectual intent. This loyalty survives theoretical changes. Even in the most internationalist moment, when our artists adhere to the values of the machine – the early 1920s –, the appeal of popular culture can be observed: "Wet, cold, rheumatized by a tradition of artistic tears, we made up our minds. Surgical operation. Removal of the lacrimal glands. The Era of the 8 Batutas, the Jazz-Band age, the era of Chicharrão, Carlito, Mutt & Jeff. The age of laughter and sincerity. The construction era. The Klaxon era."[175] The good-humored call of 1922 seems a bit old-fashioned the following year, when Tarsila and Oswald return to Brazil in December 1923. A new character – the primitive – enters the scene, properly reworked for the Brazilian environment, joining the popular element to play the dialectical game with the modern. "Poetry exists in the facts. The shacks of saffron and ocher in the green of the

Favela, under the Cabralin blue, are aesthetic facts,"[176] says Oswald de Andrade on March 18, 1924, inaugurating the *Pau-Brasil* movement. During this second stage in Brazilian modernism, with the Oswaldian manifestos occupying a strategic position, nativist and primitivist themes are added to the initial modernizing commitment of the modernist avant-garde. Klaxon gives Tupi a lift.

Tarsila's paintings, informed by national and avant-garde trends, codify the new art, which must be both Brazilian and modern. The paintings with typically urban scenes – *E.F.C.B.* and *Gazo*, from 1924; *São Paulo (135831)* and *A gare* (*Train station*), from 1925 – as well as the eminently rural ones – *O mamoeiro* (*Papaya Tree*), Paisagem com touro (*Landscape with a bull*) and Vendedor de frutas (*Fruit Vendor*), all from 1925 – intertwine industrial and rural elements, where the balance of colors and shapes takes pleasure in representing social harmony. In other paintings of the period, the opposite poles are perfectly balanced. In Palmeiras (*Palm Trees*) (1925), the railroad tracks and bridges challenge the stillness of the rural scene, with its hills and imperial palm trees. In *Lagoa Santa (Santa Lagoon)* (1925), plant shapes in the foreground occupy the lower half of the frame, while the upper half depicts houses and a church. The cheerful colors in rustic contrast evoke Tarsila's childhood memories, the palm trees pairing up with electricity transmission poles, the rustic paths interrupted by metal bridges, the humble popular constructions alongside train stations and gasometers, transport machines taking people to public fairs or festivities – in short, there's a whole game of accommodation of contrasts that results in a mixed human habitat, emerging between rural and urban domains. Perhaps the picture that best embodies this glimpse of earthly paradise is *Morro da favela* (*Favela Hill*), from 1924, where we see simple houses scattered on the natural terrain, with no ground leveling or street paving, the vegetation in the most diverse shapes and tones, and domestic animals. The local folk – black adults and children

– chat or have fun without a sense of haste or distress in a setting filled with peace and simplicity.[177] The mood suggests innocence and candor, deftly conveyed by Tarsila do Amaral, adapting what she learned in France to local necessities. Both the original culture and the cultivated one reside in her particular spiritual world:

> "Tarsila's relationship with Léger's work illustrates the cunning with which she analyzes the art developed in France at the time. What she absorbs from Léger's system is the use of the machine model. However, while the metaphor which Léger pursues in his work has industrial society as its object, Tarsila makes 'Brazilianness' the distinctive feature of her formulation, adopting the 'machine language' (just as Oswald de Andrade would make use of a telegraphic language) as a desire for renovation, in the sense of outlining an image of Brazil through this new perspective opened up by industrialization. [...] There is, however, in the naivety that emanates from Tarsila's paintings, an identification between childhood and modernist populism, that is, the channeling of what she lived in the old farm world, surrounded by plants, the mythology of the slaves, the colors of small town dwellings, and her goal of morphing these elements into signs."[178]

Going back to her childhood memories, Tarsila distances herself from Léger, demarcating a territory for her own poetics. According to Zílio, "the presence of this childhood universe adds to the rigor of Léger's industrial outlook the disconcerting naivety of Tarsila's bumkin, child-like vision."[179] Moving away from the French, the Brazilian painter approaches popular simplicity and also the childish world of Oswald de Andrade's poetic universe. The couple indeed shared this sensibility: *Pau-Brasil* poetry, after all, is "agile and candid" "like a child."[180] But this is no family matter: this

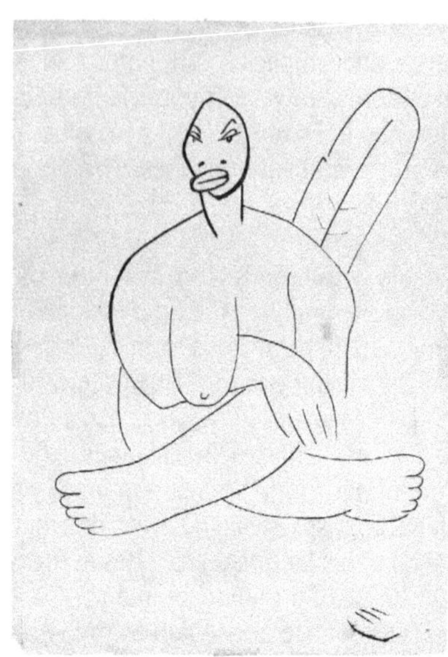

A negra (The Black Woman), study, ink on paper, 25.5 x 18.4 cm. Tarsila do Amaral, 1923. Photo by Rogério Emílio. FAMA Museum Collection

naivety in Tarsila's painting is deliberate; it emerges from modernism as developed in São Paulo, now focused on the search for national roots. In Tarsila's *Pau-Brasil* painting, there is then "the channeling of what she lived in the old farm world, surrounded by plants, the mythology of the slaves, the colors of small town dwellings, and her goal of morphing these elements into signs,"[181] in accordance with the new aesthetic and ideological agenda.

The same relationship of communicating vessels occurs during the anthropophagic period, now under the impact of Sigmund Freud's *Totem and Taboo*. In the "Anthropophagic Manifesto", besides being mentioned by name three times,[182] the Freudian text is gracefully parodied by Oswald: "We already had justice, the codification of vengeance. Science, the codification of Magic. Cannibalism. The permanent transformation of Taboo into totem."[183] The culturalist view of psychoanalysis – which draws analogies between childhood

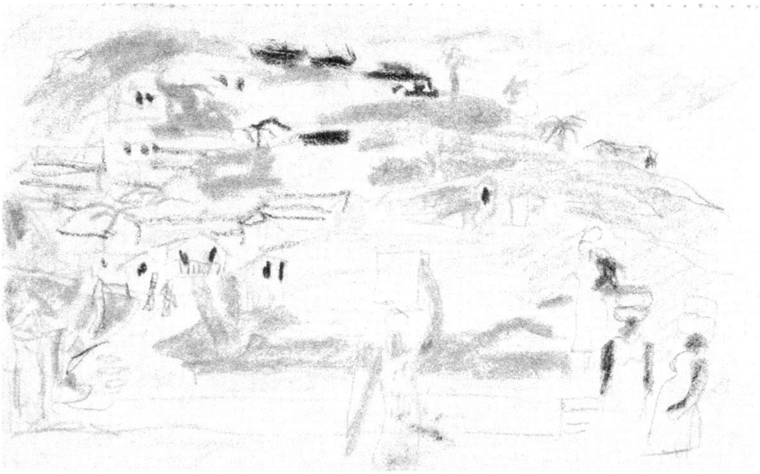

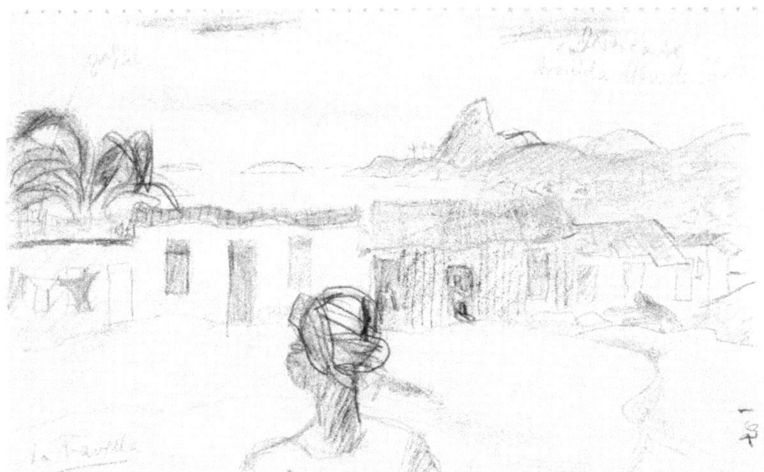

Favela (Slum), Rio de Janeiro (B4_91). Le Corbusier, 1929. Fondation Le Corbusier Collection

A favela (The Slum), Rio de Janeiro (Carnet B4_107). Le Corbusier, 1929. Fondation Le Corbusier Collection

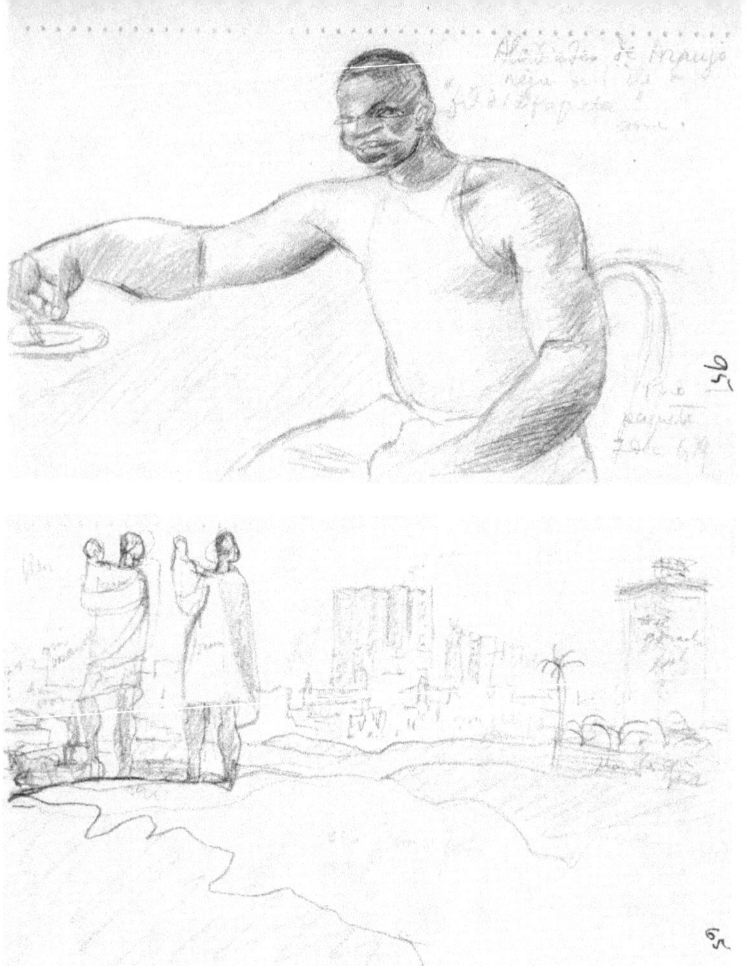

Alcebíades de Araújo in Paquetá,
Rio de Janeiro (Carnet B4_95).
Le Corbusier, 1929. Fondation Le
Corbusier Collection

Família negra e São Paulo (Black
Family and São Paulo) (Carnet B4_65).
Le Corbusier, 1929. Fondation Le
Corbusier Collection

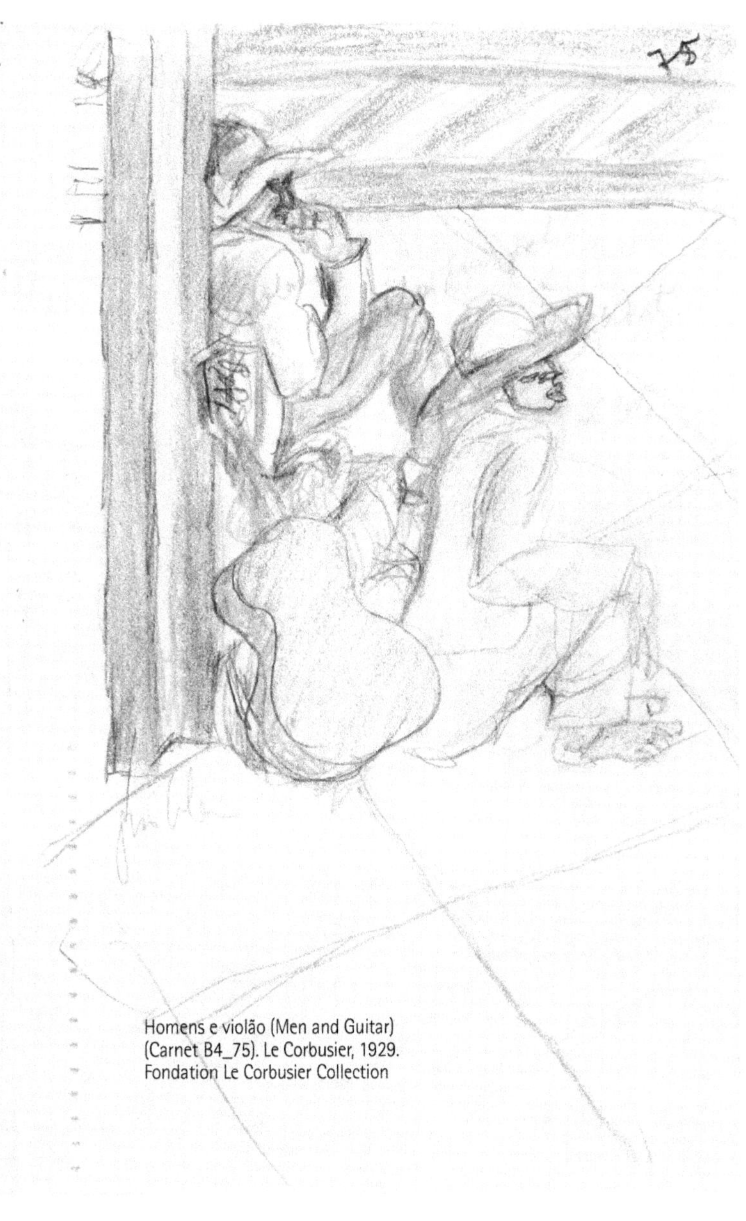

Homens e violão (Men and Guitar)
(Carnet B4_75). Le Corbusier, 1929.
Fondation Le Corbusier Collection

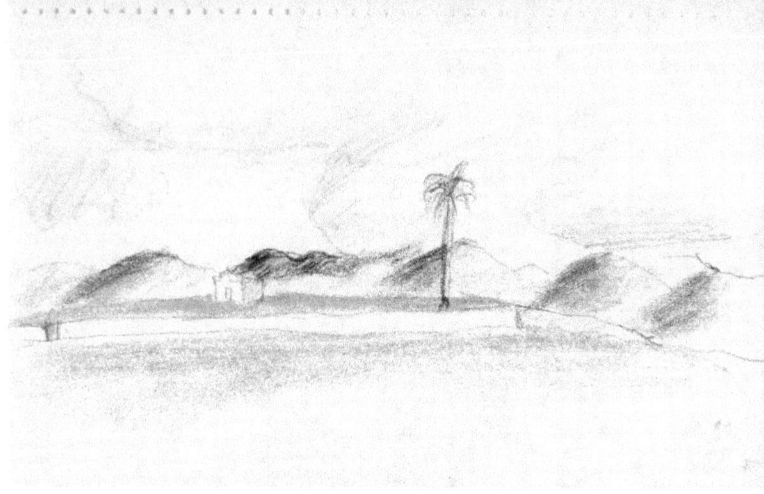

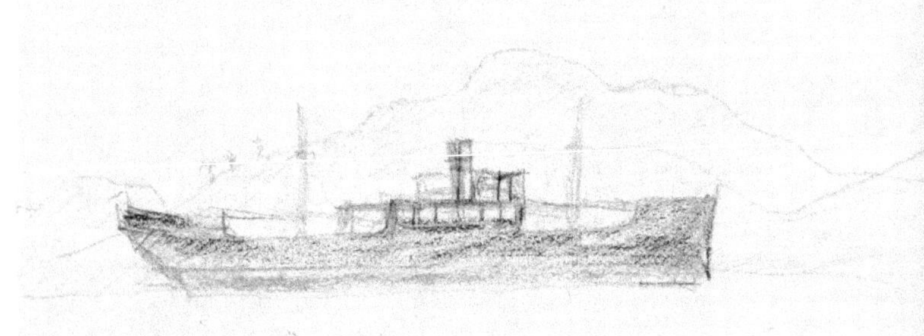

Fazenda São Martinho (São Martinho
Farm) (Carnet B4_77B); Porto de
Santos (Santos Harbor) (Carnet
B4_51); Abertura de via em São Paulo
(Opening of a Road in São Paulo)
(Carnet B4_59). Le Corbusier, 1929.
Fondation Le Corbusier Collection

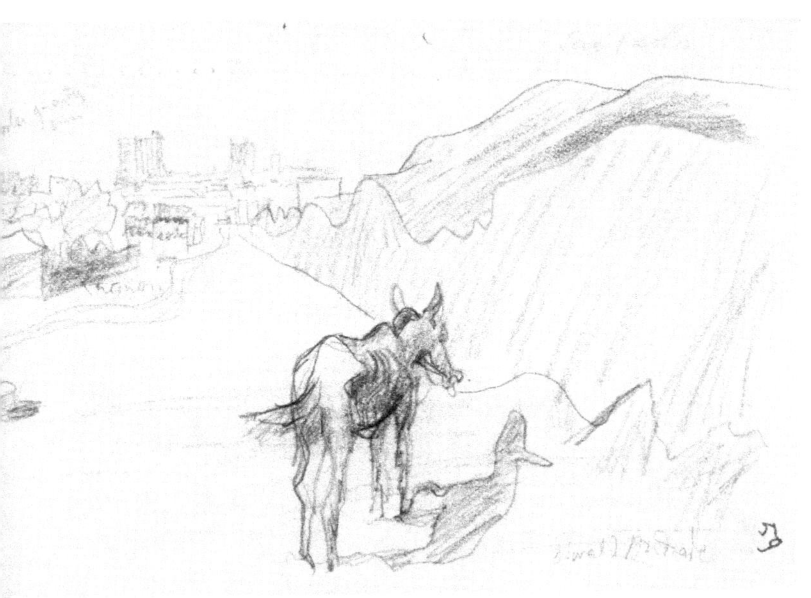

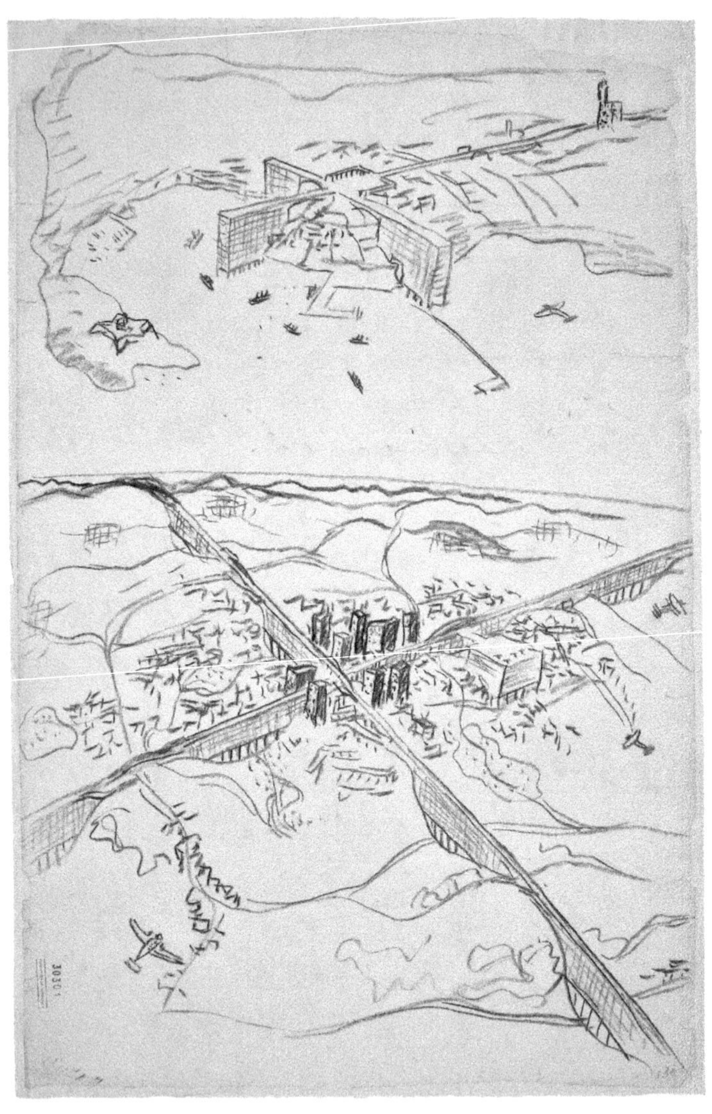

134

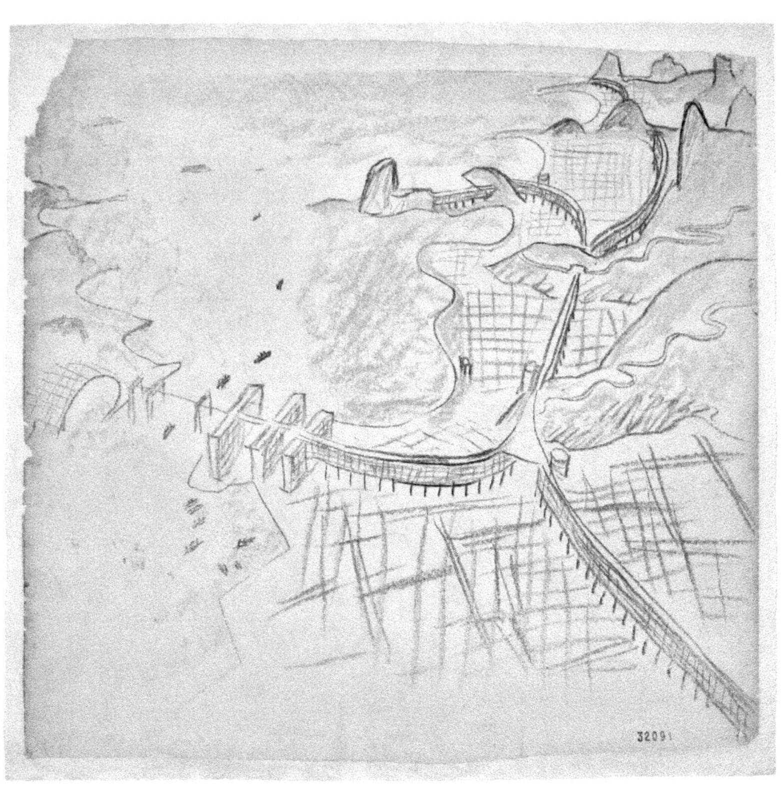

Le Corbusier, urban projects for Montevideo and São Paulo (FLC 30301); Urban Project for Rio de Janeiro (FLC 32091). Le Corbusier, 1929. Fondation Le Corbusier Collection

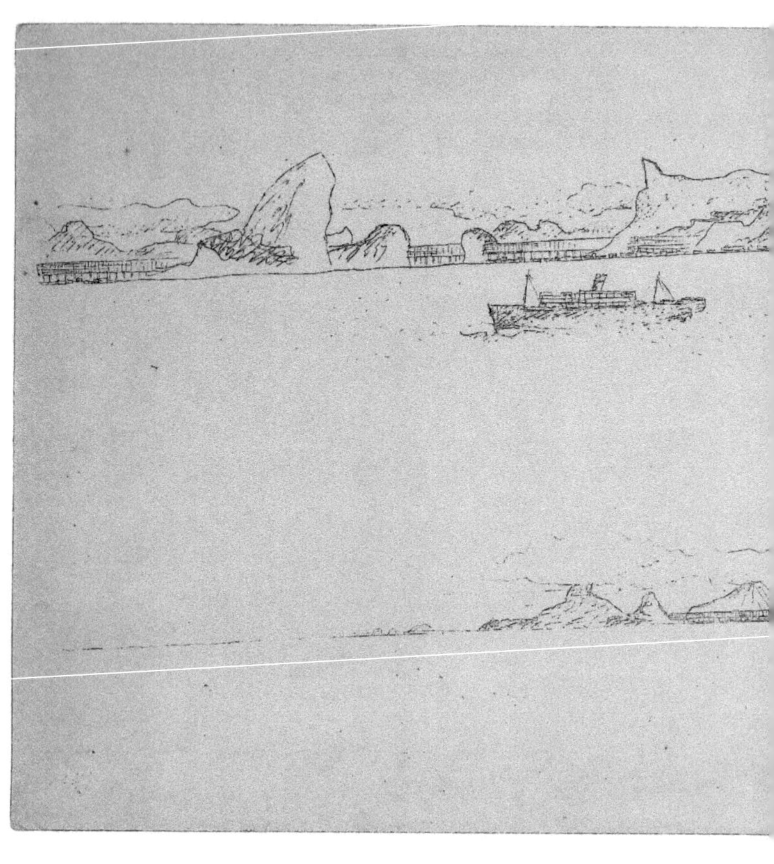

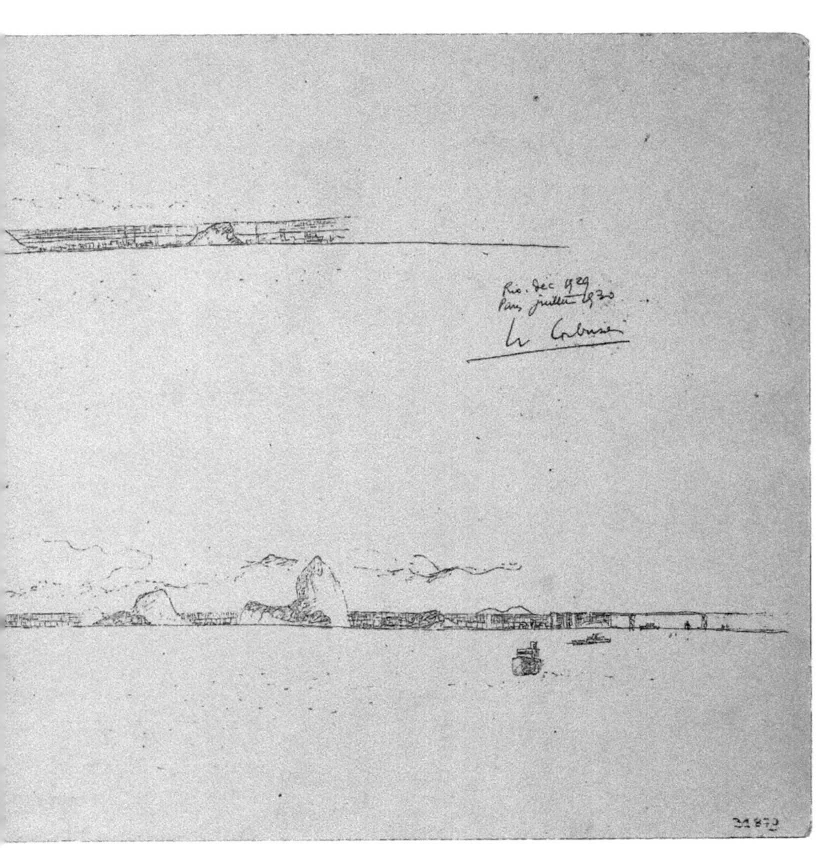

Rio de Janeiro Bay (FLC 31879). Le
Corbusier, 1929-1930. Fondation Le
Corbusier Collection

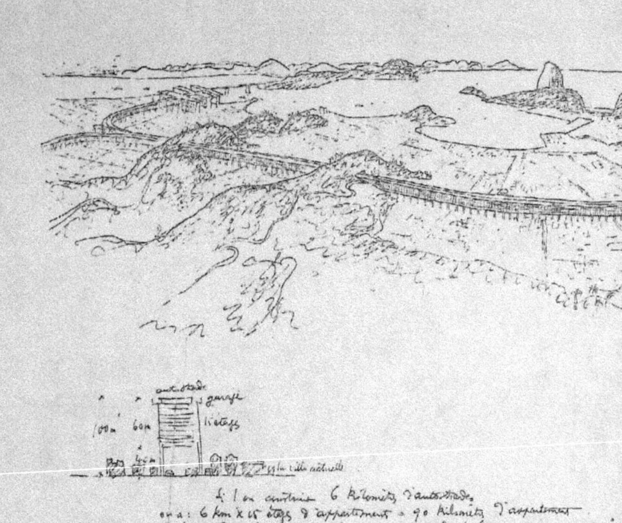

Si l'on construit 6 kilomètres d'autostrade,
on a : 6 km x 15 étages d'appartement = 90 kilomètres d'appartement
90 km à 20 m de large = 1.800.000 m² de surface
Si l'on affecte 20 m² de surface habitable par habitant on loge $\frac{1.800.000}{20}$
logés dans les conditions les plus favorables qui on [peut] une
Si on loue le m² habitable à raison de 80 francs le m², on
qui représentent à 10% un capital de 1½ Milliard
Voilà comment on peut gagner de l'argent en urbanisant
prix des

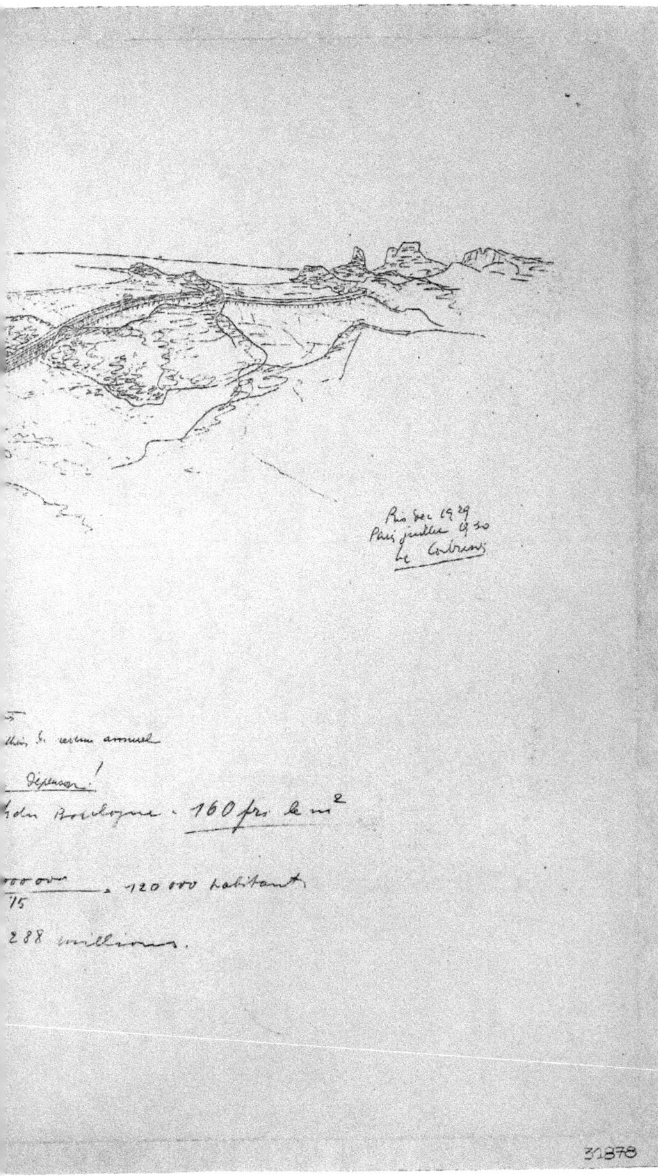

thih $\frac{}{}$ le revenu annuel

Dépenses

...du Boulogne : **160 frs le m²**

$\frac{...000\,000}{15}$ = 120 000 habitants

288 millions.

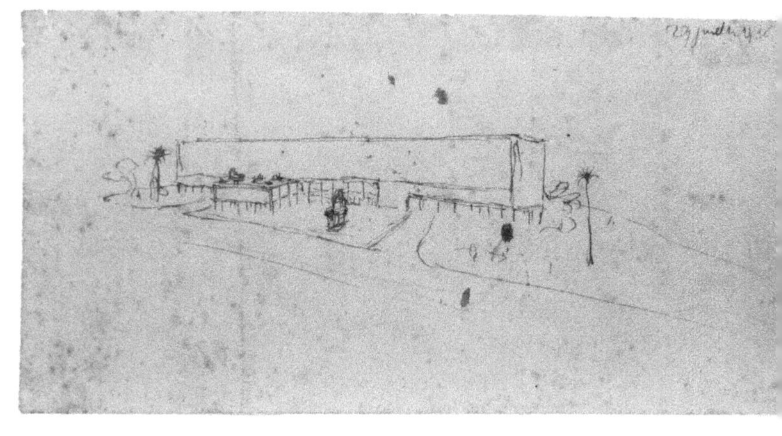

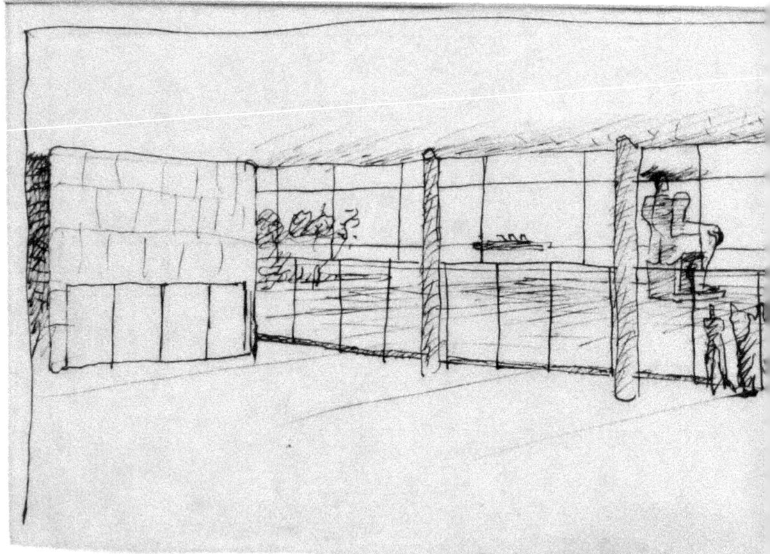

On the two previous pages
Highway Building winding through
the Rio de Janeiro landscape (FLC
31878). Le Corbusier, 1929-1930.
Fondation Le Corbusier Collection

Ministry of Education and Health,
project for the Santa Luzia site,
external perspective and perspective of
the ground floor hall, Rio de Janeiro.
Le Corbusier, 1936. Museu Nacional de
Belas Artes Collection

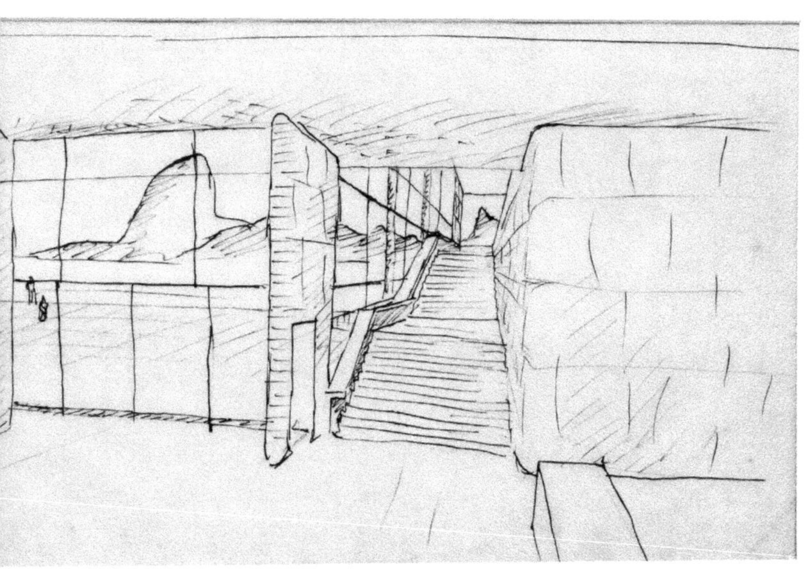

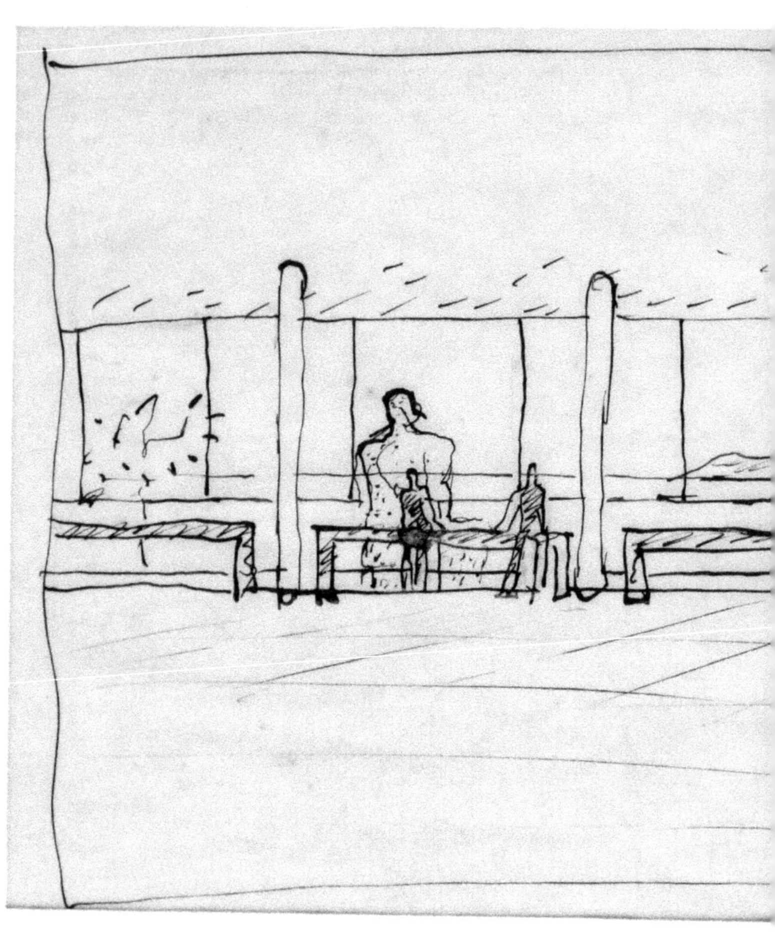

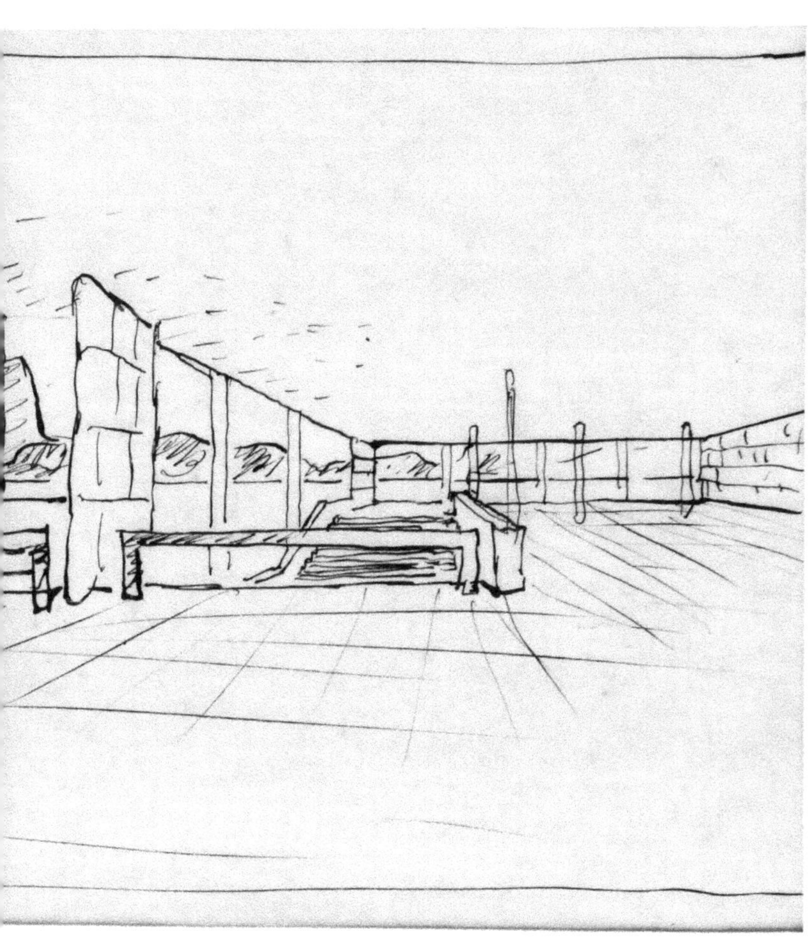

Ministry of Education and Health,
project for the Santa Luzia site, second
floor hall perspective, Rio de Janeiro.
Le Corbusier, 1936. Museu Nacional de
Belas Artes Collection

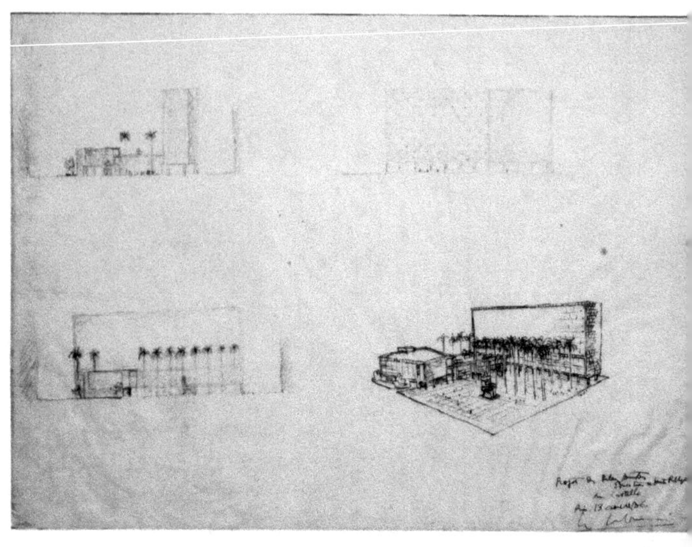

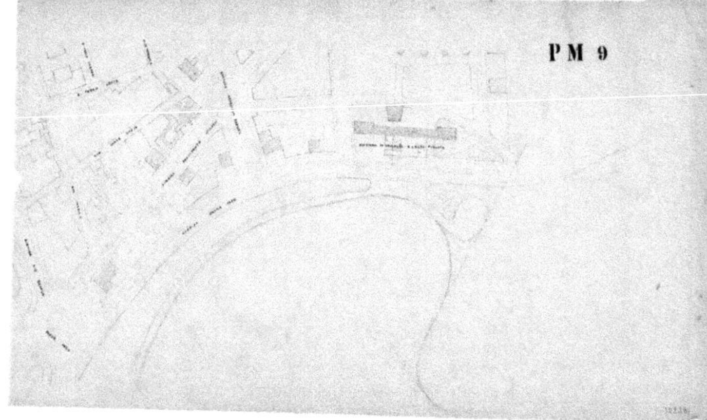

Ministry of Education and Health, project for the Esplanade of the Castle, elevations and perspective, Rio de Janeiro RJ. Le Corbusier, 1936. Museu Nacional de Belas Artes Collection

Ministry of Education and Health, project for the Santa Luzia site, implementation, Rio de Janeiro. Le Corbusier, 1936. Museu Nacional de Belas Artes Collection

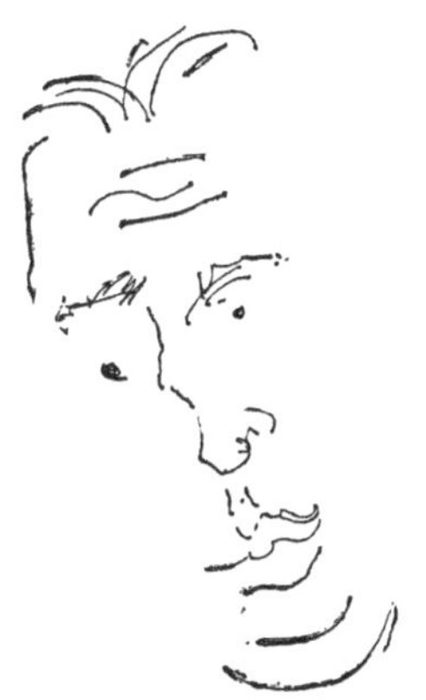

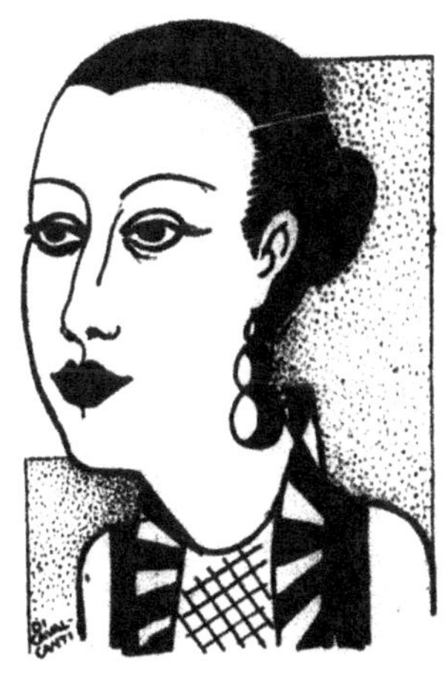

Oswald de Andrade, drawing by Nonê de Andrade, son of the writer. Correio Paulistano, São Paulo, 3rd section, June 26, 1949, 1; Tarsila do Amaral, drawing by Di Cavalcanti. *Para Todos!*, no. 554, Rio de Janeiro, July 27, 1929, 14

and the primitive universe – inspires works by Mário de Andrade (*Macunaíma*, 1928) and Raul Bopp (*Cobra Norato*, 1931) in the same period. The same is true of Tarsila, who finished two of her masterpieces during this period: *Abaporu* ("man who eats people" in Tupi-Guarani), from 1928; and *Antropofagia*, from 1929. In both paintings, the notion of the earliest beginnings expands through all the elements in the scene: humans, vegetation, the planet, the cosmos.[184] The formal stylization with the bulging of contours, the universe that boils down to sky and the sun, the simplified colors determining the organic and the inorganic, the naked bodies solidly seated on the ground, the lack of proportion between large and heavy bodies and small heads — absolutely every-thing suggests a primordial time. The origin of life is hinted upon in different ways in each painting: in *Sol poente* (*Sunset*) (1929), the shapeless plants and the crawling larvae; in *Urutu* (1928), the egg being hatched; in *Floresta* (*Forest*) (1929), overlapping eggs and trees in formation; in *O lago*

(*The Lake*) (1928), we see vegetation beginning to differentiate. Self-absorbed solitude, with a high psychological content, appears in *A lua* (*The Moon*), from 1928, and in *Figura só* (*Lonely Figure*), from 1930, an unexpected metaphysical universe along the lines of De Chirico.

Tarsila do Amaral's ideologically engaged art transcends strict aesthetic limits and becomes an important piece of a larger cultural project. Her canvases from the *Pau-Brasil* period, depicting everyday scenes from the popular universe, suggest the constitution of a *utopian Brazilian habitat* where people live happily in their everyday simplicity, and their habits and customs are perfectly adjusted to a specific way of settling down in the territory. The countryside and the city no longer exist in isolation, they merge into a single scenario where the positives of the "school" and the "forest" harmoniously coexist. The human experience is thus made possible in the tropics by the integration of human origins conveyed through the unfathomable time of nature. Tarsila's anthropophagic period, with paintings showing notable formal solutions, does not fit in so well with the current argument, but the theme of primitivity seen as the primordial relationship between humanity and nature will have significant developments for the interests driving this book.

The set of themes and approaches presented here are not restricted to the work of Tarsila do Amaral.[185] Other painters of the period portrayed the Brazilian soul, the mixture of whites, blacks and natives. Alfredo Volpi, in an early work still under the spell of the impressionist paradigm, presents a black woman with make-up and a party dress ("Sem título" / "Untitled", 1920). Emiliano Di Cavalcanti extols the sensuality and swagger of racial mixing in a popular scene filled with joy and some residual melancholy ("Samba", from 1925), anticipating the sociological vision of Gilberto Freyre and Jorge Amado's novels. Lasar Segall sets aside his Jewish background and the appeal of the introspective expressionism he brought from Europe and depicts the light and colors

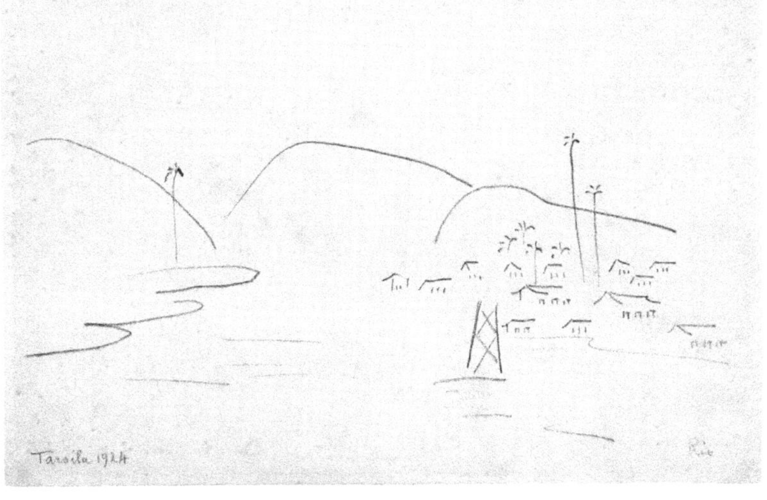

Rio com três palmeiras e casario (Rio with Three Palm Trees and Houses), graphite on paper, 16.5 x 22.8 cm.

Tarsila do Amaral, 1924. Photo Rogério Emílio. FAMA Museum Collection

of tropical vegetation enveloping dark-skinned figures, a boy and a man, both serious and secure in their moral elevation ("Menino com lagartixas" / "Boy with geckos", from 1924; "Bananal" / "Banana Grove", from 1927). The blacks and mestizos of Cândido Portinari, toiling away in the fields, rise majestically, with proud eyes set on the horizon ("Mestiço" / "Mestizo" and "O lavrador" / "The Farmer", both from 1934). Vicente Rego Monteiro exhibits his characters in scenes depicting small heroic gestures, such as the native hunting for sustenance or the *sertanejo* carrying his agricultural production on the back of a mule ("O atirador de arcos" / "The Arrow Shooter", 1925; "Sem título" / "Untitled", 1922). Among the nativist works of his first phase, there is one particular gem: "The Anthropophagous", a pencil drawing from 1921, which anticipates the anthropophagic theme of Oswald de Andrade: "this image presents us with a sculptural

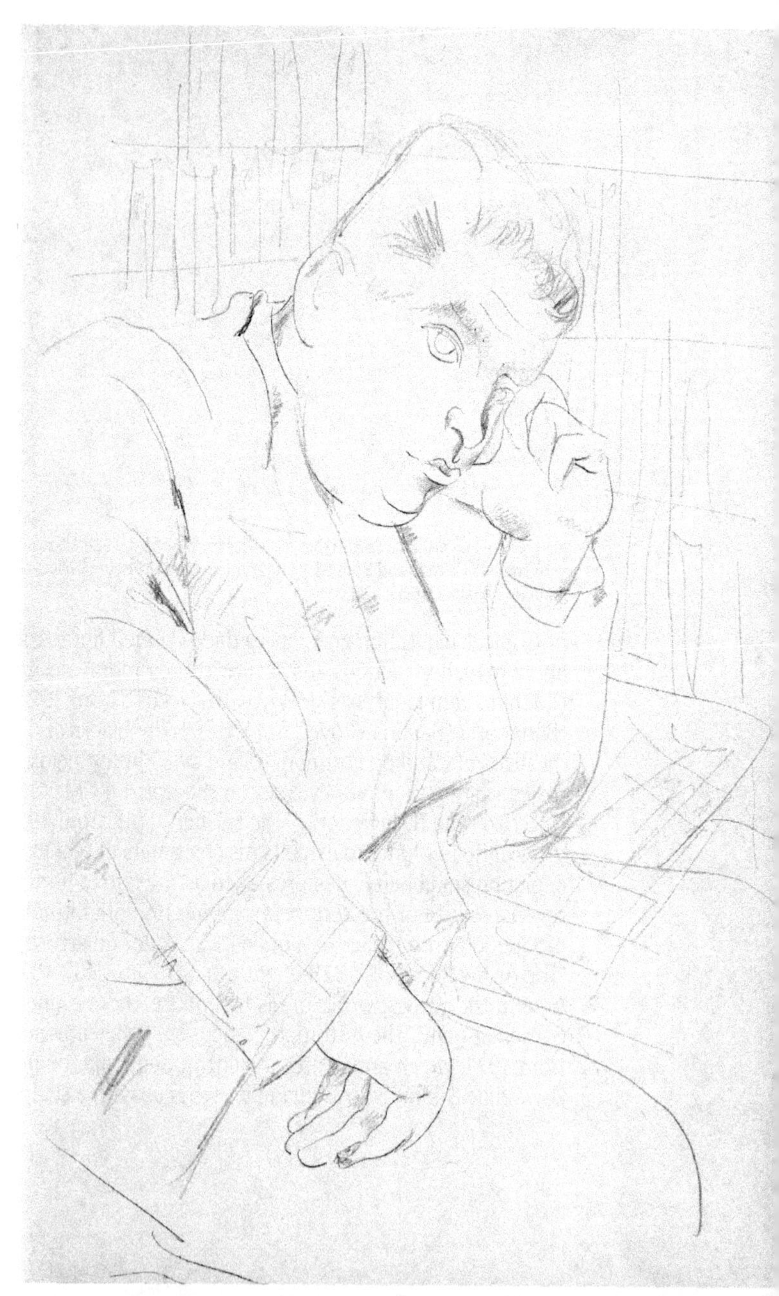

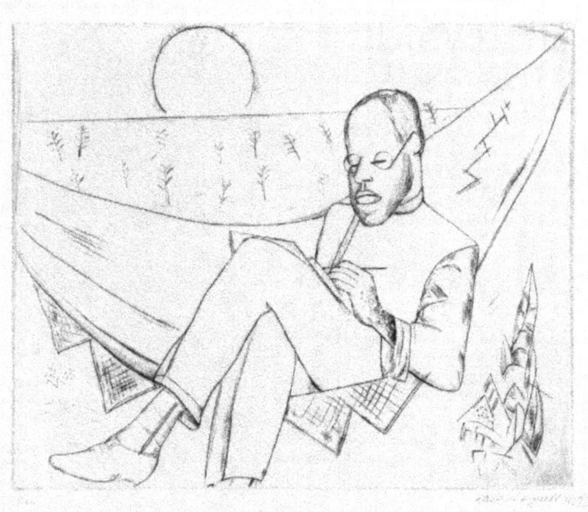

Retrato do escritor Oswald de Andrade (Portrait of the Writer Oswald de Andrade), c.1940, graphite on paper, 50.0 cm x 33.0 cm. Lasar Segall (Vilnius, Lithuania, 1889 – São Paulo, Brazil, 1957). Collection of the Lasar Segall Museum / Ibram/Ministry of Tourism

Mário na rede (Mário in the Hammock), 1929, etching, drypoint on paper, 25.5 cm x 32.0 cm. Lasar Segall (Vilnius, Lithuania, 1889 – São Paulo, Brazil, 1957). Collection of the Lasar Segall Museum / Ibram/Ministry of Tourism

native, enjoying a femur in the paradisiacal leisure that was lost with the arrival of the Portuguese in Brazil."[186] There are several Brazilian artists who, in the 1920s and 1930s, developed works in line with primitivism as seen through *Pau-Brasil* or anthropophagic lens, using stylistic techniques borrowed from the European avant-garde, particularly Cubism. However, Tarsila's work seems to embody with greater consistency and substance the search for "Brazilianness" according to the ideas forged during the 1920s.

The Paths Lead to the Countryside

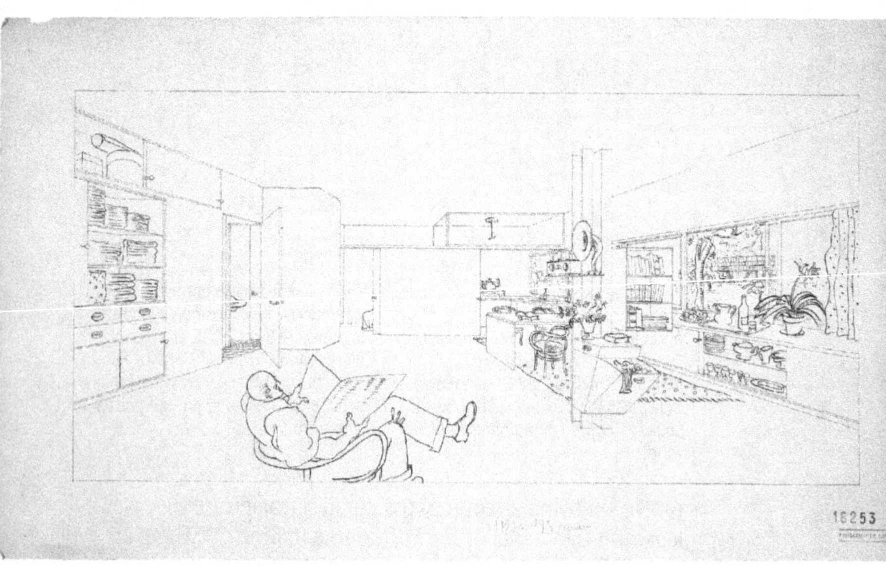

Maison Loucher, interior perspective, unbuilt project (FLC 18253). Le Corbusier, 1929. Fondation Le Corbusier Collection

Poor beast
The horse and the cart
Were stuck on the tracks
And as the driver got impatient
For he was taking lawyers to their offices
They pushed the vehicle
And the animal raced
But the quick carter
Stood up on his seat
And punished the bound fugitive
With a great whip
Oswald de Andrade, "Postes da Light," 1925[187]

In an article from 1984 where he tackles the pertinence of postmodern theoretical discussion in Brazil, architect and architecture critic Luis Espallargas caused some discomfort in the architectural milieu, which is not quite accustomed to debates, let alone criticism. Warning that "the effectiveness of a medication cannot be predicted without a diagnosis of the miseries that one intends to cure,"[188] Espallargas points to the enormous contradictions in the development of our architecture and argues that its intellectual montage, developed around the idea of national peculiarity, was established through slogans and cultural values that had little or nothing to do with actual architectural activity. The innate talent of the Brazilian architect, who allegedly nationalized European international principles, amounts – according to Espallargas – to nothing more than a rhetorical construction covering up the undeniable fact that modern architecture made in Brazil was entirely guided by the exotic model. The much-vaunted "Brazilianness" maintained vague or non-existent connections with the autochthonous traits of traditional Brazilian architecture, and its constant and compulsory rhetorical presence can only be understood ideologically. He then summarizes the tautology in which Brazilian modern architecture is entangled.[189]

"By accentuating some features, distorting a few rules
and relying on the poetics of some agents, Brazilian
architecture was based on a virtual culture of what it
wanted to be, and not on what it had actually been. [...]
The architecture of the modern movement becomes
Brazilian when it starts to point to its own modern
examples, crystallizing a style and living on stereotypes
and calligraphic corrections."[190]

Espallargas attributes to Lúcio Costa the central role
in articulating the ideology of architectural Brazilianness.
The recurrence of themes and concepts in Costa's texts –
"national genius", "national character", "Brazilianness", "modern Brazilian architecture" etc. – make him a prime target for
accusations of intellectual manipulation. Even if that was
the case – and this book, among other things, tries to point
out how the discursive montage is indeed built up through
the work of Lúcio Costa and how it gives substance to local
experiments in modern architecture –, the understanding
of this montage as a conscious deliberation restricted to a
small group of men, or even a single one, is quite limited.
The constitution of an operative discourse that manages to
be understood, accepted and shared becomes historically
possible when it gains prominence within a given social
group. The historical reliability of *a "lie" converted into a
"truth"* depends not only on the conviction or bad faith of
the person uttering it for the first time, but on the ability of
his arguments to be repeated and spread through the social
fabric, and this, of course, is only possible if that idea makes
sense for the community and meets comprehensive and collective demands. The success of Lúcio Costa's vision becomes
possible only because it reflects a vigorous intellectual current with which it maintains a fruitful exchange of meanings
and values.
But there is indeed a premonitory clarity in Espallargas'
argument, and his indictment against Lúcio Costa's discursive

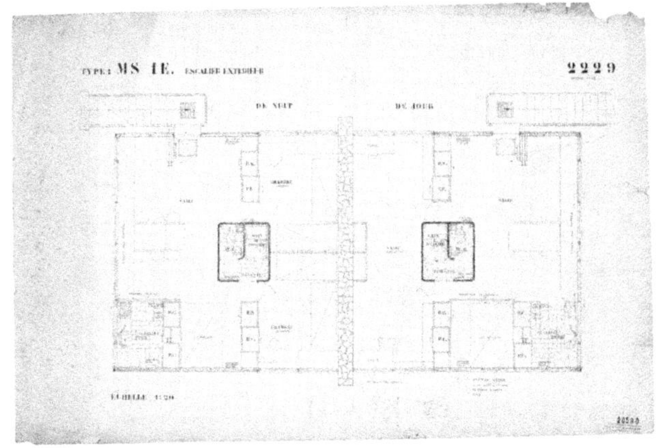

Maison Loucher, standard floor
plan, unbuilt project (FLC 20590).
Le Corbusier, 1929. Fondation Le
Corbusier Collection

montage in 1984 predates Carlos Alberto Ferreira Martins'
critique in his 1987 master's thesis. The article also has the
merit of pointing out, for the first time, a possible affiliation
for the working-class village of Monlevade, even though
his remarks do not quite address the heart of Lúcio Costa's
purposes:

> "Neither function, nor technique, nor society, the tripod
> of the modern movement, spontaneously visit culture.
> Lúcio Costa probably felt this drama with the adapta-
> tions he was forced to make in Monlevade in order to
> reconcile his fascination with the new with his respect
> for the traditional. The *Maisons Loucheurs* suffer all the
> necessary and painful transgressions so as to adjust the
> Dom-ino system to our reality, and the result is a pos-
> sible modernity that attests to the confusion between
> national culture and architectural culture: clay and bam-
> boo supported by concrete pillars."[191]

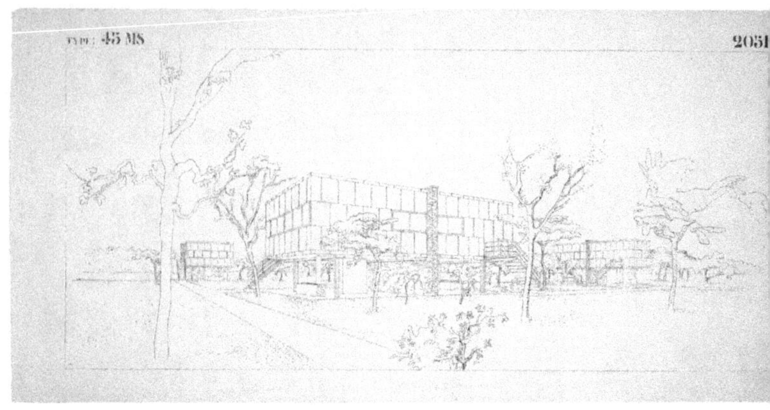

Maison Loucher, exterior perspective, unbuilt project (FLC 18.252). Le Corbusier, 1929. Fondation Le Corbusier Collection

Espallargas does not take into account that the synthesis sought by Lúcio Costa is brought about within a specific cultural context; therefore, it should not be measured with inappropriate instruments. Lúcio Costa's intellectual operation will always be seen as an impoverishment if we only consider a few core modern principles and ignore the fact that the homogeneity in the European context is less than real, as many national architectural grammars are flagrant. Taking diversity as the norm, we might talk about "deviation" rather than "transgression". In the Brazilian case, this deviation is indeed limited in its early formal and spatial gestures, but it becomes quite fertile later on, when Lúcio Costa comes up with his masterpieces – Parque Guinle and Park Hotel São Clemente in Nova Friburgo –, followed by Oscar Niemeyer, Affonso Eduardo Reidy, Rino Levi, Oswaldo Bratke, Francisco Bolonha and many others. So, instead of a *possible modernity*, perhaps it is wiser to talk about a *desired modernity*. Finally, regardless of any claims to "veracity", Lúcio Costa's premises brought about an aesthetic experimentation that, over time, having corrected initial deficiencies, delivered significant works of Brazilian architecture.

Luis Espallargas argues that the Maisons Loucheurs, conceived by Le Corbusier in 1929, are the matrix for the workers' houses in Vila Monlevade from 1934, which is a convincing argument considering dates and similarities. These similarities also exist between Monlevade and the Commune of Piacé, an urban and architectural project by Le Corbusier and Pierre Jeanneret – however, since this project was carried out in the same year,[192] it was likely unknown to Costa at the time. The Commune of Piacé seeks to implement a rural community with access to the benefits of the modern world. It's a strategy to keep people in the countryside – or return them to the countryside –, by equipping rural areas with the goods that attract people to the big cities in the first place. Conceived as a cooperative production unit, associated with small family properties, the rural village requires the state as a promoter and a new method for production management, encompassing warehouse, workshop, garage, housing unit for forty families with common services, post office, school, administration, club, conference room, party room, library, barns and silos. For smaller plots, single-family houses were planned. Everything would be built with prefabricated structures of iron and concrete, later assembled at the construction site.

The villages of Lúcio Costa and Le Corbusier are similar in size, with a few hundred inhabitants gathered to carry out a specific job (steel workers in Monlevade; peasant farmers in Piacé). The simplicity of the constructions entails perfect adequacy between means and ends, without waste of any kind. The arrangement of the facilities in the territory complies with the principles of sectorization by function. The single-family houses in the Corbusian village – derived from the *Maisons Loucheurs* –, arranged next to trees, bring about an experience similar to that provided by the semi-detached houses in Monlevade. Even the architects' sketches, where

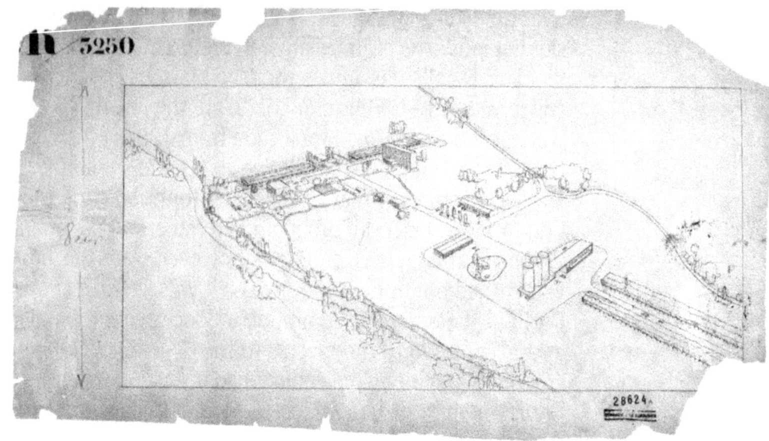

Agrarian reorganization, overall perspective, unspecified location, unbuilt project (FLC 28624B). Le Corbusier and Pierre Jeanneret, 1934. Fondation Le Corbusier Collection

we have the houses associated with leisure and rest, exhibit surprising similarities. Collective facilities – cinemas, clubs, etc. – meet the various daily needs and offer small crowds the pleasures of culture and leisure, albeit in reduced doses. The very simple buildings in both projects are even more closely related: the four-vaulted roof of the barn in the French village is very similar to the hip roof of the warehouse in the Brazilian village, both in proportions and in the structure with five rows of pilotis.

However, the differences are also blatant: while Monlevade is characterized by the dispersion of buildings across the territory, with routes only mentioned or hinted at, the Corbusian urban plan is more logical, functional and integrated, structured by roads and paths of different sizes, an overall vision made evident in drawings and models. Utility vehicles such as automobiles and tractors populate Le Corbusier's drawings, while Lúcio Costa neither records them in his drawings nor mentions them in his texts – we

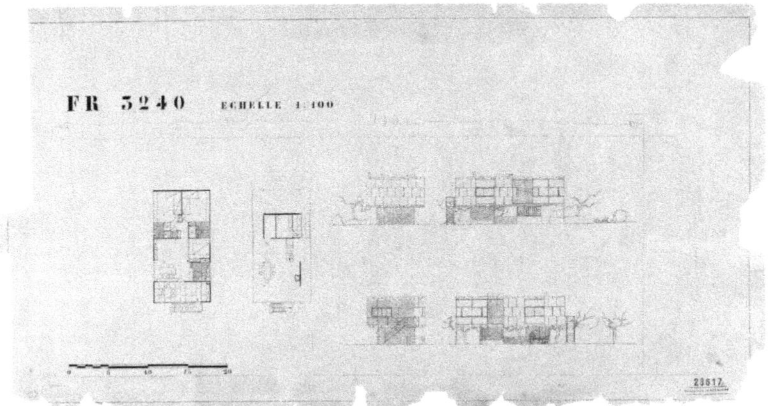

Agrarian reorganization, housing plans and elevations, unspecified location, unbuilt (FLC 28617A). Le Corbusier, 1938. Fondation Le Corbusier Collection

only find a car parked next to the market, operating as a modern counterpoint to the horses next to the pilotis on the other side of the building; references to streets and paths are always given as ambience, not as circulation. In the Commune of Piacé, the orchards formed by trees regularly displayed on the ground and the Cartesian layout of single-family houses along the road mark the rigid planning, which meets the typical territorial occupation of the French countryside, with a predominance of small properties and an extensive and intensive dominance over nature. Monlevade, on the other hand, emerges as a clearing in the midst of compact and irregular vegetation, without trying to control or subjugate nature, expressing a regressive desire for harmonic occupation of the local environment: "that row of houses that zigzags side by side along the streets and which distinguishes Brazilian small towns was deliberately disrupted in order to ensure greater privacy and relative isolation."[193]

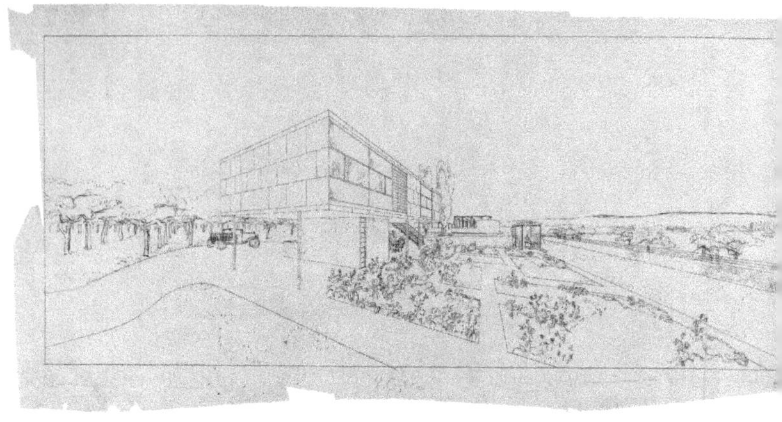

Agrarian reorganization, housing
perspective, unspecified location,
unbuilt (FLC 28621). Le Corbusier,
1934. Fondation Le Corbusier
Collection

The differences between the two village projects reflect even greater distinctions between their socioeconomic contexts. While Brazil is experiencing the first surge in industrialization and the beginning of a hierarchical turn regarding cities and the countryside, France is facing problems arising from large urban concentrations and the emptying of the rural environment. Le Corbusier will attribute the end of the isolation of the countryside to the industrial revolution and the dissemination of the artifacts of modern life – train, automobile, newspaper. Urban techniques with high functionalist content regulate the speed at which people move within the territory: the previous speed of 4 km/h restricted peasant life "to a radius of fifteen kilometers, totaling thirty kilometers for a round trip – that was therefore the explorable territory;"[194] on the other hand, the current speed could increase through mechanization, varying from 50 up to 100 km/h, calling for the restructuring of the territory. Land

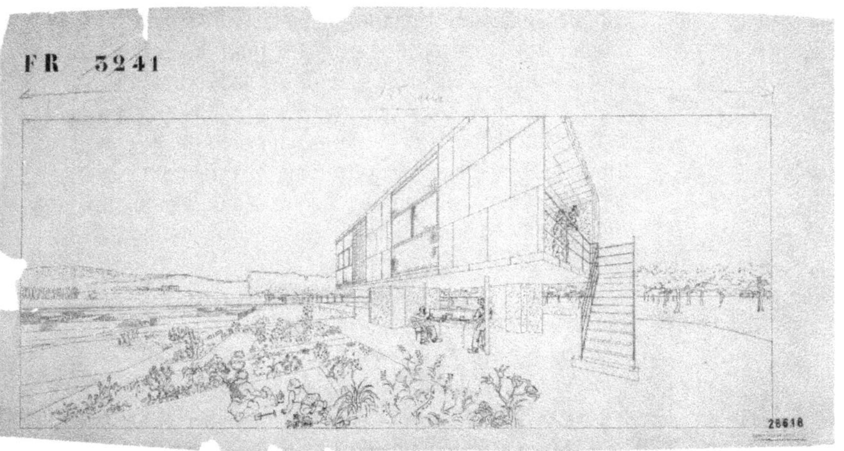

restructuring needs state interference, as the previous con-figuration is no longer adequate: "State powers feel the need to bring about a new peasant administrative unit exhibiting appropriate sizes, so that mayors, or any other administra-tors, could take charge of their responsibilities, so long as a sufficient complex of lands, people and events is entrusted to them."[195] The "cooperative center" of the new farm unit – "a modern tool that must be inserted into peasant life"[196] – is the most important element to be designed due to its role as an instrument of social transformation that avoids turmoil or upheavals:

"The *cooperative center* appears then as a technical device that brings security and hope to the peasant world. A tool to be entrusted only to alert, informed and technically developed spirits. A tool destined to forge a new conscience marked by accuracy and enthusiasm,

confidence and perseverance. Technical virtues and
moral virtues that must be extracted from the peasant
soul, where they are always latent, which is a task for
the instructor and the educator. Peasants still attached
to their traditional way of life, but nurtured by the contributions of a universal civilization. The rural school will
carry out these teachings, a school based on a program
clearly outlined and accurately measured according to
the scale of present needs."[197]

The centralization of power that evolves into educational concerns is a common point between the Commune of
Piacé and Vila Monlevade. In the rural village of Le Corbusier,
the aim is to activate the accuracy of the objects and the
enthusiasm of the inhabitants in favor of a mechanized
society devoted to work and the comprehensive control of
nature. A community reflecting the logic of speed, functional
clarity and life as an expression of work in a mechanized
civilization. When technological civilization approaches rural
archaism, the adjustment between clocks that seem to be
out of step with each other, in a present time of opposite
rhythms, will take place through the transformation of the
peasant way of life. However, the sobriety and restraint of
the ensemble and the economy of effort in each formal
solution bring us back to Kenneth Frampton's comment on a
growing primitivism in Le Corbusier's work after 1930.
In the solution given by Lúcio Costa, the residents of
the working-class village are obliged to make concessions
– to comply with the requirements regarding the use of the
house, equipment and territory, as explained in the architect's memorial –, so that the benefits of modern civilization
can be enjoyed.
However, there is room for improvisation, for irregularity, for dispersion. Introspection and restraint are valued as
suitable features for harmonious coexistence with nature.
Similar to the simple religiosity in Tarsila's *Pau-Brasil* painting

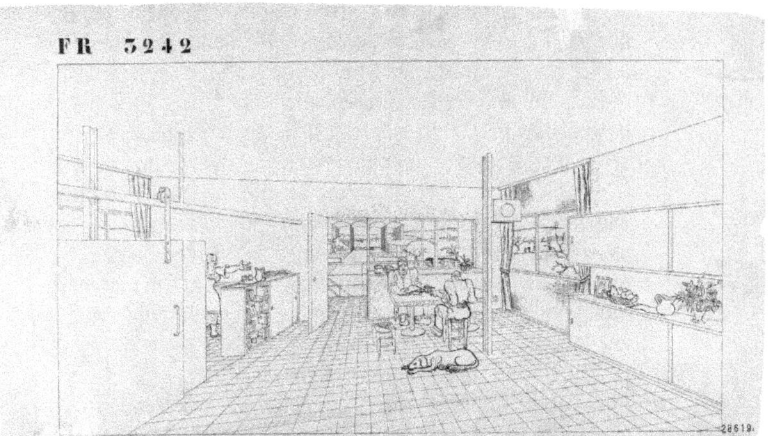

Agrarian reorganization, interior perspective of the housing, unspecified location, unbuilt (FLC 28619A). Le Corbusier, 1938. Fondation Le Corbusier Collection

("Anjos" / "Angels", 1924), the prominent presence of the church in Vila Monlevade – located on an elevated area of the plot, as seen in the historical towns of Minas Gerais – illustrates his concern to identify, codify and preserve pre-existing cultural elements that play a strategic role in social cohesion. Within an economic system whose logic and values are not even mentioned, Lúcio Costa draws a paradisiacal scenario for men in their leisure time, where physical rest and peace of mind are assured: "the only possible happiness for those who will certainly have to live in it every day, silently contributing to the well-being of so many others as well as to the ever-increasing prosperity of the Belgo-Mineira Steel Company."[198]

The Vila Monlevade project, from 1924, is the most important in a period when Lúcio Costa's convictions were being challenged. He's designing a lot, but not really building anything — sometimes he even designs with no contract or client, just for himself. The trip he made to Europe in 1926 put an end to his illusions regarding the neocolonial style as a path for the renovation of Brazilian architecture. His visit to Portugal and the first-hand experience with traditional Portuguese architecture revealed the deep gap between the original construction technique and the stylized and decorative copy that had been disseminated in the former colony. The denial of his traditional training and old academic beliefs, as well as his more recent adherence to the regionalist movement towards the neocolonial, culminates in him learning about the modern movement, which he describes as a revelation.[199]

Nevertheless, a fairly interesting study by Fernando Aliata and Claudia Shmidt[200] connects Vila Monlevade to a series of projects by Auguste Perret (1874-1954) and insists, despite his conversion to modern principles, on the survival of Costa's old intellectual convictions, particularly the academic definition of architecture as an expression of a regional character based on the "conformation of local particularities, which are the natural outcome of distinct geographical conditions."[201] According to Aliata and Shmidt, Costa's disenchantment with the neocolonial does not entail a rejection of his former academic vision; on the contrary, he learns about the debate going on among French academic groups struggling to take the lead in the process for renovation in the early decades of the 20th century. The hegemony during the 1930s fell to the "New Tradition", a sort of official State architecture, which argued for "primitivism, but with a predetermined idea of finding in it the pure and primary forms, the raw materials and the exaltation of the artisanal character of constructive systems that could unify localism and classicism."[202] The architecture of Auguste Perret follows this guideline: to shape in *modernist language* the *classic values* consecrated by tradition. Affiliated to Viollet-le-Duc and Choisy's vision of history, the Perretian style presents itself as resulting from structural truths – style being constructive rationality itself – and argues for the use of the new construction systems, especially reinforced concrete, as a settlement between architecture and modern-day techniques.

According to Aliata and Shmidt, adapting these ideas to local conditions is the solution to the dilemma Lúcio Costa was facing: unable to stand for the featureless neocolonial, but still committed to his classical convictions, the Brazilian architect seeks to adapt the European principles to the distinct cultural landscape of the former colony, an intellectual operation that allows him to continue to defend an architecture that expresses the national character, now following new propositions. As the Brazilian colonial tradition is quite different from the classical French model, Perret's experiment – a synthesis between *particularity* and technologically expressed through reinforced concrete – gains in Costa a different contour: in his equation local culture – diverse vernacular practices – was to function as the element of particularity.

As evidence for Auguste Perret's influence over Lúcio Costa, the Argentine historians present a set of warehouses built in Algeria in 1915 and the Notre-Dame du Raincy, from 1924. The former, which are also the basis for Le Corbusier's Monol Houses (as well as for the barns with four-vaulted roofs in the French town of Piacé, so it seems), would be the starting point for virtually all the institutional buildings of Monlevade – social club, school, cinema and warehouse; the latter would be the model for the church, the only building in Monlevade where the built mass overrides the constructive truth of reinforced concrete. Built in the African colony – therefore in cultural and climatic conditions similar to those in Brazil –, Perret's utilitarian buildings are a suitable model for Monlevade. Both in the Algerian warehouses as in Monlevade, the hollow and lattice elements applied to the upper part of the walls to better ventilate the internal environment imply appropriations of local vernacular techniques.

According to Aliata and Shmidt, the prototype of a semi-detached house on pilotis – an adaptation of the Loucheur Houses – were the only direct influence of Le Corbusier in this project, an observation that confirms the affiliation previously proposed by Luis Espallargas.

Finally, two comments made by Aliata and Shmidt on the mechanisms of cultural transmission are useful for our general argument. The first concerns the following steps taken by Le Corbusier regarding the incorporation of formalist ideas developed by avant-garde groups in the visual arts; here, the search for greater formal freedom entails a distancing from the constructive and technological determinations inspired by Perret. However, this was still not clear in the early 1930s, so Lúcio Costa's Monlevade emerges as a practical adherence to Perret's ideas, even though there's a simultaneous ideological alignment – much more rhetorical than theoretical – with Corbusian discourse. The second observation concerns the fact that in Monlevade nothing points to transformation of the social structure, as opposed to Tony Garnier's industrial city,[203] the most significant vision for an equivalent program at that time, where urban transformations imply a radical change in lifestyle. Lúcio Costa's stance is a reformist one, arguing for a decentralized community life where the harmonious occupation of the territory derives from a combination of art, nature and planning.[204] Thus, Monlevade assumes the continuity of the local way of life along with new facilities built with reinforced concrete.

The alignment between the ideas presented above and the arguments developed in this book calls for some clarification. Lúcio Costa's adherence to Quatremère de Quincy's defense of a national style forged over time by an anonymous production is plausible; however, over the years, even when he had the opportunity to review and rework his arguments, Costa remained consistent in defending both the production of anonymous artisans from the colonial period as the highbrow contributions of Brazilian baroque.

His notion of a spiritual affiliation between Aleijadinho and Oscar Niemeyer is the most visible aspect of this question. It is also true that Lúcio Costa, as has been said before, argues that the prevailing local culture would undergo a series of readjustments thanks to the imposition of new behaviors by modern pedagogy. Thus, by attributing Monlevade almost exclusively to the architect's classical training, Fernando Aliata and Claudia Shmidt's explanation becomes excessively limited.

The modern cultural environment in which Lúcio Costa found himself was as eclectic as his own ideas, and in this melting pot we can find justifications which are just as decisive, perhaps even more. His classical training is a necessary condition, but it alone does not explain his choices and ideas. Vila Monlevade can be considered, without exaggeration, a first iteration of *Pau-Brasil* urbanism, if we consider *Pau-Brasil* as an intellectual attitude that insists on a fusion between modernity and tradition combined with a given emotional and delicate subjectivity. The modern architecture of Perret and Le Corbusier, built upon reinforced concrete and ruled by technical precision, geometric control and standardization, contributes with formal elements which are duly softened by the use of clay, bamboo and mashrabiya. The arguments, facts and statements presented so far prove not only the intellectual proximity between Lúcio Costa and the modernist environment that existed in São Paulo, but also the personal and historical circumstances that inform this relationship. In the second part of our work, introducing new characters and ideas, we will dig deeper into the intellectual affinities between the *carioca* architect and the São Paulo avant-garde environment, especially the ideas of Mário de Andrade, of whom he became an exceptional follower.

Part 1 Notes

1. Mário de Andrade, *Macunaíma*, 23. In Mário de Andrade's rhapsody, the hammock – a presence throughout history – is a place for symbolic acts (burial; retreat before death) as well as everyday acts (sex and leisure).
2. Lúcio Costa, "Vila Monlevade," 90-99. Originally published in the *Revista da Diretoria de Engenharia da Prefeitura do Distrito Federal*, in May 1936. The text was later published again in *Sobre Arquitetura*, a collection organized by Alberto Xavier in 1962, and in *Record of an experience*, book-testament by Lúcio Costa, from 1995. Quotations are taken from this latest publication. Curiously, the first edition has the most illustrations, featuring 49 drawings; the second, by Xavier, has only 16 drawings, while the last edition has 34 drawings.
3. See: Lúcio Costa. "Memória descritiva do plano piloto," 283-297.
4. "Up until the end of 1935 [...] Lúcio Costa remained ostracized, with little work at the office and unsuccessful participation in competitions, such as the project for the city of Monlevade in Minas Gerais, ranked last". Hugo Segawa, *Arquiteturas no Brasil 1900-1990*, 79.
5. Lúcio Costa, "Documentação necessária," 459.
6. Costa, "Vila Monlevade," 99.
7. Ibid., 94.
8. A good definition of Maison Dom-Ino can be found in a master's thesis on the subject, developed a few years after the doctoral dissertation that led to this book: "In 1914, Jeanneret [Le Corbusier], together with engineers Max Du Bois and Juste Schneider, created the Maison Dom-ino Projects, in which the fundamental element was the reinforced concrete structure. The Dom-ino system became known for the dissemination of the famous image showing a basic module made up of structural elements in reinforced concrete"; "Dom-ino can be defined as a constructive system consisting of flat slabs, pillars and foundations in reinforced concrete, which proposes a rational order between its elements and its construction, through the application of organizational subsystems aiming to endow buildings that employ it with modern formal attributes, both concrete (cantilevered floors, free plan and facades, pilotis, etc.) and abstract (economy of resources, speed, rigor and precision in construction, universality)". Humberto Nicolás Sica Palermo, "O sistema Dom-ino," 43 and 7.
9. Costa, "Vila Monlevade," 94-95.
10. Ibid., 95.

11. "For the first three years of its existence, the Bauhaus was dominated by the charismatic presence of the Swiss painter and teacher Johannes Itten, who arrived in the fall of 1919. Three years earlier, he had established his own art school in Vienna under the influence of Franz Cizek. In an extremely charged environment, tinged by the anarchic anti-secessionist activities of the painter Oskar Kokoschka and the architect Adolf Loos, Cizek had developed a unique system of instruction based on stimulating individual creativity through the production of collages of different textures and materials. His methods had matured in a cultural atmosphere permeated by progressive educational theory, from Froebel's and Montessori's systems to the learning-by-doing movement initiated by the American John Dewey and vigorously propagated in Germany, starting in 1908, by the educational reformer Georg Kerschensteiner. Kenneth Frampton, *História crítica da arquitetura moderna*, 148.

12. Lúcio Costa, "O arquiteto e a sociedade contemporânea," 272.

13. Sérgio Buarque de Holanda, *Visão do paraíso: os motivos edênicos no descobrimento e colonização do Brasil*, 170.

14. Costa, "Vila Monlevade," 99.

15. Guilherme de Almeida, *Raça*, 3-4.

16. In 1947, organized by the *Anteprojeto* magazine, published by the students of the Faculdade Nacional de Arquitetura (National Faculty of Architecture), an album was published — Arquitetura contemporânea no Brasil (Contemporary Architecture in Brazil) — displaying photographs of projects and built works, seeking to outline the work of Brazilian architects, mainly from 1940 on. It is dedicated to "architect Lúcio Costa, master of traditional architecture and pioneer of contemporary architecture in Brazil". See: Edgar Graeff et al., *Arquitetura contemporânea no Brasil*.

17. Geraldo Ferraz. "Falta o depoimento de Lúcio Costa," 119-122. Entitled "Lúcio Costa's statement is missing: who is the pioneer of modern Brazilian architecture", the article was originally published in the *Diário de São Paulo* newspaper on 1 Feb. 1948 and republished on 15 Feb. 1948 in *O Jornal*, a Rio de Janeiro newspaper.

18. A few years later, in a newspaper article, Tarsila is very comfortable talking about various aspects of Warchavchik's architecture, including the difficulties the architect faced at the beginning of his career: "Warchavchik was the first to boldly implement modern architecture in Brazil, in a brave struggle against a hostile environment: war on the part of colleagues, difficulty in finding appropriate material for the new architecture, incomprehension coming from the public. It was an insane job to find the carpenter who

understood what an entirely smooth door was; it took mad patience to get a latch, a lock, a hinge that differed from the current standard. For the worker, complication had become simplicity, so that now, in order to return to the starting point and get to a real simplicity, it was necessary to re-educate the sensibilities. Warchavchik had, therefore, to think of everything, in its smallest details." Tarsila Amaral, "Gregorio Warchavchik."

19. Ferraz, "Falta o depoimento de Lúcio Costa," 120.

20. Lúcio Costa, "Depoimento," 199.

21. "However, the definitive milestone for the new Brazilian architecture, which was to become, once built, an international standard and where the doctrine and solutions advocated by Le Corbusier took shape in its monumental form for the first time, was undoubtedly the building constructed by Minister Gustavo Capanema for the headquarters of the new Ministry." Lúcio Costa, "Muita construção, alguma arquitetura e um milagre," 168. The article was originally published in the Rio de Janeiro newspaper *Correio da Manhã* on 15 Jun. 1951.

22. Mário de Andrade, "Brazil Builds." Quotations made from the original publication of the article in the São Paulo newspaper *Folha da Manhã*, 23 Mar. 1944.

23. Cf. Rui Moreira Leite, "Flávio de Carvalho: o arquiteto modernista em 3 tempos." The three articles by Mário de Andrade are: "Arquitetura moderna I," "Arquitetura moderna II," and "Arquitetura moderna III," originally published in the Rio de Janeiro newspaper *Diário Nacional*, on 2, 3, and 4 Feb. 1928.

24. Renato Anelli, Abilio Guerra, and Nelson Kon. *Rino Levi: arquitetura e cidade*, 28.

25. Agnaldo Aricê Caldas Farias, "Gregori Warchavchik: introdutor da arquitetura moderna no Brasil," 15.

26. See: José Tavares Correia de Lira. *Warchavchik: fraturas da vanguarda*; Jayme Vargas, *Gregori Warchavchik: design e vanguarda no Brasil*. In a video made available on the internet by the International Literary Festival of Paraty – Flip, it is possible to attest to the presence of Mário de Andrade at the 1930 inauguration of the modernist house on Itápolis street, a project by architect Gregori Warchavchik. The excerpt was taken from the documentary "Architectura modernista em S. Paulo", restored by the FAU USP Library: Rare record of Mário de Andrade on video, Flip. Time stamp for Mário de Andrade: 1'08".

27. Costa, "Depoimento," 199.

28. Ibid., 199.

29. João Batista Vilanova Artigas, "Semana de 22 e a arquitetura," 139-141. The article was originally published in *Módulo* magazine, in 1977. The quotes were made from the 3rd edition of the book *Caminhos da arquitetura*, by Vilanova Artigas, published by Cosac Naify.

30. João Batista Vilanova Artigas, "Os caminhos da arquitetura moderna," 35-50. The article was originally published in the São Paulo magazine *Fundamentos*, in January 1952, and the quotations were taken from the 3rd edition of the book *Caminhos da arquitetura*, already mentioned.

31. Ibid., 48.

32. Aracy Amaral writes that the aesthetic production of the Paulista modernists of the 1920s – "the modernist aristocracy, who gathered in elegant salons, English ships, cafés in Paris, at the Piolim circus in São Paulo, among objects and paintings they brought back from their recurrent trips to France" – spearheaded the hegemony exercised in the country by the rural aristocracy and the capitalist bourgeoisie, a hegemony deeply shaken by the Revolution of 1930. From then on, the main intellectuals of the group, who were at the forefront of the movement for the renewal of the arts in the country, would speak "from the margin, no longer from the center of the arena." Aracy Amaral, *Tarsila: sua obra e seu tempo*, 63.

33. Artigas, "Semana de 22 e a arquitetura," 139.

34. Ibid., 140. The expression "Brazilian roots of the universe" is attributed by Artigas to the poet Moacyr Félix.

35. Lúcio Costa, "Razões da nova arquitetura," p. 116. The quotation was taken from the 1991 *post scriptum*.

36. Lúcio Costa, *Sphan: Serviço do Patrimônio Histórico e Artístico Nacional*, 437.

37. Artigas, "Os caminhos da arquitetura moderna," 45.

38. Artigas, "Semana de 22 e a arquitetura," 139.

39. "Young architects. As you leave our beloved Faculty to face professional life, which is full of struggles and yet ridden with joys and stimuli derived from creative work, the avenues of a radiant and happy future open before you. Be certain that your future is mixed with that of our people and our country – a future of progress and happiness." João Batista Vilanova Artigas, "Aos formandos da FAU USP", 63. His speech at the graduation ceremony of the architects from FAU USP in 1955 was originally published the following year, in the May/June issue of the São Paulo magazine *AD – Arquitetura e Decoração*.

40. Artigas, "Semana de 22 e a arquitetura," 140.

41. Ibid., 140.

42. Andrade, "Manifesto da poesia Pau-Brasil," 10.

43. Yves Bruand, *Arquitetura contemporânea no Brasil*, 140.

44. Ibid., 140.

45. Ibid., 143.

46. We pursued this historiographical question in later texts, particularly in: Abilio Guerra, "O estranho ao Sul do Rio Grande."

47. Bruand, *Arquitetura contemporânea no Brasil*, 142. Bruand, on the same page, also refers to the "spiritual fusion" obtained by Lúcio Costa between ancient and modern techniques.

48. "The first steps towards the creation of a modern architecture of 'local character' are credited, in recent publications, to Lúcio Costa. However, despite the fact that his writings are as influential as his works, and that he is repeatedly praised as the theoretician of the movement and even as a pioneer in some sectors of research regarding national artistic heritage, no one has yet recognized, if I'm not mistaken, that a good deal of Brazilian architectural studies derive from the model of historical analysis that he himself elaborated. It is not by chance that these studies insist on the importance of the architect for the creation of an 'authentically' national modern architecture". Marcelo Puppi, *Por uma história não moderna da arquitetura brasileira*, 17.

49. Lúcio Costa, "Salão de 31," 71.

50. Henrique E. Mindlin, *Arquitetura moderna no Brasil*.

51. Segawa, *Arquiteturas no Brasil 1900-1990*, 102.

52. Mindlin, *Arquitetura moderna no Brasil*, 21.

53. Ibid., 32.

54. Ibid., 33.

55. Ibid., 32-33.

56. "Brazil is a country of contrasts, the result of a period of feverish speculation. Shabby shacks sprout like mushrooms in the vacant areas of the big cities and on the ridiculously expensive land on their outskirts. No balancing of the social structure and no large-scale urban planning will ever be possible unless this financial chaos is brought under control. Nevertheless, the prodigy of Brazilian architecture flourishes like a tropical plant. Sigfried Giedion, "O Brasil e a arquitetura contemporânea," 17.

57. Ibid., 17. If in Giedion the absence of a political, social and technological basis necessary for the introduction of modern architecture in our country is mentioned only incidentally, later it was one of the strongest arguments for the emergence of a more skeptical view on the part of international critics regarding Brazilian modern architecture.

58. Ibid., 17.

59. Ibid., 17, author's highlights. In our master's thesis, which was later published as a book, we have already had the opportunity to comment on how the organic metaphor is an integral part of a worldview tied to a romantic intellectual matrix, expressing various beliefs concerning a deep relationship between man, the natural environment and culture. See: Guerra, *O primitivismo em Mário de Andrade, Oswald de Andrade e Raul Bopp*.

60. "According to Gilberto Freyre, the Portuguese were the first Europeans to make the family, and not the trading companies, the basis of their civilizational enterprise. In contrast to the Anglo-Saxons, the Portuguese tradition always favored mixing with other races. The Count Keyserling observed that the unity of Brazil was established in spite of racial differences." Giedion, "O Brasil e a arquitetura contemporânea," 17.

61. Ibid., 17.

62. Mindlin, *Arquitetura moderna no Brasil*, 26.

63. Ibid., 26.

64. Henrique E. Mindlin, "A nova arquitetura e o mundo de hoje," quoted in Segawa, *Arquiteturas no Brasil 1900-1990.*

65. According to Segawa, Bruand "assimilated all the modernist prejudices against the architecture of eclecticism." Segawa, *Arquiteturas no Brasil 1900-1990*, 15.

66. Ibid., 16.

67. Oswald de Andrade, *O rei da vela*, 49. This is a line from the character Abelard I.

68. Ibid., 178-179. Photos of the building and the "simple house" can be found on pages 118 and 99 respectively.

69. Farias, "Gregori Warchavchik," 15. The modernist house and the huge garden are protected by Iphan, Condephaat, and Conpresp at the federal, state, and municipal levels. Today they constitute the Modernist Park, inaugurated in 2008 and managed by the Secretary of Environment of the city of São Paulo.

70. Even when we consider the disagreements between the Andrades, we find in all three of them an awareness of the relationship between the principles of the new architecture, present in Warchavchik's project, and structural changes in modern society. "Now Architecture also has a destiny, which does not consist in it being beautiful, but in it sufficiently sheltering, not a body, but a human being, with a body and also a soul. The Florentine souls were well clothed in the Renaissance. And the Greeks and the Chinese. And the *mamelucos* and *emboabas* of the eighteenth-century Ouro Preto, who never thought of building a church like that of São Francisco in gothic or manueline style. Well, we too, you current souls, have to shelter our souls in the current houses that you call 'modernist'. Everything else is homelessness, is self-disrespect and only serves to deceive. In a word, it's 'false'". Mário de Andrade, "Exposição duma casa modernista (considerações)": "Warchavchik's modernist house will never be lost, just as Le Corbusier will not be lost in the mass of geometric style buildings that will no doubt flood São Paulo, America, Sydney, Jaboticabal and Rouen in a few years." Oswald de Andrade, "A casa modernista, o pior crítico do mundo e outras considerações", 2. "Warchavchik's house entails a change in São Paulo: it is extra-normal, in relation to our built environment." Flávio de Carvalho, "Modernista Warchavchik," 9.

71. Farias, "Gregori Warchavchik," 18.
72. See: Costa, "Documentação necessária," 457-462.
73. Lúcio Costa, "Gregori Warchavchik," 72.
74. Gregori Warchavchik, "A primeira realização da arquitetura moderna em São Paulo."
75. Segawa, *Arquiteturas no Brasil 1900-1990*, 101.
76. "Also admirable is the collection of photographs – 'Brazil Builds' – that the Museum of Modern Art of New York – MoMA has just published, with excellent commentary by architect Philip L. Godwin. I believe this is one of the most fruitful gestures of fraternity that the United States has ever made towards us Brazilians. Because it will regenerate, as it has already done, our confidence in ourselves, diminishing the disastrous inferiority complex of mestizos that harms us so much. I have already met many Brazilians who are not only amazed, but even convulsed by this book that proves that we possess a modern architecture as good as the most advanced countries in the world. This awareness of our human normality can only be given to us by foreigners. Because we, given this inferiority complex, either react by falling into an idiotic ufanism, or into a conformist and rotten *jeca-tatuísmo*." Andrade, "Brazil Builds" quoted in Segawa, *Arquiteturas no Brasil 1900-1990*, 100. The transcription of the quote was made from the original article.
77. Lúcio Costa, "Cidade Universitária," 186.
78. Ibid.,105.
79. Bruand, *Arquitetura contemporânea no Brasil*, 105.
80. Carlos Eduardo Comas, "Arquitetura moderna, estilo Corbu, Pavilhão brasileiro," 208. Originally published in the São Paulo magazine *Arquitetura e Urbanismo*, in Oct./Nov., 1989.
81. Ibid., 207.
82. Ibid., 210.
83. Ibid., 210.
84. Ibid., 221.
85. Ibid., 221.
86. Ibid., 219.
87. As is recurrent in his interpretations of Lúcio Costa's architecture, Comas relates the tropical garden to the classical tradition in another article on the Pavilion: "Lúcio's greatest spirit of Brazilianness seems to be associated with his open ground plan, enlivened by evocative elements, the water mirror and the lattice panels. Following the Romantic classical tradition, the water mirror goes against the dominant orthogonality, as in many Brazilian parks and squares, among them the Quinta da Boa Vista park with landscaping by Auguste Glaziou in Rio de Janeiro (1880) and João Mendes Square in São Paulo (1880). The lattice imparts a certain colonial aspect to the modern forms." Carlos Eduardo Comas, "A Feira Mundial de Nova York de 1939: o pavilhão brasileiro," 66.

88.	A note in the monthly bulletin of IAB/SP from January 1954 gives a good idea of how this discussion was taking shape, often with excessive schematism and diverse ideological contours: "Architecture and nationality. The long-awaited round-table discussion on the subject was held, attended by a good number of architects and students, and the debate went on for several hours. The discussion started with the architects invited to be part of the table, namely: Flávio de Carvalho, Eduardo Kneese de Mello, Corona, Luiz Saia, Artigas; later other participants engaged with discussion. At first, Flávio de Carvalho spoke about the internationalist factors of architecture (calculation, materials, etc.) and the nationalist factors (environment, climate, social reality); he believes that architecture will be totally transformed by the new concrete calculation, a calculation in three dimensions, which will shape new forms. Artigas intervened saying that what imparts a national character to architecture is the human aspect. Corona doesn't think that our contemporary architecture was imported, because he doesn't consider the first works by Warchavchik and even Flávio de Carvalho as having a definitive influence in their time; the new phase of architecture started in Brazil in 1934, with the projects for the Ministry of Education. Artigas is of the opinion that this modern architecture had a cosmopolitan content, declaredly imported, but that it was coated with national details, taken from the architecture of the past; after the initial importation, there was always an effort to continue coating that content in this way. This is not enough to confirm this architecture as a national expression." Jorge Wilheim and Telésforo Giorgio Cristofani, "Arquitetura e nacionalidade." The IAB bulletin is from 1954, but it is inserted in the January 1955 issue of the *Acropolis* magazine. Eduardo Corona's opinion, except for the equivocation in anticipating by two or three years the date of the beginning of the MES project, is exactly the argument presented by Lúcio Costa in his polemic with Geraldo Ferraz in 1948.

89.	Comas, "Arquitetura moderna, estilo Corbu, Pavilhão brasileiro," 218.

90.	Gilberto Freyre, *Casa-grande e senzala.*

91.	Sérgio Buarque de Holanda, *Raízes do Brasil.*

92.	Philip L. Goodwin, *Brazil Builds: Architecture New and Old 1652-1942,* 194.

93.	Mindlin, *Arquitetura moderna no Brasil,* 202.

94.	Bruand, *Arquitetura contemporânea no Brasil,* 107.

95.	Comas, "Arquitetura moderna, estilo Corbu, Pavilhão brasileiro," 207.

96.	Segawa, *Arquiteturas no Brasil 1900-1990,* 93.

97.	Fernando Luiz Lara, "Espelho de fora: arquitetura brasileira vista do exterior."

98. Jorge Francisco Liernur, "The South American Way: o milagre brasileiro, os Estados Unidos e a Segunda Guerra Mundial – 1939-1943," 179-180. The article was originally published in the Argentinian magazine *Block* in 1999. The quotations are taken from the book.

99. Ibid., 212-213.

100. In the book *Pavilhões de Exposição* (Exhibition Pavilions) – which, according to the author, presents the fifty most important pavilions in the 20th century –, we find the Brazilian Pavilion for the 1939 New York International Fair, demonstrating that, if there really were a retrospective montage, it spread vigorously. See: Moisés Puente, *Pavilhões de Exposição: 100 anos*, 94-97. The book makes a mistake in attributing Thomas Price's landscape design to Roberto Burle Marx.

101. "The interest of Vargas' Estado Novo in the Pavilion was considerable, both economically and diplomatically. Brazil's participation in the Fair, decided in November 1937, was part of Roosevelt's good neighbor policy." Comas, "Arquitetura moderna, estilo Corbu, Pavilhão brasileiro," 207-208. "The 1939 calendar of events would have two high points because of the United States' effort to promote a cultural exchange between the nations, in the delicate international political panorama that eventually led to the Second War" Segawa, *Arquiteturas no Brasil 1900-1990*, 92. A new perspective on the relationship between Brazil and the United States during this period was established by Fernanda Critelli, when she investigated how Brazilian modern architecture influenced the work of Richard Neutra. Her project for scientific initiation, as well as her master's and doctoral researches, all oriented by Abilio Guerra, resulted in the following book: Fernanda Critelli, *Richard Neutra e o Brasil.*

102. Liernur, "The South American Way," 177.

103. Ibid., 179.

104. Max Bill, "Report on Brazil," quoted in Frampton, *História crítica da arquitetura moderna*, 313-314. Ciam is the acronym for International Congresses of Modern Architecture (originally in French: Congrès Internationaux d'Architecture Moderne), an organization that brought together the most important modern architects of the time and promoted a series of events to discuss principles and procedures in the various fields of architecture and urbanism. The first of its ten international congresses was held in 1928 in La Sarraz, Switzerland, when the institution was founded; the last one was held in Dubrovnik, Yugoslavia, in 1956.

105. Bill, "Report on Brazil," quoted in Segawa, *Arquiteturas no Brasil 1900-1990*, 109.

106. Another interesting note in IAB's monthly bulletin, also signed by Jorge Wilheim and Telésforo Giorgio Cristofani, reveals just how much the international critics reversed, in the 1950s, the positive evaluation that prevailed in the second half of the 1940s, probably motivated by the criticism of Max Bill and Bruno Zevi: "Under this title [The irrational in Niemeyer's work], the *Metron* magazine (Italy) published an article signed by Natalio David Firszt. [...] The author expresses the opinion that Niemeyer's work finds its deepest reasons in the egocentric character and in his rationalist conception of architecture – and not so much in the baroque tradition. Niemeyer, the author tells us, creates with extreme ease. In his most daring solutions, dominated by a kind of asymmetric frenzy, it is clear that his final objective is solely the form – form increased by a sensual egocentrism, even to the detriment of other values. It is useless, says Firszt, to try to explain this architecture through traditional methods: its psychology eludes all rules, because its only raison d'être is the development of an extraordinary plastic capacity". Jorge Wilheim and Telésforo Giorgio Cristofani, "O irracional na obra de Niemeyer."

107. Lúcio Costa, "Desencontro," 202.

108. Max Bill describes the Pedregulho housing complex as "a remarkable success, not only with regard to architecture, but also urbanism and all social problems. For me, Pedregulho is the most important example in this field, and I would be happy if there were many such achievements in Switzerland. Unfortunately, there are only a few. The human sense in Pedregulho seems to me perfect, of first order, because every time I enter a residence, I ask myself: would I want to live in this apartment? Well, my answer, as soon as I visited one of those apartments, was the following: tomorrow, if someone were to invite me, I would move with great pleasure into such comfortable apartments," quoted in Nabil Georges Bonduki, *Affonso Eduardo Reidy*, 18.

109. Costa, "Desencontro," 202.

110. Ibid., 201.

111. Liernur, "The South American Way," 190.

112. Ibid., 192.

113. Costa, "Documentação necessária," 457. There's great symmetry between Lúcio Costa's proposals for documenting colonial architecture and those of Mário de Andrade since the mid-1920s regarding popular manifestations.

114. Ibid., 458.

115. Ibid., 458.

116. "This is one of the interesting peculiarities of the project: to take advantage, in certain cases, of solutions that thirty years ago were still common among us and that are now in disuse, having been inexplicably banished – such as these verandas employed here for mass circulation." Costa, "Cidade Universitária," 177.
117. Ibid., 177.
118. Liernur, "The South American Way," 195.
119. Ibid., 206.
120. Ibid., 199.
121. Ibid., 191.
122. Blaise Cendrars, "Peixinhos", quoted in Alexandre Eulalio, *A aventura brasileira de Blaise Cendrars*, 31.
123. Carlos Alberto Ferreira Martins, "Há algo de irracional...: notas sobre a historiografia da arquitetura brasileira," 137. The article was originally published in the Argentinian magazine *Block* in 1999. Quotations are taken from the book in Portuguese.
124. Ibid., 139.
125. Geraldo Ferraz, *Warchavchik e a introdução da nova arquitetura no Brasil: 1925 a 1940*, quoted in Martins, "Há algo de irracional...," 148.
126. Gregori Warchavchik, "Decadência e renascimento da arquitetura," quoted in Martins, "Há algo de irracional...," 148. There are a few minor differences between the passage as quoted here and the one present in the article referred to in the note, for we prefer to quote directly from the original source, which was published in the newspaper *Correio Paulistano*, 5 Aug. 5, 1928.
127. Lúcio Costa, "O arranha-céu e o Rio de Janeiro," 4. We learned about this article in an unpublished collection of texts by Lúcio Costa organized by Alberto Xavier, in a typewritten volume with no general pagination. With the provisional title 'Trabalhos escritos', the volume has not been published yet
128. Martins, "Há algo de irracional...," 159.
129. Lúcio Costa, "Relato pessoal," 137. Many years later, Lúcio Costa confirmed Bruand's statement in an interview. When asked whether the use of tiles and granite in the ministry building had been a suggestion of Le Corbusier, the Brazilian architect replied: "Yes, it was his suggestion." Jorge Czajkowsky, Maria Cristina Burlamarqui, and Ronaldo Brito, "Presença de Le Corbusier: entrevista de Lúcio Costa," 146.
130. Carlos Alberto Ferreira Martins, "Arquitetura e estado no Brasil: elementos para uma investigação sobre a constituição do discurso moderno no Brasil – a obra de Lúcio Costa (1924-1952)," 89. The arguments in the article can be found especially in the chapter "Arquitetura moderna no Brasil: uma trama recorrente".
131. Ibid., 97.
132. Czajkowsky, Burlamarqui, and Brito, "Presença de Le Corbusier," 151.
133. Ibid., 144-145.

134. The three texts resulting from the trip to South America – available today in Portuguese thanks to the important research work of Margareth Silva Pereira and her associates, which resulted in the book *Le Corbusier e o Brasil* – are very revealing of the impact caused by the South American territory in Le Corbusier's worldview. See: Le Corbusier, "Corolário brasileiro;" Le Corbusier, "O espírito sulamericano;" Le Corbusier, "Prólogo americano."

135. "Attention: I am informing you that the Brazilian government has just asked Congress for the necessary funds to build the federal capital, as provided for in the Constitution. We are talking about the construction of a city of a million souls: Planaltina, in a region still virgin today! I believe that this should interest you! If that is the case, I will put you in touch with the right people." Letter from Blaise Cendrars to Le Corbusier, 13 Jul. 1926, quoted in Margareth da Silva Pereira et al., *Le Corbusier e o Brasil*, 42. This book describes, with extensive primary documentation, the various attempts by Le Corbusier to receive the commission for the urban design of the new capital of Brazil.

136. Letter from Le Corbusier to Paulo Prado, Jul. 28, 1929, quoted in Margareth da Silva Pereira et al., *Le Corbusier e o Brasil*, 44.

137. Le Corbusier, "Prólogo americano," 74.

138. The authors of *Le Corbusier e o Brasil* posit an inverted influence by which Le Corbusier would have been conditioned by the Brazilian landscape when developing his urbanistic ideas: "On this trip the architect also takes up the notion of the modern city imagined as a park, as a green city, as a place of light. Several passages in the 'South American Spirit' and the 'Brazilian Corollary' show the recurrence of these notions in the reflections from 1929 that inspire the doctrine of the Ville Radieuse. Recapture the air, the light and the green everywhere. Give the city a great purpose, a great design, a great destiny. Cities are seen from an airplane: tomorrow the airplane will be ours. Cars, steel, cement will be in our homes. The ville radieuse is a green city: without the dazzle provoked by Rio de Janeiro's nature, without the acquiescence of imagination in view of the challenge of such strength and beauty, perhaps it would not be possible for him to elaborate the doctrine underlying the Ville Radieuse." Cf. Margareth da Silva Pereira et al., *Le Corbusier e o Brasil*, 19.

139. Le Corbusier, "Prólogo americano," 76.

140. Text written at Fazenda S. Martinho during the trip to Brazil, quoted in Margareth da Silva Pereira et al., *Le Corbusier e o Brasil*, 49.

141. Spengler developed a historiography considering the vital
cycles – birth, life and death
– that are part of all civilizations. See: Oswald Spengler, *A
decadência do Ocidente*.

142. Hermann Keyserling, *El mundo
que nace*, 32. The first Spanish
edition was published by *Revista
de Occidente* in 1926, the same
year of its original publication
in German (*Die neuentstehende
Welt*). The first French edition
(*Le monde qui naît*), from 1927,
is the one consulted by both
Mário de Andrade and Oswald
de Andrade.

143. We dealt at length with this
subject and the presence of
Keyserling in Mário de Andrade's
work in our Master's thesis,
which later became a book:
Guerra, *O primitivismo em Mário
de Andrade, Oswald de Andrade
e Raul Bopp*. See especially the
subchapter entitled "O primitivismo em Mário de Andrade",
246-264.

144. The original – *Südamerikanische
Meditationen* – was published
in 1932. A volume of the
French translation, *Méditations
sud-américains*, from the same
year, can be found in Mário de
Andrade's library. Cf. Daniel Faria,
"As meditações americanas de
Keyserling: um cosmopolitismo
nas incertezas do tempo," 915.

145. Hermann Keyserling,
Meditaciones suramericanas,
26-28. Author's translation.

146. Oswald de Andrade, "Manifesto
antropófago," 14. The text was
originally published in the first
issue of *Revista de Antropofagia*,
May 1928.

147. After arguing that it is false to
point out a "barbarizing character" in modern technology,
Keyserling proposes a new
historical type: "the chauffeur.
This is the primitive type of our
age of multitudes, as in other
ages there were the priest and
the knight. The chauffeur is
the primitive man trained by
technique. His technical talent
is a quality attuned to that
faculty of self-direction, which
the savages have; technique, in
this case, is quite obvious, and
its mastery awakens i feelings
of freedom and power, the more
energetic the more primitive
man is." Keyserling, *El mundo
que nace*, 34 and 40.

148. Telê Porto Ancona Lopez, *Mário
de Andrade: ramais e caminho*,
51.

149. In the book based on our
Master's we dealt with the
pessimism inherent in our
modernism, which derived
from a debate regarding the
civilizational possibilities of
the Brazilian man, especially in
Mario de Andrade's version. See:
Guerra, *O primitivismo em Mário
de Andrade, Oswald de Andrade
e Raul Bopp*.

150. Le Corbusier, "Corolário brasileiro," 96.

151. Le Corbusier, "Prólogo americano," 83-84.

152. Ibid., 78.

153. Luis Aranha, "Drogaria de éter e
sombra," 35.

154. Aracy Amaral publishes the
drawing in a book from 1975,
which bears the following caption: "Drawing by Le Corbusier
given to Tarsila in 1936, when
she came to Rio: Panorama of
the city. On the left, 'Rio / 14
août 936 / À Madame Tarsila /
Amicalement / Le Corbusier'".
Amaral, *Tarsila*, 254.

155. Le Corbusier's positive view of
blacks and their accommodation
in the territory can be confirmed
in the architect's own text:
"When we climb up to the 'favelas' of the black people, the high
and sloping hills where they
anchor their brightly painted
wooden and clay houses, nailed
like shellfish to the rocks of the
harbor — the men are clean and
of magnificent stature, and the
women dress in a cloth adorned
with little white flowers, always
clean, being freshly washed;
there is neither street nor path
— everything is very steep — but
tracks that are at the same time
sewers and the result of floods;
scenes of popular life take place
there which are animated by
such a masterly dignity that a
school of genre painting would
enjoy a great future in Rio; the
black man almost always makes
his house on the hillside, the
front of it perched on pilotis,
the door on the back, turned
to the hill; from the top of the
'Favelas' one always sees the sea,
the basin, the ports, the islands,
the ocean, the mountains, the
estuaries; the black man sees
all this; the wind reigns, quite
handy in the tropics; there is a
haughtiness in the black man's
eye that sees all this; the eye of
a man who sees vast horizons
is more haughty, vast horizons
confer dignity." Le Corbusier,
"Corolário brasileiro." 88.

156. Le Corbusier, "Prólogo americano," 79.

157. "The young men of São Paulo
presented me with their thesis;
we are 'anthropophagous';
anthropophagy was not a
gluttonous habit; it was an
esoteric rite, a communion with
the best forces. The meal was
frugal; there were a hundred
to five hundred warriors eating the flesh of the captured
warrior. This warrior was a
valiant. He had eaten the flesh
of the warriors of his own tribe.
Therefore, by eating his flesh,
they assimilated the very flesh
of his ancestors." Le Corbusier,
"Prólogo americano," 83.

158. Frampton, *História crítica da
arquitetura moderna*, 222.

159. And also after death. It fell to
Lúcio Costa to take the body
of his deceased friend from
Roquebrune, where he drowned,
to Paris. Halfway there, they
made a stop at the convent of
La Tourette, where the most poignant scene narrated in his book
of testaments occurs: "At nightfall we arrived in Lyon, taking
the direction of the Dominican
convent of La Tourette, which
was built by him, where we
were to spend the night. It was
drizzling. The convent is on
the slope of the hillside, at the
side of the road. When the cars
stopped, those religious men, in
their traditional black and white
robes, were already waiting
and were slowly arriving. They
carried the flag-covered coffin
on their shoulders, and walked

slowly down to the road — the side span that tears the nave from top to bottom. The church is beautiful and solemn; tall, severe, conventual, the opposite of Ronchamp. They deposited the body in the central part of the nave and lined up in silence, remaining so until the superior's deep voice began the architect's eulogy." Cf. Lúcio Costa, "Roquebrune," 585.

160. And also after death. It fell to Lúcio Costa to take the body of his deceased friend from Roquebrune, where he drowned, to Paris. Halfway there, a stop at the convent of La Tourette, where the most poignant scene narrated in his book of testaments occurs: "At nightfall we arrived in Lyon, taking the direction of the Dominican convent of La Tourette, which was built by him, where we were to spend the night. It was drizzling. The convent is on the slope of the hillside, at the side of the road. When the cars stopped, those religious men, in their traditional black and white robes, were already waiting and were slowly arriving. They carried the flag-covered coffin on their shoulders, and walked slowly down to the road, - the side span that tears the nave from top to bottom. The church is beautiful and solemn; tall, severe, conventual, the opposite of Ronchamp. They deposited the body in the central part of the nave and lined up in silence, remaining so until the superior's deep voice began the architect's eulogy," quoted in Margareth da Silva Pereira et al., *Le Corbusier e o Brasil*, 211.

161. "These people do not, therefore, seem to me to deserve the characterization of savages just because they have been but very little modified by the interference of the human spirit, and have lost almost nothing of their primitive simplicity. The laws of nature, not yet perverted by the interference of our own, govern them even now, and have remained so pure that I sometimes regret that our world did not know them before, when there were men capable of appreciating them." Michel de Montaigne, *Ensaios* (chapter XXI – Dos canibais), 102.

162. "Stripping this being, thus constituted, of all the supernatural gifts which he was able to receive, and of all the artificial faculties which he only managed to acquire by a very long progress, considering him, in a word, as he must have come out of the hands of nature, I see an animal less strong than some, less agile than others, but, on the whole, more advantageously organized than all the rest. I see him feasting under an oak tree, refreshing himself at the first stream, finding his bed at the foot of the same tree that provided his repast, and thus satisfying all his needs." Jean-Jacques Rousseau, *Discurso sobre a origem e os fundamentos da desigualdade entre os homens*, 238.

163. "When Le Corbusier was in São Paulo, a mandatory stop was the party at Tarsila and Oswald's house." Cf. Amaral, *Tarsila*, 237.

164. "For his notion of the primitive man, Oswald de Andrade turned to Montaigne, Rousseau and their rebellious romantic derivations, idealizing a paradisiacal scenario where freedom, equality and absence of repression still exist as natural conditions." Cf. Guerra, *O primitivismo em Mário de Andrade, Oswald de Andrade e Raul Bopp*, 270. In this book, based on my master's thesis, we were able to trace the cultural genealogy of modernist primitivism, a concept that paid tribute to the discursive paths of evolutionism and romanticism in Brazil. The relations between Brazilian modernism of the 1920s and modern Brazilian architecture, where racial miscegenation, tropical nature and a deliberately naive vision of Brazilian culture are present, were developed later. See: Abilio Guerra, "Arquitetura brasileira: tradição e utopia."

165. Paper presented at the IV Pan-American Congress of Architecture and Urbanism and published in the São Paulo newspaper *Diário da Noite*, on Jul. 1, 1930, quoted in Luiz Carlos Daher, *Flávio de Carvalho: arquitetura e expressionismo*.

166. "As Flávio told the newspapers today, for us Le Corbusier is nothing but the last great bourgeois architect. [...] There are passages in Corbusier's 'Urbanisme' demonstrating the narrowest Christian bourgeois spirit. And it should be noted that we admire Le Corbusier very much. [...] His psychological intention in urbanism would be to standardize the dreadful mediocre hotel life. The thesis that Flávio de Carvalho reads today at the Pan-American Congress of Architects, entitled 'The city of the naked man', brings the contribution of the anthropophagic point of view to the problem. It does not lack the climatic criterion that has already produced in Brazil the great colonial architecture of yore." Oswald de Andrade, "Antropofagia e arquitetura."

167. On the origin of the expression "Pau-Brasil poetry", Oswald de Andrade explains: "Blaise Cendrars had an influence on the emergence of 'Pau-Brasil'. In 1925 I brought back from Paris, with a preface by Paulo Prado and illustrations by Tarsila, the book *Pau-Brasil*, which gave rise to a movement within our modernism. Primitivism, which in France appeared as exoticism, was for us in Brazil true primitivism. I thought, then, of creating a line of poetry for exportation instead of importation, which would be based on our geographical, historical and social ambience. Since pau-brasil

was the first of Brazilian riches to be exported, I named the movement Pau-Brasil. Its aesthetic feature coincided with the 100% exoticism and modernism of Cendrars, who, in any case, also consciously wrote Pau-Brasil poetry." Péricles Eugênio da Silva Ramos, "Depoimento de Oswald Andrade."

168. Andrade, "Manifesto da poesia Pau-Brasil," 9.

169. Le Corbusier, "Prólogo americano," 84.

170. Ibid., 85.

171. Robert Fishman, *Urban utopias in the twentieth century*, 1977, quoted in Frampton, *História crítica da arquitetura moderna*, 221.

172. Mário de Andrade, "A meditação sobre o Tietê (Lira Paulistana)," 305.

173. Carlos Zílio, *A querela do Brasil: a questão da identidade da arte brasileira – a obra de Tarsila, Di Cavalcanti e Portinari*, 79.

174. Ibid., 80.

175. Redação. "Klaxon." Republished in: Gilberto Mendonça Teles, *Vanguarda europeia e modernismo brasileiro*, 294-296. The quote can be found in the last paragraph in both versions.

176. Andrade, "Manifesto da poesia Pau-Brasil," 5.

176. Ibid., 5.

177. The paradisiacal vision present in Tarsila do Amaral's painting, where the precarious living conditions are not an impediment to a simple and happy life, well adapted to the tropical environment, gains an unexpected seal of approval from Gilberto Freyre, even if in more realistic colors: "The contrast between the dwellings of the rich and the poor in Brazil cannot be said to have always been absolute, through patriarchy and its decline, with all the advantage on the side of the sobrado, and all the disadvantage on the side of the *mucambo* or *palhoça*. One can even maintain that the dweller of the *mucambo* built on dry land, with a double roof protecting him well from the rain, was and is a more hygienically settled individual in the tropics than the bourgeois man and especially the bourgeois woman of the old sobrado. Or than the petit bourgeois of the ground floor house." Gilberto Freyre, *Sobrados e mucambos*, 301.

178. Zílio, *A querela do Brasil*, 81-82.

179. Ibid., 83.

180. Andrade, "Manifesto da poesia Pau-Brasil," 6.

181. Zílio, *A querela do Brasil*, 82.

182. "Freud put an end to the woman enigma and with the big scares of printed psychology"; "the carnal anthropophagy, which brings about the highest meaning of life and avoids all the evils identified by Freud, catechist evils"; "against the social reality, clothed and oppressive, registered by Freud." Andrade, "Manifesto antropófago," 13; 18-19; 19, respectively.

183. Ibid., 15.

184. Benedito Nunes points out how close pau-brasil thought is to philosophy and psychoanalysis. The vision of the primitive man is not based on a historical native; it is delineated rather from the supposed energetic power of the origin: "In his anthropophagic thinking, Oswald internalized the Indian, but as an image of the primitive living in a different society, and moving in an unlimited ethnographic space, resembling the unconscious of the species. On the one hand, his primitivism reproduced the modern anthropologist's critical distancing from the patterns of the society to which he is bound, from which he disengages himself; on the other hand, by retreating into a savage thought, he allied himself to the denuding of man that psychoanalysis was undertaking. Thus, the *Tupi*, or *Caraíba*, far from representing the sedimented common soul, connotes the psychic energies that animate and drive human development. Benedito Nunes. "Antropofagia ao alcance de todos," XXXVIII.

185. There were other groups in the 1920s operating along the lines of the avant-garde. Among them, perhaps the closest one with regard to theme is the Movimento Verde-Amarelo – also called Verde-amarelismo – a literary group founded by Cassiano Ricardo, Menotti Del Picchia and Plínio Salgado in 1926. A conservative movement in political and social issues, some of their works can be included in the list of primitivist works, as a counterpoint or even as confirmation of the interpretations presented.

186. Jorge Schwartz, "Tupi or not Tupi: o grito de guerra da literatura do Brasil moderno," 146.

187. Oswald de Andrade, "Postes da Light," 115.

188. Ibid., 43.

189. The epigraph of the article elucidates the author's demystifying goal: "The vast domain of the imagination is similar to that of lying [...] when imagination is abused, we fall into madness. It is a noble faculty as long as it recognizes its ideality; when it ceases to do so, it turns into madness." John Ruskin, *A lâmpada da verdade*, quoted in ibid., 35.

190. Ibid., 46.

191. Ibid., 90.

192. See: Le Corbusier, *Oeuvre Complète*, 186 and following.

193. Costa, "Vila Monlevade," 99.

194. Le Corbusier, *Os três estabeleci-mentos humanos*, 92. The French original was published in 1943 and discusses the three modern ways of settling man in the territory according to Corbusian thought at that time – "the unit of agricultural exploitation", "the linear industrial center" and the ""radiocentric city of exchanges" – considering, there-fore, an anthropic territory in its extension. The considerations regarding "the farming unit" are made from the project of the Piacé Commune, developed in the previous decade.

195. Ibid., 93.

196. Ibid., 96.

197. Ibid., 102.

198. Costa, "Vila Monlevade," 99.

199. On several occasions, Lúcio Costa highlighted the little impor-tance he gave to Le Corbusier during his 1929 lecture in Rio de Janeiro. In a letter to Le Corbusier, dated January 26, 1936, Lucio Costa described the disdain with which he saw the first visit of Corbusier to Brazil: "On the occasion of your visit to Rio in 1929, I went to listen to you: the conference was in the middle, the room was full, and 5 minutes later I left scandal-ized, sincerely believing to have encountered a *cabotino*," quoted in Margareth da Silva Pereira et al., *Le Corbusier e o Brasil*, 142. In another interview, now from 1987, Lúcio Costa presented a quite similar version of the story: "I was entirely withdrawn at the time, but I made a point of going there. I arrived a little late and the room was full. The doors to the school hall were full of people and I saw him talking. I stayed a while then gave up and went away, entirely uncon-cerned, oblivious to the pressing reality." Czajkowsky, Burlamarqui, and Brito, "Presença de Le Corbusier," 144. In the same year, in an interview with Hugo Segawa, Lúcio Costa crystallized the story: "1929 was that period in which I was withdrawn. Naturally, as everybody was talking about the conference, I went to the Great Hall of the School of Fine Arts. I got there and it had already started. The hall was full and the doors – the three doors leading to the hall from the stairs – were packed with people watching and wanting to participate. I arrived, looked around, and saw that fig-ure on the big board – they had nailed large sheets of paper that he was tearing out as he illus-trated the lecture with drawings. I only stayed a little while, for I could see almost nothing. I went to catch my train to go back to Correias, where I lived." Hugo Segawa, "Lúcio Costa: a vanguarda permeada com a tradição (interview)," 148. Lúcio Costa also recalls a contact with the American Mary Houston, who attests to his ignorance of Le Corbusier in 1927: "We were playing hangman, and she proposed a name beginning with L, and the thing went on until she hung me: it was simply 'Le Corbusier.' And to think of everything that would happen three years later, in my teaching reform." Lúcio Costa, "Mary Houston: registro de viagem," 48.

200. Fernando Aliata, and Claudia Shmidt, "Lúcio Costa, o episódio Monlevade e Auguste Perret," 239-258.
201. Aliata and Shmidt, "Lúcio Costa, o episódio Monlevade e Auguste Perret," 241. The work of Fernando Aliata and Claudia Shmidt is in tune, probably due to the proximity of their intellectual environments, with the line of historical research that has been developed for decades in Rio Grande do Sul under the leadership of Carlos Eduardo Comas and that seeks to bring to light the association between the Brazilian modern architecture as developed in Rio de Janeiro and both the academic tradition and the teaching of fine arts in that same state.
202. Ibid., 243. Italics by the author.
203. Tony Garnier, "Una ciudad industrial: estudio para la construcción de ciudades."
204. In contrast to the structural transformation of society foreseen by Garnier, Lúcio Costa's transformation proposal "involved incorporating art and nature in the planning of new cities in a general plan of decentralization and harmonious occupation of the territory" Aliata and Shmidt, "Lúcio Costa, o episódio Monlevade e Auguste Perret," 250.

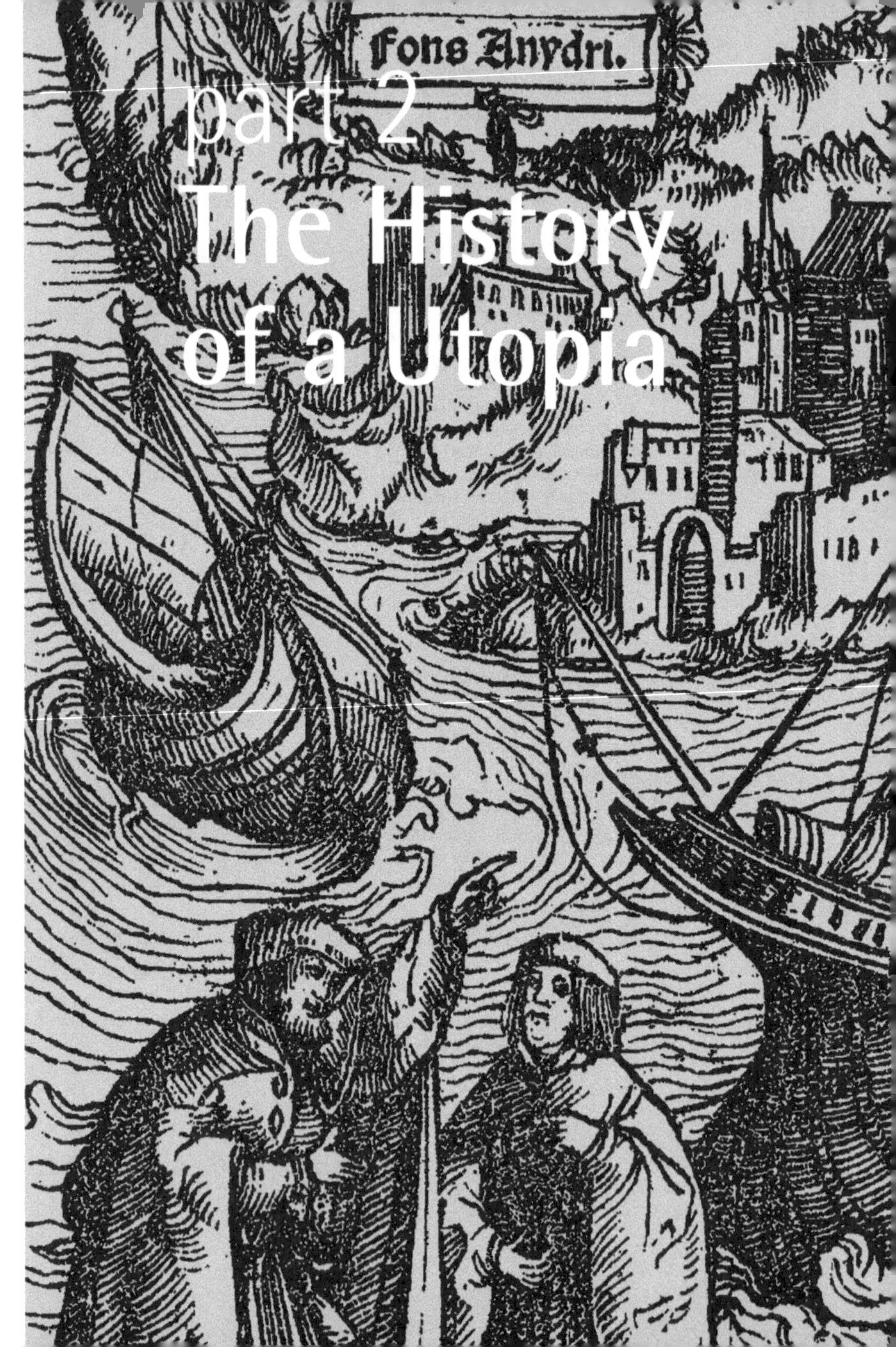

part 2
The History of a Utopia

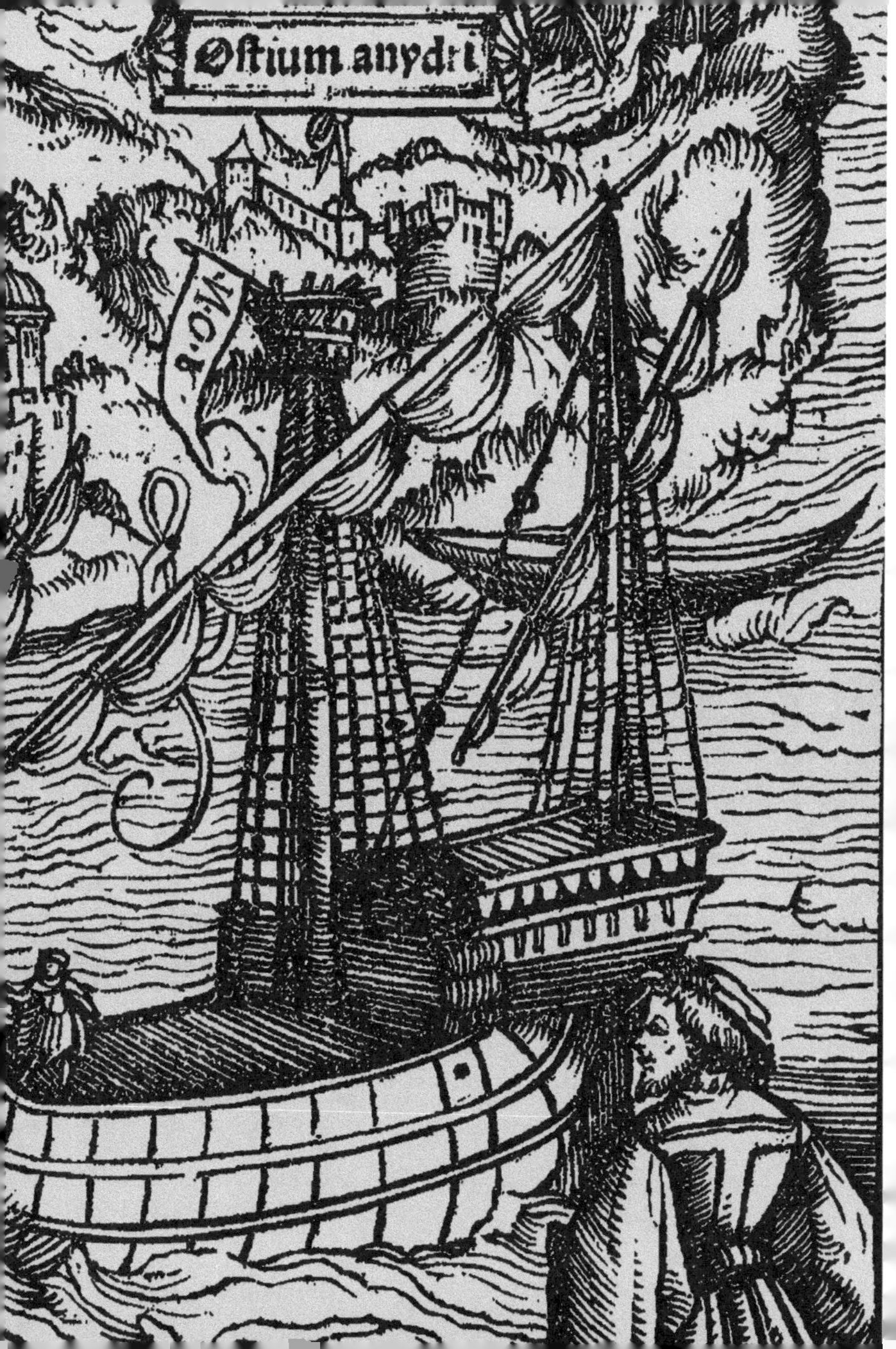
Oſtium anydri

A Countryside Balcony for the Carioca Bourgeoisie

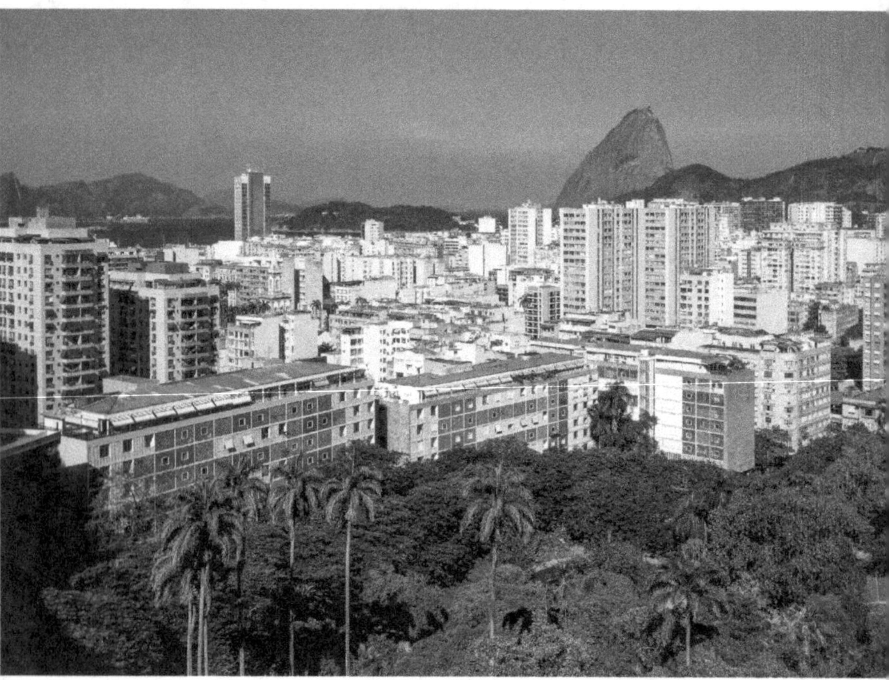

Parque Guinle, Rio de Janeiro RJ. Lúcio Costa, 1940s. Photo by Nelson Kon

On the two previous pages Island of Utopia, engraving by Ambrosius Holbein for the 1518 edition of Thomas More's book. The British Library

Ouro Preto

Let's go visit São Francisco de Assis
A church made by the people of Minas
The sexton, Maria Cana-Verde's neighbor,
let us in and shows us the neglect
Aleijadinho's pulpits
Ataíde's roof
Oswald de Andrade, "Roteiro das Minas," 1925[1]

In the late 1940s – with the ministry building fully operative, and now more experienced as an architect and builder –, Lúcio Costa had the opportunity to design a high-end housing project. The circumstance was a bit picturesque: a friend came to tell him that "the heirs of visionary and spendthrift Eduardo Guinle were facing the contingency of having to open a street in the mansion's gardens to secure an income, and they already had a building project in French style to match the palace."[2] In a playful but serious tone, Lúcio noted that building a set of houses in French style could seem like a grotesque allegory of the slave-owning relationship between *the big house* and *the slave quarters*. His answer was to shift the main focus: "I then recommended the use of a contemporary architecture more in keeping with the gardens than with the mansion."[3] In this anecdotal and involuntary way, an aristocrat in decline, driven by economic hardship and the instinct for survival, was about to become the driving force behind one of the most successful architectural ensembles built in Brazil.

The 400 x 400 meter terrain of Parque Guinle has a rugged topography — it runs upward when one walks from the entrance to the interior of the plot, with a depression in the central area. Accessibility is limited to a single entrance on Gago Coutinho Street, which runs along one of its borders for a few meters; the other borders are contiguous with other properties. The entrance is marked by the gate that dates from the early 20th century, like the family mansion,

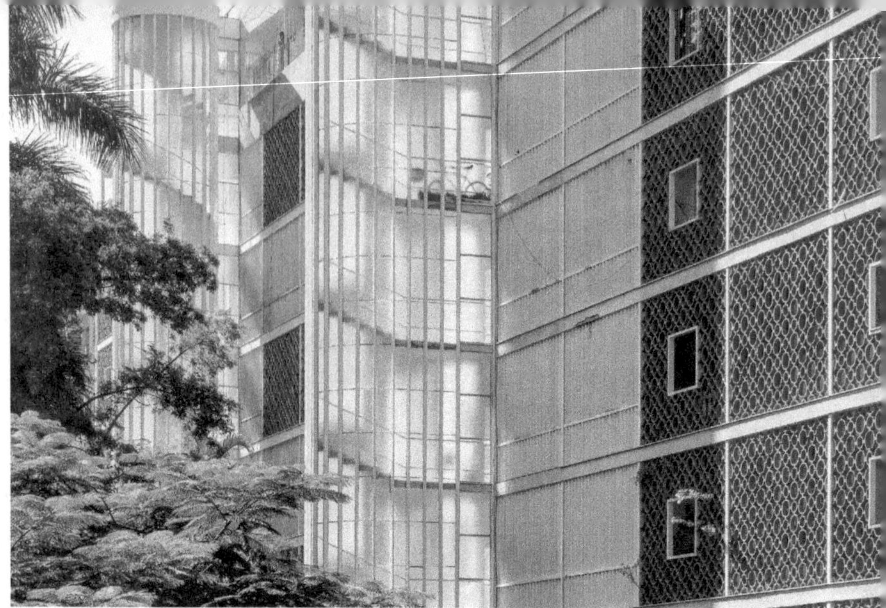

which was built in eclectic style between 1910 and 1913,
being known today as Palácio das Laranjeiras, the official
residence of the governor of the State of Rio de Janeiro. It
is located at the highest point in the property, to the left.
As the terrain is quite steep, the path that goes from the
entrance to the mansion takes a long detour in the shape
of an imperfect circle, surrounding the lower level area,
destined for "romantic gardens, with streams and artificial
lakes."[4]

Arranging the six buildings originally commissioned was
not a simple equation. Regarding the landscape, the best
location – along the border overlooking the park – would
leave the main faces of the buildings facing west, with the
undesirable incidence of the afternoon sun and its deleteri-
ous climatic consequences. The urban solution adopted – "an
amphitheater shape,"[5] the mansion functioning as the focal
point, as one critic rightly points out – would demand a

creative response to block out the sun while preserving the view; without preserving the view, this layout would make no sense. In Lúcio's words, it was important that the "elongated, six-story buildings were detached from the ground and had *loggias* along the facades, with various types of brise-soleil, as they faced the setting sun."[6] All the care in the design and precision in the construction was not enough for the set to be well received by the target audience. The apartments took a long time to be sold, due to the high cost of the property, the reticence of the bourgeoisie about inhabiting apartment buildings and even the inability of the realtors, who had in their hands a totally new product.

Only three of the six previously planned buildings were actually built;[7] Bristol and Caledonia, located inside the property, have the main rooms, bedrooms and living rooms facing the beautiful view of the park. Between the glass that seals

Previous page
Parque Guinle, Rio de Janeiro RJ. Lúcio
Costa, 1940s. Photo by Nelson Kon

Below
Parque Guinle, Rio de Janeiro RJ. Lúcio
Costa, 1940s. Photo by Nelson Kon

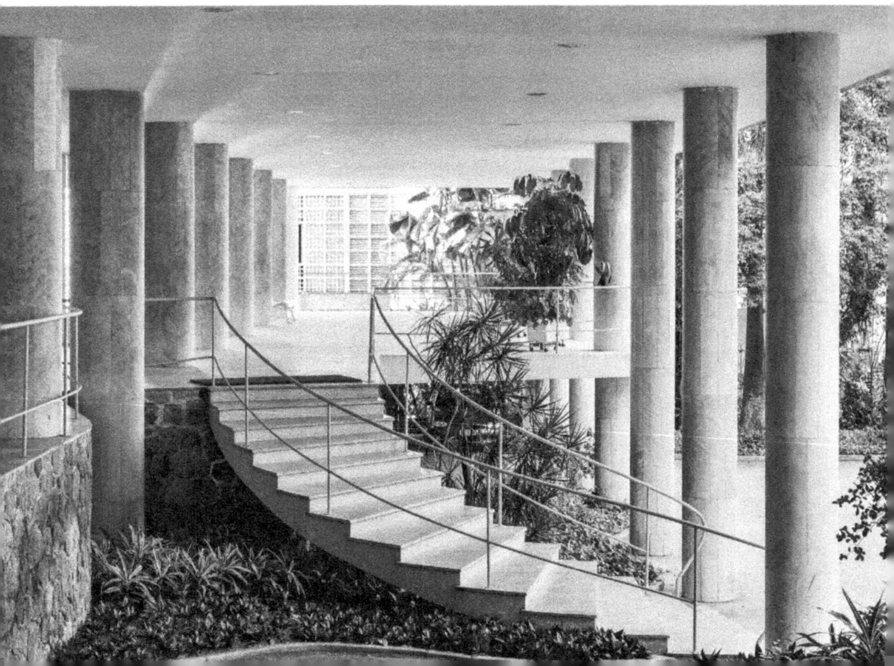

the rooms and the building's external limit, there are balconies for climatization – the *loggias*, according to Lúcio Costa –, whose external face is closed off by sun-blocking panels, which alternate rectangular wooden slats — the Corbusian brise-soleils — and hollow ceramic elements with varied designs, traditionally used in Brazil. The different textures, shapes and colors make up a vibrant and integral unit, as in a patchwork quilt. Carlos Eduardo Comas states that the solution with hollow grids has links both with Brazilian architectural tradition and with European modernity: "the references to the Luso-Brazilian mashrabiya are obvious, but the consonance with the Terragni of Casa del Fascio should also be noted."[8] However, Lúcio Costa says that his interest in the hollow element actually came from a trip to Nova Friburgo.[9]

The hollow element used by Lúcio Costa is known in several regions of the country as "cobogó". There was some debate about the origin of the expression, but Geraldo Gomes proves the regional nature of the name and its pioneering modern appearance in the work of Luiz Nunes in Recife[10]: the water tank for Alto da Sé, in Olinda, 1936, a project featured in the *Brazil Builds* catalog. Nunes' goal – a wall that would be permeable to light and wind made from preexisting elements – is already suggested in Monlevade, where wooden lattice work performs the same function – in addition to the "preservation of a certain amount of intimacy", according to Lúcio Costa. As Luiz Nunes studied at the School of Fine Arts in Rio de Janeiro at the same time as Niemeyer and Reidy, the hollow plan may be an offshoot of the adjustment of modern architecture to the tropical climate; nevertheless, the formal solution from preexisting elements has indeed a pioneering manifestation in Pernambuco's modern architecture. Besides the Parque Guinle, built in the early 1940s, the hollow element – or the "cobogó" – would go on to stamp the façade of formidable examples of Brazilian architecture over time, such as the Brazil Pavilion at the New York World's Fair, a project by

Lúcio Costa and Oscar Niemeyer (1939), the Pathological Anatomy Pavilion in Recife, by Saturnino Nunes de Brito (1940), the Sedes Sapientiae, by Rino Levi (1942), the Vital Brazil Institute in Niterói, by Álvaro Vital Brazil and Adhemar Saldanha Marinho (1942), the Pedregulho housing complex, by Affonso Reidy (1947), the villages of Amazonas and Serra do Navio, by Oswaldo Bratke (1955).[11]

Parque Guinle's *loggia* is an update of the traditional balconies of rural and urban houses from the colonial period. However, we observe a functionalist procedure in its back-to-back presence on the façade more thoroughly exposed to the sun. A Brazilian critic suggests that the solution is inspired by a typology developed by Le Corbusier: "the building is structured from the spatial module of the balconies – Le Corbusier's brise-soleil *loggias* –, which is repeated

Parque Guinle, Rio de Janeiro RJ. Lúcio Costa, 1940s. Photo by Nelson Kon

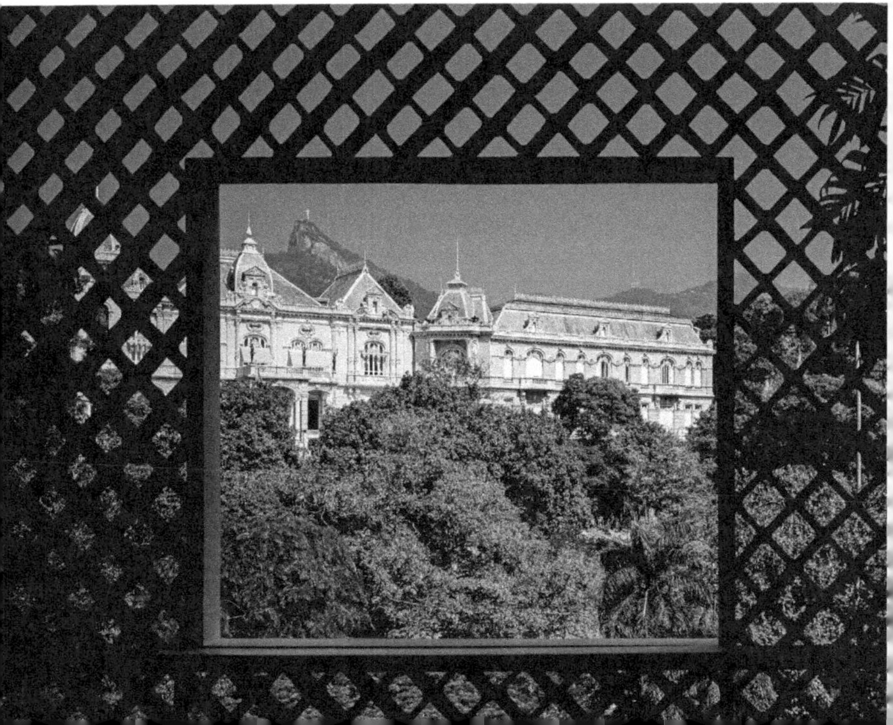

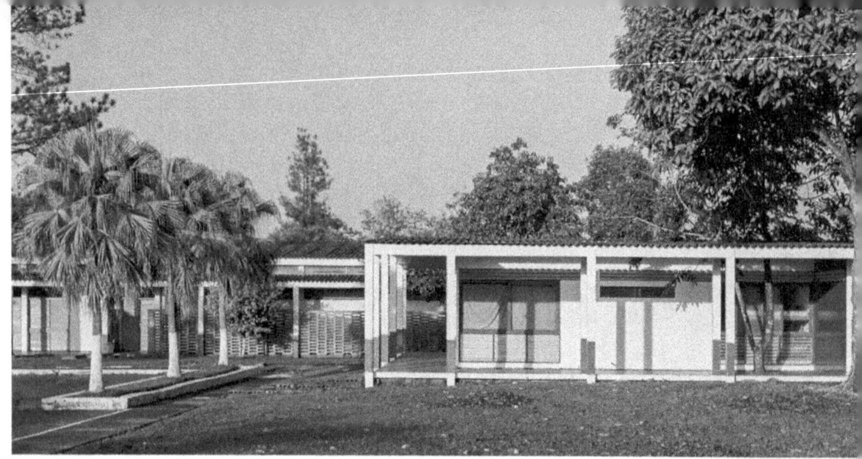

Vila Serra do Navio AP. Oswaldo
Bratke, 1956. Photo by Nelson Kon

throughout the façade of the night/day zone."[12] There is indeed some similarity between the solutions, especially the double function they fulfill – protecting the internal rooms from the sun and providing a wide view of the landscape; however, they differ in the constructive and psychological aspects. The delicacy of the hollow ceramic elements results in a renewed mashrabiya, "pierced" from time to time by rectangular openings where one can lean on to enjoy the landscape. Contrary to the transparency of the view as seen from the inside to the outside, there's opacity in the opposite direction, guaranteeing something very dear to the Brazilian architect: *intimacy and relative isolation*. In contrast, the Corbusian brise-soleil *loggia*, with hollow cement elements on the guardrail, expresses that growing roughness of the work of the Swiss-French architect in the second post-war period. The upper frame above the railing is clear, opening up a wide view of the landscape. The external face excavated by volumes along its entire length has the overall effect of a vibrant contrast of light and dark when exposed to the sun.

One episode reveals how far the *loggia* brise-soleil was from Lúcio Costa's architectural vocabulary. In 1952, he was commissioned by the Brazilian government to design a housing complex for Brazilian students – the *House of Brazil*, as he liked to say – in the Cité Universitaire of Paris. At the time, as he was staying in Europe due to personal problems, he sent his study to Rodrigo Mello Franco de Andrade, his superior at Sphan, so that he could forward it to the minister. In the letter accompanying the drawing sheets, Lúcio Costa announced the commitment he had assumed in Paris for the construction of the project: "I have already arranged things with Mr. Wogenscky, from Le Corbusier's atelier, as it seemed fair to me that the task fell to the old studio at Sèvres Street, 35, where the ideas that gave new life to contemporary Brazilian architecture were born."[13] This kindness is meant to repay Le Corbusier for the enormous impetus to the development of modern Brazilian architecture and, above all, to provide him with the much-desired Brazilian project, even if it was not in our territory (the Brazilian project

Transit housing units, brise-soleil balcony, unspecified location, unbuilt. Le Corbusier, 1944.

Fondation Le Corbusier Collection

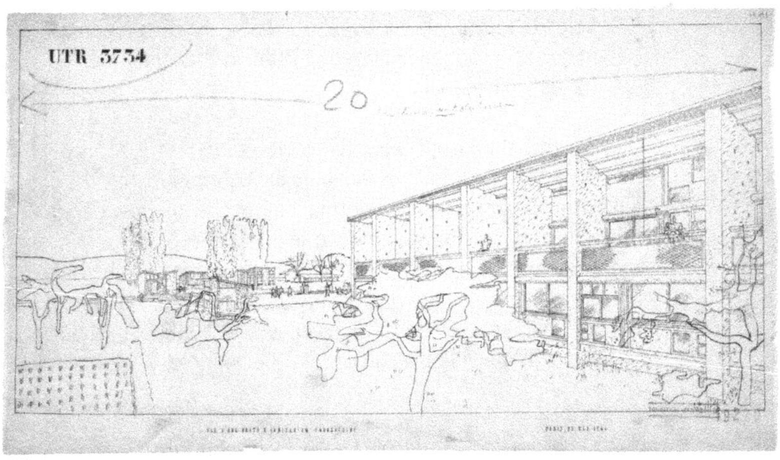

never happened, despite many efforts of Lúcio Costa and his colleagues).

The volumetry in the architect's straightforward initial study, made with his daughter's school supplies, is very close to the one that was built; however, two significant changes altered the character of the project. First of all, Lúcio Costa's detailed suggestions regarding colors and textures for the facades and interiors and the artistic panel in the students common area were not respected in the final project:

> "Regarding color, I established the following scheme just to ensure variety without undermining uniformity: ceilings and window walls, including curtains, will be white; the walls on the side of those entering the room will be gray or havana; when the wall is gray the floor will be havana, and vice versa; the opposite walls can be blue, pink, aqua green or lemon yellow; as for the covers of the beds and armchairs, they will all be gray or havana, simplifying conservation and replacement; where the floor is havana, they will be gray like the wall and havana otherwise; in the corridors, the wall of the rooms will always be gray and the opposite wall, as well as the one on the landing, will change color according to the floor, because this makes it more pleasant and helps to identify the arrival floor. I also planned a panel measuring roughly 3.20m by 7.00m, in the living room, for our Portinari."[14]

Second, the façade wall that corresponds to the rooms on all floors: "The windows will only be 1.05m high, but they will run from one end to the other, half of the window being operable and half fixed with opaque glass; in the operable half there will be a small external roller shutter; it will be of an economical and very practical type that is widely used here in Lisbon and that I have never seen elsewhere; in the fixed part there will be a curtain. On the windowsill we have

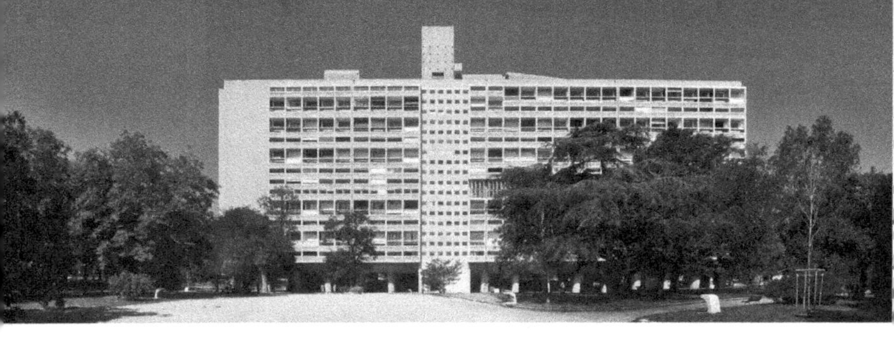

Housing Unit, Marseille, France. Le
Corbusier, 1945. Photo by Victor Hugo
Mori

a shelf and the radiator."[15] As we can imagine from such a
precise description, the facade would alternate horizontal
stripes: the sill painted with the "predominant colors in
France" and the strips of transparent and opaque glass.

Le Corbusier's team disregards the choice of colors
made by Lúcio Costa and opts for the hegemonic roughness
of exposed concrete. On the side which corresponds to the
rooms, the brise-soleil *loggias* are adopted, with the side
walls of the balconies painted, alternately and with no discernible order, in bright colors – red, green, blue and yellow;
however, the reinforced concrete rules in all elements on the
foreground: pillars, beams, hollow elements and drip pans. At
this point in Le Corbusier's work, the brise-soleil *loggia* is a
standard solution, adopted in the *unités*[16] and in the façade
corresponding to the individual cells of the Convent of La
Tourette.

Lúcio Costa does not speak out against the final product,
which had little to do with the delicate architecture that he
himself practiced during his life; however, he does dissociate himself from the authorship of the project, attributing
it almost entirely to the Parisian architects: "In view of the
upcoming opening, I wanted to define each contribution for
the purpose of the customary inscription, which should read,

197

among other things: '...built under the direction of the Atelier of Sèvres Street, 35, from an initial sketch by Lúcio Costa and project by Le Corbusier'.[17] This decision is generally seen – and several similar attitudes taken at crucial moments in his life corroborated this view – as an honest and straightforward gesture by the old master. Nevertheless, it is necessary to look at it with a bit of caution, for it seems to hide a significance that goes beyond the well-known decency of Lúcio Costa.

A clash between the two architects sheds light on the issue. When Le Corbusier claimed the authorship of the ministry project to Pietro Maria Bardi, in 1949, Lúcio Costa sent him a letter in a harsh tone, reminding him of a previous letter, from 1937, in which the Swiss-French architect made it clear that he considered the Brazilians the authors of the project. He continues: "I send you a photo of the inscription engraved on the stone cladding on the wall of the entrance hall and I will just point out ot you that the old Portuguese word "*risco*" has the same meaning as the English word "design", which differs from the meaning of the word *drawing*."[18] The photo of the entrance hall of the Ministry of Education and Health reads: "Project by Oscar Niemeyer, Affonso Reidy, Jorge Moreira, Carlos Leão, Lúcio Costa and Hernani Vasconcelos, following an original *risco* by Le Corbusier. 1937-1945". As we can see, the phrase he wants engraved in stone at the House of Brazil in the University City of Paris is a faithful adaptation of the one inscribed on the wall of the Ministry of Education and Health's headquarters building, inaugurated less than a decade earlier, in 1945. In both cases, the preliminary study becomes a "*risco*" – that is, a starting point, an inspiration. By clearly pointing out who was responsible for the Parisian project – Le Corbusier's team –, Lúcio Costa also reaffirms who the authors of the Rio de Janeiro project were: the Brazilian team.

The *cobogó* on the main faces of the buildings in Guinle Park is the traditional element that adds to the modern

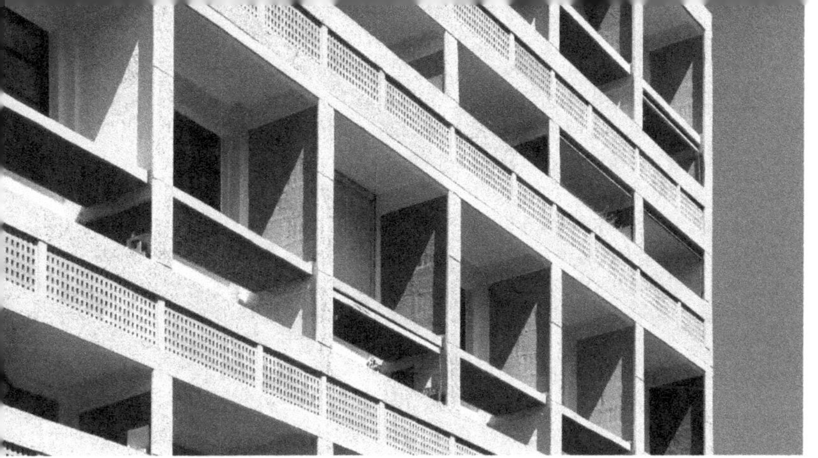

Housing Unit, brise-soleil balcony,
Marseille, France. Le Corbusier, 1945.
Photo by Victor Hugo Mori

design – the horizontal slats, measuring 65 meters in length
by 15 meters in width, and the six useful floors, which
follow the principles established by Maison Dom- Ino by
Le Corbusier: independent structural skeleton of concrete
suspended by pilotis; flat slab roof; vertical circulation with
stairs and elevators in an independent structure, partially
external to the volume; underground garage. Lúcio Costa's
concern to balance international and national elements can
also be seen on a larger scale.

The first sign of integration is the intense relation
between the vegetation and the buildings. Carlos Eduardo
Comas identifies the traditional element in the structuring
of the apartments: "there is a sprawling quality very much
in line with the Brazilian rural residence. On the other hand,
in the duplexes, suggestively arranged in the middle section
of the blocks, Costa opts for referencing the colonial town-
houses – two-story row houses –, also refraining from any
dramatic effect on the sections that could be comparable to
those of Le Corbusier in his *immeubles-villa*."[19] Lúcio Costa

himself mentions a specific typology in his effort to establish
ties with tradition: "I had imagined that these houses would
always have, near the entrance, a kind of room, an open
environment – a sort of winter garden that would be a welcoming environment, something independent of the living
room. And then another space, between the kitchen and the
bedrooms, which would correspond to a 'homely balcony'. So
the apartment would actually have two balconies, let's say,
although these were partially closed, since they were incorporated into the building – thus respecting the original propositions of the 17th century São Paulo houses, the so-called
'*bandeirista*' houses, those beautiful homes made of rammed
earth, which usually present under the same roof a central
hall, two lateral volumes with rooms and two *loggias* or
verandas wedged in the body of the house."[20]

To describe the complex more systematically, each of
the six floors of the three buildings has four apartments;
these are single apartments on the sides and duplexes in
the center, so both the areas and the number of rooms vary.
In the frontal area – which in the Caledônia and Bristol
buildings corresponds to the faces toward the park and in
the Nova Cintra building to the faces toward the street – we
have the bedrooms and living rooms arranged in rows, while
the spaces intended for services are located on the other
side. Vertical circulation in each building is concentrated in
two places, marking two autonomous buildings in the same
block, each with two apartments per floor. The internal elevators and the external spiral staircase open onto the same
hall, which then divides into "social" and "service" areas
thanks to the structure of the elevators. In the two internal
buildings, the ground floor is free and integrated into the
park, establishing collective living areas, which also facilitates
an elegant adjustment of the terrain levels that descend in
the longitudinal direction of the buildings. In the Nova Cintra
building, this bucolic character is contradicted by the urban
character of the small strip of land facing the street: the

ground floor and the mezzanine, intended for commercial establishments, give the building a commercial value, integrated to urban life. On the other hand, its external staircase is sealed with transparent glass, offering its users an unobstructed view of the park.

The overall result of Lúcio Costa's project is surprising, combining with unsuspected conviction different aspects: exemplary integration between the built volumes and the open spaces, wonderful views for practically all the noble areas of the apartments in the blocks inside the park, rationality in the appropriate climatization, aesthetic refinement in the composition of the enclosing plans, simplicity in the use of elements, adaptation of the traditional typology to contemporary use, ingenuity when translating the colonial lattice into huge ceramic "gelosias", a great sense of balance in the artisanal aspect of the vertical elements and the technical dimension verified in the reproducibility of large structures.

Lúcio Costa's Parque Guinle is a large leisure area in the midst of the endless buzz of the metropolis, perfect for spiritual circumspection and the contemplation of nature. Avoiding any flamboyance in the use of materials, formal composition or typological resources, it is marked by control in its *measurements* and a sense of *adequacy*. The spirit of the project was outlined in 1934, in the sketches and in the memorial for Vila Monlevade. Apparently, the fact that the village was not built at that time was a blessing in disguise. Without the technical resources and the enormous architectural and cultural experience, Lúcio Costa could have reached an immature and uninteresting result for Parque Guinle, a failure that would probably have prematurely aborted the development of one of the richest strands of Brazilian modern architecture.

A Second Swiss–French in the Tropics

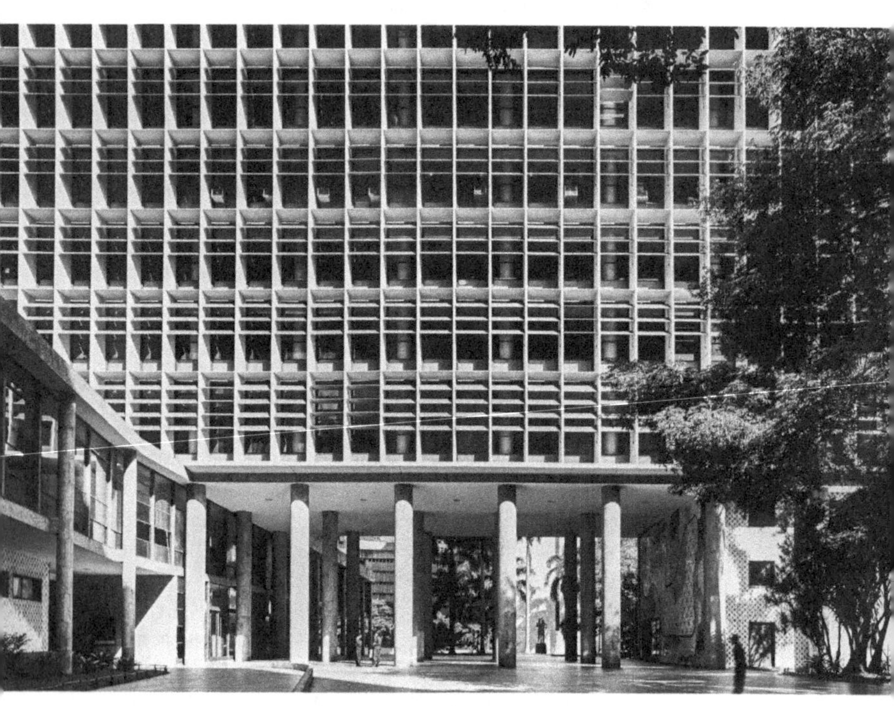

Ministry of Education and Health,
Rio de Janeiro. Lúcio Costa and team,
1936–1945. Photo by Nelson Kon

In the green thickness
of the seabed,
architecture is born,
from the lime of the shells,
from the juice of the algae,
from the life of octopuses on tentacles,
from the love of polyps
that stratify vaults,
from the avid membrane
of the red anemones
crystallizing fish,
from the salty cell
and its strange substance
that gives weight to the sea.
Shell and seahorse.
Vinicius de Moraes, "Azul e branco," 1946[21]

Regarding the Ministry of Education and Health building, the extraordinary events that took place from the 1935 contest until its inauguration in 1945 have already been narrated by several scholars. Yves Bruand gives the episode a decisive role in the development of modern architecture in Brazil, "especially due to the visit of Le Corbusier."[22] The presence of the Swiss-French architect, invited by minister Gustavo Capanema (1900-1986) at the request of Lúcio Costa, takes on an epic dimension, prompting a new state of affairs. Bruand's narrative consolidates the statements of the protagonists, especially those of Lúcio Costa, as "historical truth", meant to be repeated over time. In 1995, Lauro Cavalcanti offered a more detailed version of the events taking place behind the scenes, shedding light on the debate between distinct and antagonistic intellectual groups.[23] In the presentation of these facts, it is possible to capture the complex and contradictory narrative montage that frames the ministry building as the first example of modern Brazilian architecture. Bruand argues that, despite the Swiss-French master's ascendancy over the Brazilian disciples, "it is necessary to recognize an indisputable autochthonous plastic contribution"[24] to the final built project, which has several decisive interferences on the part of young Brazilian architects:

> "These modifications in Le Corbusier's study transformed it into a whole new project, although entirely based on the consulting architect's initial proposals and on the principles dictated by him. It is not a matter of denying Le Corbusier's fundamental contribution, fully recognized by those young Brazilians, who considered it an honor to have been able to work under the direction of the master they so deeply admired. But one should not lean towards the opposite extreme, attributing the Ministry of Education and Health exclusively to his talents. The final project, as it turned out, was the work of the Brazilian team, who gave it a peculiar development and charm not predicted by the consulting architect.[25]

Yves Bruand corroborates Lúcio Costa's version of the episode: "based on Le Corbusier's own original *risco* for another plot, motivated by prior consultation at my request, from the first proper drawing to its definitive conclusion, both the project and the construction of the current building were carried out without the slightest assistance from the master, as a spontaneous native contribution to the public consecration of the principles for which he always fought."[26] In 1980, however, Oscar Niemeyer, going against Lúcio Costa's claims, attributed the merits of the ministry building to Le Corbusier, claiming for Brazilian architects only the development of the executive project and some localized interferences that only accentuated the original concept.[27] In these opposing opinions, there is a conflict of interests: Lúcio wants to demarcate the ministry building as the origin of true Brazilian modern architecture; Oscar wants to reduce the importance of the episode and increase the value of his solo career, which begins with Obra do Berço and Pampulha.

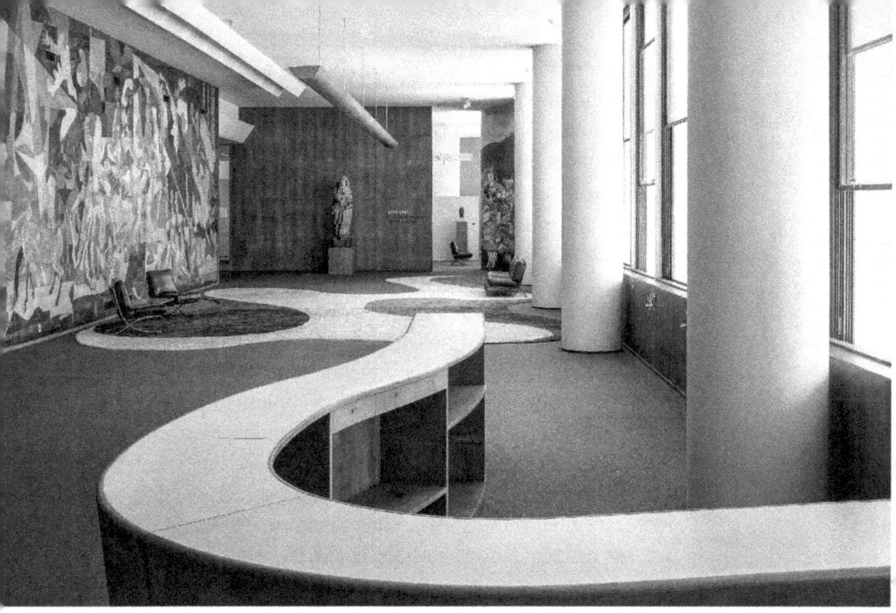

Ministry of Education and Health,
Rio de Janeiro. Lúcio Costa and team,
1936-1945. Photo by Nelson Kon

In order to defend Lúcio Costa's ideas, Bruand feels com-
pelled to explain what could justify the claim of authorship
made by the Brazilian team and – most importantly – where
the difference between the local architects and Le Corbusier
would lie – a difference that could legitimize the notion that
the ministry project and the whole series of projects that
followed it indeed belonged to a separate lineage. According
to Bruand, the modifications made by Brazilian architects –
the auditorium now sitting directly on the ground, the pilotis
going from 4 meters to 10 meters in the main block, the twofold increase from seven floors to fourteen floors – gave the
ensemble, when combined with other determinants, a special
character: "dynamism, lightness, plastic richness". These are
"undeniable contributions of the Brazilian architects, so it

was only fair that public opinion saw the Ministry as an expression of national genius, despite Le Corbusier's initial fundamental contribution."[28]

"Public opinion" here actually means the architectural milieu, which does not challenge Lúcio Costa's version. By endorsing this partial and interested view in historiography, Yves Bruand amplifies a supposedly umbilical relationship between Brazilian modern architecture and the roots of national identity, of which the ministry building would be a historical expression. Considering that the building embodies the Corbusian principles – independent structure of reinforced concrete facilitating greater versatility of plans; brise-soleil elements as architectural artifacts controlling sunlight; pilotis elevating the building and allowing for public use of the ground; glass facades resulting in greater psychological integration with the surrounding environment – and that the use of local stones and tiles, palm trees and works of art by Brazilian artists was a suggestion by Le Corbusier, Bruand resorts to argumentative gymnastics in order to grant the authorship of the building to the Brazilian team led by Lúcio Costa:

> "Le Corbusier has always planted his buildings solidly on the ground, even when employing pilotis; he never gave them a decisively aerial character, and their evolution always proceeded in the direction of mass and solidity; his plastic was always based on strength, not elegance. Now, the Ministry of Education, with its slender columns, combines these two qualities, highlighting a concern that will become one of the dominant characteristics of contemporary architecture in Brazil."[29]

Unfortunately, just as the columns are not that slender, the claim that Le Corbusier's designs lack "aerial character" is not quite accurate; the 1929 urban plan for Rio de Janeiro, with buildings hovering over the historical city, suspended by giant pilotis, invalidates this claim. The awkwardness in characterizing this particular building as the first example of Brazilian modern architecture is so blatant that Lúcio Costa never elaborated on the subject, choosing to draw attention to the fact that it was at that moment that a major talent blossomed: "It was during these short but assiduous four-week encounters that Oscar Niemeyer's incubated genius came to the fore."[30] In a furtive way, the praise for the role of the master brings with it a categorical statement: Le Corbusier does not teach, he just "awakens" something pre-existing and dormant. What is at stake here is not just the authorship regarding a building, but the very possibility of a modern Brazilian architecture. Bruand and, before him, Lúcio Costa himself, either point to issues that are external to architecture – individual or collective genius – or make use of imprecise adjectives – *dynamism, lightness, plastic richness* –, hoping to validate a much-desired aesthetic singularity.

At this point, I must digress to indulge a synapse that insists on manifesting. We have already mentioned in this elliptical narrative a character who will later gain promi-nence: Blaise Cendrars, who informed his friend Le Corbusier about "Planaltina". Many coincidences unite them: both Frédéric-Louis Sauser and Charles-Edouard Jeanneret are known by their nicknames and were born in the Swiss village of La Chaux-de-Fonds, in the French canton of Neuchâtel, in the same year of 1887; their houses were only a few hundred meters apart. According to Alexandre Eulalio, the "intriguing system of resonances" between the two friends contami-nates their texts, making it possible to establish relationships between the "poemetic breathing" in Cendrars' writings, such as "Une Nuit dans la Fôret", and Le Courbusier's "Brazilian Corollary."[31] These mirroring trajectories are also marked by the role that the two artists played in the Brazilian cultural milieu. Cendrars came to Brazil on three different occasions – in 1924, 1926 and 1927-1928 (he mentions two other trips, in 1934 and 1935, but there is no documentary evidence other than his testimony). Le Corbusier also came on three occasions – in 1929, 1936 and 1960. For their first visit, both were invited by Paulo Prado. Finally – and this is the most striking parallelism –, both helped to bring about the avant-garde renewal in Brazilian literature and architecture, only to have their roles contested or diminished later on by ungrateful children and, above all, by nationalist historians and critics. End of digression. The text takes up where it left off.

Gustavo Capanema was the fourth minister at the head of the Ministry of Education and Health, holding the position throughout the Estado Novo, from 1934 to 1945, the most authoritarian period of the first Vargas era. Capanema's liveliness gives the ministry a new drive, playing a leading role in the ideological consolidation of power. His chief of staff throughout his administration, poet Carlos Drummond de Andrade, got him in direct contact with the modernist intelligentsia. Several of its members – including Mário de Andrade, Cândido Portinari, Manuel Bandeira, Heitor Villa-Lobos, Cecília Meireles, Lúcio Costa, Gilberto Freyre, Joaquim Cardozo, Vinicius de Morais, Afonso Arinos Melo Franco and Rodrigo Mello Franco de Andrade – collaborated directly or indirectly with the new Ministry.[32] The relationship between the artists and the minister has been interpreted in different ways, but it is generally accepted that these intellectuals would not join the government if there was not an identity of purpose: the belief in the formative role of the national state. Capanema's staff is not limited to the modernist team, but these members did play a decisive role in future deliberations on the part of the minister.

Still in 1935, the city government granted the ministry an entire block on Esplanada do Castelo – a brand new area resulting from the dismantling of a hill of the same name. The public notice for the ensuing contest, insisting that the municipal urban planning laws be observed, encouraged conventional projects. Lúcio Costa later reported that "the law required the limit of seven floors squarely aligned with the internal area."[33] This imposition led the jury – formed by architects with a neoclassical background, yet another evidence that there was no previous trend towards the modern – to disqualify "33 projects that presented an 'unconventional' occupation of the plot,"[34] including those of modern inspiration. The three projects selected for the next phase of the contest were resubmitted four months later; the minutes regarding the final judgment based the choice not on the winner's own qualities, but on the shortcomings of the others. With only two votes, the victory belonged to the project by Archimedes Memória (1893-1960), which featured a "*marajoara*" style. Each project secured only one nomination for the first position. Raphael Galvão's project, an art decó composition, took second place; Gerson Pinheiro's, the only one featuring a few precepts of modern architecture – pilotis, orthogonal shapes and absence of decorative elements – took third place. Gustavo Capanema, as the fifth member of the Jury, could break the deadlock by voting in favor of Memória, but chose to assign first place to Pinheiro, forcing the second phase.

Besides the lack of conviction on the part of the jury and the dissatisfaction of the minister, there are also external reactions coming from the modern agents. Soon after the first phase, as a way of criticizing the contest's decisions, the magazine of the Directorate for Engineering of the Federal District, directed by Carmen Portinho, published two of the disqualified projects: the one by Affonso Reidy and the one by the duo Jorge Moreira and Ernani Vasconcelos, both of modern inspiration. Yet another focus of dissatisfaction arises among modern intellectuals within the cabinet of the minister. Unhappy with the result and backed by his allies, Capanema rewards the finalists, but calls off the construction of the winning project. To obtain legal support, he requests a series of analyzes from several technical departments, which are unanimous in their condemnation of the winning project.

Hence the opportunity to invite Lúcio Costa. Perhaps for feeling uncomfortable with the arbitrary decision,[35] instead of carrying the enterprise by himself, he called up a team made up of colleagues who had worked with him in the balked attempt to renew architecture education at Enba, whether as students – Jorge Machado Moreira (1904-1992), Ernani Vasconcelos (1912-1988), Carlos Leão (1906-1983) and Oscar Niemeyer – or as a professor, as was the case with Affonso Eduardo Reidy, Gregori Warchavchik's assistant in the chair of Architectural Composition.[36] Another common feature is the "high social origin of their families:"[37] three of them were born in France (Costa, Machado and Reidy) and all of them, with the exception of Niemeyer, spoke French fluently, which made dealing with Le Corbusier's works much easier. Rejected by Capanema, Archimedes Memória, a prominent member of the Carioca elite and one of the most eminent archi-tects of the neoclassical eclectic school, tried to slander the modernists, suggesting to President Vargas that the group maintained a shady connection to communism. The insinua-tion found some echo at the time, but the low blow was not enough to turn the situation around.

Lúcio Costa's team went on to develop an initial project, with a plan encompassing three "U"-shaped bodies and an auditorium on the outside of the central body. The plan was inspired by the project presented by Jorge Moreira and Ernani Vasconcelos in the ill-fated competition, both being heavily influenced by Le Corbusier's 1929 unbuilt project presented at the international competition for the Palace of Soviets, in Moscow. Minister Capanema, trying to protect himself from future accusations of having favored this particular group, requests further technical analysis. The reports are mostly positive, but they also contain a few restrictions and reser-vations which, if accepted, would detract from the modern principles of the project. According to Yves Bruand and Lauro Cavalcanti, faced with this deadlock, Lúcio Costa presented the idea – first to Capanema, then to Vargas himself – of hiring Le Corbusier as a consultant. Lúcio Costa's bold request is understandable given the network of intrigues woven by the opposing group fighting for ideological and aesthetic preferences at the time. During this period when the project by Archimedes Memória is pushed aside, Marcello Piacentini, Benito Mussolini's official architect, was trying to secure the project for the University City, which was much more important and significant than the ministry.[38]

The presence of Corbusier and his endorsement is a way for Lúcio Costa to strengthen his position and his power to pressure his superiors. "For the Brazilian architect and his group" – says Lauro Cavalcanti –, "the support of the European master was fundamental for legitimizing their work with minister Capanema and, through that, securing the opportunity to develop projects both for the ministry building and the university city, against the academics and 'neocolonials' who, in turn, courted the Italian architect Marcello Piacentini."[39] However, bringing the Swiss-French architect to the country was not quite simple, as revealed by the letters exchange between him and Monteiro de Carvalho, a Brazilian architect who lived in Paris at the time and who was assigned by Carlos Leão with the task of contacting him. In the first letter, dated March 21, 1936, the intermediary lays out a few basic facts – the commission to a team of young modern architects, the possible participation of Piacentini in the University City project and the new law that prevented the hiring of foreign architects – and presents a rather vague invitation:

> "These two (Lúcio Costa and Carlos Leão), as well as a group of modernist colleagues à la Corbusier, including Affonso Reidy, Jorge Moreira, Oscar Niemeyer, Ernani Vasconcelos etc. think that the Minister might invite you to teach a two or three-month course at the School of Fine Arts. Once here, the Minister will probably ask for your opinion on the University City, and it will be easier

to arrange things so that you can at least lead the project with the help of young Brazilian architects."[40]

On March 25 of the same year, four days after Monteiro de Carvalho's letter, Minister Gustavo Capanema officially commissioned Lúcio Costa to create a new project for the headquarters of his ministry.[41] The earlier date of Monteiro de Carvalho's letter proves that Lúcio Costa was invited, albeit unofficially, at least a few days earlier, which suggests the following situation: the team of young modernists had not yet developed the new project, so they could not have received the reports containing the objections; therefore, the invitation to Le Corbusier did not concern the ministry building, which was a promising project already secured for the modern group, but rather the university city plan, which was still pending and for which there were prominent opponents.[42] Monteiro de Carvalho's letter is quite clear on this point: he mentions the ministry building so that Le Corbusier might realize that his future hosts are prominent people. There is not even the slightest suggestion regarding his possible participation in the project already reserved for the young Brazilian architects. In his prompt answer, the European architect expresses his enormous enthusiasm for taking part not only in the University City project, but also in that of the ministry – "the essential thing is my possible participation in the construction of the new Ministry of Education."[43] Corbusier goes as far as to say that he could work in anonymity to circumvent the impeding law. As for the course, he discards it as being too extensive and proposes something more expedient.

In the subsequent letter, Monteiro de Andrade makes it even more clear the nature of the previous invitation, regarding solely the Planning Commission for the University of Brazil: "our friends Lúcio Costa and Carlos Leão told me just yesterday that they were sure that, once here, you will manage to convince the Minister, who is young and intelligent, and who will certainly find a way to use you, that is to say, to put you on the commission. As for the Ministry of Education project, they are already carrying it out."[44] The letter elicits a slanderous comment from the Swiss-French architect: "your friends Lúcio Costa and Carlos Leão seem to have reserved the development of the Ministry of Education project for themselves alone. Is that it? And is there no hope for me, despite your first letter, which made it seem like I would collaborate with our colleagues?"[45] Unfortunately, there is a gap in the correspondence, and two of Monteiro de Andrade's letters are missing. In the following messages, Le Corbusier explicitly mentions his fees for "reporting on the projects of the Ministry and the University City,"[46] but we do not know whether this entails a clever insistence on Corbusier's part or a surrender by Lúcio Costa. In any case, there is no documentary confirmation of Yves Bruand's version for this episode, which, according to him, is based on the testimonies of Lúcio Costa and Le Corbusier: "it was decided that he would be invited as a consulting architect, not only to give his opinion on the plans for the future ministry, as well as to prepare a first draft for the University City, which was intended to be built in downtown Rio de Janeiro."[47]

What followed is well-known. Le Corbusier arrived in Rio de Janeiro aboard the *Graf Zeppelin* on June 12, 1936, where he stayed for four weeks. He immediately disapproves of the project developed by the Brazilians for the ministry building – he calls it "the Mummy", making fun of the classic symmetry and the use of wings, overlooking the fact that he himself had used these features in his project for the Palace of the Soviets. He also disagrees with the location of the plot, opting for another one facing the sea.[48] Once he takes charge of the team, he outlines "with extreme spontaneity (...) a beautiful elongated low-rise building that later would be the basis for the final project."[49] The municipal government, which had donated a different piece of land for the construction of the Ministry, rejected the new request. Before leaving, Le Corbusier elaborated a final study, adapting the project from the beach to the block on Esplanada do Castelo; however, the limitations of the terrain, the legislation and his hurry to leave "resulted in a somewhat counterfeit composition, which didn't please either him or us."[50] Le Corbusier's final sketch depicts a main laminar building on pilotis, with annexes arranged orthogonally to it; the sketch becomes the main reference, the Brazilian team being responsible for tackling the proportions of the lamina, the disposition of the annexes and the implantation of the set on the plot. Corbusian principles guide every major decision, which makes it difficult to concede that the Brazilian architects actually managed to come up with something other than a Corbusian building. However, the sketches left were too schematic and the changes were many and significant, so the authorship of the final project really belongs to the young Brazilian team, which did not prevent the embarrassing controversy that would ensue a few years later.

Inaugurated in 1945, the main building features the following sentence inscribed in stone: "Designed by architects Oscar Niemeyer, Affonso Reidy, Jorge Moreira, Carlos Leão, Lúcio Costa and Hernani [*sic*] Vasconcelos, following an original *risco* by Le Corbusier. 1937-1945."[51] Niemeyer being mentioned first – regardless of alphabetical order, the hierarchy within the team and even the age scale – shows how willing was Lúcio Costa to attribute to the young architect the most important role in the development of the project. Costa believes that the credit given to the Swiss master, author of the inspiring *risco*, is fair; however, he is careful enough to place him in the "prehistory" of the project: Lúcio Costa dates the project from 1937 to 1945, while Le Corbusier's visit took place in 1936... Despite the distance between the Brazilians and the Swiss-French architect, who were an ocean apart during the Second World War, and despite the scattered news that reached France regarding the building's inauguration, Le Corbusier still felt inclined to claim authorship of the project.

The first step was to publish a sketch of the building in his complete works, in the volume dedicated to his production from 1934 to 1938.[52] The design bears a remarkable resemblance to the completed building and could indeed be taken as strong proof of authorship; however, it was an apocryphal drawing, probably made from a photo of the building under construction. The next step was a letter to Pietro Maria Bardi, director of the São Paulo Museum of Art – Masp, where the sender once again claims authorship of the project: "In 1936, I drew it myself, and had it drawn by a charming and devoted team from Rio, the plans for the Ministry of National Education (*sic*) – these plans meant a revolution in Rio as indeed in the three Americas."[53] Le Corbusier also mentions the fact that his fees were never paid,[54] complaining about the oblivion to which he was bequeathed by Brazilian architects and authorities.[55] Bardi contacts Lúcio Costa, who promptly responds to Le Corbusier, reminding him of a previous message in which the Swiss-French architect peacefully attributes the authorship of the project to the Brazilians:

> "Last night I was told about your odd behavior in a conversation with a journalist regarding the case of the Ministry of Education and Public Health building, and I would very much like to know what seems to be the matter, because your current interpretation of the facts, I am told, is no longer the one from 1937. In fact, on September 13, 1937, after having access to the definitive plans for the new project, you wrote to me: 'Your palace of the Ministry of Education and Public Health seems excellent to me. By that I mean: animated by a prescient spirit, conscious of the ultimate goals – to serve and to thrill. It doesn't feature those gaps or barbarisms that often, in modern works elsewhere, reveal that the people in charge know nothing of harmony. Can it be built, this palace? Yea? So much the better then; and it will be

beautiful. It will be like a pearl in the midst of Agachian mediocrity. My congratulations, my ok (as you ask)."[56]

In the same letter, Lúcio Costa rebuts the accusation of having buried Corbusier's participation by recalling that "at the inauguration of the building, during the war, when we had no news from you, we made a point of connecting the built project to the one you took the initiative to conceive and sketch for another plot, close to the airport, and which guided us as a compass and reference point."[57] Either consciously or unconsciously, and strengthening the Brazilian argument, the passage omits Le Corbusier's attempts to adapt that initial sketch to the plot in the downtown area. In the post scriptum, the sharpest stab: "the sketch made afterwards, based on photos of the finished building, and which you published as if it were the original proposition, made a painful impression on us all."[58] Le Corbusier, for his part, does not acknowledge any of this and appeals to his ethical conduct: "It is absolutely impossible for me to know whether my sketches were made from the model, as you seem to suggest; I do not have the slightest recollection of wanting to stir a controversy around this story. [...] My dear Lúcio Costa, you must not, in such a short *post scriptum*, suggest that I was the one who went on to commit plagiarism. This is not one of my habits."[59] Then, in his own *post scriptum*, he suddenly "remembers" to go and check the documentation: "The instinct of truth guides my hand: as I reread this page, the special issue dedicated to Brazil by *Architecture d'Aujourd'hui*, page 13, where I find the sketch, and your letter come to mind. Is this the sketch you're talking about? I have nothing to do with it; the pages 12 and 13 are from the magazine's editors. They refer (of course) to the *Complete Works L.C. – III* vol. I think the matter has now been cleared up."[60] It hadn't. The sketch published by the French magazine was taken from the complete works of Le Corbusier. Only the captions were different: while there is indeed no claim of authorship in the book,[61] the magazine attributes the design to the Swiss-French architect.[62] The book, however, is misleading: the brief text introducing the work states that the project under construction in Rio de Janeiro stemmed from a second Corbusian project and does not even mention the Brazilian architects, who appear only in a caption in the fourth and final page as "the project team". From 1956 onwards, when Henrique Mindlin published the succession of sketches, the correct evolution of the ideas for the building became public; however, Le Corbusier insisted on this ploy for quite some time.[63]

Le Corbusier's bad faith in this episode is quite evident, but it does not invalidate the crux of the matter: the unquestionable mark of Corbusian principles in the project. Lúcio Costa's attitude is ambiguous, wavering between paying tribute to the master and advancing the praise of "Brazilianness" as manifested in the building. In his letter to Le Corbusier, he first credits the foreign architect: "We wanted to irrevocably associate your name with this henceforth historic building, which is mainly due to Oscar N. Soares, but where we were able to apply for the first time on a monumental scale and with nobility of execution the constructive principles that you have established and ordered as the foundations for the new architectural and urban planning technique, created by you."[64] On at least three other occasions Costa repeats this evaluation, stressing the Corbusian affiliation of the project and its status as the first instance of this new architecture on a monumental scale.[65]

In the same letter to Le Corbusier, Lúcio Costa says: "We never failed to tie directly to you the admirable surge of Brazilian architecture: if the flowering looks beautiful, this should give you great pleasure, for the trunk and roots are yours."[66] The use of an organic metaphor – which will be dealt with in greater detail later on – stems from the romantic tradition still present, albeit in a diffuse way, in the Brazilian cultural environment at the time. It assumes an intimate relationship between national art and culture, which would

find its purest aesthetic manifestation through the national
genius (which can be understood either as an individuality
– Oscar Niemeyer, Aleijadinho – or as a collective attribute
dispersed in the collectivity and activated by an intellectual
elite). The metaphor, while linking Brazilian architecture to
Corbusian principles, also points to a future autonomy, following the typical development of all living entities. To confirm this hypothesis, here's the words of Lúcio Costa himself:

> "This building, this noble *house*, this *palace*, conceived
> in 1936 – therefore, more than half a century ago – is
> doubly symbolic: first, because it showed that the native
> genius, while absorbing and assimilating the ingenuity
> of others, is however capable not only of imparting its
> own, unmistakable connotation to this invention, but
> also of anticipating it in materialization; second, because
> the building was slowly built in a country still under-
> developed and far away, by young and inexperienced
> architects, albeit possessed of staunch passion and
> faith, at a time when a maddened world was honing its
> cutting-edge technology to raze, destroy and kill with
> maximum precision.[67]

There is a shift here, where the central object of speculation is no longer the foreign but the national: the *native
genius* is able to *absorb* and *assimilate* the *inventiveness
of others*, which is an idea in line with Oswald de Andrade's
insistence on *devouring* European civilization.

The *connotation* that Lúcio Costa imparts to Brazilian
modern architecture is precisely the material expression of
the spiritual qualities present in the *national genius* – virtualities, that is to say, awaiting historical circumstances for
their materialization. This notion of an independent path –
which Brazilians believe to be an autonomous development
of external architectural principles and which Le Corbusier
depicts as an appropriation – seems to be the source of the

enormous discontent of the Swiss-French architect, in the immediate post-war period, regarding the young architects led by Lúcio Costa. The real bone of contention does not concern the ministry, but the authorship of modern architectural principles, the Swiss-French architect's indignation being to some extent reasonable. The biting irony with which he narrates the lecture given by an unidentified Brazilian scholar during an exhibition of modern architecture sponsored by the Embassy of Brazil at the School of Fine Arts in Paris is quite symptomatic of his state of mind:

> "The exhibition features works by Niemeyer and Reidy, all from a series of pieces marked by my influence: pilotis, brise-soleil, glass facades, running floor, green city, etc. The lecturer explaining the photographs on display to the authorities (he is a Brazilian professor of the new generation and came from Rio especially for this) announces that this is Brazilian architecture, that is, Brazil's own invention. I was standing next to him greatly amused to see such a radical nationalization of my own thoughts. I said to the lecturer: 'What you said there interests me prodigiously.' He took it as a compliment."[68]

The feat of such a complex project being carried out in a peripheral and underdeveloped country while the world is shaken by the Second World War is reiterated in Lúcio Costa's testimonies. However, Le Corbusier's paternity is recurrently overshadowed by the eloquent praise of native ability. The wavering in Lúcio Costa's discourse is a symptom of the conflict encompassing two divergent points with which he and his modernist colleagues had to deal. The first is of an intellectual nature and concerns the defense of the *integration between modernity and tradition* that their historical commitment to São Paulo's modernism required them. The second is of an instrumental nature and concerns the ongoing intellectual war, in which groups fight to secure positions

within the political-ideological scenario. The influence of
Le Corbusier's postulates on the ministry is not well suited
to the defense of national capacity, but the exceptionality
of the building makes it impossible for it to be discarded.
The transparency with which we can see the ambiguity and
oscillation in Lúcio Costa's statements at that moment is
the result of the enormous difficulty in bestowing upon the
palace of education the meaning that one would want it to
carry. However, as new buildings emerge – stemming from
formal experiences that are way more compatible with the
narrative of integration and autonomy – transparency turns
into opacity.

Despite these inconsistencies, Le Corbusier's visit to Brazil
at the invitation of Lúcio Costa is quite symbolic: it expresses
the culmination of a process of aesthetic-cultural renewal
based on the synthesis between *modernity* and *tradition* and
the strengthening of the aesthetic principles of the modern
group within of a new political scenario. In the broader cultural context, it is about updating principles brought about
by an aristocratic cultural vision focused on the popular
element of the first Republic – the so-called "modernist
populism" –, in line with the new agenda established in the
post-revolutionary 1930s: the emergence of a "national
modern culture". The Vargas State tries to elevate Brazil to
the status of a technologically advanced country which goes
hand in hand with a project to outline a national identity,
following a clear fascist inspiration.

Since the beginning of the Vargas administration, sup-
porters of academic and neo-colonial values competed with
each other as well as with the modernists, seeking to impose
their principles both in terms of the necessary ties to tradition and the fundamental commitments to the future, that is,
their own conceptions of *tradition* and *modernity*. It is within
this strategic framework of cultural war that Lúcio Costa's
invitation to Le Corbusier must be understood. Corbusian discourse, grandiloquent and visionary, lent itself quite smoothly

to an association with the ideology of the Estado Novo: the faith that the new era asked for a new man; the conviction regarding the essential role of the state in bringing about social transformation while also avoiding social upheaval; the perception of the need for an official pedagogy for the education of habits and customs compatible with the new reality; the taste for the monumental and the grandiloquent; the search for homogeneity founded on the redemptive simplicity of the primitive. This is a decisive move by the *moderns* within a hostile political and cultural landscape.

Le Corbusier is the right man at the right time. The respectful and filial attitude towards the master is a constant during the early stages of modern Brazilian architecture and it lasts for quite some time, gradually diminishing in intensity and sincerity as the "children" move on to build their *wonderful works*. If the connection to Le Corbusier was convenient for external consumption, for it helped to include the young Brazilian architects in the international scene as legitimate moderns, devotion to the master meant a burden within the national context, especially in view of opponents who denounced it as submission to the foreigner. Le Corbusier's irascible genius and tortuous temper is only the tip of the iceberg in the controversy surrounding the ministry; the icy underwater mass, however, hidden in the blackness of the deep ocean, is constituted by the political interests and ideological commitments of the modern group. Save for a few exceptions,[69] despite commitments to the power structure, Brazilian modernists were able to maintain some independence, expressing their differences regarding the proto-fascist ideology in power. There is no denying, however, the enormous sense of opportunity of the protagonists, who cunningly chose to focus on the common points shared by different political visions in order to bring about the historical materialization of their aesthetic-cultural proposals.[70]

The Present Building
the Past

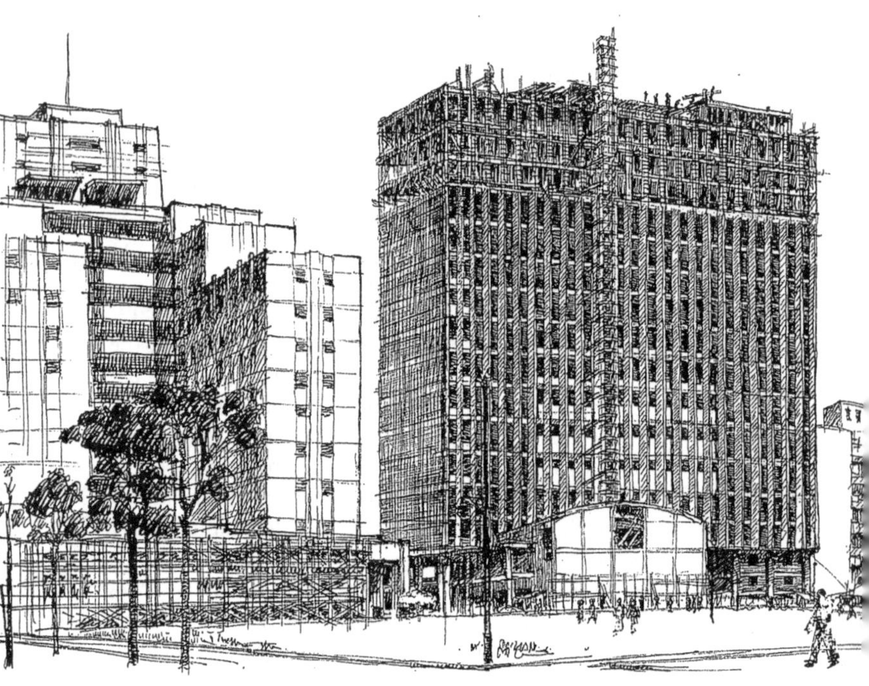

Ministry of Education and Health,
construction drawing, Rio de Janeiro.
Gèza Heller, 1938. Heller Family
Collection

Congonhas do Campo

There's a new hotel called York
And up there in the palm of the mountain
A church in the architectural circle of the Stations
Panels and paintings and effigies
Religiosity in the quiet of the sun
All of it pure like Aleijadinho
A bullock cart singing like an organ
Oswald de Andrade, "Roteiro das Minas," 1925[71]

The peculiar attention that Brazilian modern architects devote to traditional architecture is at odds with the origins of the movement in Europe, where old styles were criticized for their obsolescence. In the European scenario, there is a clear practical and theoretical division between those who promote the new architecture and those who dedicate themselves to the study and preservation of the previous architectural heritage. On the national scene, however, we find the same characters working in both areas, which concurs to Lúcio Costa's strategic vision of carrying out a synthesis between these two historical materialities.[72] In broader cultural terms, this is not an original initiative, given that it mirrors the modernist development in São Paulo. In an interview with Hugo Segawa, Costa is very aware of this: "In Brazil, the same people were insisting on the restoration of the old and the modern renovation. To incorporate the new, the São Paulo movement of 1922 even went back to anthropophagy, which was a more dramatic way of devouring the European. It was a cosmopolitan and 'anthropophagous' movement at once."[73] Lucio's clarity will be decisive in the next steps taken by him and his group.

In addition to the Ministry building, Capanema led yet another initiative that had an enormous impact on the fate of Brazilian architecture: the creation of an agency dedicated to the national historical heritage. The commission for the National Historical and Artistic Heritage Service (Sphan, in the Portuguese abbreviation) goes to Mário de Andrade, a well-known artist and intellectual with great influence over young modernists in several states. Among these colleagues, we find Carlos Drummond de Andrade, Capanema's chief of staff. Among the reasons for choosing Mário de Andrade, one must include the recommendation from this particular friend, the fact that Mário de Andrade's ideas were to some extent compatible with the nationalist ideology radiating from the Palácio do Catete as well as the fact that Mário was an active Catholic,[74] which made a big difference for Capanema: ever since his youth in Minas Gerais, he maintained close ties with traditional Catholicism, whose leaders would come to influence his educational policy.[75] In addition to Sphan, the minister's recurring requests – to outline a teaching reform for the National School of Fine Arts and the National School of Music and to produce the *Brazilian Encyclopedia* and the *Dictionary of the National Language* – prove the high regard that the author of *Macunaíma* enjoyed from Capanema.

As evidenced by the letters exchanged, despite being cordial and respectful, the relationship between Mário de Andrade and Capanema was not entirely harmonious. The most radical ideas of the São Paulo modernist are limited to highbrow initiatives, having little influence on the educational base meant to shape future generations. The authors of *Tempos de Capanema* report the tension between the two and the very ambiguity of the São Paulo modernism:

> "Modernism, of which Mário de Andrade was one of the main representatives, was sufficiently broad and ambiguous to allow for a number of different interpretations, thus avoiding a direct clash against the political and ideological program of the Ministry of Education. In some of its versions, modernism could dangerously approach European nationalist and authoritarian irrationalism, and it is not by mere chance that Plínio Salgado answers for one of the strands of the movement. What

prevailed in Brazilian authoritarianism, however, was not
the search for the most popular and vital roots of the
Brazilian people, which was Mário de Andrade's concern,
but the attempt to make traditional Catholicism and
the cult of the symbols and leaders of the homeland
the mythical basis of the strong state that was to be
constituted. Capanema was certainly much more identified with this strand than with that represented by the
author of *Macunaíma*."[76]

This tension that does not prevent a convenient relationship where both sides reap benefits:

"The point of convergence between the modernists and
the ministry undoubtedly resided in the modernists'
involvement with folklore, the arts, and particularly with
poetry and the visual arts. For the minister, aesthetic
values and culture mattered; for the intellectuals, the
Ministry of Education might open up a space for the
development of their work, through which the broader
revolutionary content they believed was implicit in their
works could be smuggled, so to speak."[77]

According to Lauro Cavalcanti, Mário de Andrade's project for Sphan has to deal with at least three focal points of
institutional resistance, where a number of groups interested
in defining and managing the national heritage converge.
The first is the National Historical Museum: the Inspectorate
of National Monuments associated with it was directed by
Gustavo Dodt Barroso, an outspoken anti-Semite who cher-
ished Arianism and the Nazi-Fascist strong state. Barroso
was also a fervent defender of the "cult of our traditions",
meaning the preservation for future generations of the "glorious objects" and "national monuments" of our common
past. Despite his outstanding performance in the field of
Museology, "Barroso did not develop a specific body of ideas

or practices regarding heritage, which the modernists did, especially Mário de Andrade, Lúcio Costa and Rodrigo Mello Franco."[78] Barroso fought to be the one to lead the creation of Sphan; failing to secure the position, he settled for the fictitious version that the new body had actually been born within his institution: "It was this Inspectorate of National Monuments that Minister Gustavo Capanema turned into the Service of the National Historic and Artistic Heritage, expanding its ranks and attributions."[79]

The second stronghold of resistance, and the most intellectually articulate, is the neocolonial movement. Emerging in São Paulo through the work of two foreign architects – Victor Dubugras, from France, and Ricardo Severo, from Portugal –, the style reached maturity in Rio de Janeiro[80] by the hand of its undisputed leader, doctor José Marianno Filho (1881-1946). Marianno was Lúcio Costa's teacher at the National School of Fine Arts and saw him as his legitimate heir, never forgiving his student for changing sides and moving on to the modern ranks. During the controversy surrounding the contest for the ministry, he took to the press to defend Archimedes Memória and denounce the coup carried out by the moderns. Exercising a lot of influence in the architectural environment – besides being the director of the National School of Fine Arts, he founded the Brazilian Institute of Architects and the Central Society of Architects in 1921, successfully merging the two in the Central Institute of Architects in 1924 –, Marianno fought to secure the neocolonial as the official style of the State, and his campaign actually succeeded for a good amount of time after the popular success of the buildings that were built for the International Centenary Exhibition in 1922. Four years later, confirming the supremacy of the movement during that period, the winning design for the Brazil Pavilion at the Philadelphia Exhibition is the one by Lúcio Costa – in neocolonial style.[81]

According to Lúcio Costa, it was his disappointment with the shallowness of the neocolonial movement that led to his conversion to the modern. His visits to Portugal and the old towns of Sabará, Mariana and Ouro Preto educated him regarding the unreasonable appropriation of constructive and formal elements from the colonial period: "I began to realize the error in the so-called neocolonial style, a regrettable mixture of religious and civil architecture, with details taken from different times and techniques, when it would have been so easy to take up the traditional experience through those elements in it which hold true today and forever."[82] In another document, Costa once again describes the neocolonial as ignorant of traditional elements and incapable of successfully tackling the past: "the lack of knowledge of the true features of traditional architecture and the resulting inability to properly take advantage of those solutions and peculiarities that are somehow adaptable to contemporary programs resulted in a big salad of conflicting forms from different periods, techniques, regions and purposes."[83] Against the pastiche that he now sees in the neocolonial, Lúcio Costa envisions the incorporation of a number of traditional features to modern architecture. Deeply disagreeing with his former student, José Marianno, a born polemicist, uses his power and his access to the press to repeatedly criticize the growing power of the moderns in the bureaucratic structure of Capanema's Ministry of Education: "these people who induced Minister Capanema to embrace the anti-nationalist doctrines of Le Corbusier..."[84]

Finally, the creation of a heritage protection agency under the control of modern intellectuals faces resistance inside the Museu Nacional de Belas Artes, which at the time was directed by "academic painter Oswaldo Teixeira" and featured Carlos Maul "as its main ideologue and promoter."[85] In an environment where neoclassical eclecticism prevailed, the main academics based their aesthetic preferences on the ideas of thinkers such as Tobias Barreto, Oliveira Vianna and Nina Rodrigues,[86] who advocated for the whitening of the Brazilian race.[87] From this perspective, the heritage that would be considered worthy of preservation bypassed the aesthetic materializations that could be associated in some way with the "stains" of racial fusion, which immediately excluded a substantial part of the colonial aesthetic production.

Although they did occupy prominent institutional and social positions, the adversaries of the modern intellectuals could not prevent the emergence of the new agency in 1937 under the directives of Mário de Andrade. The National Historical and Artistic Heritage Service – Sphan presented a comprehensive outlook on the relevant elements of the past deserving research and preservation. Its scope went way beyond the sum of the interests of the losing groups, harboring both academic and folk production from the most varied strata and periods. The archives as proposed by Mário de Andrade expressed the reach of his cultural vision: "Fine Arts; Archaeological, Ethnographic and Landscape; Historical and, the last one, that of the Applied Arts."[88] At that point in his life, Mário de Andrade had already carried out several studies and surveys and had already published articles and magazines on different cultural fields, with a special interest in popular music and folklore. His book *Essay on Brazilian Music*, published in 1928, is one of the most important records of his theory regarding an art organically articulated to the roots of nationality.[89]

Sphan began operating in 1938 with Rodrigo Mello Franco de Andrade as director and a team formed by architects Lúcio Costa, Oscar Niemeyer, Carlos Leão, José de Souza Reis, Renato Soeiro, Alcides Rocha Miranda (1909-2001) and Paulo Thedin Barreto, the only member of the team who had not adhered to modern principles. Once up and running, the original vision for Sphan gets simplified and reduced. The team of architects and the conceptual direction given by Lúcio Costa proceeded to list architectural buildings and urban sites according to an exclusionary vision, which did not consider "exotic" manifestations, such as contributions coming from neoclassical, eclectic and even neocolonial styles. The intangible historical heritage – customs and traditions in general transmitted by oral culture and performance – gets marginalized and only decades later will it be taken into account again.

The construction of the Grande Hotel in Ouro Preto is one of the first episodes where one can testify the tampering of Mário de Andrade's vision by Sphan's technical team.[90] In 1938, as a way of developing tourism potential, the Minas Gerais government asked the agency for guidelines regarding the construction of a building compatible with the colonial architecture of the former state capital. The agency took over the project and entrusted Carlos Leão with the task, whose "fundamental concern was to follow the basic typological lines of the local architecture, in order to obtain the minimum of contrast and the maximum of integration."[91] Once finished, the project, which featured a strong neocolonial content, ends up being called into question by the agency itself for its excessive submission to the local ambience and traditional architecture. The project, however, pleases the director of Sphan, Rodrigo Mello Franco de Andrade, as well as the government authorities, who immediately mobilize to obtain the resources for its construction. The internal conflict intensifies, and Lúcio Costa, even though he is in New York for the construction of the Brazilian Pavilion at the New York World's Fair, gets involved. He immediately sends Oscar Niemeyer, who was accompanying him, back to Brazil with the task of carrying out a new study for the Hotel. At the same time, architect Renato Soeiro, who was part of the technical team, proposes as an alternative the adaptation of existing buildings for hotel use.

Oscar Niemeyer's project is pretty much the opposite of Carlos Leão's. A laminar volume on pilotis, with flat slab roof, stripped of any references to tradition, the low rise nature of the building being the only concession to the guideline of adapting to the local architecture. In defense of his project, Niemeyer argues "that the new hotel, in its simple and unpretentious outlook" would stand out "as little as possible in the Ouro Preto landscape,"[92] the grass on the roof disguising its presence at a distance. Lúcio Costa, from New York, although generally approving, requests the incorporation of a few references to traditional architecture in order to better integrate the new element into the urban context. Niemeyer's first revision incorporates a gabled roof – which ended up as a flat roof in the final project – and balconies with lattice railings. As for the volume and construction technique, Costa accepts Oscar's proposal due to the similarity between the traditional and modern structures, with the use of pillars and beams in wood or reinforced concrete.[93] His opinions, expressed in a letter that would later gain the status of a guiding document,[94] are decisive. Costa does not mince words and uses the authority of his position to make Oscar Niemeyer and Carlos Leão acquiesce, with both his pupil's overstated modernity and Leão's superficial neocolonialism being replaced by the conciliation between modernity and tradition. This behavior does not fail to create fissures and dissatisfaction: Carlos Leão leaves Sphan almost immediately and Oscar Niemeyer, setting up a private office to carry out the Ouro Preto project, acts to elude the intellectual control exercised by the master, never mentioning the Grande Hotel among his favorite works.

Under the direct influence of Lúcio Costa, the Grande Hotel in Ouro Preto belongs to a particular lineage. Yves Bruand doesn't have a special name for this precious stream of Brazilian architecture; however, after praising the search for a synthesis between modern and colonial architecture, he lists typological and constructive elements, as well as traditional materials suitable for incorporation: "1) the round hip tile designs with large eaves; 2) the shutters and musharabis; 3) the balconies and external circulation galleries; 4) glazed tile walls."[95]As these are elements to some extent determined by the environment, Bruand has a very restricted view of what Lúcio Costa calls Brazilian tradition or culture. Perhaps because he is aware of this limitation, the French author mentions in one passage or another the diffuse "colonial spirit" meant to be pursued.

Starting with Vila Monlevade in 1934 and having Parque Guinle as one of its high points in the 1940s, the path proposed by Lúcio Costa – which we may perhaps refer to as *Pau-Brasil* architecture and urbanism – is joined by other projects signed by him – among them, the master-pieces Barão Saavedra Residence (Correias, 1942) and São Clemente Park Hotel (Nova Friburgo, 1944) – as well as by other architects, such as the summer camp in Tijuca, from the Roberto Brothers (Rio de Janeiro, 1944), the country house of Hildebrando Acioly by Francisco Bolonha (Petrópolis, 1949), the house of the architect Severiano Porto (Manaus, 1971), among many others. Oscar Niemeyer, in addition to the hotel in Ouro Preto, designed at least two residences featuring the characteristics defended by Lúcio Costa: the Francisco Peixoto Residence (Cataguazes, 1941) and one of the three houses he made for himself (Mendes, 1949). But it was an immigrant who insisted on becoming Brazilian, the Italian Lina Bo Bardi, who approached Lúcio Costa's formula with a very particular interpretation, greatly enriching the formal possibilities explored by the master and his followers. Her intervention in pre-existing buildings at Solar do Unhão (Salvador, 1959) and at Sesc Pompeia (São Paulo, 1977), and the Espírito Santo do Cerrado Church (Uberlândia, 1976-1982) express an effort to reconcile modern spatiality and hybrid construction techniques, where everything exudes the simplicity and authenticity of the communities that enjoy them.[96]

São Clemente Park Hotel[97] might be considered the most perfect translation of Lúcio Costa's vision. According to Bruand, "the hotel in São Clemente Park is entirely modern both in spirit and in treatment,"[98] but it is necessary to discern the programmatic character informing this instance

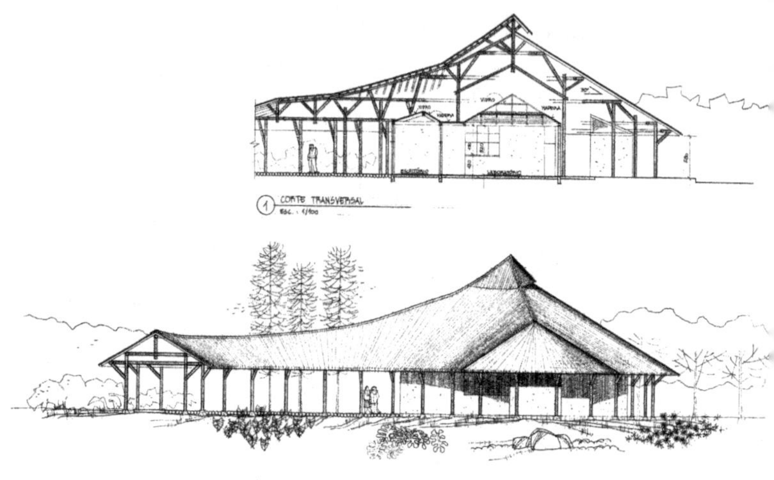

Environmental Protection Center,
Balbina, Amazonas. Severiano Porto,
1988. NPD FAU UFRJ Collection

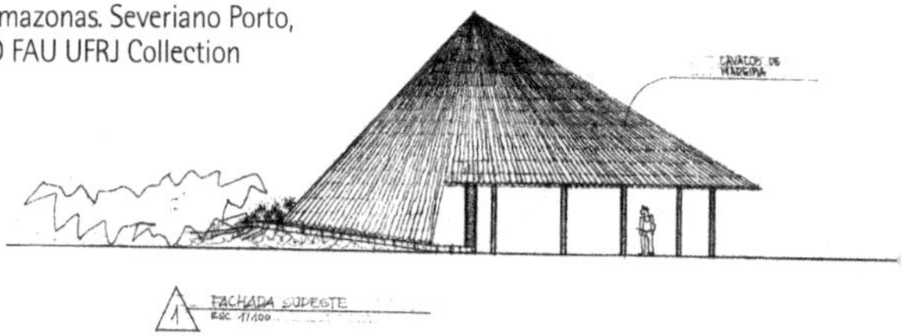

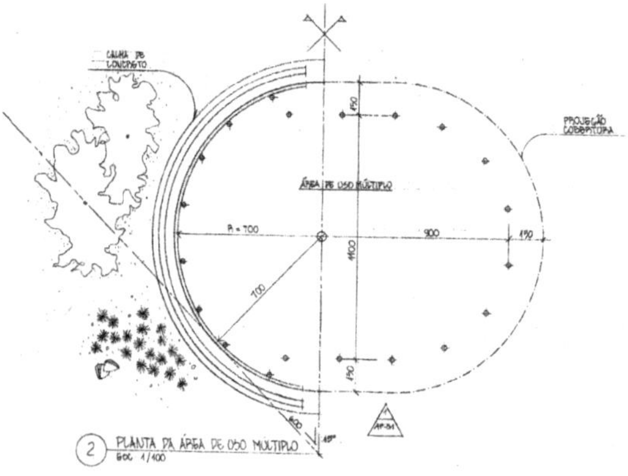

of the modern. Alcides Rocha Miranda, commenting on the work of modern architects at Iphan, a group to which he belonged, argues that "the roots of modern architecture were already in our 18th century architecture. Wooden structures freed the walls, which then could even be made of glass; in mountain towns, they ended up on stilts. Pilotis were then a normal thing for us. While dealing with these old buildings, we could see in the modern structure the ancient."[99] This understanding fits perfectly with Lúcio's vision, which is also present in several texts he wrote in the 1940s. At the Nova Friburgo hotel, his design decisions are based on this ambivalence, where the new and the old are equivalent. The wooden structure, in the form of a reinforced concrete structure, is anchored in solid stone walls, and this stability is enhanced by the bracing made of tilted, crossed wooden logs; the lightweight and translucent glass walls that house the common use area elegantly reflect towards the interior, resulting in the collective balcony on the ground floor; the functionalist layout of the row of rooms, facing the same direction and opening to the outside with individual balconies covered by a roof and protected by railings with wooden latticework. The project summarizes the elements that characterize Costa's private brand, developed since Vila Monlevade: the fused architecture (modern and traditional), the bucolic ambience (suburban area surrounded by a park) and the life style (an issue that will be discussed in more detail later on).

The episode presented above – the back-and-forth around the design and construction of the Grande Hotel in Ouro Preto – reveals some inconsistencies in the intellectual territory created by Lúcio Costa. His theoretical principles are based on a historical view of the evolution of architecture as an organic process resulting from the interaction between man and the environment. Seen from this perspective, colonial architecture should correspond to an arduous process by which Iberian architecture is accommodated in the tropical environment, entailing a victory over the problem of settling

in an inhospitable environment. However, Costa underlines
how recent the adaptation of Portuguese architecture to the
tropics within the context of Western history is:

> "Authentic regional architecture has its roots in the
> land; it is a spontaneous product of the needs and
> conveniences of the economy and of the physical and
> social environment and is developed through a tech-
> nology that is both incipient and refined, according to
> the nature and ingenuity of each people; while here the
> architecture arrived ready-made and although benefited
> by the African and Oriental experience of the colonizer,
> it had to be adapted as if it were made-to-measure
> clothing, or half-tailored clothing, to the body of the
> new land."[100]

However, this contradiction does not prevent Lúcio
Costa from going in search of the inner sap that gives life to
traditional architecture – avoiding the fake pastiche of adap-
tations lacking criteria, as in the case of the neocolonial style
– to establish a contemporary architecture organically related
to the past. There is a certain redundancy here: the proposition of continuity of a tradition only becomes intelligible
because the same tradition is being framed, retroactively, as
a noble past – therefore accepted and necessary – by the
modern authors in the present. The development is even
more contradictory: inheriting romantic vitalist principles,
modernist nationalism understands the present as organically
springing from the past, contradicting the notion of an artificial construction of the past. Lúcio Costa and his colleagues
– especially his subordinates at Sphan – began to rescue
from the past precisely those elements that could justify
the present. The same agents are on both sides of the issue:
they're championing a new architecture that is legitimized by
the umbilical cord with a traditional architecture whose value
is attested by studies carried out by the same professionals.

234

Not coincidentally, colonial and modern architecture are seen as unique and true expressions of "Brazilianness", deserving protection.

What essentially distinguishes Sphan's theory and practice from the São Paulo modernist actions during the 1920s – especially from Mário de Andrade's initiatives, whose guidelines the Sphan team purports to follow – is the ideological contamination of the Estado Novo and, above all, the power of election and transmission that the official nature of the institution allows (a situation very different from the timid performance of the São Paulo modernists in their relationship with the public authorities, the modernists securing their greatest achievements mostly in the private sphere[101]). Thus, the immediate listing of icons of modern architecture is not surprising – the Pampulha church, in 1947, the headquarters of the Ministry of Education and Health, in 1948, and the Metropolitan Cathedral of Brasília, in 1967 –, all of them made sacred only a few years after being finished or even shortly after the inauguration.[102]

By going back to the past to validate the present, the Sphan team launched "a preservationist campaign that, clearly privileging only a fragment of our history, dignifies *tradition* as a , not without attributing to it a civic function as the bearer of a truth that would contain our own essence as a Nation – an essence prior to the alleged contamination of our architecture by eclectic whims."[103] Thus, eclectic and neocolonial works do not deserve much attention in the preservationist surge that followed the foundation of Sphan. The contempt is so great that important historic buildings in Rio de Janeiro – such as the Municipal Theater, the National Museum of Fine Arts and the National Library – were only listed in the 1970s and a few others – Palácio Monroe and Solar Monjope, José Marianno Filho's residence – were demolished without any interference from Iphan. The neglect is explained by the hegemonic historical outlook, which does not count eclectic buildings as material testimony of

the *good* tradition.[104] The "villainization" of eclecticism, as
Marcelo Puppi puts it,[105] is not enough to create a vacuum
in research, but the insufficient amount of studies on these
styles is certainly due to the original prohibition resulting
from the ideas of Lúcio Costa. Paulo Santos, Carlos Lemos,
Mário Barata and Giovanna del Brenna, some of the historians who deal with these ill-fated architectures, run into the
hegemonic hold of this instrumental view of history directly
or indirectly:

> "Self-confessed champion of modern architecture", Lúcio
> Costa "was always much more interested in defending
> its cause than in the effective study of the history of
> architecture. The latter was less valuable to him as an
> object of knowledge than as a means of demonstrating
> his ideas. The form of historical study lends authority to
> the program of modern architecture: Lúcio Costa proj-
> ects it into history, reinterpreting and rewriting it solely
> and exclusively to prove the universality of the starting
> program – as the driving force of architecture in all
> times, from its earliest instances to the present day. Such
> a strategy proves to be effective, and the militant archi-
> tect will enjoy a long career as a historian."[106]

Puppi associates the ideas of Lúcio Costa with Mário de
Andrade: "It is precisely in the years 1928-30 [...] that Mário
de Andrade publishes in São Paulo his articles on architecture, drawing a parallel between modern functionalism and
the 'logical simplicity' of colonial architecture in Brazil. The
entire interpretative effort of Lúcio Costa's early texts, as we
shall see, rests on this parallel. His reservations regarding
modern architecture, expressed in 1928, did not predict the
functionalist turn in the Carioca context; this turn seems to
be explained by the impact of the São Paulo writer's ideas on
the Rio de Janeiro architect, or at least in the great proximity
between the two in those years."[107] The sudden change of

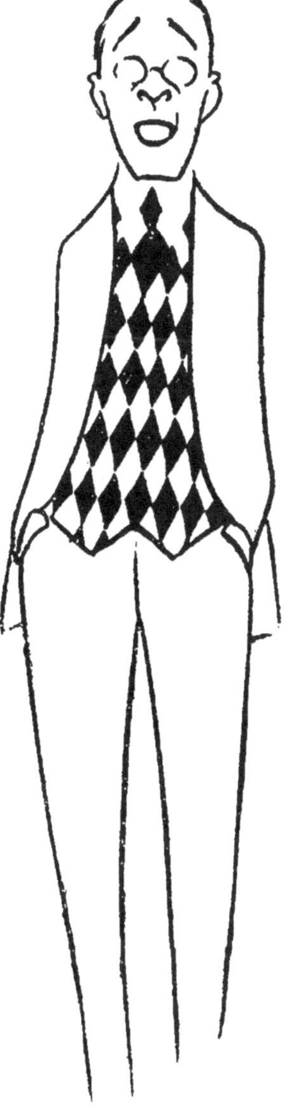

Mário de Andrade, drawing by Belmonte. *Don Quixote*, Rio de Janeiro, no. 292, December 13, 1922, 13

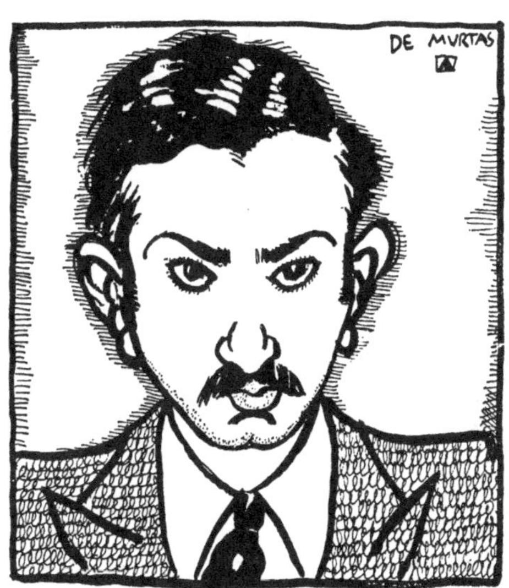

Lúcio Costa, drawing by De Murtas. *Fon-Fon*, no. 21, Rio de Janeiro, May 23, 1931, 37

heart of Lúcio Costa, who leaves the neocolonial trenches to become the greatest champion of the modern movement in Brazil, is inextricably linked to the similarity pointed out by Mário de Andrade between the simplicity of colonial architecture and European modern functionalism. More than a term, this word – *simplicity* – gains in Lúcio Costa the status of a concept.

The symmetry between Mário de Andrade's thinking and that of Lúcio Costa does not come into question, however, when Marcelo Puppi deals with the *historical method* of the latter: "the method is not, therefore, in what is said, but in what is implied: the need for a functional correspondence between form and society. In other words, according to the author, the constitution of a style in architecture only takes place when it conveys the historical and social impositions under which it is produced. The 'true' style of Brazilian colonial architecture can be found in the great mass of anonymous architecture that reacts to the impositions of the environment, and not in Aleijadinho, which is an exception to the rule."[108] Puppi discards highbrow baroque architecture, but does not elaborate on the fact that Lúcio Costa's opinion regarding Aleijadinho actually changes over the years, nor on the strategic role will the baroque master play in his definition of "artistic genius".

Another issue overlooked by Puppi is the origin of the axiom stating that the higher arts derive necessarily from popular art. This idea – widely debated, developed and conceptualized in the previous decade by modernist intellectuals – was initially proposed by Graça Aranha (1868-1931),[109] but with Mário de Andrade it gained a radical nature and a dynamism unthinkable in the conservative worldview of the intellectual from Maranhão. In the late 1920s, Mário actively encourages classical musicians, especially Villa-Lobos, to mine traditional musical expressions as the basis for their classical production; in the following decade, under the Vargas regime, as an employee of the Department of

Historic Heritage of the City of São Paulo and a consultant
to the Minister of Education Gustavo Capanema, the author
of *Macunaíma* would go on to push ethnographic research,
insisting that it would constitute the foundation on which a
national modern art would be erected.[110]

In *Essay on Brazilian Music*, published in the same year
as *Macunaíma*, Mário de Andrade argues that the only relevant classical music in any given period was always national
music inspired by folk traditions. Here one could find, as if
ingrained, the true essence of a race or a people.[111] However,
art and folklore should not be confused: "If in this early
constitutive stage, we must make frequent use of the direct
elements provided to us by folklore, we must remember that
artistic music is not a popular phenomenon, but rather a
development of it."[112] In Mário's view, classical music is quali-
tatively superior to popular music,[113] but it is in the latter that
the essential features of a race can be found. Writing truly
great musical works entails, therefore, two stages: in the first
stage, the artist must carry out a survey to pile up popular
rhythms, melodies and instrumentations; in the second stage,
he must submit the collected material to erudite elaboration.
The value of a work of art lies not in being *original*, but in
being *authentic*, and the musician must sacrifice his individuality and engage in an interested art.[114]

Once translated to the world of architecture, the
concepts and conception of art put forward by Mário de
Andrade validate two combined actions of Lúcio Costa: firstly,
the fusion between *tradition* and *modernity*; secondly, the
establishing of a set of guidelines for safeguarding the heritage in his initiatives at the head of the National Historical
and Artistic Heritage Service. *Authenticity* and *simplicity*
– attributes presented by Mário de Andrade as the general
foundation for art by the fact that they express the true
national essence – are pointed out by Lúcio Costa as characteristics of a truly Brazilian architecture.

Between Paradise and Utopia

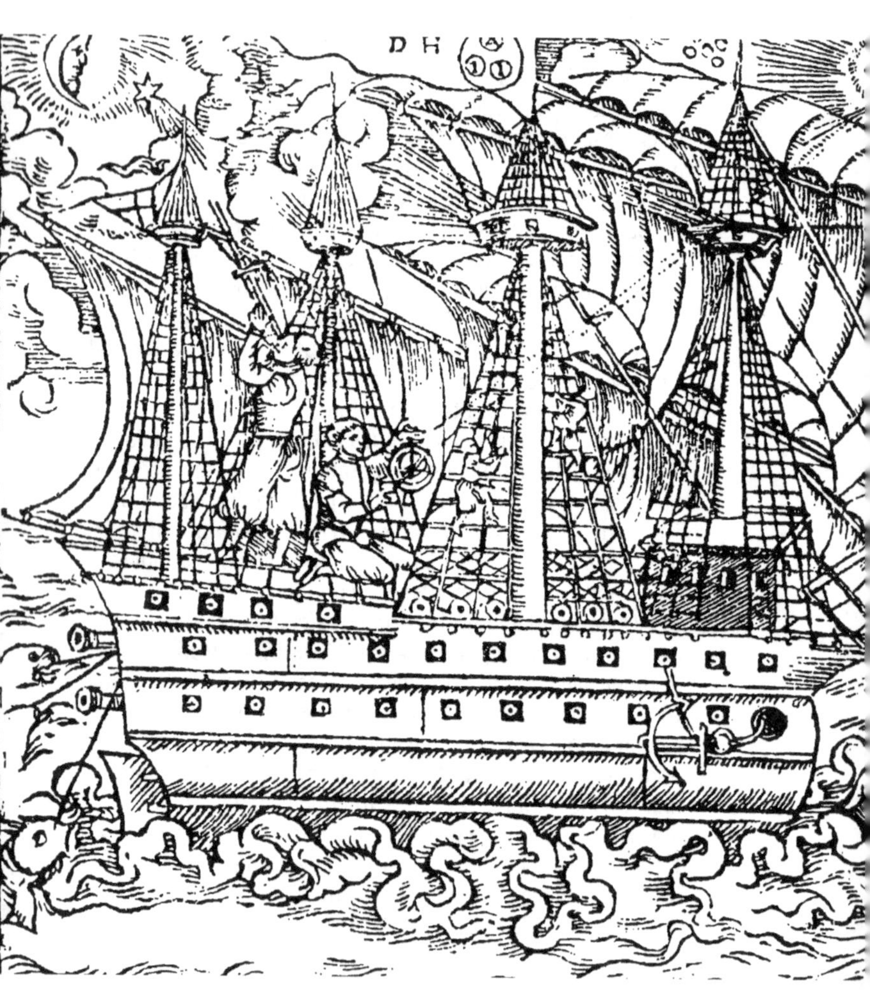

Uiara

in the country of the sun
where the sun was always shining
(it was never night)
there was a woman
with golden green eyes
dressed in the sun
the very image of the morning
she knew nothing of tomorrow
green and yet clueless
of what people say it's green
(which cannot be reached)
dressed in gold yet clueless
of what gold could even be
/ sun with no solution
woman engraved in gold
in a marajoara frieze
her hair quite green
golden eyes
Uiara was her name.
Cassiano Ricardo, Martim Cererê, 1928[115]

One of the main issues raised by Margareth da Silva Pereira, Romão Veriano da Silva Pereira, Cecília Rodrigues dos Santos and Vasco Caldeira da Silva in their formidable book *Le Corbusier e o Brazil* is the understanding of the reasons that led Le Corbusier to be chosen by the young Brazilian architects as the lighthouse that would guide them in the implementation of the new architecture in the country. The usual reasons given by critics and historians – the most repeated one being the fact that most members of Lúcio Costa's group were fluent in French – here are framed with greater precision within our cultural sphere:

> "If Corbusian ideas were so well received by Brazilians, it was because, more importantly than being modern, they captured and reinforced some of the great myths celebrated in these parts of America ever since its discovery, granting these myths a new formulation and the notion that it was indeed possible to make them come true. Myths such as the assimilation of the image of Brazil to a tropical paradise and the search for utopian visions – a search which still informs us today: the construction of an ideal society in an entirely new world."[116]

In an article from 1990 published in the magazine *Gávea*, Margareth da Silva Pereira delves further into this issue, exploring the theme of *nature* – or *landscape*, which is a recurrent synonym – in European intellectual traditions from the Renaissance to the early 20th century to demonstrate just how much the sensibilities regarding the natural environment were affected by the colonization of America. The difficulty of establishing the European man in an adverse and hostile environment is reflected in the intellectual production of a variety of fields – literature, philosophy, architecture etc. –, constituting direct or indirect reports on how those sensibilities changed. The article goes through a long period of time, weaving together two distinct visions that began to propagate after the discovery and occupation of the New World: the resumption of the myth of the original earthly paradise, now to be rediscovered in the tropical forest; and the notion of a utopia that should be built as a triumph of civilization against the powers of nature. Both visions weakened when the belief in the "long and evolutionary road that leads men from barbarism to civilization"[117] gained traction, which corresponds to the imperial period.

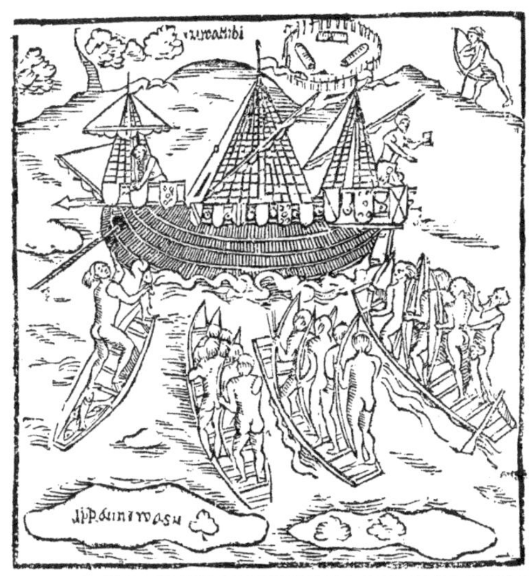

Indigenous people welcoming a Portuguese ship. STADEN, Hans. *Warhaftig Historia und beschreibung* *eyner Landtschafft der Wilden*, 1557, 94. Guita and José Mindlin Brasiliana Library Collection

Le Corbusier's presence in Rio de Janeiro, however, awakens those old visions. Facing the magnificent landscape, he evokes the words of his friend Blaise Cendrars regarding the very same scenario: "Whatever they do with their small urbanism, they will always be crushed by the landscape."[118] According to the Swiss-French architect, given the telluric forces of nature, the architect is summoned to make it artificial: "In Rio de Janeiro, a city that seems to defy all human collaboration with its universally proclaimed beauty, we are possessed by a violent desire, a mad desire perhaps, to try here, too, a human adventure – the desire to play a game for two, an *affirmation-man* game against or with *presence-nature*."[119] "Against", that is, using tools to correct the territory. "With", cunningly using the possibilities of coexistence with the environment.

According to Margareth da Silva Pereira, Le Corbusier "welded old myths that had been suffocated for more than a century by the weight of history and that now exploded again with full force. The desire to build something new and the desire to enjoy a garden – long considered antagonistic – came together in the hands of a man, an architect, to design a new story."[120] This desire for synthesis and integration seems to be one of the main reasons for the wide acceptance of Le Corbusier by the local architectural milieu. By associating the primitive and the civilized, the natural world and the city, the Swiss-French architect unknowingly said something that Brazilian architects could understand and loved to hear. It is a coincidence based on a set of values regarding the specific role of architecture in the relationship between man and landscape, which, in the Brazilian case, moves towards a broader and more ambitious field that in the previous decade had resulted in an agenda for the national culture. The location of earthly paradise in the tropics – whose ancient and vast tradition was unearthed in the 1950s by pioneer modernist Sérgio Buarque de Holanda in his fabulous book *Visão do Paraíso*[121] – is already hinted at in Oswald de Andrade's "Anthropophagous Manifesto": "We already had communism. We already had the surrealist language. The golden age."[122] It is an idea that is already explicit in the "Manifesto of Pau-Brasil Poetry", the idea of a synthesis between the desire to belong to this land and the willingness to use the powers of machine civilization: "We have a dual and present base: the forest and the school. The credulous and dualistic race and also geometry, algebra and chemistry soon after the baby-bottle and anise tea. A mixture of 'sleep little baby or the bogey-man will get you' and equations."[123] In Oswald's words, it is possible to spot an inversion of signs, quite aptly expressed by Antônio Risério:

"The Oswaldian project had its originality. He reimagined, in Brazilian terms, the European cultural adventure.

Before going to a distant civilization, Oswald delved into our own realities. And it was on this trip back, overcoming the interdictions of the dominant culture, that his thinking flourished. Instead of the *futuristic* denial of the ethnic trinity, which implied confining the non-Portuguese matrices in the undergrounds of culture, the *rich ethnic formation* emerged. Oswald then discovered that our problem was not a futuristic one, in the sense of São Paulo's fascination with novelties. He then begins to fight the repression of the cultural elements that constituted us, with modernist shots soon fired against the European facade of our social life. Furthermore, this Oswaldian project was far from being museological. It distinguished operating forces in the contemporary world. '*We have a dual and present base – the forest and the school*', he wrote. It starts from what is *barbaric* and *ours* and also from present-day technology."[124]

The *Pau-Brasil* vision is a search for a synthesis between Brazilian multiracial culture and the civilizational base borrowed from Europe. We would be particularly interested in the scientific knowledge and technology coming from the old economic and cultural metropolises – no white religion, philosophy and laws though. Oswald's radicalism – contaminated by a certain romantic naivety that Antônio Risério attributes to his lack of knowledge regarding the true native culture[125] – had the great merit of bringing about a huge change in the ideas that urban educated circles held about our origins. The "taint" of our ethnic fusion was tackled, as well as the ignorance about Brazilian traditional culture, which was enormous at the time. The scholarly tourism of the São Paulo modernists, who traveled through unknown and hidden regions across the country, was soon followed by the discoveries of a buried colonial past through the initiatives of Sphan's technical teams. Aleijadinho's elevation to the status of greatest artist in colonial Brazil, Tarsila's

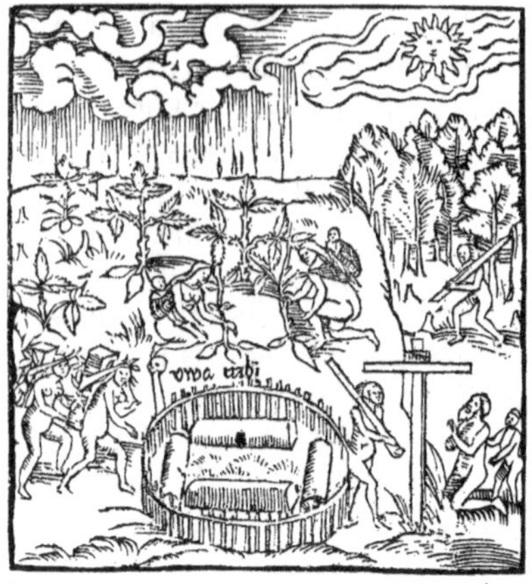

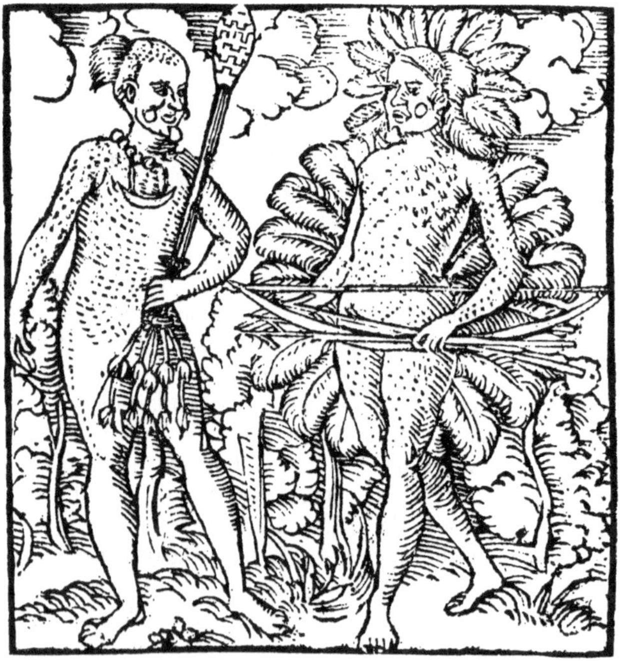

Arrival of Europeans in the New World and the daily life of the Tupinambás. STADEN, Hans. *Warhaftig Historia und beschreibung eyner Landtschafft der Wilden*, 1557, 115, 131, 140. Guita and José Mindlin Brasiliana Library Collection

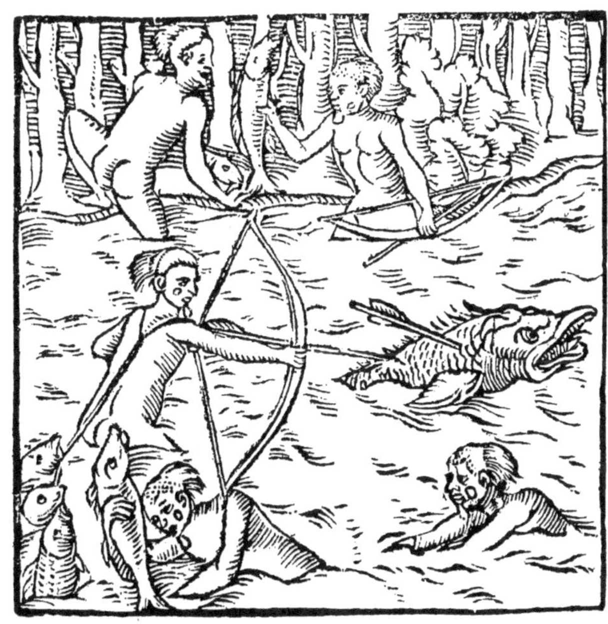

magnificent drawings depicting the interior of Minas Gerais,[126] travel diaries, Mário de Andrade's systematic ethnographic studies of regional music and folklore, historical and sociological studies by Sérgio Buarque de Holanda and Gilberto Freyre: the inventory was getting bigger and bigger and, all of a sudden, miscegenation, naivety, simplicity, primitivity ceased to be shameful aspects of our collective existence and became assets in the shaping of a a culture and an art consistent with the country's civilizational stage: "In modernist theory, primitivism is that normative and methodological value that encourages a reassessment of the national culture out of a new awareness of Brazilian reality. Particularly its underdevelopment."[127]

Oswald de Andrade goes even further. His boldness goes so far as to attribute the main libertarian aesthetic and political transgressions of modern European history to the contact with Brazilian indigenous people: "Heritage. Contact with the "*Caraiba*" side of Brazil. *Ori Villegaignon print terre.* Montaigne. Natural man. Rousseau. From the French Revolution to Romanticism, to the Bolshevik Revolution, to the Surrealist Revolution and Keyserling's technized barbarian. We push onward."[128] It was not enough to attribute the beginning of the genealogy to the primitive Brazilian; it was necessary to claim once again the leading role: "We want the *Caraiba* Revolution. Greater than the French Revolution. The unification of all productive revolts for the progress of humanity. Without us, Europe wouldn't even have its meager declaration of the rights of man."[129]

Oswald de Andrade's telegraphic and somewhat enigmatic sentence is explained almost a decade later by Afonso Arinos de Melo Franco in an interesting book published in 1937 entitled *The Brazilian Indian and the French Revolution: the origins of the theory of natural goodness.*[130] Lost in the mist of time and now largely forgotten, the book follows the adventures of the Brazilian Indian in the European scene, especially in France — both as an actual visitor and as a cultural presence. Many texts are analyzed, but Arinos sure points out the core elements of the plot he's seeking to restore: "The sober voice of Michel de Montaigne and its echo amplified centuries later in the painful cries of Jean-Jacques Rousseau constitute, in fact, the most important links in this chain of ideas that we are trying to reestablish."[131] Later in the book, he makes his reasons clear: "The influence of Montaigne's view on the Brazilian Indian was essential for the psychological and sociological conclusions that Rousseau would reach in the revolutionary part of his work."[132]

With a solid background in historical studies and proving himself to be very skilled in handling primary material – both the narratives of conquerors and travelers, as well as the texts of artists and philosophers –, the author demonstrates the straightforward relation between the Brazilian Indian and the shaping of the image of a primitive, simple and naive man, inhabitant of a *locus amoenus* where he can live naked,[133] in full harmony with nature, resting in a hammock under the leafy canopy of a tree.[134] The savage comes to incarnate the original goodness, characteristic of the state of nature, displacing the archaic figure of the animalistic, deformed and violent barbarian to the background, where it stays as a residue to be taken up later, throughout the 19th century, in degrading visions of Brazil. Arinos follows the traces left by Brazilian Indians in the daily port life and court solemnities, persuasively rebuilding the transmission mechanisms of this artificial construct, which fulfills social, religious, psychological and political demands of the European civilization. Following a scheme that for current standards might seem a bit overblown, the author periodizes the vicissitudes suffered by the "idea of natural goodness" in three different moments, corresponding to the 16th, 17th and 18th centuries: "In the first, its content was that of a philosophical and moral principle; in the second, that of a legal doctrine; in the third, that of a political theory."[135]

Among the many public presentations of indigenous people from Brazil during the 16th century in France, which were always surrounded by intense curiosity, attracting people of all social strata, the second Brazilian festival in Rouen[136] calls for special attention. In November 1562, during the festivities attended by a twelve-year old King Carlos IX – son of Henry II and Catarina de Medici –, Michel de Montaigne had his famous conversation with three Tupinambá Indians brought to court by Nicolas Durand de Villegaignon, in 1558. The encounter resulted in the essay "On Cannibals", published in 1580, where Montaigne unfolds the emotional and intellectual impact of the encounter through philosophical observations about human nature. Montaigne draws from the memories of a servant, who would have been a sailor in Villegaignon's fleet,[137] but Arinos argues that the philosopher also relies on descriptions

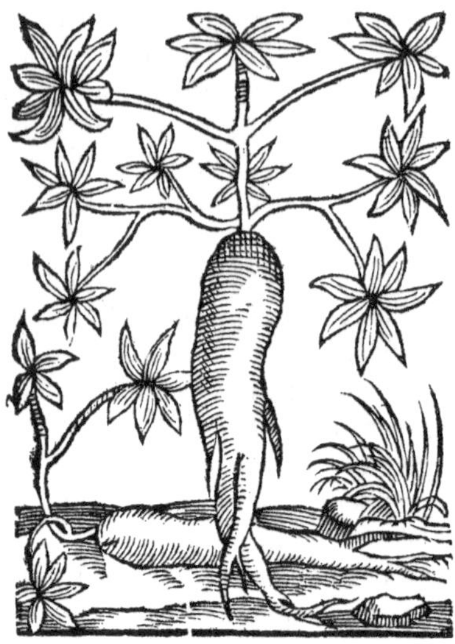

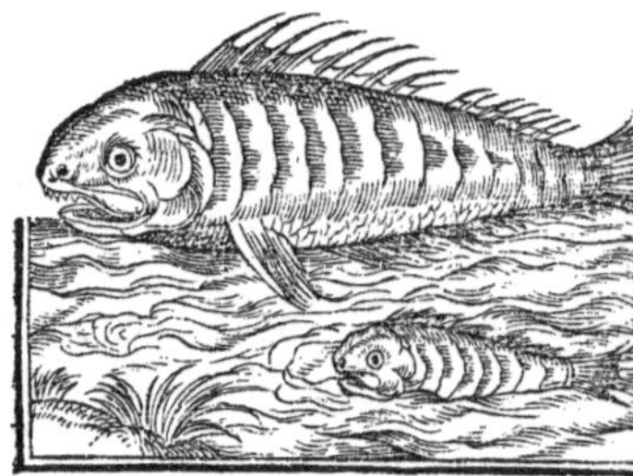

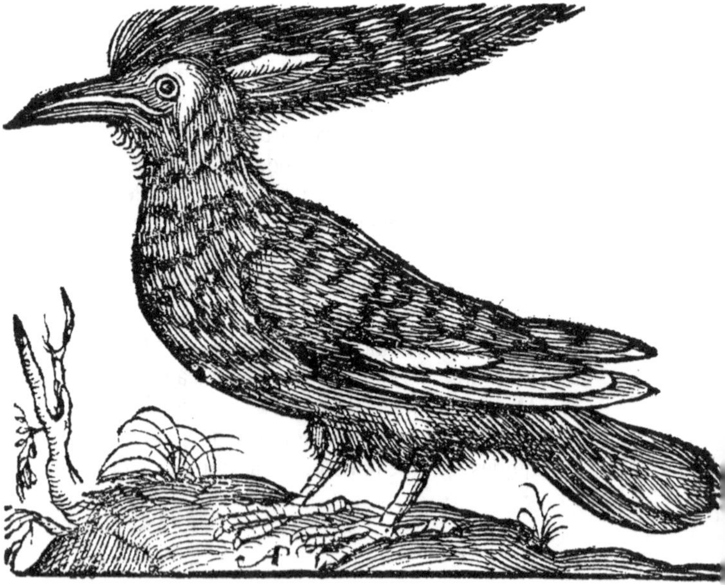

Natural world and inhabitants of the New World. STADEN, Hans. *Warhaftig Historia und beschreibung eyner Landtschafft der Wilden*, 1557, 250, 122, 253, 225. Guita and José Mindlin Brasiliana Library Collection

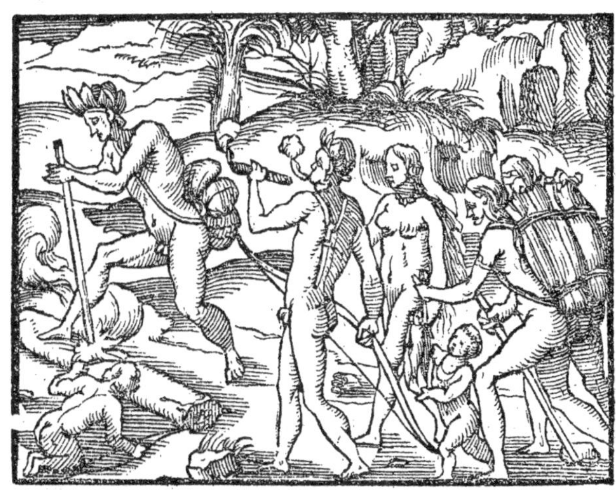

present in the narratives of two religious men — André Thevet[138] and, more keenly, Jean de Lery[139] — who visited the "France Antarctique" (1555-1570), a French enclave in Guanabara.

Montaigne's conceptual construction of the noble savage is developed by valuing primitive simplicity in opposition to the degradation of civilized customs. "It seems to me that these peoples" – says the philosopher – "are cast as savages for having been but slightly modified by the interference of the human spirit, having lost almost nothing of their primitive simplicity. The laws of nature govern them even today, almost undisturbed by ours, and thus so pure that I sometimes regret that our world did not know them before, when there were men capable of judging them better than us."[140] It's thanks to Rousseau's fanciful imagination that the abstract conception of the noble savage is embodied in a paradisiacal vision: "I see him feasting under an oak tree, refreshing himself in the original stream, finding his bed at the foot of the same tree that provided him with his food, thus satisfying all his needs."[141] Rousseau leaves no doubt about the view that both philosophers, two centuries apart, came to share: "The simple customs of early times."[142] Confirming the hypothesis of transmission of ideas and descriptions as suggested by Arinos, we have the opinion of Hugues Grotius, in the intermediary seventeenth century, who values the "great simplicity of life"[143] of the primitive man.

Oswald de Andrade takes his origin myth to the ultimate consequences: immersed in the jungle almost in a state of nature, preserved from Catholic infection and other civilized prohibitions, ruled by primitive communism, the Matriarchy of Pindorama bequeaths to Western civilization the possibilities of its own redemption. By re-engaging with the vigorous cultural current flowing through Europe during the 16th, 17th and 18th centuries, Oswald's regenerative myth transcends the insufficiencies and atavistic shortcomings imputed to native man by the foreigner and turns the civilized-primitive hierarchy upside down. The synthesis between "the desire to build something new and the desire to enjoy a garden" — Le Corbusier's proposition, according to Margareth da Silva Pereira — might be located in a broader theoretical framework, present both in Brazilian and French cultures, which nurture each other. Thomas More's Utopia ("the desire to build something new") springs from the Paradise envisioned in the New World by 16th-century navigators ("the desire to enjoy a garden"). According to Afonso Arinos, "Morus drew from the image of the Brazilian savage those traits that gave him the physiognomy of natural kindness and integrated these traits with other aspects taken from civilized man, hoping to achieve the ideal synthesis of a civilization in alliance with nature. He imagined a man who would take advantage of the progress of civilization, while not giving up his human attributes and virtues."[144] Interestingly, the tension between mutually attracting antipodes – the mythical original Edenic world and the perfect world of the future – would offer Western culture a literary work revisited by philosophical projects as different as those of Jean-Jacques Rousseau and Karl Marx:

> "Utopia is a deeply complex book. It participates in the cold revolutionary rationalism and also in the sentimentality expressed in the idea of the natural goodness of man. Its system wraps up many currents. On the one hand, there's the current which, later on, would become the nostalgic bread and butter of the romantics, of those mourning the passing of the golden age and the lost paradise."[145]

Thus, Margareth da Silva Pereira's thesis on Le Corbusier's thought finds a surprising foundation in the French-Brazilian historical-cultural framework, which explains why her words had such an impact on new Brazilian architecture. The historian explores the ambiguity present in the broader picture regarding the importation of modernism to Brazil in Lúcio Costa's own attitude towards that challenge, detecting – in his ideas and actions – both the enthusiasm of the ambition for the new and the melancholy of the reunion with nature. The proactive and confident Lúcio is remarkably revealed in the building of the Ministry of Education and Health, in the pilot plan for Brasília, in the urban plan for Barra da Tijuca and in the residences of the 1940s. However, "a certain melancholy that can be seen in some of his works is more complex to understand. This is a melancholy capable of conceiving architecture as a succession of frontiers that, ultimately, overturn the limits of artifice in face of the landscape, to the point of restoring man to the pure contemplation of nature".[146] We are dealing here with nature understood in its paradisiacal sense, which calls for "architectures that decline any ambition to permanence", which are "deliberately unfinished."[147] Some elements of the architecture, of the controlled landscape, of the selected objects – balconies, permeable partitions with trellises, palm trees, hammocks... –, present

in Parque Guinle, as they were in Vila Monlevade, which
encourage contemplation, dissolution in face of nature.
The antinomy that Margareth da Silva Pereira sees in the
work of Lúcio Costa is very opportune, for the limpidity and
clarity of some of his projects – especially the MEH, which
we have already mentioned – reaffirm a direct affiliation
with European modernism. The allusion to melancholy is
also quite suggestive, pointing to a feeling that nurtures
"architectures meticulously built to evoke paradise."[148] In the
historian's definition, the melancholy feeling results from the
human-nature interaction, when the human spirit freezes
while understanding the transience of life.[149]

The oscillation that exists in Lúcio Costa's work is an
expression of a particular subjectivity, however, it was also
perceived in the ambivalence of the cultural project idealized
by the Brazilian modernists. Marked by a series of syntheses
quite difficult to achieve – modernity and tradition, civilization and nature, progressive utopias and regressive myths
–, this project pushes Brazilian aesthetic production to a
perennial cyclothymia between joy and sadness. As in Lúcio
Costa, the same alternation of feelings could be observed
in the masterpiece of Mário de Andrade, his literary double:
Macunaíma, *the hero of our people*, is driven by an enthusiasm as great as it is inexhaustible, which doesn't prevent him
from being overwhelmed by *laziness*, by illness, by a lasciv-
ious sensuality that leads to post-coital lethargy.[150] He does
not shy away from hardship, and yet a melancholic feeling
contaminates the closing of his rhapsody: "It is always the
same lame hero who, after struggling in this unhealthy land
full of ants, got bored of everything, left and now wanders
alone in the vast fields of heaven."[151] The best expression of
this sadness can be found in this poignant paragraph from
the epilogue:

"The tribe was finished, the family had turned into shadows, the *maloca* had collapsed, undermined by ants,

while Macunaíma had risen to heaven. However, the *aruai* of the entourage from those olden days when the hero was the great Macunaíma emperor remained. In the silence of the *Uraricoera* the parrot alone kept the events from oblivion and the discourse that we could no longer hear. The silent parrot was the only preserver of the hero's sentences and deeds.[152]

Loneliness, oblivion, melancholy. Perenniality, vastness, silence. Man integrated into nature, a cultural dream that ends up canceling culture itself. There are many coincidences between Mário de Andrade and Lúcio Costa; the symmetry between their works is astounding, except for our average inability to see it. The role of ideological leadership they exercised in their respective fields was similar, as was the importance and quality of their artistic output. But they weren't identical to the point that we could swap them. In addition to the precedence of his ideas and works, Mário de Andrade had a clear advantage in the art he had chosen, after all, literature is the world of imagination, suggestion, and dreams. Through an appropriate aesthetic elaboration, incongruities and impossibilities can be transformed into qualities. Words evade the laws of physics, the principles of logic, and common sense. We couldn't say the same about architecture.

The presence of this sadness in Lúcio Costa's work does not elude the keen observation of Sophia S. Telles in an article published in 1989, where she establishes a set of similarities and differences between the ideas of Lúcio Costa and Le Corbusier. Unlike Margareth Pereira, who sees it as one of the recurring features in the old master's works, Sophia Telles tries to confine this element to Lúcio Costa's early work: "In some of his early texts, Lúcio exhibits a sense of melancholy, almost a conformism when confronted with the country's poverty and the uneducated people. At some point he even talks about the precariousness of the *race*, thinking that, deep down, culture is a matter of race."[153] The author mentions briefly the tension between atavism – a sense of the immutability of things – and faith in the "industrialization and education driven by the authority of the State,"[154] which would act as levers for social transformation. We have here, in other words, the same ambivalent dynamic between melancholic conformism towards an inevitable fate and trust in the transforming power of modern civilization. Race replaces nature, but the two terms are part of the same intellectual universe and are sometimes interchangeable; curiously, the author does not pay much attention to them, even though she refers once again to the issue of raciality in another passage.

Another thread present in Sophia Telles' argument can be used in the fabric proposed by this book: Lúcio Costa takes as a reference for a genuine national architecture the settler's house – not the churches or palaces of the colonial period – as he understands it to be the most accurate expression of the *manly element of the race*.[155] The beauty of Lúcio Costa's description, when speaking of the house that best embodied Brazilianness, is enveloped by a vapor soaked in contemplative melancholy:

> "Made of wood from nearby bushes and dirt from the ground, like animal houses, these are shelters for the whole family – toddlers, boys, older girls, the elderly –, everything gets mixed up in that sick, motionless air, waiting... [...] no one cares because they are so used to it, for that is really part of the land, like anthills, fig trees and corn plants – it's an extension of the earth... But, precisely because of that, as it is a legitimate element of the land, it has a respectable and dignified meaning for us, architects; while the *pseudo-missions* in the vicinity, either *Normans* or *colonial*, are nothing more than a mockery lacking composure."[156]

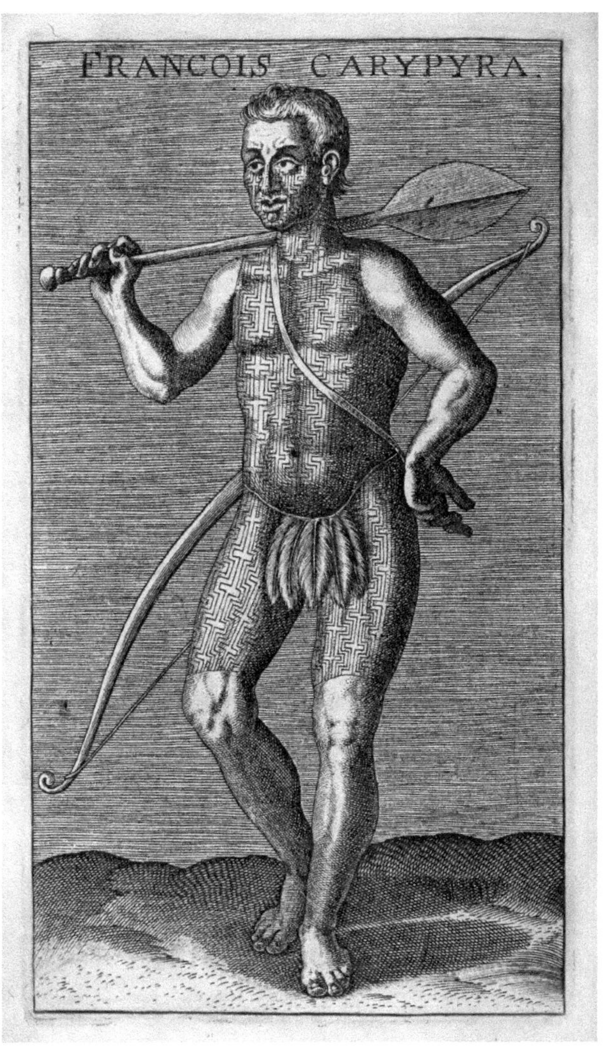

François Carypyra. D'ABBEVILLE, Claude. *Histoire de la mission des Pères Capucins*, 1614, 712.

Gallica Bibliothèque Nationale de France Collection

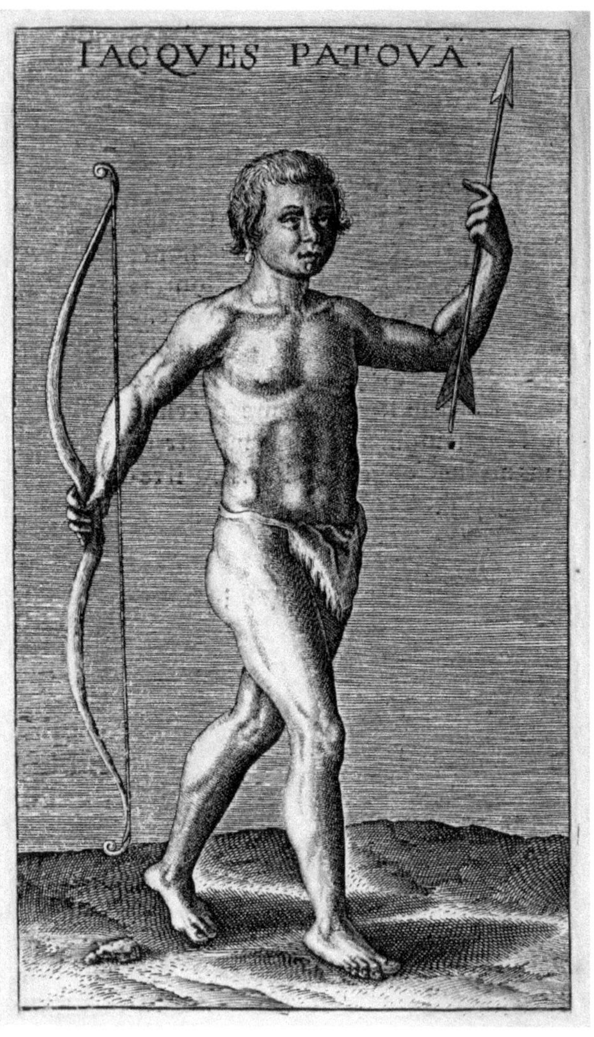

Tacques Patova. D'ABBEVILLE, Claude. *Histoire de la mission des Pères Capucins*, 1614, 728.

Gallica Bibliothèque Nationale de France

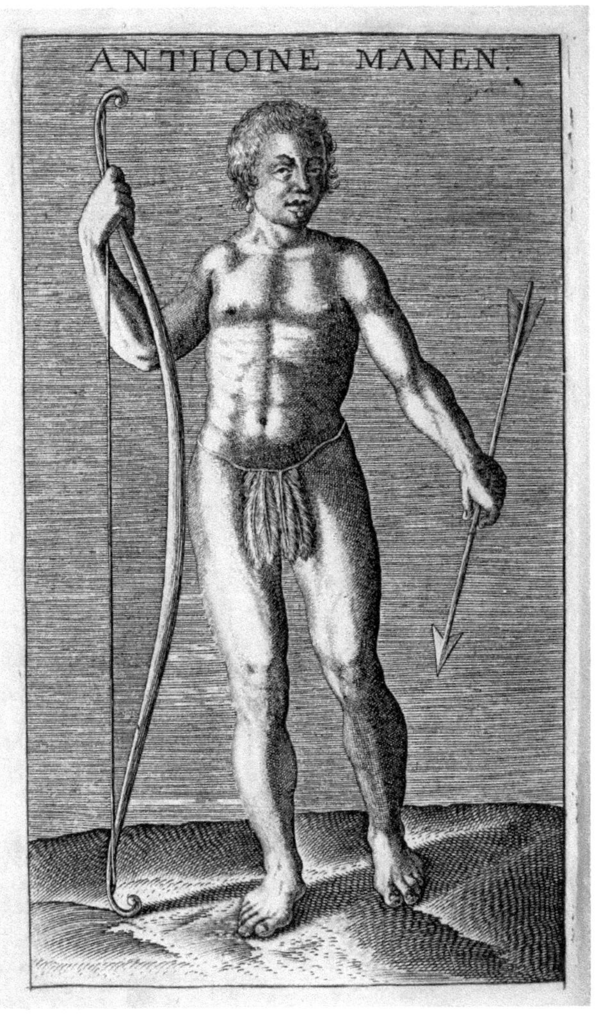

Anthoine Manen. D'ABBEVILLE, Claude. *Histoire de la mission des Pères Capucins*, 1614, 734.

Gallica Bibliothèque Nationale de France

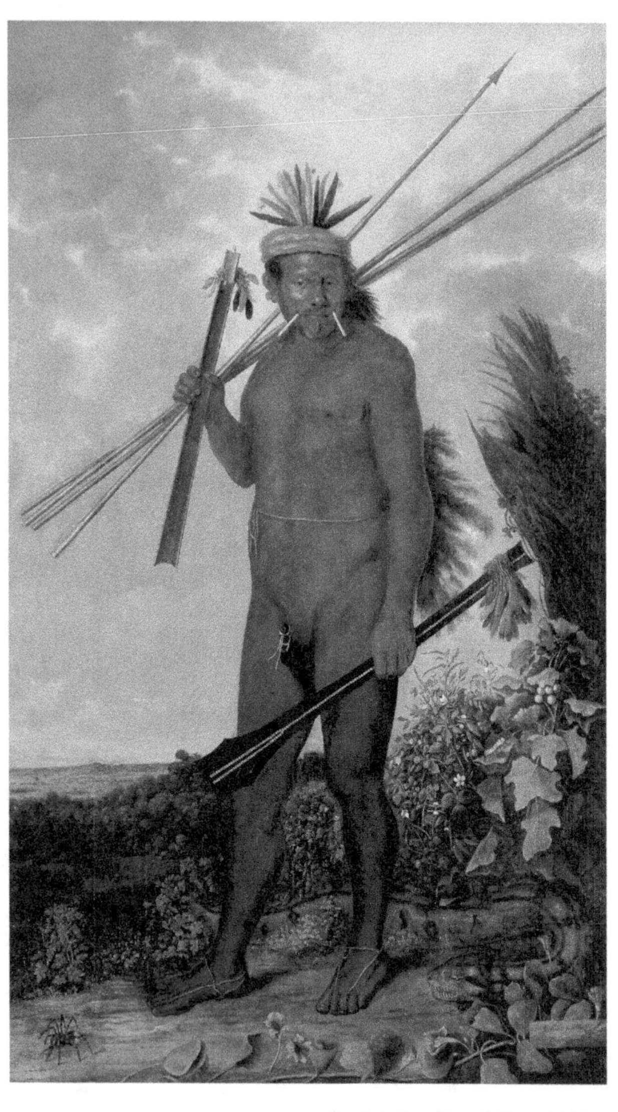

Tapuia Indian, Albert Eckhout, 1641.
Oil on canvas, 272 x 161 cm, National
Museum of Denmark

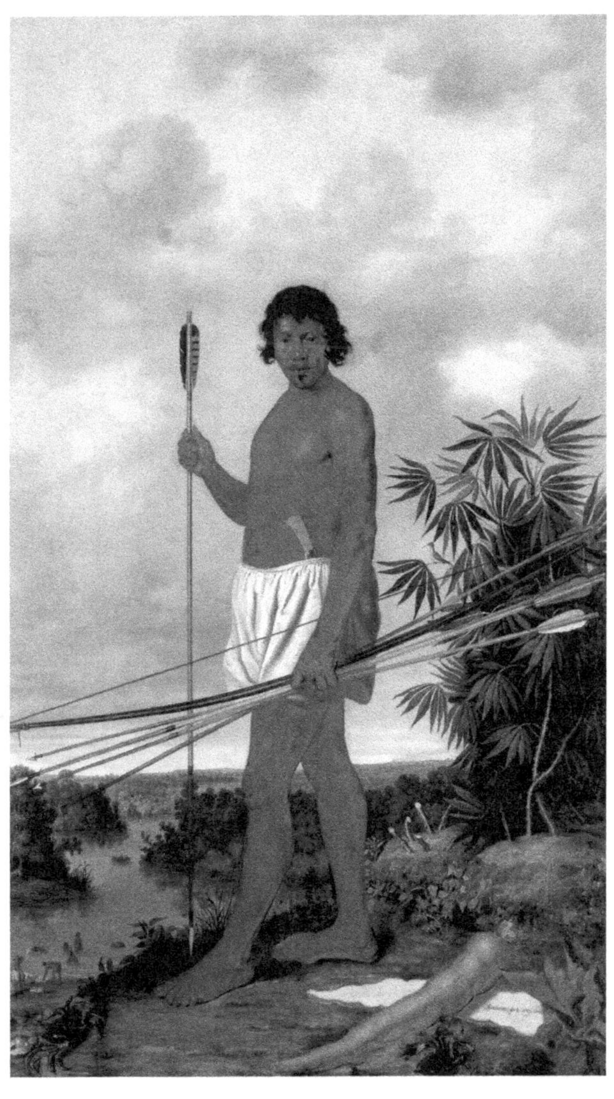

Tupi Indian, Albert Eckhout, 1643. Oil on canvas, 272 x 163 cm, National Museum of Denmark

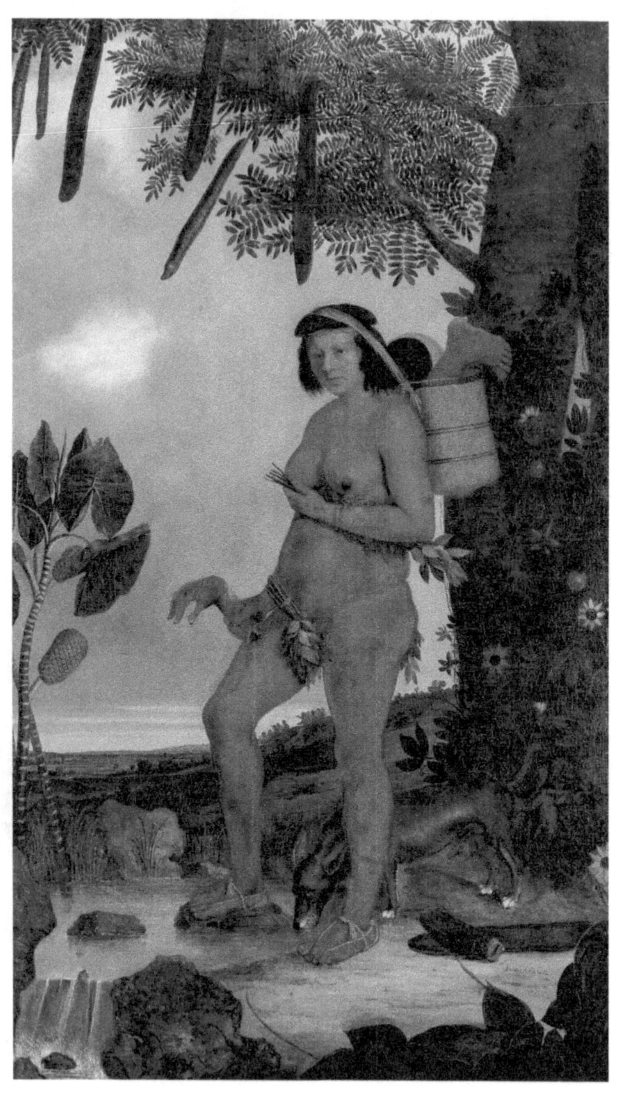

Tapuia Indian woman, Albert Eckhout,
1641. Oil on canvas, 264 x 159 cm.
National Museum of Denmark

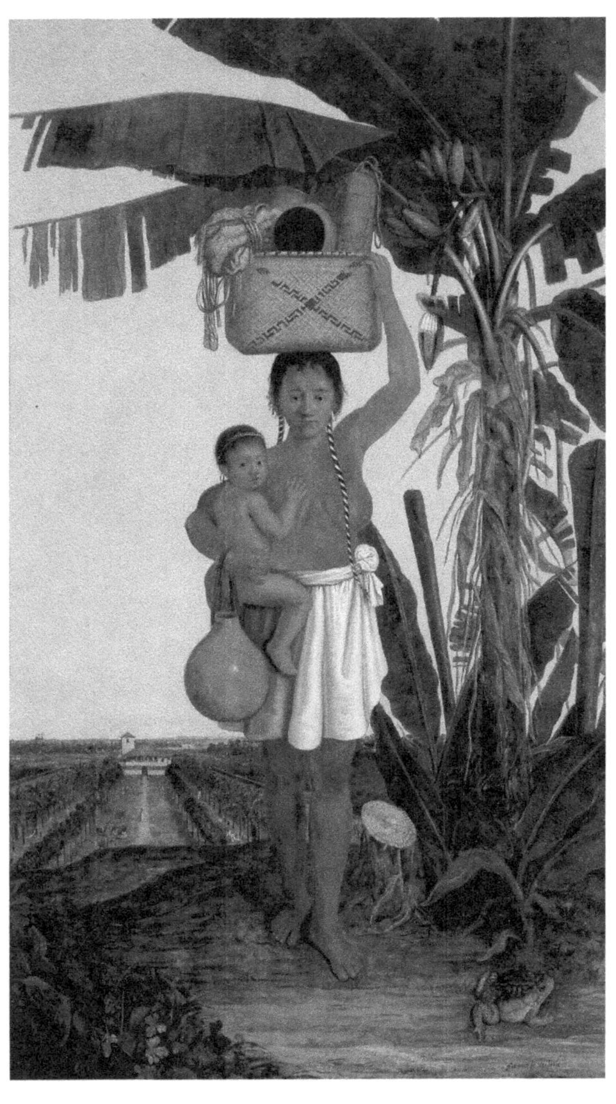

Tupi Indian woman, Albert Eckhout,
1641. Oil on canvas, 274 x 163 cm.
National Museum of Denmark

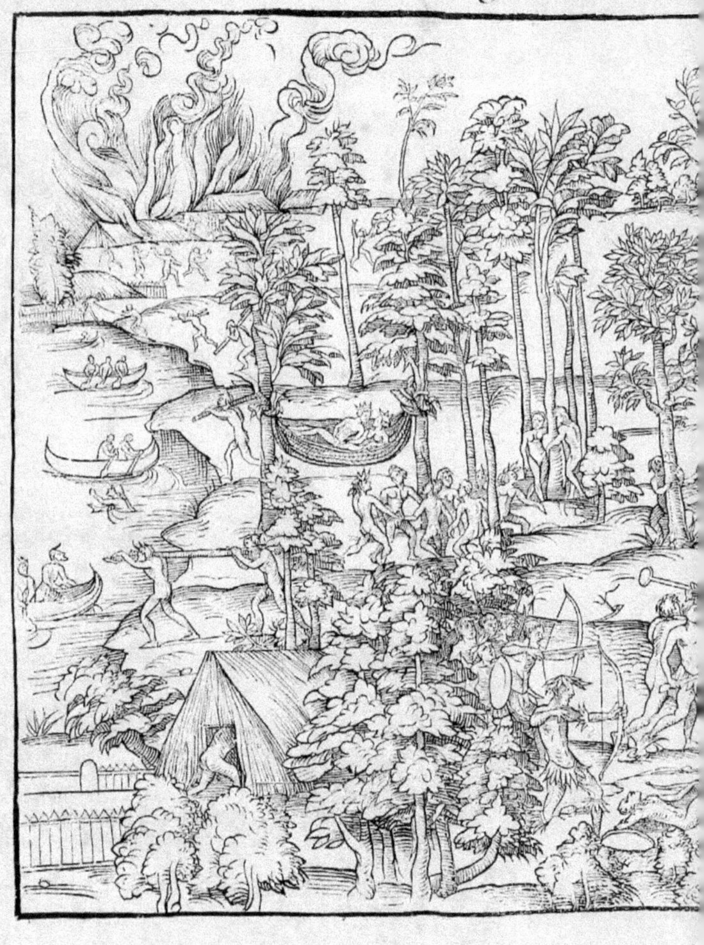

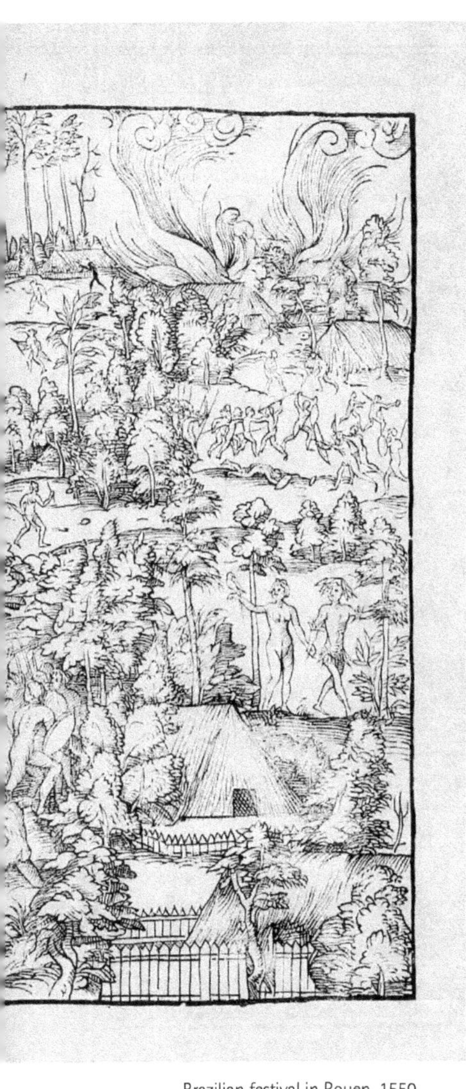

Brazilian festival in Rouen, 1550.
DENIS, Ferdinand. *Une fête brésilienne*,
volume 2, 1850, 5.

Guita and José Mindlin Brasiliana
Library Collection

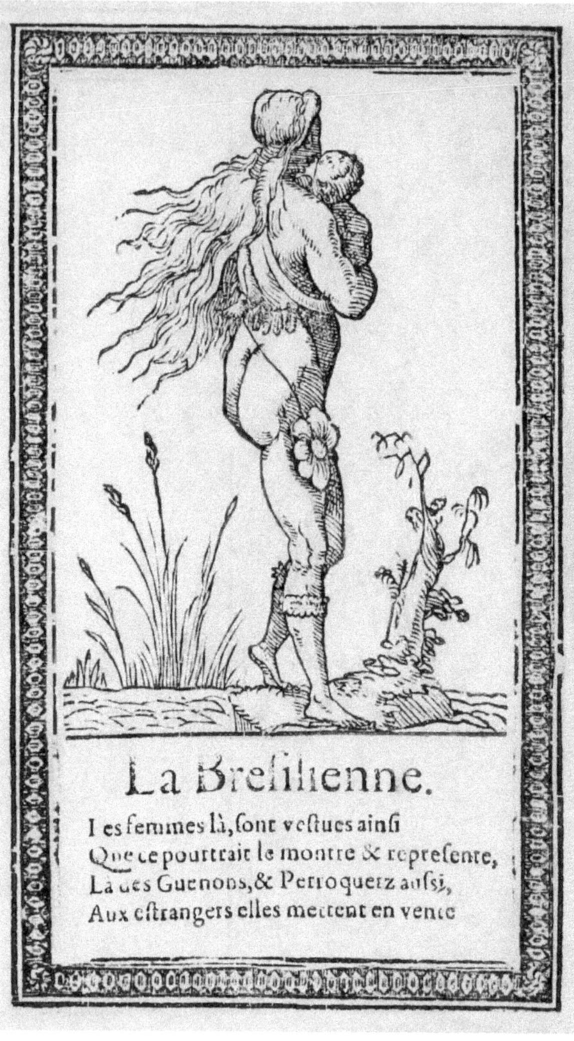

The Brazilian. DESCERPZ, François.
Recueil de la diversité des habits,
1567, 116.

Guita and José Mindlin Brasiliana
Library Collection

266

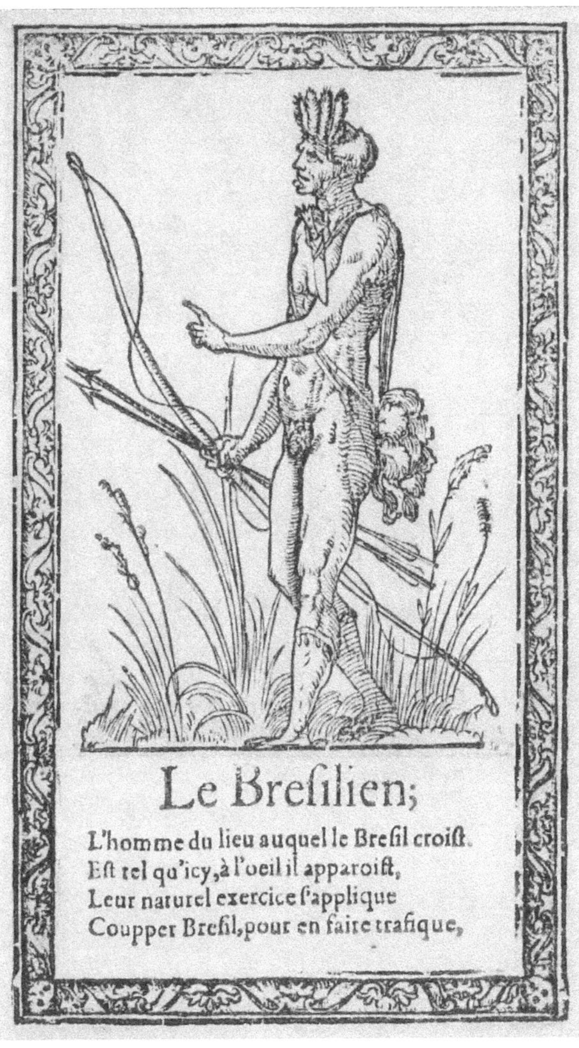

The Brazilian. DESCERPZ, François. *Recueil de la diversité des habits,* 1567, 117.

Guita and José Mindlin Brasiliana Library Collection

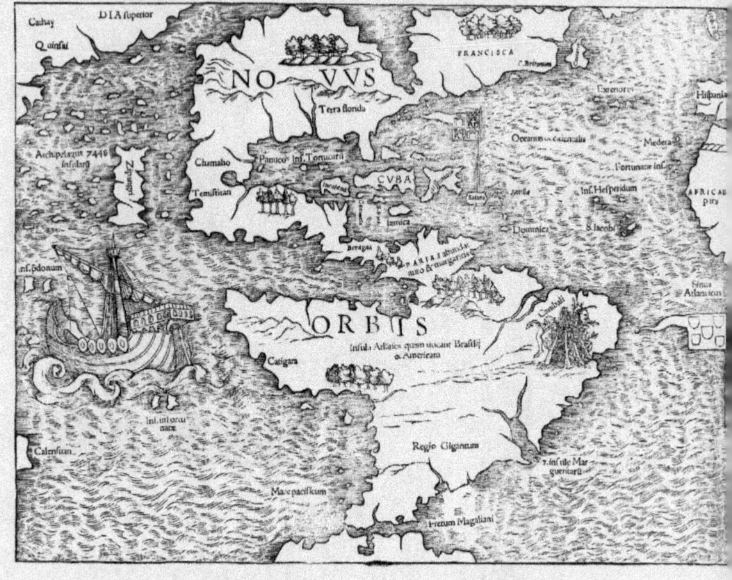

Map of the New World, Sebastian Munster, 16th century. *La Table des Isles neusues, lesquelles on appelle isles d'occident & d'Indie pour divers regardz.* Basel, c.1544. Oxford University Collection

On the next page
Inhabitants and natural world of the New World, 1558. THEVET, André. *Les singularités de la France Antartique.* Edition with notes and comments. Paris, Maisonneuve & Cie, 139, 205. Collection of the Guita and José Mindlin Brasiliana Library

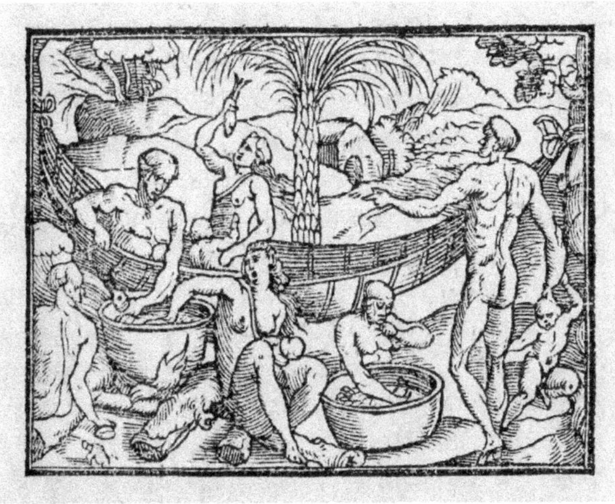

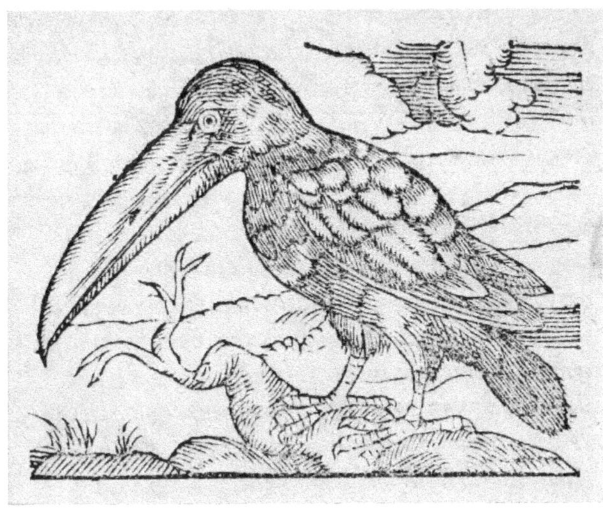

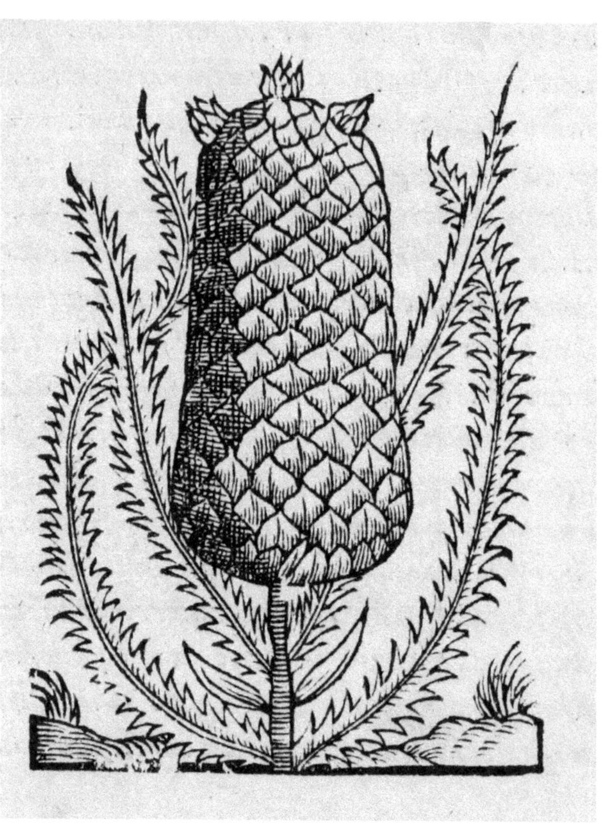

Pineapple, 1558. THEVET, André. *Les singularités de la France Antartique.* Edition with notes and comments. Paris, Maisonneuve & Cie, 202

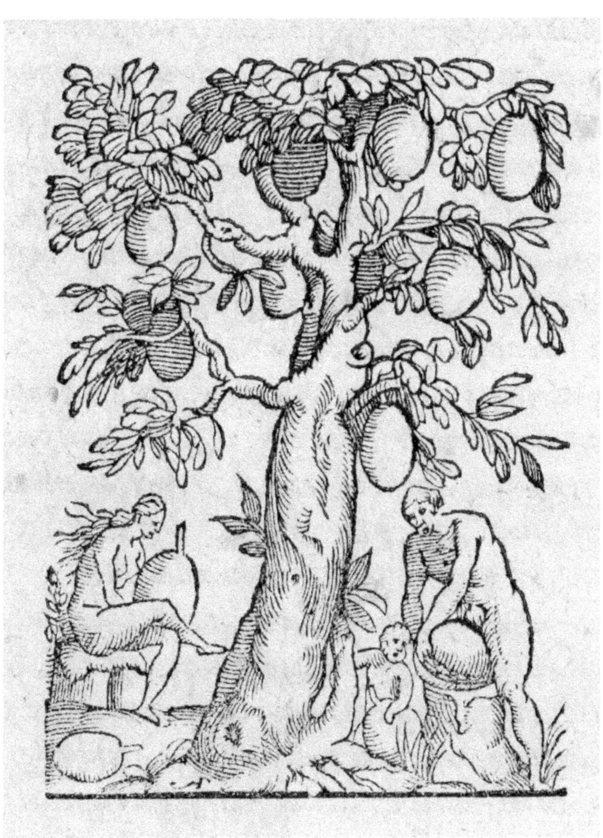

Indigenous people picking fruits, 1558.
THEVET, André. *Les singularités de la France Antartique*. Edition with notes and comments. Paris, Maisonneuve & Cie, 232

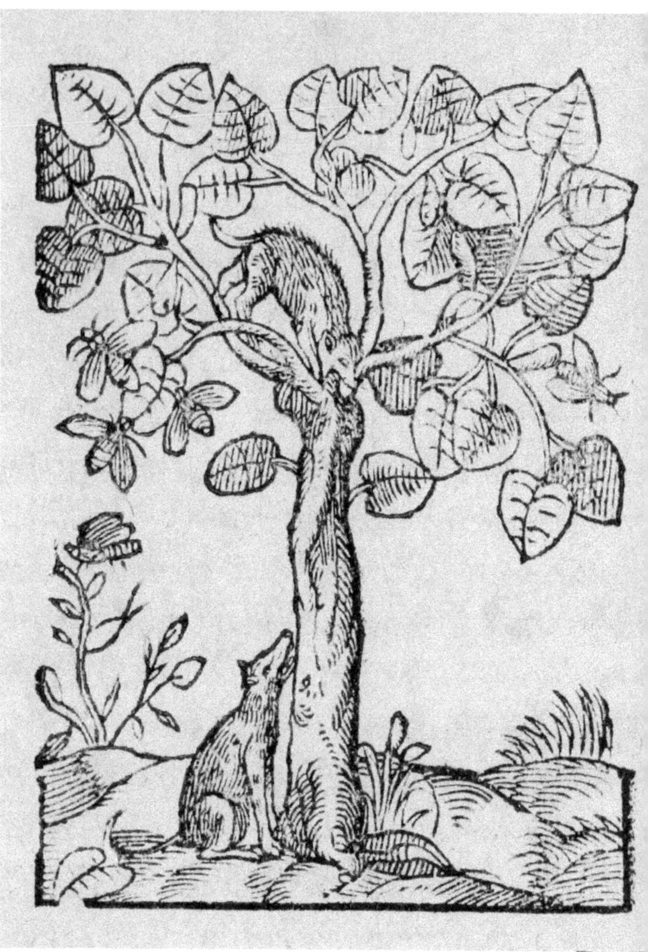

Animals in trees, 1558. THEVET,
André. *Les singularités de la France
Antartique*. Edition with notes and
comments. Paris, Maisonneuve &
Cie, 219

The association that Sophia Telles establishes between Lúcio's convictions and the French tradition starting from Viollet Le Duc, which is indeed correct, does not invalidate his ties to yet another tradition beginning a few decades earlier that seems to relate more explicitly to these issues. According to Joseph Rykwert, "the doctrine of the close correlation between art and climate, race and the moral constitution, is firmly championed by Romantic theorists, particularly by Madame de Stäel and Chateaubriand, and to a more limited extent by Hazlitt and De Quincey in England."[157] These correlations, which later crystallized into Hippolyte Taine's famous triad – *race, geographical environment and social moment*[158] –, had great penetration in Brazil during the 19th century and can be attested in a variety of cultural manifestations, as in *Os sertões*, by Euclides da Cunha, whose three sections – *land, man and struggle* – strictly follow the three Tainean concepts. References to raciality and tropical nature, far from being extemporaneous, are rather essential for understanding the primitivist worldview engendered by the modernist circle. Several theories associated with meso-logical and/or racial determinism are recurrent in most of the "portraits of Brazil" sketched in the late 19th and early 20th centuries and are incorporated by our modernism in its anthropophagic synthesis.

On several occasions Lúcio Costa refers to art and archi-tecture as expressions of an intimate correlation between man and the physical environment, but probably never as explicitly as in his project on how to teach drawing at school, originally published in 1948. According to him, it would be up to the fourth grade teacher "to recognize along with the students the impossibility of *measuring* the greater or lesser artistic beauty of works like these, which are legitimate expressions of *different* times, races, cultures, conceptions and temperaments: the fact is that that they are all beau-tiful – each in its own way."[159] The quote does not mention nature, but in another text from the 1940s and published in

1952 Lúcio Costa addresses the same issue, now adding the missing term, albeit omitting the explicit reference to race: "you can then define architecture as *building things with the intention of plastically organizing space, according to a certain time, a certain environment, a certain technique and a certain program*."[160] Finnaly, in one of his best-known texts, from 1951, Lúcio Costa returns to the theme: "The origin of art is not disinterested, for its occurrence always depends on factors that are alien to it: the physical and economic-social environment, the current times, the technique used, the resources available and the program chosen or imposed."[161] According to this intellectual tradition that goes back to Romanticism, race is a product of man's interaction with the physical environment in which he is settled. In turn, the cultural production produced by that specific man carries in his womb the basic features of his character.

Lúcio Costa highlights the distinction between the origin of the arts – precisely the conditioning exercised by the physical environment, race and the historical moment – and the essence of art – its impartial *plastic purpose*, which encompasses a moment when the artist will always be able to choose between "two colors, two tones, two shapes, two equally appropriate parties, and in this ultimate choice, art alone – *art for art's sake* – intervenes and chooses."[162] It is precisely because of these two vectors – one conditioning, the other arbitrary – that art present certain constant features in specific geographic areas, while also undergoing continuous transformation. Adopting the distinction between the *static* conception of form and the *dynamic* formal conception, conceived by German historians of the early 20th century, especially Heirich Wölfflin, was an easy step for Lúcio Costa. In the first case, dealing with a verifiable constant in Mediterranean art, there is a "predominance of geometric volumes and the continuity of surfaces exhibiting defined contours and the following sense of density, balance, containment". The second case corresponds to a particular constant where "the energy concentrated on the object seems about to be released and expand", which is typical of gothic, baroque, Hindu, Slavic, Arab, Iranian and Sino-Japanese art. Lúcio Costa adds: "for each of these formal conceptions, both the static conception and the different modalities of dynamic conception, we find a *natural habitat* at its origin."[163] Wölfflin, seeking to understand the relationship between constant and changing features in art, argues that each work is ruled by four instances: personal style, school style, country style and racial style. And he offers the following advice to scholars: "Here we come across the foundations of national sentiment, where formal taste comes into direct contact with spiritual and moral elements, and the history of art will have important tasks to carry out as soon as it starts to systematically approach the question of the national psychology through form [...] Different times produce different arts; the spirit of the age mingles with the spirit of the race."[164]

Going back to the original point – Lúcio Costa's predilection, as mentioned by Sophia Telles, for the settler's house as the most appropriate expression of the *virile element of the race* – one can now get a sense of the broader significance of this choice. Lúcio Costa's commitment to the modern in the late 1920s surreptitiously brings with it several others, and many of these contradict the new predilection. The very terms of his vocabulary – melancholy, race, tropical nature, integration, contemplation, etc. – are imported from other cultural scenes and widely used by Brazilian modernism. The "integration with nature", for instance, can be discerned in the cosmic tellurism of Graça Aranha as the main challenge for Brazilian art and was pursued by Oswald de Andrade's *Pau-Brasil* and "canibal" poetry, as well as by the right-wing nationalism of Plínio Salgado. Lúcio Costa's settler's house, therefore, is not pure materiality; it attracts implicit urban and rural indices that add up and infiltrate the interstices of culture – in language, music, landscape, habits and customs.

Bearing this in mind, perhaps now we can give a larger scope to Sophia Telles' observations regarding the meaning of the Brazilian landscape for Lúcio Costa:

"Perhaps this colonial construction belongs much less to the history of technique, as it has been seen in schools of architecture, than to the first properly modern vision of the Brazilian landscape. It's the modernist vision, which can be found in Tarsila, but also in Guignard, in the music of Villa Lobos, in the Brazilian language of Mário de Andrade, and so on. And it is the modernists who bring together civilization and the virgin forest, the automobile, the countryside, the city and nature, a long time ago. Thus, in this house with its pleasant, intimate and peaceful air, there is a completely modern vision of the Brazilian landscape."[165]

A final comment on an extremely relevant aspect addressed by Sophia Telles is in order: *the artist's role within this definition of art.* According to the historian, for Lúcio Costa, the active role of configuring the modern space is granted to technical rationality, while art is left to the task of integrating through feeling and intuition the culture of the past to the new civilization. As a result, "the artist must condense the aspirations of the people, must catalyze popular emotions, and move the hearts of the masses with his work. It is as if the artist should sum up the feeling of the country. And it is the feeling, not the judgment of art, that is at issue."[166] This somewhat romantic formulation is quite current in the 20th century in the most varied versions – "Artists are the antennae of the race," says Ezra Pound, a dictum later repeated by Glauber Rocha – and it entails a nuance of extreme importance in our modernism, which can be found, probably for the first time, in the *Essay on Brazilian Music*, by Mário de Andrade. Strongly influenced by *Totem and Taboo*, by Sigmund Freud, a book he had just read, the modernist intellectual argued that the object or content of poetry is the lyricism that pervades the collectivity – "a national art already exists in the unconsciousness of the people"[167] –, defining the social role of the artist in this context according to his innate qualities:

> "If a Brazilian artist feels in himself the strength of genius, as Beethoven and Dante felt, it is clear that he must make national music. Because as a genius he will inevitably know how to find the essential elements of nationality (Rameau Weber Wagner Mussorgsky). It will therefore have enormous social value. Without losing any of its artistic value, as there is no national genius (Rabelais Goya Whitman Ocussai) who is not incorporated to the universal heritage. On the other hand, if the artist is part of the 99 percent of artists and recognizes that he is not a genius, then he should really make national art. Because, by joining the Italian or French school, he will be just one more in the batch, while in the new school he will be valuable and necessary."[168]

For Lúcio Costa, following Mário de Andrade, both types of artists – the genius and the average artist – fulfill, within their individual possibilities, the same social role of shaping a national art. The average ones through a lower and horizontal participation, closer to the popular cultural base. The geniuses, in a higher, more artistic, more pure way and for that very reason – paradoxically – reaching closer to the soul of the people. Between the two extremes, we find different artists, occupying intermediate positions according to their personal talent. Thus, while adopting the modesty of anonymous artisans, Lúcio Costa feels justified – and obliged – to compare Niemeyer to Aleijadinho: "our own national genius that expressed itself through the chosen personality of this artist, such as already expressed in the 18th century, in circumstances, in fact, quite similar, through the personality of Antônio Francisco Lisboa, Aleijadinho."[169] Both characters play a specific role in the historical plot. In different cultural circumstances, Niemeyer and Aleijadinho carry out the task of elevating Brazilian popular culture to the status of art. In the colonial period, if baroque churches are the highest and most erudite expression of national lyricism, traditional architecture embodies the everyday pragmatism of the simple life of the people. In other words, the value of the architecture created by the anonymous masters derives from the authenticity secured by the greater proximity to popular manifestations, while the quality of Aleijadinho's architecture derives from a triage operated by the artist, that is to say, a choice, a *plastic intention*. And, following the reasoning of Lúcio Costa, it is this same plastic intention that allows Oscar Niemeyer, in another historical moment, to express the same Brazilianness.

However, if it is true that historical-cultural convergences are pregnant with potentialities, there is always the risk that the particular figure capable of capturing the latent possibilities will not emerge. For national lyricism, hitherto dispersed in the cultural base, to materialize as a superior work of art, the emergence of a genius is necessary, and his arrival will always be, to a certain extent, the product of chance. Here is the secret, the key to the enigma: the "miracle" suggested by Lúcio is the emergence of the personality of Oscar Niemeyer. A national genius, his superior sensibility managed to bring forth the latent national collective spirit through the virtual possibilities of the new technique, obtaining an unprecedented architecture that integrated the purest essence of nationality in an innovative way, expressing through the higher freedom of its forms our people and our nature.[170] Meanwhile, in a lower stratum of the cultural hierarchy, between the "so many constructions" without any interest and the brilliant "miracle", it is possible to discern "some architecture" of exceptional quality, shaping a Brazilian architecture that "stands out in the general set of contemporary production and that an outsider might identify as a manifestation of a local character, and not only because it revamps a few superficial resources peculiar to our tradition, but because it fundamentally embodies the very personality of the native artistic genius."[171]

Lúcio Costa's enormous effort to elevate Oscar Niemeyer to the pantheon was counterbalanced by his own descent into ostracism.[172] Even before his long and peaceful withdrawal from the spotlight, in the aforementioned 1948 letter/testimony addressed to Geraldo Ferraz, Costa claims for himself a role far inferior to that of Niemeyer in the constitution of Brazilian modern architecture:

"As for my contribution to the shaping of the movement, it was quite discreet. As I once clarified in a conversation with Mr. Barão de Saavedra, my initiatives were confined to the professional kindergarten, so to speak, and no one has ever seen an elementary school teacher trying to share in the glory of great men. Why, then, did a few architects, former students of the Escola Nacional de Belas Artes, responsible for the publication that now gives rise to this testimony, decide to attribute, without my knowledge, such an undue and inappropriate title? Without false modesty, and since all flattery should be despised, I attribute that initiative to the rather special position I occupied in the general events that took place at the time, and also to the fact that they wanted to point out, in some way, my indirect participation in the process which resulted in the recognition of contemporary Brazilian architecture."[173]

Tourists in their Own Country

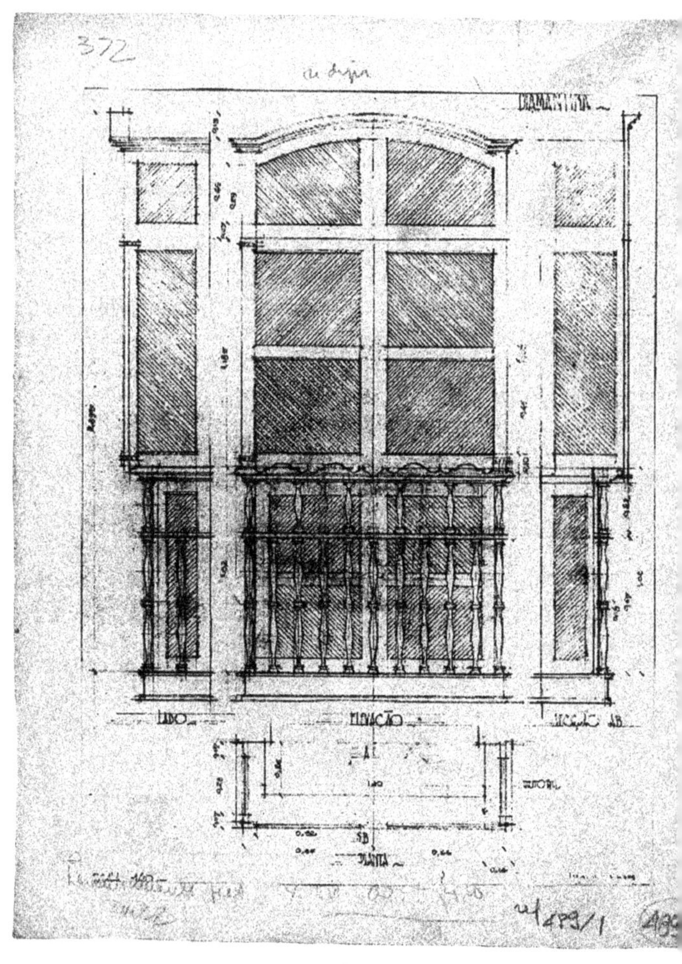

Colonial window, Diamantina MG.
Lúcio Costa, 1924. Archive of Casa da
Arquitectura

Paranapiacaba

Paranapiacaba, Serra do Mar
where the train lifted by cables overcomes the hard
mountain in several sections
All stations suspended in a vacuum
There are many waterfalls and great artwork was
needed
to shore up the crumbling mountain everywhere
Because the Serra is a rotten mountain like "les Rognes"
in Bionnassay,
but it's les Rognes covered in rainforest
The weeds that grow on the slopes, in the ditches
between the paths, are always exotic,
you don't see them in Paris except in the windows of the
great market gardens.
In one of the stations, three indolent mulattoes kept
spoiling the plants.
Blaise Cendrars, "Feuilles de Route," 1924[174]

In 1924,[175] being awarded the "Heitor de Mello" prize
by the Brazilian Society of Fine Arts and the Institute
of Brazilian Architects, Lúcio Costa visited the city of
Diamantina in Minas Gerais. The prize was created by José
Marianno Filho to reward students who stood out in the
graduation work of the architecture course at the National
School of Fine Arts, so that they could gain first-hand knowledge of traditional architecture dispersed throughout the
country, especially in the state of Minas Gerais. The train ride
to Diamantina took more than thirty hours, in addition to
the many other hours on the return journey. The creator of
Brasília would later describe the visit as follows:

"When I got there, I fell straight into the past in the
most stripped down, purest sense; a real past, which
I ignored, a past that was brand new to me. It was a
revelation: houses, churches, an inn for the muleteers, it

was all made of wattle and daub, that is, strong wooden frameworks – pillars, grid and roof beams – framing mud walls, the so-called *taipa de mão* [rammed earth that people produced with their hands], in contrast to the state of São Paulo, where the *taipa de pilão* [rammed earth made with the use of a pestle] prevailed."[176]

We can not determine the precise date for this statement by Lúcio Costa,[177] but it is unlikely that it is a record of his original impressions during the trip. The attention to constructive details is not compatible with the little experience he had at the time and especially with the neocolonial point of view to which he was then affiliated, which was more concerned with stylistic and formal issues. There's a great chance that we're dealing here with a deforming retroactive memory, given that he himself attributed the beginning of his disenchantment with the Neocolonial to his second trip to the interior of Minas Gerais – when he spent a long period convalescing in Sabará, Mariana and Ouro Preto in 1927 – and to the observations which he was able to do at that later time. His definitive break, therefore, only took place at the end of the 1920s or the beginning of the following decade, a period of self-criticism that resulted in his first major text on the modern movement, which was titled "Reasons for the new architecture."[178]

Although the psychoanalytic denial implicit in the act of "killing the father" has led modern intellectuals in general and Lúcio Costa in particular to despise it, the fact is that the Neocolonial plays a historical role equivalent to that of romanticism in literature[179] –that of looking towards our own the country: the Neocolonial "was actually the first manifestation of an awareness on the part of Brazilians regarding the possibilities of their country and its originality."[180] Architect and researcher Nestor Goulart Reis Filho sees in some architects who practiced the Neocolonial style a procedure analogous to that of the moderns, looking for essential lessons in the past that could attend to the aspirations of an architecture appropriate to a new era: "the great lesson of standard colonial architecture – constructive simplicity, which would be a guideline for modernist Brazilian architecture after 1936 – had its great precedent in the contributions of Dubugras, who carried out work of a rationalist nature, while others delved into decorativism."[181] Thus, the Neocolonial played a significant role in opposing the prejudice rooted in the national consciousness about the inferiority of the national production. More broadly, the Neocolonial fulfilled the same cultural and ideological purpose both in the United States and in several Latin American countries: it created a positive national self-image.[182]

In the same year of 1924 – while Lúcio Costa was traveling to Diamantina under the nostalgic reins of José Marianno Filho –, another troupe, this one coming from São Paulo, was also wandering through Minas Gerais. Accompanying the modernist poet Blaise Cendrars, this group of intellectuals and aristocrats from São Paulo, formed by Mário de Andrade, Oswald de Andrade and his son Nonê, Tarsila do Amaral, Olívia Guedes Penteado, René Thiollier and Gofredo Silva Telles, followed an itinerary that went through São João del Rei, Tiradentes, Mariana, Ouro Preto, Divinópolis, Sabará, Belo Horizonte, Lagoa Santa and Congonhas do Campo.[183] Mário de Andrade – who had made a similar trip back in 1916, which he recorded in a series of articles for *Revista do Brasil* – acted as the tour guide.[184] The fact that those Brazilian intellectuals did not know their own country is quite curious and surprising, as Brito Broca's sharp comment doesn't fail to point out:

"It is worth noticing the paradoxical attitude of these travelers. They were all modernists, men of the future. And to this avant-garde poet who came to visit us, creating havoc among conformist spirits, what did they choose to present? The old towns of Minas, with

their 18th century churches, their colonial and imperial palaces, in a desolate landscape, where everything
evokes the past, and one has the feeling of being among
ruins everywhere. The contradiction, however, is not
real. There was indeed an inner logic. The divorce from
the Brazilian realities in which most of our writers had
always lived made the landscape of baroque Minas
appear as something new and original, perfectly suited
for the framework of novelty and originality they were
looking for. Didn't they talk, from the onset, of a return
to the roots of nationality, searching for a path that
could lead to a genuinely Brazilian art? There, among the
ruins of Minas Gerais, they would certainly find intima-
tions of this art."[185]

Brito Broca is quite straightforward in his assessment,
which is based on the nationalist convictions assumed by
all Brazilian modernists from the mid-1920s onwards. As
defenders of a national culture, it was natural for them to
go looking for the "roots of nationality". There is, however, a
logical question lurking in the background that needs to be
clarified: why would a group of intellectuals from wealthy
families, accustomed to long stays in Paris, turn abruptly to
the heartland of the country? According to Alexandre Eulalio,
in 1923, a year before the publication of the "Pau-Brasil
Manifesto" and the visit of the Swiss-French poet, several of
them – Oswald de Andrade, Tarsila do Amaral, Di Cavalcanti,
Vicente do Rego Monteiro, Victor Brecheret, Sérgio Milliet,
Heitor Villa-Lobos and Souza Lima – were in Paris and witnessed the encounter between Oswald and Cendrars. Before
he published *Feuilles de Route*, a book of poems concerning
his trip to Brazil, with illustrations by Tarsila do Amaral, the
Swiss-French poet was a central figure in several episodes
that were crucial for the direction of the young Brazilian
modernist avant-garde. He facilitated many encounters
between Brazilians and modern artists who at the time were

flocking to Paris, such as Picasso, Cocteau and Brancusi.
It was him who introduced Fernand Léger to Tarsila, for
instance. However, it was in his revealing the "spirit of the
time" that their exchange was decisive, for here the Brazilian
group met an artist who knew how to translate exotic
experiences into poetic construction and who was used to
stripped down, colloquial writing where descriptive rationality welcomes the naivety of "primitive" customs. After
a generic question – "but to what extent would Cendrars
conveyed suggestions to these youngsters gathered in Paris?"
–, Eulalio asks a second question – now a rhetorical one –,
which reveals his opinion regarding the decisive influence of
Cendrars on Oswald[186] and the rest of the crew: "An art that
would venture to recreate with a new spirit these sometimes
rustic, sometimes suburban realities, attributing to them a
compelling lyrical aura?"[187] Cendrars, an experienced and
knowledgeable artist, outlines the travel itinerary and suggests the adoption of "travel diaries":

> "A number of particular features of the country had
> been kept in the shadows until that moment, almost
> invisible to so many talented artists; none of them had
> yet tried to unravel its significance. Now, vigorously styl-
> ized, the sharp incongruity of everyday life, its exalted,
> pure colors, the ordinary yet provocative clumsiness of
> the city and the countryside, the generous plainness of
> customs, the clear outline of the landscape, evaluated
> in both an inquisitive and lucid way, were finally tackled
> with lyrical tenderness and ironic detachment."[188]

Naturally, it was Paulo Prado, instigated by Oswald, who
invited Cendrars to Brazil. The 1924 trip is a mixture of a
friendly willingness to introduce a foreign guest on vacation
to an unknown facet of the country, and the willingness
of the guest himself to point out as an experienced artist
what deserves to be noticed. The experience becomes a kind

of study trip whose tasks are disproportionately attributed to each participant. In the works of Tarsila do Amaral and Oswald de Andrade, the syncretic religiosity permeated by popular mysticism and the everyday simplicity of men engaged in their crafts are presented in a simple setting.[189] This inclination to look at fragments of the past that have survived materially and spiritually is not driven by a nostalgic desire to capture a disappearing world, but rather by a pressing need to find elements that could be rescued for the contemporary modern world. This first *study trip* was followed by others[190] throughout the 1920s, enlisting different characters, always with the same jovial, cheerful and engaged spirit.[191] The works of art were a natural consequence of the process.

With his usual insight, Antônio Cândido engaged with the travel experiences of two of the modernists in order to grasp the meaning of their major literary works: *Macunaíma*, by Mário de Andrade, and *Serafim Ponte Grande*, by Oswald de Andrade: "Both books are based on two trips, which make them complementary despite being so different: Macunaíma's trip from Amazonas to São Paulo, ending with the return to the mythological placenta; and Serafim's trip from São Paulo to Europe and the touristic East, with the ship *El Durasno* ultimately diving into the waters of myth. These shock trips prompted the devouring of cultures and mirrored their authors: Mário, who never left Brazil and had his fundamental experience on the famous excursion to the Amazon, reported in *The Apprentice Tourist*; Oswald, who went through at least four long stays in Europe."[192] Traveling characters, traveling authors, and the culture of the Other as a menu. Lourival Gomes Machado quite aptly sums up the modernist situation after the nativist inflection: "After a first moment of rebellion, the modernists turn one eye to the colonial tradition and the other to the Parisian movement. The rediscovery follows a double route with ships departing for Le Havre and trains leading to Ouro Preto."[193]

The way in which the meaning of "primitive" as a concept or relational perception is reframed does not escape Antônio Cândido's analysis. According to Cândido, "both books promote a reassessment of values through the clash of two cultural moments. The primitive and Amazonian world of the archetypes in *Macunaíma* is reassessed on an urban scale, while the bourgeois world of *Serafim* is thrown against the cosmopolitan dimension of Europe, which guides and fascinates us, and before which we are the *primitives*."[194] The Amazonian culture – like all cultures in the interior of the country – is seen as primitive by the inhabitants of Brazil's largest cities.[195] On the other hand, in the eyes of the average European, Brazilians as a whole are the primitives, including the citizens of those big cities. In Cândido's interpretation, what really matters is not the confrontation, but the encounter between cultures as seen through specific experiences, which can be either a physical journey or a literary journey. According to Cândido, the two modernists "explored in an original way the basic theme of the cultural encounter, manipulating primitivism in different ways. *Macunaíma* not only explores the primitive world, but digs into the underground urban culture to reinterpret it in primitive terms. *Serafim*, on the other hand, approaches the Brazilian urban man as a sort of primitive in the technical era, which ends up dissolved in myth."[196] On another occasion Oswald de Andrade called this *primitive in the technical era* the "technized barbarian of Keyserling."

It was these trips by the modernists from São Paulo, and not the ones sponsored by Marianno's prize, that inspired the Sphan team to undertake recurrent prospecting journeys throughout the interior of the country – mainly to the colonial cities of Minas – from 1937 onwards. The expeditions began soon after the foundation of the agency, as pointed out by Lúcio Costa while distinguishing the trips sponsored by José Marianno Filho from those promoted by the young São Paulo intellectuals: "Marianno's actions were taken as president of the Brazilian Society of Fine Arts. It was through this thing that he financed some of the trips of several architects to Minas, three architects, actually – I went to Diamantina. But you have to take into account that, around the 'modernist' movement in São Paulo associated with the 1922 Modern Art Week and all those great figures such as Mário de Andrade, Oswald de Andrade, Tarsila – in that same year, a series of excursions to Minas and the north of the country were organized, and the goal was to seek out the roots of Brazil. To study them and get to know them. These were passionate journeys."[197] In her study on architect Alcides Rocha Miranda, Ana Luiza Nobre puts forward the same association: "Firstly, it was necessary to carry out 'first aid' actions aimed at protecting the national heritage, a task that brought together a small group of pioneers around Rodrigo Melo Franco de Andrade, to which Alcides Rocha Miranda soon joined. Through dirt roads, often long journeys by train, jeep or horseback, this small but faithful group pursued the same guiding principle of Mário de Andrade's ethnographic travels across the country, which demanded heroic efforts."[198]

The fact that our modernism fluctuates between a futuristic discourse where the machinic elements of modernization occupy a strategic role and a nativist discourse where national and regional elements take center stage reveals the broader horizon of our cultural history, wavering between local and international inclinations, as Antônio Cândido points out: "If it were possible to establish a law of evolution of our spiritual life, we could perhaps say that all of it is ruled by the dialectic of localism and cosmopolitanism."[199] According to Antônio Cândido, the condition of being a "second-rate" country – first as a *colony* and, later on, following political emancipation, as an *underdeveloped* country – has always conditioned intellectual and artistic life in Brazil to constantly borrow from an European culture always at odds with tropical life. In the aesthetic field, there is a conflict between exotic expressive means and native content, which,

regarding the psychology of the country's elites, entails an
embarrassing feeling of inferiority. For Antônio Cândido,
this sense of cultural subalternity ends up unfolding in two
antagonistic symptoms: the passive acceptance of the foreign culture, leading to an uncritical imitation of European
models and the consequent repression of the real or imaginary deficiencies of the national culture; or an emancipatory
rebellion, often on par with a mystification that denies any
historical ties to Europe. The pendulum keeps swinging, but
Cândido's assessment is unequivocal: positivity resides in the
particularist effort that seeks an autonomous national culture, even if external influences are inevitable.

Antonio Cândido argues that Brazilian modernism is a
manifestation of a localism that moves on to plunder foreign
cultures: "It inaugurates a new moment in the dialectic of
the universal and the particular, inscribing itself in the latter
with force and arrogance while making use of the weapons borrowed from the former."[200] The avant-garde period
entails both a resumption and a rupture. The *resumption*,
bringing back native themes, spiritually aligns the modern
to another particularist moment in Brazilian cultural history:
Romanticism. On the other hand, the *rupture* prompts the
emergence of historical, social and ethnic phenomena that
were repressed in the national consciousness – a series of ills
that foreigners had attributed to us through the centuries –,
and this constitutes the most original and fruitful contribution of modernism to Brazilian culture. The psychoanalytic
role played by modernism, confronting a series of issues that
had been repressed over time, had already been pointed out
by critic Lourival Gomes Machado in 1945:

> "Let us only mark the major outcome of modernism in
> the history of Brazilian culture, which was, undoubtedly,
> the elimination of the sour despairs and gloomy discour-
> agement, which revealed a somewhat incurable inferi-
> ority complex anciently imbricated in Brazil's intellectual

personality, and its replacement by a calm awareness of our true and perfectly curable inferiorities. Which – so it seems – is quite healthy.[201]

The parallel drawn between modernism and romanticism – two "crucial moments that change the course of our history and vitalize the national intelligence"[202] – does not imply, according to Antonio Cândido, a complete equivalence, for Brazilian romanticism lacked both the conviction and the investigative sincerity of the former: "It seems that modernism [...] corresponds to the most authentic current in Brazilian art and thought. In it, especially in its culmination when all its fruits ripened (1930-40), we find a fusion that encompasses the abolition of academicism, historical repression and literary officialdom; trends in political education and social reform; and the pressing need to really get to know the country."[203] This *authenticity*, which is where the seal of superior quality seems to reside, contains two different but complementary guidelines: the acceptance of one's own cultural condition – which until then was considered inferior – and the conscious and energetic work to elevate such condition to the level of autonomous art. The Brazilian intellectual, having undergone a kind of cultural therapy, is now ready to engage in emancipatory militancy, which was precisely the historical role carried out by Brazilian modernism. This reversal of expectations leads Antônio Cândido to launch a hypothesis that will enjoy a long history in the Brazilian critical scene: the primitivism Brazilian modernism argued for and disseminated, despite being imported from the European avant-garde, was much better suited to the Brazilian cultural scene than to the original context:

> "It is impossible to ignore the role that primitive art, folklore and ethnography played in defining modern aesthetics, which turned to archaic and popular elements repressed by academicism. The thing is, in Brazil,

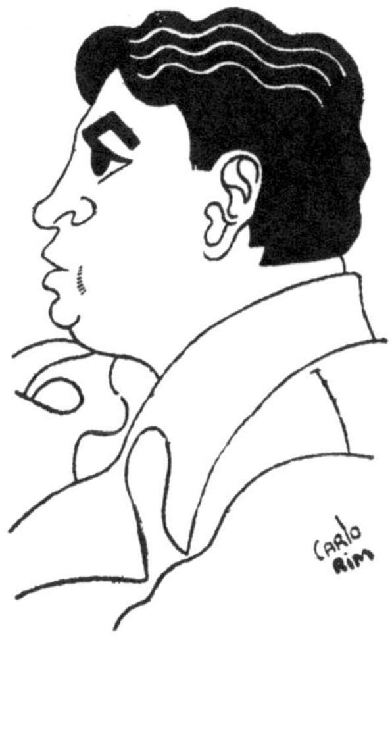

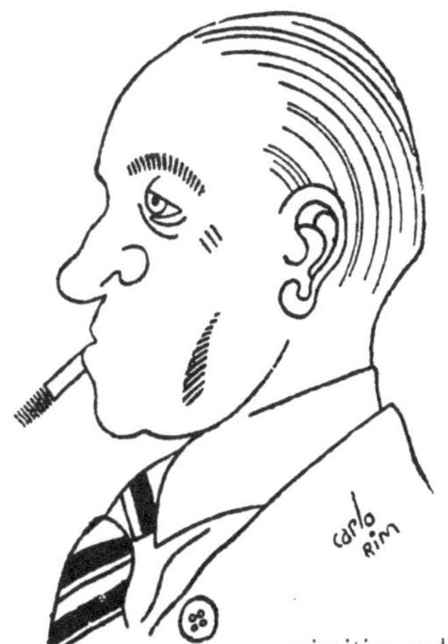

primitive cultures are either mixed with everyday life
or constitute vivid reminiscences of a recent past. The
terrible darings of a Picasso, a Brancusi, a Max Jacob, a
Tristan Tzara were, after all, more consistent with our
cultural heritage than theirs. We were used to black
fetishism, *calungas*, *ex-votos*, popular poetry, which pre-
disposed us to accept and assimilate a number of artistic
processes that in Europe represented a profound rupture
with the social environment and spiritual traditions. Our
modernists therefore quickly learned about European
avant-garde art, became acquainted with psychoanalytic
theory and shaped a type of expression that was both
local and universal, rediscovering European influence by
plunging into Brazilian detail."[204]

Deftly articulated thanks to his critical and theoretical skills, Antonio Cândido's hypothesis is not original. In 1949, Oswald de Andrade had already claimed that "primitivism, which in France stood as exoticism, was true primitivism for us in Brazil."[205] In any case, the Oswaldian vision, which Antonio Cândido elaborates into a thesis to explain the presence of primitivism in our modernism, only makes sense if we ignore the real conditions informing the intellectual production in the country. Those trips to rediscover Brazil – such a typically modernist way of getting to know our roots – only became routine in 1924, after Blaise Cendrars's first visit. At that time, primitive Brazil was as unknown to our modernist intellectuals as it was to the Europeans. What we have here is a division not only between urban and rural cultures, but also between social classes. A significant example of the precariousness of this alleged familiarity of modernist artists with Brazilian popular culture is the chapter "Macumba", from *Macunaíma*, which parodies a visit that Mário de Andrade and some of his friends made to a *terreiro* in Rio de Janeiro for the first time in their lives. Moreover, Mário de Andrade incorporated a substantial part of the habits, customs and beliefs featured in his book from a research carried out by ethnographer Theodor Koch-Grünberg — the research was published only in German, his native language, under the title *Vom Roraima zum Orinoco*.[206]

These divisions between urban and rural cultures, and between social classes, lead our argument to a thorny issue, which cannot be avoided. It's one of Antonio Cândido's most outstanding disciples, literary critic Roberto Schwarz, who will briefly guide the narrative montage of this book. Tackling the "discomfort" present in our daily lives – the widespread feeling that our cultural life is somehow fake –, Schwarz highlights the positivity of the inversion operated by our modernism, especially through Oswald de Andrade, whose style he mimics:

"Going back however to the sense of plagiarism and inadequacy that Western culture prompts in Brazil, it is clear that Oswald's program represented a shift. Now it is Brazilian primitivism that projects a modern sense to the worn-out European culture, that is, free from Christian maceration and capitalist utilitarianism. The Brazilian experience would represent a peculiar cardinal point and a utopian virtuality on the map of contemporary history (something similar is insinuated in the poems of Mário de Andrade and Raul Bopp regarding the Amazonian sloth). Therefore, the evaluative turnaround operated by our modernism was profound: for the first time, an ongoing Brazilian process is appreciated and measured in a global context as having something to offer in that chapter. Instead of gawking, Oswald put forward an irreverent cultural attitude with no feelings of inferiority, whose metaphor was the devouring of the other: it was a copy, yes, but a regenerative one."[207]

The praise has a catch though: "the passage of time brings to light the naivety and also the unreasonable nationalism in these extraordinary proposals."[208] In Schwarz's understanding, the diffuse feeling regarding the mimicking character of Brazilian culture is a false consciousness that results from a mistaken perception of reality. Such a feeling would have arisen after the country's political independence, when the question of an autonomous national culture arose. During colonial and imperial times, the adoption of European aesthetic canons and cultural values was not considered a demerit, but rather a sign of distinction. The search for an authentic national culture led to this sense of inadequacy, as there is no set of collective ideas and values that reflected the national reality and with which Brazilians could fully identify. However, this perception – the origin of the discomfort – and the search for substitutes implied a false problem:

where one sees a "cultural" issue – the lack of organicity
between popular culture and elite culture –, there is in fact
the most brutal social inequality. "The distressing feeling of
being in a mimicking civilization" – says Schwarz – "is not
produced by imitation, which is present in any case, but by
the social structure of the country."[209]

According to Roberto Schwarz, this false problem
reveals itself in the failure or mystification resulting from
the attempts to avoid imitation and secure national authenticity. The biggest paradox can be pointed out precisely in
the most radical agents: the "Pau-Brasil" denial of European
cultural values develops into a search for positive values
dispersed in colonial life; however, virtually everything one
can find is associated with a colonial experience founded on
the exploitation of slave labor. By shifting gears from nega-
tive to positive, Brazilian modernism ends up promoting an
ideological cover-up, replacing the pessimism regarding our
civilizational infeasibility with the optimistic expectation of
an unfeasible redemption in the psychological, metaphysical,
cultural and artistic spheres. Thus, anyone looking for the sap
of nationality in the "distant heartlands, far from the Atlantic
coast and its foreign associations,"[210] would come across an
anthill, which is precisely what happens to a character in
Quarup, Antônio Callado's novel.

Not far from Schwarz in her assessment of the modernists, Otília Arantes argues that Lúcio Costa's narrative scheme
seeks to reconcile the commitment to the modernizing state
of Getúlio Vargas – as with the developmentalist administration of Juscelino Kubitschek later on – and the respect
for the national historic heritage, a project that ends up in
a sort of conservative modernization that silences social
inequity. In a second turn of the explanatory screw, Otília
warns that *grace, sensuality* and *lightness* – which are the
features generally attributed to our architecture – have been
treated by national praisers and international detractors as
characteristics arising from the lack of a material basis for

the implantation of modern architecture in our tropical soil.
For the former, it is an undeniable proof of our originality,
which miraculously manages to transform a deficiency into
a quality; for the latter, it is an irrational deviation that leads
to programmatic indiscipline and formal excess, as in Max
Bill's scathing comments. According to the author, the international success of Brazilian modern architecture exposed
the very essence of international modern architecture: "It
was the distortion carried out by the copy that revealed in
the (tropical) daylight the hidden truth of the original. The
aesthetic bias praised as a national stamp ultimately exposed
the inherent formalism: the very abstraction of spaces ruled
by capital – an abstraction that was smuggled in the false
bottom of the Modern Movement."[211]

Roberto Schwarz's explanation – and, to some extent,
also that of Otília Arantes – draws from dialectical materialism to suggest that the economic infrastructure overdeter-
mines the cultural superstructure. His text, however, bumps
into Oswald de Andrade's insight: treating pre-colonial values
– prior to European interdicts, such as Christian catechesis,
restrained sexuality and erudite discourse – as utopian vectors of resistance.[212] In the ambiguities and contradictions
of the modernist movement, there is nevertheless a set of
values that, in its specific context – the nationalism of the
Vargas' administration – constitutes a real resistance against
equally real enemies. Amidst its many formulations, Brazilian
modernism converges in the identification of a crucial problem: dependence on the foreign element. If it is true that in
the 1920s modernist intellectuals proved incapable of adding
class struggle to the equation, it should also be noted that
they identified colonialist and imperialist mechanisms as the
enemy. In this specific context, the cultural and aesthetic
autonomy they were seeking at the time had a positive
value. Excavating this swampy territory is not, therefore, a
useless endeavor, if we want to understand how a vision
of Brazil was formulated that wavered between ideological

cover-up and transformative utopian promise – to some extent in the dynamic balance of a pendulum.

Another main character enters the scene for the next round of expeditions: Roberto Burle Marx (1909-1994), who traveled constantly to the most remote corners of the country. In the evolution of modern Brazilian architecture, the landscape designer will play a structuring role, not only for his recognized personal talent and innovative work, but also for his contributions in sanctioning a series of modern buildings as true *Brazilian specimens*. Throughout his extensive professional life – where he had the unique opportunity to partner up with Lúcio Costa, Oscar Niemeyer, Affonso Eduardo Reidy, Rino Levi, Vilanova Artigas and other first and second-rate stars of our architecture[213] –, Burle Marx followed many different paths, carried out different experiments, but always remained faithful to an original value: a garden must reintegrate man into his natural landscape.

The teachings he received at a very young age from Lúcio Costa were so embedded in his way of seeing the world that he seemed not to be aware of the fact. In several interviews – which are the only material available, given his refractory attitude towards the *theoretical* text –, Burle Marx's references to the old master are always sympathetic, mostly concerning his initiation in the art of landscaping and the rich experience of having had a personal relationship with Lúcio Costa. However, he never talks about intellectual influence. In an interview with Damián Bayón in the 1970s, he says: "When I was young, I lived on the same street as Lúcio Costa. He met me when I was 14 or 15, and that fact contributed a lot to my career. He saw the garden I was making in my own house and, as he was building a home for the Schwartz family at that time, he invited me to make that garden too."[214]

The decisive role played in his life by the discovery of Brazilian plants displayed as exotic specimens in a Berlin garden is recurrent in texts regarding Burle Marx's career.

According to the landscaper himself, who mentions this fact
several times, the episode was indeed crucial: "I made a trip
to Germany in 1928, when I lived in Berlin for a year and a
half. This trip influenced me a lot. In the Dahlem Botanical
Garden, which was an extraordinary garden, I saw for the
first time a large number of Brazilian plants being used for
landscaping purposes. We Brazilians did not use them, as we
considered them vulgar. At that moment, I understood that
the inspiration in my country should rely on autochthonous
species."[215] There is no way to know how reliable this memory
is, but it is unlikely that in 1928 a sudden fascination with
Brazilian autochthonous plants led Burle Marx to the conviction of a necessary use. After all, there is a step to be taken
here: it is not a plastic-landscaping valorization that leads
to an exclusivist use, but a deeper judgment as to the *desir-
ability* of such a practice, which only becomes possible in his
experience throughout the 1930s.

His first professional work, the garden for Alfredo
Schwartz's house, from 1932, brought him into close contact with Lúcio Costa at a time when the master was under
the influence of Gregori Warchavchik. The Russian architect
had already highlighted the garden in a series of residential
projects in São Paulo, with the collaboration of his wife, Mina
Klabin. Warchavchik, albeit an emigrant, was not oblivious
to the debate going on in the modernist environment of São
Paulo and dealt with the problem of Brazilianness, even if in
a subsidiary way, since he lacked the experience and deeper
understanding of the issues involved.[216] In the 1927 house on
Rua Santa Cruz, the architect mentioned both the back porch
and the garden as elements that attested to his concern for
national traditions and the native landscape. According to
Agnaldo Farias,

> "The back façade with its porch formed by the sprawling
> roof shows a certain familiarity with traditional Brazilian
> constructions, which one cannot perceive by looking

House on Bahia Street, São Paulo,
facade and veranda with hammock,
1929. Architect Gregori Warchavchik,
garden by Mina Klabin. Warchavchik
family collection

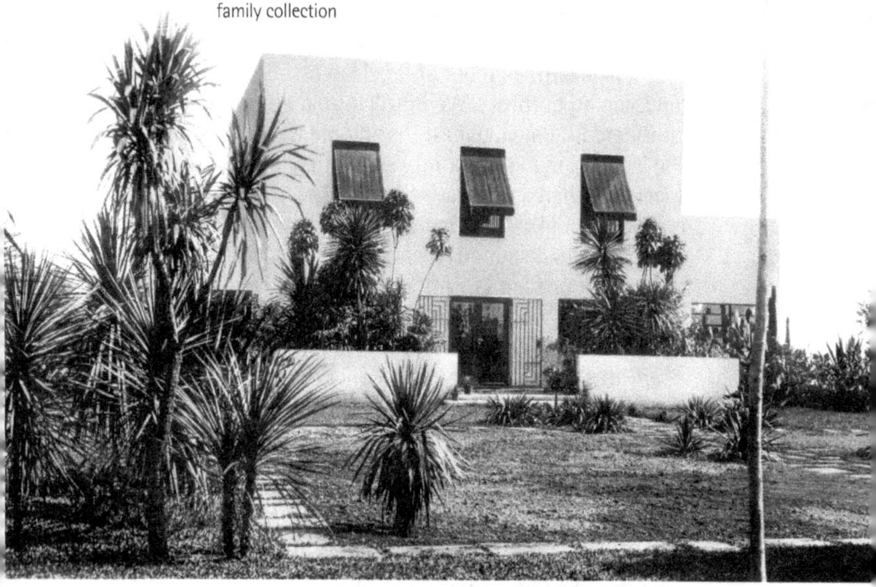

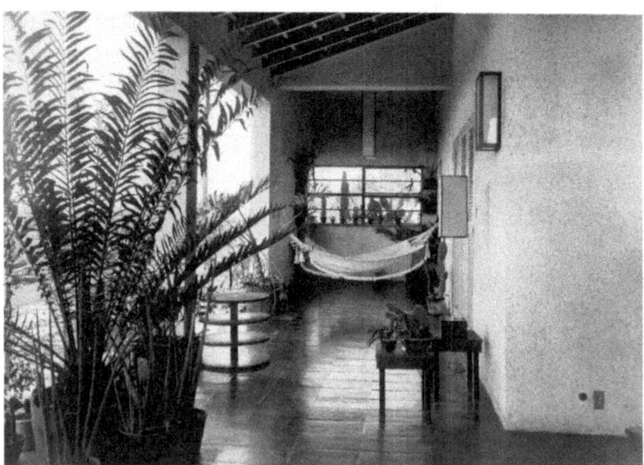

only at the main façade. Warchavchik claims that, in addition to the landscaping carried out by his wife, Mina – which, incidentally, would always be an expressive presence in his future works –, this element would be an instance of his attempt to build an architecture that incorporated the country's traditions."[217]

This concern with traditional elements will be abandoned in his later works, but not the relevance of the gardens, which he understood as a counterpoint to the geometric forms of the architectural project. In a 1930 letter sent to architect Sigfried Giedion, secretary general of Ciam, Warchavchik elaborated on the role of vegetation in his projects: "Our most efficient allies, at least in Brazil, are the tropical nature that so favorably frames the modern house – the cactus and other superb plants – and the magnificent light, which highlights the clear and crisp outline of the buildings against the dark green background of the gardens."[218] The vegetation as a tropical frame for the modern building had a limited development in the joint work of the Warchavchik couple; it seems, however, that the formulation was noticed by a young Lúcio Costa, who had just abandoned the neo-colonial hosts and had not yet found his own path within the modern scene.

The unbuilt projects from these uncertain years, called by the architect *chômage*,[219] resulted, according to him, from his systematic study of the major figures of European modern architecture: "the clientele continued to request houses of a certain *style* – French, English, *colonial* –, things I could no longer do. With no work, I began creating houses for conventional plots of twelve meters by thirty-six – *Houses With No Owner*. And I studied in depth the proposals and works of the creators: Gropius, Mies van der Rohe, Le Corbusier."[220] Examining these projects, we do not find much influence from Mies van der Rohe, but they do show that Lúcio Costa was quite familiar with the Corbusian vocabulary, especially

the use of pilotis, and also with the rigorous geometry of
Gropius,[221] although in a style quite similar to Warchavchik's:
simple, homogeneous volumes in contrast with the tropical
vegetation. In the so-called houses with no owner, which
were published in his book/testament, the presence of vegetation is obvious: in two of the drawings you can see hammocks suspended by pilotis, as in Monlevade, in 1934, and,
three decades later, in the Brazil Pavilion at the 13th Milan
Triennale, from 1964.[222] Still in the 1930s, he would design
a farm for his brother-in-law along the same lines, but now
exhibiting greater control of modern formal elements, pulling back the partition wall on the ground floor to create a
balcony, a formula repeated with great success at the Park
Hotel São Clemente years later.

Having received a double invitation from Lúcio Costa
– to become a professor at the National School of Fine
Arts and a partner in an office in Rio de Janeiro –, Gregori
Warchavchik exerts a momentary but significant influence
on Lúcio Costa, which tends to be overlooked by critics and
historians. His experimentations – the articulation between
modern architecture and the Brazilian landscape – entailed
a challenge both in the conceptual dimension and in the
required scientific knowledge, for which he was not quite
prepared and would never be. Given the intense contact
between the two, Warchavchik's intuition becomes central
to Lúcio Costa, and it is his young pupil, Burle Marx, who will
then come up with the appropriate solution. Coincidentally
or not, in order to obtain the much-desired stamp of
Brazilianness for his garden in his first landscaping project
of greater cultural significance, Burle Marx makes use of the
cactus, much appreciated by Mina Warchavchik[223] – and also
present in the paintings of Tarsila do Amaral with their stubborn *mandacarus* – to achieve the much-coveted Brazilian
identity for his garden. Interestingly, in regard to influence,
the dynamics between Warchavchik and Costa changed
direction in 1946, when the Ukrainian architect resorted to

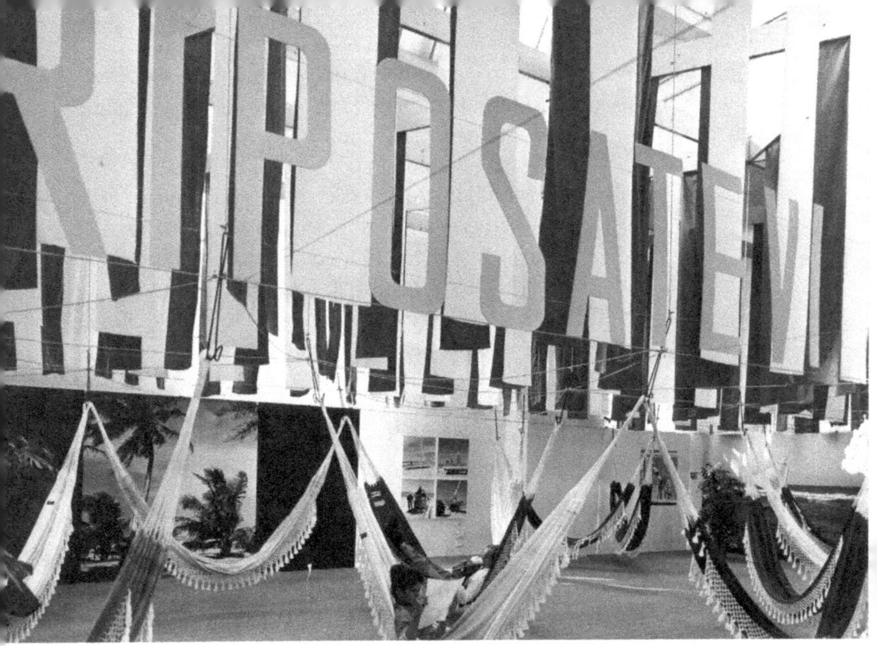

Riposatevi, Brazilian participation in
the Milan Triennial. Lúcio Costa, 1964.
Archive of Casa da Arquitectura

Marjorie Prado House, Pernambuco
beach, Guarujá SP, c.1950. Architect
Gregori Warchavchik. Warchavchik
family collection

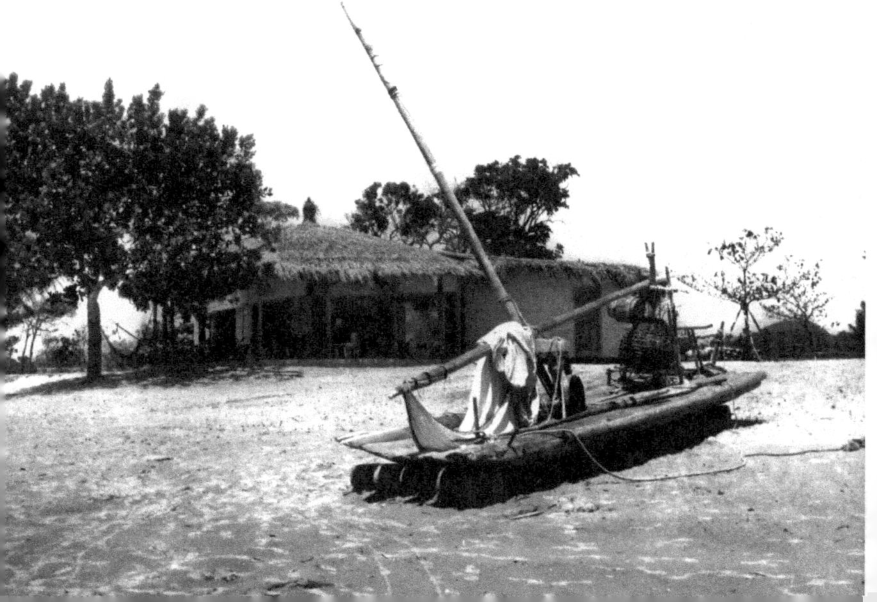

more radically nativist criteria for the design of a small social pavilion on a seaside farm on Pernambuco beach, in Guarujá, owned by Marjorie da Silva Prado.[224]

In 1935, as Director of Parks, subordinated to the Architecture and Construction Department of the city of Recife, Burle Marx designed the Cactário Madalena, an area dedicated to cacti in the Euclides da Cunha square. This and other garden proposals, while causing a stir among Recife's elites, garnered the sympathy of modern intellectuals, such as Gilberto Freyre, Joaquim Cardozo, Cícero Dias and others. The conservatives, "led by Mário Melo, from the Archaeological Institute of Recife, react to what they understand to be an attempt to send the city back to the jungle."[225] In a dispute where both sides claim to stand for Brazilianness – curiously reenacting the confrontation between moderns and neo-colonials in the previous decade –, the weapons of choice are quite different: while Melo evokes the local heroic past, which would have been offended by the removal of a monument, Burle Marx counterattacks by saying that

Euclides da Cunha Square, ink on paper, Recife PE. Roberto Burle Marx, 1935. Collection of the Instituto Burle Marx

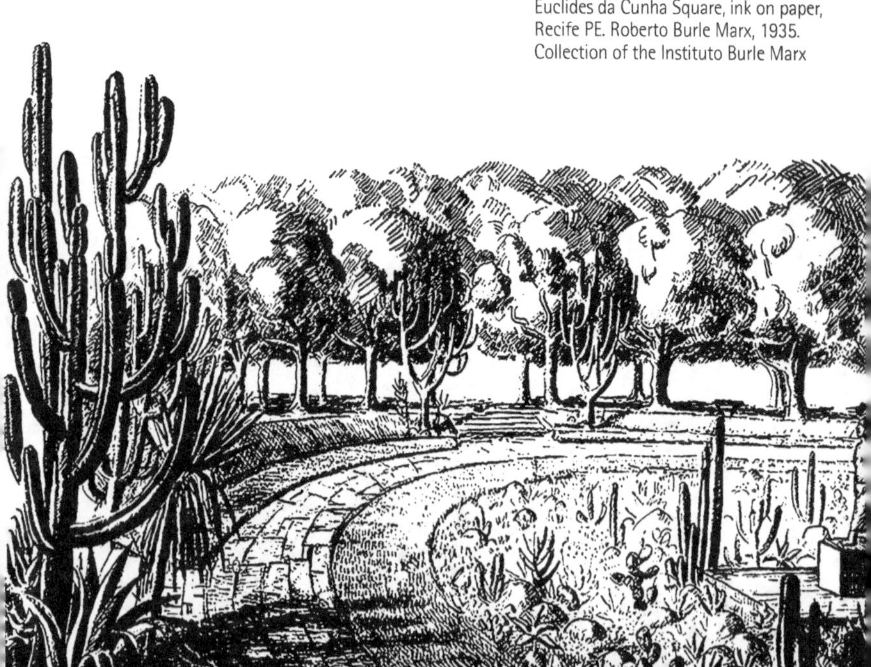

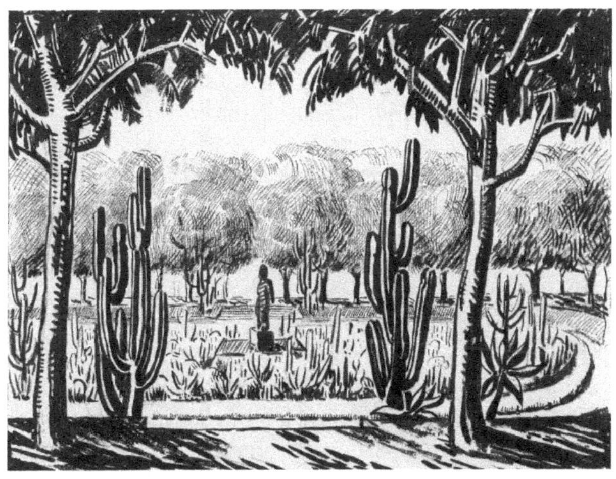

Euclides da Cunha Square, Recife PE, paper/ink, 32 x 49 cm. Roberto Burle Marx, 1935. Collection of the Sítio Roberto Burle Marx (Special Unit of the National Historic and Artistic Heritage Institute / Iphan)

he is "sowing the *Brazilian spirit* and spreading a *sense of Brazilianness*."[226]

Burle Marx's defense of the use of cactus in Recife is based on its landscaping qualities, but also on its suitability as a plant native to the region. He advocates the almost exclusivistic use of local specimens, making an exception only for situations where there is great similarity of climate between regions.[227] In Brazil, however, where the number of native species of trees and shrubs is endless, there is no reason to resort to exotic plants, whose greatest harm is the fact that they transform the *character of the landscape*.[228] His work abroad is often met with stupor, or even disappointment, for he adopts the same principle, focusing on native plants, as is the case of the garden he designed in Vienna in 1962[229] and the one for the Caracas International Exhibition (which would later become Parque del Este) in the second half of the 1950s.[230]

Reactions to Burle Marx's projects are based on ingrained preferences associating the garden to the thrill of the unknown, which is a taste encouraged by landscaping traditions that worship the exotic. The Brazilian landscaper, as a rule, avoids the unusual, so in his work you will not find an exuberant park of tropical plants in the middle of a modern city with a temperate climate or a park with European vegetation disciplined through rigid geometry in the midst of the urban chaos in some poor, populous country.[231] What appears to be a matter of preference or arbitrariness has strong motivations which are not quite visible at first glance, as such motivations cannot be found in Burle Marx's sparse statements, nor in his material output, since the final result does not make the logic underlying the equation explicit. So it is necessary to look for such motivations elsewhere.

In his creative process, Burle Marx first dedicates himself to an extensive survey of the variability of species existing in their natural state and to an in-depth research on the relationships they maintain with each other and with the environment in which they flourish. Afterwards, he moves on to formal elaboration, the aesthetic creation per se, where the raw material rises to the status of art according to the artist's subjective or objective values. The landscaper often draws an interesting analogy between his work and painting and other arts, which reveals how he understands the second stage of his practice: "I don't want to make a garden that looks like a painting. But I also cannot fail to recognize that painting had a great influence on my conceptions of landscaping. These are principles, general principles of art, which are indissolubly linked together. That's the most important thing. Knowing how to establish a contrast, how to use a vertical, the analogy of shapes, volumes, the sequence of certain values. These are principles that can be applied to music, to poetry. Without these principles, I believe, you simply cannot practice any form of art."[232]

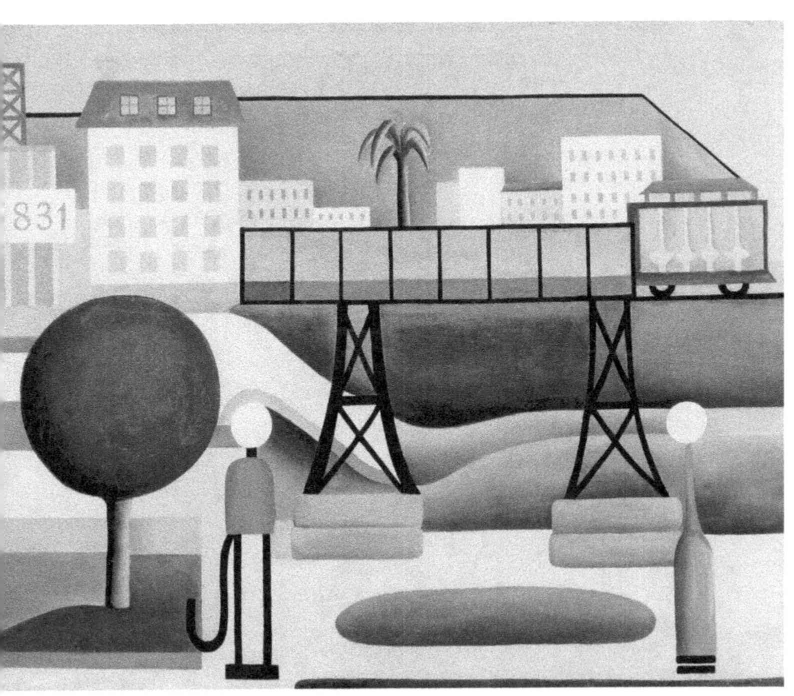

São Paulo (135831), oil on canvas,
67 x 90 cm. Tarsila do Amaral, 1924.
Pinacoteca do Estado de São Paulo.
Photo by Romulo Fialdini/Tempo
Composto

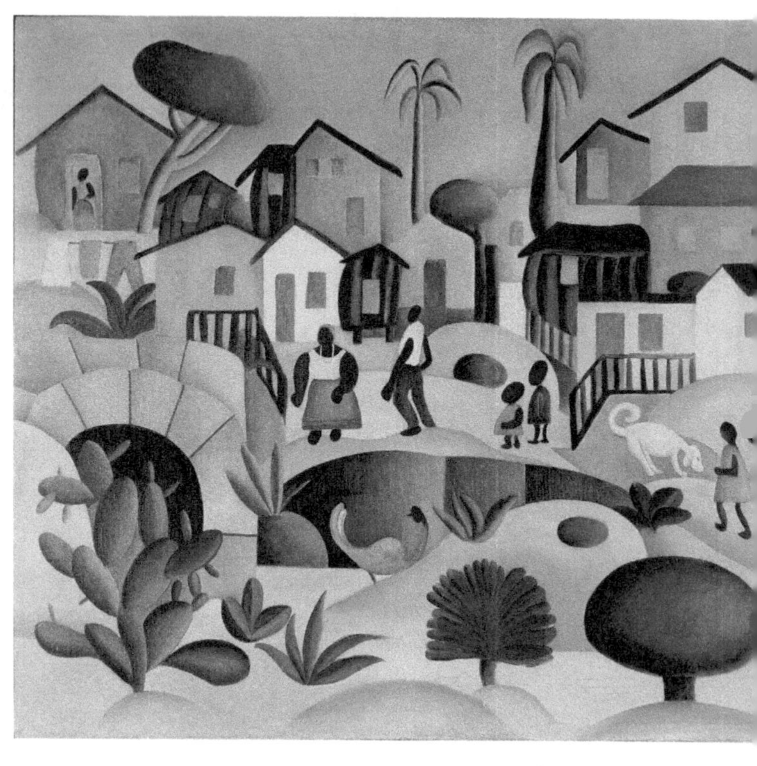

Morro da favela (Hill of the Slum),
oil on canvas, 64 x 76 cm. Tarsila do
Amaral, 1924. Private collection. Photo
by Romulo Fialdini/Tempo Composto

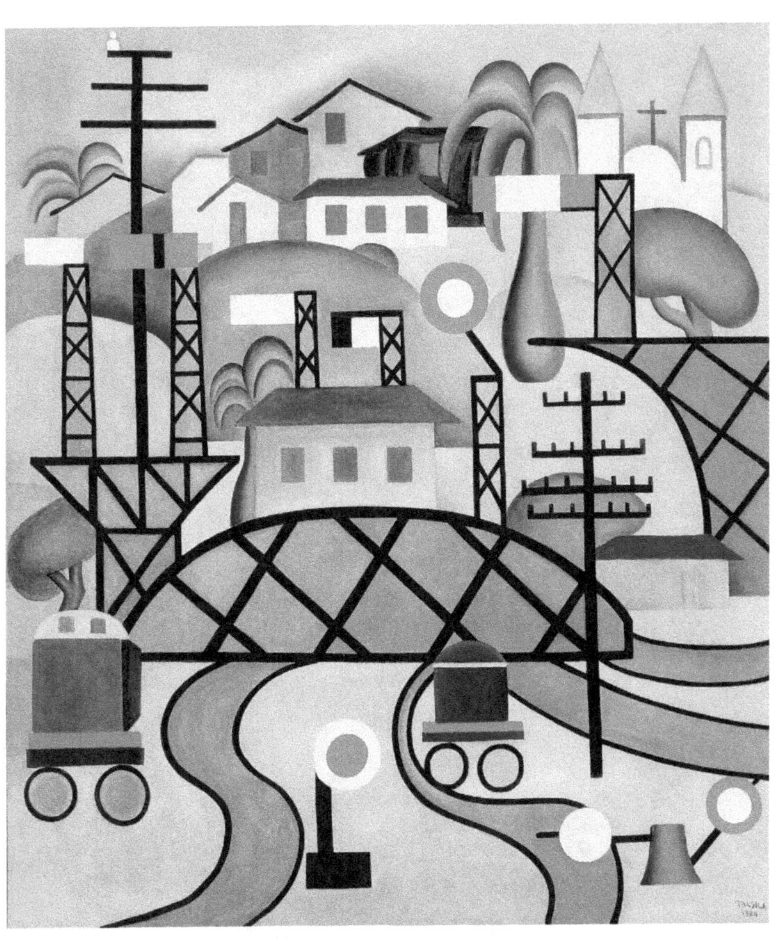

E.F.C.B., oil on canvas, 142 x 127 cm.
Tarsila do Amaral, 1924. Museum of
Contemporary Art of the University
of São Paulo – MAC-SP. Photo by
Romulo Fialdini/Tempo Composto

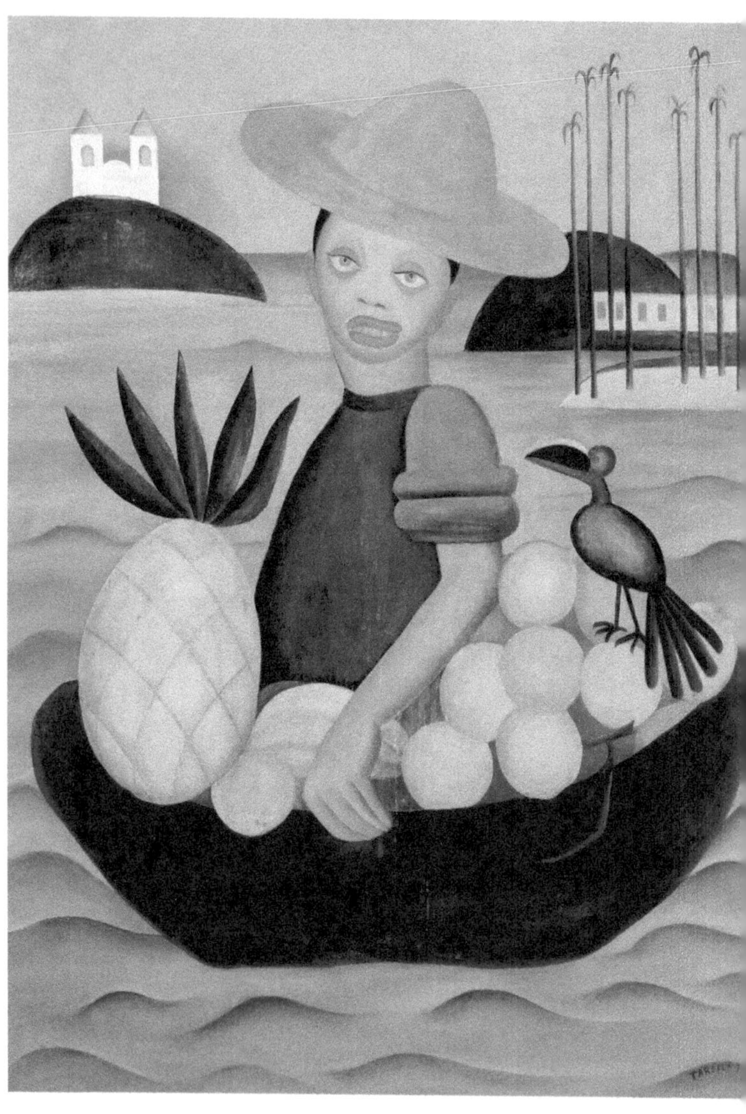

308

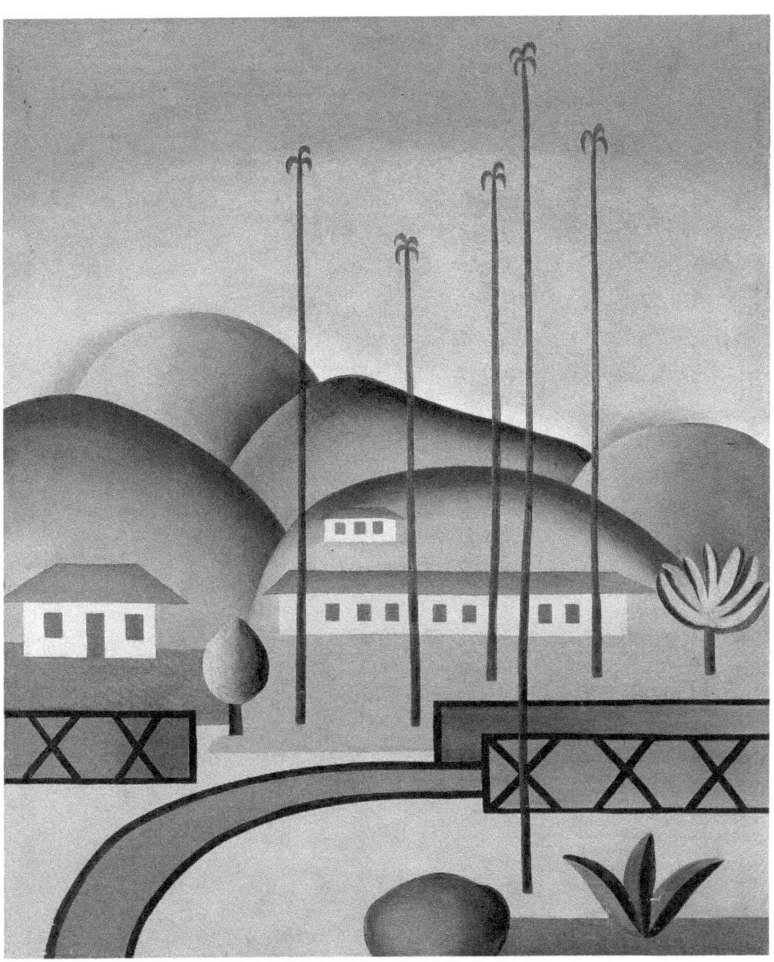

On the opposite page
Vendedor de frutas (Fruit Vendor), oil
on canvas, 108 x 84 cm. Tarsila do
Amaral, 1925. Museum of Modern Art
of Rio de Janeiro. Photo by Romulo
Fialdini/Tempo Composto

Palmeiras (Palm Trees), oil on canvas,
86 x 73.5 cm. Tarsila do Amaral, 1925.
Private collection. Photo by Romulo
Fialdini/Tempo Composto

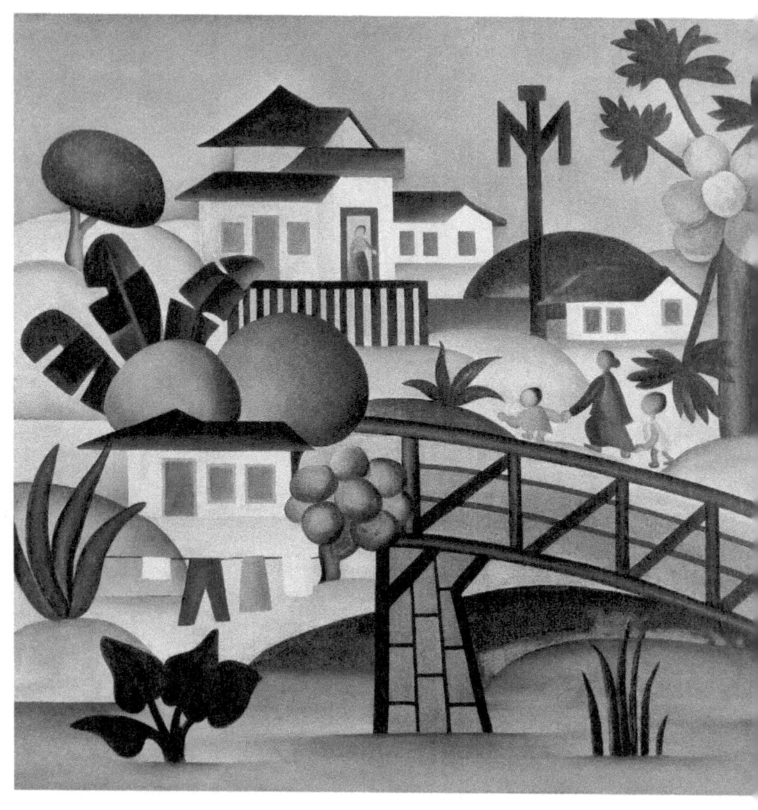

O mamoeiro (The Papaya Tree), oil on
canvas, 65 x 70 cm. Tarsila do Amaral,
1925. Mário de Andrade Collection
/ IEB USP. Photo by Romulo Fialdini/
Tempo Composto

310

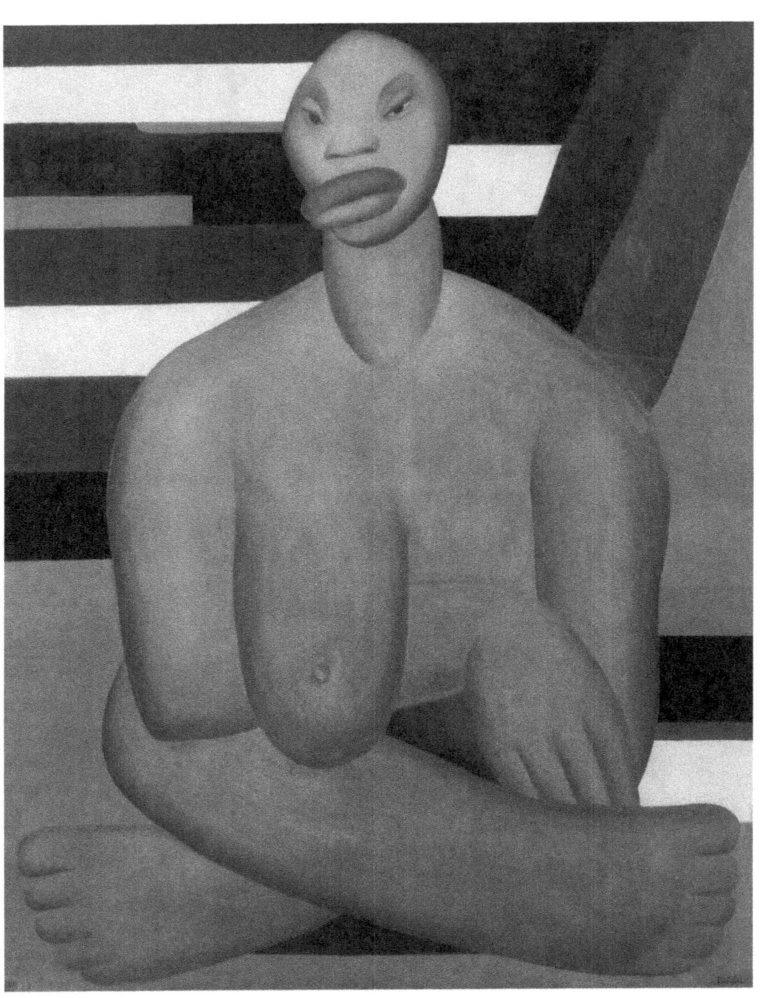

A Negra (The Black Woman), oil on canvas, 100 x 80 cm. Tarsila do Amaral, 1923. Collection of the Museum of Contemporary Art of the University of São Paulo – MAC-SP. Photo by Romulo Fialdini/Tempo Composto

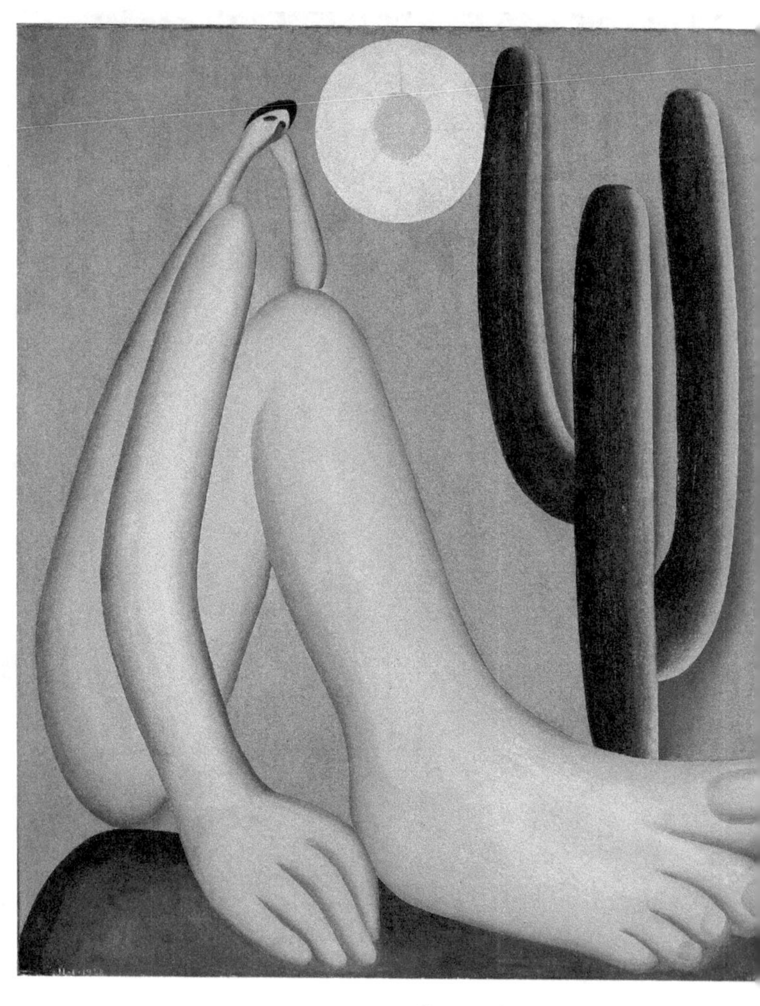

Abaporu, oil on canvas, 85 x 73 cm. Tarsila do Amaral, 1928. Latin American Art Museum of Buenos Aires. Photo by Romulo Fialdini/Tempo Composto

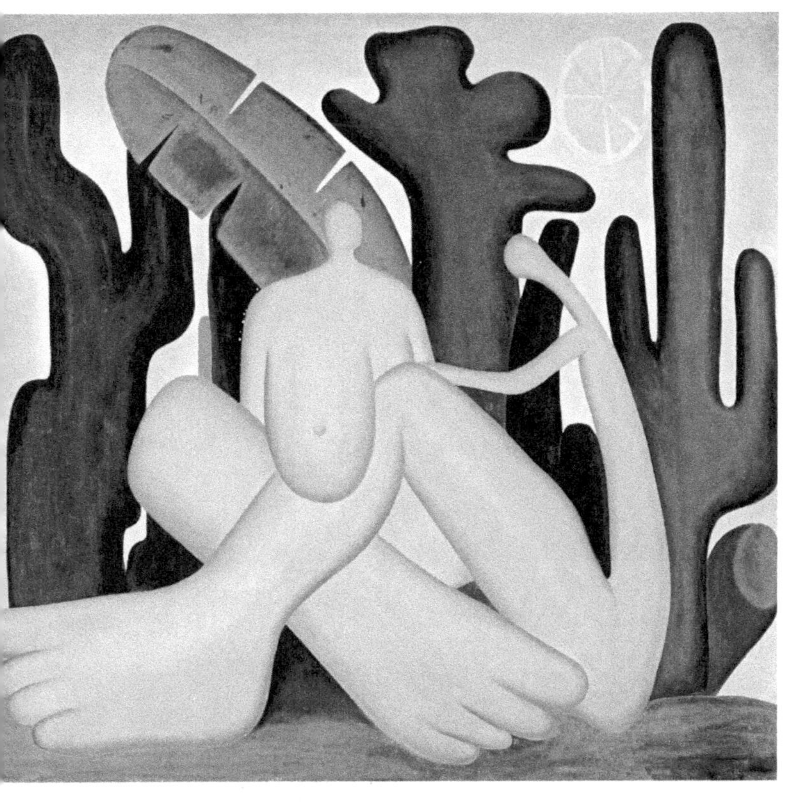

Antropofagia, oil on canvas, 126 x 142 cm. Tarsila do Amaral, 1929. José and Paulina Nemirovsky Foundation. Photo by Romulo Fialdini/Tempo Composto

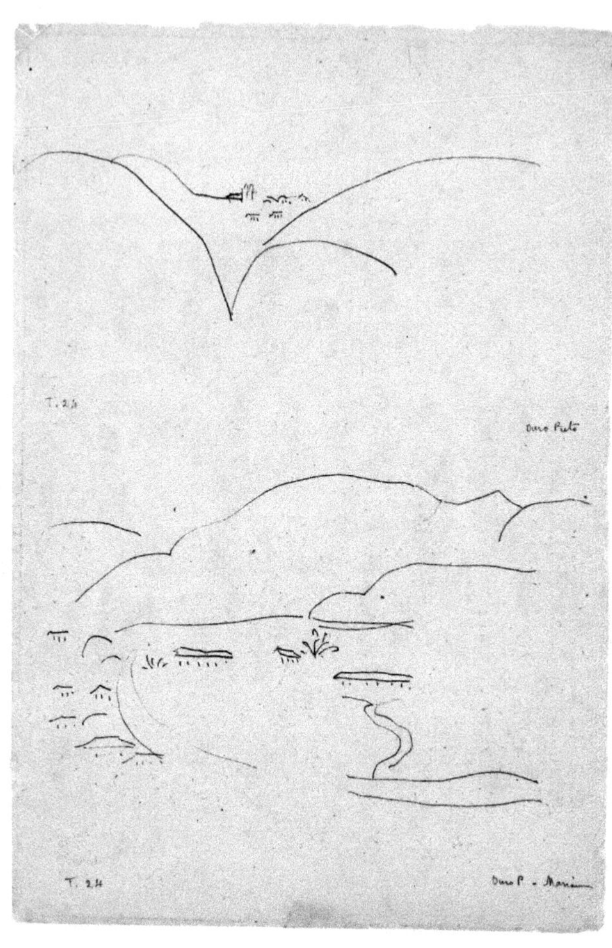

Two panoramas: Ouro Preto e Mariana,
graphite on paper, 31.6 x 21.7 cm.
Tarsila do Amaral, 1924. FAMA
Museum Collection. Photo by Rogério
Emílio

314

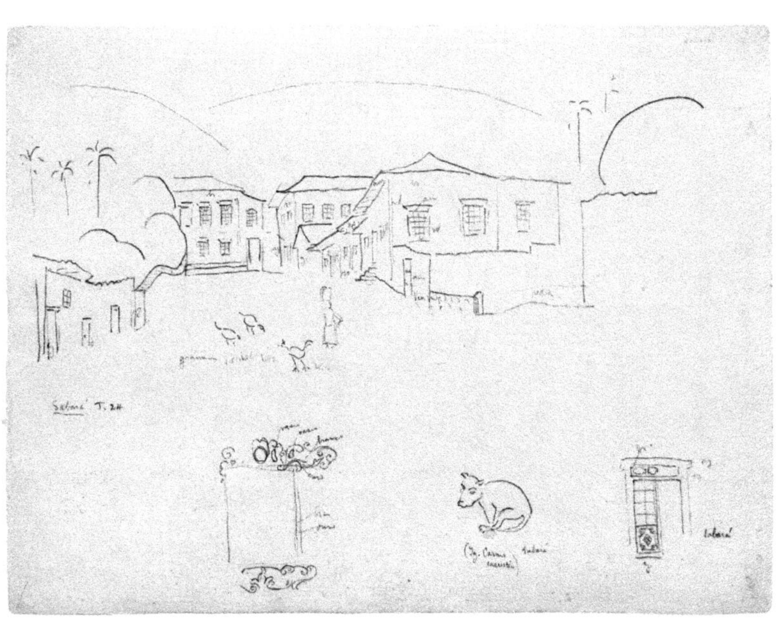

Street of Sabará: Details of
Ornamentation, graphite on paper,
21.6 x 31.8 cm. Tarsila do Amaral,
1924. FAMA Museum Collection

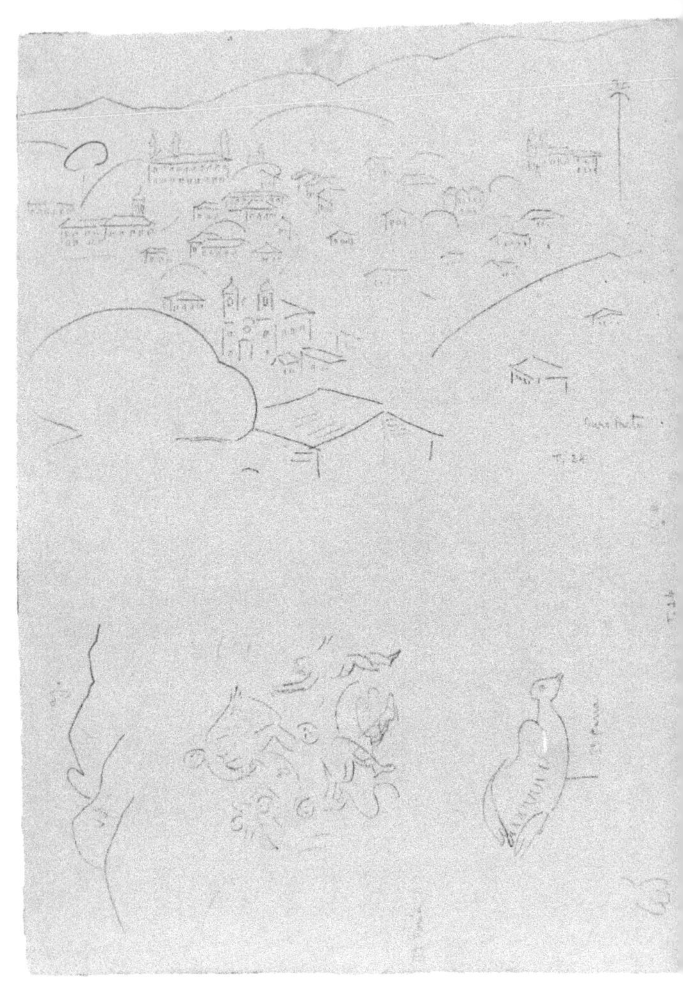

Panorama of Ouro Preto and Studies,
graphite on paper, 31.8 x 23.6 cm.
Tarsila do Amaral, 1924. Collection
of FAMA Museum. Photo by Rogério
Emílio

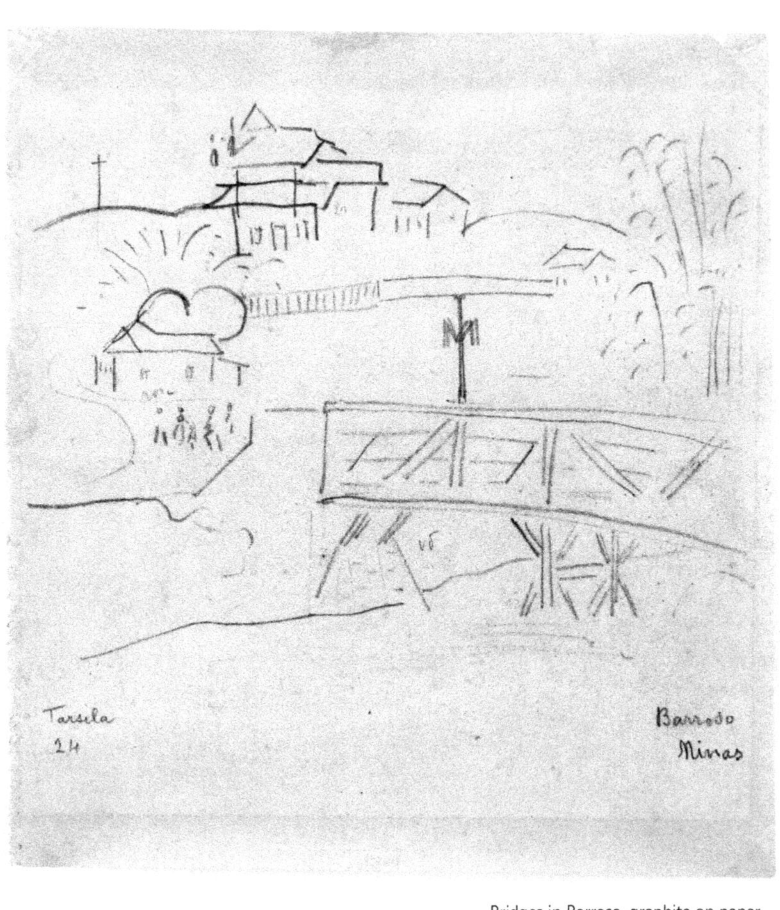

Bridges in Barroso, graphite on paper,
24 x 23.3 cm. Tarsila do Amaral, 1924.
FAMA Museum Collection. Photo by
Rogério Emílio

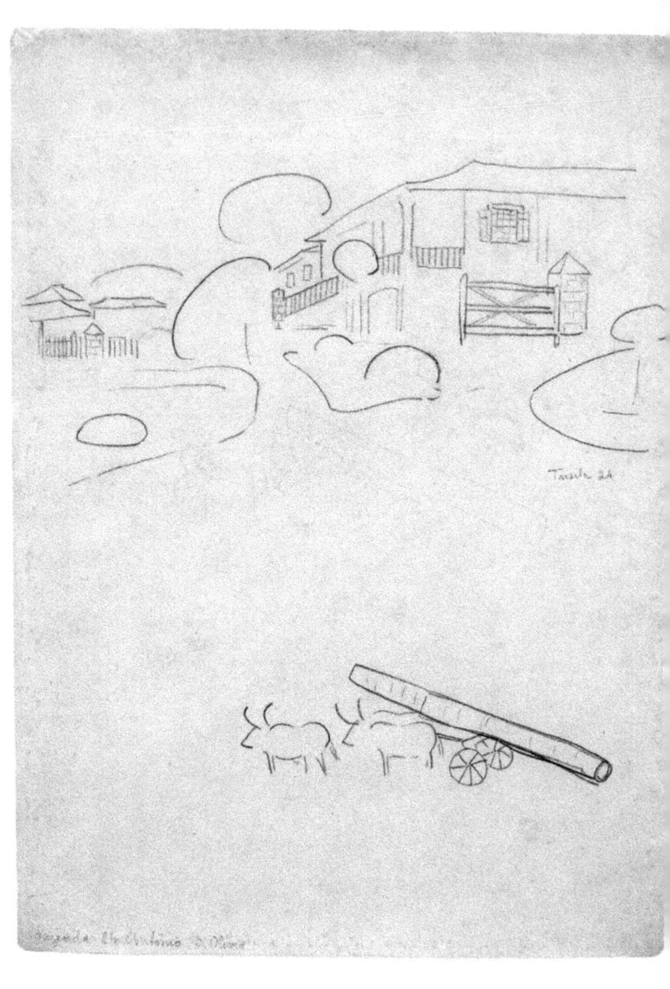

Main house and oxcart, graphite
on paper, 31.2 x 23.3 cm. Tarsila
do Amaral, 1924. FAMA Museum
Collection. Photo by Rogério Emílio

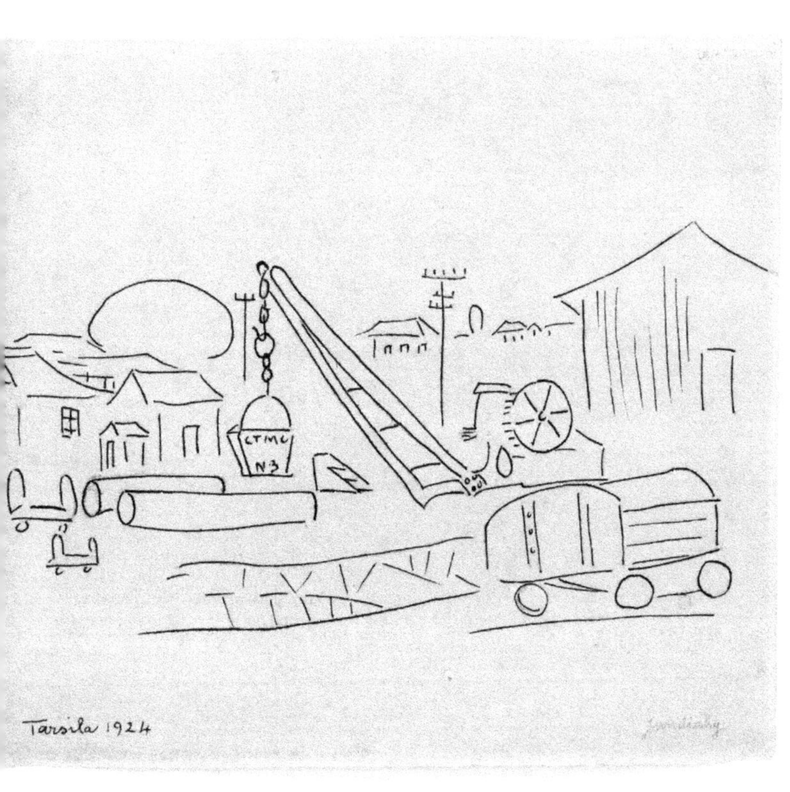

Unloading, ink on paper, 15 x 21.3
cm. Tarsila do Amaral, 1924. FAMA
Museum Collection. Photo by Rogério
Emílio

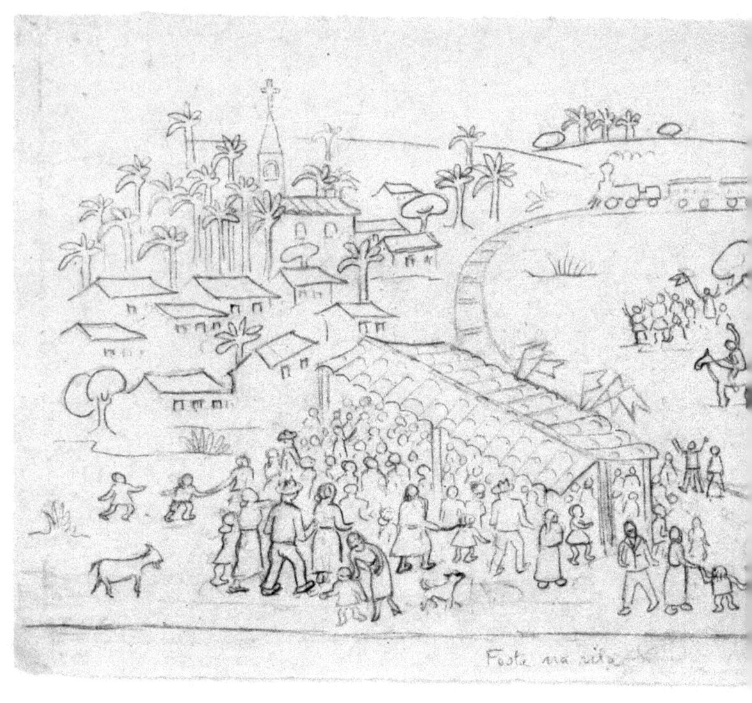

Village Festival, graphite on paper, 20 x 25.1 cm. Tarsila do Amaral, 1940s. FAMA Museum Collection. Photo by Rogério Emílio

The initial stage in Burle Marx's work is researching each biome, which forces him to take many trips where seriousness is met with enjoyment. Commenting on a scientific expedition carried out by the landscape artist to the Amazon – a trip that lasted 53 days covering, among other places, Boa Vista, Serra do Caiapó, Cuiabá, Porto Velho, Manaus and Belém –, historian Vera Beatriz Siqueira elaborates a commentary interspersed with passages taken from the expedition's report: "The main objective of the expedition is 'to expand the gardening vocabulary through the discovery of new plants', in addition to 'promoting the Brazilian flora', thus resuming the 'spirit of European travelers' from the 19th century, such as Von Martius, Saint-Hilaire and Gardner. The austere routine of observation, collection of species, documentation and cataloging, packaging of living plants, pressing and drying of material for the herbarium, combined with the habit of sleeping in camps at gas stations and having only two meals a day, contributed to intensify the scientific and adventurous feel of the trip."[233]

True to the landscaper's description, the historian does not realize how the comparison to European adventurers actually entails both differences and similarities. The voyages undertaken by foreign naturalists were scientific survey missions dedicated to the taxonomy of species; these were expeditions motivated by the botanical thinking of the time, and the goal was to expand knowledge about plants. The results fueled research in many areas, including gardening, but the purpose of the trips was more restricted. On the other hand, for Burle Marx, the trip is just a first step – the fieldwork, dedicated to collecting material; the second step, as or more important than the first, takes place on the drawing board, among drawings and sketches, and also on the actual plot where the project will be implemented. From a cultural and historical point of view, the expeditions of foreign naturalists, sponsored or promoted by central governments, constituted the civilized face of European colonialism, while the travels of the Brazilian landscape artist gained their full meaning in the design process, of which his travels are an essential part. While in the scientific and adventurous dimension the trips do share some similarities, the same cannot be said of the professional, historical and symbolic aspects.

If we are going to draw a parallel, it would be more appropriate to compare his trips to those carried out by the São Paulo modernists in the 1920s and by the Sphan architects from the 1930s onwards, the difference being that in this case the goal was not to learn about dances, customs, prayers, churches, urban residences or farms in forgotten countryside villages, but discovering orchids and bromeliads.[234] Vera Beatriz Siqueira does not associate Burle Marx's aesthetic procedures with the defense of cultural and artistic Brazilianness promoted by the artistic and architectural elite,[235] which is quite intriguing in a text in which outdoor excursions and the choice for native plants are constantly mentioned.[236] However, even though she doesn't establish such ties, the historian, resorting to a different semantic field, points out the two stages in the landscaper's work: "therefore, two procedures are articulated: the ecological and the linguistic. On the one hand, to observe and respect the plant's relationship with its habitat, its growth, germination and flowering processes; on the other hand, to transform each plant into a sign of a coherent plastic discourse."[237]

Ever since the beginning of his career, Burle Marx sought in Lúcio Costa a set of cultural values that converged to "Brazilianness". His work undergoes some changes in terms of expression, but the core remains: the choice for native plants. The initial hegemony of a more ecological vision, which has its great expression in the gardens of Recife, gradually gives way to formal concerns increasingly aligned with the evolution of modern art in Europe. In the first half of the 1940s, when he worked in the gardens for the Ministry of Education and Health, Burle Marx abandoned classical formalizations in favor of abstraction. The landscaper himself

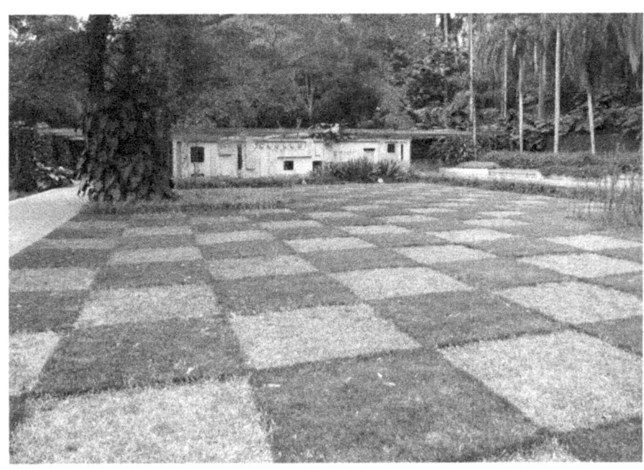

Above
Roberto Burle Marx Park, São Paulo SP.
Roberto Burle Marx, 1954. Photo by
José Tabacow

Below
Hans Broos House, São Paulo SP.
Landscaping by Roberto Burle Marx,
José Tabacow, and Haruyoshi Ono,
1975. Photo by José Tabacow

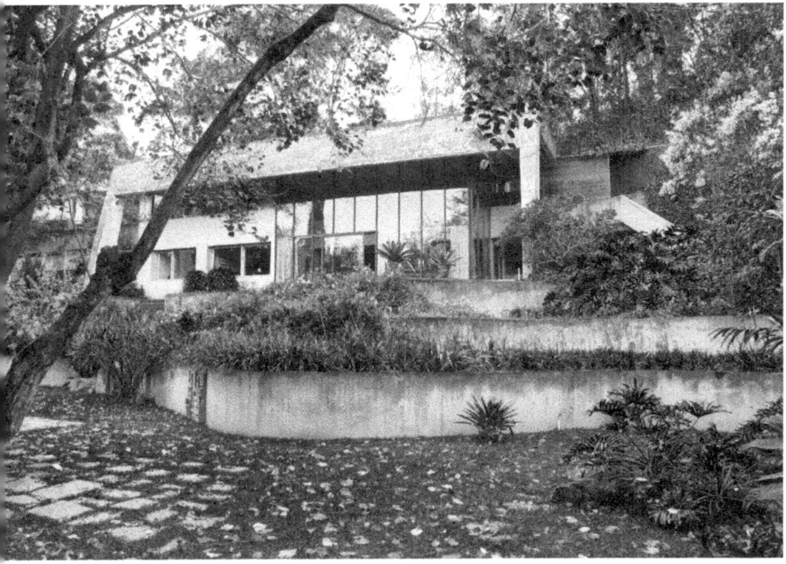

is aware of the transformation, but insists on a retroactive coherence: "Initially my gardens had an ecological focus. But this approach is quite relative. For instance, I used some very abstract stains in the MEC garden,[238] because at that time I already knew Arp. So it cannot be said that my gardens, even in the beginning, were essentially ecologically concerned."[239] Landscape architect Fernando Tábora, who collaborated for years with Burle Marx, put forward the following assessment, more in tune with the history of architecture: "His evolutionary jump from the classicism of Pernambuco to MEC's 'amoebas' is equivalent to the steps taken by the architects of the time, such as Lúcio Costa in Brazil and Villanueva in Venezuela; it's a jump from academicism to modernity. The value of Burle Marx was to have taken the leap with them."[240]

Burle Marx's landscape thinking maintains communicating vessels with ethical, aesthetic and cultural values of the modern movement, which can be attested in his works and trajectory. His assessment of the country's new capital, for which he collaborated with Lúcio Costa and Oscar Niemeyer, leaves no room for doubt: "If we compare Brasília with other Brazilian cities, the gardens are the big difference. In Brasília, constructions of all types – residential, administrative – always have green areas where people find themselves in close contact with the vegetation."[241] Regarding the park he helped to build in the Flamengo neighborhood, Burle Marx emphasized yet another purpose of landscaping, now a pedagogical one: "For me, the garden must have didactic qualities. Through the garden, many teachings can be conveyed, encouraging people to live better."[242] The structured ecological vision argues for preservation, especially in the context of a society oriented towards progress, with its great capacity for destruction: "a *Bulldozer* may very well destroy in one hour the work that nature took millions of years to finish."[243] The correct structuring for open areas in large cities is not the restitution of a natural state that has been lost, but the elaboration of an artificial space that integrates the designed

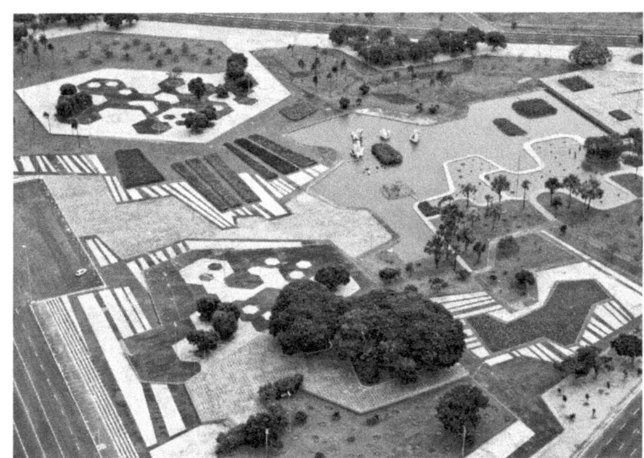

Above
Army Ministry, Brasília DF. Roberto Burle Marx, 1970. Photo by Nelson Kon

Below
Flamengo Park, Rio de Janeiro RJ. Affonso Eduardo Reidy and Roberto Burle Marx, 1964. Photo by Nelson Kon

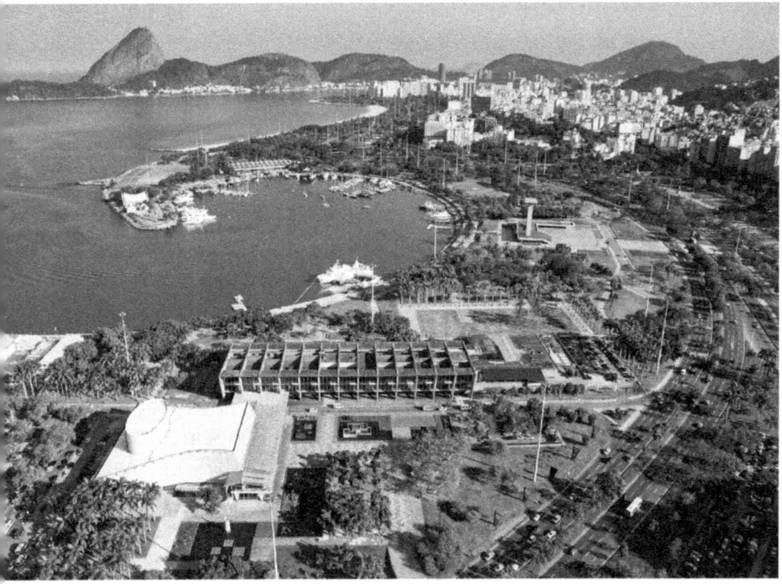

landscape and modern man, offering peace of mind, intellectual elevation and a sense of duty regarding the preservation of nature, of which the park is just a simulacrum.[244]

Mário Pedrosa, an important Brazilian art critic, dedicated at least two articles to landscape architecture that are of interest to our argument. In "Landscape Architecture in Brazil", published in *Jornal do Brasil* on January 9, 1958, Pedrosa takes up themes and arguments developed by José Lins do Rego in his article "The man and the landscape": "The fact is that this original nature, tropical and exuberant, was not well regarded by our Portuguese ancestors or even our grandparents. One was afraid of it – or, perhaps, ashamed".[245] During the long arc that goes from the colonial period to the Empire, the gardens the Portuguese planted in Brazil mirrored the inadequacy and lack of intimacy of the colonizer with our tropical nature. The gardens were "pedantic and artificial, lacking strength and vigor, without the soul of the earth that bursts forth, thriving and luxuriant, in the local bushes and plants, in the wild flowers of the fields and forests, which sometimes would approach the margins of the paths, getting pretty close to the garden fences."[246]

In Pedrosa's argument we find the same evaluative inversion observed in Lúcio Costa when he sees vernacular architecture no longer as a bundle of deficiencies of all sorts, but as a legitimate expression of the accommodation of the Brazilian man in a hostile territory. Now it is the vegetation, consistently rejected throughout history on account of its insubordination to civilizing order, that is reassessed as legitimate and desirable, for it sprouts organically in the land that shelters Brazilian society. What is questionable in the exotic gardens are not the textures, colors, masses, volumes or the odors they harbor, but the inadequacy between the man who inhabits the territory and the landscape expressed by these gardens. The method Mário Pedrosa identifies in the work of Burle Marx is similar to those adopted by Mário de Andrade and Lúcio Costa for literature, music and architecture: a first step is dedicated to researching the native flora, which involves practical and scientific knowledge founded on first-hand experiences with the biomes, which is only possible through expeditions;[247] then there's a second step dedicated to the processing of the discovered and collected specimens, which requires the technical knowledge and artistic skill necessary for the artistic design of the gardens.

Just as the knowledge of colloquial language and regional folklore contributed to the elaboration of a superior literary expression, the inventory of *modinhas* and popular songs led to the invention of a higher Brazilian music and the research on vernacular architecture, long abandoned in the interior of the country, served as the basis for a vigorous lineage of Brazilian modern architecture – the exemplary cases of Mário de Andrade, Heitor Villa-Lobos and Lúcio Costa –, the systematic and comprehensive knowledge of the flora and its ecological and climatic specificities would constitute a necessary condition – even if not a sufficient condition – for the elaboration of a relevant and adequate landscape art. Landscaping, when thought of as an art, entails a form of expression and is not restricted to the application of recent specialized knowledge coming from sciences such as botany, biology and ecology, or ancestral practices such as horticulture and gardening. The landscaper, in Mário Pedrosa's view, is the right combination between the researcher and the artist; in Brazil, this figure is represented by Burle Marx: "It was then that Burle Marx showed up; he was young, robust, native, revolutionary, and put an end to to all these prejudices. Thanks to him, Brazilian modern architecture found its environment, its integration with nature. And the plebeian national plants, such as the native crotons, of which we have more than a dozen varieties in the most beautiful and transparent shades, were granted permission to enter the new gardens. The painter in Burle Marx soon saw in the richness of these tones the ideal material to inaugurate a true landscape art in the country."[248]

Earthly Forces of Brazilian Nature

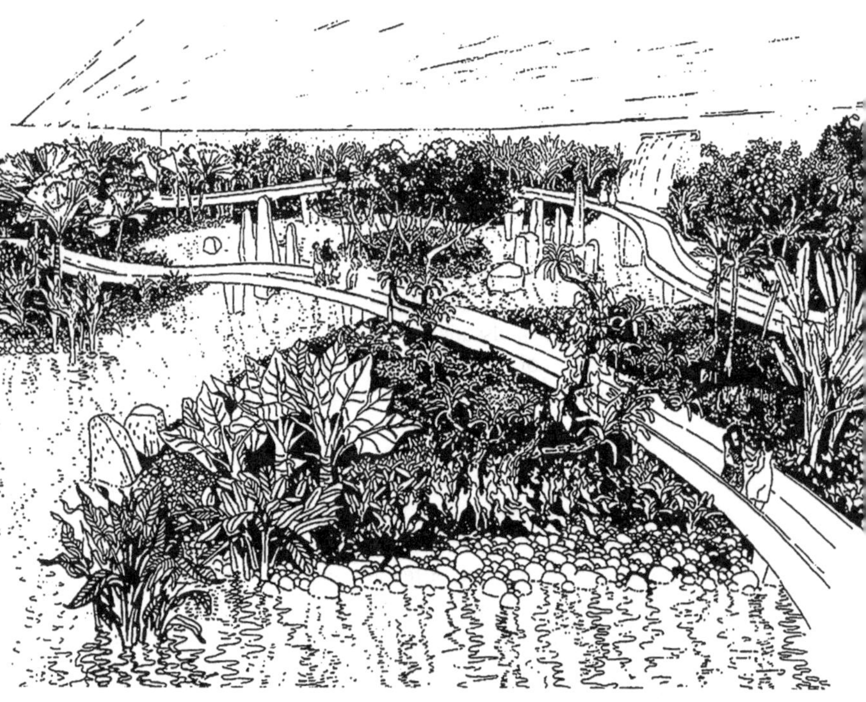

Flamengo Park, view of the Aquarium garden, not built, Rio de Janeiro RJ. Roberto Burle Marx, 1969. Burle Marx Institute Collection

I walk over the edge of a swamp
A slimy plasma crumbles
and floods the shores hemmed with mud
I'm drilling through great walls of stone
I fall deep in a forest
swollen alarmed haunted
I hear whistles and crashes
There are people welding sawing sawing
Looks like they're making earth
Huh! They're really making earth
Raul Bopp, "Cobra Norato," 1931[249]

In 1954, one of the main architectural magazines in the world – *L'Architecture d'Aujourd'hui* – published another special issue on Brazilian architecture.[250] By that time, Brazilian modern architecture – which had been gaining prominence with an expressive production since the beginning of the 1940s – had already obtained the recognition of international critics, who saw in the artistic creativity of Oscar Niemeyer's generation a counterpoint to the harshness of the second post-war period of reconstruction in Europe. The issue of the French magazine was one of several special issues dedicated to our architecture by European specialized periodicals. Interestingly, this issue features the article "The man and the landscape,"[251] by José Lins do Rego (1901-1975), a writer generally associated with the so-called second generation of Brazilian modernism, when the initial concerns about simplicity and originality had pushed the experimental literature of the 1920s towards solutions that were more accommodating to the many regionalisms. In his French article, José Lins do Rego denotes an unsuspected conviction about the nature of art, both in terms of its insertion in the cultural context and its social purpose. Far from expressing a merely personal view, his text – whose erudition makes evident a series of connections that in other authors seem more diluted – points to a broader worldview, shared not only by those intellectuals connected to the European modern movement, but also by the most expressive group of Brazilian intellectuals of the first half of that century.

In his article, Rego goes back to the well-known episode of Le Corbusier's visit at the invitation of Lúcio Costa to explain the emergence of this new architecture in Brazil, which culminated in the construction of the first Corbusian "skyscraper" in the world. Although he mentions the fact that the paternity of this new movement might be attributed to the Swiss-French architect, Lins do Rego insists on the Brazilianness of our modern architecture: "Le Corbusier was, therefore, the starting point for the new school of Brazilian architecture to express itself with great spontaneity and come up with original solutions. Like the music of Villa-Lobos, the expressive force of a Lúcio Costa and a Niemeyer was a creation intrinsically ours, something that sprang from our own life. The return to nature, and the way in which the landscape is valued as a substantial element, saved our architects from what could be considered Le Corbusier's formalism."[252] José Lins do Rego's explanation intertwines two previously mentioned arguments: that of Lúcio Costa, in his duel with Geraldo Ferraz, four years earlier; and that of Oswald de Andrade and Antonio Cândido, in their texts from 1949 and 1950. From the first comes the conviction that our architects, despite the direct influence of the Swiss-French master, were able to produce something characteristically ours; the second, the indication that the aesthetic-formal principles of European primitivism would be much more adequate to the Brazilian context. As we can see, the "miracle" pointed out by Lúcio also has the ability to multiply infinitely.

José Lins do Rego describes the accommodation of man in the Brazilian territory from the discovery and colonization by the Portuguese up to the arrival of the Swiss-French architect. In his view, the impossibility of harmony is a constant in the relationship between man and landscape throughout Brazil's history: "man was opposed to nature;"[253]

"in a permanent struggle with the landscape"; "no affection at all for the land"; "they never sought fraternal intimacy with nature."[254] Given the hostility of the environment, the majesty and exuberance of the tropical forest and the fear of the native Tapuia, the human habitat becomes a refuge, a sort of locus separated from the overwhelming natural forces. "It was therefore necessary to live in permanent struggle with the landscape, which filled us with terror. In the beginning, the Brazilian house was not an abode, but a sort of trench."[255] The "terror" provoked by the hostile environment, which was a constant in the life of the settler, causes a feeling of perennial estrangement; this is expressed in a way of settling in the territory that is a faithful reflection of the psychic dimension, with sites protected by palisades, walls and ramparts.

At the beginning of the 19th century, the arrival of the royal family with their luggage filled with artificialities further expanded the division. The transplanted aristocratic society, instead of engaging with the diverse environment they found, chose to double down on the separation, repressing the natural autochthonous influxes. "Did the fear of the original forest still remain?", asks José Lins do Rego. Then adds: "Our Second Reign reached the utmost refinement as to gardens, but almost always excluded what was truly original in our landscape. Having conquered the forest, man then sought to impose a different one, his own, with the same attitude with which he would choose slaves for his service and pleasure. It was a top-down solution, when the solution had to come from the earth, the deep roots."[256]

The refractory attitude of a disgruntled Portuguese nobility, which came here to avoid a clash with Napoleon Bonaparte, is completely at odds with the generosity, confidence and vigor demonstrated by Le Corbusier on his visit to the tropics. His ongoing search for a regeneration of the relationship with the environment through a more harmonious accommodation of man in the territory found in the immensity and virginity of large areas of the country a suitable stage for his speculations. His ideas – "the house, for him, was not a way of isolating ourselves from the world, a leper colony, a refuge from nature. He seeks for architecture a more ecological solution, consequently more human, more poetic, more profound" – seduced the attentive ears of the young architects led by Lúcio Costa: "And that's when the new school of architecture emerged in Rio. Le Corbusier had found followers in the land of the sun."[257]

Rego's argument implies a comprehensive understanding of the discursive context in which he is operating. The articulation between two semantic fields – the *biological* metaphor and the *psychologizing* terminology – explores the allegorical and literal potential of their meanings and coherently contemplates a *specific notion of culture* that pays tribute to the discussions carried out by the young modernists during the 1920s. When talking about our emerging modern architecture, the writer barely mentions the aesthetic-formal aspects; his main goal is to discern the historical and cultural significance rooted in our tradition – that is, to what extent this architecture represented an original contribution of Brazilian culture. In what seems to be a curious exposition by a non-specialist made for foreigners, one can spot deep connections with the theoretical conceptions that engendered the birth of *Brazilian modern architecture*.

José Lins do Rego reduces (or perhaps expands?) the essence of architecture to the peculiar relationship that each society establishes with the territory it chooses to live in. As for Brazil, he points out the centuries-old dispute between man and landscape, which will be mitigated by the emergence of a new *sensibility* where man and nature reconcile. This sensibility is ruled by a collective psyche that, for more than four centuries, had been marked by an atrocious terror in its relation with nature. After the establishment of modern Brazilian architecture, however, this acute fear would have finally metamorphosed into *intimacy* with the natural world:

"Houses, palaces, churches, it all becomes an extension
of the forest, the very fruits of it sprouting from the
ground. Instead of threatening the natural world around
them, these man-made structures write a symphony
with it. Man and house, man and forest, man and beast
no longer face each other as enemies. The beaches and
coconut trees, the mountains of *ipês* and *quaresmeiras*,
the banks of rivers, the hills, all the landscape provides
architects with elements that allow them to attend to
our needs with more beauty, more effectiveness and
even more humanity. Today a Brazilian might sleep on
the tenth floor of a skyscraper with his doors open, the
room surrounded by backwoods plants. The scent of
the countryside invades the house, and he feels deeply
connected to the world, more of a creature of the land,
even at such height. The house becomes a powerful vital
element. It is no longer a fortress against the environment, but a poetic reduction of nature. The house opens
its windows, protects itself from the light, makes use of
rivers, goes up and down mountains. It is the Brazilian
house that turns to the landscape where it finds all
the essential elements to be original, pleasant and
beautiful."[258]

The challenge was won, the cosmic terror defeated.
Modern architecture is the historical culmination of a process of accommodation of the Brazilian man in the tropical
territory. This abrupt transformation has something miraculous about it. Following Lins do Rego's reasoning, the abyssal
dread – resulting from the primary consciousness awakened by the portentous and inclement nature (only slightly
repressed at the time of the artificial transfer of aristocratic
society in the 19th century) – is fully abolished through the
spiritual confrontation that only the moderns were able to
carry out. This confrontation entailed the courage to integrate and accept the insurmountable barriers of atavistic

forces. The Brazilian man, in order to remain *authentic*, cannot be "enslaved by earthly forces, but must learn to extract a kind of eternity from things."[259] Such reconciliation calls forth a possible utopia. The Brazilian man, in order to be more human, has to blend in with the landscape. Moreover, the Brazilian artist – the architect, the landscaper, the painter, the writer –, in order to save this landscape, must "fertilize it with his creative genius."[260] Lins do Rego's writing, which evokes a centuries-old tradition depicting an engulfing Brazilian nature overpowering the startled man, calls to mind the lyrical and emotional text of Graça Aranha:

> "The rainforest is the splendor of the forces of disorder. Trees of all sizes and shapes, trees that rise, trying to match their peers and sketch the line of an ideal order, while others stretch and break the symmetry, bending down and sprawling across the floor their rich canopies. If a reptile runs off through the dry leaves pilling on the ground, then a slight rustling cuts through the sweet combination of silence; there is a fleeting movement in the air, like a lightning bolt, and a shudder runs through the nerves of the whole bush; travelers passing by, filled with august solitude, turn restless, feeling the electric and instantaneous cold of dread in their bodies."[261]

It is in the pages of *Aesthetics of Life*, published in 1921, that we find the intellectual basis for the historical reality described by José Lins do Rego. The book is little known, and yet it is crucial for understanding the Brazilian intellectual universe in the first half of the century. Author Graça Aranha wrote *Canaã*, an immigration novel, at the beginning of the century. Acclaimed by critics and the public, the book ended up catapulting him to a chair at the Brazilian Academy of Letters, a seat he resigned when he joined the modernist hosts on the eve of the Modern Art Week, of which he became one of the stars. Like the São Paulo writer

and journalist Menotti del Picchia – who in the pages of the
Correio Paulistano gave a step- by-step account of the surge
of modernism in São Paulo[262] –, Graça Aranha is conveniently
welcomed by the original modernists, as both brought with
them intellectual recognition and penetration into the
general public. Later, however, both would be scorned, in a
typical psychoanalytic repudiation through which young
intellectuals get rid of embarrassing parents who are seen as
"outdated".

At the turn of the year in 1922, Graça Aranha receives
a unique tribute from the modernists: a special issue of
the *Klaxon* magazine, with articles by Ronald de Carvalho,
Renato Almeida, Cândido Motta Filho, Rubens de Moraes,
Luiz Annibal Falcão and poems by Mário de Andrade,
Guilherme de Almeida, Luis Aranha and Sérgio Milliet.[263]
The "Extra Texts", two loose sheets enclosed in the copy,
are signed by Tarsila do Amaral – a black and white portrait
of the honoree – and Heitor Villa-Lobos – a score of the
first part of the "Sextetto mystico", dedicated "to Graça
Aranha."[264] The unsigned dedication on the last page registered the enthusiasm and respect with which the modernists
treated him:

> "This issue of Klaxon is dedicated to Graça Aranha. It
> is meant to convey all the joy of having found such a
> beautiful and high spirit willing to smile at us, lending
> us a little of his enthusiasm to multiply our own. Graça
> Aranha is a delightful companion, who has traveled
> a lot through life and knows how to tell those travel
> adventures that are more properly ours. A companion
> always cheerful, always happy, younger than any of us, a
> sensitive soul and a universal spirit, with the brain of an
> artist and philosopher, a chemist of the Brazilian dream,
> Rouget de L'Isle of Brazilian literature. This Klaxon issue
> is more voluminous than the others, so that we can hug
> Graça Aranha harder and longer."[265]

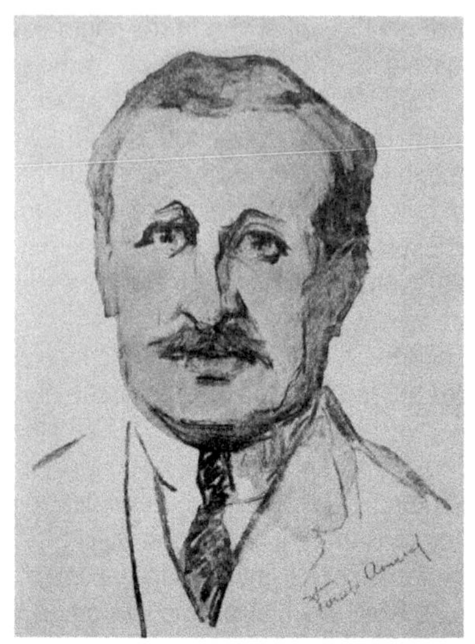

Graça Aranha. Tarsila do Amaral, 1922;
Score of Sexteto Místico, tribute to
Graça Aranha. Heitor Villa-Lobos, 1921.
Klaxon, no. 8-9, Dec. 1922/Jan. 1923

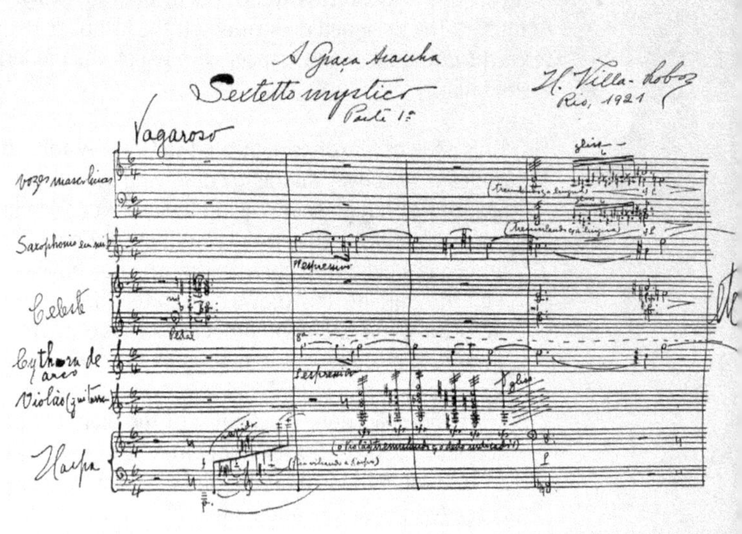

The contributions are all enthusiastic. In the words of Motta Filho, it was Graça Aranha "who, with more ingenuity, greater philosophical sense, greater stylistic vigor, managed to express the Brazilian soul in its many aspects,"[266] which gives a certain measure of how the aesthetic vision of Graça Aranha was carefully read by the young writers associated with the Modern Art Week. Rubens de Moraes carries out a long survey of the critical reviews and tributes received by Graça Aranha in France, attributing to him the merit of having been the only one among Brazilian writers to "shine in other countries" and "the first to enrich us by incorporating thought, philosophy, and metaphysical urge to the novel."[267] Renato de Almeida highlights the coalition between Brazilianness, man and natural environment that characterizes the writer from Maranhão: "Graça Aranha pulled the figure of Malazarte from the depths of our popular soul – that subtle demon like Mephistopheles, although less academic and more irreverent – and created a symbol of the imagination through which he justifies the pantheistic unity of the Universe as outlined in the philosophy of *The Aesthetics of Life.*"[268] In a grandiloquent tone, Luiz Annibal Falcão comments on *The Aesthetics of Life*: "The innate optimism regarding the destiny of the race, the magic of the stately performance, the synthetic power of its thought, all these features merge, and Brazil, its nature and its people are incorporated into the work."[269] Ronald de Carvalho is also not lacking in grandiloquence: "Graça Aranha, epic poet of the Race, Creator of Enthusiasm!"[270] Finally, anticipating the telegraphic style and the urban-rural themes of *Pau-Brasil* poetry, the verses of "Mormaço (for Graça Aranha)", by Guilherme de Almeida:

Heat. And the fans of the palm trees
and banana trees swaying slowly,
uselessly, in the perpendicular light.[271]

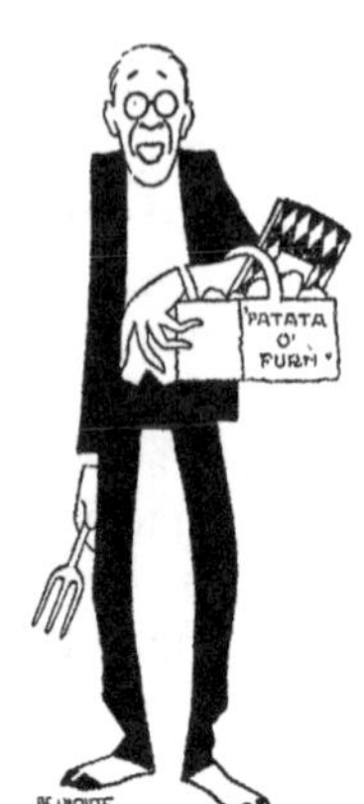
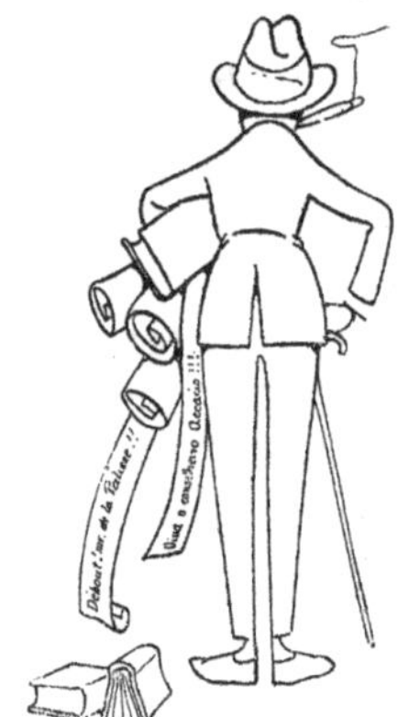

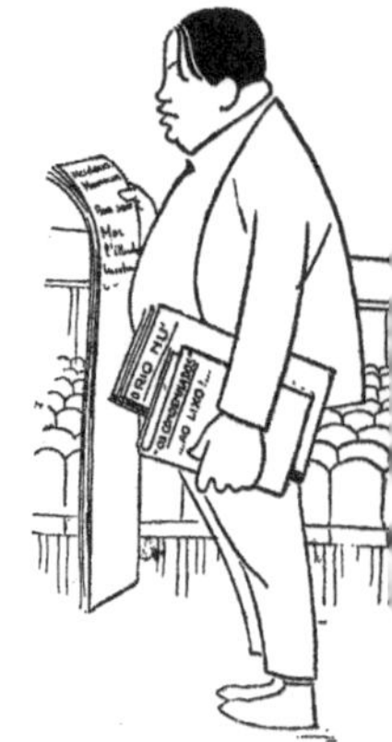

Mário de Andrade, Motta Filho, and Oswald de Andrade. Drawing by Belmonte. *Don Quixote*, Rio de Janeiro, no. 327, Aug. 15, 1923, 11

The enthusiasm of the *klaxists* for Graça Aranha was gradually replaced by a growing disdain, especially on the part of Oswald de Andrade, always prone to polemics, and Mário de Andrade, who was eager to consolidate an increasing influence over his companions. In 1954 Oswald published an article in *Anhembi* magazine, number 49, where he sarcastically describes the figure of Graça Aranha as "generally confused and talkative, son of an abominable 19th century philosophical background, but a great national man who belonged in our Academy of Letters, author of a taboo book, *Canaã*, which nobody read and everyone admired."[272] However, in his retrospective assessment, Oswald de Andrade recognizes the institutional benefits obtained with such a relationship: "It was evident that for us the official support of Graça Aranha meant a gift from heaven. With his endorsement, people would take us seriously. Otherwise, it would have been difficult. Without Paulo Prado's intelligence and understanding, nothing would have been possible. He was

338

the active link between the group that was being formed
and the renowned Graça Aranha."[273] In a letter to Manuel
Bandeira written a decade earlier, Mario, generally fairer than
Oswald in his assessments, expressed a very similar albeit
more affectionate opinion:

> "On the subject of Graça [Aranha] I still think that you
> and Couto [de Barros] were wrong not to honor the
> man. You see, as much as he puts himself in front of
> us, as much as people there, in the North, in the South,
> and even Antônio Ferro in Portugal, say that he started
> Brazilian modernism, all we have to do is check the
> dates. And the works. Now what no one will deny is his
> importance to the viability of the movement, and his
> personal worth. Of course: even if Graça did not exist, we
> would still be modernists, and others would follow us,
> but it made our implementation easier and faster. Today
> we exist. If there were no Graça Aranha, we would exist
> just for us, and now we exist for almost everyone."[274]

In 1958, historian Mário da Silva Brito adopts the
assessment of Mário de Andrade and Oswald de Andrade in
his famous book on the *History of Brazilian Modernism* and
emphasizes that the contribution of the author of *Aesthetics
of Life* – who had returned from Paris in 1921, when the
movement was already articulated – was restricted to the
endorsement given to the young modernists. "Graça Aranha
would lend the importance of his name to the success of the
enterprise carried out by the intellectual youth, and this was
his main role in the events that would take place in the year
in which Brazil celebrated a century of political autonomy."[275]
This sentence was extracted from the last paragraph of the
last subchapter in the book, entitled "The presence of Graça
Aranha": symptomatically, the writer from Maranhão gets
nothing but a quick reference in the epilogue, when everything had already happened.

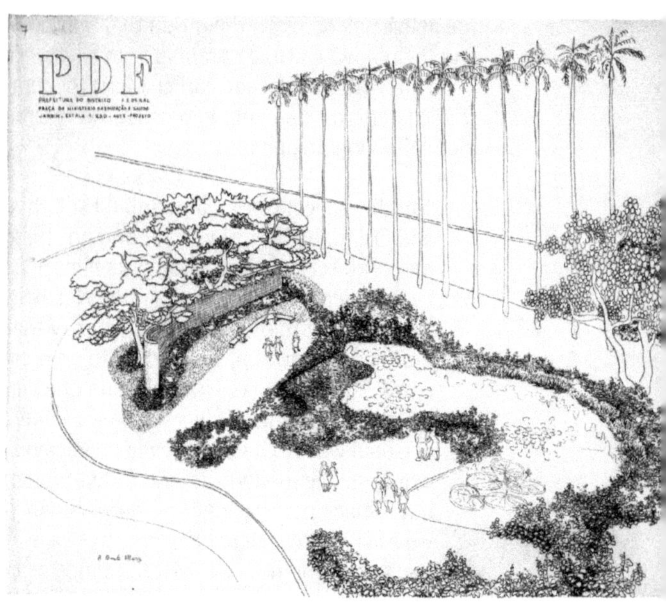

Ministry of Education and Health, unbuilt public garden, Rio de Janeiro RJ. Roberto Burle Marx, undated drawing. Photo by Andrés Otero. Burle Marx Institute Collection

The minor role of Graça Aranha in the intellectual structuring of São Paulo modernism was in a way corroborated by his withdrawal from the movement during the period of consolidation. Adding this to the fact that he really was an intellectual formed in another cultural context, it is understandable that most critics and historians, voluntarily or involuntarily adopting the official version propagated by the modernists themselves, accepted the strategic importance of Graça Aranha in the emergence of Brazilian modernism, while at the same time reducing his intellectual relevance – often to the point of almost erasing him –, especially the influence of his ideas on later developments. The exception here is Wilson Martins – always suspicious of the rationalizations perpetrated by the unconscious, prompted by obscure desires – who makes an interesting comment on the intriguing influence of the writer on the modernists, especially Mário de Andrade, even insinuating the psychoanalytic murder of the father:

> "Thus, *hating* Graça Aranha for the unshakable influence he exerted on him and, mysteriously, on the modernist group as a whole, despite all the conscious divergences, trying to prevent such hostility from showing in his behavior and gestures, it is possible that it manifested psychoanalytically and that Macunaíma, *the hero with no character*, was the antithetical and somewhat late response to the man, who actually was quite *cheerful*, sporty, healthy and full of *character*."[276]

It would be an exaggeration to attribute a major intellectual status to the work of Graça Aranha. *Canaã* is a verbose book filled with confused ideas, awkwardly pretending to be a fictional novel. *The Aesthetics of Life* is a big pastiche of ideas from different origins – Darwinian ethnology, romantic philosophy, different mesologies, positivist sociology, etc. –, all fused together in a bland style. Pretentious in their approach and conclusions, these texts often get lost in metaphysical ramblings trapped in a hermeticism that is difficult to understand. His style feels quite outdated when compared to early modernist writings from the same period.[277]

Nevertheless, the erasure of Graça Aranha's influence on the modernists is counterproductive: it obscures the strong intellectual ties connecting the works of Oswald de Andrade, Mário de Andrade and other modernists to the immediately preceding Brazilian cultural context. The privilege of rupture, which in the formal-expressive dimension is quite evident, has as a counterpart the erasure of a dynamic cultural context, the hybridity of which is attested by the curious coexistence of incompatible worldviews, indicative of the absence of a consolidated tradition. Thus, the importance of Graça Aranha lies not in the intellectual status of his work – his relevance as a philosopher, critic or esthete – but in the penetration of his ideas in the Brazilian intellectual universe; his presence was so profound that a writer of the stature of José Lins do Rego turns to him in 1952 to explain the birth of modern Brazilian architecture.

Graça Aranha's anthropology[278] implies an evolution of the human species concomitant with the emergence of national particularities forged in the relationship between peoples and the physical environments they inhabit. Referring to physiological and psychic heredity, Graça Aranha's ethnic ideas include both a Darwinian evolutionism – touched by positivist notions as in the work of the English philosopher Herbert Spencer –, as well as romantic conceptions along the lines of Herder and Madame de Stäel. It's a broad synthesis that also incorporates different explanatory hypotheses from the 19th century, such as the mesology of Thomas Buckle, the explanatory triad of Hippolyte Taine and the ideas regarding geographical determinism and ethnic atavisms defended by the Count of Gobineau in the 19th century. Graça Aranha's repertoire enompasses the same references of several relevant Brazilian intellectuals from the turn of the century, especially those who orbited around the Recife School – Silvio Romero,[279] Clóvis Beviláqua, Tobias Barreto, Artur Orlando, Martins Júnior and others.[280] In the studies carried out by the group, the search for a synthesis results in several interdisciplinary views of the historical-cultural phenomenon. The effort in question brings to light not only the different conceptual orientations at play, but also the broad spectrum of issues being debated:

"The philosophical discussions involved sometimes criticism of religion, sometimes problems of cosmology and therefore of physical sciences; literary studies were articulated around anthropological, ethnographic and comparative considerations. Legal studies often involved political theory, and sociology meant, on the one hand, an interest in biology and history in the broadest sense, and on the other hand, projections about economics, social doctrines, financial, demographic, hygienic issues."[281]

In Graça Aranha, the effort of synthesis turns towards understanding the *integration* of man in his *natural physical environment*, with all the repercussions in the mental, social, cultural and artistic spheres. Man's spiritual production maintained a subtle link with a deep node of his mental existence, that is, with his *character*. If intelligence, sensualism, the metaphysical spirit and transfigured faith characterize, respectively, the French people, the Italian people, the German people and the Spanish people, "in Brazil, the collective characteristic feature is the imagination. [...] The distant roots of this imagination are found in the soul of the different races that merged in the wonder of tropical nature. Each people brought their own melancholy."[282] The characteristic Brazilian imagination results from the cultural and psychological fusion of three melancholic races in the tropical environment, where the tragic representation of nature in the souls of blacks and natives outlined a frightened and misty psyche: "everything is hallucination, dread, melancholy in the wild soul that generated them."[283]

The founding moment of humanity, according to Graça Aranha, is the fracture in the harmonious integration of man in nature, a moment in which the world takes on a strange and inexplicable aspect, which is the seed for the emergence of consciousness, only possible when man perceives himself as an entity distinct from the world.[284] The *cosmic terror* of a helpless man is the source of his urge to understand the world, the deepest foundation of all explanatory modes for existence, be it religion, art, metaphysics or science. Graça

Aranha connects this explanatory logic, systematized by Auguste Comte and fundamental in Levy-Bruhl's philosophical anthropology and in Freudian phylogenesis,[285] to naturalist and romantic components.

Human expression in its many modalities reveals the peculiar character of the soul of each people, reflecting the different physical environments where they achieved their emancipation from nature. Myths, legends, folklore, art, language, rituals and festivities would express the differentiated origin of each group. The original mark, the atavism of races and peoples, going through particular historical evolutions and shaping the national character and collective cultural expressions, arise from those primordial impressions instilled in man by his natural habitat. As Maria Cecília de Moraes Leonel points out, "blinded by biological determinism, the writer is incapable of discerning in political, economic and social problems the reasons for the situation in the country – a country that, according to him, was given over to mestizos and now languished, invaded by foreigners."[286]

In Graça Aranha's anthropological theory, the splendor, magnificence and potency of our tropical landscape are the essential cause of Brazilian intellectual primitivism, giving rise to a barbaric metaphysics ruled by an exalted and melancholic imagination. Lethargy, lustful frenzy, and mystical exaltation were the spiritual reflections of an overpowering nature. Overcoming this barbaric metaphysics is the essential task of the Brazilian man in order to overcome his paralyzing fatalism. But this task becomes impossible if we cannot overcome nature. It is not, however, a matter of a material conquest, the civilizing domination over the telluric forces through the superiority of the machine; the cosmic dread, the malignant product of the individual-universe split and the resulting egoic formation, cannot be extinguished by science; the latter exercises its dominion only in the phenomenal world, which makes it incapable of addressing the deepest questions of being. This achievement must be essentially spiritual, with the defeat of the frightening ghost that inhabits the collective soul. The reconciliation between man and nature will only take place, in Graça Aranha's view, with the adoption of an aesthetic conception of life and the intellectual acceptance of the uncontrollable *fieri* of existence. Blending contradictory elements, Graça Aranha's cultural project proves to be radically aestheticizing.

Going back to our original point, there is no perfect parallelism between Graça Aranha's ideas and the arguments presented by José Lins do Rego. When he's examining the Brazilian house in the colonial period, Rego is concerned with the Portuguese colonizer – the white man of European origin who settles in the tropics. When he speaks, therefore, of the fear instilled in this man by our tropical nature, he's not following the same reasoning as Graça Aranha, who attributes this atavistic component of our psyche to blacks and natives.[287] Instead of applying a "theory", what we have here – which, by the way, is quite common in ours as well as in other intellectual environments – is a free appropriation of ideas that best suit the author's interests. Due to their reiterative aspect, these ideas, adjusted to new explanatory contexts, end up establishing a worldview that dominates Brazilian cultural life at least until the mid-20th century. Three structural pillars of this worldview are worth highlighting:

First, *tellurism as a cultural determinant.*[288] Each and every human manifestation within the scope of the human spirit results from the specific relationship between man and landscape. For José Lins do Rego, that which is fundamental for the birth of our modern architecture is not the invention of typologies or the adaptation of innovative techniques, but the disappearance of our collective fear towards nature. From then on, "the house opens its windows, protects itself from the light, takes advantage of rivers, goes up and down mountains. It is the Brazilian house that turns to the land-scape where it finds all the essential elements to be original,

pleasant and beautiful."[289.]When the writer, thinking about
our peculiar relationship with the environment, defines Brazil
as the "country of the sun ", he's not alone. Besides Graça
Aranha, he has many other illustrious comrades. In several
writings, Mário de Andrade speaks of a "solar civilization",
of the "primitive of a new era" – that is, the Brazilian man;
in a 1924 letter to Tarsila do Amaral, he even argues that
the "*mata-virgismo*" ("woodland virginitism") would be the
aesthetic solution to the impasses of our modernism. Oswald
de Andrade, in turn, spoke of "vegetation", of the "country of
Cobra Grande" (Big Snake), of Brazilians as "children of the
sun" and of "*Pau-Brasil* poetry" as the panacea for our artistic indigence.

Second, as a direct result of tellurism, *art as a collective
and original product of a people*. It is an idea of romantic
extraction that has had a deep penetration in our modernism, expressed through a particular semantics. In this reasoning, which is present in Lins do Rego and in many other
intellectuals and artists in the first half of the last century,
the *biological* metaphor and the *psychologizing* terminology
are quite visible, building through the mutual articulation
of their meanings a *specific notion of culture*. Now, organic
metaphors such as "coming from the earth", "deep roots",
"sprung from our own lives" and other equivalent terms
bring about a language that implies a natural development
of powers that would be intrinsic to our being. This notion is
complemented by terms borrowed from the sphere of sensi-
tivity, which would reveal the *spontaneity* and the *expression*
of our collective character. In this context, expressing what
we are translates into expressing our specific relationship
with the environment. As this equation has multiple components, and as the man-landscape interaction takes place in
time and space, the cultural materialization of the collective
spirit will have *originality* as its major token and *authenticity*
as its greatest quality.

Thirdly, following directly from the two previous aspects, the artist as a catalyst of cultural virtualities dispersed within the collectivity, responsible for the aesthetic-formal renovations and transformations. In the extensive horizontal base, the collective character is constituted as a result of the spontaneous manifestations of the community through rites, prayers, music, dances, language. At the upper end of the social structure, however, it is up to the artist – having as his sole and exclusive object the collective character – to apply color, shape, volume, texture, rhythm, creating the superior manifestations of the collective spirit. The artist, while unable to forge the collective psychology or character of his people, nonetheless has the mission of shaping up a superior form for the culture dispersed through the social fabric. If he proves himself incapable of producing his work in obedience to this truth, no matter how perfectionist the artist may be, the result obtained will never be an art of historical value.[290]

A community's reckoning with its environment, carried out by a group of intellectuals properly prepared for the challenge, becomes a cultural project. Rallying Brazilian artists to take part in the historic task of reconnecting with the country and with themselves, Graça Aranha made it clear that this would only be possible through a collective commitment and a search for an essence and a character that transcended individual subjectivity. As stilted as his writing style may be, it is possible to glimpse in his ideas that which would become the very core of the modernist cultural project:[291]

"Thus, our intelligence, in order to be released from barbaric elements, turned culture into a gesture of bad taste and cowardice, producing a colorless literature devoid of superior works, where the idealism of our metaphysical spirit never found its proper symbols, nor life its ideal creations. And yet those barbaric elements of our spiritual formation and our nationality demanded, before their total disappearance, their own poets and writers. That which is grandiose, enormous, monstrous, amorphous, infantile, even obsolete, in nature and in each collectivity, demands, nevertheless, its epic. Some tried to be the poet, the bard of all this wilderness. Nature made them barbarians, therefore equipped with the necessary unconsciousness. The rudimentary culture they acquired, however, put them out of balance with their true *homeland*. Pedantry killed the intimate wildness in them. They stopped expressing themselves unconsciously and started to see and explain. Such writers never came to terms with the things they were writing about."[292]

Between the primitive roar of Graça Aranha in 1921 – when virtually all of our modernists were under the spell of the urban icons of the machine age, the same ones the European avant-garde celebrated in prose and verse (without rhyme!) – and the serene realization, present in the retrospective carried out by José Lins do Rego in 1952, that the mission had been accomplished, we have the emergence, development and consolidation of Brazilian modernism.[293] In 1922, young Futurists were placing their bets on popular culture, but from 1924 onwards this vision became much more radical with the incorporation of those "barbaric elements of our spiritual formation" present in the relationship between man and landscape. Brazilian culture and nature are then spoused by Tarsila do Amaral, Oswald de Andrade, Heitor Villa-Lobos, Mário de Andrade, Raul Bopp, Oscar Niemeyer, Burle Marx and others, not only as a background for the staging of contemporary life, but also with all its conceptual implications, encompassing race and culture.

Tropical nature is much more than a scenographic element; it constitutes the very essence of the life of the Brazilian man who settled in it. A simple, sensitive and cheerful man, improving his existence and his presence in the territory with new civilizational acquisitions. Reconciliation with

the physical environment, according to the cultural project
set up at the time, entailed rediscovering and accounting for
the historical problems of raciality and, as a result, the rediscovery of a forgotten tradition. Since then, these notions
have vigorously delivered aesthetic achievements of the
highest quality and in the most varied artistic areas – literature, music, painting, architecture, theater –, despite the
constant risk of getting trapped in arid, schematic formulas
of a sterile nationalism[294] that ignores the anthropophagic
hunger, which must always be greedy: "I am only concerned
with what is not mine. Law of man. Cannibal Law."[295]

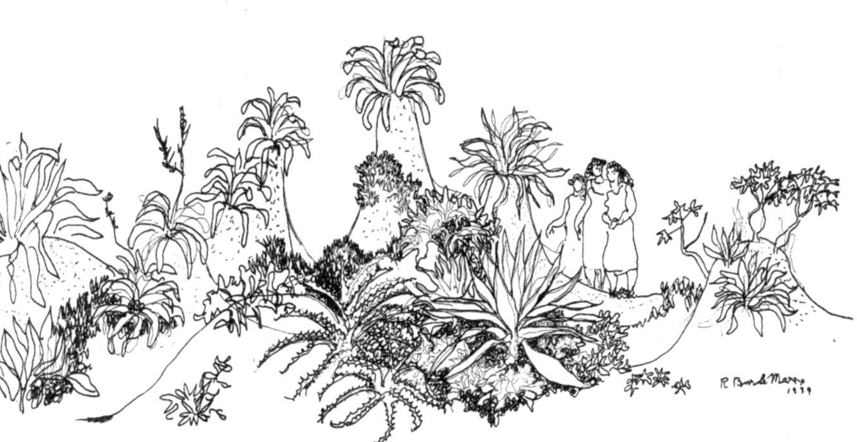

Vargem Grande Farm, garden, Areias
SP. Roberto Burle Marx, José Tabacow,
and Haruyoshi Ono, 1979. Burle Marx
Institute Collection

Part 2 Notes

1. Oswald de Andrade, "Roteiro das Minas," 135.
2. Lúcio Costa, "Parque Guinle," 205.
3. Ibid., 205.
4. Patrimônio – Patrimônio Cultural Brasileiro. Rio de Janeiro: Palácio das Laranjeiras.
5. Mauro Neves Nogueira, "Parque Guinle. Reinterpretação das 'unités d'habitation'," 92.
6. Costa, "Parque Guinle," 205. On another occasion, Lúcio Costa stated that "these were buildings oriented towards the sun, the west, so we had sun in the afternoon. Thus, it was necessary to have a structure that would work as a sunbreak, absorbing the insolation." Segawa, "Lúcio Costa," 150.
7. Later on, a single building was built in a nearby plot, designed by MMM Roberto.
8. Carlos Eduardo Comas, "A racionalidade da meia lua: apartamentos do Parque Guinle no Rio de Janeiro, Brasil, 1948-52."
9. "Going through the city, one fine day I saw, in the basement of a building from the previous century, a partition wall on the ground-floor facing the street with that grid, as if it were a ceramic lattice made of 'eights' of clay, each piece with two juxtaposed squares and a certain depth." Segawa, "Lúcio Costa," 150.
10. Geraldo Gomes Silva, "Marcos da arquitetura moderna em Pernambuco," 21. In the introduction to the facsimile edition of the *Dicionário de Arquitetura Brasileira*, Carlos Lemos comments on the message he received about the error committed in the meaning of the entry in the original edition: "The first collaboration was sent by architect and professor Geraldo Gomes da Silva, from Recife. It was a small sheet, filled out front and back. The text corrected the origin given by our dictionary for the term *cobogó* or *combogó*, whose affiliation we mistakenly attributed 'to the perforated bricks of North African constructions, as suggested by the sound of the word, which is evidently black.' According to Gomes, using the testimony of engineer Antônio Bezerra Baltar as a source, the origin of the name is much more prosaic, showing the only error recognized in our work so far. The file forwarded by him contained an excerpt from an article written by the engineer, which describes the circumstances that led to the creation of the term, actually an acronym: 'It is worth mentioning, first of all, the use of the popular cobogós, i.e., cement and sand bricks with 0.50m x 0.50m x 0.10m and square holes with 0.05m sides, originally used by a company from Pernambuco to build walls. These hollow elements would then, when necessary, have their holes filled with mortar. The name *cobogó* is formed by joining the initials of the names of the partners of the factory that

produced these bricks: 'co' from Coimbra, a Portuguese master builder, 'bo' from Boeckmann, a German blacksmith, and 'go' from Antônio de Góis, an engineer who would become mayor of Recife." Eduardo Corona, and Carlos Lemos, *Dicionário da arquitetura brasileira*, XV.

11. See: Hugo Segawa, and Guilherme Mazza Dourado, *Oswaldo Arthur Bratke*; Benjamin Adiron Ribeiro, *Vila Serra do Navio. Comunidade urbana na serra amazônica: um projeto do arquiteto Oswaldo Arthur Bratke*.

12. Nogueira, "Parque Guinle," 98.

13. Lúcio Costa, "Casa do estudante. Cité Universitaire, Paris," 231.

14. Ibid., 234-235.

15. Ibid., 234.

16. *L'Homme et l'Architecture*, n. 11-12-13-14,

17. Lúcio Costa, "Casa do Brasil em Paris," 291.

18. Letter from Lúcio Costa to Le Corbusier, Rio de Janeiro, Nov. 27, 1949, quoted in Lúcio Costa "Mise au point," 140. The episode will be further discussed below along with the project for the Ministry of Education and Health.

19. Ibid.

20. Segawa, "Lúcio Costa," 151.

21. Vinícius de Moraes, "Azul e branco," 172. In the preamble to the poem, Vinícius attributes the tagline "Concha e cavalo-marinho" (Shell and seahorse) to Pedro Nava, referencing one of Cândido Portinari's tile panels on the first floor of the Ministry of Education and Health building.

22. Bruand, *Arquitetura contemporânea no Brasil*, 81.

23. Some years after the completion of the thesis on which our book is based, we had the opportunity to publish the monumental research carried out by Professor Roberto Segre and his team, which resulted in the most comprehensive research on the building of the Ministry. See: Roberto Segre, *Ministério da Educação e Saúde: ícone urbano da modernidade brasileira – 1935-1945*. Lauro Cavalcanti himself would later publish a book on the project, mixing history and fiction. See: Lauro Cavalcanti, *Dezoito graus: a biografia do Palácio Capanema*.

24. Bruand, *Arquitetura contemporânea no Brasil*, 88.

25. Ibid., 89.

26. Costa, "Muita construção, alguma arquitetura e um milagre," 168. Or in this passage: "We were all still young and inexperienced – Oscar Niemeyer, Carlos Leão, Afonso Eduardo Reidy, Jorge Moreira, Ernani Vasconcelos; However, we acted as if we were the owners of the work"; "Whatever the case, however, the truth is that after those four weeks in 1936 there was no more interference from Le Corbusier, who only came to know the finished building a few years before his death, when he returned here to design the French Embassy in Brasília". Costa, "Relato pessoal," 136 and 138.

27. Documentary produced by
TV Cultura, São Paulo, 1987.
Duration: 53 min. Video collec-
tion of the Audiovisual Center of
the Faculty of Architecture and
Urbanism of PUC-Campinas.

28. Bruand, *Arquitetura contemporânea no Brasil*, 93.

29. Ibid., 92.

30. Costa, "Relato pessoal," 136.

31. Alexandre Eulalio, "Prefácio a
'Lembrança de Le Corbusier.'" In
*A aventura brasileira de Blaise
Cendrars*, edited by Carlos
Augusto Calil, 428.

32. Cf. Lauro Cavalcanti, *As preocupações do belo*, 205.

33. Costa, "Muita construção,
alguma arquitetura e um
milagre," 169. Also cited in:
Cavalcanti, *As preocupações do
belo*, 57.

34. Ibid., 58.

35. Regarding the episode, Yves
Bruand has said: "It was a
cautious attitude, dictated by
a sense of justice and, perhaps, by a certain insecurity".
In a footnote, he adds: "Lúcio
Costa would act in the same
way three years later, when he
designed the Brazilian Pavilion
at the New York International
Exposition". Bruand, *Arquitetura
contemporânea no Brasil*, 82.
Bruand's hypothesis is coherent
and presents Lucio Costa's
much-vaunted modesty through
different lens.

36. Cf. Ibid.

37. Cavalcanti, *As preocupações
do belo*, 66. The intellectual
and class proximity must
have been an important factor in the group's cohesion.
Acquaintanceship ties were,
however, decisive for the choice
of Lúcio Costa: "I called Carlos
Leão, a cultured and fine person,
because he was my partner
and friend. Afonso Reidy and
Jorge Moreira, colleagues of
mine at Enba, presented good
projects. Moreira said he would
only accept to collaborate if we
accepted Ernani along with him.
Oscar, a collaborator of mine,
argued that he also deserved
to be in the group," quoted in
Cavalcanti, *As preocupações
do belo*, 66. Also in another
text: "I did not invite Oscar to
collaborate in the project right
away, but when Jorge Moreira
asked me for the participation of
Ernani Vasconcelos, his partner,
he demanded his inclusion as
well, on equal terms with the
others." Lúcio Costa, "Oscar
Niemeyer: prefácio para o livro
de Stamo Papadaki," 195-196. At
another point, Lúcio Costa mentions participation in the original competition as a criterion,
but then he himself disproves
the idea right away: "I gathered
a group of young architects
who had participated in the
competition: Affonso Eduardo
Reidy, Jorge Moreira, Carlos
Leão – who did not compete but
was my friend. Later on Oscar
Niemeyer and Fernando (sic)
Vasconcelos were also included."
Haifa Sabbag, "A beleza de um
trabalho: percurso, síntese da
tradição e da modernidade
(entrevista com Lúcio Costa)," p.
16.

38. An interview from August 1935 with Gregori Warchavchik in a Rio de Janeiro newspaper gives us a good idea of the ongoing clash. Lúcio Costa's former partner praises the architect Marcello Piacentini, who was soon to come to Brazil. The IAB itself shows a submissive posture regarding the fate of the Cidade Universitária (University City) project. In a separate box next to the main article, entitled "Cidade Universitária", we find the following text: "Having the Minister of Education requested from the Institute of Architects of Brazil a list of five Brazilian architects of recognized culture and technical competence, so that His Excellency could choose among them the collaborators who will work with architect Marcello Piacentini, a board meeting on the 16th of this month elected for this purpose the following architects: F. Fernandes Saldanha, Carlos Henrique de Oliveira Porto, Ângelo Bruhns, Lúcio Costa e Paulo Ferreira dos Santos". See: Redação. "A construção da 'Cidade Universitária'. A personalidade do arquiteto Marcello Piacentini na opinião do Sr. Gregorio Warchavchik."

39. Cavalcanti, *As preocupações do belo*, 70.

40. Letter from Monteiro de Carvalho to Le Corbusier, Mar. 21, 1936, quoted in Margareth da Silva Pereira et al., *Le Corbusier e o Brasil*, 134.

41. Cf. Cavalcanti, *As preocupações do belo*, 75.

42. "The construction of the University City, however, would not start during Capanema's administration. A decree from 1944 (no. 6.574, of June 8) transferred the location of the future University City to Vila Valqueire, formerly Valqueira farm; another one, from May 21, 1945 (no. 7.566) transferred yet again the site to the island of Fundão, where the headquarters of the Federal University of Rio de Janeiro would finally be built, ignoring everything from the projects of Piacentini or Le Corbusier". Cf., Simon Schwartzman, Helena Maria Bousquet Bomeny, and Vanda Maria Ribeiro Costa, *Tempos de Capanema*, 105. Jorge Machado Moreira, a member of the team of Brazilian architects responsible for the ministry, was in charge of the overall coordination of the University City project, which is, in a way, a victory for the moderns, even if a late one.

43. Letter from Le Corbusier to Monteiro de Carvalho, Mar. 30, 1936, quoted in Margareth da Silva Pereira et al., *Le Corbusier e o Brasil*, 135.

44. Letter from Monteiro de Carvalho to Le Corbusier, Apr. 8, 1936, quoted in ibid., 136.

45. Letter from Le Corbusier to Monteiro de Carvalho, Apr. 17, 1936, quoted in ibid., 137.

46. Letter from Le Corbusier to Monteiro de Carvalho, May 5, 1936, quoted in ibid., 137.

47. Bruand, *Arquitetura contem-porânea no Brasil*, 83. Yves Bruand warns that the version should be considered with caution as "the documentation concerning the negotiations that preceded Le Corbusier's arrival and stay in Brazil is quite restricted. Capanema's personal archives could provide much data, but they are not accessible." Ibid., 82 (note 10).

48. According to a 1975 text by Lúcio Costa, Le Corbusier "immediately considered the land unsuitable, for it would soon be surrounded by insignificant buildings. It seemed to him that the building should face the sea and the Pão de Açúcar fixing itself in the area before the second embankment, which corresponds to the one where the MAM is located." Costa, "Relato pessoal," 136. According to Lauro Cavalcanti, the plot would be where the Casa di Italia and the Maison de France were built. Cavalcanti, *As preocupações do belo*, 72. However, in an interview with Haifa Sabbag, Lúcio Costa reiterated the version that Le Corbusier "rightly argued that it should be situated elsewhere, overlooking Guanabara Bay and the Pão de Açúcar, in the direction where the Museum of Modern Art stands today." Sabbag, "A beleza de um trabalho," 16.

49. Costa, "Relato pessoal," 136.

50. Ibid., 136.

51. Costa "Mise au point," 141.

52. Le Corbusier, *Oeuvre Complète*, 81.

53. Letter from Le Corbusier to Pietro Maria Bardi, Paris, 18 Oct. 1949, quoted in Margareth da Silva Pereira et al., *Le Corbusier e o Brasil*, 198.

54. As previously mentioned, Le Corbusier came to Brazil as a lecturer and consultant, receiving corresponding fees. His stay in Brazil was only four weeks. On this question, Lúcio Costa reminded Le Corbusier himself: "But if this is about money, allow me to bring to your attention that during the four weeks of your stay here, you received more than the rest of us received during the six years of construction, because we were six architects, and although the individual contributions were unequal, the fees were always divided equally among us." Letter from Lúcio Costa to Le Corbusier, Rio de Janeiro, Nov. 27, 1949, quoted in Margareth da Silva Pereira et al., *Le Corbusier e o Brasil*, 140. We have adopted the translation from the second source, the original being in French.

55. "Years 46/48, I try to make the Brazilians I meet - the ones living in Paris or passing through - understand my great surprise at having been left clueless as to the construction of the building"; "1948 or 1949 (?), the Brazilian Embassy sponsors a Brazilian Exhibition of modern architecture in the great amphitheater of the School of Fine Arts in Paris. I am not invited by the Embassy, but by the Order of French Architects." Letter from Le Corbusier to Pietro Maria Bardi, Paris, Oct. 18, 1949, quoted in Margareth da Silva Pereira et al., *Le Corbusier e o Brasil*, 198.

56. Letter from Lúcio Costa to Le Corbusier, Rio de Janeiro, Nov. 27, 1949, quoted in Costa "Mise au point," 140. Pietro Maria Bardi's participation in the episode is quite ambiguous, since in the first moment he took the Swiss-French architect's side: "I immediately started engaging with people with the purpose of obtaining the moral satisfaction and the monetary compensation that are due to you. There is no doubt about the authenticity of your 'paternity' regarding the drawings and sketches for the Ministry… I ask you, dear Le Corbusier, to tell us approximately what would be your fees for the services rendered to the Brazilian government." Letter from Pietro Maria Bardi to Le Corbusier, São Paulo, 17 Nov. 1949, quoted in Margareth da Silva Pereira et al., *Le Corbusier e o Brasil*, 123. In his book about Le Corbusier, Pietro Maria Bardi completely omits his original reaction — offering to represent the architect in the battle for his fees — and points to a more restrained and cautious performance, which evidently did not happen: "Although I did not know Brazil very well at that time, I thought it was yet another absurdity from our friend, or at least a misunderstanding. Everyone knew about Gustavo Capanema's correctness. In any case, through Gregori Warchavchik, Lúcio Costa got interested in the matter and went on to investigate the case. Just as I thought, the Calculator had forgotten that he had received what was agreed upon in the contract, and that he had written the corresponding receipt." Cf. Pietro Maria Bardi, *Lembranças de Le Corbusier: Atenas, Itália, Brasil*, 107. When writing the book in 1984, Bardi did not consider the possibility that he might be contradicted, and that's precisely what happened three years later with the publication of his letter in *Le Corbusier e o Brasil*. Ironically, the book was published by Masp, the art museum he himself ran.

57. Letter from Lúcio Costa to Le Corbusier, Rio de Janeiro, Nov. 27, 1949, quoted in Costa, "Mise au point," 140.

58. Ibid., 140.

59. Letter from Le Corbusier to Lúcio Costa, Paris, Dec. 23, 1949, quoted in Margareth da Silva Pereira et al., *Le Corbusier e o Brasil*, 203.

60. Ibid., 203.

61. "Adaptation sur le terrain adopté en dernière heure, des aménagents du projet de la page 78". Le Corbusier, *Oeuvre Complète*, 81. On page 78 was the sketch made indeed by Le Corbusier for the plot on the beach.

62. "Second projet de Le Corbusier, adapte au terrain definitivement choisi". *Architecture d'Aujourd'hui* (special issue on Brazil), vol. 18, n. 13-14, Sep. 1947, 13.

63. "Le Corbusier receives the final design for the ministry building in July 1937 and congratulates the team in response. Between 1937 and 1939, his gestures to secure some project in Brazil multiply without success. Frustration grows into resentment from 1945 on. Claims for authorship and fees regarding the Ministry become frequent, and personal relations are strained. Even in 1956, when he was closer to Lúcio Costa and in charge of the Casa do Brasil project in Paris, the subject came up again. Lúcio points out the difference between the 'elongated building, situated on another site' and the 'project built during the war', with no further contact between the Brazilian team and the French architect, and rebukes him again, for the sketch he had published to suggest the authorship of the definitive project constituted "a false testimony, made a posteriori from the photographs of the finished building or the scale model". Carlos Eduardo Comas, "Le Corbusier: os riscos brasileiros de 1936," 31.

64. Letter from Lúcio Costa to Le Corbusier, Rio de Janeiro, Nov. 27, 1949, quoted in Costa "Mise au point," 140.

65. "This beautiful Ministry building is, as I have already said, a historical and symbolic landmark. Historic, because it was the first time architecture was adapted to the new construction technology of reinforced concrete on a monumental scale, including the façade made entirely of glass, the *pan de verre*; previous experiences had always involved smaller buildings. When, with the construction of its structure already underway, I went with Oscar Niemeyer to take care of the Brazil Pavilion at the 1939 International Fair, there were no buildings in New York with those translucent façades that now characterize the city, the so-called curtain walls or *murs rideaux*. They all came later. And it is symbolic because, in a still socially and technologically underdeveloped country, it was built with optimism and faith in the future, by young and inexperienced architects, while the world was engaged in self-flagellation." Cf. Costa, "Relato pessoal," 138; "They say that the 'International Style' was born in the United States, but it is not true, because the first great building with glass facades was that of the Ministry. Both Gropius and Mies had already used these concepts in Europe, in smaller buildings. The American architects came to Brazil to see the Ministry, Pampulha. Then they started to adopt the style in the United States. The Lever House project is a replica of the Ministry, a new, lighter version. The Ministry is more solid, more Doric. It is perfect." Cf. Sabbag, "A beleza de um trabalho," 17; "I took Oscar Niemeyer to New York in 1938 to design the Brazilian Pavilion for the International Exhibition, there was no building there with glass façade, and the Ministry of Education was already under construction, so

Brazil anticipated the innovative application of the so-called curtain wall or *mur rideau, pan de verre*, as the French say". Cf. Segawa, "Lúcio Costa," 148.

66.	Letter from Lúcio Costa to Le Corbusier, Rio de Janeiro, Nov. 27, 1949, quoted in Costa "Mise au point," 140.

67.	Lúcio Costa, "Ministério da Educação e Saúde," 128. In the interview with Haifa Sabbag, Lúcio says: "This architecture was born in Europe, and had its first monumental expression here, in an underdeveloped country, brought about by young, inexperienced architects, with the support of a minister who trusted them." Sabbag, "A beleza de um trabalho," 17-18.

68.	Letter from Le Corbusier to Pietro Maria Bardi, Paris, Oct. 18, 1949, quoted in Margareth da Silva Pereira et al., *Le Corbusier e o Brasil*, 198-199. The special issue dedicated to Brazil by the French magazine *L'Architecture d'Aujourd'hui*, Sep. 1947, published, among others, the following projects: Brazilian Pavilion at the New York World Fair, Pampulha ensemble, Obra do Berço, Park Hotel São Clemente, ABI's headquarters building, Sedes Sapientiae. Besides Lúcio Costa, Oscar Niemeyer, Roberto Brothers, and Rino Levi, authors of these projects, we also find works by Attílio Correa Lima, Álvaro Vital Brazil, Francisco Bolonha, Affonso Eduardo Reidy, Jorge Moreira, Eduardo Kneese de Mello, Aldary Henriques Toledo, Sérgio Bernardes, Roberto Burle Marx and others. If we take this publication as our reference, the projects presented in Paris probably gave a very representative picture of the enormous Corbusian influence in Brazil. *Architecture d'Aujourd'hui* (special issue on Brazil), vol. 18, n. 13-14, Paris, Sep. 1947.

69.	Cândido Portinari is an example of subservence to power: "Capanema had a much more instrumental view of art, as his correspondence with Cândido Portinari reveals. In fact, the minister had very definite ideas about what the painter should do." Schwartzman, Bomeny and Costa, *Tempos de Capanema*, 95.

70.	We use here the term "opportunity" in the sense of the word *kayros*, from the Greek archaic period, that is, the historical understanding of *timely* action.

71.	Andrade, "Roteiro das Minas," 135.

72.	"The originality of the Brazilian contribution consists precisely in this singular fact, namely, that in our country the moderns were the first (as well as the most authorized and equipped) to commit themselves to the recovery and preservation of traditional architecture, so that the same people who championed modern renovation were also engaged with older forms. They are thus first of all modern instead of passadists (that is, academics) and precisely because they were modern, they were the first to reengage (through a different register) with tradition." Otília Beatriz Fiori Arantes, "Resumo de Lúcio Costa," 264.

73. Segawa, "Lúcio Costa," 149.
Otília Arantes, commenting on
Lúcio Costa's conversion to the
modern, argues that his adherence to the thought of Mário
de Andrade was not motivated,
but the result of chance: "These
are some of the accidents that
would have made Lúcio Costa
modern. But the premises of
what, in his, or in our, architecture, ended up (unintentionally) becoming the modernist
commandment – the need to
'traditionalize' our past, according to Mário de Andrade – were
already given." Arantes, "Resumo
de Lúcio Costa," 261.

74. With all the irreverence that
was peculiar to him, Oswald de
Andrade ridiculed this aspect of
Mário de Andrade's life for years.

75. "The church was already seeking
to carve out a space in the
new regime, with Francisco
Campos trying to make the
connection. In December 1930,
Alceu Amoroso Lima would
find some place for God among
the revolutionaries, when he
affirmed that there was among
them 'a rational, traditional and
Christian current' in opposition
to another one, 'demagogic,
libertarian that would fatally
lead to communist materialism
and the persecution of Christian
tradition. [...] The magazine
The Order calls on Catholics to
struggle for the position of the
Church in society, and states:
'the revolution will be inefficient
as long as the Church is not
given its due supremacy.' The
government responds positively.
A month later the decree is
promulgated allowing religious
instruction in public schools,
which had been abolished
since the Constitution of 1891."
Schwartzman, Bomeny and
Costa, *Tempos de Capanema*, 55.

76. Ibid., 80.

77. Ibid., 81.

78. Lauro Cavalcanti, ed.,
Modernistas na repartição, 12.

79. Ibid., 11. The same quote can be
found in Cavalcanti, *As preocupações do belo*, 139.

80. "Although the neocolonial
movement began in São Paulo
in 1914, thanks to the personal
initiative of Ricardo Severo, soon
followed by Victor Dubugras,
it was not in São Paulo that it
achieved a major expansion and
importance in historical terms."
Bruand, *Arquitetura contemporânea no Brasil*, 54. Dubugras,
who had a career marked by
profound stylistic changes, is
considered by some historians as a precursor of modern
architecture in Brazil. According
to Nestor Goulart, "in 1906 the
architect made the project for
the Mayrink station in concrete, which became famous
as a modern work when it was
publicized. The project was
both plastically and technically
modern." Nestor Goulart Reis
Filho, *Racionalismo e proto-racionalismo na obra de Victor
Dubugras*, 61.

81. A more recent study further details what happened: "In 1925 Brazil received an invitation to participate in the Sesquicentennial Philadelphia Exposition, celebrating the 150th anniversary of the declaration of independence of the United States. The Brazilian government then launched a design competition to choose its pavilion, and more than twenty projects were submitted, all in neocolonial style, since the public notice required the adoption of this style. The projects were evaluated by the jury after the United States had already communicated that it was revoking the international character of the exposition, withdrawing the invitation it had extended to Brazil. This situation led to prizes being awarded to the three best projects, in no order of distinction. The winners, who shared the prize money, were, in order of mention: Lúcio Costa, Nerêo de Sampaio & Fernandes, and Angelo Bruhns. Lúcio Costa's project for the Brazilian Pavilion in Philadelphia followed a rigorous model in keeping with the colonial tradition of Brazilian architecture, and from the considerations in the judgment minutes, it seems to have been the work that pleased the jury the most. Samuel Silva de Brito, "Pavilhão do Brasil na Exposição de Filadélfia: 1925," 1.

82. Lúcio Costa, "À guisa de sumário," 16.

83. Costa, "Muita construção, alguma arquitetura e um milagre," 165.

84. See: Cavalcanti, *As preocupações do belo*, 144.

85. Ibid., 145.

86. See: Oliveira Viana, *Raça e assimilação*; Nina Rodrigues, *Os africanos no Brasil*.

87. We have already dealt, on another occasion, with the debate regarding the whitening of the Brazilian race, as well as with authors Oliveira Vianna and Nina Rodrigues. See: Guerra, *O primitivismo em Mário de Andrade, Oswald de Andrade e Raul Bopp*.

88. Cavalcanti, *As preocupações do belo*, 141.

89. For Mário de Andrade, the reasoning used to forge a Brazilian music that was truly articulated with the roots of nationality is similar to his conception of a Brazilian literature that would draw its expressive vigor from the Brazilian language as actually spoken by the people.

90. "The theoretical basis of the retranslation of values, with the objective of shaping a new 'national identity', was elaborated, in the architectural field, by Lúcio Costa, in consonance with the 'modern' postulates established by the literary vanguard of the time – Oswald de Andrade and Mário de Andrade also advocated the marriage of an erudite vanguard with traditional and popular elements." Cavalcanti, *As preocupações do belo*, 77

91. Ibid., 155.

92. Ibid., 161.

93. See: Carlos Eduardo Comas, "O passado mora ao lado: Lúcio Costa e o projeto do Grande Hotel de Ouro Preto, 1938/40."

94. "The letter acquires a much broader scope than the mere case of the Ouro Preto hotel, becoming, in the field of Heritage, a kind of charter of principles for new construction in historic sites." Cavalcanti, *As preocupações do belo*, 166.

95. Bruand, *Arquitetura contemporânea no Brasil*, 148.

96. See: Marcelo Carvalho Ferraz, ed., *Lina Bo Bardi*.

97. See: Carlos Eduardo Comas, "Arquitetura moderna, estilo campestre. Hotel, Parque São Clemente."

98. Bruand, *Arquitetura contemporânea no Brasil*, 132.

99. Alcides Rocha Miranda, Testimony of Alcides Rocha Miranda to the author, Jun. 8, 1995, quoted in, Ana Luiza Nobre, "O passado pela frente: a modernidade de Alcides Rocha Miranda," 43.

100. Lúcio Costa, "Tradição local," 451. The first sentence is very similar to the closing line in an unpublished text written certainly before 1970, and that can be considered a prototype for the text that came to be published: "While the formation of the various modalities of regional architecture took place gradually in other places, as a logical consequence of the function for which they were intended and of the impositions of the physical and social environment, in American countries the process was reversed: the colonizers brought finished solutions that had to be adjusted like ready-made clothes — or, to be more precise, 'half-made', as they now say, to the body of new land." Lúcio Costa, "Raízes da arquitetura colonial brasileira," 4.

101. The frustrated initiative to set up an institution dedicated to preservation in São Paulo in the 1920s was conceived by Blaise Cendrars with private promotion. See; Carlos Augusto Calil, "Sob o signo do Aleijadinho: Blaise Cendrars, precursor do patrimônio histórico."

102. Brasilia's Cathedral is an exemplary case, for it was inaugurated and listed at the same time (the listing was registered in the Livro das Belas-Artes, vol. 1, folio 088, inscription 485-A, Jun. 1, 1967). "Catetinho", President Juscelino Kubitschek's building/hostel in Brasília, was listed even before the city was built (registered in the Livro Histórico, vol. 1, folio 055, inscription 329, of Jul. 21, 1959). Brasilia's urban complex corresponding to Lúcio Costa's Pilot Plan took a little longer: it was listed in 1990 (as recorded in the Livro Histórico, vol. 2, folio 017, inscription 532, of Mar. 14, 1990).

103. Nobre, "O passado pela frente," 50.

104. Lúcio Costa's well-known expression was written in this context: " is up to us now to retrieve all this lost time, extending a hand to the master builder, always so scorned, to the old 'portuga' of 1910, because - say what you will - it was he who, alone, kept the good tradition." Cf. Costa, "Documentação necessária," 462. Also see: Silvana Barbosa Rubino, "Gilberto Freyre e Lúcio Costa, ou a boa tradição."

105. Puppi, *Por uma história não moderna da arquitetura brasileira*.

106. Ibid., 17-18.
107. Ibid., 22 (note 7).
108. Ibid., 21.
109. See: José Pereira Graça Aranha, *A estética da vida*.
110. In a letter dated April 30, 1935, responding to an informal request from Capanema for suggestions regarding the reform of higher education in the arts, Mário made the following remarks: "There are however a few disciplines that immediately encompass all the arts. Aesthetics (in its philosophical conception), the History of Arts and Ethnography." Letter from Mário de Andrade to Gustavo Capanema, quoted in Schwartzman, Bomeny and Costa, *Tempos de Capanema*, 362.
111. "Brazilian popular music is the most complete, the most totally national, the strongest creation of our race so far. For it is by intelligently observing our folklore and taking advantage of it that artistic music will develop"; "The same soft sweetness, the same throatiness, the same malinconia, the same ferocity, the same touchy sexuality, the same cry of love rules the creation of national music from north to south." Mário de Andrade, *Ensaio sobre a música brasileira*, 73 and 109. In the writing of the doctoral thesis, the third edition of the book, from 1972, was used, but the references to this book were made from the excellent critical edition organized by Flávia Camargo Toni and published by Edusp in 2020.
112. Andrade, *Ensaio sobre a música brasileira*, 85. According to Gilda de Melo e Souza, "is the textbook for the nationalist project in music. Published in 1928, it calls forth musicians to bring about a highbrow transposition of folklore elements as a starting point for the establishment of a specifically Brazilian music." Gilda de Mello e Souza, *O tupi e o alaúde: uma interpretação de Macunaíma*, 31 (note 16).
113. This is probably why Mário de Andrade paid little attention to the developments of popular music towards samba. This fact becomes evident if we compare his research on musical traditions and the initiatives of Blaise Cendrars while visiting Brazil in 1924: "Cendrars, who had published a Black Anthologia in 1921, warns his Brazilian friends about the contribution that blacks could give – and were already giving – to the process of consolidating a spontaneous popular culture, free from patterns of imitation. His interest in the *favelas*, which he visited aboard a hospital ambulance, and in the music produced by black people, who were forging a new rhythm, the samba, and also his acquaintance with composer Donga, whom he introduced to Rio intellectuals, led Gilberto Freyre to recognize, with a hint of surprise and spite, that in the movement for the valorization of blacks, which he was then initiating, he found traces of Cendrars' passage. Carlos Augusto Calil, "Tradutores de Brasil," 331.

114. Cf. Guerra, *O primitivismo em Mário de Andrade, Oswald de Andrade e Raul Bopp*, 248-249.

115. Cassiano Ricardo, *Martim Cererê*, 10.

116. Margareth da Silva Pereira et al., *Le Corbusier e o Brasil*, 12.

117. Margareth da Silva Pereira, "A arquitetura brasileira e o mito," 241.

118. Blaise Cendrars, quoted in Le Corbusier, "O espírito sulamericano," 71.

119. Le Corbusier, "Corolário brasileiro," 89.

120. Pereira, "A arquitetura brasileira e o mito," 243.

121. See: Holanda, *Visão do paraíso.*

122. Andrade, "Manifesto antropófago," 16.

123. Andrade, "Manifesto da poesia Pau-Brasil," 9.

124. Antonio Risério, "A dupla modernista e as realidades brasileiras."

125. Antônio Risério's statement can be put into perspective through Antonio Cândido's interpretation of a common point between Mário and Oswald de Andrade in the two texts in question, *Macunaíma* and *Serafim Ponte Grande*: "Let us remember, also, that this primitivism – defined by a character in *Chão* as the search for the natural man through the 'bad savage', not the 'good' one – meant in both authors a kind of showy aggressiveness that undoes the bourgeois line of decorum and measure. It is a different kind of shock, breaking away from the balanced style of authors such as Machado de Assis and the advent of certain forms of excess — the grotesque, the erotic, the obscene, which only appeared in a repressed way in our literature, quite used to other excesses: the sentimental, the pathetic, the grandiloquent." Antonio Cândido, "Digressão sentimental sobre Oswald de Andrade," 86.

126. Aracy Amaral affirms that these drawings are the direct result of her studies in Paris between 1922 and 1923, especially with André Lhote and Albert Gleizes, who taught her how to control the line: "And it was precisely the mastery of the line that allowed the artist to produce drawings like those of the 1924 trip to Rio de Janeiro and the historic cities of Minas Gerais". Aracy Amaral, and Regina Teixeira de Barros, *Tarsila: estudos e anotações*, 17. Renata Teixeira de Barros, in the same exhibition catalog, says that "the excursion to Minas, in turn, resulted in about a hundred drawings, studies and sketches of rural and urban landscapes [...]. In this rich material, it is possible to discern fragments of paintings such as Morro da favela, Carnaval em Madureira and Barra do Piraí, from 1924, and Mamoeiro, Lagoa Santa and Passagem de Nível, from 1925." Regina Teixeira de Barros, "Sobre os desenhos de Tarsila," 27.

127. Sílvio Castro, *Teoria e política do modernismo brasileiro*, 111.

128. Andrade, "Manifesto antropófago," 14.

129. Ibid., 14.

130. Afonso Arinos de Melo Franco, *O índio brasileiro e a Revolução Francesa: as origens da teoria da bondade natural*. Oswald de Andrade's quote would be the perfect epigraph for the book; however, Arinos, who was born in Minas Gerais and lived most of his life in Rio de Janeiro, never mentions the writer from São Paulo — an intriguing fact considering the friendly relationship between the two. In his inaugural address at the Brazilian Academy of Letters, on November 26, 1999, Afonso Arinos recalled that, "whenever they came from São Paulo, Recife and Porto Alegre, Mário and Oswald de Andrade, Gilberto Freyre and Érico Veríssimo would visit our home". Afonso Arinos de Melo Franco, *Discurso de posse*.

131. Franco, *O índio brasileiro e a Revolução Francesa*, 165.

132. Ibid., 198.

133. Nudity is recurrently mentioned by travelers, artists and theorists in association either with the tropical climate or moral features – innocence, purity, naivety, simplicity –, as is the case of Rousseau: "The savages of America, who walk around completely naked and who only live on the product of their hunting, have never been subjugated; indeed, what yoke could be imposed on men who need nothing?". Jean-Jacques Rousseau, *Discurso sobre as ciências e as artes*, 335.

134. The Tupi-Guarani hammock, so ubiquitous in Brazilian art - including architecture, as seen earlier -, shows up in prints, paintings and reports by Europeans that portray the Portuguese colony during the 16th century, as highlighted by Affonso Arinos when mentioning that the hammocks used by the Indians appear in Montaigne from his reading of Jean de Léry. Cf. Franco, *O índio brasileiro e a Revolução Francesa*, 181.

135. Ibid., 275.

136. The first Brazilian festival, arranged in honor of the King of France Henry II and Queen Catarina de Médici, which took place in 1550, was taken up again in 1850 by Ferdinand Denis, based on the report "Suntuosa visita", attributed to Maurice Sève and published in 1551, in Rouen. See: Ferdinand Denis. *Une fête brésilienne célébrée à Rouen en 1550, suivie d'un fragment du XVIe siècle roulant sur la théogonie des anciens peuples du Brésil, et des poésies en langue tupique de Christovam Valente*.

137. "I had with me for a long time a man who had stayed ten or twelve years in that new world which has been discovered in this century, in the place where Villegaignon landed and which he named France Antarctique". Montaigne, *Ensaios*, 100.

138. Andrew Thevet, *Les singularités de la France Antarctique*.

139. Jean de Lery, *Histoire d'un voyage faict en la terre du Brésil*.

140. Montaigne, *Ensaios*, 102.

141. Rousseau, *Discurso sobre a origem e os fundamentos da desigualdade entre os homens*, 238.

142. Jean-Jacques Rousseau, "Julie, ou la nouvelle Heloise," quoted in Franco, *O índio brasileiro e a Revolução Francesa*, 319.

143. Hugues Grotius (1768), "Le droit de la guerre et de la paix," quoted in Franco, *O índio brasileiro e a Revolução Francesa*, 210.

144. Franco, *O índio brasileiro e a Revolução Francesa*, 149.

145. Ibid., 138.

146. Pereira, "A arquitetura brasileira e o mito," 246.

147. Ibid., 247.

148. Ibid., 247.

149. Knowingly, psychoanalysis takes euphoria and melancholy as facets of the same psychological type: the manic-depressive. In the European tradition, from which Sigmund Freud drew his primary materials, euphoria and melancholy are features repeatedly present in biographies and critical analyses of artists. See: Rudolf Wittkower, and Margot Wittkower, *Nascidos bajo el signo de Saturno: genio y temperamento de los artistas desde la Antigüedad hasta la Revolución Francesa*. Erwin Panofsky offers an interesting record of Michelangelo's artistic life in the Florentine Neoplatonic milieu, where melancholic anguish, or inertia of spirit, is the major attribute of artistic genius. See: Erwin Panofsky, "O movimento neoplatônico e Miguel Ângelo."

150. According to Alfredo Bosi, the ambiguity of feelings is, in *Macunaíma*, the very ambiguity of the national character: "Macunaíma loses the muiraquitã, loses the protection of Ci Mãe do Mato and of Vei a Sol, gets soft with a Portuguese woman, but not even then does he acquire a fixed, white and civilized identity. His destiny, in fact, comes to be precisely this: never to establish any constant identity". Alfredo Bosi. "Situação de Macunaíma," 180. Cavalcanti Proença points to the inconsistency present in the ethnicity-psychology relationship: "Macunaíma, who is born both Indian and black, gets blue eyes when he reaches the upland area; as for his brothers, one becomes Indian and the other black. And they all remain brothers. Macunaíma, however, does not acquire a European soul. He is white only in his skin and habits. His soul is a mixture of everything." Manoel Cavalcanti Proença, *Roteiro de Macunaíma*, 19-20.

151. Andrade, *Macunaíma*, 166.

152. Ibid., 168. It is interesting to note that talking birds have been associated with the paradisiacal locus since antiquity. "But it is in a certain description by Arnoldo of Bonneval, mentioned by Patch, that the parrot is clearly inserted into the Edenic setting. All the stereotypes of this landscape as it was constituted during the Middle Ages are present in the text: the mildness of the place corresponds well to the notion of man made in the image of God; no snow or hail is known there, and nothing is sad or corrupt; with no fever there is the antidote, and, with no defects in Nature, remedies emerge. Winter horror

and bad weather are absent;
spring prevails constantly,
and everything is improved
by the harmony of time itself.
Completing the picture, atop
the cedar and other trees, sing
both the ever-living phoenix
and the parrot, and innumerable
birds sing in harmony, each in its
own way praising and jubilantly
celebrating the Creator. Cf.
Holanda, *Visão do paraíso*, 208.
With parodic inversion as one of
the fundamental stylistic mechanisms of his rhapsody, Mário
de Andrade places the parrot as
the narrator of an uninhabited
paradise.

153. Sophia S. Telles, "Lúcio Costa:
monumentalidade e intimismo,"
181. Article originally published
in the São Paulo magazine
Novos Estudos, in October 1989.
The quotations were made from
the book. Sophia Telles refers, in
this passage, to the following
text: Costa, "O arranha-céu e o
Rio de Janeiro."

154. Telles, "Lúcio Costa," 181.

155. Ibid., 175-177. The passage
referred to by Telles reads as
follows: "Now, in Portugal, popular architecture presents, in our
view, a greater interest than the
'erudite' – to use the word Mário
de Andrade applied when distinguishing the art of the people
from the so-called 'learned' art.
It is in its villages, in the virile
aspect of its rural constructions,
at once rough and welcoming,
that the qualities of the race
are best shown. Cf. Costa,
"Documentação necessária,"
457. It's quite extraordinary
the extent to which Mário
de Andrade determines Lúcio
Costa's ideas.

156. Costa, "Documentação
necessária," 458-459. For a
better understanding of what is
at issue, we made a larger cut
than Sophia Telles.

157. Joseph Rykwert, *A casa de Adão
no paraíso: a ideia da cabana
primitiva na história da arquitetura*, 43.

158. See: Hippolyte Taine, *Historia de
la literatura inglesa*.

159. Lúcio Costa, "Ensino de desenho,"
156.

160. Lúcio Costa, "Considerações
sobre arte contemporânea," 246.

161. Costa, "Muita construção,
alguma arquitetura e um milagre," 166. It might go unnoticed
by the distracted reader the
reference to an "interested art",
a recurring expression in Mário
de Andrade's texts.

162. Ibid., 166.

163. Costa, "Considerações sobre arte
contemporânea," 247.

164. Heirich Wölfflin, *Conceitos
fundamentais da história da
arte: o problema da evolução
dos estilos na arte mais recente*,
8-9.

165. Sophia S. Telles, "Pequena
crônica," 117.

166. Telles, "Lúcio Costa," 182.

167. Andrade, *Ensaio sobre a música
brasileira*, 63.

168. Ibid., 66.

169. Ibid., 199.

170. "He loves beauty. Women
fascinate him, and nature moves
him." Oscar Niemeyer, *Meu sósia
e eu*, 11. Oscar Niemeyer said
several times in his life that his
architecture was inspired by the
mountains of Minas Gerais as
painted by Guignard and by the
curves of Brazilian women.

171. Costa, "Muita construção, alguma arquitetura e um milagre," 170.
172. Lúcio Costa closes his book-testament with a sort of riddle. It is a small text, soaked in melancholy, where immobility perhaps symbolizes death: "Unusual: 'unused; unknown; strange; new.' Someone gave me this shuttlecock as a gift in February. It is pink, with green, yellow and white feathers; it is bright and light — but it has a latent charge. Since then it has been sitting on the table, waiting. Just waiting for a gesture." Lúcio Costa, "In extremis: a inusitada peteca," 597.
173. Lúcio Costa, "Carta depoimento," 125-126.
174. Translated from French by Patrícia Galvão (Pagu), published in the Santos newspaper *A Tribuna*, on Sep. 9, 1956: "Le Paranapiaçaba est la Serra do Mar / C'est ici que le train est hissé par des câbles et franchit la dure montagne en plusieurs sections / Toutes les stations sont suspendues dans le vide / Il y a beaucoup de chutes d'eau et il a fallu entreprendre de grands travaux d'art pour étayer partout la montagne qui s'effrite / Car la Serra est une montagne pourrie comme les Rognes au-dessus de Bionnasay mais les Rognes couvertes de forêts tropicales / Les mauvaises herbes qui poussent sur les talus dans la tranchée entre les voies sont toutes des plantes rares qu'on ne voit à Paris que dans les vitrines des grands horticulteurs / Dans une gare trois métis indolents étaient en train de les sarcler". Blaise Cendrars, "Feuilles de route," 233.
175. In one of the texts of his book/testament, Lúcio Costa mentions the year 1922 as the date of his trip. This is either an editorial error or an oversight by the author, as evidenced by the letter of introduction signed by Juscelino Dermeval da Fonseca, Mayor of Diamantina, dated May 10, 1924, and published as an illustration for the text itself. Lúcio Costa, "Diamantina," 27. Lúcio Costa graduated in 1922, a necessary condition to receive the distinction and perhaps this is the origin of the confusion regarding the dates. Cêça de Guimaraens also points to 1924 as the correct date of the trip. Cêça de Guimaraens, *Lúcio Costa: um certo arquiteto em incerto e secular roteiro*, 22.
176. Costa, "Diamantina," 27.
177. The text ends with the following sentence: "And little did I know that, 30 years later, I would be designing our capital city for a boy my age, born there." Ibid., 27. In other words, the text was written at least in the 1960s, but we should not rule out the hypothesis that it was produced for his book-testament, Record of an experience, from 1995.
178. The text "Reasons for the new architecture" was published two years later, in the magazine *Revista da Diretoria de Engenharia da Prefeitura do Distrito Federal*, in Jan. 1936. In the same year there was the public clash with José Marianno Filho, triggered by the competition for the ministry's headquarters building, when Lúcio Costa was treated by his opponent as a traitor to

the neocolonial cause. Alberto Xavier, in his 1962 collection *Sobre a Arquitetura*, dates the text as having been written in 1930. In the 1995 book/testament *Lúcio Costa: registro de uma vivência*, the article appears as being from 1934. Lúcio Costa, in another opportunity, makes the following comment: "Invited by Celso Kelly, I taught – and that eas the only time I did so – together with Prudente, Gilberto Freyre, Portinari and many others at the unjustly extinct University of the Federal District, conducting a course based on the study 'Reasons for the new architecture'". Costa, "À guisa de sumário," 17. The courses were taught in the short period from Jul. 1935 to Jan. 20, 1939, when it was extinguished by a decree signed by Getúlio Vargas. Cf. Schwartzman, Bomeny and Costa, *Tempos de Capanema*, 210. Lúcio Costa's performance as director-intervenor of the Escola Nacional de Belas Artes during the period 1930-1931 proves that his adhesion happened well before the publication of his first important text on modern architecture, making Xavier's dating credible. If we take into account Lúcio Costa's habit of rewriting texts and using passages previously written in new ones, we can hypothesize that 'Reasons for the new architecture' went through a long gestation process before being published.

179. "In Brazilian literature, there are two decisive moments that change the course and vitalize the entire intelligence: Romanticism, in the 19th century (1836-1870) and the movement we still call modernism, in the present century (1922-1945). Both represent culminating phases of literary particularism in the dialectic between the local and the cosmopolitan; both are inspired, nevertheless, by the European example." Antônio Cândido, "Literatura e cultura de 1900 a 1945," 112.

180. Bruand, *Arquitetura contemporânea no Brasil*, 52.

181. Reis Filho, *Racionalismo e proto-racionalismo na obra de Victor Dubugras*, 75.

182. See various articles present in: Aracy Amaral, ed., *Arquitectura neocolonial: América Latina, Caribe, Estados Unidos*.

183. Cf. Aracy Amaral, *Blaise Cendrars no Brasil e os modernistas*, 46; Eulalio, *A aventura brasileira de Blaise Cendrars*, 39.

184. Cf. Amaral, *Blaise Cendrars no Brasil e os modernistas*. See chapter "Viagem a Minas", 45 and followers.

185. Brito Broca, "Blaise Cendrars no Brasil, em 1924." *A Manhã*, Rio de Janeiro, May 4, 1952, quoted in Amaral, *Blaise Cendrars no Brasil e os modernistas*, 47.

186. In his 1924 manifesto, Oswald explicitaly takes on the advice of the Swiss-French poet: "A suggestion of Blaise Cendrars: you have the train loaded, ready to leave. A negro churns the crank of the turn-table beneath you. The slightest carelessness and you will leave in the opposite direction to your destination." Andrade, "Manifesto da poesia Pau-Brasil," 6.

187. Eulalio, *A aventura brasileira de Blaise Cendrars*, 29.
188. Ibid., 29-30.
189. "Tarsila was registering the scenes and situations she observes on her train trip through Minas. These inspire paintings, as well as poems by Mário de Andrade, Oswald de Andrade, Blaise Cendrars. And they pile up in a notebook that the artist carries in her purse: it is the phase in which she draws with a simplified, simple stroke, which suggests much of the atmosphere of the places she passes through. Nádia Batella Gotlib, *Tarsila do Amaral, a modernista*, 92. Haroldo de Campos goes a step further: it is not only the landscape of Minas Gerais that inspires Cendrars, but the pau-brasil poetics itself: "Everything seems to indicate that the Swiss poet (who was not ignorant of Portuguese, by the way) would have had knowledge of Oswald's unpublished productions, through the author himself, becoming infected by them or by his spirit. Edgar Braga states: 'Oswald de Andrade still had time to see not only his autochthonous landscape theme being assimilated but also the structure used in his own poems'. And he cites as an example the poem 'Fernando de Noronha', published by Cendrars in 1928". Haroldo de Campos, "Uma poética da radicalidade," 33.
190. Besides the already mentioned excursion to the interior of Minas Gerais in 1924, in 1927 he led an excursion to the northern region in the company of the aristocrats Olívia Guedes Penteado, Margarida Guedes Nogueira and Dulce do Amaral Pinto, Tarsila's daughter. In 1929 he went alone to the northeast, where he would meet many intellectuals - Ascenso Ferreira, Cícero Dias, Antônio Bento de Araújo Lima, Ademar Vidal — from the various states of the region he visited: Pernambuco, Alagoas, Rio Grande do Norte and Paraíba. Telê Porto Ancona Lopez, "Viagens etnográficas de Mário de Andrade," 16 and followers.
191. Mário de Andrade, less well-off than his friends, travels less, but the profound impact of his travels on his literary and critical work reveals the density and depth of his immersion in the territories visited. "His travels, rare but fundamental, are three in total and all lead him to the pith of Brazil. After the 'baroque trip' to Minas Gerais, in 1924, the great trip was the one through the Amazon, from May to August 1927. Finally, in late 1928 and early 1929, he made the ethnographic journey through the northeast of Brazil (Alagoas, Rio Grande do Norte, Paraíba and Pernambuco), with the aim of recording folkloric elements. The visual result of these last two tours totals more than 800 photographs." Schwartz, "Tupi or not Tupi," 147. The records of his trips to the Northeast and the Amazon become a fundamental book, published after his death: Mário de Andrade, *O turista aprendiz*.
192. Cândido, "Digressão sentimental sobre Oswald de Andrade," 85.

193. Lourival Gomes Machado, "Sobre a influência francesa na arte brasileira," 64, quoted in Amaral, *Blaise Cendrars no Brasil e os modernistas*, 2-3.

194. Cândido, "Digressão sentimental sobre Oswald de Andrade," 85-86.

195. That's how Euclides da Cunha sees Antônio Conselheiro e Canudos in his masterpiece *Os Sertões*.

196. Cândido, "Digressão sentimental sobre Oswald de Andrade," 85.

197. Segawa, "Lúcio Costa," 149.

198. Nobre, "O passado pela frente," 64.

199. Cândido, "Literatura e cultura de 1900 a 1945," 109.

200. Ibid., 119.

201. Lourival Gomes Machado, *Retrato da arte moderna do Brasil*, 91, quoted in Affonso Ávila, ed., *O modernismo*, 17.

202. Cândido, "Literatura e cultura de 1900 a 1945," 112.

203. Ibid., 124.

204. Ibid., 121. The intertwining of historical times presented by Antônio Cândido has a curious symmetry with Caio Prado Jr's text: "A trip through Brazil is often [...] an incursion through history, going back a century and more. A foreign professor once told me that he envied Brazilian historians who could personally witness the most vivid scenes of their past." Caio Prado Jr., *Formação do Brasil contemporâneo*, 11.

205. Ramos, "Depoimento de Oswald Andrade," quoted in Lígia Morrone Averbuck, *Cobra Norato e a revolução caraíba*, 31.

206. "In 1931, in the open letter 'To Raimundo de Moraes', Mário de Andrade, when answering the subtle accusation of plagiarism, 'defending Macunaíma from the slanderers' who denounced the presence of Theodor Koch-Grünberg's book, *Vom Roraima zum Orinoco*, makes a point of stressing that the very nature of the rhapsody had required the convergence of many authors and works to the text. And Mário is not concerned with the erudite presence, mentioning there those who, in some way, had offered him elements of popular culture. Of Amerindian legends and Brazilian particularity. Among so many authors, publicly recognized and proclaimed as sources, he attributes the greatest importance to *Vom Roraima zum Orinoco*, where he discovered the myths, legends and tales of the Taulipangs and Arekunás, as well as the god without character, Macunaíma, always in conflict with an antagonist, Piaimã. This discovery had, in fact, already been discussed, since 1927, in letters to his friend Manuel Bandeira." Telê Porto Ancona Lopez, "O texto e o livro. 1. Vínculos Makunaíma/Macunaíma," 311. Wilson Martins treats Roquette Pinto's Rondônia as a forgotten source of Macunaíma: "Because of its deliberately simple style and realistic observations of everyday details, Rondônia is already a 'modernist' book, and it is not surprising that the modernists recognized themselves in it (when one speaks of the erudite sources of Macunaíma,

which is perfectly correct, this 'literary' and psychological source is generally forgotten)." Wilson Martins, *História da inteligência brasileira – 1915-1933*, 40.
207. Roberto Schwarz, "Nacional por subtração," 37-38.
208. Ibid., 38.
209. Ibid., 46.
210. Ibid.,. 33.
211. Arantes, "Lúcio Costa e a *boa causa* da arquitetura moderna," 128-129.
212. The argument around the utopic vector present in the modernism from São Paulo, and which developed into the architectural lineage inaugurated by Lúcio Costa, was developed later. See: Guerra, "Arquitetura brasileira: tradição e utopia."
213. After this work, I had the opportunity to act as advisor in two master's researches on the relationship of Roberto Burle Marx with other architects beyond the scene of Rio de Janeiro. The dissertation by Marília Dorador Guimarães and Fernanda Rocha surveys the participations of the landscape designer in São Paulo works by Rino Levi, Marcello Fragelli, Miguel Juliano, Hans Broos, and Ruy Ohtake. The second deals with the gardens designed by Burle Marx in Fortaleza, in partnership with architects Acácio Gil Borsoi, Luiz Fiuza, Delberg Ponce de Leon, Fausto Nilo and brothers Francisco and José Nasser Hissa. See: Marília Dorador Guimarães, "Roberto Burle Marx: a contribuição do artista e paisagista no Estado de São Paulo;" Fernanda Cláudia Lacerda Rocha, "Os jardins residenciais de Roberto Burle Marx em Fortaleza: entre descontinuidades e conexões."
214. Roberto Burle Marx, "Depoimento," 307. Text originally published in Spanish in the book *Panorâmica de la arquitectura latinoamericana*, organized by Damián Bayón. The quotes are from the first edition of *Arquitetura moderna brasileira: depoimento de uma geração*, organized by Alberto Xavier (Hunter Douglas Project). In an interview with Ana Rosa de Oliveira, many years later, he repeated almost the same version: "I was lucky because Lúcio Costa lived on the same street as my family. I've known him since I was nine years old. If today I am 82, he is 90. This shows you what living with people who know... An architecture lesson from Lúcio is the lesson of a master." Cf. Ana Rosa de Oliveira, "Roberto Burle Marx e o jardim moderno brasileiro."
215. Marx, "Depoimento," 306. On another occasion, he said almost the same, but giving credit to the botanist in charge: "In Berlin, I frequented the Dahlem Botanical Garden assiduously. The collections of plants, grouped there by Engler under geographical criteria, were for me living lessons in botany and ecology. It was there that I could appreciate for the first time, in a systematic way, many specimens of the typical Brazilian flora. They were beautiful species almost never used in our gardens," quoted in Ana Rosa de Oliveira, "Bourlemarx ou Burle Marx?".

216. The idea that Roberto Burle Marx's thought is directly linked to the encounter and partnership between Lúcio Costa and Gregori Warchavchik – and, by extension, with Mina Klabin's landscape practice – was developed by us in an article that was published in three situations: Abilio Guerra, "Lúcio Costa, Gregori Warchavchik e Roberto Burle Marx: síntese entre arquitetura e natureza tropical."
217. Farias, "Gregori Warchavchik," 16.
218. Quoted in Ferraz, *Warchavchik e a introdução da nova arquitetura no Brasil*, 51.
219. *Chômage*, in French, means both the unemployment situation and the state of inactivity. Lúcio Costa impinges on the word a meaning quite close to the idea of "creative leisure", which Mário de Andrade and Oswald de Andrade argued for.
220. Lucio Costa, "Chômage," 83.
221. Walter Gropius, *Bauhaus: novarquitetura*.
222. Guilheme Wisnik makes an interesting observation on the presence of hammocks in the Brazilian Pavilion for the Milan Triennial: "The hammock, in Brazil, is at the same time a place of rest and reflection. It is also one of the finest handcrafted objects: its texture denotes a patient and rigorous constructive knowledge. Suspended through the tension of cables, it seems to reveal, like a *ready-made* turned inside out, the possibility of an artistic place in which gratuity means both commitment, and in which *chômage* means production and creativity." Guilherme Wisnik, *Lúcio Costa: entre o empenho e a reserva*, 49. Eduardo Rossetti's considerations about this project are in line with the current argumentation: "The Brazilian pavilion in this Triennial seems to suggest an alternative to the practices of technological progress and the dynamics of industrial society, maintaining its heterogeneity and uniqueness, juxtaposing socio-cultural values, technical procedures, rhythms and ways of life. It explores the contrast between the industrial, dynamic, urban and pressing rhythm that builds Brasília and a calm, telluric, popular and simple rhythm suggested by the act of lying down in a hammock. The country's technical, social and aesthetic vicissitudes are presented with great force and clarity: we may build 'Brasílias', but we still retain archaic cultural knowledge, with latent values, as our hammocks and rafts demonstrate." Eduardo Pierrotti Rossetti, "Riposatevi, a tropicália de Lúcio Costa: o Brasil na XIII Trienal de Milão."
223. "The cactus, together with the thrifty vegetation of Mina Warchavchik's landscaping, would always enhance the architect's works. Functioning as sculptures, with organic rigidity and a rough appearance, they contrast with the geometric asepsis of the architectural work, as is the case of this residence located on Rua Itápolis, projecting the jagged ink of its shadows onto the clean and white surfaces". Farias, "Gregori Warchavchik," 19.

224. José Lira highlights the surprising quality of Warchavchik's project; however, he also points out its fake character, when one takes into account the social position of the owners: "This alliance between geometric and functional discipline and vernacular values, adapted to the semi-rural or tropical context, would come to fruition in the shameless primitivism of the social pavilion designed by Warchavchik in 1946 for Marjorie da Silva Prado, on her seaside farm on Pernambuco beach, in Guarujá. [...] A mix of modern arbour and stylized sales stand, the rustic solution of the small pavilion located on the edge of the immense plot of land, somewhere between pop and populism, evoked the charm of the seasonal huts of fishermen on the Brazilian coast while also expressing the eccentricity and boldness of its owners, whose real estate investment, by the way, was absolutely indifferent to the indigenous uses of the beach. In terms of architecture, one can see Warchavchik's resourcefulness in the use of different materials, such as wood, thatch, true grass, leather, raw cement, stone, and exposed masonry, in the construction method, in the finishes and in the decoration, as well as in the expressive use of handicrafts, which added to the expressionist reinterpretation of the thatched hut's single roof plan, with its rooms, levels and accesses to the outside defined centrifugally by the rotation around the central pillar. Inside there was the kitchen, living room, bar and changing rooms, and outside a gazebo-terrace developed under the smoothed wooden structure of the thatched roof. Everywhere the rustic furniture and fixtures contributed to the poor ambience of the architecture." Lira, *Warchavchik: fraturas da vanguarda*, 431-434.

225. Vera Beatriz Siqueira, *Burle Marx: paisagens transversas*, 18.

226. Ibid., 18.

227. "The magnolia grandiflora is a tree from North America. You can use it in Argentina because there are some plants that go well with the climate and that give the impression that they have always existed in the landscape". Marx, "Depoimento," 309.

228. Ibid., 309.

229. "I remember a garden I made in Vienna in 1962. People were disappointed because they thought I was going to make – in the heart of Europe – a tropical garden. That I was going to come up with orchids in the aspens, jungle vines climbing through the pines. Of course, I didn't do any of that, because I'm convinced that each climate has its own flora, the use of which has to be in accordance with the physical environment". Ibid., 309.

230. "I remember that, when I was working in Parque del Este, in Venezuela, there were people who would come to take a look, and their only comment was: 'But this is nothing but weeds!'". Ibid., 311.

231. "I believe that, in order to make a garden, we have to start by understanding the environment. If I make a garden for the Amazon, that same garden cannot be used for Rio de Janeiro or São Paulo. We have to understand that we must use plants from nature and, with them, build gardens made by and for man". Idem, ibidem, p. 310.

232. Ibid., 307-308.

233. Siqueira, *Burle Marx*, 7. In italics, passages taken from Burle Marx's original report; in quotation marks, passages taken from the author's text.

234. The series of trips through Brazil, which took place in three cycles – intellectuals from São Paulo in the 1920s, architects at Iphan from 1937 onwards, and landscape designers led by Roberto Burle Marx from the 1940s onwards – have a justification, explained in Mario de Andrade's *Essay on Brazilian Music*: the need to collect the raw material to be used in artistic production from the popular base – and it is very simple to transfer the issue to literature, architecture, landscaping or other arts. In another text published later, we developed these similarities a little bit: Lopez, "Viagens etnográficas de Mário de Andrade."

235. Unless we are mistaken, Mário de Andrade is absent from the book and Lúcio Costa is mentioned only once, when he narrates the invitation to the garden at the Schwartz house. Siqueira, *Burle Marx*, 11.

236. During the research that resulted in the thesis that is the basis of this book, we published a book that touches upon the friendship between Rino Levi and Burle Marx, in addition to the importance of the study and collection trips they took together. "With basic notions of botany, Levi made several exploratory trips, in which, accompanied by Burle Marx, he studied the Brazilian flora, collecting specimens that he cultivated in the garden of his house, which became a small laboratory. He thus builds a kind of ideal Brazilian nature, a synthesis of our plant species that he found most interesting". See: Renato Anelli, Abilio Guerra, and Nelson Kon. *Rino Levi: arquitetura e cidade*, 90. In September 1965, during a botanical expedition in Morro do Chapéu, in the interior of Bahia, the landscape designer witnessed the death of the São Paulo architect.

237. Siqueira, *Burle Marx*, 33.

238. "The Ministry of Education and Public Health was created by Decree n. 19,402 of Nov. 14, 1930. Law 378 of Jan. 13, 1937, drafted by Gustavo Capanema, defined it as the Ministry of Education and Health. Later, with the creation of the Ministry of Health, it became the Ministry of Education and Culture – MEC (Law 1.920, from Jul. 25, 1953). In 1960, the building was renamed Palácio da Cultura (Palace of Culture). With the Decree n. 91.144, Mar. 15, 1985, the Ministry of Culture – MinC was created, and the building came to be identified as Palácio Gustavo Capanema, as it is called until today". Segre, *Ministério da Educação e Saúde*, 98 (note 5).

239. Oliveira, "Roberto Burle Marx e o jardim moderno brasileiro."

240. Interview with Fernando Tábora by Ana Rosa de Oliveira, Jan. 8, 1997, quoted in Oliveira, "Bourlemarx ou Burle Marx?".

241. Ibid., 306.

242. Ibid., 311-312.

243. Ibid., 311.

244. "By the sap of the plants and the vigor of the colors, Burle Marx's gardens are still part of nature, although they already participate in the life of the house and serve to alter its spatial rhythm. Their function is now to enlarge it, to make it spill over into the open spaces." Mário Pedrosa, "O paisagista Burle Marx," 285.

245. Mário Pedrosa, "Arquitetura paisagística no Brasil," 282.

246. Ibid., 283.

247. The revaluation of the Brazilian flora, according to Pedrosa, is directly related to field research: "The colonialist solution that condemned the great imperial palm tree did nothing more than copy the romantic gardens, *avant la lettre*, of the end of the 18th century. Burle Marx showed the false character of this so-called solution to go get the material he needed in the true sources, that is, in the Brazilian vegetation of inexhaustible resources, from the Amazon rainforest, where he brought us specimens in all the splendid vigor of its savagery, to the backyards of the caboclo's little houses or the side of the roads, where he went to pick plants and flowers abandoned, despised, but familiar to the ambience of the Brazilian countryside, like stray dogs without owners, wandering through backyards." Pedrosa, "O paisagista Burle Marx," 286.

248. Pedrosa, "Arquitetura paisagística no Brasil," 283.

249. Raul Bopp, "Cobra Norato," 17.

250. The French magazine *L'Architecture d'Aujourd'hui* has dedicated some special issues to Brazilian architecture: n. 13/14 of Sep. 1947; n. 42-43 of Aug. 1952; n. 90 of Jun./Jul. 1960 (special issue on Brasilia); n. 171 of Jan.-Feb. 1974 (special issue on Oscar Niemeyer); and n. 396 of Jul./Aug. 2013 (special issue on Brazil).

251. José Lins do Rego, "O homem e a paisagem," 302-304.

252. Ibid., 303.

253. Ibid., 300.

254. Ibid., 301.

255. Ibid., 301.

256. Ibid., 302-303.

257. Ibid., 303.

258. Ibid., 303-304.

259. Ibid., 304.

260. Ibid., 304.

261. José Pereira Graça Aranha, *Canaã*, 50-51.

262. See: Yoshie Sakiyama Barreirinhas. *Menotti del Picchia, o gedeão do modernismo: 1920/22.*

263. The double issue 8-9 of Klaxon magazine, for the period from December 1922 to January 1923, was dedicated to Graça Aranha. The diversity of perspectives present in the texts and poems give an idea of the importance of the intellectual to the modernist generation.

264. The chamber work "Sexteto Místico" was composed by Heitor Villa-Lobos for flute, oboe, saxophone, guitar, celesta,

and harp. There is controversy regarding the work's dating, but researcher Humberto Amorim found "a manuscript from 1917 and another incomplete one from 1921, both with differences when compared to the edited version", "published in 1957 by Max-Eschig". Allan Kolodzieiski, "Intertextualidade no Sexteto Místico de Heitor Villa-Lobos," 2. Villa-Lobos' dedication, therefore, boils down to the score of the opening bars of the piece.

265. Redação, "Sem título," 32.
266. Cândido Motta Filho, O psicólogo da raça, 6.
267. Rubens de Moraes, "Graça Aranha e a crítica europeia," 9.
268. Renato Almeida, "A estética de Malazarte," 3-4.
269. Luiz Annibal Falcão, "Assim ele compõe," 11.
270. Ronald Carvalho, "Graça Aranha, criador de entusiasmo," 3.
271. Guilherme Almeida, Mormaço (para Graça Aranha), 11.
272. Oswald de Andrade, "O modernismo," 123.
273. Ibid., 123.
274. Letter to Manuel Bandeira, São Paulo, Nov. 22, 1924, 153-154, quoted in Marcos Antonio de Moraes, ed., *Correspondência Mário de Andrade & Manuel Bandeira*. In his statement on the modernist movement — a sardonic and sullen text demolishing the group's facts and heroic deeds —, Mário de Andrade is less polite in his jokes: "And then the famous Graça Aranha, bringing his 'Estética da vida'=' from Europe, came to São Paulo, and tried to meet us and group us around his philosophy. We laughed a bunch at the 'Estética da vida', which by the way attacked certain European moderns that we admired, but we frankly adhered to the master." Mário de Andrade, "O movimento modernista," 234. The same ambiguity of love and hate in relation to Graça Aranha and the same retrospective strategy of emptying his intellectual importance by inflating the institutional dimension can be verified in the episode of the foundation of the modernist magazine *Estética*: "Prudente de Moraes Neto and Sérgio Buarque de Holanda were looking for a name for the magazine and were thinking of writing the article-program together, when they met Graça Aranha, who, learning about the problem, solved it immediately. He chose the name: *Aesthetics*, and offered to write the introductory article. The young editors hesitated at first, but eventually accepted. Sérgio Buarque leaves no doubt that the title, 'which to some may seem to be the fruit of a supposed avant la lettre inclination towards the aestheticism of our current post-modernists, was purely his suggestion'. And he clarifies: 'I am almost certain that we agreed to it somewhat against our will and for lack of anything better. Prudente's justification complements his colleague's: 'It was, at least, a name of immense prestige to endorse our adventure." Maria Cecília de Moraes Leonel, *Estética e modernismo*, 46.

275. Mário da Silva Brito, *História do modernismo brasileiro 1: antecedentes da Semana de Arte Moderna*, 322.

276. Wilson Martins, *O modernismo*, 152. He is an author of great insight and, in the volume dedicated to modernism in his monumental research on Brazilian intellectuals, there are many findings when dealing with the relationships between the characters. See: Martins, *História da inteligência brasileira – 1915-1933*.

277. The fictional writing of Oswald de Andrade, according to the well-founded opinion of Haroldo de Campos, expresses in its form the strength of demystifying criticism: "Oswald's parody catches these same bad habits in their rhetorical dilution, it is a fierce criticism of what Paulo Prado, in his important preface to Oswal"s first book of poems (*Pau-Brasil*, 1925), would call 'the evil of a fatuous eloquence that drags on', 'one of the great evils of the race'" According to Campos, it is a "parodistic sketch of a far-fetched and false language and, through it, the satirical characterization of the status of a determined urban social group of academic graduates to whom it served as an emblem and caste jargon." Haroldo de Campos, "Miramar na mira," XIX; XVII.

278. "Graça Aranha (1868/1931), a Recife graduate (1886), in the early period of his activity was an ardent disciple of Tobias Barreto and a partisan of evolutionist monism, as can be seen in his preface to Fausto Cardoso's work, Concepção monística do universo." Antonio Paim, *A filosofia da escola do Recife*, 71-72.

279. Among the members of the "Recife School", literary critic and historian Sílvio Romero is the one who gained more projection in the 20th century, thanks to Antonio Cândido'dissertation, defended in 1945 and later turned into a book. Cândido takes pains to demonstrate the intellectual's autonomy before the limits imposed by the methods he had adopted: "The application of determinism to literature was a consequence that would not be long in coming. Its most perfect and happy form, the Tainian triad, seemed to chain the hitherto capricious expansion of the human spirit to a system of causal links and inescapable determinants. The work of Sílvio Romero was, in Brazil, the first and most complete expression of this tendency". Antônio Cândido, *O método crítico de Sílvio Romero*, 97.

280. "The effort at synthesis, which we saw in Tobias [Barreto] as a rejection of eclecticism and as a hidden attempt to bring Kant and Haeckel together; which in Silvio [Romero] had given primacy to Spencer; which in Arthur Orlando sought to stand between the manias of monism and the rigidity of positivism." Nelson Saldanha, *A escola do Recife*, 60.

264. Ibid., 92.

265. Aranha, *A estética da vida*, 86.
Completely immersed in the
modernist universe of São Paulo,
Paulo Prado, one of the promoters of the Modern Art Week
of 1922, notes the relationship
between man and environment
where the words of Graça
Aranha resound: "In the equato-
rial zone of Brazil, the constantly
hot and humid climate develops
vegetation of incomparable
strength and violence. It is the
Amazon Hylean, covering the
largest expanse of land in the
universe with trees, more than 3
million square kilometers, where
man's imperfect senses can
barely grasp and fix the disorder
of branches, foliage, fruit and
flowers that sands him." Paulo
Prado, *Retrato do Brasil: ensaio
sobre a tristeza brasileira*, 16.

266. Aranha, *A estética da vida*, 107.

267. These are the ideas, widespread
in the 19th century, that
support Sigmund Freud in the
construction of his hypothesis
on the constitution of the
primitive ego, the first moment
of psychic separation of the
individual in relation to the
outside world. "A first separation
would thus be established, on
the background of the psychic
continuity between the baby
and the breast, compared in a
note of the 'Two Principles' to
the little chicken in the egg, to
signify that the libido circulating
in this system is the libido of
self-investment. It is from this
state, in which what is going
to be subject and what is going
to be world are still indistinct,
that Laplanche and Pontalis
derive the primitive phantasm,

in which the subject occupies all
places at the same time". Renato
Mezan, *Freud, pensador da
cultura*, 360.

268. Sigmund Freud looked to the
symmetry between ontogenesis
and phylogenesis proposed by
Haeckel as inspiration for his
analogy between the infantile
and the primitive developed
in some of his major cultural
texts, such as 'Totem and
Taboo', 'Civilization and Its
Discontents', and others. "Taken
from Haeckel's materialism,
the 'fundamental biological
law' postulates that, in a given
species, each individual during
its embryological development
reproduces in an abbreviated
(and therefore deformed)
manner the stages of the
species' evolution. [...] The myth
of the primitive horde is invoked
repeatedly, not only in the
context of individual psychology,
but also to account for the
phenomena of the multitude in
'Psychology of the Masses', the
origin of monotheism in 'Moses
and the Monotheistic Religion',
and the extraordinary power
of religious representations in
'The Future of an Illusion'. Myth
thus takes on proportions as
an essential heuristic principle,
acting both in the individual
unconscious and in the genesis
of social formations and the
origin of social contents of the
utmost importance." Cf. Mezan,
Freud, pensador da cultura,
434-435. There is no indication
that Graça Aranha knew Freud's
work, so any similarities must
be attributed, at least until
more systematic studies prove

otherwise, to the intellectual influences suffered by both, especially the evolutionist ideas derived from Haeckelian biological monism and conceptions of psychic atavism, of romantic origin. In any case, Mário de Andrade and Oswald de Andrade suffer the impact, which can be verified in their works, of reading Freud.

269. Leonel, *Estética e modernismo*, 48.

270. Paulo Prado presents another interpretation based on Thomas Buckle's conception of mesological determinism, where local and exotic elements are combined. In *Retrato do Brasil* (Picture of Brazil), from 1928, he explores the role of the lasciviousness of the tropics in the consolidation of the national character, marked by sadness. "Allied in the adventurer were the seduction of the land and the hastiness of adolescence. For men coming from a policed Europe, the ardor of temperament, the amorality of manners, the absence of civilized modesty – and all the continuous voluptuous tumescence of virgin nature – were an invitation to a loose and unruly life in which everything was permitted. The native, on the other hand, was a lustful animal, living without any constraint in the satisfaction of his carnal desires. Nature-induced lust leads to sadness: "From the weakening of physical energy, from the absence or diminution of mental activity, one of the characteristic results in men and in communities is undoubtedly the development of the melancholic propensity.

Post coitum animal triste, nisi galus qui cantat, as stated in the old medical adage. Later, the Negro, inserted in this social framework, also contributed to the conformation of the melancholic character of the Brazilian with his sexual exuberance: "Evil, however, gnawed deeper. The slaves were terrible elements of corruption within the families. The black and mulatto women lived in the practice of all vices. As children – says Vilhena –, they began to corrupt their young masters by giving them the first lessons in libertinism. The little mulattos were very pernicious. They transformed the houses, according to the consecrated and precise phrase, into true dens of depravity." Prado, *Retrato do Brasil*, 33, 23 and 141.

271. Our phrase is not without some redundancy, after all, according to the *Aurélio* dictionary, telurism is the very "influence of the soil of a region on the customs, character, etc., of the inhabitants".

272. Rego, "O homem e a paisagem," 304.

273. Aranha, *A estética da vida*, 121. In complete disagreement with Graça Aranha's vision about the insertion of Machado de Assis' work in our cultural history, Roberto Schwarz will see in the "illusion" and in the "irony", as well as in the imported intellectual models, an acute conscience of the imitative character of the Brazilian culture and a subtle way to bring to surface the alienating Brazilian social reality. By reiterating Machado de Assis' denunciation of the

"affectation" of Brazilian intellectual life, which results from the incompatibility between "local conditions" and "imported values", Schwarz highlights the mismatch between the "center" and the "periphery", placing the problem of literature and intellectual production in general in the field of ideology, that is, of false consciousness and domination. See: Roberto Schwarz, *Um mestre na periferia do capitalismo: Machado de Assis*.

274. We share the hypothesis proposed by Eduardo Jardim de Moraes: "our hypothesis is that the barbarian elements that are an integral part of Brazilian culture are not simply rejected by Graça Aranha, but thought of as data to be transformed in the process of accommodation of the Brazilian soul to nature." Eduardo Jardim de Moraes, *A brasilidade modernista: sua dimensão filosófica*, 34.

275. Which is what happened, according to Graça Aranha, with one of the most important Brazilian writers, who "dissimulates and ignores the great cosmic element in which the Brazilian spirit lives. The cleverness of Machado de Assis, deceiving the existence of a tropical nature that crushes him, and freeing himself from its oppression through irony, does not solve the primordial problem of Brazilian intelligence, which is to overcome the terror of the physical world and incorporate nature. Culture will free our spirit". Aranha, *A estética da vida*, 117-118.

276. In our master's thesis, which became a book, we discussed at length the hypothesis that a substantial part of our modernism is umbilically linked to the tradition of Brazilian thought, even if its formalization, strongly marked by the European modernist aesthetics, apparently contradicts this statement. See: Guerra, *O primitivismo em Mário de Andrade, Oswald de Andrade e Raul Bopp*.

277. In 1967, at the III Festival da Música Popular Brasileira (Brazilian Popular Music Festival) which took place at Teatro Paramount, in São Paulo, Gilberto Gil and the Mutantes group, led by Arnaldo Baptista and Rita Lee, were forbidden to present the song *Domingo no Parque* accompanied by electric guitars; according to the organization, the instruments were incompatible with an authentically national music. Over the years, Gilberto Gil came to be, with guitars and everything else, one of the icons of the so-called MPB, reworking the issue again in the line of the modernist tradition. There is no doubt that Oswald de Andrade would approve of the synthesis in question.

278. Andrade, "Manifesto antropófago," 13.

Unfinished Epilogue

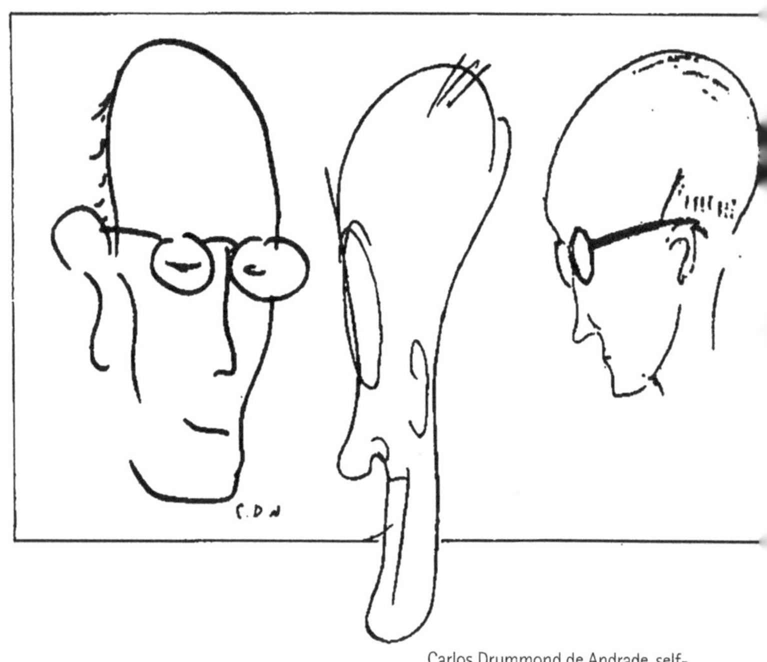

Carlos Drummond de Andrade, self-portraits. *O Povo*, Fortaleza, Aug. 23, 1987, 4

The most superb bridges and buildings,
that which we elaborate in the workshops,
that which was thought and soon reaches

a distance greater than thought,
the earth's resources brought under control
and the passions and the impulses and the torments

and everything that defines the earthly being
or that extends to the animals
and enlists the plants so as to soak

in the resentful sleep of minerals,
that which goes around the world and engulfs itself
again
in the strange geometric order of everything,

and the original absurdity ridden with riddles,
its truths, higher than so many
monuments erected to the truth

and the memory of the gods, and the solemn
sense of death, which blooms
in the trunk of the most glorious existence,

everything was presented to me in a glimpse
and called me to its august kingdom,
finally offered to human sight

Carlos Drummond de Andrade, "A máquina do mundo,"
1951[1]

In one of his books, Josep Maria Montaner suggests that America is a "laboratory" for European social and urban experiments: "the importance of landscape is one of the defining features of America, and that is how Europe conceived it: it represents the survival of a natural landscape that Europe sacrificed on the other side of the ocean, prompted by the industrial revolution. From the European point of view, America, where adventurers seek wealth, a shelter for exiles and a territory for the exploration of utopias, becomes the American laboratory."[2] Long before that, Oswald de Andrade developed a similar argument, but with an irreverent, anarchic inversion in which Europe greatly benefits from the Tupi-Guarani worldview, actually owing to it its great libertarian achievements: "Without us Europe would not even have its poor declaration of human rights."[3] Today, when the contemporary world is faced with the civilizational deadlock presented by the risk of extinction, Amerindian thought once again surges as a repository of valuable contributions to a new social thought. According to Michael Hardt and Antonio Negri, the Brazilian Eduardo Viveiros de Castro "presents the Amerindian perspective as an inversion of a series of conventional modern philosophical positions, to draw the consequences from the fact that Amerindians conceive animals and other non-humans as people, as human types, in such a way that human interactions with what would normally be called *nature* are conceived as something like *social relations*."[4] Both appropriations of indigenous thought in such different moments of our national trajectory represent the extremes of a full arc of exchanges where the myth of an earthly paradise and the history of a utopia meet and mix. These are real phenomena in the realm of ideas, imagination and social attitudes, resulting from the encounter of different cultures and civilizations, something that at times seems barely perceptible, like an underground stream. It is a story of many defeats, but also of survival of hope.

The discernible history of Brazil in the 20th century is the result of the hegemonic belief in the forces of modernization and progress, a kind of anti-utopian vector that sweeps inland territories – our *hinterland* –, gaining symbolic expression with the construction of Brasília. Since the construction of the Madeira-Mamoré Railroad in the first two decades of the 1900s, this immense territory began to be understood as a reserve full of resources to be explored by the urban center, which went on to design miraculous projects encompassing government agencies and private initiatives, both national and foreign. In this context, the native peoples were treated either as cheap labor – with the constant incorporation of their knowledge about the forest and rivers rarely acknowledged – or as an obstacle to be overcome, depending on the subservience or bellicosity of each native community. The exploitation of natural resources – wood, rubber, minerals – and deforestation for crops and cattle farming resulted in the destruction of the natural environment, a process that expanded exponentially during the military regime, with the planned occupation of the Amazon (Transamazonian highway, Manaus Free Trade Zone), the agricultural fronts in the Midwest and the large multinational mining and logging corporations, which keep harassing and destroying the great forest.

The ambivalence between progressive thinking and civilizational forces becomes quite evident in some concrete cases of territorial occupation. When the steel companies Companhia Siderúrgica Belgo-Mineira, Companhia Brasileira de Metalurgia e Mineração – CBMM and Indústria e Comércio de Minérios – Icomi (associated with the North American Bethlehem Steel) set up shop in Minas Gerais and Amapá to explore iron deposits in Monlevade, niobium in Araxá and manganese in Serra do Navio, respectively, they hired important architects to design the projects for the workers' facilities. The architects' awareness or intuition regarding the destruction to come is revealed in the form

of projects that represent the antithesis of unbridled exploration: Vila Monlevade, by Lúcio Costa, 1934; Vila Serra do
Navio, by Oswaldo Bratke, 1956; and the housing complex
for CBMM workers in Araxá, by the Technical Office Rino Levi,
designed by architect Paulo Casé and landscaper Fernando
Chacel, in 1979. All these projects seek environmental and
social harmony, as if trying to compensate for the inevitable ecological and social damages intrinsic to extensive
and intensive exploitation of mineral deposits. In the two
projects that were actually built, one may find many urban
qualities, but there is no denying that such projects do little
to mitigate the widespread destruction when we observe the
endless craters eating up the landscape.

Brazilian modernism took notice of predatory mining
activities. Carlos Drummond de Andrade, one of Capanema's
greatest allies and a close friend of Mário de Andrade, dedicates a good chunk of his work to this theme. José Guilherme
Wisnik's acute reading points out how Drummond's poetry
entails a personal testimony of his anguish regarding the
disappearance of the Cauê peak, a mountain that marked
his childhood, against the backdrop of the unfair and inglo-
rious clash between the modernizing forces of international
capital and the unprotected local popular culture, a central
theme of Brazilian modernism:

> "Itabira's gifts encompass the intersection between
> the modernizing bet on industrialization and the relics
> of a past that one does not want to lose sight of. The
> relationship between them calls into question the fate
> of Brazilian modernization, a central issue that haunts
> other luminaries of our literary modernism, particularly
> Mário de Andrade, who hoped that Brazil's adherence
> to international industrialization would not destroy the
> accumulated and decanted testimony of traditional
> culture. Considering this cultural context, the iron stone
> of the 'Confidência do Itabirano', exhibited among

other gifts, seems like an anomalous object out of place between the artisanal past and the industrial horizon – something like a Muiraquitã stone endowed with national-developmental powers, but also doomed to failure, like the Macunaíma's stone."[5]

In this anti-utopian process of economic development, in which mining is included, there are also major infrastructure works. After the construction of the Anchieta Highway in the 1940s, several temporary encampments built in the middle of Serra do Mar to house the construction workers became permanent villages, known as Cota 95/100, Cota 200, Cota 400 and Cota 500, in which the numbers correspond to the altitude of each village in relation to sea level (*cota* meaning spot height). Precarious and quite similar to urban slums, these small settlements became controversial after the creation of the Serra do Mar State Park and its listing by Condephaat in 1985.[6] The authorities' decision to extinguish the villages inside the park,[7] based on federal environmental legislation, was indeed justified, given the risk to the lives of its inhabitants, for the land there was susceptible to landslides. Nevertheless, when about to leave the place where he was born and where he had always lived, retiree Carlos Guilherme Campos Costa – echoing the simplicity and authenticity that modernist poets always coveted – converted his pain into spontaneous poetry. In "Remoção" (removal), he wrote:

"I'm from here. I was born here, here I grew up.
Here I was a child, went to school, got a family.
Suddenly someone quite strong wants to take me away,
remove me from my place, from my people,
people who made my story,
who take part in my dreams
and share my pain,
people who celebrate my love and drink to my victories.

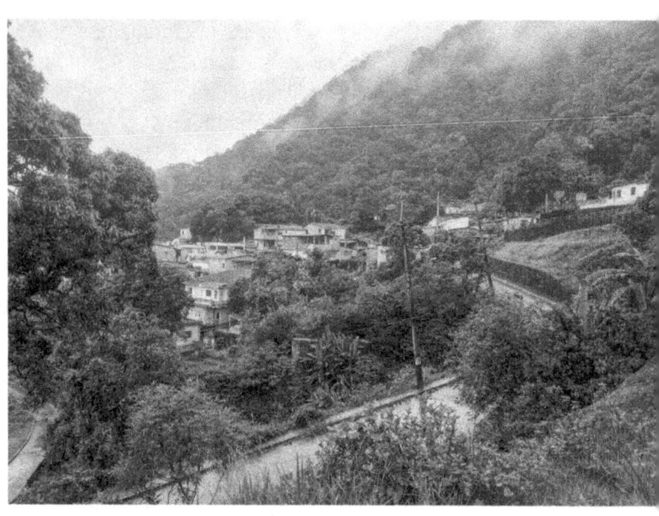

Cota 200 neighborhood, Serra do Mar, Cubatão SP. CDHU, 2008-2014. Photo by Abilio Guerra

They want to take me away. They talk about removals,
but they do not listen to my heart.
I don't want to live in an apartment.
I want to live in freedom,
the same freedom I feel now being taken from me.
I want to see the forest, the birds, and the mountains.
I don't want luxury, buildings, asphalt,
I just want to stay in my own little corner, listening to
the birds,
the dogs barking, I want to get up in the morning,
go to work and long for the time to come back.
My shack is so small
and my hope is so great
and in this dark, almost black body,
lives an old man who only believes in children."[8]

The resistance finds resonance with the public authorities, and the government of the State of São Paulo decides to take in consideration the bonds already established between the residents and Serra do Mar and the trauma that the removal of thousands of families would represent. "Between eliminating every human settlement within the Serra do Mar State Park and accepting unrestrained occupation, which is dangerous for both communities and the ecosystem, the government opted for a moderate, reasonable solution: urbanization whenever possible, and negotiated removal followed by resettlement when necessary."[9] Most of the 7,500 families that lived in Serra do Mar in 2009 were resettled in the Rubens Lara and Bolsão IX housing projects after long negotiations.

About 750 families are still living in the park, however, all of them in the so-called Cota 200, the only community that had part of its area on more stable land.[10] This contingent benefited from the guidelines established in 2006 by the State Environmental Council – Consema, which defined a series of zoning regulations as well as programs to be implemented in the remaining inhabited areas: development and implementation of water, sewage and drainage networks, paving of streets and sidewalks, creation of public squares and observation decks, slope stabilization, street lighting and a single access viaduct to the community. It was up to the Housing and Urban Development Company – CDHU to define the urbanization project and commission the works. The negotiation between a conciliatory public power and a participatory community made it possible to develop affirmative actions, such as the creation of the Community Communication Center along with training programs aimed at generating income. Among the actions carried out between public authorities and the community, one deserves special attention:

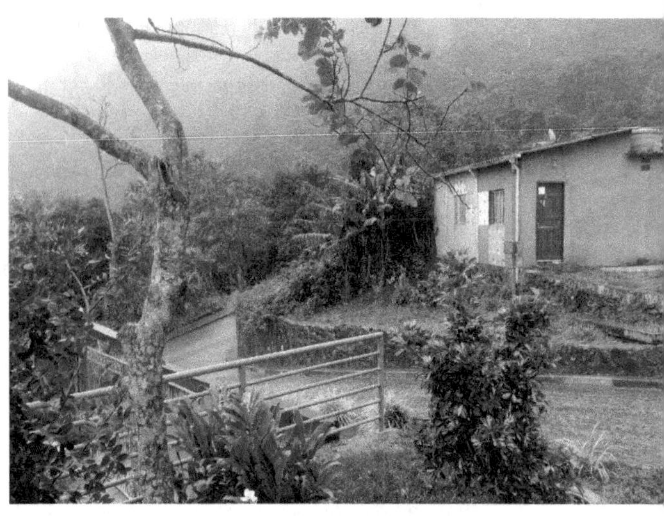

Cota 200 neighborhood, Serra do Mar,
Cubatão SP. CDHU, 2008-2014. Photo
by Abilio Guerra

"Most of the inhabitants are descendants of northeast-
ern migrants who, coming from another ecosystem,
did not inherit or receive any environmental education.
The Cota Viva Project was launched in 2013 by CDHU
precisely to fill this gap and promote environmental
competence among residents, starting with children and
adolescents. The objective is to teach sustainability values and prepare them to help in the recovery and con-
servation of Serra do Mar and the ecosystems involved.
It aims to reforest degraded areas, promote practical and
educational environmental actions and act in the reveg-
etation of the Atlantic Forest."[11]

The remaining dwellings, now in a harmonious relationship with the local vegetation, were renovated, most
of them receiving colorful paintings adorned with floral

or geometric motifs designed by the residents themselves, thanks to the action of Ateliê Arte nas Cotas, inspired by the work of Mônica Nador," an internationally recognized artist who makes her work a form of social activism."[12] This *Pau-Brasil* architecture and urbanism laboratory, even on this small scale, is auspicious. The respectful action of the public power for the benefit of an underprivileged, yet tough and resilient community, resulted in a viable human settlement installed in an environmental protection area. A light ecological footprint becomes possible by means of a thoughtful arrangement of the infrastructure, with a layout that obeys the impositions of the natural environment.

Now, as to unravel the thread that leads this argument to its end, it is important to say that in the uncertain limits between the process of modernization and the social and environmental ills that accompany it, there is a blurred fringe where it is possible to discern the fine line of the utopian dream. As in an anamorphosis, one must look from a specific point of view for this blurry vision to become intelligible. In that which we see a possibility of redemption, many see an ideology that hides our subordinate condition in the world stage and the oppressive violence of the ruling classes. We largely share this diagnosis, but we also believe in the transforming power of discourse. Thus, it is possible to find potential contributions in the vigorous tradition of a "particularist" modernism (Antonio Cândido) awaiting to incarnate into historical reality that is indeed committed to the intellectual development of the country. In the beauty of José Lins do Rego's text, we can see this commitment that turns to the past and to the future, seeking conciliation between man and landscape: "From the moment we start to make music, poems, paintings, sketches, we must not, if our goal is to remain authentic, allow ourselves to be enslaved by those telluric forces; what we need is to learn to extract a kind of eternity from things. Roberto Burle Marx went into the heart of the forest and rescued it to his gardens, where we can find the vegetation of the *caatinga*, the *serrado*, the mountains and the beaches,"[13] with the landscaper creating from his elective affinities or unconscious preferences. A sort of imaginary space created by the dialogue between the ideas and works of Mário de Andrade, Oswald de Andrade, Tarsila do Amaral, Lúcio Costa and many others, also with the aid of foreigners, such as Blaise Cendrars and Le Corbusier, both duly incorporated and transformed.

In this imaginary space, ideas and works of art mirror each other and multiply in shapes and colors within a magical kaleidoscope called culture. Everything is so mixed up, you no longer know what belongs to whom, so it's a common enterprise, a diffuse property that belongs to all. Thus, we have every right to suppose that this powerful imagination might bring about a real place, embedded in the territory and developed over time, a place where one finds ambitious visions of a common, genuine, egalitarian life, a kind of paradisiacal locus with mild temperatures, where a simple man lives his peaceful days under the shade of *ipês* and *jacarandás*, stretched out in a tupi-guarani hammock reading the daily newspaper. In this leisure, which he rightfully deserves, he enjoys the music being played on his smartphone, talks about the past, thinks about the future – or declaims mockingly: "I am a Tupi playing a lute."[14] A bucolic yet civilized habitat, where the humble dwellings of each citizen is rooted in a lush garden that emulates, on a reduced scale, the glorious and unfathomable nature. It would be a sort of Vila Monlevade.

"*Pau-Brasil* Poetry is a Sunday dining room with birds singing in the condensed forest of cages, a thin fellow writing a waltz for flute and Maricota reading the newspaper. The present is all there in the newspaper."[15]

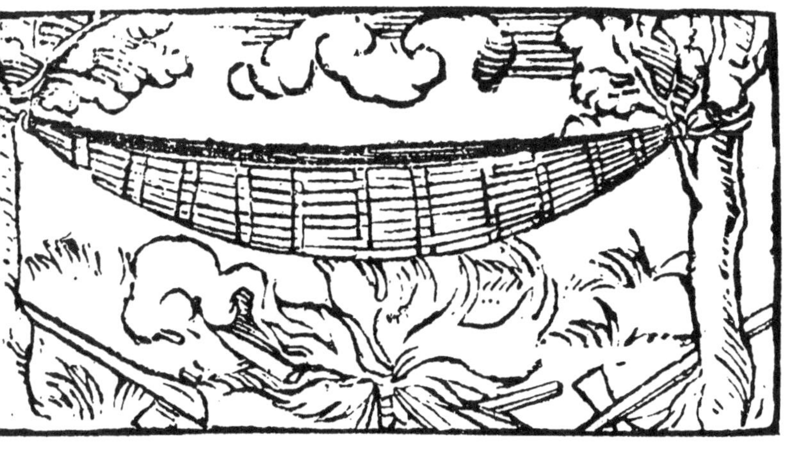

Tupinambá hammock. STADEN, Hans.
*Warhaftig Historia und beschreibung
eyner Landtschafft der Wilden,*
1557, p. 139. Guita and José Mindlin
Brasiliana Library Collection

Epilogue Notes

1. Carlos Drummond de Andrade, "A máquina do mundo," 123.
2. Josep Maria Montaner, *Arquitetura e crítica na América Latina*, 22.
3. Andrade, "Manifesto antropófago," 14.
4. Hardt and Negri, *Bem-estar comum*, 145.
5. José Miguel Wisnik, *Maquinação do mundo: Drummond e a mineração*, 105.
6. The listing of Serra do Mar, promoted by the Council for the Defense of the Archeological, Artistic and Tourist Heritage – Condephaat, was decreed by Resolution n. 40, of 1985, signed by the State Secretary of Culture Jorge Cunha Lima, and published in the State Official Gazette on Jun. 15, 1985.
7. A court decision from the 4th Civil Court of the City of Cubatão/SP (case no. 944/99, from September 1999), arising from the civil public action filed by the State Public Ministry, obliges the State of São Paulo and the Municipality of Cubatão to "physically extinguish all the neighborhoods or settlements that have been formed within the Serra do Mar State Park". Program for the socio-environmental recovery of the Serra do Mar and the Atlantic Forest mosaic system. (BR-I1241), 6.
8. Carlos Guilherme Campos Costa, "Remoção," 131.
9. Lorette Coen, *Serra do Mar: as cores da urbanidade*, 145.
10. Em seu estudo sobre as paisagens culturais no entorno do Parque Nacional Cavernas do Peruaçu, no norte de Minas Gerais, Ana Carolina Brugnera aponta que a proteção integral da área de proteção ambiental desconsidera as comunidades tradicionais, descendentes de povos indígenas e africanos, que ali habitam há gerações, em relação harmoniosa com o meio ambiente. Segundo a autora, "tanto a conservação da natureza como a valorização da cultura das comunidades tradicionais são de extrema importância para a manutenção das paisagens culturais"., Ana Carolina Brugnera, "Rumo às comunidades criativas – as articulações entre natureza e cultura na gestão sustentável das paisagens culturais do Peruaçu, Brasil," 155.

11. Coen, *Serra do Mar*, 190.
12. Ibid., 186.
13. Rego, "O homem e a paisagem," 304. Burle Marx's personal triumph takes place in a broader cultural spectrum: "The Europeans, who fear the jungle, think that everything in it is dangerous. The Brazilians, even though they have indeed mastered it, still harbor a few traces of resentment towards it. But this terrible resentment is about to disappear. A renewed contact has made it possible to make peace. Man and landscape are no longer enemies. Painters are no longer ashamed of our colors, nor of our luminosity. A Cícero Dias, even while living abroad, puts on his canvas the green of the sea of Boa Viagem, the blues, yellows, and reds of the flowers of Pernambuco. Thousands of miles away, a man carries in his blood the authenticity of his native land." Ibid., 304. Our emphasis.
14. Mario de Andrade, "O trovador (Pauliceia desvairada)," 33.
15. Andrade, "Manifesto da poesia Pau-Brasil," 9.

Bibliography

Aliata, Fernando, and Claudia Shmidt. "Lúcio Costa, o episódio Monlevade e Auguste Perret." In *Textos fundamentais sobre história da arquitetura moderna brasileira: parte 2.* Edited by Abilio Guerra. São Paulo: Romano Guerra, 2010, 239-258.

Almeida, Guilherme. "Mormaço (para Graça Aranha)." *Klaxon*, n. 8-9, São Paulo, Dec. 1922/Jan. 1923, 11.

Almeida, Guilherme de (1925). *Raça.* 2nd edition. Rio de Janeiro: José Olympio, 1972.

Almeida, Renato. "A estética de Malazarte." *Klaxon*, n. 8-9, São Paulo, Dec. 1922/Jan. 1923, 3-4.

Amaral, Aracy, ed. *Arquitectura neocolonial: América Latina, Caribe, Estados Unidos.* São Paulo: Memorial da América Latina/ Fondo de Cultura Economica, 1994.

Amaral, Aracy *Artes plásticas na semana de 22.* 5th edition. São Paulo: Editora 34, 1998.

Amaral, Aracy, and Regina Teixeira de Barros, *Tarsila: estudos e anotações.* São Paulo: WMF Martins Fontes/Fábrica de Arte Marcos Amaro, 2021.

Amaral, Aracy. *Blaise Cendrars no Brasil e os modernistas.* São Paulo: Martins, 1968.

Amaral, Aracy. "Tarsila: estudos e anotações." In *Tarsila: estudos e anotações,* 11-21.

Amaral, Aracy. *Tarsila: sua obra e seu tempo.* São Paulo: Patroc/ Tenenge, 1986.

Amaral, Tarsila. "Gregorio Warchavchik." *O Jornal,* section 4. Rio de Janeiro, Dec. 6, 1936, 1 <https://bit.ly/3IqXnAN>.

Andrade, Carlos Drummond de. "A máquina do mundo." In *Claro enigma,* by Carlos Drummond de Andrade, 10th edition. Rio de Janeiro: Record, 1995, 121-124.

Andrade, Mário de. "Arquitetura moderna I." *Diário Nacional,* Rio de Janeiro, Feb. 2, 1928, 2 <https://bit.ly/3nNwAqF>.

Andrade, Mário de. "Arquitetura moderna II." *Diário Nacional,* Rio de Janeiro, Feb. 3, 1928, 2 <https://bit.ly/3nNwRdb>.

Andrade, Mário de. "Arquitetura moderna III." *Diário Nacional,* Rio de Janeiro, Feb. 4, 1928, 2 https://bit.ly/3rDhiFX>.

Andrade, Mário de. "Brazil Builds." *Folha da Manhã,* São Paulo, Mar. 23, 1944, 7 <https://bit.ly/340MyXb>.

Andrade, Mário (1944). "Brazil Builds." *Arte em Revista,* n. 4, São Paulo, CEAC, Aug. 1980, 25-26.

Andrade, Mário de (1928). *Ensaio sobre a música brasileira.* Critical edition by Flávia Camargo Toni. São Paulo, Edusp, 2020.

Andrade, Mário de (1928). *Ensaio sobre a música brasileira.* 3rd edition. São Paulo/Brasília: Martins/INL, 1972.

Andrade, Mário de. "Exposição duma casa modernista (considerações)." *Diário Nacional,* São Paulo, Apr. 5, 1930, 6 <https://bit.ly/33yUHm2>.

Andrade, Mário de (1928). *Macunaíma: o herói sem nenhum caráter.* Edited by Telê Porto Ancona Lopez. Florianópolis: UFSC/Unesco, 1988.

Andrade, Oswald de. "Manifesto da
poesia Pau-Brasil." *Correio
da Manhã*, Mar. 18, 1924, 5
<https://bit.ly/3HncXh1>.

Andrade, Mário de (1942). "O movimento modernista." In *Aspectos
da literatura brasileira*, by Mário
de Andrade. 5th edition. São
Paulo: Martins, 1974, 231-255.

Andrade, Mário de. *O turista aprendiz*.
2nd. edition. Edition, introduction and notes by Telê Porto
Ancona Lopez. São Paulo: Duas
Cidades, 1983.

Andrade, Mário de. *Poesias completas*.
3rd edition. São Paulo: Martins/
MEC, 1972.

Andrade, Mário de (1945). "A meditação sobre o Tietê (Lira
Paulistana)." In *Poesias completas*, 305-314.

Andrade, Mário de (1922). "O trovador
(Pauliceia desvairada)." In *Poesias
completas*, by Mario de Andrade,
32-33.

Andrade, Oswald de. "A casa modernista, o pior crítico do mundo e
outras considerações." *O Jornal*,
Rio de Janeiro, Apr. 9, 1930, 2
<https://bit.ly/3tQ7U4L>.

Andrade, Oswald de. "Antropofagia
e arquitetura." *Diário da Noite*,
Rio de Janeiro, Jun. 28, 1930, 1
<https://bit.ly/3AnJeSs>.

Andrade, Oswald de. *Do Pau-Brasil
à antropofagia e às utopias:
manifestos, teses de concursos
e ensaios*. Complete works, v.
6. Rio de Janeiro: Civilização
Brasileira/MEC, 1972.

Andrade, Oswald de (1924). "Manifesto
da poesia Pau-Brasil." In *Do
Pau-Brasil à antropofagia e às
utopias*, 1-10.

Andrade, Oswald de (1928). "Manifesto
antropófago." In *Do Pau-Brasil
à antropofagia e às utopias*,
11-19.

Andrade, Oswald de. "Manifesto
antropófago." *Revista de
Antropofagia*, n. 1, São Paulo,
May 1, 1928.

Andrade, Oswald de. *Memórias sentimentais de João Miramar /
Serafim Ponte Grande*. Complete
works, v. 2. Rio de Janeiro:
Civilização Brasileira/MEC, 1972.

Andrade, Oswald de. "O modernismo."
In *Estética e política*. Edited by
Maria Eugenia Boaventura. São
Paulo: Globo, 1992, 120-127.

Andrade, Oswald de (1937). *O rei da
vela*. Complete works. 8th edition. São Paulo: Globo, 1999.

Andrade, Oswald de. *Pau-Brasil*.
Edited by Haroldo de Campos.
Complete works. 2nd edition.
São Paulo: Globo/Secretaria de
Estado da Cultura de São Paulo,
1990.

Andrade, Oswald de. "Postes da Light."
In *Pau-Brasil*, 115.

Andrade, Oswald de. "Roteiro das
Minas." In *Pau-Brasil*, 135

Anelli, Renato, Abilio Guerra, and
Nelson Kon. *Rino Levi: arquite-
tura e cidade*. São Paulo:
Romano Guerra, 2001.

Aranha, José Pereira Graça. *A estética
da vida*. Rio de Janeiro: Livraria
Garnier, 1921.

Aranha, José Pereira Graça. *Canaã*. 3rd
edition. Rio de Janeiro: Nova
Fronteira, 1981.

Aranha, Luis (1921). "Drogaria de éter
e sombra." In *Cocktails poemas*.
Edited by Nelson Ascher e
Rui Moreira Leite. São Paulo:
Brasiliense, 1984, 25-41.

Arantes, Otília Beatriz Fiori (1996). "Lúcio Costa e a *boa causa* da arquitetura moderna." In *O sentido da formação: três estudos sobre Antônio Cândido, Gilda de Mello e Souza e Lúcio Costa.* Edited by Arantes, Otília Beatriz Fiori, and Paulo Eduardo Arantes. São Paulo: Paz e Terra, 1997, 115-133.

Arantes, Otília Beatriz Fiori. "Resumo de Lúcio Costa." In *Textos fundamentais sobre história da arquitetura moderna brasileira: parte 2*, 259-278.

Artigas, João Batista Vilanova (1977). "Semana de 22 e a arquitetura." In *Caminhos da arquitetura.* Third edition, São Paulo: Cosac Naify, 1999, 139-141.

Artigas, João Batista Vilanova. "Os caminhos da arquitetura moderna." *Fundamentos*, n. 24, São Paulo, Jan. 1952, 20-25.

Artigas, João Batista Vilanova. "A Semana de 22 e a arquitetura." *Módulo*, n. 45, Rio de Janeiro, 1977, 20-23.

Artigas, João Batista Vilanova. "Aos formandos da FAU USP." *AD – Arquitetura e Decoração*, year 4, n. 17, São Paulo, May./Jun. 1956.

Artigas, João Batista Vilanova. *Caminhos da arquitetura.* 2nd edição. São Paulo: Fundação Vilanova Artigas/Pini, 1986.

Artigas, João Batista Vilanova. *Caminhos da arquitetura.* 3rd edition. São Paulo: Cosac Naify, 1999.

Artigas, João Batista Vilanova. "Os caminhos da arquitetura moderna." In *Caminhos da arquitetura*, 35-50.

Artigas, Rosa, ed. *Vilanova Artigas.* São Paulo: Instituto Bardi/Fundação Vilanova Artigas, 1997.

Averbuck, Lígia Morrone. *Cobra Norato e a revolução caraíba.* Rio de Janeiro: José Olympio/INL/Pró-Memória, 1985.

Ávila, Affonso, ed. *O modernismo.* São Paulo: Perspectiva/Secretaria da Cultura Ciência e Tecnologia, 1975.

Bardi, Pietro Maria. *Lembranças de Le Corbusier: Atenas, Itália, Brasil.* São Paulo: Nobel, 1984.

Barreirinhas, Yoshie Sakiyama. *Menotti del Picchia, o gedeão do modernismo: 1920/22.* São Paulo: Civilização Brasileira, 1983.

Barros, Regina Teixeira de. "Sobre os desenhos de Tarsila." In *Tarsila: estudos e anotações*, 23-33.

Bayón, Damián. *Panorâmica de la arquitectura latino-americana.* Barcelona: Blume, 1977.

Bill, Max. "Report on Brazil." *Architectural Review*, out. 1954, 235-240.

Bonduki, Nabil Georges. *Affonso Eduardo Reidy.* São Paulo/Lisboa: Instituto Bardi/Blau, 1999.

Bopp, Raul (1931). "Cobra Norato." In *Cobra Norato e outros poemas*, by Raul Bopp. Introductory note by Antônio Houaiss. 13th edition. Rio de Janeiro: Civilização Brasileira, 1984, 1-88.

Bosi, Alfredo. "Situação de Macunaíma." In *Macunaíma: o herói sem nenhum caráter*, 171-181.

Branco, Ilda Helena Diniz Castello, Luiz Carlos Daher, Maria Cecília Naclério Homem, and Carlos Alberto Cerqueira Lemos. *Warchavchik, Pilon, Rino Levi: três momentos da arquitetura paulista.* Catálogo de exposição. São Paulo: Funarte/Museu Lasar Segall, 1983.

Brito, Mário da Silva. *História do modernismo brasileiro 1: antecedentes da Semana de Arte Moderna.* 5th edition. Rio de Janeiro: Civilização Brasileira, 1978.

Brito, Samuel Silva de. "Pavilhão do Brasil na Exposição de Filadélfia: 1925." *Anais do III Encontro da Associação Nacional de Pesquisa e Pós-graduação em Arquitetura e Urbanismo.* Tema "Arquitetura, cidade e projeto: uma construção coletiva". São Paulo: Enanparq, 2014 <https://bit.ly/3FDck0Z>.

Broca, Brito. "Blaise Cendrars no Brasil, em 1924." *A Manhã*, Rio de Janeiro, May 4, 1952.

Bruand, Yves (1981). *Arquitetura contemporânea no Brasil.* 2nd edition. São Paulo: Perspectiva, 1991.

Brugnera, Ana Carolina. "Rumo às comunidades criativas – as articulações entre natureza e cultura na gestão sustentável das paisagens culturais do Peruaçu, Brasil." PhD diss., FAU Mackenzie, 2020.

Calil, Carlos Augusto. "Quem foi Blaise Cendrars, franco-suíço que se encantou por Aleijadinho e influenciou Oswald e Tarsila." *Folha de S.Paulo*, Caderno Ilustríssima. São Paulo, Jan. 23, 2021 <https://bit.ly/3AD9qs4>.

Calil, Carlos Augusto. "Sob o signo do Aleijadinho: Blaise Cendrars, precursor do patrimônio histórico." *Arquitextos*, year 13, n. 149.05, São Paulo, Vitruvius, Oct. 2012 <https://bit.ly/3GGe8YI>.

Calil, Carlos Augusto. "Tradutores de Brasil." In *Brasil 1920-1950: da antropofagia a Brasília.* Edited by Jorge Schwartz, 325-349.

Campos, Haroldo de. "Miramar na mira." In *Memórias sentimentais de João Miramar / Serafim Ponte Grande*, XIII-XLV.

Campos, Haroldo de. "Uma poética da radicalidade." In *Pau-Brasil*, 7-53.

Cândido, Antônio (1950). "Literatura e cultura de 1900 a 1945." In *Literatura e sociedade*, by Antônio Cândido. 7th edition. São Paulo: Companhia Editora Nacional, 1985, 109-138.

Cândido, Antônio (1970). "Digressão sentimental sobre Oswald de Andrade." In *Vários escritos*, by Antônio Cândido. 2nd edition. São Paulo: Duas Cidades, 1977, 56-87.

Cândido, Antônio. *O método crítico de Sílvio Romero.* São Paulo: Edusp, 1988.

Carvalho, Flávio de. "Modernista Warchavchik." *Arte em Revista*, n. 4, São Paulo, CEAC, August 1980, 9.

Carvalho, Flávio de. "Modernista Warchavchik." *Diário da Noite*, São Paulo, Jul. 8, 1930.

Carvalho, Ronald. "Graça Aranha, criador de entusiasmo." *Klaxon*, n. 8-9, São Paulo, Dec. 1922/Jan. 1923, 2-3.

Castro, Silvio. *Teoria e política do modernismo brasileiro.* Petrópolis: Vozes, 1979.

Cavalcanti, Lauro, ed. *Modernistas na repartição.* Rio de Janeiro: UFRJ/Paço Municipal/Tempo Brasileiro, 1993.

Cavalcanti, Lauro. *As preocupações do belo.* Rio de Janeiro: Taurus, 1995.

Cavalcanti, Lauro. *Dezoito graus: a biografia do Palácio Capanema.* São Paulo: Olhares, 2018.

Cavalcanti, Lauro. "Henrique Mindlin e a arquitetura moderna brasileira." In *Arquitetura moderna no Brasil,* by Henrique E. Mindlin. Rio de Janeiro: Aeroplano, 1999, 11-16.

Cendrars, Blaise (1924). "Feuilles de route." In *Du monde entier au cœur du monde: poésies completes,* by Blaise Cendrars. Paris: Gallimard, 2009, 189-269.

Coen, Lorette. *Serra do Mar: as cores da urbanidade.* Projeto Com Com (collaborator). São Paulo: Ipsis Gráfica e Editora, 2017.

Comas, Carlos Eduardo. "A racionalidade da meia lua: apartamentos do Parque Guinle no Rio de Janeiro, Brasil, 1948-52." *Arquitextos,* year 01, n. 010.01, São Paulo, Vitruvius, Mar. 2001 <https://bit.ly/3qhheMA>.

Comas, Carlos Eduardo. "A Feira Mundial de Nova York de 1939: o pavilhão brasileiro." *Arqtexto,* n. 16, Porto Alegre, p. 56-97.

Comas, Carlos Eduardo. "Arquitetura moderna, estilo campestre. Hotel, Parque São Clemente." *Arquitextos,* year 11, n. 123.00, São Paulo, Vitruvius, Aug. 2010 <https://bit.ly/3nV8iv5>.

Comas, Carlos Eduardo. "Arquitetura moderna, estilo Corbu, Pavilhão brasileiro." In *Textos fundamentais sobre história da arquitetura moderna brasileira: parte 1.* Edited by Abilio Guerra. São Paulo: Romano Guerra, 2010, 207-225.

Comas, Carlos Eduardo. "Arquitetura moderna, estilo Corbu, Pavilhão brasileiro." *Arquitetura e Urbanismo,* São Paulo, n. 26, Oct./Nov. 1989, 92-101.

Comas, Carlos Eduardo. "Le Corbusier: os riscos brasileiros de 1936." In *Le Corbusier. Rio de Janeiro 1929 1936.* Edited by Yannis Tsiomis. Rio de Janeiro: Centro de Arquitetura e Urbanismo do Rio de Janeiro, 1998, 26-31.

Comas, Carlos Eduardo. "O passado mora ao lado: Lúcio Costa e o projeto do Grande Hotel de Ouro Preto, 1938/40." *Arqtexto,* n. 2, Porto Alegre, 2002, 6-19.

Constituição da República Federativa do Brasil de 1988. "Texto constitucional promulgado em 5 de outubro de 1988, com as alterações determinadas pelas Emendas Constitucionais de Revisão n. 1 a 6/94, pelas Emendas Constitucionais n. 1/92 a 91/2016 e pelo Decreto Legislativo n. 186/2008." Brasília: Senado Federal/Coordenação de Edições Técnicas, 2016 <https://bit.ly/3gfenhG>.

Corona, Eduardo; and Carlos Lemos. *Dicionário da arquitetura brasileira.* 2nd edition. São Paulo: Romano Guerra, 2017.

Costa, Lúcio. "Anteprojeto para a Vila Monlevade: memorial descritivo." *Revista da Diretoria de Engenharia da Prefeitura do Distrito Federal,* v. III, n. 3, Rio de Janeiro, May 1936, 115-128 <https://bit.ly/3GiGAyv>.

Costa, Lúcio. *Lúcio Costa: registro de uma vivência.* São Paulo: Empresa das Artes, 1995.

Costa, Lúcio (1982). "À guisa de sumário." In *Lúcio Costa: registro de uma vivência,* 11-19.

Costa, Lúcio (1952). "Casa do estudante. Cité Universitaire, Paris." In *Lúcio Costa: registro de uma vivência,* 230-236.

Costa, Lúcio (1936-1937). "Cidade Universitária." In *Lúcio Costa: registro de uma vivência*, 172-189.

Costa, Lúcio (1932-1936). "Chômage." In *Lúcio Costa: registro de uma vivência*, 83- 89.

Costa, Lúcio (anos 1940). "Considerações sobre arte contemporânea." In *Lúcio Costa: registro de uma vivência*, 245-258.

Costa, Lúcio (1948). "Depoimento." In *Lúcio Costa: registro de uma vivência*, 198-200.

Costa, Lúcio (1953). "Desencontro." In *Lúcio Costa: registro de uma vivência*, 201-202.

Costa, Lúcio. "Diamantina." In *Lúcio Costa: registro de uma vivência*, 26-29.

Costa, Lúcio (1938). "Documentação necessária." In *Lúcio Costa: registro de uma vivência*, 457-462.

Costa, Lúcio. "Gregori Warchavchik." In *Lúcio Costa: registro de uma vivência*, 72-73.

Costa, Lúcio. "In extremis: a inusitada peteca." In *Lúcio Costa: registro de uma vivência*, 597.

Costa, Lúcio. "Mary Houston: registro de viagem." In *Lúcio Costa: registro de uma vivência*, 48.

Costa, Lúcio (1957). "Memória descritiva do plano piloto." In *Lúcio Costa: registro de uma vivência*, 283-297.

Costa, Lúcio (1936). "Ministério da Educação e Saúde." In *Lúcio Costa: registro de uma vivência*, 122-130.

Costa, Lúcio (1949). "Mise au point." In *Lúcio Costa: registro de uma vivência*, 139-141.

Costa, Lúcio (1951). "Muita construção, alguma arquitetura e um milagre." In *Lúcio Costa: registro de uma vivência*, 157-171.

Costa, Lúcio (1952). "O arquiteto e a sociedade contemporânea." In *Lúcio Costa: registro de uma vivência*, 268-275.

Costa, Lúcio (1950). "Oscar Niemeyer: prefácio para o livro de Stamo Papadaki." In *Lúcio Costa: registro de uma vivência*, 195-196.

Costa, Lúcio (anos 1940). "Parque Guinle." In *Lúcio Costa: registro de uma vivência*, 205-213.

Costa, Lúcio (1934). "Razões da nova arquitetura." In *Lúcio Costa: registro de uma vivência*, 108-116.

Costa, Lúcio (1975). "Relato pessoal." In *Lúcio Costa: registro de uma vivência*, 135-138.

Costa, Lúcio. "Roquebrune." In *Lúcio Costa: registro de uma vivência*, 582-585.

Costa, Lúcio. "Salão de 31." In *Lúcio Costa: registro de uma vivência*, 70-71.

Costa, Lúcio (1970). "Sphan: Serviço do Patrimônio Histórico e Artístico Nacional." In *Lúcio Costa: registro de uma vivência*, 437.

Costa, Lúcio. "Tradição local." In *Lúcio Costa: registro de uma vivência*, 451-454.

Costa, Lúcio (1936). "Vila Monlevade." In *Lúcio Costa: registro de uma vivência*, 90-99.

Costa, Lúcio. "Muita construção, alguma arquitetura e um milagre." *Correio da Manhã*, Caderno Construções e Urbanismo (newspaper's fiftieth anniversary supplement). Rio de Janeiro, Jun. 15, 1951, 2 <https://bit.ly/3fQeAaB>.

Costa, Lúcio. "O arranha-céu e o Rio de Janeiro." *O País (O Paiz)*, Rio de Janeiro, Jul. 1, 1928, 1 and 4 <https://bit.ly/32HfKSW>; <https://bit.ly/3re3GCh>.

Costa, Lúcio. *Sobre arquitetura*. Edited by Alberto Xavier. Porto Alegre: Centro dos Estudantes Universitários de Arquitetura, 1962.

Costa, Lúcio (1948). "Carta depoimento." In *Sobre arquitetura*, 123-128.

Costa, Lúcio (1959). "Casa do Brasil em Paris." In *Sobre arquitetura*, 290-291.

Costa, Lúcio (1948). "Ensino de desenho." In: *Sobre arquitetura*, 129-160.

Costa, Lúcio (1929). "O Aleijadinho e a arquitetura tradicional." In *Sobre arquitetura*, 12-16.

Costa, Lúcio (1934). "Razões da nova arquitetura." In *Sobre arquitetura*, 17-41.

Costa, Lúcio (1936). "Vila Monlevade." In *Sobre arquitetura*, 42-55.

Costa, Lúcio. *Trabalhos escritos*. Edited by Alberto Xavier. Brasília: UNB, 1970 (mimeo).

Costa, Lúcio (1928). "O arranha-céu e o Rio de Janeiro." In *Trabalhos escritos*, 6 pages (mimeo, no overall pagination).

Costa, Lúcio. "Raízes da arquitetura colonial brasileira." In *Trabalhos escritos*, 4 pages (mimeo, no overall pagination).

Costa, Carlos Guilherme Campos. "Remoção." In *Serra do Mar: as cores da urbanidade*, 131.

Critelli, Fernanda. *Richard Neutra e o Brasil*. São Paulo: Romano Guerra, 2022.

Czajkowsky, Jorge, Maria Cristina Burlamarqui, and Ronaldo Brito (1987). "Presença de Le Corbusier: entrevista de Lúcio Costa." In *Lúcio Costa: registro de uma vivência*, 144-155.

Daher, Luiz Carlos. *Flávio de Carvalho: arquitetura e expressionismo*. São Paulo: Projeto, 1982.

Espallargas Gimenez, Luis (1984). "Pós-modernismo, arquitetura e tropicália." In *Textos fundamentais sobre história da arquitetura moderna brasileira: parte 1*, 35-62.

Espallargas Gimenez, Luis. "Pós-modernismo, arquitetura e tropicália." *Projeto*, n. 65, São Paulo, Jul. 1984, 87-93.

Eulalio, Alexandre (1978). *A aventura brasileira de Blaise Cendrars*. Edited by Carlos Augusto Calil. 2nd edition. São Paulo: Edusp/Imesp, 2001.

Eulalio, Alexandre (1984). "Prefácio a 'Lembrança de Le Corbusier.'" In *A aventura brasileira de Blaise Cendrars*, 428.

Falcão, Luiz Annibal. "Assim ele compõe." *Klaxon*, n. 8-9, São Paulo, Dec. 1922/Jan. 1923, 10-11.

Faria, Daniel. "As meditações americanas de Keyserling: um cosmopolitismo nas incertezas do tempo." *Varia Historia*, v. 29, n. 51, Belo Horizonte, Sep./Dec. 2013, 905-923.

Farias, Agnaldo Aricê Caldas. "Arquitetura eclipsada: notas sobre história e arquitetura a propósito da obra de Gregori Warchavchik, introdutor da arquitetura moderna no Brasil." Master diss., IFCH Unicamp, 1990.

Farias, Agnaldo Aricê Caldas. "Gregori Warchavchik: introdutor da arquitetura moderna no Brasil." Óculum, n. 2, Campinas, FAU PUC-Campinas, Sep. 1992, 8-22.

Faye, Jean-Pierre. *Los lenguajes totalitarios*. Madrid: Taurus, 1974.

Ferraz, Geraldo (1948). "Falta o depoimento de Lúcio Costa." In *Sobre arquitetura*, 119-122.

Ferraz, Geraldo. Depoimento do arquiteto Lúcio Costa sobre a arquitetura moderna brasileira. *O Jornal*, Rio de Janeiro, Mar. 14, 1948, 2 <https://bit.ly/3ltKVAA>.

Ferraz, Geraldo. "Falta o depoimento de Lúcio Costa: quem é o pioneiro da arquitetura moderna brasileira." *O Jornal*, Rio de Janeiro, Feb. 15, 1948, 2 <https://bit.ly/3Kvwvl8>.

Ferraz, Geraldo. *Warchavchik e a introdução da nova arquitetura no Brasil: 1925 a 1940*. São Paulo: Museu de Arte, 1965.

Ferraz, Marcelo Carvalho, ed. *Lina Bo Bardi*. 5th edition. São Paulo: Instituto Bardi/Romano Guerra, 2018.

Frampton, Kenneth. *História crítica da arquitetura moderna*. São Paulo: Martins Fontes, 1997.

Franco, Afonso Arinos de Melo. *Discurso de posse*. Rio de Janeiro: Academia Brasileira de Letras, Nov. 26, 1999 <https://bit.ly/3nN1JtW>.

Franco, Afonso Arinos de Melo. *O índio brasileiro e a Revolução Francesa: as origens da teoria da bondade natural*. Colection Documentos Brasileiros. Rio de Janeiro: José Olympio, 1937.

Freyre, Gilberto. *Casa-grande e senzala*. São Paulo: Círculo do Livro, 1987.

Freyre, Gilberto. *Sobrados e mucambos*. 15th edition, 2nd reprint. São Paulo: Global, 2012.

Garnier, Tony. "Una ciudad industrial: estudio para la construcción de ciudades." In *Origenes y desarollo de la ciudad moderna*, by Carlo Aymonino. Barcelona: Gustavo Gili, 1972, 215-284.

Giedion, Sigfried. "O Brasil e a arquitetura contemporânea." In *Arquitetura moderna no Brasil*, 17-18.

Goodwin, Philip L. *Brazil Builds: Architecture New and Old 1652-1942*. Nova York: MoMA, 1943.

Gotlib, Nádia Batella. *Tarsila do Amaral, a modernista*. São Paulo: Senac, 1998.

Graeff, Edgar; Marcos Jaimovitch, José Duval, and Slioma Selter. *Arquitetura contemporânea no Brasil*. Rio de Janeiro: Gertum Carneiro, 1947.

Gropius, Walter. *Bauhaus: novarquitetura*. 3rd edition. São Paulo: Perspectiva, 1977.

Guerra, Abilio, ed. *Textos fundamentais sobre história da arquitetura moderna brasileira: parte 1*. São Paulo: Romano Guerra, 2010.

Guerra, Abilio, ed. *Textos fundamentais sobre história da arquitetura moderna brasileira: parte 2*. São Paulo: Romano Guerra, 2010.

Guerra, Abilio. "Arquitetura brasileira: tradição e utopia." *Revista IEB*, n. 76, Aug. 2020, 158-200 <https://bit.ly/34JWOUj>.

Guerra, Abilio. "Lúcio Costa, Gregori Warchavchik e Roberto Burle Marx: síntese entre arquitetura e natureza tropical." *Arquitextos*, year 03, n. 029.05, São Paulo, Vitruvius, Oct. 2002 <https://bit.ly/3zqv6Ht>.

Guerra, Abilio. "Lúcio Costa, Gregori Warchavchik e Roberto Burle Marx: síntese entre arquitetura e natureza tropical." *Revista USP*, n. 53, São Paulo, mar./mai. 2002 <https://bit.ly/3zr6VJ5>.

Guerra, Abilio. "Lúcio Costa, Gregori Warchavchik e Roberto Burle Marx: síntese entre arquitetura e natureza tropical." In *Textos fundamentais sobre história da arquitetura moderna brasileira: parte 2*, 299-325.

Guerra, Abilio. *Lúcio Costa, modernidade e tradição: montagem discursiva da arquitetura moderna brasileira*. Campinas: IFCH Unicamp, 2002.

Guerra, Abilio. "Modernistas na estrada." *Arquiteturismo*, year 01, n. 008.02, São Paulo, Vitruvius, Oct. 2007 <https://bit.ly/3fjalPh>.

Guerra, Abilio. "O estranho ao Sul do Rio Grande." In *Richard Neutra e o Brasil*, 6-23.

Guerra, Abilio. "O homem primitivo: origem e conformação no universo intelectual brasileiro (séculos 19 e 20)." Master diss., IFCH Unicamp, 1990.

Guerra, Abilio. *O primitivismo em Mário de Andrade, Oswald de Andrade e Raul Bopp: origem e conformação no universo intelectual brasileiro*. São Paulo: Romano Guerra, 2010.

Guerra, Abilio. "O primitivo modernista em Mário de Andrade, Oswald de Andrade e Raul Bopp." Óculum, n. 2, Campinas, FAU PUC-Campinas, Sep. 1992, 43-59.

Guimaraens, Cêça de. *Lúcio Costa: um certo arquiteto em incerto e secular roteiro*. Rio de Janeiro: Relume Dumará, 1996.

Guimarães, Marília Dorador. "Roberto Burle Marx: a contribuição do artista e paisagista no Estado de São Paulo." Master diss., FAU Mackenzie, 2011.

Gutiérrez, Ramón, ed. "Architettura e società: l'America Latina nel XX Secolo." *Dicionário enciclopédico*. Milão: Jaca Book, 1996.

Hardt, Michael, and Antonio Negri. *Bem-estar comum*. Rio de Janeiro: Record, 2016.

Holanda, Sérgio Buarque de (1936). *Raízes do Brasil*. 3rd edition. Rio de Janeiro: Livraria José Olympio, 1956.

Holanda, Sérgio Buarque de (1959). *Visão do paraíso: os motivos edênicos no descobrimento e colonização do Brasil*. 4th edition. São Paulo: Companhia Editora Nacional, 1985.

Patrimônio – Patrimônio Cultural Brasileiro. Rio de Janeiro: Palácio das Laranjeiras <https://bit.ly/3g6LC6N>.

Jacques, Paola Berenstein. *Pensamentos selvagens: montagem de uma outra herança, 2*. Salvador: EDUFBA, 2021.

Janeiro, Brasil, 1948-52. *Arquitextos*, year 01, n. 010.01, São Paulo, Vitruvius, Mar. 2001 <https://bit.ly/3qhheMA>.

Keyserling, Hermann (1926). *El mundo que nace*. 2nd edition. Madrid: Revista de Occidente, 1929.

Keyserling, Hermann. *Meditaciones suramericanas*. Madrid: Espasa-Calpe, 1933.

Kolodzieiski, Allan. "Intertextualidade no Sexteto Místico de Heitor Villa-Lobos." Speech given at XXIII Congresso da Associação Nacional de Pesquisa e Pós-Graduação em Música. Natal: ANPPOM, 2013 <https://bit.ly/35gSYST>.

Kopenawa, Davi, and Bruce Albert, *A queda do céu: palavras de um xamã yanomami*. São Paulo: Companhia das Letras, 2015.

Krenak, Ailton. *A vida não é util*. São Paulo: Companhia das Letras, 2020.

Krenak, Ailton. *Ideias para adiar o fim do mundo*. São Paulo: Companhia das Letras, 2019.

Lara, Fernando Luiz. "Espelho de fora: arquitetura brasileira vista do exterior." *Arquitextos*, year 01, n. 004.07, São Paulo, Vitruvius, Sep. 2000 <https://bit.ly/3nhRoGo>.

Le Corbusier (1929). "Corolário brasileiro." In *Le Corbusier e o Brasil*, by Margareth da Silva Pereira, Romão Veriano da Silva Pereira, Cecília Rodrigues dos Santos, and Vasco Caldeira da Silva. São Paulo: Tessela/Projeto, 1987, 87-96.

Le Corbusier (1929). "O espírito sulamericano." In *Le Corbusier e o Brasil*, 68-71.

Le Corbusier (1943). *Os três estabelecimentos humanos*. 2nd edition. São Paulo: Perspectiva, 1979.

Le Corbusier. *Oeuvre Complète*. Vol. 3, 1934/38, Zurique: Girsberger.

Le Corbusier (1929). "Prólogo americano." In *Le Corbusier e o Brasil*, 72-86.

Leite, Rui Moreira. "Flávio de Carvalho: o arquiteto modernista em 3 tempos." Óculum, n. 2, Campinas, FAU PUC-Campinas, Sep. 1992, 25-34.

Leonel, Maria Cecilia de Moraes. *Estética e modernismo*. São Paulo/Brasília: Hucitec/INL/ Fundação Nacional Pró-Memória, 1984.

Lery, Jean de (1578). *Histoire d'un voyage faict en la terre du Brésil*. Introduction and notes by Paul Gaffarel. Paris: Alphonse Lemerre, 1880.

Liernur, Jorge Francisco. "The South American Way: el 'milagro' brasileño, los Estados Unidos y la Segunda Guerra Mundial – 1939-1943." *Block*, Buenos Aires, Universidad Torcuato di Tella, n. 4, dez. 1999, 23-41.

Liernur, Jorge Francisco. "The South American Way: o milagre brasileiro, os Estados Unidos e a Segunda Guerra Mundial – 1939-1943." In *Textos fundamentais sobre história da arquitetura moderna brasileira: parte 2*, 169-217.

Lira, José Tavares Correia de. *Warchavchik: fraturas da vanguarda*. São Paulo: Cosac Naify, 2011.

Lopez, Telê Porto Ancona, *Mário de Andrade: ramais e caminho*. São Paulo: Duas Cidades, 1972.

Lopez, Telê Porto Ancona. "O texto e o livro. 1. Vinculos Makunaíma/Macunaíma." In *Macunaíma: o herói sem nenhum caráter*, 311-337.

Lopez, Telê Porto Ancona. "Viagens etnográficas de Mário de Andrade." In *O turista aprendiz*, 15-23.

Machado, Lourival Gomes. "Sobre a influência francesa na arte brasileira." *Revista Acadêmica*, Rio de Janeiro, n. 67, Nov. 1946, 64.

Maillard, Robert, ed. *Diccionario universal del arte y de los artistas: arquitectos*. Barcelona: Gustavo Gili, 1970.

Martins, Carlos Alberto Ferreira. "Há algo de irracional...: notas sobre a historiografia da arquitetura brasileira." In *Textos fundamentais sobre história da arquitetura moderna brasileira: parte 1*, 57-70.

Martins, Carlos Alberto Ferreira. "Hay algo de irracional...": apuntes sobre la historiografia de la arquitectura brasileña. *Block*, n. 4, Buenos Aires, Universidad Torcuato di Tella, Dec. 1999, 8-22.

Martins, Carlos Alberto Ferreira. "Arquitetura e estado no Brasil: elementos para uma investigação sobre a constituição do discurso moderno no Brasil – a obra de Lúcio Costa (1924-1952)." Master diss., FFLCH USP, 1987.

Martins, Carlos Alberto Ferreira. "Identidade Nacional e Estado no projeto modernista." Óculum, Campinas, Faculdade de Arquitetura e Urbanismo da PUC-Campinas, n. 2, Sep. 1992, 71-76.

Martins, Wilson (1965). *O modernismo*. 3rd edition. São Paulo: Cultrix.

Martins, Wilson. *História da inteligência brasileira – 1915-1933*. São Paulo: Cultrix, 1978.

Marx, Roberto Burle (1977). "Depoimento." In *Depoimento de uma geração*. Edited by Alberto Xavier. Hunter Douglas Project. São Paulo: Abea/FVA/Pini, 1987, 305-313.

Mattar, Denise, ed. *Flávio de Carvalho: 100 anos de um revolucionário romântico*. Rio de Janeiro: Centro Cultural Banco do Brasil, 1999.

Mezan, Renato. *Freud, pensador da cultura*. 4th edition. São Paulo: Brasiliense, 1986.

Mindlin, Henrique E. "A nova arquitetura e o mundo de hoje," (speech given at the Mackenzie Engineering School, Aug. 30. 1945). In *Arquiteturas no Brasil 1900-1990*, by Hugo Segawa. São Paulo: Edusp, 1998, 105.

Mindlin, Henrique E. *Arquitetura moderna no Brasil*. Rio de Janeiro: Aeroplano, 1999.

Mindlin, Henrique E. *Modern architecture in Brazil*. Rio de Janeiro: Colibris, 1956.

Montaigne, Michel de (1580). *Ensaios* (chapter XXI – Dos canibais). Colection Os pensadores. 4th edition. São Paulo: Nova Cultural, 1987, p. 100-106.

Montaner, Josep Maria. *Arquitetura e crítica na América Latina*. São Paulo: Romano Guerra, 2014

Moraes, Eduardo Jardim de. *A brasilidade modernista: sua dimensão filosófica*. Rio de Janeiro: Graal, 1978.

Moraes, Marcos Antonio de, ed. *Correspondência Mário de Andrade & Manuel Bandeira*. São Paulo: Edusp/IEB, 2000.

Moraes, Rubens de. "Graça Aranha e a crítica europeia." *Klaxon*, n. 8-9, São Paulo, Dec. 1922/Jan. 1923, 7-9.

Moraes, Vinícius de (1946). "Azul e branco." In *Antologia poética*, by Vinícius Moraes. 2nd edition. Rio de Janeiro: Editora do Autor, 1960, 171-173.

Motta Filho, Cândido. "O psicólogo da raça." *Klaxon*, n. 8-9, São Paulo, Dec. 1922/Jan. 1923, 5-7.

Niemeyer, Oscar. *Meu sósia e eu*. Rio de Janeiro: Revan/Memorial da América Latina, 1992.

Nobre, Ana Luiza. *Carmen Portinho: o moderno em construção*. Rio de Janeiro: Relume Dumará, 1999.

Nobre, Ana Luiza. "O passado pela frente: a modernidade de Alcides Rocha Miranda." Master diss., Departamento de História PUC-RJ, 1997.

Nogueira, Mauro Neves. "Parque Guinle. Reinterpretação das 'unités d'habitation." *Arquitetura e Urbanismo*, n. 38, São Paulo, Oct./Nov. 1991, 92-98.

Nunes, Benedito. "Antropofagia ao alcance de todos." In *Do Pau-Brasil à antropofagia e às utopias*, XI-LIII.

Oliveira, Ana Rosa de. A construção formal do jardim em Roberto Burle Marx. *Arquitextos*, ano 01, n. 002.06, São Paulo, Vitruvius, Jul. 2000 <https://bit.ly/3fd4iB9>.

Oliveira, Ana Rosa de. "Bourlemarx ou Burle Marx?" *Arquitextos*, year 02, n. 013.01, São Paulo, Vitruvius, Jun. 2001 <https://bit.ly/3HUAJka>.

Oliveira, Ana Rosa de. "Roberto Burle Marx e o jardim moderno brasileiro." *Entrevista*, year 02, n. 006.01, São Paulo, Vitruvius, Apr. 2001 <https://bit.ly/3fffZHK>.

Paim, Antonio. *A filosofia da escola do Recife*. 2nd edition. São Paulo: Convívio, 1981.

Palermo, Humberto Nicolás Sica. "O sistema Dom-ino." Master diss., Propar UFRGS, 2006 <https://bit.ly/35fLCiv>.

Panofsky, Erwin. "O movimento neoplatônico e Miguel Ângelo." In *Estudos de iconologia: temas humanísticos na arte do renascimento*, by Erwin Panofsky. Lisboa: Estampa, 1986, 153-199.

Papadaki, Stamo. Prefácio de Lúcio Costa. *Oscar Niemeyer: works in progress*. Nova York, Reinhold, 1955.

Pedrosa, Mário. *Dos murais de Portinari aos espaços de Brasília*. Edited by Aracy Amaral. São Paulo: Perspectiva, 1981.

Pedrosa, Mário (1958). "Arquitetura paisagística no Brasil." In *Dos murais de Portinari aos espaços de Brasília*, 281-283.

Pedrosa, Mário (1958). "O paisagista Burle Marx." In *Dos murais de Portinari aos espaços de Brasília*, 285-287.

Pereira, Margareth da Silva, Romão Veriano da Silva Pereira, Cecília Rodrigues dos Santos, and Vasco Caldeira da Silva. *Le Corbusier e o Brasil*. São Paulo: Tessela/Projeto, 1987.

Pereira, Margareth da Silva. "A arquitetura brasileira e o mito." *Gávea*, n. 8, Rio de Janeiro, Dec. 1990, 2-21.

Pereira, Margareth da Silva. "A arquitetura brasileira e o mito." In *Textos fundamentais sobre história da arquitetura moderna brasileira: parte 1*, 227-250.

Prado Jr., Caio (1942). *Formação do Brasil contemporâneo*. São Paulo: Companhia das Letras, 2011.

Prado, Paulo. *Retrato do Brasil: ensaio sobre a tristeza brasileira*. 2nd edition. São Paulo: Duprat-Mayença, 1928.

Proença, Manoel Cavalcanti. *Roteiro de Macunaíma*. 4th edition. Rio de Janeiro: Civilização Brasileira/INL, 1977.

Puente, Moisés. *Pavilhões de exposição: 100 anos*. Barcelona: Gustavo Gili, 2000.

Puppi, Marcelo. *Por uma história não moderna da arquitetura brasileira*. Campinas: Pontes/CPHA-IFCH, 1998.

RAMOS, Péricles Eugênio da Silva. "Depoimento de Oswald Andrade." *Correio Paulistano*, São Paulo, Jun. 26, 1949, 1-2 <https://bit.ly/3qWu8jz>; <https://bit.ly/3rErApq >.

Redação. "A construção da 'Cidade Universitária'. A personalidade do arquiteto Marcello Piacentini na opinião do Sr. Gregorio Warchavchik." *O Jornal*, Rio de Janeiro, Aug. 21, 1935, 1 <https://bit.ly/3AnTWs5>.

Redação. "Klaxon." *Klaxon*, São Paulo, n. 1, May 1922, 1-3.

Redação. "Sem titulo." *Klaxon*, São Paulo, n. 8-9, Dec. 1922 – Jan. 1923, 32.

Rego, José Lins do (1952). "O homem e a paisagem." In *Depoimento de uma geração*, 300-304.

Reis Filho, Nestor Goulart. *Racionalismo e proto-racionalismo na obra de Victor Dubugras*. São Paulo: 3rd Bienal Internacional de Arquitetura/ Fundação Bienal de São Paulo, 1997.

Ribeiro, Benjamin Adiron. *Vila Serra do Navio. Comunidade urbana na serra amazônica – um projeto do arquiteto Oswaldo Arthur Bratke*. São Paulo: Pini, 1992.

Ricardo, Cassiano (1928). *Martim Cererê*. 13th edition. Rio de Janeiro: José Olympio, 1974.

Risério, Antonio. "A dupla modernista e as realidades brasileiras." *Folha de São Paulo*, Caderno Letras. May 26, 1990, F7 <https://bit.ly/3rhVrVD>.

Rocha, Fernanda Cláudia Lacerda. "Os jardins residenciais de Roberto Burle Marx em Fortaleza: entre descontinuidades e conexões." Master diss., Minter Mackenzie/ Unifor, 2015.

Rodrigues, José Paz. *Hermann Keyserling, criador da Escola da Sabedoria*. Santiago de Compostela: Associaçom Galega da Língua – AGAL, Feb. 6, 2019 <https://bit.ly/34eMCCW>.

Rodrigues, Nina. *Os africanos no Brasil*. 5th edition. São Paulo: Companhia Editora Nacional, 1977.

Rossetti, Eduardo Pierrotti. "Riposatevi, a tropicália de Lucio Costa: o Brasil na XIII Trienal de Milão." *Arquitextos*, year 06, n. 068.02, São Paulo, Vitruvius, Jan. 2006 <https://bit.ly/34Uekpe>.

Rousseau, Jean-Jacques (1754). *Discurso sobre a origem e os fundamentos da desigualdade entre os homens*. Colection Os pensadores, 3rd edition. São Paulo: Abril Cultural, 1978, 201-320.

Rousseau, Jean-Jacques. *Discurso sobre as ciências e as artes*. Colection Os pensadores, 2nd edition. São Paulo: Abril Cultural, 1978, 329-352.

Rubino, Silvana Barbosa. "Gilberto Freyre e Lúcio Costa, ou a boa tradição." Óculum, Campinas, FAU PUC-Campinas, n. 2, Sep. 1992, 77-80.

Rykwert, Joseph. *A casa de Adão no paraíso: a ideia da cabana primitiva na história da arquitetura*. São Paulo: Perspectiva, 2003.

SABBAG, Haifa. "A beleza de um trabalho: percurso, síntese da tradição e da modernidade (entrevista com Lúcio Costa)." *AU – Arquitetura e Urbanismo*, n. 1, São Paulo, Jan. 1985, 15-19.

Saldanha, Nelson. *A escola do Recife*. 2nd edition. São Paulo: Convívio/Pró-Memória/INL, 1985.

Schwartz, Jorge, ed. *Brasil 1920-1950: da antropofagia a Brasília*. São Paulo: Cosac Naify, 2002.

Schwartz, Jorge. "Tupi or not Tupi: o grito de guerra da literatura do Brasil moderno." In *Brasil 1920-1950*, 143-158.

Schwartzman, Simon; Helena Maria Bousquet Bomeny, and Vanda Maria Ribeiro Costa. *Tempos de Capanema*. Rio de Janeiro/São Paulo: Paz e Terra/Edusp, 1984.

Schwarz, Roberto. "Nacional por subtração." In *Cultura brasileira: tradição contradição*. Edited by Gerd Bornheim, Alfredo Bosi, José Américo Pessanha, Roberto Schwarz, Silviano Santiago, and Paulo Sérgio Duarte. Rio de Janeiro: Jorge Zahar/Funarte, 1987, 91-110.

Schwarz, Roberto. *Que horas são?* São Paulo: Companhia das Letras, 1993.

Schwarz, Roberto. *Um mestre na periferia do capitalismo: Machado de Assis*. 3rd edition. São Paulo: Duas Cidades, 1998.

Secretaria De Meio Ambiente. Programa de recuperação socioambiental da Serra do Mar e do sistema de mosaicos da Mata Atlântica (BR-I1241). São Paulo, Banco Interamericano de Desarrollo/Governo do Estado de São Paulo, Oct. 5, 2009 <https://bit.ly/3ICtVHS>.

Segawa, Hugo; and Guilherme Mazza Dourado. *Oswaldo Arthur Bratke*. São Paulo: ProEditores, 1997.

Segawa, Hugo. *Arquiteturas no Brasil 1900-1990*. São Paulo: Edusp, 1998.

Segawa, Hugo. "Lúcio Costa: a vanguarda permeada com a tradição (entrevista)." *Projeto*, São Paulo, n. 104, Oct. 1987, 145-154.

Segre, Roberto. "Carmen Portinho (1903-2001): sufragista da arquitetura brasileira." *Arquitextos*, year 02, n. 015.00, São Paulo, Vitruvius, Aug. 2001 <https://bit.ly/3fex9VF>.

Segre, Roberto. *Ministério da Educação e Saúde: ícone urbano da modernidade brasileira – 1935-1945*. São Paulo: Romano Guerra, 2013.

Silva, Geraldo Gomes. "Marcos da arquitetura moderna em Pernambuco." In *Arquiteturas no Brasil: anos 80*. Edited by Hugo Segawa. São Paulo: Projeto, 1988, 19-27.

Siqueira, Vera Beatriz. *Burle Marx: paisagens transversas*. São Paulo: Cosac Naify, 2001.

Souza, Gilda de Mello e. *O tupi e o alaúde: uma interpretação de Macunaíma*. São Paulo: Duas Cidades, 1979.

Souza, Jessé. *A elite do atraso: da escravidão à lava jato*. Rio de Janeiro, Leya, 2017.

Spengler, Oswald. *A decadência do ocidente*. 3rd edition. Rio de Janeiro: Zahar, 1982.

Taine, Hippolyte. *Historia de la literatura inglesa*. 9th edition. Buenos Aires: Americalee, 1945.

Teles, Gilberto Mendonça. *Vanguarda europeia e modernismo brasileiro*. Petrópolis: Vozes, 1986.

Telles, Sophia S. "Lúcio Costa: monumentalidade e intimismo." In *Textos fundamentais sobre história da arquitetura moderna brasileira: parte 1*, 173-206.

Telles, Sophia S. "Lúcio Costa: monumentalidade e intimismo." *Novos estudos*, n. 25, São Paulo, Cebrap, Oct. 1989, 75-94.

Telles, Sophia S. "Pequena crônica." *AU – Arquitetura e Urbanismo*, n. 38, São Paulo, Oct./Nov. 1991, 117 (special issue on Lúcio Costa).

Thevet, Andrew (1558). *Les singularités de la France Antarctique*. Paris: Maisonneuve & Cie, 1878.

Vargas, Jayme. *Gregori Warchavchik: design e vanguarda no Brasil*. São Paulo: Olhares, 2019.

Viana, Oliveira. *Raça e assimilação*. 4th edition. Rio de Janeiro: José Olympio, 1959.

Viveiros de Castro, Eduardo. *Arawete: os deuses canibais*. Rio de Janeiro, Zahar/Anpocs, 1986.

Viveiros de Castro, Eduardo. O recado da mata. In *A queda do céu*, 11-41.

Warchavchik, Gregori. "A primeira realização da arquitetura moderna em São Paulo." *Correio Paulistano*, São Paulo, Jul. 8, 1928, 3 <https://bit.ly/331erOF>.

Warchavchik, Gregori. "Decadência e renascimento da arquitetura." *Correio Paulistano*, São Paulo, Aug. 5, 1928, 4 <https://bit.ly/3zqJWOC>.

Wilheim, Jorge; and Telésforo Giorgio Cristofani. "Arquitetura e nacionalidade." *Boletim mensal do IAB São Paulo*, n. 13, Jan. 1954. In *Acrópole*, n. 196, São Paulo, Jan. 1955, 2.

Wilheim, Jorge; and Telésforo Giorgio Cristofani. "O irracional na obra de Niemeyer." *Boletim mensal do IAB São Paulo*, n. 14, Mar. 1955. In *Acrópole*, n. 197, São Paulo, Feb. 1955, 3.

Wisnik, Guilherme. *Lúcio Costa: entre o empenho e a reserva*. São Paulo: Cosac Naify, 2001.

Wisnik, Guilherme. "Plástica e anonimato: modernidade e tradição em Lúcio Costa e Mário de Andrade." *Novos Estudos Cebrap*, n. 79, São Paulo, Nov. 2007 <https://bit.ly/3L3AUwO>.

Wisnik, José Miguel. *Maquinação do mundo: Drummond e a mineração*. São Paulo: Companhia das Letras, 2018.

Wittkower, Rudolf, and Margot Wittkower. *Nascidos bajo el signo de Saturno: genio y temperamento de los artistas desde la Antigüedad hasta la Revolución Francesa*. 3rd edition. Madrid: Catedra, 1988.

Wölfflin, Heirich. *Conceitos fundamentais da história da arte: o problema da evolução dos estilos na arte mais recente*. São Paulo: Martins Fontes, 1984.

Xavier, Alberto, ed. *Depoimento de uma geração: arquitetura moderna brasileira*. Hunter Douglas Project. São Paulo: Abea/FVA/Pini, 1987.

Zílio, Carlos. *A querela do Brasil: a questão da identidade da arte brasileira – a obra de Tarsila, Di Cavalcanti e Portinari*. 2nd edition. Rio de Janeiro: Relume Dumará, 1997.

Special issues of periodicals

Architecture d'Aujourd'hui, n. 13-14, Paris, set. 1947 (special issue on Brazil).

Architecture d'Aujourd'hui, n. 171, Paris, jan./fev. 1974 (special issue on Oscar Niemeyer).

Architecture d'Aujourd'hui, n. 396, Paris, jul./ago. 2013 (special issue on Brazil).

Architecture d'Aujourd'hui, n. 42-43, Paris, ago. 1952 (special issue on Brazil).

Architecture d'Aujourd'hui, n. 90, Paris, jun./jul. 1960 (special issue on Brasília).

Arquitetura e Urbanismo – AU, n. 2, São Paulo, abr. 1985 (special issue on Brasília).

Arquitetura e Urbanismo – AU, n. 38, São Paulo, out./nov. 1991 (special issue on Lúcio Costa).

Klaxon, São Paulo, n. 8-9, dez. 1922/ jan. 1923 (tribute edition to Graça Aranha).

L'Homme et l'Architecture, n. 11-12-13-14, Paris, 1947 (special issue on Unité d'Habitation).

Videos

Documentary produced by TV Cultura, São Paulo, 1987. Duration: 53 min. Video collection of the Audiovisual Center of the Faculty of Architecture and Urbanism of PUC-Campinas.

Rare video record of Mário de Andrade, Flip <https://bit.ly/33QHnJj>.

Latin America: Thoughts
Romano Guerra Editora
Nhamerica Platform
Management Coordination
Abilio Guerra
Fernando Luiz Lara
Silvana Romano Santos

Pau-Brasil Culture
When Lúcio Costa Met Mário de
Andrade, Oswald de Andrade and
Tarsila do Amaral
Abilio Guerra
Brasil 8
Editor
Abilio Guerra
Fernando Luiz Lara
Silvana Romano Santos
Graphic Design and Formatting
Dárkon V Roque
Translation
Odorico Leal
Translation Review
Noemi Zein Telles
Irene Nagashima

This book received funding from
the Proex Program / Edital Portaria
Capes no. 34/2006, grant number:
0425/2021, process number:
no. 23038.006765/2021-64, awarded
by Programa de Pós-Graduação
em Arquitetura e Urbanismo da
Universidade Presbiteriana Mackenzie

Acknowledgements
Casa da Arquitectura (Nuno Sampaio
e José Fonseca), Casa de Lúcio
Costa (Julieta Sobral e Maria Elisa
Costa), FAMA Museu (Stefanie Klein),
Tarsila do Amaral Licenciamento
e Empreendimentos Ltda (Heitor
Estanislau do Amaral, Paulo Henrique
do Amaral Studart Montenegro e
Maria Goretti Amaral), Foundation
Le Corbusier (Brigitte Bouvier e
Arnaud Dercelles), Musée national
d'art moderne – Centre de création
industrielle / Centre Pompidou (Olivier
Cinqualbre e Valentina Moimas),
Instituto Burle Marx (Isabella Ono),
Instituto Tomie Ohtake (Vitória Arruda),
Family Warchavchik Collection (Carlos
Warchavchik), Associação Cultural
de Amigos do Museu Lasar Segall
(Marcelo Monzani Netto, Marlene
Thomann, Jonatan Pereira, Sandra
Britto e Ademir Maschio), Sítio
Roberto Burle Marx / Iphan (Jéssica
Santana e Claudia Maria Pinheiro
Storino), NPD FAU UFRJ (João Claudio
Parucher da Silva e Andrés Passaro).

Alberto Ricci, Alecio Rossi, Andrés
Otero, Aracy Amaral, Dina Uliana,
Elisabete França, Hugo Segawa, José
Tabacow, Malu Gomes, Mario Lasar
Segall, Nelson Kon, Odorico Leal,
Tarsilinha do Amaral, Victor Hugo Mori

Support

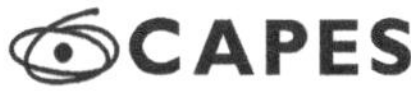

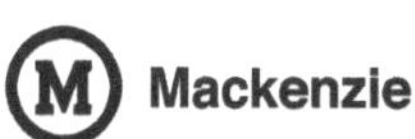

© Abilio Guerra
© **Romano Guerra Editora**
© Nhamerica Platform
1st edition, 2023

Pau-Brasil Culture
Abilio Guerra, 2023
ISBN 978-65-87205-12-0
(Romano Guerra)
ISBN 978-1-946070-47-0
(Nhamerica)

Portuguese Version
Cultura Pau-Brasil
Abilio Guerra, 2022
ISBN 978-65-87205-17-5
(Romano Guerra)
ISBN 978-1-946070-45-6
(Nhamerica)

Ebook Version
Cultura Pau-Brasil
Abilio Guerra, 2022
ISBN 978-65-87205-13-7
(Romano Guerra)
ISBN 978-1-946070-46-3
(Nhamerica)

Cover image
J. Borges, A vida do preguiçoso (The Life of the Lazy), 2016. Woodcut, reproduction on paper, 63.3 x 48.2 cm.

Guerra, Abilio
Pau-Brasil Culture
When Lúcio Costa Met Mário de Andrade, Oswald de Andrade and Tarsila do Amaral
Abilio Guerra

1ª edição São Paulo, SP:
Romano Guerra;
1st edition Austin, TX:
Nhamerica Platform
2023

412 p. il.
(Latin America: Thoughts: Brasil, 8)

ISBN 978-65-87205-12-0
(Romano Guerra)
ISBN 978-1-946070-47-0
(Nhamerica)

1. Modern architecture – 20th Century
2. Modernism – Brazil
3. Cultural Heritage – Brazil
4. Costa, Lúcio 1902-1998
5. Andrade, Mário de 1893-1945
6. Andrade, Oswald de 1890-1954
7. Amaral, Tarsila do 1886-1973

I. Title

CDD 724.981

Catalog sheet prepared by librarian
Dina Elisabete Uliana – CRB-8/3760

Quinn sighed. "Murray sure knows how to pick 'em. You're very good. Okay, kiddo. If you can stand a ride with a snake, I can stand it." He gestured toward the cab. "After you, ma'am."

"Thank goodness." She walked forward, put her packages in the back seat and closed the door. Then she climbed in the front.

Quinn closed the street-side back door and paused before he got in the cab. He really didn't want to climb in there with that snake, but he didn't want Murray to get the upper hand, either. Besides, if Murray was behind all this, the snake was harmless. And maybe it had already slithered out.

He rested his hands on the roof of the cab and leaned down to peer inside. "It's customary for the fare to sit in the back."

"I've never liked that custom," she said. "It seems downright unfriendly. Out west we—"

"Oh, yeah. That's right. You're from the wild and woolly west. Central Park West, most likely."

"Listen, could you continue weaving your fantasies while we drive? I'm running out of time to chat."

Quinn surveyed the floor in the front. "Did you, uh, notice the snake by any chance?"

"No, but if I sit up here, I can protect you better."

That did it. Damned if he'd let this woman insinuate that he was a wuss. He slid into the seat with all the confidence he could muster. "A little snake doesn't bother me. I just wouldn't want you to be startled."

"I've faced timber rattlers with bodies as thick as your forearm."

Quinn laughed as he started the car. "That's a good line. Next you'll be telling me about the grizzly bear who lives in the hills up above your ranch."

"Actually, there are two."

"Oh, I'll bet there are." Quinn pulled into traffic, noticing as he did that she filled the cab with a nice fragrance. "So what name are you going by for this caper?"

"The name I always go by. My own. Jo Fletcher."

"Short for Josephine?" Quinn didn't believe for a minute that was her name, but he decided to play along and see what sort of whopper she and Murray had dreamed up. It also took his mind off the snake.

"Well, yes. After my great-aunt Josephine. Which is why she left me the ranch, I guess. Well, that and the fact I'm the only member of the family who knows diddly about horses."

"You and Murray must have stayed up nights concocting this story. I'm impressed. Ticked off, but impressed. The guy will do anything to win a bet."

"I don't know anybody named Murray and I certainly don't know anything about a bet."

Quinn gave her a superior smile. "Right."

She cocked her head and looked at him strangely. "Did anybody ever tell you that you look exactly like Brian Hastings, the movie star? Even the smile."

"Only a couple of million people."

"Ah. So you get that a lot."

"Yeah. I'm pretty sick of it, which is probably why Murray asked you to bring it up, just to needle me."

"I don't know Murray. But if you're sensitive about the Brian Hastings thing, we can drop the subject. It's just that you really do look like him."

He swerved around a delivery van. The job took reflexes he hadn't used in years, and he liked knowing they were still there. "But I'm taller than Hastings. You can't tell that on the screen because they use camera angles to make him look tall, and he stands on a box if he has a tall costar."

"I'd heard that he was on the short side. So what? People are too hung up on how tall a guy is. Being taller doesn't make you a better man."

"I didn't say that."

"You sort of did, Quinn."

"Aha!" He thought he had her this time. His name had popped right out of that luscious red mouth of hers. "How do you explain the fact that you know my name? Wiggle out of that little slip, if you can." He liked the mental picture of Jo wiggling. At least Murray had provided a beautiful woman as part of the joke. Quinn wondered if she was dating anybody.

"You told me your name."

"Did not."

"Did, too. You said, 'just trying to throw old Quinn a curve.'"

"Oh."

"Anyway, I loved Brian Hastings in *The Drifter*. Did you see that?"

"Nope. I pretty much don't go to his movies. I pretty much boycott them, as a matter of fact." Two kids in purple hair jaywalked in front of him, and he gave them the horn. Except for the box of snakes, he'd had fun today. More fun than he'd been having recently planning investment strategies, to be honest.

"But why don't you go to Hastings' movies?" Jo asked. "He's a good actor, and now he's into directing. I think he's very talented."

Quinn recognized that tone of adulation. "Meaning you think he's sexy."

"Well, yes, I do. What, are you jealous because women find him sexy? Is that why you don't go to his movies?"

"No, I'm not jealous." It was more as if the guy had usurped his identity.

"Then why boycott his movies?"

"Think about it. I show up at a Brian Hastings movie looking like Brian Hastings. I've had women throw themselves into my arms, rip off pieces of my clothing, follow me for blocks."

"Poor baby."

"You think it would be fun, don't you?" He pulled over to let a fire engine roar past, siren screaming. "It's not fun. And besides that, they're not after me, Quinn Monroe, investment banker. They're after Brian Hastings, Hollywood star. So it means nothing."

"Investment banker? You must not be very good at it if you have to drive cab on the side."

Quinn glanced at her. She acted as if she had no idea he'd agreed to drive cab for one day on a dare. She just sat there gazing at him with an innocent look in those big brown eyes that would be hard to fake. For the first time he wondered if she was legit. "Either you're an incredible actress or you're telling the truth about this ranch in Montana."

"I can't act my way out of a paper bag."

"Would you be willing to show me your driver's license?"

"No, I would not."

He nodded, smiling. "Just as I thought. Your driver's license isn't from Montana, is it? I'll bet your name isn't even Josephine Fletcher."

"All right! I'll show you the damned license." She unzipped her purse and pulled out her wallet. "But you have to promise not to laugh at my picture. I look like an escaped convict." She flipped the wallet open and held it up.

He stopped at a red light and glanced at the license. Josephine Fletcher stared at him from the picture, unsmiling, grim even, but still beautiful. The license had been issued by the Montana Department of Transportation.

<u>2</u>

Jo watched amazement spread over Quinn's face as he glanced from her to the license and back again. He really was a cutie, with his laser-blue eyes and movie-star looks.

She flipped the wallet closed and stuffed it in her purse. "Is that proof enough, or would you like to see my maxed-out Visa card, too?"

"If you're really Jo Fletcher, then I guess you have horse sperm in that cooler."

"Of course I do! Do you think I'd make up a thing like that?"

"If you were part of Murray's big plan, you would."

"But I'm not." They crossed the Queensboro. Bridge, linking Manhattan with Long Island, and Jo glanced at the skyline. She might never fly here again, which was why she'd stocked up on extra souvenirs for Emmy Lou. No use crying over it now, though. She turned to Quinn. "Since I've proven I'm not part of some intricate plot, would you kindly tell me who this Murray person is?"

"My best friend since the second grade and the owner of a fleet of cabs. He's convinced I've turned into a stuffed shirt who couldn't handle a day in one of his cabs, so finally I bet him I could. When the guy showed up with a shoebox full of snakes I wondered if Murray had somehow engineered that. A cooler full of horse sperm was so outrageous I decided you were also in on the campaign to rattle me and make me lose the bet."

"I see." Jo had caught a glimpse of the little snake twice. It was just a harmless garter snake, but she'd suspected from the beginning of this adventure that snakes sent Quinn into a panic. She'd decided to try to catch the snake with a minimum of fuss so he wouldn't wreck the cab. Then she'd suggest they let it go in one of the open fields near the airport.

"Now it's your turn," Quinn said. "What's with the horse sperm?"

"It belongs to my friend Cassie's stallion, Sir Lust-a-Lot. Cassie was my college roommate, and I worked at her family's stable in upstate New York after graduation. Then I inherited the ranch, and we established a spring tradition — I take the red-eye to New York, shop all morning, meet Cassie for lunch at Tavern on the Green and leave with the sperm."

"Are you telling me you don't have horse sperm in Montana?"

"Sure, we do, but this is a connection with Cassie, and besides, Sir Lust-a-Lot has extremely viable sperm. Good little swimmers. My mares get pregnant like *that*." She snapped her fingers for emphasis, then glimpsed the snake easing out from under her seat. She kept an eye on it and said nothing.

"Is that what you raise on your ranch? Horses?"

"No. We try to raise cattle." Jo sighed as she was reminded of her heavy debt load, most of it accumulated since she'd inherited the Bar None. She might be good with horses, but she was financially challenged. She should have followed her great-aunt's advice and taken more accounting courses, but they'd given her a migraine, and she'd really had no idea Josephine would will her the ranch. "We lost quite a chunk of the herd this past winter. I'm already behind on my payments to the bank, so I'm not sure what the future holds."

"I guess it's tough to be a small ranching operation these days."

"It is tough. And when the ranch is such a little gem and has been entrusted into your care by your favorite great-aunt, you'd do almost anything to keep it going." She glanced at him. "I'm sorry you're not Brian Hastings. One of his advance men came by the ranch last fall and said they were looking for a location for his next film. If you were Brian Hastings, I'd fall to my knees and beg you to use the ranch in your movie."

He smiled at her. "And if I were Brian Hastings, I would use your ranch in my next movie."

"Thanks." She really liked that smile of his. Actually she thought it was sexier than Brian's, but she probably shouldn't say so. They were only going to be sharing a cab ride, after all. No point in starting anything, especially with a guy whose roots were in New York City. Despite her money problems, she'd discovered a kinship with Montana. Even losing the ranch might not force her to leave. But she intended to find a way to keep the Bar None. Somehow.

"I take it you haven't heard any more from the Hastings organization?"

"Nope. But I shamelessly told the bank that the movie deal was a sure thing. It's kept them off my back temporarily, but if Brian Hastings never shows, the bank will start demanding money again."

"I don't know if it's a good idea to stake everything on the whim of a movie star," Quinn said.

"Probably not." Jo watched the snake ease out a little more and poised herself to lean down and snatch it. To distract Quinn from what she was doing, she kept talking. "Considering the shaky condition of my finances I shouldn't have made the sperm run this year, but Cassie's decided to geld Sir Lust-a-Lot this spring, so this is my last chance to breed my mares to him, unless we get into freezing sperm, which is too complicated and expensive for me."

"Gelding. Is that where they cut off—"

"Let's just say he'll lose the ability to be a family man."

"Why would she do that?"

"Because he's a pain in the butt and useless as a saddle horse. Gelding should mellow him out. I don't blame her. She's the one who has to put up with his testosterone fits, not me."

"So you're carrying Sir Lust-a-Lot's last stand?"

Jo laughed. "I guess you could say that. The sperm's packed in dry ice, and it's always stayed fresh for the plane flight home, but I don't want to miss that plane and risk having it go bad."

Quinn stepped on the gas. "Then let's make sure you don't." He started weaving through traffic like a man on a mission.

Jo smiled. Some men took castration of male animals personally. Apparently Quinn was one of those who did. Maybe that was a good thing, because as long as he was thinking about Sir Lust-a-Lot's fate he might forget about the snake, which was almost within her reach. "So you're really an investment banker?" She leaned slowly down, straining slightly against the seat belt.

"Yeah, I really am."

She made a grab for the snake and missed. "Damn!"

"Sorry I'm not something more exciting, like a movie star."

"It's not that." She tossed her hat in the back seat and unbuckled her seat belt as the snake moved quickly to Quinn's side of the car. "Slow the car, get in the right-hand lane and hold still."

"Oh, God. The snake." Quinn eased his foot off the gas.

"Yep. He's just a little guy, which makes him harder to catch." She got to her knees on the floor of the passenger side and reached toward Quinn's ankle.

"He's down there? Right by my foot?"

"Don't be afraid. He won't hurt you,"

"I'm not afraid, dammit! I'm just..." He paused and made a strangled sound. "What's that?"

"Hold still. He's trying to climb up your leg."

"Up my *leg*? What for?"

"Maybe it's a girl snake, and she's curious." Jo clamped an arm around Quinn's thigh, noting he had great muscles, and reached under his pants leg.

"Oh, my God. What's happening?"

"Don't look down here! Watch where you're going, Quinn!"

"Holy sh—" Quinn's voice was drowned out by the loud thunk of metal against metal.

<u>**3**</u>

Jo clutched Quinn's thigh to keep from being thrown against the dashboard as the cab lurched from the impact. The jolt dislodged the small snake, and she grabbed it behind its head. "Got him!'

"Jo!" Gasping, he clutched her shoulder. "God, I'm sorry. Are you okay?"

"I think so." She released his thigh and pushed herself upright. "See?" She dangled the snake in front of him. "Real small."

Quinn didn't look so good. In fact, he was breathing hard and looked ready to pass out.

"Quinn, are you hurt?"

"No." He kept staring at the snake. When someone started knocking on his window, he reached around and rolled it down without taking his eyes off the snake.

A man peered into the cab. "We got a problem here, buddy. You want to call the police?"

"Uh, sure." Quinn didn't move.

Jo figured if she didn't get the snake out of the cab he would stay frozen in that position forever. She looked around and discovered they weren't far from JFK. The vacant lot beside the expressway would have to do. She glanced at the man looking in the window. "Sir, I'm going to take this snake over to that field. In the meantime, Quinn, you can call the police and also call me another cab."

Quinn nodded, but he didn't take his attention off the wiggling snake in her hand.

Keeping a firm hold on it, Jo climbed onto the seat and opened the passenger door. As she got out she called to Quinn over her shoulder. "Move my stuff over to the other cab while I'm gone, okay? I don't want to miss that plane!"

She climbed the knee-high metal railing beside the road and sidestepped down an embankment. "After all this I want to get you far enough away from the road that you won't get run over," she said to the snake. "This looks like a good field. There ought to be plenty of bugs, and when you're bigger you might even find a mouse or two."

After hiking about thirty yards through clumps of wild grass, she slowly lowered the snake to the ground. "There you go. Stay away from the road. Have a good life."

The snake darted away without so much as a thank-you. But Jo felt immensely better as she walked toward the road. Holding the snake had been like a moment from home, where she'd learned to appreciate all creatures. She'd grown up in a city — her father and stepmother still lived in Chicago — but cities were no longer home to her. Maybe they hadn't been for a long time. Her summers with Aunt Josephine at the Bar None had probably ruined her for city life by the time she was ten.

When she reached the expressway, the police and a second cab had arrived on the scene. Quinn was standing beside the damaged cab waving his arms and looking upset. Even upset he looked damned good — broad shoulders, lean hips. He really was attractive. Too bad he lived in New York.

She climbed the railing and walked to the group. The man whose car Quinn had hit glanced at her suspiciously before turning to the police officer.

"There was something kinky going on in that vehicle, I tell you. I was riding along next to them, and they were going really slow, so I got curious and went slow. Then they started swerving all over the road, and then she got down and put her face in his lap, if you get my meaning."

"She was trying to get a snake out of my pants!" Quinn bellowed.

The man glanced at the officer. "So who drives to the airport with a snake in his pants?"

"Nobody!" Quinn's jaw worked. "I'm sure my friend Murray is behind this snake thing. He probably paid the guy with the snakes."

The officer cleared his throat and gazed at Jo. "Would you like to tell us your version?"

She glanced at her watch and gauged the distance to the airport. "I would love to, but I'm warning you that unless I catch my plane, my sperm will spoil."

Quinn groaned.

Jo realized she should have phrased the sentence differently as soon as it left her mouth. "I was referring to horse sperm, Officer, which I am transporting, with all the necessary health department papers, to Montana. Quinn's previous passenger left a snake in his cab, and I was indeed trying to catch it when the incident occurred. I just released the little fellow in that field over there."

Quinn stepped forward. "Look, she really had nothing to do with the accident. I'll vouch for that. The cab company will assume all liability for this." He turned to the owner of the other car. "The sperm she's carrying is from a stallion that's being castrated, maybe right this minute. She has to get on that plane to Montana so the poor horse can have one last shot at immortality, okay?"

The man's belligerent expression evaporated. "Oh, well, in that case..." He turned to the officer. "Never mind the kinky thing. Just a routine fender bender. I'm sure the cab company will handle everything. This poor slob should be fired, though."

"I'm sure I will be," Quinn said.

"So I'm free to go?" Jo asked.

"After I get some basic information," the officer said.

Jo gave him what he needed and turned to Quinn. "I guess this means you lose your bet with Murray."

"Afraid so. Jo, I'm sorry about this. It's just that—"

"You're petrified of snakes."

He flashed her a little-boy grin. "Yep."

"There are worse flaws," Jo said. "Listen, I gotta go. Is all my stuff in the other cab?"

"Bill transferred it as soon as he pulled up. I think he consolidated a few things so it'd be easier to carry up to the gate."

"That was nice of him."

Quinn stuck out his hand. "Good luck with the ranch."

"Thanks." She liked the feel of his hand — warm, strong, secure. "Good luck with Murray." With a smile she released his hand and hurried to the waiting cab.

Approximately thirty-five minutes later, as she was checking into the gate, she realized that the cooler of horse sperm was nowhere to be seen.

<u>4</u>

Quinn didn't find the cooler of horse sperm on the floor of the back seat until the tow truck arrived. Just before the cab was winched on the flatbed, Quinn put in a quick call to Bill and had him pick him up.

Bill grinned as Quinn climbed into the cab. "You're lucky you caught me. I was next in line for a fare at the airport."

"You're lucky I caught you, too." Quinn held up the cooler. "You forgot to transfer this. It belongs to Jo, the woman you just took to the airport. We have to try and catch her before she boards that plane."

Bill gunned the engine and zipped into a break in traffic. "I thought that was your lunch, man!"

"It's sperm from a stallion that is probably being castrated even as we speak."

"Get outta here!"

"I know it sounds crazy, but she came to New York to pick this up and take it back so she can give it to her mares in Montana."

Bil shook his head. "Me, I don't believe in those methods. I know a guy who donated to a sperm bank. Now what fun is that?"

"Don't know. Never tried it."

"Me, neither." Bill glanced at Quinn. "How do you figure they do it with stallions?"

Quinn had been wondering the same thing ever since Jo had convinced him she was really transporting horse sperm. "Let's not even go there. Listen, drop me at the airline where you let her off."

"Good luck, but I really don't think you can make it. She was running behind. She thanked me for getting her packages all organized, and I guess she thought the cooler was in one of the bags."

"Yeah, well, it's been a crazy day."

"No kidding. Everybody knows about your little brush with the law, by the way. Murray's busting a gut laughing."

"I knew it! I knew he was behind that snake thing."

"No, he wasn't, swear to God! He said he couldn't have planned a better day for you if he'd tried." Bill maneuvered next to the curb. "Should I wait?"

"Nope."

"Yeah, but if you don't catch her, what are you gonna do? You can't follow her to Montana."

Quinn stared at Bill as he considered the idea for the first time. He hadn't planned his next step if he missed the plane, but he'd been mostly to blame for this whole mess, and Jo would be bitterly disappointed to lose Sir Lust-a-Lot's sperm on top of all her financial problems. He didn't like to think about her being bitterly disappointed, especially if it was his doing. And it wasn't as if he couldn't get away from the office for a few days.... "Sure, I can."

* * *

Driving a back road miles from Bozeman, Quinn felt as small as a flea on the back of a woolly mammoth. The headlights of his rental car cast the only light for miles around, not counting the moon and stars overhead. The mountains loomed threateningly around him, pitch-black except for a pale topping of moonlit snow. There was so much space in Montana. If his rental car broke down, he could imagine waiting for days before another vehicle came down this two-lane highway.

Belatedly he wished he'd brought food and water, a sleeping bag, a... a *rifle*. He'd never shot a gun in his life, but this was the sort of country that seemed to require firearms. And it was Jo's country. His estimation of her grit and determination rose with every bend in the increasingly lonely road.

He hoped to God he was on the right lonely road. While he'd waited for his flight he'd asked his personal assistant to call every chamber of commerce in Montana until she found somebody who recognized the name Bar None. Fortunately she'd hit pay dirt within the first half hour of phoning. Unfortunately it was located near a town named Ugly Bug, on the banks of Ugly Bug Creek. After snakes and lizards, Quinn listed bugs as his third least favorite creature.

If he was on the right road, he might miss the turnoff to the ranch, but at least he'd eventually get to Ugly Bug. If he was on the wrong road he'd probably drive until he ran out of gas, and then a bear would eat him.

He'd always been fascinated with the West, but he realized that his picture of it had been highly romanticized. Cowboys around a campfire, the comradery of a roundup, card games in the local saloon. His image of the West had been cozy, quaint and not nearly big enough. This country was enormous.

He rounded another bend and saw a spark of light nestled in a valley. Checking his odometer, he decided it could be coming from the Bar None. Maybe he'd defied the odds and found the place. Maybe they wouldn't find his bleached bones lying beside a dried-up watering hole.

A few more bends in the road, and sure enough, on his right stood a big wooden gate. Two upright poles supported a crossbeam, and from that dangled a sign. Quinn couldn't read it in the dark, but he'd bet it said Bar None.

He shone his car's headlights on the gate and got out to open it. The thing was wired together instead of padlocked, which was fortunate for him. The barbed wire fence on either side of the gate wasn't something he wanted to tangle with. He drove through and went back to hook the gate closed again.

Driving slowly down the dirt road toward the cluster of lights he assumed was the ranch, he noticed dark shapes scattered across the moonlit landscape. Either cows or bears, he concluded. He remembered Jo mentioning timber rattlers with bodies as thick as his forearm, and he shuddered. With luck, none of those would be hanging around the front porch of her house tonight.

Finally he arrived at a cluster of buildings and corrals. With his limited knowledge, he figured the two-story white clapboard one was the main house, the rust-colored structure was a barn and the third, also rust-colored, was probably a bunkhouse. Light spilled from the ranch-house windows onto the front porch with its wide swing and two rocking chairs.

The whole arrangement was right out of a Brian Hastings movie. Cowboys were making a comeback these days, and Hastings was cashing in on the new craze. Quinn hoped to hell Hastings would contract with Jo for the use of her ranch. Any woman who could keep her cool under fire the way Jo had today deserved a break.

Taking the cooler from the passenger seat, Quinn got out and closed the car door. A plump woman of about forty opened the door and peered out. Such a thing would never happen in the city, Quinn thought, remembering his triple-locked apartment door.

He smiled at the woman. "Hello, I'm—"

"Glory, hallelujah." The woman gazed at him as if she were witnessing the second coming.

Quinn figured she must have recognized the cooler he carried, but even so he was a little taken aback at the woman's worshipful expression. "Hey, glad to be of service. It's the least I could do, under the circumstances."

"You know about our circumstances?"

"Some of it. Listen, is Jo around? I'm—"

"I know who you are." The woman's grin put big dimples in both cheeks. "And I'm tickled spitless to see you. We'd about given up hope. Come in, come in. I'm Emmy Lou, the housekeeper. Have you eaten? I can warm up the leftover chicken."

It was a most gratifying welcome. Quinn decided he'd done the right thing. "Chicken sounds wonderful." He followed the woman into a small entry hall. "I figured Jo would be worried. I came as soon as I could."

"Jo has been worried, all right. Poor woman takes her responsibilities very seriously, although between you and me, I think she needs someone to give her good financial advice. Maybe you could recommend someone. But the main thing is, you're here. I wasn't sure you'd show up."

"Well, a lot is at stake. And a stud deserves to have his last shot count."

"Last shot?" Emmy Lou's smile was coy as she looked him up and down. "I hardly think so."

"Well, that's what Jo said this would be."

"How rude of her!" She peered at him. "When did you discuss this with Jo?"

"In New York." Quinn was becoming a little confused by the conversation.

"That little dickens. I need to have a talk with that girl. She may be getting a little too big for her britches."

Quinn thought Jo fit her britches just fine.

"Anyway, you're here now." Emmy Lou led him into a country kitchen filled with the scent of chicken and baked apples.

Quinn's mouth watered.

"Sit yourself down and take a load off," the woman said. "I'll run and fetch Jo. She's upstairs. She'll be *so* glad to see you."

"Okay." Quinn felt extremely pleased with himself. Maybe this sperm-delivery trip would improve his image after his sorry performance with the snake this afternoon. And if Jo truly needed financial advice, maybe he could help her there, too.

He set the cooler on the floor beside his chair. After Jo got over the shock of seeing him, he'd bring it out as a special surprise. He wondered how she'd react. Maybe she'd hug him in gratitude. That was a nice prospect.

Emmy Lou left the kitchen and walked down the hall. "Jo!" she called up the stairs. "You'll never guess who's here!"

Quinn smiled with pleasure. Despite the snake, he must have made a decent impression on Jo if she'd told her housekeeper all about him. He'd planned to head straight back for New York, but with this kind of welcome he might be convinced to stay a little longer.

5

Jo came to the head of the stairs. "Who?"

Grinning like a politician at a barbecue, Emmy Lou motioned her down, and Jo descended the stairs, eyebrows lifted.

When Jo was two steps away, Emmy Lou leaned forward and delivered her news in a stage whisper. *"Brian Hastings."*

"You're kidding." Jo's heart rate kicked up a notch.

"Nope. Sitting right in my kitchen."

Technically it was Jo's kitchen, but she didn't correct Emmy Lou. If possession was nine-tenths of the law, Emmy Lou owned the kitchen. "He just showed up at the door? Nobody's with him?"

"He probably enjoys getting off by himself once in a while, away from all those screaming women. Why I decided I wouldn't even ask him for a button off his shirt. At least not yet."

"Go slow on the button thing." Jo glanced toward the kitchen, and her chest tightened. As much as she'd prayed for this moment, she realized she'd never negotiated a movie contract. It probably wasn't a job for someone with math anxiety, either. She'd have to concentrate really hard and make sure she counted the zeros, although she had no idea how many there should be when someone wanted to rent your ranch. Lots, she hoped.

"It's really going to happen, Jo." Emmy Lou's voice trembled with excitement. "The Bar None will rocket to stardom, and we'll be able to pay the bank. Not to mention having Brian Hastings around for weeks. Do you think I should ask him for a part in the movie yet?"

"No!" Jo whispered. "And don't you ask about that darned button, either! This might still be a preliminary visit. We might have made the shortlist or something." She ran her fingers through her hair and glanced at the torn jeans and old T-shirt she wore. She could either meet a famous movie star looking like this or go upstairs and change, which would keep a famous movie star waiting. She decided to go with the outfit she had on and headed for the kitchen. A man used to starlets probably wouldn't give an ordinary woman a second look no matter what she had on.

She paused outside the kitchen door and took a deep breath. He was only a man, she reminded herself. But herself wouldn't listen. Her heart was leaping like a rodeo bronc at the idea of coming face-to-face with the very person commonly referred to as the sexiest man alive. And she couldn't blow this interview. The future of her ranch might depend on the impression she made in the next minute.

Closing her eyes, she counted to ten. Then she walked into the room.

Quinn Monroe smiled at her. "Surprise."

"Damn! It's you!"

His smile faded.

"Josephine Sarah Fletcher!" Emmy Lou said. "Is that any way to treat Mr. Hastings? Apologize this instant!"

"I'm sorry," Jo said. "In more ways than one. Emmy Lou, this isn't Brian Hastings."

"What do you mean, he isn't Brian Hastings? You're talking to a woman who saw *The Drifter* fourteen times! And *this*—" she gestured dramatically toward Quinn "—is Brian Hastings."

Quinn winced. "As a matter of fact—"

"I would know this man anywhere." Emmy Lou marched over to Quinn and took his face firmly in her hand. She lifted his chin. "Look at those sensuous lips." She brought his chin down again. "Look into those intense blue eyes. And the profile!" She whipped Quinn's head abruptly to one side. "There! Are you trying to tell me that's not the profile of Brian Hastings, love god?"

Jo sighed, "That's the profile of Quinn Monroe, investment banker. I couldn't say whether he's a love god or not."

"Only on alternate Thursdays," Quinn said.

Emmy Lou frowned and turned his head until she could look into his eyes. She fluffed his hair and stared at him some more. "Smile for me."

"I can't. You're digging your thumb into my cheek."

Emmy Lou released him. "Now smile."

Quinn obliged.

"You see? It's the Brian Hastings I'm-too-sexy-for-my-shirt smile! Only in real life it's even better." She patted him on the cheek. "You should make more public appearances. You look good close up. Not all actors do."

While Emmy Lou was talking, Jo's brain began working overtime. She was fascinated with the housekeeper's conviction that Quinn had to be Brian Hastings, despite Jo and Quinn denying it. Fascinated and intrigued. She might have been convinced herself if she hadn't seen him driving a cab, but logic had told her that Brian Hastings wouldn't get his kicks driving a cab in New York City.

"I'm here to deliver the sperm," Quinn said.

Emmy Lou gasped. "Young man, I know Hollywood's filled with sin and debauchery, but you're in Montana now, and we don't talk like that out here. You work up to that — a few dates, a few stolen kisses, a little fondling. And the term is *making love*, not *delivering sperm*."

"You brought it?" Jo asked. Now that was something to be happy about.

Quinn reached beside his chair and lifted the cooler onto the table. "I figured you might still be able to salvage it if I caught the next flight to Bozeman. So I just came. On the spur of the moment."

"That's really...amazing. Thank you, Quinn. Let me stick it in the refrigerator." Jo's disappointment that Brian Hastings wasn't here to rent her ranch dimmed as she realized what a sacrifice Quinn had made. After putting the cooler inside the refrigerator, she turned to Emmy Lou. "Remember the cabdriver who was afraid of snakes? This is him. I just forgot to tell you he looks like Brian Hastings."

Emmy Lou crossed her arms and surveyed Quinn. "Maybe Brian Hastings went undercover in New York City in order to get away from the pressures of making movies."

Jo shook her head. "Give it up, Em. He's not Brian Hastings, and all the wishing in the world won't make it so. But he's done me a very big favor, and I appreciate it." She glanced at him nervously as she thought about what a plane ticket had probably cost him. "I need to reimburse you for your ticket."

"No, you don't. I'm the one who made you lose the sperm." He glanced at Emmy Lou. "Does the offer of chicken still stand even if I'm not Brian Hastings?"

"Of course! I feed any poor hungry soul who comes through that kitchen door, no matter who it is."

"Thanks, I think."

"But I still can't believe you're—what was the name?"

"Quinn Monroe."

"Any proof?"

"As a matter of fact, I have the chauffeur's license I had to get before I could drive one of Murray's cabs." Quinn reached in his back pocket and pulled out his wallet. Then he glanced at Jo. "But you have to promise not to laugh. The picture makes me look like an escaped convict."

"I'll bet it makes you look like Brian Hastings." Emmy Lou studied the license for a long time. Finally she handed it back to Quinn. "Okay, so you're not him, but you could pass for him any day of the week."

"Yeah, I know that."

Emmy Lou stood and headed for the refrigerator. "Come to think about it, I read that Brian Hastings is a vegetarian. Are you a vegetarian, too?"

"Nope. I'd be willing to bet there is almost nothing about me that is the same as Brian Hastings."

Emmy Lou shook her head. "What a shame."

"Now, Emmy Lou," Jo said. "You sound as if Brian Hastings sets the standard for all men. That's a little extreme."

Emmy Lou pulled some containers from the refrigerator. "Not for me."

Jo sat at the table and smiled at Quinn. "You'll have to excuse her. She's been a real fan for ten years."

"I'm pretty much used to it by now."

"I'm sure you are." *And if you're so used to it...* Jo couldn't help herself. A plan was forming—a daring, audacious plan. And it just might save her bacon.

Jo decided to wait until Quinn had some of Emmy Lou's home cooking in his stomach before she hit him with her proposition. Still, she could do some preliminary spadework. "Is there a problem with you being away from your office for another day or so?" she asked.

"Not a huge problem. My personal assistant knows where I am. I thought I'd call her in the morning and see if anything major is going on I need to deal with."

"What time is your flight?"

He hesitated. "I didn't book a return because I didn't know exactly how long it would take me to find you. I can take care of it in the morning."

Excitement built within her. "Have you ever been to Montana?"

"Nope. First trip."

"Then as long as you've come all this way, how about staying for a few days? Spring is a great time of year in this country. You arrived in the dark, so I'm sure you didn't get the full impact. We have wildflowers galore, and all the trees are greening up. It's beautiful."

He looked interested, but cautious. "I'd hate to inconvenience you."

"No problem!" Jo liked her plan more and more. It might save the ranch and give her more time with this guy, and that was a good thing. Physically he appealed to her, but more than that she was charmed by his humanness. He might be afraid of snakes, but he'd traveled all the way to Montana to return a cooler of horse sperm. Although she wasn't bold enough to say so, Quinn interested her far more than the macho image projected by Brian Hastings.

Emmy Lou turned from the stove. "Betsy and Clarise are fixing to foal any day now."

"The miracle of birth," Jo said. "How many Wall Street investment bankers have seen a mare bring a foal into the world?"

"Certainly not this investment banker," Quinn said.

"You just said he was afraid of snakes," Emmy Lou pointed out. "They're starting to come out now. It's snakes and more snakes this time of year."

Jo smiled at Quinn, who was looking doubtful at the mention of snakes. "Will you excuse me a minute?" She walked to the stove, put her arm around Emmy Lou and leaned down to murmur in her ear. "Will you work with me here? I have a stupendous idea. And besides, I think he's very cute."

"I can see that he's cute," Emmy Lou said under her breath, "but you need a greenhorn like him around like you need an alligator in the stock tank."

"Maybe I should go back to New York tomorrow, after all," Quinn said.

"Just taste Emmy Lou's cooking first," Jo said. "And then tell me if you wouldn't like to stay a few extra days. One bite of her chicken, and I promise she'll have you moaning in ecstasy."

<u>6</u>

Quinn could think of another scenario that would have him moaning in ecstasy. Not that Emmy Lou's cooking wasn't melt-in-his-mouth perfect, especially considering how hungry he was by the time he bit into her fried chicken, but it wasn't the housekeeper's skills at the stove that had him considering a stay on the ranch.

Of course there were the snakes to consider, and he still worried about how the town of Ugly Bug got its name. Maybe he could just stay inside a lot. Jo awakened basic urges in him, and basic urges were best investigated inside, anyway. He'd started fantasizing what it would be like to hold her in his arms, kiss those cherry red lips, touch her soft skin. But her physical attributes weren't the only draw. He was also a sucker for a woman in distress.

At first he'd only been concerned with getting the horse sperm to her on time, but now that he'd seen the ranch, he couldn't help thinking what a shame it would be for her to lose it. He didn't know a damn thing about ranching, but he knew a fair amount about money management. If he stayed a few days he might be able to suggest some things that would get Jo out of the bind she was in.

He doubted that she'd accept a personal loan, and he didn't have enough liquid assets to make that sort of gesture, anyway. But he might be able to arrange a new bank loan with one of his contacts or find her some investors. He mainly wanted to loosen the grip of this local guy and set her on a better course than the one that seemed to be leading her into trouble.

But he'd have to hang around a while and win her trust. The minute he'd seen her walk through the kitchen door, no matter how disappointing her reaction had been, he'd been inclined to do just that.

While he ate, he answered Emmy Lou's questions about New York. She'd never been there and had a fixation on the place, apparently. She proudly trotted out all the souvenirs Jo had brought her over the years, and Quinn made a mental note to send her something special when he got back to the city.

Finally he finished off the chicken and potato salad and pushed away his plate with a sigh of contentment. "That was delicious. Thanks."

Apparently his knowledge of New York and his appreciation for her cooking had warmed up the housekeeper considerably. "You have to have a piece of apple pie to top it off," she said.

He grinned at her. "Twist my arm, Emmy Lou."

She flushed and put a hand over her heart. "Land sakes, but you look like Brian Hastings when you do that. Makes my heart go pitty-pat."

"Maybe it'll also make you serve him some of your famous pie," Jo said.

Quinn had noticed that Jo was being terrifically friendly and obliging. He'd love to think it was his manly charm causing her to be so nice, but he also had the feeling she might be fattening him up for the kill. He just wasn't sure what sort of kill.

"Would you like ice cream on top?" Emmy Lou asked as she popped the slice of pie in the microwave.

"Sure, why not?" A piece of pie à la mode wasn't going to turn him into a mush brain, he decided. He'd navigated the tricky world of high finance without getting his butt kicked. Surely he could handle whatever this pair of women had in mind.

Jo watched him eat the pie with far too much interest. And every time she caught his eye she smiled a secret sort of smile. Something was definitely up.

He glanced at her. "Want a bite?"

"Oh, no, thanks. I just love to see a man enjoy his food."

Quinn polished off the pie. "I'm afraid the show's over. But I have to say that was the best piece of apple pie I've ever had, and I've eaten at some pricey restaurants. They could serve this pie with pride at the Waldorf-Astoria."

Emmy Lou looked enraptured. "I would love to see the Waldorf."

"I've offered to take you on my sperm runs," Jo said.

"No, no, not like that. It would break my heart to fly in and out on the same day. I want to see the lights, feel the city's pulse, breathe in the rich aromas." She closed her eyes and took a deep, dramatic breath.

"You might want to give the rich aromas a miss," Quinn said. "New York's rich aromas can be overwhelming, especially on garbage pickup day."

Emmy Lou grinned at Jo. "Spoken like a man who's never cleaned out a chicken coop. You'd better keep him away from shovel duty while he's here."

"I had no intention of putting him on shovel duty."

"Anyway," Emmy Lou said as she turned to Quinn. "I don't want to give anything a miss. I want to hear the noise, taste a hot pretzel, mingle with the crowd in Times Square, give my regards to Broadway. I don't want a tiny bite of the Big Apple." She spread her arms wide. "I want to have it all."

Quinn curbed his impulse to immediately invite her there as his guest. It would be a real kick to watch her revel in the sights and sounds of the city. But he had no business inviting Emmy Lou Whatever to New York. He didn't even know her last name. The sugar must be affecting his brain for him to even think of doing such a thing.

Jo leaned forward, her dark eyes sparkling. "So, Quinn, are you ready to extend your visit a few days? I think we're having pot roast tomorrow night."

Logic warned him to use caution. She was a little too eager. But his libido reacted to that sparkle in her eyes in a very primitive fashion. And he did love a good pot roast. "I think it could be arranged."

"What about your job?" Emmy Lou asked.

"I can keep in touch by phone. With the help of Erin, my personal assistant, I can probably take care of anything critical from here." Quinn began to anticipate what it might be like living in the same house with Jo, or more appropriately, sleeping in the same house with Jo.

"Great," Jo said. "Because I have the most amazing idea. As long as you're going to be here, what if you told everybody you were Brian Hastings?"

Quinn groaned and buried his face in his hands as his fantasies dissolved. There it was. The catch.

Emmy Lou clapped her hands together. "Josephine, you're brilliant."

Quinn took his hands away from his eyes and leaned toward Jo. Damn, but she was beautiful. And treacherous. He lowered his voice. "But you see, I'm not Brian Hastings."

"You could fool them. You fooled Emmy Lou. And if everyone around here thought Brian Hastings was visiting my ranch, I could hold off the bank a while longer."

With a sigh of deep regret, he leaned back in his chair. Like too many of the women he'd known, she was only interested in him because he looked like a famous movie star. "And then what happens when Hastings never shows up? You're in the same fix as before."

"But by the end of the summer I'll have some money, and I can make a partial payment. I need to keep the bank at bay until then."

"There may be other ways around this. It's possible I could arrange for a line of credit from—"

"No!" She held up her hand like a traffic cop. "I don't want anyone else getting involved in my financial problems. If I go down, I'll go down alone.'"

"That's very noble but totally unnecessary. Jo, this is what I do for a living. I don't know why I didn't suggest consulting with you about it before, during the cab ride."

"Consulting?" She raised her eyebrows. "I'm sure you don't do that for free, Quinn."

"Not normally. But we could work something out."

"I'd rather struggle along on my own. If you'd just agree to be Brian Hastings for a week, that's all I ask."

"All?" Quin stared at her. "The guy's a movie star and a director, so he knows the Hollywood scene inside and out. Besides that, he's a worldwide sex symbol. Do you realize how intimidating that would be for an ordinary guy like me?"

"Nonsense," Emmy Lou said. "You can do the sex symbol part with both hands tied behind your back. Just give the ladies that killer grin, throw in a wink or two, and they'll drop like flies."

Maybe, but he knew that when women found out for sure he wasn't really Brian Hastings, they had a tendency to turn nasty, and he'd be in constant fear they'd find out. Besides that, he was sick of never being evaluated on his own merits, and he wanted no part of this scheme, no matter how nice it would be to spend time with Jo. As far as he was concerned, this wasn't the way to handle her money problems, either. It was only a Band-Aid when she needed a tourniquet.

"As for the movie lingo, we can fake that," Jo said. "Emmy Lou has seen every interview that Brian Hastings ever gave — Barbara Walters, Larry King, Oprah Winfrey. She can coach you on the show biz angle."

Quinn shook his head. "Sorry. The whole idea goes against the grain. I've hated being mistaken for Hastings, and I sure as hell don't want to deliberately bring that kind of chaos down on my head. Listen, Jo, don't reject my financial advice out of hand. I might be exactly who you need. I could—"

"No, thank you. I appreciate the offer, but I have no guarantee I'll come out of this with the ranch intact. I don't want to risk your good name."

"You won't ruin my good name, and even if you did, I'd rather involve myself that way than pawn myself off as some two-bit version of Hastings."

"You're not giving yourself credit. You'd be at least a four-bit version," Emmy Lou said.

"That's what you think." The more closely Quinn evaluated this stunt, the more impossible it sounded. "He's not only a Hollywood insider, he's a cowboy. I can't ride, I can't rope, and if you put boots and spurs on me, I'd probably trip and fall down before I walked two feet into the local saloon. Let me do what I do best, which is manipulate money."

Jo looked sad but determined. "I can't let you get involved with my messy finances, Quinn. I just can't."

"And I have no interest in masquerading as Brian Hastings."

"Then I guess that's that," Jo said. "But you're welcome to stay."

He hated like hell to turn her down, but he could see that a few days at the Bar None would be a nightmare as people continued to mistake him for Hastings. He pushed back his chair. "Thanks, but I'd better leave first thing in the morning. In the rush of coming out here to deliver Sir Lust-a-Lot's last legacy I forgot about your Brian Hastings connection. Chances are everyone would react the way Emmy Lou did. I'd rather not put myself through that."

Jo nodded. "I understand. Emmy Lou, would you please show Quinn his room? I need to go out and check on Betsy and Clarise before bedtime."

"Come along, Quinn."

Under Emmy Lou's reproving glance, Quinn felt like a misbehaving schoolboy. He silently followed her up the stairs.

" I don't think it would kill you to do what Jo's asking," she said in a very schoolmarmish tone.

"That's because you've never been surrounded by a hoard of women who wanted to rip your clothes off."

Emmy Lou sniffed as she continued up the stairs. "I'm sure you're exaggerating. Why, I thought you were Brian Hastings up until recently, and I never once considered ripping your clothes off. All I wanted was a button from your shirt."

"See? It starts with the buttons. What harm's in that? Then we run out of buttons, so somebody wants a sleeve. Then somebody wants my belt. Then it's strip city. It only takes one person to start it off, and before I realize it I'm surrounded. I try to tell them they have the wrong guy, but do they listen? Not when they're in their Brian Hastings crazed mode.

There are at least twenty women walking around this world with a button or a sleeve or a back pocket of my pants, and all of them think their souvenirs came from Brian Hastings."

"And I suppose this all happened in New York?"

Quinn followed her down the hall. "That's where I live."

Emmy Lou stopped in front of a doorway and turned to him. "Well, there you go. It's the too-many-rats-in-a-cage theory. They start eating their young or stripping their celebrities, whatever is handy. Out here we have room to stretch out. We're not so snappish."

"You just admitted you wanted one of my buttons!"

"Well, not now! Who wants the button off the shirt of an investment banker?"

Quinn was irritated. He couldn't decide which was worse, the loss of privacy when he was mistaken for Hastings or the blow to his ego when women finally accepted that he was only Quinn Monroe, investment banker. "I don't understand what women want with those trophies, anyway. Do they mount that button and shine a spotlight on it? Do they frame that piece of sleeve? Do they arrange my back pocket in a vase on the coffee table? I don't get it."

Emmy Lou cleared her throat and glanced at the ceiling. "Some might sew the button on a piece of velvet and embroider the person's name under it and frame it. If that someone really had a button from Brian Hastings' shirt, that is."

"Like you, for instance? I suppose your wall is full of framed buttons."

"No, it isn't. We don't get many celebrities out this way. And it was just dumb luck that Georgina Mason was in the ice cream parlor when Robert Redford came in. She claims he gave her the button, but it would be like her to pop it right off his shirt when he wasn't looking."

Quinn couldn't help smiling. "That'd be hard to do."

"Not for Georgina. She's the sneaky type. And she's such a showoff — has that framed button over the fireplace, where the whole world can see it." Emmy Lou gestured toward the doorway. "So here's your room, Benedict Arnold."

"Emmy Lou, nobody would believe me after the first five minutes! In New York it's different, because there are no horses for me to fall off of or cows for me not to rope."

"Cattle. Brian Hastings wouldn't say cows."

"That's my point!"

"We could teach you. Jo and I could whip you into shape in no time."

"Forgive me if I don't relish the sound of that."

"Okay. Be a coward. Bathroom's across the hall. If you were staying I'd hunt you up a change of clothes down at the bunkhouse, but I guess that won't be necessary."

Quinn vowed he wouldn't be baited into saying something he'd deeply regret. "Why couldn't you just take one of my buttons and claim it came from Brian Hastings' shirt?"

Emmy Lou looked shocked. "Because it would be dishonest!"

"Dishonest? You and Jo want to tell the entire town of Ugly Bug that I'm Brian Hastings, and you're worried about fudging on a button?"

Emmy Lou clucked her tongue in disapproval. "It's not worth lying just to spite Georgina Mason. But I'd lie from now until doomsday to save the Bar None for Jo." Her pointed stare indicated that she thought he should have the same missionary zeal. "Why, I—" She paused and cocked her head. "Somebody's downstairs with Jo."

Quinn heard the voices, too. Jo was talking to a guy, and from the sound of her voice, she wasn't too happy about the conversation.

"It's that Dick!" Emmy Lou said, almost spitting out the words.

"Would that be a first name or a description?"

Emmy Lou's eyes twinkled at him. "I do like you, Quinn."

"I like you, too."

"Dick Cassidy is Jo's ex. One of the worst things she ever did was marry him, and one of the best was to divorce him. All he wanted, besides the obvious, was access to Ugly Bug Creek so he could water his cattle."

Quinn didn't like thinking about some guy enjoying the obvious with Jo. "The creek the town's named after is on this ranch?"

"Yep. At least the best stretch of it, and none of it runs across the Cassidy ranch next door. He put her through hell during the divorce proceedings while he tried to hang on to that water. We can't prove it, but we think Dick had something to do with so many of the cattle dying last winter. I think he was stealing the hay she put out for them. Besides that, he might have made off with some money, but Jo's not the best bookkeeper in the world, so she's not sure."

Quinn's protective instincts surged to the fore. He tried to tamp them down, knowing they'd get him into trouble. "So why did she even let him in the door?"

"Oh, he always has some good reason he has to be let in. Last time, he came to report a break in her fence line, which I think he created. The time before that, his truck had broken down on the main road. The code of the west says you help out your neighbors, so Jo helped him. I say he's finding excuses to nose around and see how bad Jo's hurting. He's already offered her a lowball figure for the ranch."

Quinn glanced through the door into his bedroom, taking note of sturdy oak furniture and what looked like a handmade quilt on the bed. "Okay, you've shown me where I'm sleeping." As the voices downstairs rose in volume, he glanced at Emmy Lou. "What do you say to a cup of coffee before I turn in?"

Emmy Lou beamed in approval. "I'd say that's a great idea." She led the way downstairs.

As they approached the kitchen, Quinn could make out the conversation much better.

"That section of fence was fine yesterday," Jo said, an edge to her voice. "Somebody's cutting that wire."

"Now who would do a thing like that? You think I want your bull trampling my cook's garden?"

"If it means I have to pay restitution for your specially ordered designer veggie plants, yeah, I think you'd love to have my bull running around in your cook's garden!"

Give him hell, Jo. He stepped into the kitchen behind Emmy Lou, but the five-foot-something housekeeper didn't block his view of the proceedings. Dick Cassidy faced the door, while Jo stood rigidly with her back to it. Cassidy had soft, fleshy features that might have been cute when he was a kid and would look ridiculously juvenile in another ten years. Quinn hated him on sight.

Cassidy's reaction to Quinn was exactly the opposite, however. His eyes widened, and he broke into a goofy grin. "Well, I'll be damned. You're a sly one, Jo."

Jo turned toward the door and caught sight of Quinn and Emmy Lou standing there. Then she glanced at Dick. "It's not what you think. This is—"

"As if you have to introduce the guy." Dick pushed past her and stuck out his hand. "Dick Cassidy. I live on the neighboring ranch. I'd like you to come over and take a look. You might even like it better than the Bar None. The buildings are newer, and we've been able to keep up with painting and such better than Jo has. Well, you have to excuse her. A woman alone can't be expected to stay on top of everything."

"I like the rustic look." Quinn even hated Cassidy's handshake, which felt clammy.

"Then we can sand some of that paint off!" Cassidy said. "You name it, and we'll do it."

"Dick, let me explain," Jo said. "I know what you think, but this is—"

"Brian Hastings, of course." Dick pumped his hand. "I've seen all your movies. Damn good flicks, if you ask me."

Quinn had about three seconds to decide whether he could live with himself if he allowed this sorry excuse for a man to continue to ride roughshod over Jo. He decided in two. "That's good to hear," he said. "Which one did you like the best?"

7

Jo had never felt so much like hugging a man in her life. Thank God for Dick, jerk that he was. Apparently his appearance had tipped the scales in her favor and made Quinn decide to help her.

"It'd be real hard to pick a favorite movie," Dick said. "Which one did you like the best?"

"Couldn't say. Never see my own films."

Emmy Lou hovered nearby. "Except for the daily rushes, of course. I'm sure you see those."

"Well, yeah." Quinn gestured vaguely. "The daily rushes and sometimes the weekly rushes, but I don't bother with the monthly rushes."

Dick stared at him. "Monthly rushes?"

"Hollywood!" Jo threw up her hands. "Who can keep up with the funny little terms they use? Hey, I don't know about the rest of you, but I crossed two time zones twice today and I've had no sleep for twenty-four hours, so if you don't mind, I think I'll turn in." She glanced at Quinn. "Brian? You look pretty bushed, yourself. I'm sure you'll find the guest bed comfy."

Dick's jaw dropped. "He's staying here?" He turned to Quinn. "But where are the rest of your people? Your what d'ya call it... entourage?"

Quinn flexed his shoulders and looked bored. "I sent 'em off to Bimini, told 'em to relax, catch some rays. I need to be here alone, get in character."

"Wow. I never knew you guys were so dedicated. That's impressive, Brian. Is it okay if I call you Brian? You can call me Dick."

"I sure will, Dick."

"How many Oscars have you won, anyway?"

"You know, Dick, it's easy to lose track of things like that, after the first few." Quinn glanced quickly at Emmy Lou, who discreetly held up three fingers. "Three."

"Dick, I hate to be rude." Jo linked her arm through Quinn's. "But Brian's so polite he'd stay here answering your questions all night, when he really needs to get some sleep. I've appointed myself as his personal watchdog, to make sure he takes care of himself. Stars become so involved in their art that they sometimes neglect the essentials, like food and sleep."

She loved watching Dick try to hide his jealousy. He hated seeing her getting cozy with this movie star, but he also wanted to suck up to that same movie star. Jo hadn't counted on this little perk when she'd created her plan. It was a nice bonus.

The warmth of Quinn's body next to hers was a pleasant extra, too. She had an idea she'd enjoy working with him. He had lots to learn about being a Hollywood cowboy, and teaching him promised to be fun.

"Then I guess I'll be going," Dick said with obvious reluctance. He started toward the entry hall but paused. "Listen, I know people probably ask you this all the time, but seeing as how we're neighbors, in a manner of speaking, I was wondering if there'd be a part in this movie for me? I ride and rope real good."

Quinn took his time giving Dick the once-over. Jo caught Emmy Lou's glance and had to turn away and bite her lip to keep from laughing.

Finally Quinn nodded. "There might be," he said.

"Hey, that would be great. I really—"

"If..." Quinn said, and paused dramatically.

"If?"

"If you lose some of that flab. You're soft in the middle, Dick. Can't have that. I suggest lifting weights, an exercise bike, maybe a little jogging."

"Jogging? An exercise bike? Cowboys don't jog, and they sure as hell don't ride no exercise bike!"

Quinn shrugged. "Up to you. I'm just throwing out suggestions as to how you can become more acceptable for the role. You can do it or not."

Dick sighed. "Hell, I'll do it. I just hope none of my men see me. I'll be the laughingstock of the county. When will you start shooting?"

"When it's time."

"Huh?"

Jo choked back a burst of laughter.

"It's all about light, Dick," Quinn continued. "I have to wait until we have the perfect light. I'll know it when I see it. Might take months, might be in two weeks. Better buy that exercise bike and start jogging."

"Yeah. Guess so. Well, see you around, Brian.

"See you, Dick. Oh, and about your vegetable garden. Do you think, under the circumstances, that you could—"

"Hey, I don't really give a damn about the garden. I'm a meat and potatoes man, myself."

Quinn lifted an eyebrow. "And it shows. I'd suggest you switch to broccoli and carrots if you want to lose that spare tire."

Dick reddened. "I guess the cook can plant another garden. It was probably too early, anyway. No problem. Forget it, Jo."

"Don't worry, I will." Jo managed to contain herself until Dick closed the front door and headed toward his truck. Then she collapsed into a chair and clutched her stomach while she laughed until the tears came.

Emmy Lou joined her, stopping every now and then to pound on the table with glee.

Finally, Jo glanced at Quinn, her voice choked with laughter. "You've just given me the best laugh I've had in months. Thank you."

He smiled. "You're welcome."

"If I ever get depressed, I'll just think of Dick pedaling away on that exercise bike to get rid of his spare tire. And forcing down broccoli."

Emmy Lou took off her glasses and wiped her eyes. "Or jogging in his boots. I'm sure that boy doesn't own a pair of running shoes." She chuckled. "Good thing Dick doesn't know any more about making movies than Quinn, here. Monthly rushes. I almost lost it." She shook her head. "Here's my first bit of advice, Quinn. Don't ad-lib. Before you go to bed I'll get you some of my back issues of *Premiere* magazine to study."

"I think your best bet is to keep me mostly out of sight. I can do mysterious."

"That's no fun!" Jo said. Then she gazed at him. "I really do appreciate this, you know. I realize you didn't want to do it."

"I still don't, but I couldn't resist going a couple of rounds with your ex. Don't take this personally, but if he's any indication, you have lousy taste in men."

"I like to think I was having an out-of-body experience when I agreed to marry him."

Jo felt a noble impulse coming. Try as she might, she couldn't sidetrack it. "Quinn, you can still leave tomorrow morning if you want. Now that at least one person believes you were here, I can use that to convince the bank the deal is on. I'll just say you were suddenly called away."

Quinn rubbed the back of his neck and stared into space. Finally he met her gaze. "I'll stay a few more days."

"Spoken like a true hero," Emmy Lou said.

Jo had to agree. And heroes had been in short supply in her life recently. As she looked into Quinn's eyes her heart took on a jerky rhythm she hadn't felt in a long, long time. She wondered if she was risking more than she realized, if in the process of trying to save her ranch she was in danger of losing her heart. "I promise we won't be too rough on you," she said.

"Oh, I can take rough." He grinned. "The way this is shaping up, I'm just hoping I make it through alive."

<u>8</u>

Quinn woke with a start. The house was dark, but somebody was knocking on a door across the hall, which must have been what woke Quinn in the first place.

"Jo!" called a man in a loud whisper.

Quinn threw the covers back and got out of bed. He'd heard that locking the house wasn't always done out here in the neighborly west, so maybe neighbor Dick was back. Maybe Dick didn't know the meaning of the term *ex-husband*. Jo was probably out like a light after being up so many hours straight. Emmy Lou slept in a bedroom downstairs, but this joker had obviously slipped right past her. Jo's safety was in Quinn's hands.

Treading softly, he opened his door as quietly as possible and peered into the hall. Sure enough, a man was opening Jo's bedroom door. Talk about nerve.

Quinn crept across the hall and through Jo's bedroom door just as the creep leaned over Jo. "Oh, no, you don't, lizard breath." Quinn launched himself at the intruder's knees.

The guy let out a screech, followed by a loud yell from Jo as both men tumbled into bed with her.

"Don't worry, Jo!" Quinn wrestled with the guy as best he could, considering it was very dark and he wasn't sure which arms and legs belonged to which person. "I've got him!"

"I think you've got me!" Jo yelled. "How many of you are there? Let go! Ouch!"

"Help!" cried the man, flailing wildly. "Help, murder, police!"

"Murder sounds like a great idea," Quinn said, gasping. He made a grab for where he thought the guy was and encountered warm bare skin. Wonderful soft skin. "Whoops. Sorry, Jo." He tried for the intruder again and caught the guy's leg.

"What in hell is going on?" Panting, Jo struggled away from both of them.

"I'm protecting your honor." Quinn got hold of the guy's belt as he tried to squirm off the bed. "And where do you think you're going, buster? What makes you think you can—oof!" Quinn lost his grip as the guy kicked him in the privates. Groaning, he sprawled across Jo's legs.

The overhead light flashed on. "Everybody freeze or I'll shoot!" Emmy Lou bellowed.

"Go ahead," Quinn said. "Put me out of my misery. But save a bullet for your friendly neighbor, here."

"Don't shoot, Emmy Lou!" the guy cried.

"She can't, Benny." Jo sounded thoroughly disgusted. "That shotgun's not even loaded."

"You're not supposed to tell anybody that," Emmy Lou said.

"It's okay to tell Benny," Jo said.

Quinn's pain subsided enough for him to lift his head and gaze at Jo. She wore a plaid flannel nightshirt, which had become sort of twisted around as he'd tried to save her, and the effect was rumpled and very sexy. "Who's Benny?"

"Me," the guy said.

Quinn raised himself on one arm and glanced to the other side of the bed where someone who was definitely not Dick lay half on, half off the bed, staring at Quinn apprehensively. "Who the hell are you?" Quinn asked.

The guy flinched. "Benny," he said again. "Emmy Lou, can I move now?"

"You can all move," Jo said. "I don't remember inviting a single one of you to join me in bed this evening."

"I thought Benny was Dick," Quinn said. "I was saving you."

"That's very sweet. But Benny is not Dick. Benny is my wrangler."

"And Fred's the foreman," Benny said. "He's got a beard."

"Thanks for the info," Quinn said. "If he happens to show up at your door tonight I'll know who he is."

Jo glanced at Benny. "So I've figured out that Quinn is here because you're here. But why are you— oh, my God!" She threw back the covers and jumped from the bed. "I'll bet it's Clarise!"

Benny nodded. "It's Clarise. Fred sent me. He said you told him to get you if it was time. I didn't know you had a movie star in your house."

"He's not a movie star, Benny. His name is Quinn. But I want to be with Clarise. Thank you for coming to get me."

Emmy Lou snapped into action. "Foaling time. I'll make coffee." Shouldering the shotgun, she headed downstairs.

"I'll go help Fred," Benny said. He glanced at Quinn. "You sure look like a movie star. Sorry I kicked you in the—"

"It's okay, Benny." Quinn had figured out the guy was somewhat of a lightweight in the brains department. Quinn almost felt bad for scaring him, except that he had a kick like a mule, which took the edge off Quinn's regret.

"I'll just go downstairs, okay? Keeping a wary eye on Quinn, Benny eased out the door and pounded down the stairs.

Quinn climbed off the bed, suddenly aware that he wore only his briefs. "I, uh, really thought—"

"I'm sorry he kicked you." Her gaze drifted to that part of his anatomy. "Are you... okay?"

"I'll live." In fact, as she continued to look him over, his injured parts became full of life.

"I imagine you will live, at that." She looked at him with amused tenderness. "You thought somebody was about to do me wrong, didn't you?"

"Yeah."

"So with no weapon, and having no idea what you might be up against, you came charging in here to protect me?"

"Yeah."

Her gaze warmed even more. "I haven't had a man risk his own safety for my sake in a long time. It feels nice."

His pulse started to hammer.

She sighed. "We'd both better put on some clothes. My mare is about to foal, and I want to be there."

He was encouraged by that sigh and the interest in her brown eyes. "Of course."

"It's worth seeing, Quinn."

"I wouldn't miss it for the world." With one last look into those wonderful eyes of hers, he turned and headed out of the room. "Meet you downstairs in two minutes."

<u>9</u>

The birth of a foal always stirred Jo's blood, but with Quinn leaning over the stall door in rapt attention, the event seemed more emotional than usual. No doubt she was still affected by their encounter in her bedroom. The picture of Quinn standing there in his briefs would stay with her a long time. She'd never realized bankers could look like that. About her only experience with bankers was Mr. Doobie at First National in Ugly Bug. She'd never seen him in his briefs, but she could imagine it wouldn't be pretty.

Quinn, on the other hand, had made her tremble and quicken with desire. If she hadn't had Clarise on her mind…

"Get ready. I think we're close," Fred said.

"We're ready," Jo said. She and Benny stood behind the mare's rump, available to help deliver the foal, if necessary. Fred stood by her head, stroking her neck and talking to her in the gentle way he had with all animals. Some people were intimidated by Fred's size, his bushy gray beard and his gruff manner. Jo had known him since she was a kid, and when she'd inherited the ranch from Aunt Josephine she'd been thrilled when Fred had offered to stay on.

Unfortunately, his arthritis made riding painful for him, which left certain ranch chores strictly to Jo and Benny. That was how she'd ended up accepting help and advice from Dick, who'd even loaned her a couple of his men during roundup. But there had been strings attached. Actually more like steel cables attached. She'd felt shackled by Dick for way too long. Having Quinn step in tonight and torque Dick around had soothed her soul.

A couple of times in the past half hour she'd glanced up and caught him watching her. She wondered if he could soothe other parts of her, too.

The thought filled her with trepidation, because of how Dick had made her feel about herself sexually. Dick's method of intimidation was to subtly belittle a woman until she began to doubt her worth. She'd divorced him before he could do a thorough job on her, but she still felt insecure about a few things. Like whether she was any good in bed.

Clarise snorted and shifted her hindquarters.

"Here it comes!" Benny said.

"Yep." Jo's heart pounded with excitement as the mucus-covered nose and forelegs of the foal poked out between Clarise's haunches. "Good girl, Clarise. Keep pushing."

The mare groaned and sank to her knees as more of the shimmery foal emerged.

Fred groaned, too, as he knelt beside her. "You and me both, Clarise. After this I'm having a shot of whiskey."

Jo watched anxiously as the process seemed to stall. She clutched Benny's arm. "Do you think she needs us to pull?"

"I think she's doin' fine. Just fine." Benny's eyes shone.

Jo loved Benny like the little brother she never had, even though he was a few years older than she was. His mental slowness made him seem forever young, but when it came to ranch duties, Benny knew his stuff.

Sure enough, Clarise gave another mighty heave, and the foal slipped out.

Benny leaned forward to clean its nose so it could breathe. "It's a colt," he announced proudly.

"Wow," Quinn murmured.

"Wow is right." Jo couldn't take her gaze away from the new baby.

"What do you do about the glop it came in?" Quinn asked.

"Watch," Jo said. "Do your thing, Clarise."

The mare turned and began to lick her baby clean.

"Ugh," Quinn said. "I'll never eat oysters Rockefeller again."

Jo laughed. "Yeah, I know. If human mothers had to do this, I'd probably opt out of having kids."

Benny gazed at her with worship in his gray eyes. "You'd make a real good mommy, Jo."

"Thanks, Benny." She gave him a smile.

"So when are you gonna be one?"

Fred snorted as he got slowly to his feet. "Benny, you ask too many questions."

Benny looked troubled. "I don't mean to. But it'd be fun to have some little kids around."

"Yeah, it would." Jo stretched her stiff muscles. Too many hours on a plane and not enough sleep had taken their toll. "But a mother needs a daddy."

Benny grinned and jerked a thumb at Quinn. "How about the movie star? I'll bet he'd do it."

10

Quinn had joined in the laughter following Benny's remark, but under cover of the joking that followed, he'd checked out Jo's pink cheeks and the sparkle in her eyes. He decided she didn't hate the idea, no matter how embarrassed she was.

He didn't hate the idea, either, which was amazing. As the child of divorced parents, he was wary of the whole marriage and fatherhood thing. He'd promised himself he'd live with a woman for a long time before he even proposed, and as for kids, he hadn't thought he wanted any.

Yet watching Jo serve as one of the midwives for her mare, he'd had some very unfamiliar yearnings. Murray had two kids, and he'd raved about the delivery room scene. Quinn hadn't been able to relate... until now. Maybe it was the sugar in the apple pie still affecting his brain, but he'd found himself wondering what it would be like to be a proud father at the moment of birth. He'd probably imagined Jo in the role of the mother because she was handy.

"Stand back, everybody," Fred said. "She's going to get that little fella on his feet."

"No way." Quinn surveyed the colt's spindly legs and couldn't picture it. "I don't think he has the engineering for it yet."

"He has to," Jo said. "It's the only way he can nurse."

"He's not up to it, I tell you." Quinn grew agitated as the mare hauled herself to her feet. "Make her lie down and drag him to the right spot."

Jo walked to the stall door and stood near Quinn. "You can't interrupt nature like that," she said gently. "In the wild, a horse's survival depends on getting upright as soon as possible. This has been going on for centuries."

"Well, I don't like it." Quinn folded his arms across the top of the stall door and frowned as the mare started pushing the colt with her nose. "She's expecting too much, too soon."

"She's acting on instinct," Jo said.

"She's pushy, is what she is." Quinn breathed in the sweet scent of Jo's hair. It looked as mussed and tangled as it had in the bedroom. She probably hadn't bothered to comb it in her rush to get to the barn. When she shifted her weight, tendrils of it brushed his bare forearm. If he moved his hand a fraction, he'd be able to wind a lock around his finger.

But he didn't want such a tame experience. He wanted to grab handfuls of her hair and let the rich silkiness flow between his fingers. He wanted to comb her hair over her naked breasts so that she looked like a brunette version of Lady Godiva. He wanted—

"See? He's up."

"I'll be damned." To Quinn's astonishment, while he'd been fantasizing about a sensuous experience with Jo's hair, the colt had somehow balanced itself on those four matchstick legs and was sucking vigorously on his mother's teat.

"He's going to fall, I tell you. You should prop something under him. A stepladder would probably work."

Emmy Lou walked over and patted Quinn's arm. "Relax. These folks know what they're doing. We've had lots of foals born on the Bar None, and not a one of them ever needed to be propped up with a stepladder. Now if you'll all excuse me, I'll bring us some coffee."

Benny turned from his inspection of the colt. "And chocolate chip cookies?"

"Of course. What would foaling be without a batch of my chocolate chip cookies? Before we came down here I took them out of the freezer."

"Good thing." Quinn grinned at her. "I can't stand a foaling without chocolate chip cookies, myself."

Emmy Lou gazed at him and sighed. "Are you sure you're not Brian Hastings?"

"Matter of fact, I am. Until somebody blows the whistle on me."

"That reminds me." Jo turned to Fred and Benny. "I need to let you two in on what's happening. In spite of what you might think, this man is not Brian Hastings."

Fred stuck a plug of tobacco under his lip. "Who's Brian Hastings?"

Quinn smiled. He'd found a friend.

Benny pointed to Quinn. "He is."

"No, he's not," Jo said.

"Makes no never mind to me." Fred put his can of tobacco in his back pocket. "He can be Donald Duck for all I care. A man's name's not important. It's how he conducts himself."

Jo glanced at Quinn. "Fred doesn't go to the movies, and he hates TV."

"I gathered,"

She turned to Benny and Fred. "Remember when that guy came by the ranch last fall looking for a place to shoot a movie?"

Benny looked blank.

Fred scratched his beard and finally shook his head. "Guess he didn't make no impression on me."

"He was an advance man for Brian Hastings, who is the top box office draw in the country."

Fred spit tobacco juice into a can. "Whoop-de-doo."

Quinn was liking this guy more every minute.

"The thing is," Jo continued, "I told Mr. Doobie at the bank that Brian Hastings definitely would use the ranch, and we'd be able to make a big payment on our loan soon, so he gave me an extension. Only Brian Hastings hasn't ever come here."

"But he did," Benny said. "We were all in your bed together."

Fred almost swallowed his chaw. "What did you say?"

"Benny, this is not Brian Hastings. He just looks a lot like him." She glanced quickly at Fred, who had developed a dangerous gleam in his eye. "Now don't look like that, Fred. This very nice man is Quinn Monroe, from New York."

"I don't give a damn where he's from. He'd better stay the hell out of your bed. Benny, you and me need to have a talk. You ain't ever been to the big city, and these city slickers got some tricky ways about them. You gotta be on your guard."

Judging from Fred's expression, Quinn was afraid he'd just lost his new best friend. And if he valued his life, he'd shelve his fantasies about Jo. "I was only trying to save her," he said.

"Yes, that's true," Jo said. "He saw Benny coming into my room tonight, and he didn't know it was about Clarise. He thought Benny was Dick, up to no good. So he tackled him, and we all ended up rolling around on my bed until Emmy Lou arrived with the shotgun."

Fred glared at Quinn. "Likely story."

Quinn tried to salvage Fred's goodwill. "Would you believe I've agreed to impersonate this Brian Hastings character so the bank will get off Jo's back?"

Fred pointed a gnarled finger at Jo. "Don't you be getting too grateful, Josephine Sarah. You see what gratitude got you with a Dick Cassidy type."

Benny jumped into the conversation and pointed at Quinn. "But he's not a Dick," he said brightly.

Fred scowled at Benny. "Go up to the house and help Emmy Lou bring the coffee and cookies down."

"Okay." Benny opened the stall door, and Quinn stood aside to let him out. Benny peered at Quinn. "Who are you, anyway?"

"Benny, I'm losing track of that myself."

Benny nodded as if he understood the problem completely and sauntered out of the barn.

Jo turned to Fred. "I haven't wanted to worry you, but we're not in good financial shape."

"I could figure that out on my own. If I coulda done more riding this winter I mighta been able to catch Cassidy doing some of his dirty work. We shouldn'ta lost all them cattle. But the only way to catch him would be sneak up on horseback. The truck makes too much noise, and that's all I was using this past winter."

"I tried to catch him," Jo said. "Never could. But that's water over the dam. Right now, Quinn is my best hope. If Mr. Doobie believes Quinn is Brian Hastings, then he won't heckle me for money. If I could get Doobie signed up as an extra in the movie, he might not ever heckle me again."

"So I'll sign him up," Quinn said.

Fred held up his hand. "Wait a minute. You're not a movie star or director or nothin', but you're gonna sign Doobie up for a movie?"

Quinn shrugged. "Sometimes movies don't get made. The money dries up. I don't know much about it, but I figure a lot can go wrong when you're trying to raise millions of dollars to make a picture."

Fred's eyes widened. "*Millions?*" He turned to Jo. "If this Hastings really rented the ranch, how much would you get?"

"I don't know. The important thing is that Doobie doesn't know, either. He's willing to let my note ride until after the movie's shot."

"But Hastings never came back." Fred shifted his wad of tobacco to his check. "There might never be a movie."

"I know, but Quinn's agreed to buy me some time. So for the next few days, if anybody asks if Brian Hastings is staying on the Bar None, say yes."

"I can do that, but this may be way too complicated for Benny to figure out."

Jo nodded. "I realize that now, but I can't lie to Benny. If I'd told him Quinn was a movie star and Benny found out later it wasn't true, I'd feel awful."

Fred patted her shoulder. "Yeah, we all feel that way about Benny. I'll see if I can explain it to him."

"Oh, and Fred, I have a favor to ask."

"Yeah?"

"The real Brian Hastings is a cowboy star. He knows how to ride and rope and everything. Quinn's the greenest greenhorn you'll ever run across."

Quinn stood up straighter. "Hey, I wouldn't go that far."

"I'm telling you, Fred, he doesn't have the foggiest idea about that stuff. He doesn't even have the right clothes. I'd like to turn him over to you for..." She smiled at Quinn. "For cowboy school, I guess you'd call it."

Quinn's stomach felt as if he'd eaten cement, and he didn't trust the gleam of relish that flashed in Fred's eyes. Didn't trust it one bit. Fred looked Quinn up and down like he might be sizing him for a coffin.

Finally the big man spoke. "I think he'll fit into Benny's duds. As for the rest—" He grinned, showing tobacco-stained teeth. "Leave him to me."

A shiver of dread ran down Quinn's spine.

"Now if you'll keep an eye on Clarise, I'm gonna head down to the bunkhouse and get my whiskey."

"Could you bring an extra glass?" Quinn asked. He had a feeling he needed some fortification.

Fred smiled again. "Real cowboys don't need no glass," he said. "They drink straight from the bottle."

After Fred left, Quinn leaned against the stall door, which still separated him from the delectable Jo. Jo the turncoat. "I thought you were going to teach me how to be a cowboy."

"I was." She looked disappointed. "I was really looking forward to it."

"You weren't the only one."

"But then, while Clarise was giving birth to her foal, I started thinking."

"Yeah, me, too."

"About what?"

"You first." This didn't seem like the time to tell her he'd started thinking how nice she'd look pregnant.

"Here's the deal." She moved a little closer to him. "I like you. I like you a lot."

"Is that why you're turning me over to Grizzly Adams? Because, gosh darn, you sure do like me?"

"Yes." She trailed a finger along his forearm. "Because if I did all the teaching, I'm afraid we'd get involved."

"And what a disaster that would be." So what if her touch affected his breathing? He could work around that. The one bright spot in this whole episode had been wiped out, almost as if Fred had hit it dead center with a stream of tobacco juice.

"It would be a disaster." Jo's expression was sweet and serious as she continued to draw imaginary lines over his arm. "Now that you're going to be Brian Hastings, you have to play your part and hightail it out of town before anybody's the wiser. You can never set foot in these parts again. It'd be too risky."

He was beginning to get her point. He didn't like it, but he was getting it. He captured her hand. She had strong hands, but warm and so soft. She must slather them with lotion to keep them that way. "And you're not the kind of woman who wants a fling with a guy who can never set foot in these parts again."

"I wish I could be, Quinn. If I could be that kind of woman, you'd be the very guy I'd choose to have a fling with."

"That's such a comfort." He brought her hand up to his lips and kissed her knuckles one by one.

Her eyes darkened to the color of chocolate. "Are you the kind of guy who would have a fling with a woman you could never see again?"

Under the glow of that gaze he began to fidget. He looked away. His conscience wasn't as clear on this score as hers apparently was. There was that time in Rio, when both he and the woman had known the relationship would go nowhere, yet they'd had a damned good time for a few days. And then there was the woman he'd met on the subway. She'd come to New York for a convention and had flown home to Paris three days later. Even though the time together had been great, neither of them had felt committed enough to uproot their lives to be with each other. Both times he'd suspected the women were pretending he was Brian Hastings, but that was another matter.

"I guess you are that kind of guy," Jo said quietly. She tried to pull her hand away.

He held it tight and met her gaze. "Okay, I'll admit I've been willing to do that in the past. Not often, but it's happened. I'll also go out on a limb and say that I wouldn't want that sort of arrangement with you."

"Because you think I would get hurt?"

He stroked the back of her hand with his thumb. "Because I think we could both get hurt."

Her gaze softened. "Thank you. You're a kind man, Quinn."

Not kind. Right now he wanted to come into that stall and push her down on the fragrant hay at her feet. "Just telling it like it is. I hadn't thought this through as completely as you have. You're right. Now that I'm going to impersonate Hastings, we really shouldn't let anything develop between us." He hated saying that, but it was true.

Jo sighed wistfully. "You sure look good with no clothes on, though."

Quinn's body tightened even more. "You sure felt good—whatever part of you I got a grip on when I was wrestling with Benny."

"My thigh. You grabbed my thigh."

"Mmm." Probably another spot she slathered lotion on. An ache began to build in the vicinity of his groin. He should end this conversation while he could still walk. "I said I was sorry. I wasn't really."

"That's okay." She sounded breathless. "Maybe we should get all these comments out in the open, now that we're not going to... do anything. I think you look lots sexier than Brian Hastings. It's just my personal opinion, of course."

"That's the opinion that counts." He kissed her palm and felt the shiver that ran up her arm. "I've been wishing I could run my fingers through your hair. I love your hair."

She drifted closer, until they would have been nestled against each other if they hadn't been separated by the stall door. "And I love your eyes." Her voice grew husky. "Such a deep blue. I've heard Brian Hastings wears contacts."

"How do you know I don't?"

"Do you?"

God, but he wanted to kiss her. "No. Do you?"

She shook her head. "No contacts, no capped teeth, no breast implants."

He glanced down and noticed she'd skipped putting on a bra under her T-shirt. Her nipples pushed at the soft material. He looked into her eyes. "I wanted to comb your hair over your naked breasts."

Her breath caught. "And I wanted to feel your chest muscles flex. Do you... work out?"

"Not much." Desire thickened his vocal cords. He sounded as if he had strep. "Mostly I go out to Murray's house on Long Island and help him with his projects." Only one project interested Quinn at the moment, and that was finding a quiet place where they could both get naked. "He's always adding a room or something."

"You can do handyman stuff?" Her breasts touched his chest as she leaned closer.

"Hey, I'm very macho." He ached to kiss her, but he didn't dare. Instead he ran a forefinger gently over her lower lip until she closed her eyes and sighed, surrendering to the caress. "Forget teaching me to ride and rope," he murmured. As he eased his finger between her slightly parted lips, his erection pressed against the rough wood of the stall door. "I'll impress the population of Ugly Bug by hammering a couple of boards together. Then for an encore I'll saw a plank in half."

"Coffee and cookies, anyone?"

Quinn and Jo leaped away from their respective sides of the stall door. Then Quinn quickly plastered himself to the door again, grimacing at the impact of the wood against the body parts most affected by Jo.

"Hi, there, Emmy Lou. Hey, Benny." Jo blushed furiously. "We were just—"

"Were they kissing?" Benny asked Emmy Lou.

"Not quite." Emmy Lou set a wooden tray on a leather trunk in the aisle between the rows of stalls.

"We were talking," Jo said.

Emmy Lou poured a mug of coffee and handed it over the stall door to Jo. "Honey, no explanation necessary. You already told me you thought he was cute. " She filled a second mug and gave it to Quinn.

Quinn's embarrassment turned to delight, "She did?"

"I just meant in a general sense," Jo said, blushing.

"But you did say it."

"Yes, she really did." Emmy Lou patted him on the arm. "I think you're cute, too."

"Well, I don't think he's so damned cute," Fred said as he walked into the circle of light by the stall door carrying his bottle. "How're momma and baby doing?"

"Sleeping," Jo said.

Quinn glanced guiltily at the mare and foal. They could have been dancing the tango for all he knew. Once everyone had left he'd forgotten the horses and become completely immersed in Jo.

"Whatcha gonna name him?" Fred asked.

Jo gazed at the little foal curled up against his mother. "Well, if people hear that Brian Hastings was present for the birth, they'll expect this colt to be named Brian, probably."

"Aw," Fred said. "Don't do that. That don't sound like a horse name. And don't be calling him Hastings, either. That sounds like a butler."

"Then I guess I'll call him Stud-muffin," Jo said.

Fred groaned.

"I think it's clever," Emmy Lou said.

"What's it mean?" Benny asked.

"Never mind, Benny," Fred said. "So is that it, Jo?"

"That's it."

"Then if it's official, I can drink to it." He uncorked his bottle. "Here's to—" He grimaced. "Stud-muffin. Long may he live." He took a swig and wiped the top on his sleeve. Then with a rascal's glint in his eye, he handed the bottle to Quinn.

Quinn took it. "I'll bet you think I've never swigged whiskey from a bottle before, don't you?"

Fred nodded. "That would be my guess, city boy."

"You'd be wrong." It had been a few years, but he'd done it. Once. "Here's to Stud-muffin." Quinn took a big swallow from the bottle and choked, spilling coffee on himself in the process. The whiskey burned its way to his stomach. The coffee on his shirt seared his chest. He whimpered.

"Give me that!" Emmy Lou grabbed the bottle out of his hand and sniffed it. Then she glared at Fred. "What do you think you're doing, giving that boy some of your hundred-and-fifty-proof home brew? You want to kill him before he has a chance to do this Brian Hastings thing?"

"Jo said I was supposed to turn him into a cowboy!"

"She didn't tell you to turn him into a lush, now, did she?"

Fred stuck out his chin. "A real cowboy can hold his liquor!"

Quinn had recovered enough to set his coffee mug on the wooden tray. "Give me that bottle, Emmy Lou."

"Nope."

Quinn knew his smile could accomplish most anything with Emmy Lou, and he used it. "Come on, Em. Let a guy salvage his pride."

Jo leaned over the stall door. "Forget your pride, Quinn. That stuff would burn a hole right through the floor of this barn."

"You're all a bunch of pansies," Fred muttered.

Quinn motioned for the bottle. "Give it here."

"Don't drink it," Benny said. "It rots your innards."

Quinn glanced at Fred. "He's still standing."

"You can't go by him," Emmy Lou said. 'His insides are galvanized steel."

"Emmy Lou. The bottle."

"Oh, give it to him," Jo said. "It's a guy thing. Might as well get it over with."

Emmy Lou surrendered the bottle with obvious reluctance. "Just so you know, we don't have a very up-to-date medical clinic in Ugly Bug."

"I won't need a medical clinic." Quinn met Fred's piercing gaze. Then he slowly raised the bottle to his lips and took another drink, a slightly smaller one this time. Damn, but it was strong. Tears sprang to his eyes, but he lowered the bottle and smiled at Fred. "Good stuff," he said hoarsely. "You make this yourself?" His whole chest was on fire.

"I do."

Quinn wiped the bottle on his sleeve and handed it back. "Thanks."

"Any time."

"I'll remember that." Quinn looked into Fred's eyes and was rewarded with a gleam of exactly what he'd been hoping for—respect.

11

Jo woke at six-thirty, which was late for her, and heard rain drumming on the roof. She flopped back on the pillow. Rain was good, making the hay grow that she'd use to feed her cattle next winter. If she still had the ranch next winter. But rain meant mud as she went about her chores. Mud wasn't so good.

She turned her head and looked at the picture of her great-aunt Josephine sitting on her dresser. Aunt Josephine had believed in past lives, and she claimed that Jo was a reincarnated pioneer woman, which Aunt Josephine said explained everything.

Jo's mother had died when she was thirteen, and her father had married a woman who didn't seem to like Jo much. Aunt Josephine had been Jo's salvation, and she'd dreamed of helping run the ranch someday. But her great-aunt had insisted she go to college instead of moving directly to the ranch after high school, and there Jo had met lovable, bossy Cassie.

Jo smiled. When Cassie got an idea in her head, most people went along, including Jo. So after graduation she'd worked with Cassie at her family's stables for a year, always thinking she could eventually join Aunt Josephine in Montana. Then an unexpected heart attack claimed her seemingly ageless great-aunt, and suddenly the Bar None belonged to Jo.

"Heels down! Back straight! Grab some mane! That's it!"

That sounds like Fred. Jo threw back the covers and hurried to the window. Her breath fogged the glass, and she rubbed a clear place to look through.

Sure enough, Fred had somebody up on Hyper, and from the way the rider was bouncing around Jo knew who it had to be. God, what had she done?

As she pulled on her jeans, she hopped one-legged to the window to see if Quinn was still aboard Hyper. Trust Fred to give him the acid test, just like he had with the whiskey. And in the rain, no less. Everything was slippery in the rain, including saddles.

Still buttoning her shirt, she took the stairs at a rapid clip.

Emmy Lou was in the kitchen frying bacon. "Fred came to get Quinn at five-thirty," she called as Jo headed for the door.

"Why the hell didn't Quinn tell Fred to get lost?" Jo clamped her hat on her head and grabbed a yellow slicker from a peg by the door.

"I think he wants to be your knight in shining armor," Emmy Lou said.

"I don't know what to do with one of those," Jo said. "I never had one before."

Emmy Lou came to the door. "You were on the right track last night in the barn."

Jo shook her head. "That would completely louse up the plan."

"Then maybe you need a new plan."

Jo flung open the door. "Can't think about that now. I have to go save Quinn before Fred breaks every bone in his gorgeous body."

She ran toward the corral, splashing through puddles along the way, but she wasn't in time. As she arrived, Hyper slid to an abrupt halt, haunches down, and Quinn popped right out of the saddle. The corral was a sea of mud, so there was no question he'd land in it. Fortunately it was butt-first instead of headfirst.

Jo stormed up to Fred, who was leaning against the top rail, the brim of his hat creating a mini waterfall in front of his face. He didn't turn. "Mornin', Jo."

Jo would never publicly chastise anyone who worked for her, but it took an effort for her to keep her voice down so Quinn couldn't hear her. "It's raining, Fred. A real trash mover."

"I did notice that."

Jo nodded. "Okay. I guess we'll move on to my next point. Quinn's riding Hyper."

"I noticed that, too."

"Why is he riding Hyper, Fred?"

"That was the horse he wanted."

"Of course he did!" Jo heard herself getting loud and lowered her voice. "That's the horse everybody wants, because he's beautiful. I'll bet you didn't tell him that horse is a spoiled brat, did you?"

"'Scuse me a minute, Jo." Fred made a megaphone of his hands. "Your hat's over yonder!"

he called to Quinn. "Grip harder with your thighs next time."

"I don't want there to be a next time," Jo said.

Fred turned to her at last, a challenge in his gray eyes. "Wanna take over?"

"No, I want you to take it easy on him! At this rate he'll end up in the hospital, which is not fair considering he's only doing this as a favor to me."

"I don't think he'll end up in the hospital."

"No? I've already seen him take one tumble. The next one could be—"

"He's hit the mud four times already." Fred sounded proud of the fact.

"*Four?*"

"Whoops. Make that five."

Jo whipped around to take stock of the newest disaster. What she saw made her go cold. Quinn lay facedown in the muck. "God, Fred, you've killed him." Jo ducked through the rails of the corral and ran toward Quinn. "Are you okay? Please be okay!" She crouched beside him. At least he seemed to be breathing. "Quinn! Speak to me!"

Slowly he rolled to his back and glanced at her, his face grimy with mud. He grinned. "Well, damn. I thought I'd have this riding thing figured out before breakfast. It may take a little longer than that."

"Don't move." Jo wiped a glob of mud from his chin with a trembling hand. If he was really hurt she'd never forgive herself. "You may have a concussion. A broken back. Broken neck. Broken ribs."

"Nah. Besides, I can't just lie here. The way the rain's coming down, I'll drown."

Jo leaned closer, her conscience kicking her six ways to Sunday. "You don't have to do this," she said in an undertone. "I'll tell Fred I've changed my mind about having you impersonate Hastings. Go get cleaned up, have Emmy Lou's famous ranch breakfast and drive out of here."

His blue gaze, usually so easygoing, slowly took on the look of tempered steel. "Nope. Can't do it."

"Why not? Surely you're not trying to prove something to Fred. I could have throttled you last night with that stupid posturing about the whiskey."

Quinn smiled and eased to a sitting position. "It did taste a lot like the muck in this corral." He turned his face away and spit.

"Go back to New York, Quinn. Please."

He looked at her. "You don't want me around anymore?"

"I didn't say that."

"Then I'm staying." He jerked a thumb at Hyper. "Is it true that horse slept in your bed?"

So Fred had explained that she was the one who had spoiled Hyper. "He was tiny. Premature, and an orphan. So cute and lonesome. Fred told me I'd be sorry."

Quinn gave her a sly grin. "You said I was cute, and I'm feeling kinda lonesome."

She tried to ignore the leap in her pulse rate. "I don't make those mistakes anymore. You see how Hyper turned out." She stood. "Come on, I'll help you up, and we'll go inside."

He ignored her outstretched hand and got to his feet by himself. "I told you I'd do this, and I'll do it."

She noticed him wince and caught his arm. "You were never supposed to learn to become a real cowboy! I thought you could pick up a few things and fake it."

He leaned down and retrieved his muddy hat, obviously a loan from Benny. The mud-spattered jeans and shirt looked like Benny's, too, and the worn boots. Mud-spattered or clean, Benny had never looked so good in these clothes. Quinn might be a lousy rider, but he was born to dress in snug jeans and broad-shouldered Western shirts.

He settled the hat on his head and glanced at her. "There's something I forgot to tell you. Faking it isn't my style." He tipped his hat. "Excuse me, ma'am." There was a definite drawl in his voice. "I need to go catch your spoiled-rotten horse."

As he ambled away, Jo stared at him with her mouth open. "What's with the drawl? You're from New York! New Yorkers don't drawl."

Quinn laughed. "I bit my tongue on that last go-round. Drawling feels better than talking fast."

"And where'd you get that bowlegged walk? That's not your normal walk, either."

He kept going, headed for the dark bay standing in a corner of the corral. "I always wondered why cowboys walk this way. After banging around in that saddle a few times, I get it."

"Quinn, stop this!"

He kept walking.

Jo stalked to Fred. "We have to make him quit."

"Now, Jo, have you ever known a cowboy you could talk out of something once he's set his mind to it?"

"Read my lips—*he's not a cowboy.*"

Fred shrugged, "I wouldn't be so sure. I thought he shouldn't ride this morning on account of the rain. But he wanted to."

"You're kidding."

"Nope. He just asked if rain would be bad for the horse."

"But you should have talked him out of riding Hyper."

"I tried. He said if he could ride Hyper he'd know he'd really learned how to ride. Said he'd keep at it until he could stay on. And look at that. Damned if he don't have old Hyper figured out."

Jo gazed across the corral. Hyper started out with his usual crow hops, but Quinn gripped with his thighs and held on. Jo could tell that he was gripping with his thighs because of the way the wet denim moved. Not that she was looking at his thighs on purpose. And she was definitely not looking at the spot between his thighs, the place that had taken so much punishment from the saddle this morning. He'd probably appreciate an ice pack for that area. She cringed as Quinn's butt came partially off the saddle and slammed down again.

But, God, he had a great butt. And he was keeping it mostly in the saddle this time. He dug his heels into Hyper's ribs, and the gelding took off at a lope. Quinn's hat flew off, and for a second Jo thought he would tumble into the mud again, but he corrected his position by using those spectacular thigh muscles.

As Hyper and Quinn rounded the curve of the corral, Quinn let out a whoop. "Coming through," he yelled. "I still can't steer worth a damn!"

Jo scrambled through the fence barely ahead of the thundering hooves.

"Yee-haw!" Quinn shouted as Hyper made another circuit, flinging mud everywhere.

Jo turned to stare at Fred. "Yee-haw?"

"We'll work on that," Fred said. "He probably thinks that's what you're supposed to say at a time like this. Can't expect him to get everything right at first. He's from New York."

Jo gazed at Quinn sailing around the corral in the rain, a big old grin on his face. "Let me get this straight. This whole circus this morning was Quinn's idea, not yours?"

"I've seen how you look at him, Jo. I wouldn't deliberately do the boy wrong."

Jo pulled her slicker closer around her. "I don't look at him any certain way."

"Okay. Whatever you say. And he don't look at you no certain way, either. I'm an old coot and I don't know what I'm talking about."

Jo sighed. "You sound like Emmy Lou."

"Well, she's an old lady, just like I'm an old coot. Our eyesight's no good, and besides, we can't remember what it's like to have them feelings, so don't pay us no mind."

Jo had a sudden flash of insight. She began putting together isolated incidents and finally decided she had a case. "Fred, are you sweet on Emmy Lou?"

The part of Fred's cheeks not covered with his bushy gray beard grew red. "Now what makes you say a darn fool thing like that? Emmy Lou and me have been working on this ranch together for years, been giving each other hell for years, too. We've known each other too long, and we're too danged sensible for such goings-on."

Jo grinned. "I'll be damned. You are sweet on her. Does she know?"

"She don't know because there's nothing to it!" Fred turned abruptly and made a megaphone of his hands again. "Hey, Quinn, how about finding the brake on that nag? I need me some breakfast!"

"You go ahead. I'll be fine."

"You will not be fine. Don't go getting cocky on me. In case you hadn't noticed, you're on a runaway horse. Hyper's got the bit in his teeth, and if you weren't in this here corral, he'd be taking you on a trip to the high country, and you wouldn't have any say about it at all."

"I'll bet I could stop this horse whenever I want."

Fred exchanged a glance with Jo and sighed. "Ain't that just like any other cowboy in the world? A little success, and he gets to bragging on himself."

"Fred, he's not a cowboy."

"He sure as hell acts like one." He raised his voice. "Let's see this control you've got over that horse, cowboy. And don't go jerking the reins and hurting his mouth. Go easy."

"Okay." Quinn started pulling as he rounded the curve coming toward Jo and Fred. Nothing happened. He frowned and pulled harder.

Fred folded his arms. "We're waiting on you, cowboy. Try yelling *whoa*."

Quinn put more muscle into it. "Whoa!" he yelled. When Hyper still didn't respond, he leaned back on the reins. "Dammit, stop!"

"I'll get him not to say *dammit stop* when I mention the *yee-haw*," Fred said.

"Good idea. Look out, here he—"

Hyper slid to a stop right in front of Jo and Fred, spraying mud all over them.

"—comes," Jo finished, holding out her arms and surveying her yellow slicker, now polka-dotted with mud. At least her clothes were protected by the slicker. Fred would have to start over before he appeared at the ranch house.

"Wow. Just like a New York street sweeper." Quinn sat in the saddle staring at them. "Sorry about that."

Jo glanced at him and saw the sparkle of mischief in his blue eyes. "Funny, but you don't look sorry," she said.

"Oh, but I am." He leaned on the saddle horn and grinned at her.

Amazing, Jo thought. At this moment every obnoxious, sexy, devilish inch of him screamed out cowboy. But he wasn't quite cowboy enough to know he should keep his feet in the stirrups until he was ready to dismount.

Taking note of that, Jo slipped through the rails of the corral. "Let me help you get off that beast."

"Oh, that's okay." He patted the horse's neck. "Me and Hyper, we're getting along fine. You have to know how to deal with him. He just needs a firm hand."

"I'm sure you're right. What was I thinking? Thanks for telling me." She hoped Hyper remembered the trick she'd taught him when he was still a colt. She grabbed his reins and gave a soft, low whistle.

On cue, Hyper reared, and Quinn slid neatly down the horse's rump into the mud.

"It's a good idea to keep your feet in the stirrups when you're sitting in the saddle," she said with a sweet-as-pie grin. "You never know what might happen if you don't." She led Hyper out the gate Fred held open.

"Good job," Fred said, smiling in approval as he took the reins from her. "I'll walk him a little and give him a rubdown." He glanced at Quinn, who still sat in the mud as if he couldn't quite believe he'd ended up there after his grand finish. "Come on down to the bunkhouse for a shower before breakfast, cowboy," he said. "You're not fit to sit at Emmy Lou's table looking like that." He walked Hyper toward the barn.

Quinn continued to sit in the mud with the rain pouring down on him.

Jo stood by the open gate. "Are you coming out?"

"You did that on purpose," he said, a note of surprise in his voice.

"Somebody had to. You were getting way too big for your britches." She stepped a little closer, hoping her little maneuver hadn't been too rough on him. "Are you okay?"

"What if I'm not?"

Instantly she regretted her impulsiveness. She hurried toward him. "Oh, Quinn, I didn't mean to hurt you. I only wanted to prick a hole in your pride before it got out of control." Anxiety twisted in her stomach. "Can you stand?"

"I don't know."

Dammit, why had she allowed herself that moment of revenge? "Where do you hurt?"

His head drooped. "All over. I don't think there's a single inch of me that doesn't hurt."

"Oh, Quinn." She dropped to her knees in the mud beside him and put her hand on his mud-caked shoulder. "Did you twist your ankle? Is that why you're afraid to stand up? What can I do?"

His head lifted slowly. She had the space of a heartbeat to see the wicked gleam in his eyes before he grabbed her and wrestled her to the mud. She shrieked and fought, but he unsnapped her slicker and started smearing mud down the front of her shirt.

"Stop that! I'll kill you, Quinn Monroe!"

"Devil woman," he said, laughing as he rolled with her in the muck. "How dare you make that horse rear? You turned him into a regular water slide."

"How dare you tell me how to handle him? Let me up!"

He pinned her to the ooze and proceeded to rub mud all over her. "Not until you're as covered with this goo as I am. Dump me in the dirt, will you?"

"You were getting too cocky!" Her breathing became labored as she struggled to free herself. Or maybe it was the other sensation, the one of having his hands all over her, that was causing her to gasp for breath.

"I deserved to be cocky." His chest heaved as he gulped in air. "I got up at the crack of dawn and busted my butt, literally, on that spoiled horse of yours. And by God, I rode him."

"I think it was more like he took you for a ride!" She continued to squirm away from his touch, but her heart wasn't in it. In fact, the squish of the mud was beginning to feel sort of good. And she was feeling a bit warm and oozy inside as well as outside.

"That horse knew who was boss." His hand grazed her breast as if by accident. "I was in control the entire time."

"Were not."

"Was, too." He grabbed her wrists and held them as he rolled on top of her.

Surely she hadn't meant to make a cradle of her hips. Surely he hadn't meant to ease himself between her thighs. Surely neither of them had intended to end up in the perfect position for her to discover that he was fully aroused.

"Were not," she whispered, looking into his eyes.

"Was, too." His eyes darkened as his gaze searched hers. "Jo..."

Her heart beat like a rabbit's. "Don't kiss me, Quinn."

"Okay, I won't." He lowered his head.

"You are." She was quivering. "You're going to kiss me."

"No. Brian Hastings is going to kiss you. Think Brian Hastings."

When his mouth found hers, she didn't think at all. She sure did feel, though — cool lips that quickly warmed against hers and shaped themselves into the soul of temptation in no time, a tongue that told her exactly what Quinn would be doing if they didn't have two layers of denim between their significant body parts. She liked everything about this kiss, even the mud that squished between them as he eased his chest to press against her breasts.

The only thing she didn't like was that he stopped kissing her. "More," she whispered, keeping her eyes firmly closed.

"Can't."

"Can so."

"If I kiss you some more, I'm liable to unzip your jeans and start getting serious about this maneuver."

Reluctantly she opened her eyes. At least he looked as frustrated as she felt. "Oh, Quinn, what are we going to do?"

He gave her a crooked grin. "I'm moving to the bunkhouse."

12

"Tarnation, boy, don't they feed you in New York City?" Fred stared at Quinn as he served himself a second helping of biscuits and gravy.

"Not like this." Quinn dove in while Emmy Lou beamed. He'd never been a breakfast eater in New York. Coffee and toast did the trick. But he wasn't in New York anymore, and he polished off enough bacon, eggs, biscuits and gravy to make him embarrassed, except that everyone else ate almost as much. None of the people sitting around the table was plump except Emmy Lou, and on her it looked nice.

Nobody was rude enough to mention the ice pack Quinn had positioned against his crotch. Emmy Lou had noticed the way he was walking and had suggested it. After a few minutes the ache had gone away and he just felt numb down there, which was probably a good thing considering the direction his thoughts took every time he glanced across the table at Jo.

The topic of conversation turned to Quinn's impending move to the bunkhouse. Jo didn't say much, just got pinker and pinker as the discussion continued. Her hair was damp from her shower, and she wore no makeup. Quinn had always loved the stage in a relationship when a woman became comfortable enough to appear in front of him fresh from the shower without doing her hair or putting on makeup.

Of course this didn't count as a stage, because he wasn't involved with Jo. Wouldn't be involved with Jo. Dammit. Maybe he should strap an ice pack permanently to his crotch.

"People will think it's terrible if we make Brian Hastings sleep in the bunkhouse," Emmy Lou said. "I think you should stay up at the house, Quinn. The bunkhouse is grungy."

"No, it ain't!" Fred said. "Just because I won't let you clean it every five minutes and put doilies around on whatever don't move, you—"

"It's a pit," Emmy Lou said to Quinn with a smile. "Fred and Benny act like it's their clubhouse or something. All I did was try to vacuum one day and rearrange a few things, and you'd think I'd burned the place to the ground."

"You Hoovered the ace of clubs out of my lucky deck of cards, woman!"

Emmy Lou leaned over and patted Quinn's hand. "Stay up at the house. Don't you agree he should, Jo?"

"Well, I—"

"Emmy Lou," Fred said, pointing at her. "Don't be forgetting that Jo's a divorcée."

"So what?" Emmy Lou said.

Fred acted as if he were explaining a simple fact to a three-year-old. "People think a certain way about divorcées. They'll think there's hanky-panky going on between him and Jo if he sleeps in the house."

And they would be right. But it had nothing to do with her being divorced. Jo would tempt him single, divorced, even virginal.

"That might be the way your mind works, Fred," Emmy Lou said. "But everybody doesn't automatically think like that."

"Wanna bet?" Fred pointed at Emmy Lou. "Try hanging out in the Lazy Bones Saloon sometime."

Emmy Lou glared at him. "I've been meaning to try that. But first you'd better teach me how to chew and spit. Honestly, Fred. As if I care about what a bunch of old booz—"

"Watch yourself, woman," Fred said.

Benny's eyes widened. "You're gonna learn to chew and spit, Emmy Lou?"

"Not really, Benny." Emmy Lou smiled at him. "I think it's a perfectly disgusting habit, don't you?"

Benny glanced uncertainly from Fred's scowl to Emmy Lou's smile. "I think... I want some more biscuits."

"Well done, Benny," Jo said. "It doesn't pay to get in the middle of a lovers' quarrel, you know." Then she looked stricken. "Oops. I didn't mean to say that. I really didn't. Must be the stress getting to me. I'm sorry."

Quinn stopped chewing as silence descended over the table. He looked at Jo, who sat gazing anxiously at Fred and Emmy Lou. Then he glanced at Fred, who had a murderous gleam in his eye, and Emmy Lou, who had turned the color of the tomatoes ripening on the windowsill.

Finally Emmy Lou cleared her throat. "I have no idea what you're talking about, Josephine." She stood and started collecting dishes. "I wouldn't take up with that old goat for all the tea in Japan."

"It's China!" Fred muttered. "And that goes double for me." He pulled his napkin from where he'd tucked it into his shirt and tossed it on the table. "I got chores to do."

"You don't have to hide it!" Jo cried. "I didn't mean to spill the beans and embarrass you both, but I think it's wonderful if you two have something going!"

"Me, too!" Benny said. "What do they have going, Jo?"

"Not a dad-blasted thing," Fred said. He started out of the kitchen just as the doorbell rang. "I'll get that."

Jo walked to the sink and put her arm around Emmy Lou. "Em, I'm sorry. I didn't even figure it out until this morning, and then—damn, I just opened my mouth and out it came."

Emmy Lou squirted a large stream of dishwashing liquid in the sink and turned the faucet on full blast, creating mounds of foam. Then she began washing furiously. "If that man said anything to you I'm going to hang him by his... thumbs."

"No! It was just the way he made a certain comment, and I asked if you two were sweethearts, and he got all red, like you're doing now. Em, you and Fred are like parents to me. This feels perfect, the two of you in love."

In her agitation Emmy Lou slopped water and soapsuds on the floor. "Who said anything about love?"

"It's perfectly obvious, the way you two fight, that you're in love."

Quinn sipped his coffee and watched in fascination. For so many years he'd lived by himself in Manhattan. Sure, he had buddies, and twice he'd had a live-in girlfriend for a few months, but aside from occasional trips to Murray's house, he hadn't been in a family setting in a long time. That's what this morning felt like, and he was loving the hell out of it.

Fred appeared in the kitchen doorway. "It's that fool Doobie and his scrawny wife, Eloise. I parked them in the living room. I imagine they want to get a look at Brian Hastings."

Quinn tensed. Last night's performance with Dick had been a reflex action, and Dick hadn't been inclined to be skeptical. Quinn remembered that Doobie was president of the local bank. In his experience, bankers were born skeptics. He glanced at Jo.

"It's up to you," she said. "You don't have to see them. In fact, you don't have to see anybody. You can be as reclusive as you want."

"Yeah, but this is your banker. I'm supposed to offer him a part in the movie, remember?"

"You don't have to." Ever since they'd squirmed together in the mud this morning, she'd had a captivating shyness in her eyes whenever she looked at him.

Quinn smiled at her. Hell, didn't she know he'd do just about anything for her? Only a guy who was wrapped around a woman's little finger would voluntarily suggest that he move to the bunkhouse after she'd announced that they shouldn't become sexually involved.

"I'm sure we can find a part for him somewhere," he said. He'd never wished that he could be Brian Hastings, but at the moment he almost wanted to be, just so he'd have the power to shoot a movie here and help her cause. He set down his mug and pushed back his chair. "Come and introduce me." He stood up, and the ice pack dropped to the floor.

Jo blushed as she glanced at the ice pack and at his crotch. "Um, are you better?"

Quinn leaned down and picked up the ice pack. "Good as new."

"I'm glad. I mean, that's good. I mean…"

Fred coughed. "Maybe you should drop that particular topic, Jo."

"Good idea." Jo swallowed. "Come on, Quinn. Let's go meet my banker."

"I'll come in with some coffee and arsenic in a little bit." Emmy Lou continued washing dishes without turning.

Fred snorted with laughter. Then he snuck a look at Emmy Lou and glanced quickly away again. "Benny, you and me got stuff to do. Let's get a move on."

Emmy Lou kept her back to Fred while she washed and rinsed dishes with a vengeance. "I was hoping you men would clear out of my kitchen and let me get my pot roast in the oven," she said. "Can't accomplish a dad-blasted thing when you're underfoot."

Jo winked at Quinn.

He winked back and followed her out of the kitchen. "How long do you think it's been going on?" he said in a low voice.

"Probably years. I was just too wrapped up in my own problems to notice, but when Fred started talking this morning I got this flash, and all sorts of things began to click in my brain." She walked into the living room, where a skinny man and his wife sat on a worn leather sofa. "Mr. and Mrs. Doobie! May I introduce you to Brian Hastings?"

Doobie popped up from the sofa and came forward, hand outstretched, but Mrs. Doobie looked as if she might pass out. Her mouth opened and closed several times, but she made no sound.

"Mr. Hastings," Doobie said in an unfortunately high voice. The few strands of long hair he'd combed over his bald head quivered as he pumped Quinn's hand vigorously. "This is quite an honor."

Definitely not a speaking part. "I feel lucky to be here," he said. "This is the perfect location to film *The Brunette Wore Spurs.*" Yeah, that was a good title. Amazing what he could come up with on short notice.

Jo stared at him in astonishment. "That's a working title, right?" She gave him a slight nudge with her foot.

"Guess so. Works for me."

"It sounds a little like a film that would be in the adult section at the video store." Jo chuckled and nudged Quinn again. "But, as we all know, film titles get changed all the time."

"They do?" Quinn had never thought about that. "I mean, yes, they certainly do. Why, Julia told me—you all know Julia Roberts, right?"

Jo looked wary, but Doobie and his wife nodded enthusiastically.

"Well, Julia told me that *Pretty Woman* was almost called *Pretty Prostitute*. And the other day I was talking to Bob Redford, and he said that—"

"Coffee!" Emmy Lou announced. "Hello there, Doobies! So good to see you up so bright and early this morning. What do you think of our celebrity guest, Eloise?"

Eloise licked her thin lips and twisted her hands in her lap. "Mr. Hastings, was that really your fanny in that nude scene?"

"Eloise!" Doobie blanched.

Quinn gulped. He hadn't seen a Brian Hastings movie in years. He didn't know the guy had shot a nude-fanny scene. He wished he had known before he'd agreed to impersonate the guy.

"Of course it was him." Emmy Lou calmly poured coffee from a silver urn into a china teacup. "You think anyone else would have a tush that cute? Here you go, Eloise. Sugar and cream's on the coffee table there."

"I've always wondered," Eloise said. She took the coffee but continued to stare at Quinn as if she might ask him to strip down and prove it was his fanny in the scene. "The lighting wasn't very good. You were mostly in shadows."

Thank God. Even though he hadn't been the one naked in front of the cameras and half the free world, he was pretending to be that guy. He hoped there had been lots of shadow.

Doobie turned to his wife. His face had gone from pale to quite pink. "You told me you closed your eyes at that part."

"I lied, Cuthbert."

"You know I don't approve of a married woman seeing another man's naked... parts."

Eloise sat up straighter. "And I've obeyed you all the years of our marriage, until I found out there would be a nude scene in *Rogue's Reward*. When we saw it at the Lyric Theater I closed my eyes to please you, but I left them open a little slit, like this." She demonstrated her peeking technique. "Then I bought the video," she added bravely.

"And watched that scene again without me?" Doobie looked scandalized. "Eloise, how could you?"

"Brian Hastings is the only man who could tempt me to break my vow to you, Cuthbert." Eloise gazed adoringly at Quinn. "Two hundred and six times."

Doobie made a little choking sound.

"Well, that certainly must be a record!" Jo said brightly. "I don't know how many people watch the same movie two hundred and six times. You should be very flattered, Brian."

"Oh, I didn't watch the whole movie." Eloise took a dainty sip of her coffee. "Only the nude-fanny scene. I keep the tape permanently rewound to that section."

Quinn couldn't look at Doobie. The poor little man seemed about to have a fit, and Quinn couldn't say he blamed him. He wouldn't be too happy to discover such a fact about his wife, if he had one. He glanced at Jo. "What did you think of that scene?"

"It was pretty hot, Brian. Some of your better work." She looked as if she might burst out laughing any minute.

He didn't think it was so damn funny, and he didn't much like the idea that she'd been drooling over Hastings' butt, too. "Did you buy the video?"

She pressed her lips together, as if that was the only way she could keep from laughing. She shook her head.

"I did," Emmy Lou said. "And since you never watch your own movies, you might like to take a look sometime."

"Yeah. Yeah, I'd like to see that, uh, scene."

"It's wonderful," Eloise said with a sigh. "All the girls think so."

"Girls?" Doobie squeaked. "What girls?"

"The Ugly Bug Garden Club. We always close the meeting with a showing of that scene."

"Oh, my God," Doobie wailed. "My wife's peddling porn in the sanctity of our home."

"Get a grip, Cuthbert," Emmy Lou said. "It's one scene, for crying out loud. And it's not pornography, it's art."

"We're all hoping you'll do another," Eloise said to Quinn. "Any chance of that in *The Brunette Wore Spurs*?"

"No."

"That's too bad." Eloise set down her cup and saucer. "Mr. Hastings, the ladies of the garden club would consider it a great honor if you would—"

"*What*?" Quinn wasn't aware he'd backed up until he bumped into a leather wing chair in the corner of the room.

"—speak to our group," Eloise said. "Goodness, what did you think I was going to ask?"

"Uh, nothing." Quinn cleared his throat and took a deep breath. "I'd love to do that, of course." Not. He couldn't imagine speaking to a bunch of women who ended every meeting ogling his bare butt. Or Hastings' bare butt, which nearly amounted to the same thing. "But I'll be pretty busy investigating the area and figuring out..." He racked his brain for what a filmmaker might need to know about a location. "I have to decide where we can plug in our lights."

Jo turned to him with a puzzled expression.

But he'd hit upon a way to work in something he knew about, which was home improvement, and he decided to go with it. "Yep, electricity's a big concern with these things. I look around at Jo's ranch, and I like what I see, but I have to ask myself, are there enough outlets? When you're filming, you can never have too many outlets."

"Or *generators*," Jo said, rolling her eyes.

"Well, there's that option, too," Quinn said casually. "Personally I like lots of outlets."

"So I guess the Brian Hastings town festival is out of the question," Doobie said, sounding relieved.

Jo turned to Doobie. "What Brian Hastings town festival?"

"Dick Cassidy brought it up last night when he was buying rounds of drinks at the Ugly Bug Saloon. I guess he's pretty set up about getting a part in the movie. Word got back to the town council, and the mayor asked me to come out this morning and ask about it, considering that I have a close relationship with Jo, here."

"Do you?" Quinn asked. From what he'd heard, Doobie could hardly wait to foreclose on the Bar None.

"Absolutely." Doobie smiled at Jo. "She's like the daughter I never had."

Eloise bounced out of her seat. "Cuthbert Doobie, you have a daughter, and she's given you nine lovely grandchildren. It's not her fault that none of her husbands have been able to hold a job."

Quinn decided it was time to stroke old Cuthbert's ego. "I've been thinking about something ever since I walked in here." He pointed a finger at the skinny banker. "You're the perfect Pierre."

Doobie blinked. "Pierre?"

"A French character in the movie. You have that same worldly look, that same sophistication."

Doobie preened. "Maybe so, but I don't speak French."

"No problem. It's not a speaking role."

"Then how do we know that he's sophisticated and worldly if he never says anything?"

"Trust me. The minute you walk in front of the camera, everyone will know the kind of person you are."

Doobie nodded and looked wise. "I see your point. Then certainly, I'll do it. How about a dance?"

Quinn's jaw dropped. "You want to dance with me, Cuthbert?"

"No, no." Doobie laughed, and his dentures slipped a little. "I meant we could have a dance, just a simple dance on Saturday night, instead of the town festival. Or say, even better, a small rodeo in the afternoon, followed by the dance. If you could possibly see your way clear to participate, the people of Ugly Bug would be very appreciative."

Quinn glanced at Jo, and she shrugged, letting him know it was up to him. A dance sounded relatively harmless. He was a decent dancer. But a rodeo would expose him as a fraud, for sure. "You don't want me to perform in the rodeo," he said. "The liability, you know. If I got hurt, the resulting suit would bankrupt the town."

"Oh! Then of course we don't want you to be in the rodeo. You can be the guest of honor."

"All right."

"Wonderful! Then—"

"Cuthbert, if we hold these events, we have to make a rule," Emmy Lou said. "Women are not allowed to grab at Brian's clothes or pinch his tush. No button popping, no pocket ripping. None of that."

"Certainly not!" Doobie looked offended at the very idea. "Well, then, I guess our mission is accomplished, Eloise. Come along."

Eloise didn't move. She stood gazing at Quinn, a dreamy smile on her face. "Save me a dance," she said.

"Sure."

"Oh, *thank you*." She sighed and clasped her hands together. "I'll be counting the hours."

Doobie snorted and took his wife's arm. "Don't make such a big deal out of it, Eloise. It's just a dance."

"Just a dance? Just a *dance*? I think not, Cuthbert." She kept her gaze fastened on Quinn as her husband dragged her to the entry hall. "Why, dancing with Brian Hastings is more important than winning best garden of the year, more important than giving birth to our darling Primrose, more important than our *wedding night*. Which reminds me. I know you think you're a great—"

"Thanks for the coffee!" Doobie called as he hustled his wife out the door.

After they left Jo grinned at him. "You've done it again. First Dick, and now that weasel Doobie. Thanks, Quinn."

"I loved it, Eloise's tush fetish and all." Emmy Lou gathered coffee cups.

"Don't remind me about that part," Quinn said.

"Oh, she's harmless," Emmy Lou said. "But he's not. Can you believe he had the nerve to say you were like a daughter to him? Just last week when you asked for an extension on your loan he said you might as well sell out and go back east, where you belong. Quinn, you were magnificent." She smiled at him. "Brian Hastings couldn't have done it better. Well, he might not have spouted all that nonsense about electrical outlets, but otherwise, good job." She left the room carrying the tray.

"Doobie really said that to you last week?" Quinn wished he'd been a little rougher on the guy.

"Well, to be fair, I am pretty far behind on my payments."

"Listen, Jo, I—"

"Nope." She held up both hands. "I shouldn't have brought it up. Forget I said anything."

Quinn gazed at her. "If you say so." He longed to get his hands on her books. Okay, he'd rather get his hands on her, but she'd put the skids on that program. But if he could look over her accounts and have her explain the ranching business to him, he knew he could help.

"Don't you need to call your office?"

"Guess I do."

"While you're doing that, I'll go down to the barn and check on Clarise and Stud-muffin. See you in a little while, then."

"Right." Quinn noticed she hadn't suggested he use her office phone, probably because she didn't want him in there, period. So he made his call on the phone in the hallway.

As he was hanging up, Jo came in and hooked her slicker on a peg by the door.

"Everything okay at the barn?" he asked.

"Great." She looked damp, pink and very kissable. "How's your office?"

"No problems. What's next on the schedule?"

Jo shook her damp hair. "It's still raining. I called the vet before breakfast, and she can't come out to inseminate Lullabelle and Missy until tomorrow." She looked at Quinn. "We're sort of at loose ends today."

"What do you usually do when it rains like this?"

"Oh, paperwork in my office."

Exactly. "Jo, don't be so damned stubborn. Let's go into your office and you can give me a rundown on your financial situation."

"Nope, nope, nope."

Emmy Lou appeared in the doorway with a tape in her hand. "Here's *Rogue's Revenge* anytime you want to take a peek. I have some others, but it sounded like this was the one you were interested in."

"Hey, we can watch that!" Jo seized the opportunity. "You really should see one of your—I mean, Brian's—movies and get an idea of his personal style before you show up at the rodeo and dance on Saturday."

He couldn't argue with her reasoning. And he'd be dumb to turn down a chance to sit on the sofa with her and watch a movie. "Okay. We can do that."

She walked into the living room and opened the oak cabinet that housed the television set. "Sit down, sit down. You're about to be able to see yourself without hordes of screaming women interfering with your viewing enjoyment."

"I can hardly wait." He wouldn't mind one particular woman interfering, he thought as he sat on the sofa.

After shoving the tape into the VCR, she picked up the remote and started toward the sofa.

Okay. How close would she sit?

At the last minute she veered toward a wing chair. "Maybe I'll sit over here, for good measure."

"Hey, Emmy Lou's right in the kitchen. What could happen?"

"I suppose you're right." She sat on the sofa, but put a good three feet between them.

The movie started, and Quinn had to admit it was eerie how much Hastings looked like him, except that he seemed completely at home in a Western setting. "He's a good rider."

"You'll be fine with a little more practice. If all you do is attend that rodeo and dance, you might not ever have to demonstrate your riding to anyone."

He looked at her. "You mean I tortured my privates for nothing?"

She glanced at his crotch, and her cheeks grew pink. Then she looked at the television screen. "Watch the movie, Quinn."

He'd rather watch her, but he dutifully turned his head toward the TV.

Emmy Lou appeared in the doorway pulling on a raincoat. "The pot roast's in the oven, and I have to run into town for a few groceries."

Jo grabbed the remote and hit the pause button. "Want some company?"

"No, thanks. I'm taking the truck and I need the space for the bags. I'll be back in a couple of hours.

Quinn's heart began to pound. A couple of hours. He glanced at Jo.

She got up and moved to the chair. "Just to be on the safe side," she said.

Quinn didn't think there was any safe side to this situation.

13

On her way to the chair, Jo glanced out the window and saw Fred climb in the truck with Emmy Lou. So that's what Emmy Lou had in mind, Jo thought with a smile.

"What's going on out there?" Quinn asked.

"Emmy Lou's taking Fred to town."

"No wonder she didn't want you along."

"Yeah." Still smiling, Jo sat in the chair and punched the remote to restart the movie.

"But Benny's still around?"

"Oh, sure, and he's great with the horses, if you were worried about Clarise and Stud-muffin being alone down there. And if Betsy goes into labor, I'm sure he'll come up and get us."

"Glad to hear it."

"Now watch the movie, Quinn." Her pulse wouldn't settle down. She didn't think for a minute that he was worried about who was watching Clarise and Stud-muffin or whether Benny would alert them when Betsy went into labor. He wanted to know exactly how alone they were and how much temptation lay before him.

She wasn't about to explain that although Betsy was due any day, she showed absolutely no signs of going into labor. Benny wasn't the type to pop into the house for no reason, and Jo was sure Fred had told him to stay in the barn and keep an eye on the new baby. The chances of Benny showing up before lunch were practically nonexistent. She knew how alone they were, and it made watching the movie very difficult.

"I don't sound exactly like Hastings," Quinn said after a while.

"No, you sound better." Whoops. She hadn't meant to say it like that.

"What do you mean, better?"

Now she'd done it. "I happen to like a deeper voice on a guy, that's all."

"Oh." He sounded pleased with her answer.

"I don't think it's a problem that your voice is a little deeper than his. Nobody's mentioned your voice being different. In fact, they're all so gaga they don't notice anything different. They're prepared to believe you're him."

"I guess so."

But Jo could already tell big differences, and the advantage was in Quinn's favor. His eyes were a deeper blue, and his mouth had a more sensuous curve to the lower lip. And she liked Quinn's hands better. The fingers were longer, the back of his hand broader. Of course that was probably because Quinn was taller, bigger all over. And then she wondered if he was bigger all over. Her mouth grew moist.

The movie was quickly approaching the famous scene in the mining shack, the one that had made Eloise Doobie break her promise that she wouldn't look at another man's naked parts. The heroine, played by superstar Cheryl Ramsey, had already taken refuge in the shack while a terrible storm raged. She was conveniently in the process of taking off her wet clothes by candlelight while sitting on a cot.

"He's going to show up, isn't he?" Quinn said.

"Yep." Jo was becoming embarrassingly aroused being in the same room with Quinn during this sexy movie. She was so glad she wasn't a man. The poor guys couldn't hide their sexual interest at all.

"We're getting down to it, aren't we?"

"Yep." She didn't dare look at Quinn to find out if his sexual interest was beginning to show, but she'd bet it was. She could hear him breathing, and he kept shifting on the seat cushions. She wondered if getting an erection was painful after the punishment of his morning ride. "Are you okay?"

"How do you mean?"

"Um, are you... uncomfortable?"

"Yeah." His voice was dry. "Any suggestions?"

"I could get another ice pack for your—"

"No, thanks."

Jo tried to concentrate on the movie instead of the state of Quinn's private parts. Cheryl Ramsey was quite beautiful and quite naked. Jo really didn't like Quinn looking at her, but it couldn't be helped.

Brian Hastings opened the door of the shack. The woman glanced up. The look that passed between the two of them made Jo quiver. Then, without saying a word, Hastings unbuttoned his shirt.

Jo remembered thinking he looked pretty damned good when she first saw the scene, but that was before she'd been treated to Quinn Monroe in his briefs last night. Still, watching Hastings peel off his shirt and reach for the buckle of his belt reminded her of the joy of watching a well-put-together man undress. Quinn had been right about Dick's physique—he was soft in the middle.

She gripped the remote as Hastings, standing partially in shadow with his back to the camera, took off his jeans and his underwear in one movement. No wonder the Ugly Bug Garden Club closed out their meeting with this scene. Her gaze was riveted to the screen. But she'd wager that Quinn's behind looked even better than this.

Hastings walked over to Cheryl and sank to his knees before her. That simple, knightly gesture was the sort of thing that had made Brian Hastings number one at the box office, in Jo's estimation. She held her breath as Hastings kissed Cheryl — her mouth, her throat, her breasts. Jo's breasts felt tight and feverish.

As the music swelled, Hastings guided Cheryl to the cot, and the soft light illuminated their bodies as he moved over her.

Jo moaned softly and gripped the remote.

The scene froze in place.

"Did you mean to do that?" Quinn's voice was strained.

"No!" Jo glanced at the remote and punched it, but her hand was shaking so much she kept missing the play button.

"Fast forward through that scene, dammit," Quinn ordered tightly.

"I'm trying!" She stood and pointed the remote at the VCR while she stabbed at the buttons with trembling fingers.

"I'll do it." Quinn half rose from his seat and made a grab for the remote in her hand.

"I've got it!" She backed up and stumbled. The remote flew out of her hand and plopped between the cushions of the sofa.

"Oh, for crying out loud." Breathing hard, Quinn dropped to one knee and started fumbling for the remote.

"I've got it, I've got it." Jo sat on the sofa and shoved her hand in the space.

He pushed her hand aside. "Get out of there and let me. This cushion is the deepest—" The VCR clicked and whirred.

"You must have hit something. I think it's rewinding!"

"We're sure as hell not going to see that again!"

"Whoops, now it's going forward. Whoops—"

"Move your tush so I can reach under here and—damn, but leather is slippery. You paused the tape on purpose just when they were doing it, didn't you? You're just like those garden club ladies."

"No, I swear! It was an accident!"

"Quit jiggling around. Okay, I've got it." He leaned forward, and his cheek bumped her breast.

"Oh." She couldn't help it. She was on fire.

Quinn went very still. Slowly he lifted his head and looked into her eyes while the movie rewound behind him. "Don't look at me like that," he murmured.

"How?" She drifted closer to him as if pulled by an invisible string.

"Like you want me to rip your clothes off."

"Oh." She was breathing hard. "Okay, I won't." She closed her eyes.

"Dammit, that's worse. Open your eyes."

She did as he asked.

He groaned. "No help there."

As her gaze shifted to his sensuous mouth, she couldn't seem to help the downward tilt of her head, bringing her closer and closer. "It's because of the movie. We're just worked up because of the—"

"Speak for yourself." He cupped the back of her head and kissed her.

But she couldn't speak for herself when he kissed her like that. She couldn't even think for herself with her heart pounding so loud. Vaguely she heard a click and whirr as the movie surged to fast forward again. Quinn must have abandoned the remote, leaving it to fend for itself. As if she cared.

A girl couldn't be worried about remote controls when being kissed by a man who knew how to use his tongue the way Quinn did. When he started unbuttoning her blouse she let him do it. She even helped with a button or two. When he fumbled with the front catch of her bra, she pushed his hand away and unhooked it herself.

After all, a man who could kiss like that would know what to do when presented with a woman's aching, needy breasts.

Quinn knew.

Jo arched her back and moaned as he showed her the full extent of his knowledge. After stroking her for several delicious moments, he slid up on the sofa and leaned her back over the armrest. She'd never been caressed so fully or with such murmured appreciation. She barely noticed as the movie switched from rewind to fast forward with every abandoned movement she made. She began to respond in other ways, becoming very moist at the point where the denim seam of her jeans started to pinch. The tender spot cried out for his attention.

He was panting by the time he kissed his way back to her mouth. He plunged his tongue in deep, letting her know what he wanted, and then slowly drew back. "I'm in agony," he said, gasping. "We need a decision, here. Either unzip my jeans or button your blouse."

She cradled his face in her hands. "I'm in agony, too."

His smile looked strained. "Yeah, but you weren't bouncing on a horse for an hour this morning."

"Oh! Poor Quinn."

"Poor Quinn is right." He slid his hands under her bottom and fit his erection tight against her. "I'm being tortured here, Jo."

"Oh, Quinn." She pressed closer.

He pushed back with a groan. With a whirr and click the VCR reversed direction.

She rocked against him and closed her eyes. Whirr, click. "I don't know if—"

"I know I'll be permanently impaired in another minute. God, Jo." He shoved harder. Another click from the remote was followed by a loud snap and a frantic spinning noise from the VCR.

Quinn turned his head toward the television. "What the hell?"

Jo stared at the snow on the screen. "I think we killed the movie."

"We didn't touch it!"

"But we bounced on the remote, Quinn. We pushed its little buttons, back and forth, back and forth, until snap! It came apart."

He gazed at her. "You are certainly pushing mine back and forth, back and forth, Josephine, and I am definitely ready to come apart."

She didn't let many people call her that, but she had a feeling Quinn had become one of the select few. "I'm getting scared, Quinn. This has the potential to be bigger than both of us."

"That's what the bulge in my jeans feels like."

"Do you want some ice?"

"No." He looked at her with frank admiration. "I want you. I want to take off your jeans, undo mine and finish what we started."

Her heart hammered as she pictured them doing exactly that. "I want you, too. So, I guess there's only one solution."

His hand went to the buckle of his belt. "Live for today and to hell with tomorrow?' he suggested hopefully.

"No. I'll tell Dick and Mr. Doobie that you're not really Brian Hastings. I'll say we were playing a practical joke and they should forget the whole thing."

He sighed and took his hand away from his belt buckle. "Nope. Absolutely not. Those two would never let you forget it. Doobie would probably foreclose on this ranch immediately, and Dick would snap it up so he could have Ugly Bug Creek." Looking very much in pain, he eased slowly to the end of the couch.

"Quinn, I'm sorry." She pulled her blouse together, not wanting to make his condition worse. Or hers. But his sounded more critical.

"No, you're right," he said. "It's either tell everybody the truth or stop fooling around." He sat on the end of the couch and rested her booted feet on his knees. "Be careful with your feet. One of these pointed toes in the wrong place would probably kill me."

"Maybe I could find you some sweats. That would give you more room."

"And maybe I should just stay away from you and Brian Hastings movies. Can we replace the tape?"

"We could have bought a new one at the video store yesterday, no problem. Today, big problem. I'll bet now that the word's out on you, there's not a Brian Hastings movie for sale in the entire town of Ugly Bug."

He shifted position and winced. "Then I'll just call my PA and ask her to overnight a copy of the tape."

"That would be wonderful."

"Yeah, I can autograph it for Emmy Lou."

"Oh, my God. Autographs. We need to find a copy of his signature for you to practice on."

"Or sprain my writing hand."

"A fake sprain, you mean."

"Oh, no, I want a real sprain. Something major to take my mind off my... other problem."

"Quinn, we're not going to deliberately injure you. I'm sure Emmy Lou has something with his signature on it. You can practice. I can't believe I didn't think of autographs. The trouble is, I keep forgetting that you're supposed to be Brian Hastings."

"You do?" He turned to her, and his gaze was steady. "I thought that's what was going on just now. You had me confused with him."

"You thought that?" She tightened her grip on her blouse. "You thought I was like those women who rip your clothes off because they think they're getting a piece of Brian Hastings? You thought I'd parked my brain somewhere?" She *had* parked her brain somewhere, which explained her rash actions, but she'd never for a minute fantasized that Quinn was Brian Hastings. Quinn was powerful enough for any woman's fantasy.

"Well, we were watching one of his movies, and you were getting turned on."

"So were you! Does that mean you imagined I was Cheryl Ramsey?" she asked, suddenly worried.

"No." He propped a hand on the back of the sofa and leaned over her. "It means that the movie inspired me to think of what we might be doing. Power of suggestion. And to be honest, when I'm in the same room with you I need very little of that. This movie was overkill."

"So it wasn't seeing that beautiful naked woman that got you worked up?"

"Not by a long shot. It was the thought of seeing this beautiful naked woman."

Her pulse raced as his gaze traveled over her. "And for the record, it wasn't seeing Brian Hastings' butt that got me worked up, either," she said.

He looked into her eyes. "Thank you." He gave her a wry smile. "But I would have taken that. I want you so much I don't care who you think I am if you'll let me touch you."

"Me, too," she murmured. "I don't care if I'm substituting for a glamorous movie star."

Desire flared in his eyes. "You're not. She wouldn't be a fit substitute for you."

"That's sweet. I don't believe it for a minute, but—"

He leaned closer, and his hand went to his belt again. "Want proof?"

"Oh, Quinn, I—uh-oh, I hear the truck coming up the road."

Quinn moved to his end of the sofa and grimaced as his jeans tightened across his crotch. "Better go upstairs and put yourself back together."

Jo sat up. Under her cushion the remote clicked again, and snow crackled on the television screen.

"Easy." Quinn gently lowered her feet to the floor.

"Would it help if you stood up?"

"Yeah. I'll do that in a minute. Go on."

"I hate to leave you to explain the broken tape to Emmy Lou."

"I'm a big boy."

She couldn't resist. "So you said."

His gaze was challenging. "Looks like you'll have to take it on faith."

"Yep." Jo couldn't help glancing at his crotch and remembering what he'd felt like pressed against her. She had some idea of what she was giving up, which didn't make the sacrifice any easier. A little bit of knowledge could be a terrible thing. She stood on rubbery legs. "I'm sorry I put us in this position," she said, starting past Quinn. "It won't happen again."

He reached up and gripped her thigh. "I'm not sorry," he said, gazing at her. "I love this position."

"Okay, so do I."

He gave her thigh a squeeze. "If it happens again, I'll make no noble guarantees about my behavior. I'd take you on any terms. Any terms at all."

Warmth rushed through her. "I'll keep that in mind."

"See that you do." He released her.

She wanted to stay, wanted to make love to him more than she'd ever wanted that with any man. The slamming of the truck's door propelled her reluctantly up the stairs.

<u>**14**</u>

Quinn's emotions were in a shambles, but he could pick one truth out of this mess. He should never make Jo choose between him and the Bar None. Maybe in a moment of sexual weakness she'd choose him and hate him forever for causing her to lose this ranch.

Emmy Lou made a lot of racket coming into the house. Quinn suspected she was giving notice in case he and Jo were in the middle of... exactly what they'd been in the middle of.

"I'm back!" the housekeeper announced in a loud voice as she closed the front door with a bang and bustled into the kitchen with a paper sack in each arm.

"Need any help?" Quinn called. He was almost in shape to render aid. Almost.

"I've got it, thanks." She sounded breathless.

Quinn flashed on an old memory—coming home from a hot date and discovering his mother still up watching a movie on television. He'd responded to her greeting in that same breathless way before hurrying to his bedroom to see whether his shirt was buttoned up wrong or he had lipstick smeared across his mouth. Sure enough, once Emmy Lou dumped her bags in the kitchen, she scurried down the hall toward her bedroom. Apparently everyone had some repair work to do.

Quinn took his time standing, then turned his back to the door to adjust himself. He'd had uncomfortable erections before, but nothing to compare with the pain of being saddle sore and aroused at the same time. He had new respect for cowboys who could ride all day and make love all night. They must be tough in places he'd never considered needed toughening.

Finally he was able to crouch and lift the seat cushion to retrieve the remote. As he reached for it, he noticed a movement next to his foot. He leaped back, knocking over the coffee table in the process.

"What on earth is going on in here?" Emmy Lou appeared in the doorway, her plump cheeks flushed.

"Stay back!" Quinn glanced around for a weapon and settled on the shovel from the fireplace tool set. By the time he had it in his hand, the creature had scuttled under the sofa.

"What is it?" Emmy Lou put her hand to her throat. "A rattlesnake?"

"It's not a snake." Quinn's insides were flipping around, but he'd die before admitting it. He'd been raised to be a protector. He had to slay this beast.

"Then what is it, for heaven's sake?"

Quinn thought of Jo lying on the sofa, her soft skin exposed, and shuddered. Then he thought of what might have happened if he'd unzipped his jeans, and he nearly passed out.

"Quinn, tell me what you've found."

"I don't know." He gripped the shovel and raised it over his head as he crept slowly toward the sofa. "But it's a monster," he said, his voice quivering.

"A rat?" Emmy Lou asked.

"You have rats out here, too?" Quinn wondered how anybody in Montana slept at night.

"Well, of course."

"Well, it's not a rat or a mouse. It had a bunch of legs."

"Oh, a bug." With a chuckle, Emmy Lou took off her shoe and walked to the sofa.

"Stay back!" Quinn warned. "I'll handle this."

"If you whack that bug with the fireplace shovel you'll spray soot from here to kingdom come. Put that thing down and I'll take care of this, whatever it is."

"It had fangs."

"Really? How many legs, exactly?"

"Too many."

"Probably a wolf spider," Emmy Lou said.

"A *wolf* spider?" Quinn's hands grew clammy. "It attacks wolves?"

"No, no." Emmy Lou looked as if she was trying hard not to laugh, for which Quinn was grateful. "They just look ferocious. They're not poisonous or anything, and they keep the other insects under control."

Quinn got a bad feeling in the pit of his stomach. "What other insects?"

Emmy Lou gazed at him, a twinkle in her eye. "You know, it's really sweet of you to offer to defend me, considering you're so scared of bugs."

"I'm not, either! That's no bug. Bugs are things like flies and mosquitoes and ladybugs. Moths, butterflies, caterpillars. This is... prehistoric."

Emmy Lou smiled. "How did you think the creek and town got named?"

"I tried not to think about it, if you must know." He had a horrifying thought. "You mean these things are common around here?"

"Sure. You get used to them." A wicked little gleam appeared in her eye. "You're more likely to find them down at the bunkhouse than up here."

Quinn caught his breath. For one wild minute he thought of reconsidering his sleeping arrangements. Then Jo appeared in the living room doorway, and he knew he'd have to stay in the bunkhouse, ugly bugs and all. She'd combed her hair and fastened her clothing so she looked perfectly proper, but he remembered all too well how she'd helped him unbutton her blouse. And how she'd unhooked her bra for him. And then lifted those spectacular breasts, pressing them into his waiting hands.

"What's going on?" Jo asked, gazing at the sofa cushion tossed aside, the coffee table capsized and the fireplace shovel in Quinn's hand. "Spring cleaning?"

"Sort of," Quinn said. "Don't come in here, Jo. Wolf spider."

"Really? Cool! Where is it?"

He couldn't believe her reaction. "Under the sofa," he said ominously. "You know, under the *sofa*." He wondered how long it would take her to realize the monster could have attacked while she was lying there exposed.

"Then let's move the sofa," Jo said, totally nonchalant about the whole thing.

"Don't, Jo. It's huge."

"They usually are," Jo said, walking toward the sofa.

"Suit yourself, Red Riding Hood." Quinn folded his arms, but he kept hold of the fireplace shovel. "Move that sofa and take a look at that big old wolf spider. Don't say I didn't warn you."

Emmy Lou started out of the room. "Hold on. I'll get a glass and see if we can catch it and put it outside."

Quinn almost dropped the shovel. "You're going to what?"

"Try to catch it. You know, put a glass down on top of it and then slide a piece of cardboard underneath."

"Are you crazy?"

"No. I've done it before."

Quinn rolled his eyes. "Then you'd better bring a punch bowl and a piece of plywood! We're not talking about Charlotte here, ladies. We're talking big. Very, very big. Spiderzilla."

Emmy Lou smiled at him. "I've discovered that men tend to exaggerate the size of things." She left the room.

Jo let out a very unladylike snort of laughter, and Quinn glared at her.

She tried to compose herself but was obviously having trouble. "Did you tell her about the tape?"

"Not yet. I—"

"Well, this should work." Emmy Lou came in holding a water glass and the back of a cereal box.

"For one leg," Quinn muttered darkly. "But if you women are determined to do this reckless thing, I'll ride shotgun. If it starts to attack, I'll be here."

"They don't attack," Jo said. "Okay, Em. I'll move the sofa just a bit, and you stand ready with that glass."

"Right."

"And I'll stand ready to whack it when you two run screaming out of the room," Quinn said, raising the shovel over his head.

Jo moved the sofa a few inches, and the spider ran right at Quinn.

The women didn't scream, but he was afraid he might have as he started banging the shovel everywhere, stirring up clouds of soot as the spider raced around the room.

"Quick, over by the door, Em!" Jo cried.

Emmy Lou pounced with her glass. "Got him!"

"Or her," Jo said. She crouched as Emmy Lou slid the cardboard under the glass and expertly flipped the whole thing over. "Nope, it's a him."

Quinn stared at the two women in horrified fascination. "How can you tell? And why would you want to?"

"Spiders are fascinating," Jo said. "His sex organs are right by his mouth, an arrangement certain people might envy. Want to see?"

"That's okay." Quinn was sweating like crazy. Sure enough, the monster fit in the glass, but he wouldn't have bet on it. "I'll take your word for it."

"This is a pretty big one," Emmy Lou said. "That body looks almost two inches across, so with the legs and all, it's—"

"Gigantic, like Quinn said," Jo finished, giving Quinn an understanding smile. "Bigger than his fist."

"I'll take him outside and let him go," Emmy Lou said.

Quinn tried to sound casual. "Uh, where would that be, exactly?"

"Out in my veggie garden. He'll like it there. He'll probably stay."

"Oh." He rolled his shoulders and made a mental note to never, ever offer to pick vegetables for Emmy Lou. "I'll, uh, pick up around here, then."

"I'll help," Jo said.

"Thanks." Quinn grabbed the small broom hanging with the fireplace tools and turned to find Jo looking at him with great tenderness. "What?" he asked.

"It's just that you're so adorable," she said.

"*Adorable?*" He preferred words like virile and manly, himself. Adorable was for kids. He used the shovel like a dustpan as he swept up the soot.

"A big strong man like you who's afraid of snakes and bugs." She set the coffee table on its feet. "And trying so hard not to be. It's very sweet."

Quinn felt his face heat up. He kept sweeping to avoid looking at her. "I had an older cousin who used to tease me, shoving wiggly things in my face."

"Shame on him," Jo said.

"It was a girl," Quinn said, his cheeks on fire.

"Then shame on her." She walked over to touch his arm. "But you know, it's possible to get over things like that."

"I doubt it. Been that way ever since I was four."

"You can desensitize yourself. It would be easy around this place, because you'll always be coming in contact with creepy-crawlies. Soon you'd barely notice them."

He glanced at her hand. His arm already tingled where he felt the light pressure of her fingers. He looked into her eyes. "Think that would work with you, too?" he asked in a low voice. "Because I'd sure love to try."

She jerked her hand away and stepped back.

"If the concept works, it should work for anything," he said, closing the gap between them. "Maybe if I kiss you enough, eventually I won't get so aroused when I do it."

Jo swallowed. "I don't think... we have that much time."

"I don't think we'd ever have that much time," he murmured.

"So," Emmy Lou said from the doorway, "how did you two enjoy the movie?"

Quinn cleared his throat and glanced at Jo. "I broke it."

"No, we broke it together." Jo turned toward Emmy Lou. "We're both to blame."

Emmy Lou looked confused. "Broke it?"

"Yeah." Quinn dumped the shovel of soot in the fireplace and put the tools back in the holder.

"The tape snapped. Don't worry. I'll have my PA send a new copy right away."

"How much did you get to see before it broke?"

Jo tapped her chin. "Let's see. Was it before the train robbery? Or was it after that scene in the miner's shack?"

Quinn didn't dare look at her. "The miner's shack scene, I think. Anyway, a new tape's practically on the way. I'll make a—"

"Oh, don't buy me a new one." Emmy Lou blushed. "I know why it broke."

"You do?" He wondered if she'd somehow figured out what had been going on.

"It's all that pausing and rewinding."

"How did you know about that?" Quinn asked before he could stop himself.

Emmy Lou's eyes widened, and then she clapped a hand over her mouth. A smothered giggle slipped out anyway.

Jo's cheeks grew pink. "You mean you paused and rewound the tape a lot at that spot."

Emmy Lou nodded, her eyes bright. "Plus it was a rental tape I bought on sale at the video store. I'm sure it was already weak right there. I guess you two weakened it a little more."

Quinn's ego had suffered enough. First he was revealed as bugophobic, and now Emmy Lou thought he was some sort of voyeur who'd had to replay a nude scene over a hundred times to get his kicks. "It was by accident that we kept rewinding it," he said. "The remote fell between the sofa cushions, and..." He realized the quagmire he'd stepped in about the same time he caught the dismay in Jo's eyes.

"You know, that pot roast smells a little too good," Jo said. "Maybe you should check on it, Emmy Lou. I think you might need to turn down the heat."

Emmy Lou put her hands on her hips and glanced from Jo to Quinn and back to Jo again. "I believe I could say the same thing to you."

"The thing is," Quinn began, determined to find a way out of this, "I lost my balance and—"

"Did I hear the dinner bell?" Fred asked, coming through the front door.

"We don't have a dinner bell," Emmy Lou said.

"Well, I didn't think we had one, but then I was out in the yard and I heard all this clanging and banging that sure sounded like a dinner bell. So I figured I'd just wash up and come in to find out if it was time for lunch yet."

"Why, as a matter of fact, it is," Jo said. "I'm starving. How about you, Quinn?"

"Starving," Quinn agreed.

Emmy Lou glanced at them both with a smile on her face. Then she picked up the remote, pointed it at the television and flicked off the power. "Then let's eat."

"What was that clanging sound, anyway?" Fred asked as they headed toward the kitchen.

Quinn wondered if Emmy Lou would tell on him. Fred could make his life a real hell if he knew about Quinn's fear of bugs and snakes.

"You must have heard me banging around with my cast iron pans. I got in the mood to rearrange them," Emmy Lou said.

And with that single statement, Emmy Lou won Quinn's loyalty forever.

<u>15</u>

The rain let up that afternoon, and Jo spent the hours between lunch and dinner riding the fence line with Benny, checking for downed wire, while Fred kept watch on the new foal and taught Quinn something about roping. Jo wasn't pleased to admit it to herself, but she also spent the afternoon missing Quinn.

She wanted to be the one to teach him how to rope, although that would be a disaster in the making, and she knew it. Whatever time she spent with Quinn was filled with danger, and she wanted to be with him twenty-four hours a day. She had a gigantic crush on the guy.

She had plenty of time to analyze why Quinn affected her so deeply, and she nearly had it nailed down. Any woman would be attracted to a guy who looked like Quinn, which explained the physical draw he had for her. But what had really hooked her was his ability to make bold, generous gestures coupled with his very human weaknesses. He'd flown all the way from New York on impulse to return the horse sperm, yet he was so frightened of creepy crawlies he'd wrecked the cab. He'd gallantly decided to move to the bunkhouse to keep a safe distance between them, but when faced with temptation, he'd crumbled, just as she had. Crumbled in a very delicious way. She still tingled at the thought of those moments on the sofa.

"Say, what's that yonder?" Benny asked, pointing to a far hillside.

Jo squinted into the distance. "It looks like a man running."

"Then somethin's wrong," Benny said. "People don't run out in the middle of nowhere. Unless they lost their horse or somethin's after them."

"I'll check." Jo reached to her saddlebag and pulled out a scarred pair of binoculars that had belonged to Aunt Josephine. She focused on the small figure running up the hill and grinned. "It's Dick. I think he's jogging."

"Jogging? I wanna see."

Jo handed the binoculars to Benny and leaned over to rest her forearms on her saddle horn while she gazed at the tiny figure pumping madly up the hill. In jeans and boots. She loved it.

"I can't figure out what he's tryin' to catch. There ain't no horse around, or cattle, neither." Benny seemed totally mystified by the concept of a man running for no visible reason.

"Actually he's trying to lose something."

"Ain't nothin' chasing him, neither. No bear or nothin'." Benny continued to stare through the binoculars. "He looks plum possessed. I ain't never seen him so red in the face."

"Let me look again." Jo knew that revenge was a mean-spirited emotion, and she shouldn't be indulging in it. Well, she'd have to get saintly some other day. Watching Dick jog was too damn much fun to miss.

She adjusted the focus so she could see Dick's red face. He was panting like a freight engine, too. Unlike Benny, she'd seen him that red in the face before during the divorce proceedings when the judge had upheld her right to fence off Ugly Bug Creek so Dick's herd couldn't water here as they had been during the two-year span of Dick and Jo's marriage. At that point old Dick was back to hauling water, and he hadn't liked it much.

"Do you reckon we should go over there?" Benny asked. "Somethin' could be wrong."

"I think something's finally right," Jo said. Her heart lifted at the knowledge that Dick could be bested that easily, and she vowed she'd no longer be his victim. "Thanks to Quinn Monroe."

"Are you sure that's his name?"

"Yes." Jo tucked the binoculars away. "That's his name. Did Fred explain our plan?"

"He tried, but I got mixed up. You know I get mixed up."

Jo's heart squeezed at the forlorn look on Benny's face. "I know you're the best wrangler a gal could have."

"I wish I was smarter."

"You're smart where it counts, Benny. Now let me try and explain this situation as best I can."

All the way home Jo did her best to untangle Benny's confusion regarding Quinn Monroe and Brian Hastings. She thought she'd succeeded until Benny asked if he could be in the movie.

"There may not be a movie, Benny."

"But Dick and Mr. Doobie are gonna be in it."

"Quinn was only pretending about the movie when he told them they could be in it."

"If there's a movie, I wanna be in it," Benny insisted stubbornly.

"Okay," Jo said at last. "If there's a movie, I'll do my best to get you in it."

"But I ain't running up no hill."

"No, Benny." Jo smiled again at the memory. "That's a special thing only Dick has to do."

Benny grinned. "He looked like a dork, didn't he?"

"Yep, he looked like a dork." Jo was in an extremely good mood as she rode toward the ranch buildings in the light of the setting sun.

And the catalyst for her good mood stood in an empty corral, twirling a loop over his head. With a beat-up Stetson shading his eyes, leather gloves on and a rope in his hand, he looked a lot like a cowboy. Jo's heart picked up the pace. She wondered if buried under all that Wall Street conditioning was a man who could learn to love wide-open spaces and tolerate bugs and snakes.

Then she remembered why that was a dumb thought. No matter how much Quinn adapted to life as a cowboy, he couldn't stick around, even if he had a notion to. The person everyone believed to be Brian Hastings couldn't very well take up permanent residence in Ugly Bug.

Fred was nowhere to be seen, and Jo decided he must have coached Quinn on the basics and left him to practice. Quinn twirled the loop one more time, and with a snap of his wrist he let it go. It floated out in a beautiful arc and settled nicely over the post he had been aiming for.

"Yes!" he shouted, cinching it tight. "Finally!"

"Nice throw, cowboy," Jo called.

He glanced over, shoved his hat to the back of his head and grinned at her. "Thanks, ma'am."

Jo gulped. Damn, but he looked good. Almost like he belonged here. She nearly tripped dismounting because she couldn't stop staring at him. "Of course that post isn't moving," she said. "Most things don't stay still when you try to rope them."

"That's a fact."

He'd even started sounding like a cowboy.

"I'll put the horses up, if you want to go talk to Mr. Hastings," Benny said.

Jo groaned. Apparently she hadn't gotten through to Benny on this double identity deal. "No, that's Quinn over there, Benny."

"His name's Quinn Hastings?"

"No, it's—" She decided if she kept this up pretty soon she'd be as confused as Benny was. She handed the reins to him. "Never mind. Thanks for taking care of Cinnamon for me."

"No problem. I love it."

"And that's why you'll have a place here as long as I own the Bar None."

"I know." With a shy smile, Benny tipped his hat and led the horses away.

Benny was another reason she needed to hang on to the ranch. A new owner might only notice Benny's mental deficiencies and not give enough credit to his instinctive bond with the animals. And then there was Fred, who was getting too crippled with arthritis to do as much as he once had. If Fred was fired, then Emmy Lou would leave the ranch. All three of them depended on her to keep the place going.

Jo looked at the corral as Quinn neatly roped the post again. The golden light from the setting sun touched his broad shoulders as he coiled the rope for another try. He was learning that skill for her, just as he'd been determined to ride Hyper this morning so that he'd do a credible job as Brian Hastings. If she managed to hang on to the ranch, much of the credit would go to Quinn for agreeing to her wild idea.

He'd abandoned his own work so he could get saddle sore, plagued with giant spiders and probably mauled by the townspeople during Saturday's rodeo and dance. All to help out a lady in distress. Other than the satisfaction of a good deed, he wasn't getting anything out of the deal.

A girl should be grateful when a man put himself out like that, Jo thought as she watched Quinn form a loop and twirl it over his head. Unfortunately, gratitude had landed her in hot water once before, when she'd been stupid enough to think she owed Dick the favor of marrying him after all the help he'd given her running the Bar None. But Quinn wasn't asking for her hand in marriage or a chunk of the ranch. All he wanted was to make love to her.

God, that would be tough to take, she thought with a wry smile. But it wasn't the lovemaking part that worried her. That would be glorious. No, what kept her from rushing into his arms and into his bed was not the loving. It was the leaving.

<u>16</u>

Quinn had loved watching Jo ride in. She'd tied her hair back with a scarf and worn an old brown hat that gave her a rough-and-tumble tomboy look he thoroughly enjoyed. She sat straight in the saddle, her tummy in and her breasts thrust forward as she laughed and talked with Benny. Nice.

Years of riding had obviously made her feel completely at home in the saddle. He doubted she was the least bit worried about falling off. He'd spent a little more time on Hyper this afternoon, and he'd been constantly worried about falling off. With good reason. He had bruises on top of bruises.

Wondering if he'd ever achieve that relaxed look on a horse, he studied the way Jo sat and how she gripped with her thighs. Then he had to stop studying her. Focusing on her while her thighs were open and her hips rocked gently in response to the horse was not a good idea.

He'd really done himself in this time. He couldn't back out of his agreement because Jo might lose the ranch and he'd feel guilty for not helping her. Yet the longer he stayed at the Bar None the more desperately he wanted to make love to her. Tomorrow was the rodeo and dance, and by Sunday he'd probably need to hit the road. His head understood perfectly that he should keep his hands off of her until then. The rest of him wanted to argue.

Thinking about Jo had screwed up his usually excellent concentration on the task at hand. Consequently, as she'd returned to the ranch, he had yet to rope the post. Fred had told him not to quit until he lassoed that sucker at least once, and he'd begun to wonder if he'd be out here after dark with a flashlight, still trying after everyone else had turned in. He wanted to have some roping ability in case something came up during the rodeo, but he seemed to have no talent for it.

Then he had an inspiration. Squinting at the post, he imagined it was Jo standing there, daring him to throw a loop around her. The concept took some effort, because Jo had interesting curves that the post lacked and a waterfall of fragrant hair and... okay, so the concept took *tremendous* effort. But finally he stared at the post so long it became Jo—saucy as you please, head thrown back, a taunting look in her brown eyes, a smile on those full lips.

Quinn took a deep breath. Now this he could get into. Twirling the rope over his head, he concentrated on the image of settling a rope around those lovely shoulders and pulling Jo closer and closer and... Flick. He sent the rope sailing as he'd done a hundred times this afternoon. And he roped the post.

Better yet, Jo had seen him do it and had called out some encouragement. Of course she also had to mention that the post wasn't moving, a fact he knew very well. He had to perfect this stage before he could advance to moving targets.

He decided to try again. This time he added an embellishment and imagined Jo standing in the corral, impudent as hell, with no clothes on. He roped the post even more competently than before. Apparently all he needed was the appropriate goal. Smiling, he loosened the rope from around the post and coiled it again.

"Looks like you made some progress this afternoon."

Quinn turned to see Jo walking into the corral. In a few seconds she'd be the same distance from him as the post, but a little to the left of it.

"I'm learning." He built his loop and swung it over his head again. "It's harder than I thought it would be."

"Chances are nobody will expect you to perform tomorrow."

"I know, but I'd still like to have the basics down." He twirled the rope and thought about his next move. If he missed he'd look really stupid. So he wouldn't miss.

"I hate to tell you, but the basics won't do you much good if somebody wants you to demonstrate your roping skills. They'll expect you to rope something alive, not a post planted in the ground."

"Maybe all I need is a little more practice." He turned toward her, took a split second to gauge the distance and tossed the loop.

She stared at him, openmouthed, as the loop dropped over her head.

Using every new skill he'd gained, plus some instinct he didn't know he had, he pulled at exactly the right moment, and the rope tightened around her arms, pinning them to her body. With a quick movement he cinched it.

"Quinn!"

Keeping the line taught, he went hand over hand toward her, watching her intently the whole way. She did her best to look indignant, but the effect was spoiled by the eagerness in her eyes. Finally he stood next to her. "How's that?"

"Very clever, Monroe." Her breathing was quick, urgent. "You can let me go now."

"I guess I could." He kept the rope taut with one hand while he pulled the glove off his other hand with his teeth. He loved the way her eyes darkened and flashed as she watched him. He tucked the glove in his belt. "Then again, I've never roped a woman before. Shouldn't I get a prize for that?"

"I've never heard of one. In Montana the men don't generally go around roping women."

"Maybe they should try it." He'd acted on impulse, not realizing how secluded the corral was. Benny and Fred would have no reason to pass on their way to the house for dinner. "It gets the women hot." He took off her hat and set it on the post. Then he took off his and dropped it on top of hers.

"Does not."

He loosened the scarf from her hair, pulled it over her curls and stuffed it in his back pocket. "Does, too." He brushed his knuckles over her throat and down the V in her blouse, taking great satisfaction in the shiver he produced. "You want me to kiss you so bad you can hardly stand it."

"Listen to you." She sounded breathless. "One lucky toss and your head's swelled up like a balloon."

"That's not the only part of me swelling up, honey-bunch." He tunneled his fingers through her hair and cupped the back of her head. "But I have the feeling you're getting mighty stirred up, too."

Her lips parted in anticipation. "Your macho routine doesn't do a thing for me."

He leaned closer, keeping his grip firm on the rope. "Oh, I think it does."

"Wrong," she whispered.

His lips hovered over hers. "Let's see," he said softly, and took his prize.

If every roping session ended with this sort of reward, he'd give up his banking career. He took everything her ripe mouth offered, and she was offering plenty. She wasn't just hot, she was steaming. He shifted the angle of his mouth, then shifted again, trying to get deeper, trying to touch the essence of her.

She responded with a hunger that took his breath away. With a groan he tugged on the rope, snugging her against him. As he pressed his body to hers, he remembered how her hips had moved rhythmically as she rode in this afternoon. He remembered her passion this morning — the velvet of her breasts, the erotic taste of her. And he wondered if not making love to her, not ever making love to her, would drive him crazy.

Fear of that prompted him to finally lift his mouth from hers and loosen the rope. It dropped to the ground at her feet. "I've tried not to want you, Jo." He gasped for air. "It's not working."

She lifted her arms and wound them around his neck as she rested her head on his shoulder. "I've tried, too. I thought about you all afternoon."

"Good." He continued to cradle her head as he stroked her back with his gloved hand.

"Not good. This can go nowhere, as you very well realize. Unless, of course, I blow your cover."

"Don't do that. Just make love to me. I'm developing a condition."

"A condition?" She lifted her head to look into his eyes. "What condition?"

"Denim-tightis. It's fatal if left untreated."

A smile twitched at the corners of her mouth. "I offered you sweats."

"Cowboys don't wear sweats." He cupped her bottom and brought her tight against him. "They take care of the problem so their jeans fit right again."

Her voice grew husky. "Do you think it's that simple?"

"Probably not." His aching erection sought her heat. "My jeans may never fit when I'm around you. But it's worth a try. I really don't think Brian Hastings would wear sweats to a country dance, do you?"

"No." Amusement and desire flared in her eyes. But gradually her expression grew serious. "What I meant was that making love is not a simple solution to the problem in any sense. Just suppose we make love tonight."

"I like supposing that." His heart hammered as he rocked gently against her hips. "Let's do suppose that. Let's seriously suppose that."

"Quinn, quit joking around. I'm—" She paused and cleared the huskiness from her throat. "I'm trying to make a point."

"So am I. Going to bed may not be a permanent cure for my condition, but I'm willing to settle for symptomatic relief."

"And then what? Tomorrow's Saturday."

"Fortunately followed by Saturday night." He leaned forward and nibbled on her earlobe. "Another opportunity to treat my potentially fatal problem." He ran his tongue around the pink inner shell of her ear.

She moaned. "The point is—"

"Yes?" He loved the way she turned into a rag doll in his arms, so supple, so willing. He considered scooping her up and carrying her into the barn, except that Benny and Fred might still be in there, and what he had in mind required privacy.

She took a deep breath and attempted to push him away, but it was only a halfhearted effort. Her words came out in a determined rush. "The point is that Saturday's your big coming-out party, which means it would be very advisable for you to leave on Sunday, before people get suspicious."

He had no wish to think about the leaving-on-Sunday part. "Tonight could be the granddaddy of all coming-out parties, with your participation."

"Quinn, will you stop thinking about your... problem and listen?"

"It's hard." He lifted his head and waggled his eyebrows at her. "Very hard."

Breathless laughter trembled on her lips. "Honestly, you act as if you've never been sexually frustrated before in your life. Has every woman except me tumbled directly into your bed?"

"Not by a long shot. But this is not mere sexual frustration. This is sexual torture. To be more specific, I could represent my previous sexual frustrations by, say, a gnat, and my present one by, say, a wolf spider."

"Really?" She looked sort of pleased with the news.

"I'm afraid so."

"Why do you think that is?"

"I've asked myself the same thing, Josephine. I don't know. All I know is that if I'm forced to drive away from here on Sunday without ever making love to you, I might have to throw myself off the top of the Empire State Building."

Her cheeks grew pink, and her eyes sparkled. "How you exaggerate. Besides, they've put up barriers so people can't throw themselves off the Empire State Building."

"Then I'd have to tie a cement block to my feet and jump off the George Washington Bridge. And I'd probably land on a garbage scow and sink over my head into the muck, like Luke Skywalker in Star Wars, only I wouldn't ever come up again. I'll die covered in slime." He kneaded her firm bottom with his gloved hand. "I'm sure you don't want that on your conscience."

"You sure know how to treat a girl, Quinn." Her chin had a saucy tilt, but her bedroom eyes gave her away. "First you rope her and then you whisper sweet nothings about garbage scows and slime."

"It's a gift." He smiled. "Take pity on me, Jo. I'm a desperate man."

"But this is all we'd ever have."

"I know." His smile faded. "And I know that's a problem for you. It could be a problem for me. If I could find the off switch on this obsession I'd use it. That was my plan, to shut down that part of me. Turns out I'm not as strong as I thought I was."

"I need some time to think."

Quinn glanced around. Dusk was upon them. After dusk came night, and it might be the longest, most frustrating one of his life if Jo shut him down. She thought he was kidding about the Empire State Building and the George Washington Bridge. And he was, sort of. But he'd never wanted any woman like this, and he wasn't sure life would be worth living if he'd never know the ecstasy of holding Jo's warm, responsive and totally naked body in his arms. "How much time?"

"You can see my bedroom window from the bunkhouse."

"I guess. I never checked."

"Well, take my word for it. You can. By eleven tonight everyone will be asleep."

"Not everyone."

"Everyone *else*, then. I'll turn my light out at ten-thirty. If I flash it twice at eleven, meet me at the barn. I'll bring a blanket."

"We're doing this outside?" Quinn got a quick picture of all sorts of creatures slithering around and decided he'd have to deal with it. "Hey, outside's fine. Outside's terrific. I love outside."

"I was thinking the hayloft."

That was only marginally better in Quinn's estimation, but he smiled, trying to demonstrate extreme confidence. "Fine. The hayloft it is. Sounds great. A roll in the hay. I'm there. I'm—"

"But if I don't flash my light twice, then that means I think it would be better if we stay with our original plan and not make love while you're here."

Quinn had temporarily forgotten that she hadn't committed to the plan. The realization hit him like a medicine ball in the gut. "Oh." He was afraid he looked like an abandoned cocker spaniel as he gazed at her. This craving was turning him into a pathetic shadow of his former self. "Please flash."

"I still think we'd be making a terrible mistake, Quinn. You're thinking short-term."

"Very short. Like from now until eleven tonight. What if you fall asleep and forget?"

"No chance." She stood on tiptoe and brushed her lips across his. "Watch my window," she whispered. Then she eased out of his arms, retrieved her hat and headed in the direction of the house.

Quinn stood in the shadows and knew exactly how Samson must have felt when bewitched by Delilah. Marc Anthony when captivated by Cleopatra. A woman had never wielded this much power over him, had never turned him into a beggar.

He picked up the rope and walked away from the post. He could barely see it in the darkness, but that made his new technique easier. He hardly had to squint to mentally turn the post into Jo. *Rope me, and*

I'm yours for the night, cowboy. He twirled the rope, let it sail and neatly roped the post.

<u>17</u>

Sitting across the table from Quinn and contemplating her decision regarding the evening ahead, Jo could barely eat Emmy Lou's delicious pot roast. Quinn appeared to have no trouble, though.

"You sure seem to be enjoying your meal," Jo commented with some irritation as he forked up a second helping of meat. She thought it was highly unfair that nothing ever seemed to take away a man's appetite, while women's stomachs were affected by every little bit of stress.

"I love pot roast." He gave her a dazzling smile before tucking into the meal once again.

Emmy Lou beamed from the end of the table. "It's a pleasure to watch you eat, Quinn."

Fred snorted. "Why, I'm covered with goose bumps at the sight, myself."

"You are?" Benny stared at him. "I don't see nothin'."

"Oh, Fred, you're just jealous," Emmy Lou said, "because you can't put away food the way you used to when you were younger."

"Who says I can't?" Fred held out his plate. "I'll take another helping of that pot roast."

"I'm not serving you seconds." Emmy Lou pushed his plate aside. "You'll be up all night with heartburn and you know it."

Quinn glanced up in alarm. "Yeah, and the rodeo and dance are tomorrow. I'm sure we all need a good night's rest."

"Oh, we certainly do," Jo said, covering a smile with her hand.

"I damn well know what's happening tomorrow, and I'll have another helping, Emmy Lou." Fred thrust his plate in her direction again.

Emmy Lou rolled her eyes. "Okay, you stubborn old goat." She placed more meat and vegetables on his plate. "Don't blame me when you're walking the floor at three in the morning."

Quinn gripped Fred's arm. "You know, Fred, I'll bet that would taste even better for lunch."

Fred glared at him. "Listen here, greenhorn. I was eating Emmy Lou's pot roast while you were still in diapers, so don't be telling me the time of day when I can enjoy it. Now take your mitts off my arm."

"Well, I'll tell you what, my eyes were bigger than my stomach." Quinn pushed his plate away. "I'm stuffed. Couldn't eat another bite. Just one more mouthful and I'd have heartburn for sure. I'm saving this for lunch. And you know, Fred, if we put cellophane over our plates, we could heat them in the microwave and save Emmy Lou the trouble of making us lunch tomorrow before we leave for the rodeo. What do you think of that?"

Fred shrugged. "Suit yourself. Emmy Lou knows she don't have to bother about my lunch if she's too tired. I'm capable of building a sandwich."

"Is that a fact?" Emmy Lou gazed at him. "I'm glad you told me, Fred. And when was the last time you built yourself a sandwich? When Nixon was president?"

Fred looked down the table and winked at her. "I do believe Johnson was in the White House at the time. Now if you'll excuse me, I have a meal to eat."

Now that she understood the true nature of it, Jo was fascinated by Fred and Emmy Lou's relationship, which could turn from gruff to lighthearted in a split second. She assumed that was the mark of an enduring partnership, but she'd never been around a couple who'd had such a long and apparently loving association. She hadn't known either set of grandparents well, and Aunt Josephine had stayed single all her life.

How sweet it would be to know someone that well, she thought with a pang of longing. Irrationally she thought of Quinn, the man she was destined to know for less than a week. Funny, but he was exactly the sort of man she could imagine creating a long-term partnership with. She could picture them thirty or forty years from now, sparring with each other the way Emmy Lou and Fred did, with a deep respect and love underlying every teasing word.

Love. Oh, my God. Jo glanced quickly at Quinn, as if he might have been able to read her thoughts. She couldn't love him. She hadn't known him long enough. She'd never met his family, his friends. She didn't know if he had a dog, or maybe a cat, or precisely what he did for a living, except that it had to do with money, a subject that had always confused her.

Of course she hadn't been thinking that she did love him, only that she *could* love him, in some other circumstance, after they'd become friends and spent lots of time in each other's company—years, maybe. Love was a tricky emotion. She'd talked herself into loving Dick, and that hadn't worked at all.

Now it seemed she was talking herself out of loving Quinn. She hoped that worked a little better. Quinn was definitely the wrong man for her to fall in love with, unless she wanted to give up her ranch and send Emmy Lou, Fred and Benny into the street. Good thing she'd had this little mental chat with herself, so she didn't allow her heart to do something really, really stupid.

"Who wants dessert?" Emmy Lou asked.

Quinn patted his flat stomach. "Couldn't possibly."

"What is it?" Benny asked.

"Cherry cobbler."

"I'll have some," Fred said, finishing the last of his pot roast. "Warm, with ice cream on top."

Emmy Lou shook her head. "Frederick, I do hope you have a good book to read, because you aren't going to be doing any sleeping tonight."

"Ah, I'll sleep like a baby," Fred said.

"Babies wake up constantly," Emmy Lou replied.

"I could run into town for some sleeping pills," Quinn said. "Or those tablets that fizz, or maybe that pink stuff that coats your stomach, or maybe it's white. I don't know. I'll buy it all. Whatever you need. I think sleep is important. Very important."

Fred gazed at him. "You seem mighty interested in getting me to sleep tonight. Any particular reason?"

Quinn reddened. "Just looking after your health, Fred."

Fred nodded, but there was a gleam of mischief in his eyes. "That's what I thought."

<u>18</u>

After dinner Jo excused herself from the table and headed for her study to figure out which bills she should pay and which ones she could stuff back in the shoe box. She'd never completely understood Josephine's bookkeeping system, so she'd come up with one of her own, but even she had to admit it wasn't adequate. She should have stuck with those accounting classes, but it was a little late to worry about that now.

The process of bill paying always left her stomach in knots, but it was her responsibility. After an hour of figuring and refiguring, she kept coming to the same conclusion. She needed some quick cash, and one of her best mares had produced an outstanding foal. She had to sell Clarise and Stud-muffin.

She wrote down the decision so it felt irreversible. Sherry, the vet who was coming out early the next morning to inseminate the mares with Sir Lust-a-Lot's sperm, had mentioned she had a buyer for Clarise once she'd foaled successfully. Sherry knew Jo's financial problems well — the vet had let bills slide many times in the past. Keeping Clarise and Stud-muffin was selfish and financially irresponsible, Jo decided, and she couldn't afford either behavior.

With the decision made she got up from her desk and paced the small room while she tried to come to grips with losing one of her favorite mares. Aunt Josephine had taught her not to get sentimentally attached to the cattle, but even tough-minded Josephine had hated selling a horse, including the ones who misbehaved or who were too old and swaybacked to carry a rider.

Someone tapped on her study door. Drawing an unsteady breath, she walked over and opened it.

Quinn took one look at her and reached out a hand to cup her cheek. "What is it?"

She forced a smile. "Nothing. Ranch business."

He combed her hair over her ear. "I thought you were probably in here wrestling with your finances. I wish you'd be willing to discuss the situation with me."

"I did." Her emotions lay close to the surface, and his gentle touch threatened to bring tears. She stepped out of reach. "I told you I needed to stall Doobie until September, when I could make another payment on my loan."

He allowed his hand to fall to his side, and there was a flash of hurt in his eyes. "I'm sure there's more to the problem than that." His glance flicked to the shoe box. "If you'd tell me what's going on, I might be able to help you work through it."

"Quinn, you can't be my financial adviser, even if I wanted you to, which I don't. You're leaving on Sunday."

"So what?" He motioned toward the telephone sitting on her desk. "That's the connection I have with my clients, for the most part."

She stared at him for several seconds. Then she lowered her voice. "Quinn, you can't have it both ways. You can't beg me to make love to you one minute and offer to provide long-distance financial counseling the next. The two just don't go together."

He studied her. Finally he shook his head. "You're right, dammit. If we make love tonight—"

"Shh." Jo glanced into the hall before pulling him inside the room and closing the door. "For heaven's sake. It's an old house. The walls have ears."

"Then let's stop talking." He pulled her into his arms and kissed her thoroughly. "Mmm. That's better," he said, lifting his head.

Well, at least he'd taken her mind off her troubles, she thought as warmth surged through her. "Are you..." She stopped to catch her breath. His kisses packed a wallop. "Are you trying to influence my eleven o' clock decision?"

He studied her face for several long seconds. "I don't know what I'm doing."

"Could have fooled me."

"I came in here to see if I could help you with your books."

She wound her arms around his waist and fit herself against the jut of his obvious erection. "Uh-huh."

"Honest. And now you tell me the only way I can possibly help is if we don't make love tonight." He stroked her cheeks with his thumbs. "You sure know how to hurt a guy."

"I don't want you to help me with the books." But he could help her forget that she'd soon be selling Clarise and Stud-muffin.

"You should want me to. I'm very good at it."

"Yeah, well, maybe I'm more interested in finding out what else you're very good at." She rubbed sensuously against him and kissed the hollow of his throat. What she'd never admit to him was that she was embarrassed to have him look at her books and discover they were in total disarray. A professional like Quinn would probably go into shock if he could see the mess she'd made. She'd rather shock a stranger, if it came to that.

No, she didn't want Quinn's financial advice, but if she'd allow him to, Quinn could certainly get her through this rough patch. By impersonating Hastings, he was postponing her financial crisis, and by making wonderful love to her he could make her forget her worries, at least for a little while, and that was worth quite a bit.

Quinn groaned. "Damn, but you make it tough to be noble." He took her by the shoulders and gently pushed her away. "But I'm going to give it a shot. Show me your ledgers."

She couldn't admit that she wasn't sure what ledgers were, exactly, so she reached for the top button of her blouse. "I'd much rather show you my—"

"No." He gripped her hand and closed his eyes. "I can't believe I'm stopping you from unbuttoning your blouse. I must be out of my mind." He held her hand tighter and opened his eyes to gaze at her intently. "Jo, this is for your own good. Forget sex."

"Have you been drinking?"

"Not yet. I may start on Fred's rotgut after this conversation. Listen, forget everything I said to you out in the corral. Think about your commitment to the ranch. I can help you keep that commitment. Use my services. Please." He released her hand and stepped away from her. Although a muscle in his jaw twitched as if the effort was costing him, he kept his arms at his sides.

He was magnificent. As much as he wanted her, he'd deny himself in order to help her achieve her goals. "Why are you doing this?" she murmured.

For a moment he looked confused. "Because I—because that's the best thing for you."

"But not for you," she said softly.

"My needs aren't as important as yours right now."

She wondered if he knew he was falling in love with her. Just as she was falling in love with him. Their relationship would be short and intense, but at least it would exist. She wasn't going to squander this chance at a moment of happiness for the possibility of straightening out some dry old ledgers, if she even had ledgers, which she doubted.

She took a long, shaky breath. "I absolutely refuse to allow you to get involved in my financial affairs," she said.

"Jo, don't—"

"But I'm looking forward to our brief but significant love affair. Never mind all that signaling nonsense. I'll be at the barn at eleven with a blanket.

Now go on out to the bunkhouse before Emmy Lou begins to wonder what we're doing in here so long with the door closed."

He shook his head, but his ragged breathing indicated he was greatly tempted by her offer in spite of his noble intentions. "You're making a mistake. Please reconsider."

She shook her head. "You don't have to show up at the barn, though, if it would compromise your principles."

His laugh was dry as he gazed at her with fire in his eyes. "Sweetheart, I'm not that strong. I'll be there."

<u>**19**</u>

Quinn didn't intend to give up the idea of helping Jo create a workable financial plan before he left. But obviously the straightforward approach wasn't going to work. He'd have to be more devious.

He walked into the bunkhouse to find Benny and Fred playing a game of what Quinn used to call War when he was a kid. It was a simple game, the kind Benny could probably understand, and Quinn thought it was decent of Fred to play it with him.

Fred glanced up. "Hey, Quinn."

"Hey, Fred."

"Hi, Mr. Hastings," Benny said before returning his attention to the game.

Quinn decided not to correct Benny about his name. Instead he faked a huge yawn. Yawns were supposed to be contagious. "Aren't you guys tired?"

Benny yawned, right on cue. "Guess so. You tired, Fred?"

"Nope." He glanced at Quinn. "Go on to bed if you want. We'll be quiet."

"Okay, believe I will."

"I'm going to bed, too," Benny said.

Fred shrugged. "Okay. I'll play solitaire."

One down and one to go, Quinn thought as he sat on the bunk assigned to him and pulled off his borrowed boots. The bunkhouse reminded Quinn of the cabin he'd been assigned to at Camp Washogee twenty years ago. He experienced no nostalgia — for a kid who hated wiggly things, summer camp had been a nightmare.

The metal beds looked exactly the same as the ones at camp. There were four of them lined up against opposing walls, two on a side. A scarred dresser topped by a mirror was against the end wall between the beds.

A table and four captain's chairs took up most of the opposite end of the bunkhouse, and a door in the far wall opened into a small bathroom. Nails driven into the walls held jackets, hats, a rope or two and a bridle Fred was repairing in his spare time.

Fred wasn't working on the bridle at the moment, Quinn noticed as he shucked his pants and shirt and pulled back the blanket on his bed. Fred's belt was undone, and the guy looked uncomfortable. Emmy Lou obviously knew Fred's digestive system well.

Quinn's stomach felt fine, but the rest of him was a little beat-up. He groaned softly as he climbed into bed. Between bruises and sore muscles, he could be pretty well crippled by tomorrow, especially considering the activity he had planned for tonight. He took off his watch and set it on the windowsill next to the bed, where he could see the time by turning his head. An hour and a half before he was supposed to meet Jo.

His groin tightened. In less than two hours, assuming he could sneak past Fred, he'd have Jo in his arms. He wondered what she'd wear to their rendezvous and if she'd bother with items like underwear. Underwear could be very erotic, but getting it off might take up valuable time. Quinn decided he'd rather she didn't wear any.

Maybe he wouldn't wear any, either, although you had to be damn careful with the zipper in a case like that. Too careful, come to think of it. He'd wear his briefs. Considering how much he wanted Jo, he'd be shaking like a leaf, and sure as the world, he'd get something important caught in the zipper.

Then he wondered if he should wear his hat to the barn. Of course he didn't *need* that Stetson on his head, considering it would be dark and he was planning to climb to the hayloft and make love all night. But in another way he did need the hat. Wearing it made him feel more like a cowboy, and damned if that didn't seem to add a certain something to his self-confidence.

He also liked the idea that he'd meet Jo looking like a seasoned ranch hand, a devil-may-care stud of a wrangler. Maybe he ached all over from today's activities, maybe he couldn't sit a horse like a pro or rope a wild bull yet, but he could project the image darn well when he put on that Stetson. He knew because he'd checked it out in a mirror.

Yeah, he'd wear the hat, maybe even keep it on while he took his other clothes off. He hoped Jo would keep her outfit simple. A pair of pull-on shorts and a T-shirt sounded perfect to him. He could strip those off in no time, leaving Jo lying on the blanket, waiting....

And then Quinn went cold. He had no condoms. He had no reason to expect Jo to be using any form of birth control, and besides, a stud didn't show up at the appointed place with no protection for his lover. Dammit, what to do? Benny wouldn't have any, but Fred... Fred might. But he couldn't ask. He'd have to snoop, and if he hit pay dirt, he'd have to swipe. Normally he wasn't a swiper, but this was an unusual situation.

"You asleep, Mr. Hastings?" Benny whispered from across the room.

"Not yet, Benny."

"I can't sleep from thinking about the movie."

Quinn sighed. "I don't think there will be a movie, so just relax and go to sleep, okay?"

"I think there will be a movie. And I want to be in it."

"Benny, I'd give up the idea if I were you. Chances are—"

"Will you promise me, if there is a movie, I'll get to be in it?"

Quinn hated to make a promise like that to a guy as trusting as Benny. What if the real Brian Hastings showed up some day? What if the damned movie actually got made? Dick and Doobie could go hang, but Quinn didn't want Benny to be disappointed. "I don't think I can make that kind of promise."

"Yes, you can. Jo did."

"She did?" Quinn thought about that for a minute. All along he'd been hoping that Hastings would come back and make the movie so Jo would get the money. Yet he suddenly pictured Hastings hanging out at the Bar None, interacting with Jo and granting her favors like giving Benny a part in the movie. If Jo was attracted to Quinn, who was a poor woman's version of Hastings, then she'd probably fall head over heels for the real thing. Quinn felt a little sick to his stomach imagining Hastings putting the moves on Jo. With a guy like that, it would probably be an automatic reaction to a beautiful woman.

"So can I be in it?" Benny asked again.

"I guess so," Quinn replied, feeling depressed. "If there is a movie."

"There will be," Benny said with complete confidence.

Quinn grimaced. Damn, he really wanted that movie to be filmed at the Bar None, for Jo's sake. Of course he did. This morning she'd insisted that looking at Hastings' bare butt hadn't been the reason she'd jumped Quinn's bones. Quinn wanted to believe her, but Hastings was America's sexiest leading man. *People* magazine had said so. Quinn wondered why every single thing that would be good for Jo turned out to be the worst thing that could happen to him.

"Night, night." Benny yawned. "Sleep tight."

"Thanks, Ben."

"Don't let the bugs bite," Benny added in a sleepy voice.

Quinn stiffened. "What bugs?"

Benny's reply was barely audible. "Dunno. People just say that." Soon afterward he began to snore.

Quinn lay rigid as a corpse and tried not to think about wolf spiders as big as his fist creeping under his bed, on his bed. Finally he cleared his throat. "Fred?" he called softly.

"Yeah, Quinn."

"You get many of those wolf spiders in here?"

Fred chuckled. "Ugly sons of bitches, ain't they?"

"I guess."

"That's how the creek got named, they say. Then the town after that. I picture some old prospector waking up in the middle of the night with one of those suckers sitting right by his nose. Musta scared the crap outta him."

Quinn swallowed. "Yeah, probably. I bet you don't see them much anymore, though. Like in the bunkhouse and stuff."

"Oh, sure, we do. This place was built in nineteen-ten, and it's not real tight. We get all kinds of critters in here. Last week it was a small rattlesnake."

"No kidding?" Quinn realized his voice had squeaked and deliberately lowered it. "That's interesting."

"You're turning into a regular chatterbox, aren't you, Quinn? I thought you said you was real tired."

"I am. Good night." Quinn didn't want to discuss critters with Fred anymore. He lay there wondering what he was doing surrounded by poisonous snakes and ugly bugs. In Manhattan he could swim with the sharks, or face a bear market without blinking. In Manhattan he could be a hero.

But Jo wasn't in Manhattan. She was in Montana, and so, for the moment, he had to do his best to be a hero in Montana.

He stared at his watch and willed Fred to go to sleep. Not only did he want to slip out of the bunkhouse so he could meet Jo, he also wanted to spend the night somewhere besides a place with cracks big enough to drive a truck through, or at least a herd of wolf spiders.

After what seemed like eternity squared, Fred began to snore in his chair. Quinn leaned over and checked the floor before swinging his feet down. He dressed in record time but left his boots off. He took the blanket off the spare bed and rolled it up before arranging it under his own blanket to approximate the bulk of a person lying in the bed. Then he padded to the dresser.

The top two drawers belonged to Fred. Quinn figured the top drawer was his best bet. He eased it open and felt cautiously among the socks, briefs and T-shirts. Nothing. Finally, in a back corner, his fingers closed over some foil packets.

He counted four. Decided to take two. If and when Fred discovered the loss, he might chalk it up to losing track of his inventory. Feeling like a seventeen-year-old raiding his dad's supply, Quinn shoved the condoms in his pocket with a little prayer that they were the right size.

There was just enough light from the lamp on the table for him to see a shadowy version of himself in the rippled old mirror over the dresser. He put on his Stetson, gave it a rakish tilt and headed out carrying his boots. He would have given his best Armani suit for a flashlight.

<u>20</u>

Jo changed clothes eleven times between ten o'clock and ten forty-five. Quinn was probably used to fancy lingerie and soft little dresses that came undone with a quick pull on an invisible tie. At least that was the way Jo imagined a Manhattan woman dressed for a late-night meeting with a lover.

She didn't have anything like that. Cotton underwear made sense when you lived in jeans and Western shirts. In winter she wore thermal long johns, even less romantic. She had exactly two dresses, one full-skirted for dancing and the other a sedate linen thing that buttoned up to her neck. Neither of them qualified for a secret rendezvous.

Dammit, when Quinn looked back on this episode she didn't want him to think of it as the night he spent with the hayseed. She rummaged through all her drawers, tossing things on the bed. Then she went through her closet one more time, swishing hangers along the rod in her impatience. At the far end of the closet she found a box she couldn't remember putting there. She opened it and started to laugh. Perfect.

In an abortive attempt to put some romance into her relationship with Dick, she'd bought herself red silk boxers and a chemise. But before she'd had a chance to try them out, Fred had seen Dick kissing a waitress at the Ugly Bug Tavern and forced him to confess he was having an affair. Jo had filed for divorce and had forgotten all about the sexy outfit.

The silk felt good against her bare skin. She'd have to wear something over the outfit, of course, or she'd freeze to death walking to the barn. The slicker hanging by the front door would work. She stood in front of the mirror and admired herself in the red silk while she imagined Quinn's reaction. Her breath quickened.

Smoothing the material over her breasts, she closed her eyes. She craved his touch so desperately it scared her. Maybe meeting him tonight wasn't the wisest thing she'd ever done, but logic wasn't in charge at the moment. Deep in her heart she knew that if she didn't make love to him before he went back to New York she would regret it for the rest of her life.

She slipped on a pair of sneakers and picked up a folded quilt before creeping downstairs. As she made certain to avoid the steps that squeaked, she shivered as much from excitement as the chill in the air. The house was dark and quiet as she made her way to the front door and took down the slicker. She picked up the flashlight they kept on the entry hall table and reached for the knob of the front door.

As she started to turn it, she felt resistance, as if... as if someone was turning the knob from the other side.

Heart pounding, she stepped away from the door. Maybe Quinn had become impatient and decided to come to the house to get her. After the incident with Benny, he knew they didn't lock doors at the Bar None.

The door opened, but the man silhouetted by the glow from the porch light wasn't Quinn. He squinted in the darkness. "Jo, is that you?"

Jo pulled the slicker tight around her and swallowed. "Hi, there, Fred."

She didn't know who was more embarrassed, her or Fred. She was glad the light wasn't very good, because she was sure her face was bright red. They both started a sentence of explanation at the same time, then stopped and stared at each other.

"I, uh, thought I'd get something for my upset stomach," Fred said, his usual bluster completely gone.

"I... wanted to go check on Betsy." It was a transparent fib. She'd checked on Betsy two hours ago, and the mare had shown no signs of going into labor. Fred knew that as well as she did.

But he nodded as if that was a brilliant idea. "Sure."

"There's... there's probably some of that pink stuff in the downstairs bathroom," Jo said.

"I figured." He glanced at the blanket. "How long you planning to, uh, spend time with Betsy?"

"Well, I wasn't sure." He probably knew what the blanket was for, she decided, but she wondered what he thought of her slicker. It wasn't raining. "A couple of hours?"

"Sounds about right."

"Then I guess I'll be getting on down there." She had no idea if Quinn would be waiting. With Fred prowling around, Quinn might have decided to stay put until the coast was clear.

"Yeah, might as well get on down there. Check on Betsy," Fred said.

"Fred, you're blocking the door."

"Oh!" He came all the way into the house, and they sashayed around each other in the narrow hallway like two people do-si-doing at a square dance.

"See ya," Jo said as she hurried out of the house.

"Yep." Fred closed the door quietly behind her.

Once she was headed down the porch steps, Jo began to grin. Shoot, those folks had probably been carrying on like this for years. Josephine might have known about it but couldn't find a good way to inform her young grand-niece. Jo wondered why they'd never made their romance public and gotten married.

But she could guess. Fred might enjoy having Emmy Lou nearby, and she no doubt felt the same, but Jo couldn't picture Fred becoming domesticated enough to live in the house, which would probably mean giving up his chewing tobacco and his occasional trips to the Ugly Bug Saloon.

Jo swept the ground with her flashlight, checking for snakes. She didn't expect to find any. The nights were still too cold for them to be out and about at eleven o'clock. Finding nothing, she started around the house toward the barn and glanced quickly at the entrance lit by a dusk-to-dawn light.

No Quinn.

Although Jo told herself he was probably waiting until he was sure Fred wouldn't see him, her self-confidence slipped a notch. Maybe he'd reconsidered and wasn't coming, after all. Or even more humiliating, maybe he'd fallen asleep, his ardor for her forgotten once his head touched the pillow. She'd rather be rejected outright than forgotten like some dentist's appointment.

The more she considered it, the less she liked the idea of hanging around the front of the barn for God knew how long before Quinn decided to show up, assuming he would show up and wasn't sawing logs at this very minute. Quinn wasn't following the script. He was supposed to be so excited that he'd arrive early. Eager and nervous, he would then pace back and forth until the appointed time. When he first glimpsed her, he'd rush to meet her, and she would drop the quilt and flashlight (gracefully) and run to meet him, except the moment would be drawn out in slow motion, with appropriate background music.

Instead Quinn was late. He would arrive, if he arrived at all, to see her standing in the unflattering glare of the dusk-to-dawn light wearing her yellow slicker and clutching an old quilt. She probably looked like a refugee. Or a flasher.

On impulse she stepped into the shade of a large oak. When she saw him coming, she could hurry forward as if she'd just arrived, as if she'd lost track of the time and had suddenly realized that it was past eleven. Yes, that was a good line. She'd say she'd been reading a wonderful book and hadn't realized how late it was. That should put Mr. Quinn Monroe in his place.

Assuming he showed up at all.

If not she'd have to stay here for two hours because she'd subtly promised Fred she wouldn't interrupt him and Emmy Lou any sooner than that. From Jo's perspective Fred and Emmy Lou had the ideal relationship. It sure beat marriage, from what Jo had seen of that institution. She envied their comfortable, no-strings arrangement. This standing out in the cold waiting for some guy to meet you was for the birds.

She used to play in this tree when she was a kid, she remembered. The trunk branched off about three feet from the ground, providing a crotch that was a perfect place to put your foot and heave yourself into the tree for a good climbing experience. The oak had leafed out in the past couple of weeks, and it provided dense enough shade to camouflage her until Quinn arrived or... he didn't. If the rat didn't show, she'd find some way to get revenge.

Strong arms came around her from behind, and she yelped. The quilt and flashlight plopped to the ground.

"How come you didn't come over to the front of the barn, where you said you'd be?" Quinn murmured in her ear as he pulled her hard against him.

"Because you were late!" she whispered hoarsely, her heart going like crazy. "I decided to wait here until you managed to get yourself out of the bunkhouse!"

"I wasn't late." He nibbled her earlobe as he held her tight and began unsnapping her slicker with one hand.

"Were so." Even through the slicker she could feel his erection pressing against her, rock hard and ready.

"Was not. I stayed in the shadows so there was no chance Fred would see me. I watched you coming toward me and decided I'd wait until you got right to the door of the barn before I showed myself, in case anyone was watching." His teeth raked the lobe of her ear as he slipped his hand inside her slicker. "Except for some reason you changed your mind and decided to hide under this tree. So I had to come and get you."

She gasped as he reached under the silk chemise and cupped her breast. Cool air touched her skin through the open slicker. She should suggest they go into the barn, but his hand felt so good she didn't want to move just yet. In a minute they could move. He kneaded her breast with his strong fingers. In another minute. "I... met Fred coming in the house as I went out," she said.

Quinn's breath was warm against her ear, his voice husky and deep. "And what did you tell him?" He rubbed his thumb back and forth across her nipple until the ache inside her became almost unbearable. Perhaps it was knowing that they would finally make love tonight that had touched some basic cord, making her vibrate so she could barely stand.

"I told him I was... oh, Quinn, I can't think when you do that."

"That's okay." He continued to knead her breast while he slid his other hand beneath the elastic of her boxers. His words rasped in the darkness. "I don't really care what you told Fred." Boldly he

tunneled his fingers through her moist curls. "I just—
" He caught his breath as he probed deeper.

She moaned and leaned back in his arms.

"Ah, Jo." He caressed her with a gentle, rhythmic motion that soon had her quivering. "You're drenched, sweetheart," he whispered. "Why did you hide from me?"

This was crazy, letting him touch her this way with only the darkness to conceal them. But for the life of her she couldn't ask him to stop.

He kissed her neck, then nipped playfully as he slowed his strokes, drawing out the exquisite pleasure. "Why, Jo?"

She could barely breathe as she reached for the summit. Almost there. Just a little more. "Playing it... cool."

"Oh."

She could feel his smile against her skin as he paused, his finger lightly touching her throbbing flash point. She thought she'd go crazy. "But I'm not cool," she said, her words a breathless plea.

"No?"

She trembled on the brink of ecstasy. "Quinn, have mercy. Do something."

"Like this?" He pushed deep and pressed down on that aching, needy spot with the heel of his hand.

Her world came apart, and the rest of the world would have known all about it if he hadn't taken his other hand from her breast and gently covered her mouth, muffling her cry of release. She arched in his arms as the quakes took hold of her. She felt tumbled about like a pebble in the rapids of a stream, and through it all Quinn held her, supported her, whispered sweetly in her ear.

At last she shuddered and was still, drooping in his arms as she gasped for breath. "Wow."

"Good?" His voice sounded hoarse.

"Oh, yeah."

He eased his hand out of her boxers and slowly turned her to face him, holding her firmly by her shoulders as if he realized without his strong grip she'd fall flat on the ground. "I'm glad."

She gazed at him. "I feel as if I've had too much to drink."

"I know the feeling. I'm pretty high myself."

"Yeah, but you're still standing. You may have to carry me to the barn."

He gave her a lopsided grin. "I'm not sure I can walk that far." He guided her a couple of steps backward until she felt the trunk of the oak against her back. "Let's rest a minute before we decide." He took off his Stetson, hung it on a nearby twig and leaned down and covered her mouth with his.

She didn't find his kiss at all restful. One thrust of his tongue and the ache began to build again as if he hadn't just given her the most dramatic climax of her life. She'd never experienced lovemaking like this. There seemed to be no quenching the fire inside. When she thought it had burned itself out, Quinn breathed the embers to life again.

His hands found their way under her chemise, cupping her breasts, coaxing her nipples to quivering tautness. Then he lifted his mouth from hers, pushed the chemise up and leaned down to draw one nipple into his mouth. Without the tree's support she would have definitely crumpled to the hard ground as he lavished her breasts with attention.

She was guilty of pulling the chemise higher, so it wouldn't flutter down and get in his way. And she arched her back to make it easier for him to do all those marvelous things with his mouth and tongue that she remembered from their session on the couch.

"Oh, Quinn, I want you so much," she cried softly.

"Undo my jeans," he murmured against her tongue-dampened breasts.

"Here?"

"Right here, sweetheart. I need your hands on me in the worst way."

She gasped as he resumed fondling her. "Then you'll have to stop... doing that."

She wondered if he'd heard her, but he must have, because eventually he kissed his way to her throat and nuzzled the sensitive skin beneath her ear as he continued to stroke her breasts.

"And that," she said breathlessly.

"What can I do?" He squeezed her breasts gently. "I want to touch you. I need to touch you."

She moaned with pleasure. "But I can't concentrate when you touch me. So stop. Just stand there."

With a husky sigh he drew back and braced his hands on the tree's two main branches.

Taking a long, shaky breath, she leaned forward and unfastened his belt with trembling hands. As she started to ease the zipper over his rigid shaft, she looked into his shadowed face, her heart pounding with anticipation. "You're sure you want me... to do this here?"

"Oh, yes."

"But—"

His voice was tight with desire. "No one can see. I wouldn't have known you were under this tree if I hadn't watched you slip back here. And I'll never make it to the barn, Jo. I'd wreck myself trying."

She unzipped his jeans carefully. His harsh breathing drowned out the crickets as she followed his lead and slid her hand beneath the elastic of his briefs. Her hand closed around enough warm, rigid male to make any woman very happy. Her body reacted with an intense, hollow ache and a rush of moisture.

She caressed him and he groaned, but it was muffled, as if he'd clenched his teeth to keep from crying out. That low, desperate sound made her heady with her own power to please. And the quilt was almost within reach. "Stay here."

"I couldn't move if you shoved a stick of dynamite up my—"

"I'll be right back." She released him, ducked under his arm, grabbed the folded quilt and dropped it at his feet. "There."

"What are you doing?"

"This." She knelt on the quilt and wrapped her fingers around his sizable erection once again. Damn, he was impressive. And he was all hers. When she took him into her mouth, a massive shudder went through him.

"Jo... I didn't mean that you... oh, Lord." He began to quiver.

She lifted her head and gazed at him while she stroked his sensitive tip with her thumb. "Want me to stop?" She barely recognized her voice, which had become throaty and seductive.

He struggled for breath. "No."

"Good." She replaced her thumb with her tongue. The more she loved him, the more insistently her body demanded his presence deep inside her. She'd never felt this way, as if the world wouldn't make sense anymore unless she received that elemental connection with this particular man. Only with this man.

Quinn gasped and trembled. "Jo. Jo, stop now. Please."

She took her time about releasing him and gave him one last sensuous stroke before rising to her feet. "I need you now," she said, her voice thick with longing. "Right here, right now. On the quilt, in the dirt, I don't care. Now, Quinn."

His laugh was shaky. "I hate it when you're indecisive. Get off the quilt a minute."

She stepped aside, and he picked up the quilt. She thought he'd spread it on the ground and pull her down with him, but instead he kept it folded and settled it into the crotch of the tree. Excitement rose in her, hot and wild.

He turned to her and guided her close to the tree. Then he slipped his thumbs under the elastic of her silk boxers. "I like these," he murmured, tugging them down. "But they gotta go."

Impatient and aching, she started to help him.

He pushed her hands away. "Oh, no. My job."

He went to his knees in front of her as he pulled the boxers down. He kissed her navel, flicking his tongue inside the indentation. Need shot through her, and she cried out.

"Shh," he whispered, drawing her boxers over her knees as he kissed her damp curls.

She could barely breathe from the pressure of wanting him, yet he was moving at a snail's pace. "Are you... going to make a big... production out of taking those off?" she asked.

"Yep." Steadying her with one hand, he grasped her ankle and lifted, so that she stepped out of one leg of the boxers. Then, before she quite realized his purpose, he'd cupped her behind and tilted her pelvis so that he could give her a very intimate kiss indeed.

She gasped, and her knees buckled as pleasure surged through her. She felt the quilt brush the small of her back. Trembling, she leaned weakly against the padded crotch of the tree as he had his way with her. She was helpless against the onslaught of his tongue as he urged her pulsing, tightening body to enjoy, enjoy, enjoy.

Gripping the rough branch arching beside her, she pressed the back of her other hand to her mouth as the explosion came, rocking her against the tree. Her muffled cry sounded like the keening of a wild creature — the wild creature he had set loose within her.

And she wanted him still. Even as the shock waves continued, she wanted him. She took her hand from her mouth. Her plea was choked with emotion, but he couldn't possibly mistake what she needed.

He didn't.

He eased her gently against the tree and steadied her with one hand as he reached in his pocket. She made a real effort and managed to stay upright when he released her so he could put on the condom. Slipping it over his erection, he made a noise low in his throat, as if even that contact challenged his control.

Then he was back, his hands under her bottom, lifting her to the wide crotch of the tree, holding her there. She braced her hands against the outstretched branches, leaned into the cradle of his cupped hands and opened her thighs.

With her slicker draped protectively around them, he stepped closer and probed gently, his breathing ragged. "Don't let me hurt you."

She moaned in frustration. "I want all of you, Quinn. Every last rigid inch."

He eased inside a little more. "Okay?"

Oh, he was big, but she wanted big. She wanted to be filled, at long last, with everything this man had to offer. She panted with need. "Not enough."

He pushed slightly deeper.

"More," she whispered.

He gave her a fraction more, but he was obviously holding back, obviously had a hangup about being too big.

"Oh, Quinn." In one swift motion she wrapped her legs around his hips and pulled him in tight. "Oh, *Quinn*."

Apparently he couldn't control his growl of satisfaction, but then he went right back to being the soul of concern, although his voice was a little rough around the edges. "I'm hurting you."

"That was not hurt you heard in my voice," she said breathlessly. "That was heaven. My body is singing, Quinn, singing the praises of your big beautiful—"

"Okay. I get it." He covered her mouth with his.

His kiss might be all it would take, her heart pounding as he explored thoroughly with his tongue while still locked against her. He might not have to move that astounding equipment at all, since it filled her so totally, making contact in all the right places.

Then he began to move, and she decided moving might be a good thing. Moving might be a great thing. Moving might be a really spectacular thing.

He lifted his mouth from hers. "Ah, Jo. I've never... this is so good."

"So very good." She absorbed another soul-filling moment as he buried himself deep, eased back and pushed home again.

"As if this is what we're meant for." He nibbled at her lower lip.

"Oh, yes." She welcomed another thrust, treasuring each and every one.

"We fit." He kissed her chin, the hollow of her throat, all the while holding her steady as he eased his hips back and forth, bringing her joy with every stroke.

"Like a sword in a sheath." The quickening that had started with the first glorious full contact had intensified with each rhythmic motion. She wanted it to last forever, but knew they had only seconds to go, knew from the subtle way Quinn increased the pace, the slight change in his breathing.

Faster still. Exquisite friction. So right. There. *Yes. Now. Quinn. Oh, Quinn. Love me. Love me, love me, love me.*

He kissed her hard, forcing the cry into her throat, smothering the groan rumbling from his chest. Holding her tight and deeply impaled, he absorbed her convulsions and drank her whimpers of delight until his own release gripped him.

For the first time in her life, she felt the joy of another's climax as if it were her own. And as he shuddered helplessly in her arms, gasping her name, she knew that no matter how much heartbreak it brought her, she would never regret this night of loving Quinn.

<u>21</u>

Quinn had decided to make love this way because he'd figured that lying on the ground was just asking for interference from snakes and bugs. However, the experience had turned out to be much better than he could have imagined. He'd go so far as to say he'd never known anything to equal making love propped against an oak tree on a chilly spring night in Montana.

With Jo, he quickly added. Jo, the most perfect sexual partner he'd ever known. The funniest, sweetest, sexiest woman he'd ever known. He kissed her eyes, her cheeks, her hair. Gathering her close, he savored the recent ecstasy of being enclosed by her warmth.

If this wasn't love, then he didn't understand what love was all about. He not only wanted to spend the rest of the night with her, he wanted to spend days, months, years with her. "Maybe I could dye my hair blond," he murmured, nestling her head against his shoulder.

"*What*?" She roused herself and stared at him. "Quinn, you make love like no man I've ever known, but your after-the-loving conversation needs work. This is not the time to discuss hair treatments."

He chuckled, and as he gazed at her he felt as if someone had poured warm melted butter over his heart. Yeah, he probably loved her, loved her strong enough to last clear into doddering old age. "Or I could shave my head. That's popular these days."

"I'm not wild about that look, if you're really determined to discuss this now. And blond won't go with your skin tones as well as dark brown does. What's this about?"

"I'm trying to figure out how I could sneak back to see you again after I leave town. I think the blond hair would work. And maybe a mustache and glasses."

She cupped his face in both hands. "Let's just tell everybody you're not Hastings."

"No. I can't let you do that."

"Well, I can't let you dye your hair. Your friends and clients would wonder what on earth was going on. I don't want to be responsible for making you look dumb in front of everybody. Let's tell."

"No. I'll dye my hair."

"No." She combed her fingers through his hair. "I love it this color. That's partly what makes your eyes look so incredibly blue — your skin is a nice bronze color." Her voice grew soft and wispy. "The contrast is, wonderful," she murmured, drawing him down to her waiting lips.

Incredibly he began to get hard again. He deepened the kiss and kneaded Jo's firm bottom, just to see where that would take him. Sure enough, it took him right back to where he'd been when he'd first lifted her to the perfect level for this activity.

Maybe it was the wildness of making love to a woman sitting in the crotch of a tree that was causing him to feel randy as a seventeen-year-old who'd just lost his virginity. Or maybe it was simply Jo, the scent of her, the taste of her, the feel of her.

And judging from the way her breathing had changed and the hungry way she opened her mouth to his kiss, she also wanted him again, and that was another small miracle. Heart soaring, he gave thanks for his foresight and prepared to enter paradise a second time. How he loved the supple feel of her muscles beneath his palms as she moved in response to his thrusts.

He longed to see her face, but even though he lifted his head to gaze at her, the shadows were too deep. "I wish I could look into your eyes," he murmured, his voice already rough and trembling, his climax hovering near.

"Do you?"

"Yes." He heard the quiver in her voice and knew she was on the edge, too. How quickly they could excite each other. Like lightning.

"Why?"

"Because." He pushed in again, listening for the catch in her breath that meant she was ready. When it came, he slowed, wanting to draw the moment out this time. "I want to see how your eyes change when you're close, like now."

"Are you...?"

"Yes." He drew back ever so slowly and slipped in with practically no force at all. Easy, easy. "Very close."

She trembled in his grip. "I want to see your eyes, too."

"It's too dark." He held back, but even his lazy strokes were going to get them there very soon, no matter how much he wanted to draw out the process.

"I know how your eyes look." She gasped as a tremor shook her. "Like blue flames."

"And yours are like warm chocolate." She was there, and he couldn't keep himself from going with her, moving faster, pushing deeper, trying to touch that part of her that would make her his. "So rich... so hot."

"Quinn." His name was a moan on her lips. "Kiss me, or the world will hear how I feel right now."

He took her mouth with some regret. Maybe the world shouldn't hear just yet, but he'd like to. When he carried her once more into the whirlwind, he wished he could listen as she moaned and cried out his name. He wanted all the sounds he'd helped create as she trembled in his arms.

Because those sounds might include the words, "I love you."

<u>22</u>

Jo clung to Quinn for many long moments, savoring the closeness and the incredible pleasure. But at last he eased back and lifted her gently to the ground. She leaned against the tree, feeling weak and just the slightest bit bowlegged, while he turned and got himself together.

When he turned back to her, he had picked up her silk boxers from the ground. "Want some help putting these on?" he said with a smile in his voice.

Incredibly, considering all she'd experienced, a shiver of desire went through her. "No, thank you." She took the boxers from him and put them on. If she let him help, he might begin to think she was insatiable. Which she might be, but she still didn't want him thinking she was. Besides, as it was, she'd have trouble sitting a horse tomorrow. Much more of Quinn's loving and she'd be crippled. Happy, but crippled.

"Stay there," he said. "I think I heard Fred leave the house. I'll go make sure." Quinn left the shadow of the tree and crept around the house.

Once he was no longer holding her, kissing her, making her forget everything but his loving, she had the unwelcome chance to think about their situation. He sounded really serious about disguising himself so he could come back and see her. The trouble was, she didn't want him to be an occasional visitor, she wanted him to be a full-time, old-fashioned husband.

There, she'd finally admitted it to herself. She loved him, and not only because he was, as the saying went, hung like a horse. That was a nice bonus, but she'd fallen in love before she discovered that pleasant reality. She'd fallen in love with his courage, his generosity and his sense of fun. To have him drop in once in a while would break her heart.

It could very well break his, too. The man she loved wouldn't be happy with that arrangement for long, but he was an investment banker, not a cowboy. He might want her, in fact he obviously wanted her very much, but he didn't want this life-style full of creepy-crawlies, belligerent horses and saddle sores. She couldn't ask him to sacrifice his career to live with her in Montana, but if she didn't cut their relationship off right now, he might get in deep enough to consider such a move only to regret it later. She hated the thought of hurting him, but it was the only way.

Quinn walked to the tree. "He's gone back to the bunkhouse," he said. "The coast is clear." He slipped his arms beneath her slicker and pulled her close, resting his cheek against the top of her head. "But I don't want to let you go. Listen, maybe I could use colored contacts and glasses. And a beard."

She drew back and gazed at him. Maybe it was just as well she couldn't see his face in the darkness. That made it easier to say what must be said. "Forget the disguise idea, Quinn. It wouldn't work."

"That's what you think. You'd be amazed what facial hair can—"

"No, I mean it wouldn't work for me. I don't know if I'll ever find another man to love, but if I do, he needs to be somebody who belongs in this country, somebody I can share ranch life with. If you keep showing up, I'll naturally keep wanting you, but you belong in New York, not out on some remote Montana ranch. We both need to cut our losses, Quinn."

He gasped and stepped back as if she'd slapped him. He seemed to struggle with his breathing for a moment, and then he finally spoke. "Okay, if that's the way you see it." His voice was raw with hurt. "I guess I thought we'd created something worth hanging on to."

"I will hang on to it," she said softly. "I'll never forget this night as long as I live."

"But you never want another one?"

She braced herself against his agonized plea. "Not when it means I have to keep watching you head to New York when it's over. And you have to do that, Quinn. We both know it. That's what you're trained for, what you're used to."

He turned away from her. "Yeah. That's me. Wall Street or bust."

She touched his arm. "Please understand how much you mean to me. How much what we've shared means to me."

"Yeah." His voice was thick with sorrow.

Oh, God. If Quinn started getting emotional, so would she. She'd be bawling her eyes out in a minute if she didn't get out of there. "I'd better get back to the house."

"Okay.

She gave his arm one last squeeze, grabbed the blanket and ran to the house. The quick movement told her she would indeed be very sore tomorrow. But it would be nothing to equal the pain in her heart.

* * *

Quinn stood in the shadows feeling as if somebody had come after him with a bullwhip. He knew he wasn't much of a cowboy, but she didn't have to be so brutal about it. Apparently he was so bad that she never even considered he might someday be of use on this ranch. She thought he was so hopeless that even she and Fred couldn't teach him enough to make his sorry ass worth something around here.

Nope, she was sending him right back to New York where he belonged. And she would look for a real cowboy. Like Hastings. Quinn gritted his teeth. He'd never met Hastings, and the guy was probably a decent human being, but Quinn was really beginning to hate the bastard.

He started to the bunkhouse and tripped over something. He picked up the flashlight she'd dropped when he'd grabbed her from behind. Damn, but her breasts were silky, and her... no. He couldn't think about any of that or he'd go crazy.

He glanced at the flashlight and remembered seeing it on the table in the hallway.

Maybe he should quietly return it so it wouldn't become a topic of discussion. Tomorrow would be weird enough without having to explain the mysterious roving flashlight.

When he reached the porch he took off his boots so he wouldn't make noise. The unlocked door still amazed him, but with all the nocturnal comings and goings around the place, a key would be a nuisance. And he supposed being surrounded by all these acres of rangeland kept the threat of crime very low.

He stood in the darkened entryway and battled temptation. Despite what Jo had said, if he went up those stairs and climbed into her bed, she wouldn't refuse him. He might be out of condoms, but there were plenty of other ways to find mutual satisfaction, and his hunger for her still raged. But that plan wouldn't come to pass as long as he had a shred of pride left.

He started to set the flashlight on the small table by the door when another thought occurred to him. He had a flashlight, so he wouldn't have to turn on a lamp and risk having Fred or Benny notice it. Okay, so he wasn't a cowboy, but he was a hell of a good hand with figures. If Jo didn't lock her front door she sure as hell didn't lock her desk.

He had a few hours before daybreak. It might be enough time to work some magic with Jo's books.

<u>23</u>

Quinn didn't show up for breakfast, which was fine with Jo. Despite the open kitchen window that Emmy Lou had raised to let in a warm spring breeze, the air was thick with tension as Emmy Lou and Fred exchanged looks, and Benny, clueless, chattered away about the day's events. Finally Fred suggested that Benny go polish the tack in preparation for the rodeo, and Benny breezed happily off to do his chores.

"I'll be getting down to the barn, myself." Jo pushed back her chair. "Sherry will be here for the insemination any minute." She'd never blushed when she'd talked about such matters before, but she blushed now. Dammit.

"Hold on a second, Jo," Fred said.

Jo sat down. "Listen, if it's about last night, that's none of my business. I'm happy for both of you. I—"

"It's about last night." Emmy Lou cradled her mug of coffee. "But not what you think. We're not kids, and we won't ask for your permission. If our behavior isn't to your liking, then we'll hire on somewhere else, right, Fred?"

Fred stared at her. "You'd leave this place on account of me?"

"Amazing, isn't it?" Emmy Lou grinned. "Don't let it go to your head."

"I just never thought..." He shook his head, a smile lifting the corners of his gray mustache.

"We were going to broach another subject, weren't we, Fred?' Emmy Lou prompted.

"Yeah." Fred hunkered over his coffee. "Yeah, we were. Jo, you know we didn't think much of Dick."

Emmy Lou cleared her throat. "Except to imagine him swinging by his—"

"Em" Fred sent her a look of warning.

"I'll bet Jo's thought of that, too," Emmy Lou said a touch defensively.

"I have."

"Anyway," Fred continued, "we think you should hang on to this one."

"This one?"

"The greenhorn," Fred said. "He has heart, Jo. More'n Dick ever dreamed of. I know he can't ride a lick or rope worth a damn, but he's got guts, and that's what counts. We could teach him — at least, I think we could. He's not real talented, but he's determined. And I have to say I was impressed because he had sense enough to... uh, use protection last night." Fred gulped his coffee and choked.

Emmy Lou pounded on Fred's back while Jo sat there getting very red and wondering how Fred could possibly know such an intimate thing. Surely Quinn hadn't left evidence lying around.

Once Fred calmed down, Emmy Lou glanced at Jo. "Quinn borrowed from Fred's supply," she said gently. "Fred noticed because he was down to four, and two were missing."

"Oh, my God." Jo buried her face in her hands. "I can't believe I'm having this discussion with you two."

Fred still sounded a little wheezy, but he seemed to want to get his message across. "It ain't always easy to talk about. But Emmy Lou and me saw you make one mistake by takin' up with Dick, and we don't want to see you make another one by lettin' the greenhorn go."

Tears pushed at the back of Jo's eyes. "That's the sweetest, most considerate and wonderfully protective attitude, and I thank you both. But there's a tiny problem. Quinn doesn't want to live here and be a cowboy."

Fred looked astonished. "Why not?"

"Because he's a New York investment banker. He chose that, the same way you chose to work on ranches. He wouldn't mind coming to see me once in a while, but he's not interested in moving to the Bar None."

"He said that?" Fred scratched his head, still not comprehending.

"Not in those words, but it's very obvious. I think it's a bit too primitive for him."

"What's primitive?" Quinn asked from the doorway.

Jo glanced up and couldn't seem to remember what she'd been saying. He looked tired, but still gorgeous. Despite everything she'd told herself, she wanted to walk straight into his arms.

Fred stood. "I got business at the barn. Sherry'll be here soon."

"And I have to check on something in my garden," Emmy Lou said, leaving the table on Fred's heels. "There's coffee and toast and a few hash browns left. I'm sure Jo could scramble you some eggs." She hurried out of the room.

Quinn glanced after them as the front door closed. "I sure know how to clear a room."

"I need to get going, too." She pushed back her chair.

"Before you do, I have something to talk to you about."

"What?" Her heart began to pound. Maybe he wanted to make some sacrifices so they could be together. She couldn't imagine how it would work, but then she didn't know exactly what investment bankers did. Maybe he could investment bank in Bozeman.

"Well, I—"

"Yo, Brian!' The shout came from the front yard.

Jo groaned. She did not feel like facing Dick this morning.

Quinn walked over to peer out the window. "He's riding a bike."

"You're kidding." Jo got up to look. Sure enough, Dick was riding back and forth in front of the porch on—Jo could hardly believe it—a pink girl's bike that was too small for him.

"Hey, Brian! Got a minute?" Dick called. "My heart rate's up, and I need to keep it elevated, buddy.

It ain't time for my cooldown, or I'd stop riding and come on in. But I gotta talk to you."

"Coming!" Quinn called through the window. "I'd better go or he's liable to ride around out there forever."

"He might," Jo agreed. "He functions on about a sixth-grade level."

"Come with me?"

When he gave her that look she couldn't deny him anything. "Okay."

Quinn walked out on the porch, and Jo followed. "Nice bike, Dick," Quinn said.

"Found it at a garage sale. It'll do until the Nautilus equipment arrives."

"Nautilus?" Jo asked. "You're getting a home gym?"

"Sure am." Dick grinned at her as he pedaled across the yard, his knees sticking out awkwardly. "After people see me in this movie, I might be getting other offers. Gotta stay buff, you know. 'Course, I don't ride this thing where my men can see me."

"Of course not," Quinn said. "What's on your mind, Dick?"

"Me and Doobie got to thinkin'."

"There's a scary thought," Jo muttered.

"Yeah?" Quinn said. "About what?"

"We understand you can't be in the rodeo and all, on account of you being such a valuable property, but we figured it wouldn't hurt for you to lead off the grand parade."

Jo remembered Quinn's wild ride on Hyper and smelled disaster in the air. "Oh, you know, Dick, that's a wonderful idea, but Brian really shouldn't be on a horse right now."

"Why not?"

Jo thought quickly. "Well, he recently spent some time in the tropics and went swimming in questionable water that gave him a real bad case of jock itch."

"I'll do it," Quinn said, glaring at her. "I'm completely cured."

"Don't be a hero," she said, glaring back at him. "You know you're not a hundred percent."

"Close enough," Quinn said.

"You're sure?" Dick asked. "That's nasty stuff. I remember one time I got it, and I tell you, I scratched till I thought my—"

"I'll be fine," Quinn said. "Plan on me doing it."

"Great. Well, gotta get on down the road. Still got my lifting program to do. Until the Nautilus stuff comes I'm using a broomstick with a six-pack strapped on each end. Oh, and I drink a glass of raw eggs every morning."

Jo grimaced.

"Good idea," Quinn said.

"I thought so. See you." Dick pedaled off, humming the theme from *Rocky*.

Quinn gazed after him. "So you don't think I can ride well enough to lead the grand parade?"

"Maybe. Depending on the horse you choose. But you're taking a big chance, Quinn. I think you'd be better off if you—"

"Said my jock itch flared up again?" He sounded testy.

"I'm sorry. It was the first thing I thought of, and I couldn't very well say you were saddle sore, could I?"

"And what makes you think I am?"

"The way you walked out on this porch."

"You're walking with a certain amount of care yourself this morning," he said.

Her cheeks warmed.

"Will you be riding in this grand parade?" he asked.

"Yes. All of the contestants ride in it, and I always do the barrel racing event."

"Barrel racing, huh? And how will that feel after... last night?"

She couldn't look at him. "I admit that I'm a little tender."

"Then I guess we'll suffer together. Because I'm going to lead that grand parade regardless of my delicate condition."

"Okay, then I'd recommend riding Butternut. He's—"

"Thanks, but I'll pick my own horse."

Jo groaned. "Don't tell me."

"Yep. I'll be lookin' good. I'm riding Hyper."

24

His crotch hurt like hell. Quinn sat atop a restless Hyper at the entrance to the small rodeo arena outside Ugly Bug and wished he'd used the jock itch excuse, after all. But when Jo had automatically assumed he couldn't even lead a sedate little parade, he'd taken offense. He'd decided he had something to prove to her before he left on the red-eye tonight.

Besides, after watching people steer horses down Fifth Avenue during parades in New York City, he figured there was nothing to it. This would be even easier because it was contained inside a fence.

He hadn't counted on the fact that the leader had to carry an American flag big enough to wrap a body in. And he hadn't counted on wind.

Hyper jumped sideways with every snap and billow of the massive flag. And with each jump, Quinn was painfully reminded of his manly attributes. Jo was somewhere behind him in line, along with Benny, Dick and a bunch of other real cowboys and cowgirls. Mostly they'd behaved themselves, and only a couple had asked for autographs, which he'd politely postponed until after the parade. With luck he'd sprain his wrist in the next twenty minutes, because he'd never gotten around to practicing Hastings' signature.

The other residents of Ugly Bug, however, weren't behaving themselves. Whistling, stomping and calling out his name, or rather Hastings' name, they jammed the modest bleachers. Camera flashes popped constantly, even though it was the middle of the day. At least ten homemade signs waved in the crowd. The more conservative ones said things like Brian Hastings for President, or We Love You, Brian, but one held by a rowdy band of high-school-age girls was covered in huge lipstick kisses with red, glittery letters that spelled out Take Me, Brian! Take Me Now!

A couple of Western lawmen types had positioned themselves at either end of the bleachers. Quinn appreciated having them there, but if the mob decided to rush him, even Marshal Matt Dillon wouldn't be able to control this crowd.

Quinn swallowed. If he survived the parade, he was supposed to sit in a special section smack-dab in the center of those bleachers. The roped-off area already held Doobie and his tush-fixated wife, along with several other middle-aged couples. Jo had wrangled a place in that section for Fred and Emmy Lou, thank God. Maybe they'd help protect him.

As Quinn waited for the gate to open, sweat dampened the black Western shirt with pearl buttons that Benny had insisted he wear. Benny had also donated his best black Stetson, and Fred had brought out silver spurs that winked in the sunlight. Hyper's coat shone like polished mahogany, and his mane and tail were braided with red ribbon. The horse looked great, just as Quinn had imagined. All Quinn had to do was stay on him.

A wizened old cowboy swung open the arena gate, and members of the Ugly Bug High School Band swung into a fast-paced march. Quinn mentally reviewed his instructions. Once around the arena, then straight up the middle to face the grandstands. The other riders would fan out on either side of him, forming a line facing the bleachers as the band played the national anthem. Then he'd lead the riders around to the exit. Taking a firm grip on the flag, he nudged Hyper in the ribs with Fred's silver spurs, and the crowd surged to its feet, applauding loudly.

With a piercing whinny, Hyper reared.

Quinn grabbed at the saddle horn with his free hand and by some miracle hung on, but by the time Hyper's front feet hit the ground, the horse had the bit in his teeth.

Quinn felt the gelding's muscles bunch. "Whoa!" he yelled.

Hyper wasn't listening. He shot through the gate and in three strides was in a dead run. Quinn's hat sailed off, and he lost his stirrups, but he kept his grip on the flag, which streamed dramatically over his shoulder. The grandstands, filled with cheering people, passed in a blur, then passed in a blur again as Hyper turned the arena into his private racetrack.

As Quinn whizzed past the gate, the other riders waved their hats and whistled. Quinn would bet Jo wasn't whistling. And if Hyper kept up this merry-go-round much longer, she might even ride out and pull him to a stop. God, how humiliating.

"Whoa, dammit!" he yelled. He was afraid to let go of the saddle horn to pull back on the reins, and if he dropped the flag so he could grab the reins, then everyone would know he was involved in a major screwup instead of the dramatic flourish they were giving him credit for. Worse yet, they might begin to wonder if he was really Brian Hastings.

He tried to remember what Fred had taught him. Oh, yeah. Grip with your thighs. You could even steer with your thighs, assuming your thighs didn't feel as if somebody had set fire to them, which Quinn's pretty much did.

He gritted his teeth as he flashed by the stands again. Hyper was young and strong. He could probably run for quite a long time, especially when he had the impression he was being chased by an American flag. So Quinn couldn't hope the horse would get tired. And he definitely didn't want Jo to ride out and save him.

The only solution was to get the horse through the gate somehow. After that Hyper would probably continue to run, but maybe they'd get far enough away that Quinn could safely drop the flag and try to establish control. Then again, maybe he and Hyper would see a great deal of the Montana countryside together.

Quinn figured that if he shifted his weight and used his tortured thigh muscles, he might be able to get Hyper to swerve through the gate instead of sailing past it. Bracing himself against the pain, he started leaning and squeezing as Hyper went into the straightaway and headed in the direction of the gate. Twice before the horse had veered left and continued around the arena. Quinn vowed he wouldn't do it again.

Apparently Hyper didn't care where he ran as long as he could keep doing it. He stampeded right through the gate as riders waiting beside it scattered in front of his pounding hoofs. Ahead was the parking lot, and beyond that, open country.

Quinn hung on as Hyper veered headlong between rows of pickup trucks. Once out of the parking lot, Quinn figured he'd drop the flag and try to put an end to this wild ride. Then he heard hoofbeats behind him and looked over his shoulder. Sure enough, Jo was in hot pursuit, with Benny behind her. Maybe it was just as well. He was nearly at the edge of the lot, and he really didn't want to ride this nag all the way to Idaho.

As he faced forward again, a long white vehicle pulled across the empty space at the end of the lot. Quinn squinted, not quite believing what he saw. A limo? In Ugly Bug?

Hyper didn't slow his pace as the limo stopped, blocking the horse's path.

Quinn dropped the flag and seized the reins in both hands. "Whoa, you sorry nag! Whoa, goddammit! You're gonna hit the car, you idiot horse!" When Hyper didn't respond, Quinn braced himself for one hell of a collision.

Instead, Hyper gathered himself and sailed gracefully over the limo. Unfortunately Quinn didn't make the trip with him. Falling sideways, he hit the roof of the limo and rolled down the windshield, coming to rest facedown on the hood.

In seconds, Jo was leaning over him. "Don't move! Did you hit your head? Where are you hurt? Oh, Quinn, speak to me!"

He was having trouble drawing a breath, but he was at least able to register the concern in her voice. Well, good. She cared for him a little. "Don't call me Quinn," he muttered. "I'm Brian Hastings."

"That's funny," said another voice. "So am I."

25

"Not yet, you're not," Jo said, barely giving the man a glance as she leaned over Quinn, her chest tight with fear. So Brian Hastings was here. So what? "Talk to me, my darling. Does anything feel broken?"

"I don't think so. Where's Hyper?"

"Benny went after him."

"Boss, you need anything?" said the uniformed driver as he climbed out of the limo.

"Not right now, Sid," Hastings said. Then he turned to Jo. "What do you mean, not yet? I've been Brian Hastings ever since the studio changed my name from Bernard Hilzendeger. I made it legal ten years ago. Listen, do you want me to call 911?'

"Yes," said Jo.

"No," said Quinn. "I'm okay." He pushed himself slowly to his hands and knees. "But I dented the limo."

"It appears you did," Hastings said

"Call 911," Jo said as she gazed into Quinn's beloved face. Fred had said the greenhorn had heart, and Fred sure knew what he was talking about. "He's in shock."

"No, don't call 911," Quinn said, looking at Hastings.

"My God." Hastings stared at Quinn. "It's like looking in a mirror."

"Don't you wish." Jo didn't spare the movie star a glance as she stroked Quinn's cheek. "I'm so sorry I put you through this, sweetheart. Please forgive me. I should have found a better way to raise the money than having you impersonate this guy. If you're seriously hurt I'll never forgive myself."

"Hold it." Hastings frowned at Quinn. "You've been pretending to be me? Trading on my fame? Well, I hope you have a damned good lawyer, mister, because you have a lot more to worry about than a dented limo hood."

Jo whirled toward him, glad to be able to focus her anger on someone besides herself. "Don't you dare threaten him! He nearly killed himself for me, and all because you wouldn't get off the dime!"

Hastings' square jaw dropped. "This is my fault?"

"It certainly is." She shook her finger in his handsome face. "Your advance man came by my ranch and was so enthusiastic he got my hopes up that you would actually use my ranch in your movie!"

Hastings adjusted his sunglasses. "Actually, I was thinking I'd—"

"But did you show up to close the deal?" Jo barreled on. "No, you did not. Well, you may have millions, but some of us struggle along from one payment to the next, trying to live the American dream, while our ex-husbands sabotage us at every turn."

"But, you see, that's why I'm—"

"And then, when we finally find a decent guy who's willing to go that extra mile for us, willing to risk life and very attractive limb to make our dreams come true, along comes some millionaire movie star threatening to sue the pants off him!"

"And these aren't even my pants," Quinn added.

Hastings propped his hands on his hips and gazed at Quinn. Then he looked at Jo. "I still don't get it."

Jo took a deep breath. "It's very simple. If my banker thought Brian Hastings was staying at my place, he'd assume the movie deal was on and that at some point in the future I'd be able to make a sizable payment on my loan so he wouldn't foreclose."

"But then, if the movie never gets made...?"

"By this fall, especially if the price of beef goes up, I should be able to make a payment that will satisfy him."

"I have a couple of other ideas, too, Jo." Quinn climbed off the hood and came to stand beside her. "You don't have to sell Clarise and Stud-muffin. Instead you should shop around for a better insurance rate, for one thing. What you're paying is outrageous."

She turned to him, her eyes wide. "You snooped in my books?"

"Yeah, as a matter of fact, I did. I set up a basic bookkeeping system you should have no trouble following, and in the process found some cost-saving—"

"I can't believe this!" Jo cringed at the thought that he'd seen the chaos of her financial affairs. "That is extremely private!"

"Dammit, Jo, it's my area of expertise. And I thought we'd arrived at a point where I could—"

"You think because of what happened in that tree you now have the right to invade my private financial records and make all sorts of recommendations? Well, let me tell you, Mr. Quinn Monroe, investment banker, that I—"

"Excuse me, Jo," Hastings said. "That is your name, right?"

"That's my name." Jo still glared at Quinn.

"Jo, I have a comment to make. I'm not sure what went on between you and this Hastings look-alike in the tree, but if he's willing to give you some free financial advice as a result, I suggest you take it. I hate to tell you what I pay my accountant, but it's worth every penny. I'm not good with numbers, and obviously, neither are you."

Jo lifted her chin. "I've been managing."

"Oh, yeah? Then what was that speech about the American dream and loan payments and sabotaging ex-husbands all about?"

"I got... carried away."

"Okay, but it's hard-won advice I'm passing out. And these guys hardly ever work for nothing. That tree experience must have been something else." Hastings folded his arms and glanced across the roof of the limo. "Here comes the horse you rode in on, Monroe."

Jo looked over to see Benny leading Hyper toward them. Then she glanced toward the arena and noticed a small contingent of people, led by Emmy Lou and Fred, coming toward them. She had to find a way to stall them until she figured out what to do.

Benny reined in his horse and stared at Quinn and Hastings. "Separated at birth," he said in an awed voice, shaking his head.

Jo hurried to him. "Not quite. Listen, Benny, I need you to do something for me. See Emmy Lou and Fred coming over here with all those people?"

Benny nodded.

"I want you to ride over and tell them that Brian Hastings has a big surprise planned, and everyone has to remain in their seats, or it will be ruined."

Benny frowned. "Okay. But the flag's on the ground."

Jo snatched it up, shook it off and handed it to him. Benny had always longed to carry that flag. "You take it back, Benny. You're the flag bearer and the messenger, okay? I'm counting on you."

Benny grinned. "You bet." He kicked his horse into a fast trot to make the flag ripple as he rode toward the approaching crowd, and Hyper followed docilely behind.

Jo heaved a sigh and turned to Quinn and Hastings. "Now, where were we?"

Hastings gazed at her. "I was about to ask if you want to negotiate the terms for my use of your ranch, or are you going to be smart and turn it over to Mr. Investment Banker, here?"

Jo's heartbeat quickened. "You really want the ranch?"

"Yep. I drove out there just now, and it's perfect. But nobody was home, so I came into town, saw all the commotion and decided to investigate."

Jo glanced from Hastings to Quinn. "That's great. Really great. But we have this tiny problem." She looked at Hastings. "People around here think Brian Hastings has already arrived."

Hastings stroked his jaw and looked at Quinn. "Think we could make the switch?"

"Maybe," Quinn said.

Jo shook her head. "No way."

"Why not?" both men said at once.

"Because you really don't look anything alike," Jo said. "Quinn's eyes are much bluer, and he's taller, and his shoulders are broader. His hair's thicker, and he's got that cute little freckle on his cheekbone, and everyone may not notice, but when he smiles, one of his eyeteeth is slightly crooked, which gives him a rakish air you can't get with caps."

"I don't have caps," Hastings said stiffly. He glanced at Quinn. "But maybe I need the name of your stylist. To be honest, I haven't been all that happy with Antoine recently."

"My barber's in New York."

"No problem. Maybe he'd like to relocate."

Quinn's expression turned belligerent. "If you're going to steal the first decent barber I've found in six years, I'm not telling you his name."

"Guys. Could we get back on track? I don't think it will work to switch one of you for the other, so what else have we got?"

"We could say it was all a joke," Quinn said.

Jo looked doubtful. "But you promised people parts in the movie."

Hastings groaned. "Oh, boy. Here we go. Not speaking parts, I hope?"

"No," Quinn said. "I wasn't specific, except I told this one guy, Jo's banker, that he'd be perfect for this French character."

Hastings shook his head. "I'll get with the scriptwriters. The last thing I want is bad publicity because some local guy thought he'd be in the movie and he's not." He hesitated, as if afraid to ask the next question. "Did you... tell them what it was about?"

"No," Jo said.

"That's a relief."

"I only gave them the title," Quinn said.

"The title?"

"Yeah. *The Brunette Wore Spurs*."

"Ye gods and little fishes. That's *awful*."

Quinn looked hurt. "I sort of liked it."

Hastings gave him a disparaging look. "Which is why you're in investment banking and I'm in filmmaking. Okay, we can deal with that. I'll tell them we had some fun with that title, thought of turning this into a Mel Brooks type spoof, but the producers didn't think it would suit my image. You didn't know that when I sent you out to Ugly Bug."

"You sent me? Wait a minute, you didn't—"

"Work with me here, Monroe. I'm trying to get you out of trouble, sport. Now, picture this." Hastings glanced around to make sure they weren't being overheard. "I met you in New York. That's where you're from, right?"

"Yep."

Hastings nodded. "Good. I go there all the time. So I met you and noticed the striking resemblance." He sent Jo a challenging look, but she only shrugged. "I've been looking for a stand-in, so I asked you if you were interested. You agreed to give it a try, so I sent you to Ugly Bug as a test, to see if people would believe you were me. It worked. I'm ready to hire you."

"But I don't want the job."

"I'm not really offering you the job! Hell, you probably can't even act!" Hastings shook his head. "Damn, but bankers can be literal. So I offer you the job, you turn it down, and we go on from there. Do you love it?"

Quinn nodded. "It might work."

"Might work?" Hastings threw his hands in the air. "It's brilliant! Improv at its finest! It's so hard to get any honest appreciation these days."

"I appreciate it," Jo said. "You've just found a way to save my reputation in Ugly Bug. Thank you."

"That reminds me," Hastings said. "Where'd that dumb name come from?"

"You don't even want to know," Quinn said.

"Maybe not. We're sure not using it in the script, that's for sure. I even hate to put it in the credits, but I guess we'll have to." Hastings motioned to the limo. "Shall we?"

Jo eyed the limo dubiously. "Where are we going?"

Hastings smiled his perfect smile. "Straight into the arena, my friends. If there's one thing Brian Hastings knows how to do, it's make an entrance."

Jo glanced at Quinn. "You'll have to go some to top the last one."

<u>26</u>

Quinn watched Hastings maneuver his way through the rodeo festivities and the dance that evening, and by the end of it he had to admit Hastings was a hell of a guy. He handled crazed fans with a finesse Quinn envied, but of course he'd had plenty of practice. For the first time Quinn understood that being a star in the spotlight required boundless energy. Hastings was on the go constantly from the moment he stepped out of the limo in the middle of the rodeo arena to his late-night tour of the Bar None ranch buildings.

Quinn used the time Jo and Fred were showing Hastings around to change into his city clothes and lay his borrowed ones in a neat pile on his bunk. He hadn't told anyone about reserving a seat on the red-eye, figuring he'd make his goodbyes short and sweet when the time came. Finally he walked to the house, where a light shone from the kitchen window and he could see people gathered around Emmy Lou's table, probably swapping stories of the day and sampling one of her pies.

Quinn felt very sorry for himself. Not long ago he'd sat in that kitchen enjoying the same treatment Hastings was getting, being fed like a king and hailed as Jo's savior. Now she had a new hero.

Come to think of it, she'd never really needed Quinn. Salvation had arrived only a few days after he was pressed into service. If Hastings hadn't turned out to be an understanding guy, Quinn's presence even might have ruined the movie deal. He'd been worse than useless—he'd been in the way.

At least he wouldn't make the mistake of hanging around. He walked up the steps to the porch just as Jo came out the front door.

"There you are! I've been wondering where you—" She paused and surveyed his outfit. "Why are you dressed like that?"

"I'm taking the red-eye, Jo."

"Tonight?" Her face paled. "You're leaving right now?"

He nodded. "I was coming in to say goodbye to everyone."

"I see." She swallowed. "Well, let me say, while we're out here by ourselves, that I'm very grateful for all you've done." She twisted her hands in front of her. "I can't... thank you enough."

Gratitude was beggar's wages. He wanted love from her, not a polite thank-you. But she needed a cowboy to love. "It turns out I didn't do a damn thing. Hastings was on his way."

"We didn't know that. You stepped into the breach, Quinn. I'll never forget... that."

He figured she would forget it, and him, eventually. He wasn't part of her world and never could be. But standing here and not reaching for her, no matter how dumb the gesture would be, was the most difficult thing he'd ever done.

"I, um, guess you need to come in so you can get going," she said.

"Yeah." His voice was husky with sadness.

"I'll... I'll be right down. I need to... check on something." She turned and fled, letting the screen door bang after her as she ran upstairs.

With a heavy sigh, Quinn walked into the house and entered the cheerful kitchen, the kitchen he'd never see again.

Conversation stopped, and Fred glanced up from his plate. "Where've you been, boy? I know how you crave Emmy Lou's cooking."

"It's been one of the best things about this trip," Quinn said, smiling at Emmy Lou. "Thank you for feeding me so well."

Emmy Lou frowned. "That sounded like a goodbye thank-you, to me."

"And you got your own clothes on for a change," Benny said.

"I'm catching the red-eye for New York tonight," Quinn said.

Benny leaped from his chair. "I'll be right back. Don't leave yet."

"I've got a few minutes left," Quinn said. Funny how emotional he felt at this moment. Like he was leaving his own family.

"Does Jo know?" Emmy Lou asked.

"Yeah. I met her on the porch."

"So that's why she pounded up those stairs like a skunk was after her," Fred said.

Quinn cleared his throat. "I wanted to say that you've been great, all of you." He glanced at Hastings, who sat at the table with his chauffeur, Sid.

Hastings had a button missing from his shirt. Emmy Lou had scored her trophy, after all. "You, too, Brian," Quinn said. "You could have nailed me for this little stunt. Thanks for letting it go."

Hastings grinned and leaned back in his chair. "Hey, I love a challenge. Figuring out how to explain you to the good folks of Ugly Bug was the most fun I've had in years. Just don't go trying to be me anymore, okay?"

Quinn returned his smile. "I never wanted to be you in the first place."

"You didn't?" Hastings pretended great shock. "Who wouldn't want that?"

"I sure as hell wouldn't," Fred said. He got up to come over and shake Quinn's hand. "It's been a pleasure."

Quinn's conscience nagged him about the swiped condoms. "Uh, Fred, I—you might notice sometime that you—"

"I already did." Fred winked at him. "Forget it."

Not likely, considering what I used them for. Quinn nodded. "Thanks."

Emmy Lou pulled Quinn into a big hug. "Come back, you hear?"

"I... we'll see."

Emmy Lou stood back and gazed at him with tears in her eyes. "How about a button off your shirt?"

Quinn laughed in surprise. "I'm no celebrity."

"You are to me. I've never known a New York investment banker before. Can I have one?"

Quinn shrugged, more touched by the request than he wanted her to know. '"Why not?" He stood patiently while she found some scissors and snipped off the button nearest his collar.

Then she patted his chest. "I mean it. Come back."

He was sure she knew that wasn't going to happen, or she wouldn't be fighting tears. "I'll try."

Benny came charging into the kitchen, his black Stetson in his hand. He shoved it at Quinn. "Here."

"Benny, I couldn't take this. It's your best hat."

"It looked good on you today. Well, until Hyper started running and it fell off. Wear it in New York. Go on. Take it."

Quinn recognized the gift as a gesture of friendship that meant as much to Benny as it did to him. "Thank you. I'll wear it with pride." God, it would be tough leaving these people. He put on the hat and adjusted the brim while Benny beamed at him. Another couple of minutes and Quinn was afraid he'd be bawling. "Well, folks, I'd better get on the road."

"I'll walk you out," Hastings said, pushing back his chair.

Uh-oh. Quinn wondered if Hastings was as laid-back as he'd seemed about the impersonation thing. Maybe he wanted Quinn to sign an affidavit promising never to repeat the stunt. Or maybe he was planning to press charges after all. "Okay."

After a last round of goodbyes, handshakes and hugs from Emmy Lou, Quinn walked to his rental car with Hastings, his eyes moist. It took him a few seconds before he trusted himself to speak. "So, what's on your mind?" he asked as they reached the car.

"The more appropriate question is, what's on yours?"

Quinn stood by the driver's side of the sedan and turned to Hastings. "What do you mean?"

"Are you really as stupid as you're acting right now, or do you have some master plan you're not telling anyone?"

Quinn stared at him.

Hastings sighed and shook his head. "So you're stupid. So stupid you're going to leave that woman, even though she loves you to pieces."

"Jo?"

"No, Meg Ryan." Hastings snorted. "Yes, Jo! Lord love a duck, but you're dense. I was thinking of hiring you for a couple of financial deals I'm working on, but if this is how you are, forget it. Jo is crazy about you. Genuine crazy, not the starstruck stuff I get most of the time. She loves you deep down to the bone. A guy finds that maybe once in a lifetime, if he's lucky, and you're walking away from it. You're an idiot, Monroe."

"She wants a cowboy. She said so."

"Oh, my God. So be a cowboy."

"I'm no good at it."

"Trust me, she won't care. All you really need to pull it off is a Stetson and a smile. Benny just gave you the Stetson, and according to Jo, and I quote—" Hastings slipped into falsetto "—when he smiles, one of his eyeteeth is slightly crooked, which gives him a rakish air." Hastings rolled his eyes. "That's love talking, sport. L-U-V, love. She looks at you as if you're the most expensive thing on the menu, something she'd give anything to have, but she's afraid she doesn't have the money to pay for."

Quinn's brain whirled as he wondered if he dared believe what Hastings was saying. "But if she really wants me—"

"She's scared to say, because of your big important job. Are you married to that hotshot position in New York, or could you see yourself moving to Montana? Montana's not so far from California, and if you can convince me you have at least a few brain cells working, I could probably scare you up some Hollywood clients. They're flaky, but they're rich. But then, you're flaky. It should work out."

"I'm not flaky."

"Oh, sure. I've heard enough to think otherwise. You hop on a plane to bring the lady horse sperm, and then you parade around here pretending to be a big star when you're clueless about the film industry, and then you climb on some spoiled-rotten horse and go tearing around a rodeo arena in front of the good people of Ugly Bug when you can't even ride, let alone ride and carry a flag. I'm gonna hook you up with Steve Martin. You two are soul mates."

"You've got me pegged wrong." Maybe he used to be like that when he was growing up in the Bronx with Murray, but he'd changed.

Hastings grinned at him. "Have it your way. I've spent years studying how character is revealed, and I know this cold. You're a wild man. I'm not even going to ask what went on in that tree, but news flash,

Quinn, baby—tight-assed guys don't make love in trees."

"I was just trying to stay away from snakes!"

"Are you kidding? Snakes can climb trees!"

Quinn could have lived without that factoid. "Okay, okay. What do you think I should do?"

"I have to tell you? Put away your car keys and go upstairs!"

"But everybody's in the house. It's an old house. I don't want—"

"I see your point. Okay. Especially considering your wild streak. Sid and I will take everybody for a moonlit limo ride. I can give you an hour, maybe an hour and a half. But if you can't get your business done in under sixty minutes, you're not the banker for me."

27

Jo knew she was being cowardly, but she couldn't go back downstairs and watch Quinn leave. Besides, no amount of makeup or eyedrops would be able to disguise that she'd been crying buckets. She'd closed her door and muffled the sound with pillows so they wouldn't be able to hear her downstairs, but with all those people in the house talking and laughing, they probably couldn't hear her, anyway.

Through her sobs she listened to everyone filing out of the house. No doubt they'd all gone to wave goodbye as Quinn drove away. He'd been a popular guest. The sound of a car engine drifted up to her window, and a fresh wave of tears engulfed her. He was really gone.

When she heard her bedroom door open, she moaned. "Go away, Em. And don't tell me I'm stupid to cry over him." She sniffed. "I already know that."

Footsteps approached the bed.

"Please, Emmy Lou. There are some things a girl has to get through alone. I should never have allowed myself to care about him, but I did, so now I get to pay the consequences."

The bed sagged.

"Dammit, Emmy Lou. I don't need mothering, I need—" She lifted her head and stared into Quinn's blue, blue eyes.

"Loving?" he murmured, smoothing her tousled hair from her damp cheeks.

She buried her face in the pillow, mortified that he'd heard her babble about him and especially that he saw her like this, weeping like a dope because he'd left. "What are you doing here?" she mumbled into the pillow. "You'll miss your flight."

"Guess so." He stroked her hair.

"Why are you wearing Benny's hat?"

"He gave it to me. He likes me."

"Well, I don't. And don't you dare stay here because you feel sorry for me! I'm not crying over you, anyway."

"You're not?" He kicked off his shoes, took off his hat and scooted down next to her on the bed. "Then what are you crying for?"

"None of your beeswax."

He curved his arm around her waist. "I haven't heard that since fourth grade."

"Don't touch me, either."

"Why?" He nestled closer and pushed her hair back so he could nibble at her ear. "Because I have cooties?"

"Exactly." She didn't want to like his arm around her, or his warm breath on her ear. Maybe he wasn't leaving tonight, but he would leave tomorrow. And she'd have to go through this all over again.

"But you like bugs."

Apparently she'd cried so hard she'd sapped her strength. That was the only explanation for why she allowed him to roll her onto her back. And before she knew it, he'd plastered himself on top of her. And her stupid body was getting all hot and bothered about it, too. "Go away." The words came out in a croak.

"No." He began to kiss her eyes and her cheeks.

"Don't kiss me. I probably look like hell."

He grinned. "No, you don't. Just a little red and puffy."

"You missed your plane just so you could tell me that? What a guy."

His grin faded. "No, I didn't miss my plane so I could tell you that. I missed my plane so I could tell you this. I love you."

The world stopped. She stared at him, her mouth open.

"Breathe, Jo."

She gasped.

"That's it. Now keep breathing. In, out, in, out. Good."

She struggled to do as he asked, but it wasn't easy. "Sorry," she said in a strained voice. "But that's not the sort of thing I hear every day."

He gazed at her with loving concern. "I sure hope not."

She looked into his eyes. She'd suspected he was falling in love with her, but she'd never in a million years expected him to say so. "Why are you telling me this?" she asked.

"In hopes I could get you to say the same thing back to me."

"And then what?"

He nudged her gently with his arousal. "We have an hour before the group comes back from their moonlit limo ride."

"No."

The light in his eyes dulled. "No, you don't love me?"

"Yes, I love you, but no, we won't be frolicking in the sheets for the next hour."

The gleam returned to his eyes. "Why not?"

"Because this love talk is bad enough, but if you throw in a session with your talented and very large equipment, I won't be able to survive your leaving tomorrow, that's why."

He leaned down and brushed his lips across hers. "Which means I have to stay."

Her breath caught at that sweet contact. "Don't be ridiculous. You can't stay. You'll ruin your career."

"My career will be fine." He feathered a light kiss on her mouth. "I'm just afraid I'll be in the way around here. I can handle your ledgers like no one you've ever seen, but as you know, I can't ride and I can't rope and I'm scared of snakes and big ugly bugs."

"You think I care about that?"

He lifted his head to gaze at her. "I thought you did, yeah. I thought I wasn't cowboy enough for you."

"Oh, *Quinn*." She pulled his head down and proceeded to kiss him until the press of his arousal became very prominent indeed.

Gasping, he levered himself away from her. "Is that a yes?"

"I don't recall you asking a question."

"I didn't? Damn. Okay, let's make it a two-parter. First part — will you marry me? And second part — can we get rid of these clothes and get to it before that limo pulls up in front of the house?"

She smiled at him, her heart brimming with happiness. "Here's a one-part answer to your two-part question. Yes."

"Hallelujah." Quinn began unbuttoning her blouse at a furious pace.

"Oh, Quinn, we haven't talked about children!"

"Do we have to right now?" He tugged off her jeans and panties in one motion. "We only have about forty-four minutes left." He pulled his shirt over his head without unbuttoning it.

"We certainly do have to talk about children, unless you came prepared for this encounter, which I seriously doubt, because I happen to know Fred's supply was nearly exhausted last night."

Quinn paused, his pants half off. "He told you I swiped?"

"Yes, and he's about out by now. So, are we having kids or not?'

"That's up to you." Quinn pulled a foil-wrapped square from his pocket before letting the slacks fall to the floor.

"Are you taking Fred's last one?"

"Nope. He has a backup stash. And this time I didn't have to swipe it. He offered."

Jo's cheeks heated. "So everybody knows what we're doing up here?"

"Pretty much. So what'll it be?" He leaned down and wiggled the packet in front of her face. "I happen to like kids, myself."

Jo's embarrassment lost out to a powerful surge of desire. "I like kids, too," she said, her voice husky.

Quinn straightened, tossed the packet over his shoulder and took off his briefs.

Jo looked at him standing before her in all his glory. He was perfect, but one little detail would make him even more perfect. "Quinn, do me a favor?"

"Anything."

She picked up the Stetson from where he'd laid it on the bedside table. "Humor me and put this on."

Quinn chuckled as he took the hat. He set it on his head and pulled it low over his eyes. "Damned if Hastings wasn't right."

"About what?"

"Nothing, sweetheart. Nothing at all." Then he smiled that heart-stopping smile, the one that made her knees weak and her pulse race.

Her heart brimming with happiness, Jo opened her arms. "Come here, you big, beautiful cowboy."

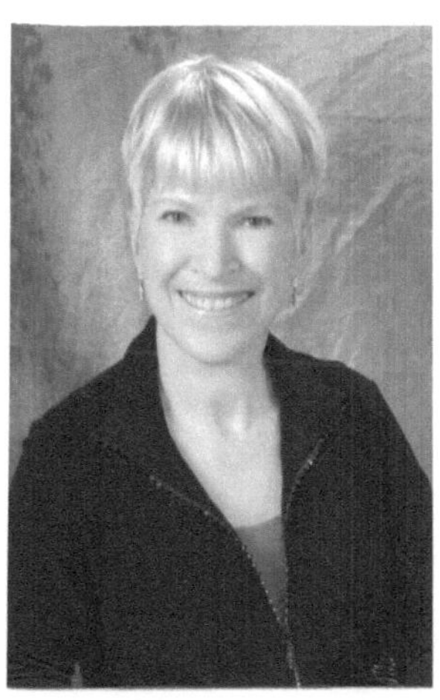

New York Times bestselling author Vicki Lewis Thompson's love affair with cowboys started with the Lone Ranger, continued through Maverick, and took a turn south of the border with Zorro. She views cowboys as the Western version of knights in shining armor, rugged men who value honor, honesty and hard work. Fortunately for her, she lives in the Arizona desert, where broad-shouldered, lean-hipped cowboys abound. Blessed with such an abundance of inspiration, she only hopes that she can do them justice.

For more information about this prolific author, visit her website and sign up for her newsletter. She loves connecting with readers.

VickiLewisThompson.com